The
Interview:

Skills and Applications

William C. Donaghy
University of Wyoming

Scott, Foresman and Company   **Glenview, Illinois**

Dallas, Texas   Oakland, New Jersey   Palo Alto, California   Tucker, Georgia   London, England

An Instructor's Manual to accompany *The Interview* is available through a Scott, Foresman representative or by writing to Speech Communication Editor, College Division, Scott, Foresman and Company, 1900 East Lake Avenue, Glenview, Illinois, 60025.

Cover photos: (top right) Jean-Claude Lejeune; (center right) Jacqueline Durand; (center left) Courtesy Ralston Purina; (middle) Carole Dugan; (lower middle) Jacqueline Durand. All interior photos by Carole Dugan.

Library of Congress Cataloging in Publication Data
Donaghy, William C.
   The interview.
   Bibliography: p. 405–429.
   Includes index.
   1. Interviewing.   I. Title.
HV41.D64   1984   158'.3   83-11506
ISBN 0-673-15736-9

1 2 3 4 5 6 - MPC - 88 87 86 85 84 83

Credits

Credits continue on page 436.

From "Focus group interview: Consumers Rap About Today's Shopping, Buying." Reprinted with permission from the March 3, 1975 issue of *Advertising Age*. Copyright © 1975 by Crain Communications, Inc.

From *Study of Values*, Third Edition, by G. W. Allport, P. E. Vernon, and Gardner Lindzey, 1960. Reproduced by permission of The Riverside Publishing Company.

From "The 1980 Census Questionnaire" from *American Demographics* Magazine, April 1979. Copyright © 1979 by American Demographics, Inc. Reprinted by permission.

Arthur S. Aubry, Jr., and Rudolph R. Caputo, *Criminal Interrogation*. Springfield, Illinois: Charles C. Thomas, Publisher, 1965, pp. 75, 94–95, 103.

From *Improving Interview Method and Questionnaire Design* by Norman M. Bradburn and Seymour Sudman. Copyright © 1979 by Jossey-Bass, Inc., Publishers. Reprinted by permission.

From *The Craft of Interviewing* by John Brady. Copyright © 1976 by John Brady. Reprinted by permission of Writer's Digest Books.

Alfred Benjamin: *The Helping Interview*, 3rd edition. Copyright © 1981 by Houghton Mifflin Company. Used by permission.

"Consultation Problem for Attorneys: Memorandum" from *Client Counseling Competition: Explanation and Consultation Situations* by Louis M. Brown, 1981–82 Client Counseling Competition Chairperson. Copyright © 1979 by Louis M. Brown. Reprinted by permission of Louis M. Brown and the Law Student Division of the American Bar Association.

From *A Technique for Evaluating Interviewer Performance* by Charles F. Cannell, Sally A. Lawson, and Doris L. Hausser. Copyright © 1975 by The University of Michigan, all rights reserved. Reprinted by permission of the Survey Research Center of the Institute for Social Research, The University of Michigan.

Cooperative Study in General Education, *General Goals of Life: Inventory H-Alb*. Washington, D.C.: American Council on Education, 1942.

William H. and L. Sherilyn Cormier, *Interviewing Strategies for Helpers*. Monterey, California: Brooks/Cole Publishing Company, 1979, p. 308.

From *Mail and Telephone Surveys* by Don A. Dillman. Copyright © 1978 by John Wiley & Sons, Inc. Reprinted by permission.

From *Professional Interviewing* by Cal W. Downs, G. Paul Smeyak, and Ernest Martin, pp. 223–224. Copyright © 1980 by Cal W. Downs, G. Paul Smeyak, and Ernest Martin. Reprinted by permission of Harper & Row, Publishers, Inc.

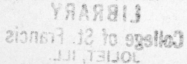

Preface

The importance of interviewing skills has increased dramatically in recent years: managers and employees are eager to conduct fair and productive business interviews; the information explosion has put more pressure on research interviewers to collect representative and accurate data; and the growth of media-related fields has placed greater demands on informative (especially journalistic) interviews. The increasing importance of interviewing skills along with the growing body of interviewing research led to the writing of *The Interview: Skills and Applications*. The book is solidly grounded in current interviewing theory, but it emphasizes the acquisition of skills and the practical application of those skills in a variety of typical interviewing situations. This commitment to skills is reflected by *The Interview*'s numerous exercises and activities, which encourage students to practice analyzing and conducting interviews.

The Interview is designed for Interviewing courses usually offered at the sophomore level by communication departments. It is also well suited to courses offered by business, journalism, sociology, political science, and psychology departments. The variety of fields that consider interviewing an integral part of their discipline demonstrates the universality and importance of these skills.

The Interview emphasizes the acquisition of a set of skills which are then applied to a variety of situations; these contexts range from journalistic to diagnostic, from persuasive to managerial settings. Part I is devoted to the eight basic interviewing skills: preparing, developing interview guides, opening, questioning and responding, probing, listening, recording, and concluding. Part II applies these skills to ten specific interview situations: information, research, selection, counseling, diagnostic, performance, persuasion, discipline, termination, and group interviews. I have attempted to blend concepts and skills in a readable style accessible to freshman and sophomore students. The photographic program was designed to enhance text concepts; the photographs were taken specifically for use in *The Interview*.

Several applied features ensure that students have ample opportunity to practice their skills and become familiar with different interviewing situations:

- Numerous exercises, all previously tested, are included *within* chapters to help students understand key concepts. Some exercises have answers at the end of the chapter; others are designed for classroom/workshop discussion. Exercises include interview analyses, fill-in activities, and discussion questions.
- Three activities are presented at the end of each chapter for in- or out-of-class application. These include practice interviews, interview preparation, recording, case studies, role plays, and discussions with professional interviewers.
- Each chapter includes a comprehensive summary to help students review key concepts.
- For those who want to pursue specific areas in greater depth, an extensive bibliography is provided at the end of the text. It offers students a range of source materials, both books and journal articles.
- Samples of various forms such as resumes, interview guides, performance appraisal forms, and termination questionnaires are presented throughout.

Many people contributed to the completion of *The Interview*. My students and all the professional interviewers I have spoken with taught me most of what I know about interviewing. They inspired me to write this book by showing me the importance of application. I am also indebted to the many interview scholars who have written before me. I have recognized their contributions and influence, in part, by quoting from them at the beginning of each chapter. I would also like to thank my typists who helped prepare the book, and the Scott, Foresman staff, Michael Anderson, Barbara Muller, and Patricia Rossi.

I am particularly indebted to the critics who read the manuscript and provided helpful suggestions for improvement: Anita Covert, Michigan State University; Lois Einhorn, State University of New York at Binghamton; Susan Hellweg, San Diego State University; Steve Price, Colorado State University; Debra Strugar, University of Arizona; and George E. Tuttle, Illinois State University.

Finally, those who suffered most throughout this project are the members of my family; their love and encouragement have sustained me. Especially my wife, Carole, recognized my strong desire to write this book and took up the parental slack. To Carole, Kelly, Brian, Scott, and the rest of you who helped make this book possible, I thank you all.

I now commend this book to those of you interested in the "how to" as well as the "who, what, when, where, and why" of interviewing.

William C. Donaghy

Contents

Part 2   The Applications of Interviewing

Introduction

*An architect commissioned to design a building creates sketches, draw-
ings, blueprints, and a three-dimensional model, allowing clients to
picture the building so they can make a decision about cost, traffic flow,
space, aesthetic appearance, and functional usage. Like the architect, an
interviewer needs to construct a model that pictures the total interviewing process and shows the relationships of its parts. (Olson, 1980,
p. 15)*

This is a book about *communication* . . . a very special type of communication.
It takes place hundreds of thousands of times a day throughout the world in
shops, offices, schools, government agencies, homes, hallways, lunchrooms, and
even on street corners. It is used by merchants, industrialists, doctors, supervisors, social workers, psychiatrists, educators, nurses, personnel directors, lawyers, homemakers, salespersons, pollsters, journalists, politicians, and almost
every man, woman, and child in their daily activity. It is reasonably safe to say
that everyone in the world has taken part in this form of communication at least
once. To use Bingham's (1931) classic definition, the type of communication
examined in this book is simply, "conversation with a purpose"—the interview.

Your obvious question at this point is, "Why, if this is something I have done
all my life, do I need a book to tell me how to do it?" By asking that question you
have started an interview. Inquiry and response is a primary means of information exchange which differentiates interviews from other forms of communication. Since you are asking the question, you have taken on the role of inquirer or

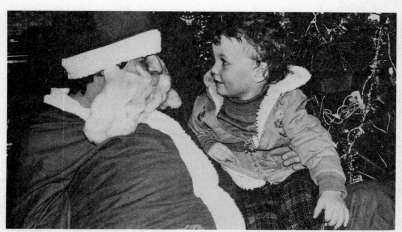

Interview participants come in all sizes and shapes.

1

interviewer. The person who answers your question assumes the role of respondent or interviewee. Although it would be an exaggeration to say that every time a question is asked an interview is taking place, it would not be an exaggeration to suggest that any time an inquiry is made the principles of interviewing apply.

Now, to answer your question: No, you *don't* need this book to tell you how to take part in an interview. You need this book to tell you how to be a *skillful* interviewer or interviewee. Everyone who takes part in interviews is not skillful, and, even those who are often become that way only through the painful trial-and-error method. This book is designed to help you avoid the "painful" and "error" part. Nothing can take the place of "trial." You must practice the concepts discussed in this book to become a truly skillful interview participant, and you will find many suggestions and exercises to help you. If this does not answer your question then you will either have to read *The Interview* to get a complete answer or throw it away and keep taking part in interviews as you have done in the past. If you choose the latter and are lucky, you still might become a skillful interview participant, but the former approach is more efficient and less risky.

CHARACTERISTICS OF AN INTERVIEW

Bingham's definition of an interview as a "conversation with a purpose" is good, but isn't specific enough. Instead of a long-winded definition, however, here are ten general characteristics of interviews: (1) a serious purpose, (2) planned interaction, (3) oral interaction, (4) face-to-face interaction, (5) dyadic interaction, (6) inquiry and response, (7) objective and subjective information, (8) role differentiation, (9) alternating roles, and (10) multiple measures of success. No one of these characteristics is the exclusive possession of an interview, and all need not exist in all interviews, but taken together they should help better understand the term, "interview."

Serious Purpose

In social conversation, chit-chat, or small talk, there is little purpose involved other than the pleasure of the conversation itself. An interview, on the other hand, must have a serious purpose, at least in the mind of one of the participants. The same purpose does not necessarily exist in the minds of both participants. The purpose is usually in the mind of the individual initiating the interview. Hence, when an interview is referred to as either interviewee or interviewer initiated, you will usually know which person had the serious purpose.

Interview purposes can be as broad as wanting to give information, wanting to get information, solving a problem (for either participant), or persuading another person. These are the *general* purposes of an interview. Most interviews also have one or more *specific* purposes such as gathering information to hire, promote, or fire; solve a medical, legal, or work problem; or give information to get a story published, sell a product, or receive counseling advice. The specific purpose describes the exact nature of the interview and information involved. If an employee is frequently late to work, the specific purpose would restrict the interview to dealing with only information relevant to that problem, not to information about vacation preferences, current duties, golf handicap, or childrens' ages, unless of course, you suspect or discover that this information relates to the specific purpose. Every interview, then, has a serious general and specific purpose.

As an interview progresses, both the general and/or the specific purpose can change. In some interviews a change of purpose is actually planned. In a hiring or selection interview, for example, interviewers often plan to seek information from applicants at the beginning of the interview and then give information about the organization toward the end of the interview. In other situations, information can come up which will modify, change, or add to the interview purpose. For example, in a work performance interview, the respondent might bring up a policy inconsistency which was not anticipated, thus modifying the interview purpose. But under no circumstances can an interview exist without a serious purpose. This is the first and most important interview characteristic.

Planned Interaction

Because interviews have a definite purpose, the interaction is usually planned prior to the interview. Think about the last time you had an interview with your doctor or lawyer about a problem. You probably went over what you were going to say and what you expected to hear many times beforehand. Professional interviewers, such as doctors and lawyers, are also well prepared for such interviews. You have seen the health record forms and other written guides used by doctors and nurses to conduct diagnostic interviews. Professional interviewers have such plans for the interaction, if not written out, then at least in their heads.

Interaction planning is what helps interview participants achieve their purpose(s). Throughout this book, a great deal of emphasis is placed on interview preparation. The more planned the interaction content, the greater the likelihood that the interview will be successful. Even in interviews with no conscious formal planning, there is some measure of mental planning. A child who sees a parent doing something and wants to find out how to do it must determine at each stage what is not understood and plan questions to gain the necessary information. Unlike other forms of communication where people often don't know what they are going to say until they hear themselves saying it, in an interview one participant usually planned what type of interaction will take place.

Oral Interaction

A third characteristic of interviews is that they are usually oral. The word "conversation" in Bingham's definition implies this. Very few people would think of holding a memo or letter interview. The single exception to the characteristic of *oral* interaction is the *questionnaire*. A questionnaire is a written list of

Nonverbal behaviors communicate valuable information.

questions to be answered in writing by respondents. It represents the ultimate in interview planning. Questionnaires are most often used by research interviewers. There is very little difference between a research interview where questions are asked orally in a completely planned and structured manner and one where the questions are presented to respondents in written form. Questionnaires are included in this book as a research interview technique.

Face-to-Face Interaction

The characteristic of face-fo-face interaction implies that the interview participants are not only able to hear but also to *see* each other. There is one exception to the face-to-face characteristic of interview interaction—a telephone interview. It occurs most often in research interviewing, because of the expense of interviewing large numbers of people face-to-face as well as some other factors. In so doing, however, telephone interviewers lose many of the benefits of a face-to-face interview.

The main value of conducting an interview face-to-face is the amount of information that can be gained by observing the behavior, as well as hearing the words, of respondents. This is usually referred to as *nonverbal communication*—or popularly as "body language." Nonverbal communication consists of all the ways people transmit and receive messages through means other than spoken or written words (Donaghy, 1980, p. 2). A person's physical appearance, posture, facial expression, eye movement, gestures, clothing, and much more are all extremely important means of gaining information. In a counseling interview, for example, a respondent's trembling hands or rapid shifts in body position can often be more important than the words that are spoken. And this information is lost when interviews are not conducted face-to-face.

Dyadic Interaction

Dyadic interaction means that the interview usually involves two people rather than a group or audience. Because most interviews involve only two people, the interaction is generally more intimate both in terms of the messages sent and the responses received. It is much easier for participants in a dyadic interaction to share meanings and mutually influence one another. This ability to mutually influence one another has been studied in recent years and is called the *transactional approach*. The following is a typical description of this approach:

We mean that the communicators are interrelated, that we can't consider one of them without considering the other or others. We mean that one perception of a communicator can't be considered apart from all his other perceptions. We mean that the external environment and the internal state of each person in the communication are interrelated. And finally we are saying that a communicator cannot be considered apart from the world he knows and perceives. By transactional approach we mean that all elements in the communication process are interrelated and interdependent.

(Sereno/Bodaken, 1975, pp. 8–10)

The transactional approach is a reaction to the traditional one-way approach to the study of various forms of communication. The one-way approach assumes that a message sender transmits information to a receiver, but that the receiver has little or no effect on the sender. In the interview context, this would imply that interviewees have no effect on the quantity or quality of questions asked by interviewers. This isn't true. Throughout an interview both participants are adapting to and are influencing one another. Even when interviewers plan the same interview for different interviewees, the interviews turn out differently.

Each interview is a unique transaction which cannot be understood by looking at either participant in isolation. Once any two people interact, either verbally or nonverbally, a transaction or interdependent relationship is formed. As one person speaks, the other responds and affects the first instantaneously and simultaneously. Many types of transactional relationships can exist in an interview, depending upon such factors as the age, sex, attitudes, attributes, beliefs, status, and behaviors of the participants. To understand a dyadic interview, you need to understand the relationship. Although interview relationships can change, each dyad interview relationship is unique.

The group interview is the single exception to the two-person or dyadic interview. There are two types of group interviews, when there are several interviewers and one interviewee, and when there are several interviewees and one interviewer. As you might suspect, the more people involved in the interview, the more problems. Although the group interview is becoming more common, most interviews are still conducted between only two people.

Inquiry and Response

As was said earlier, inquiry and response are the primary means of information exchange which differentiate interviews from other forms of communication. They are the normal means of completing an interview. All inquiries, however, do not necessarily end with a question mark. As a matter of fact, Benjamin (1974), a noted counseling interviewer, actually challenges the use of questions in an interview.

> By initiating the question-answer pattern, we are telling the interviewee as plainly as if we put it into words that we are the authority, the expert, and that only we know what is important and relevant for him. . . . I am convinced that the question-answer pattern does not create the atmosphere in which a warm, positive relationship can develop; in which the interviewee may find a valuable experience; in which he may discover more about himself, his strengths and weaknesses; in which he has the opportunity to grow.
>
> (Benjamin, 1974, p. 66)

Benjamin's objection is not really to inquiry in its broadest form, but to the interrogative nature of questions. Silence can be as strong a form of inquiry as words or sentences which end with a question mark. Silence can also be a response. A nod of the head; shrug of the shoulders; direct or averted eye gaze; or utterance such as "go on," "well," "um-hum," and "I'm not sure I understand" are all forms of inquiry and response which do not carry authoritarian implications. In this book the term "question" will be used interchangeably with "inquiry" to mean all forms of information request and not just an interrogative.

In most interviews the purpose of inquiry and response is to exchange information with little or no desire on the part of either participant to influence or persuade the other. Some interviews, however, start out in this manner but eventually shift to a persuasive and/or argumentative style of interaction. These include persuasion, discipline, appraisal, and counseling interviews. In these interviews the interaction may appear to remain one of unbiased inquiry and response, but underneath the surface one or both of the participants wants to influence the other. So long as the primary mode of interaction remains one of inquiry and response, regardless of whether there is a persuasive purpose, the label, "interview," still applies.

Objective and Subjective Information

Two types of information can be collected in an interview: objective and subjective. *Objective* information includes unbiased and testable facts. Names, dates, locations, and circumstances are examples of objective information. *Subjective* information includes personal feelings, attitudes, and beliefs of an individual. An interview participant's positive or negative feelings regarding an event would be an example of subjective information. One of the primary values of an interview is that it facilitates not only the gathering of objective information but also subjective information. The best way to do this is in face-to-face interaction. Some interviews, such as a research interview, are primarily geared to gathering objective information while others, such as counseling interviews, focus on subjective information. Most involve the collection of both types of information.

It is often hard to separate objective from subjective information. Feelings and beliefs can appear in both inquiries and responses without the speaker even being aware of them. You are dealing with people, not machines, and people tend to confuse and intertwine objective and subjective information. What appears to be objective information may not really be completely "objective." In most interviews what is really important is what the participants *think* is "real," "accurate," or "objective," not the actual facts. In termination interviews, for example, it does not really matter if an employer is treating respondents poorly or not. What does matter is that the employees *think* they are being treated poorly. A resignation has the same result regardless of the "true" facts. Unless you are a mind reader, inquiry and response is still the best way to gather both the objective facts and subjective feelings in another person's head.

Role Differentiation

Earlier, the terms, "interviewer" and "interviewee" were used to refer to interview participants. These terms identify the roles individuals play in an interview. A *role* is a set of expectations people have about themselves and others with whom they interact. These expectations normally involve people's perceptions of their own power and status with regard to others. Each role carries with it certain acceptable and unacceptable, expected and unexpected, and natural and unnatural behaviors based on that power and status estimate. In an interview, for example, it is acceptable, expected, and natural for the interviewer to inquire and the interviewee to respond.

It would be a mistake to think of either the interviewer or interviewee role as being more important. In an interview the power and status of each role is reflected in the type of control each possesses. In most cases, the interviewer possesses *directional control*, that is, control over what topics will be discussed, when a topic is completed, what inquiries will occur for each topic, and so on. Interviewees, on the other hand, possesses *informational control*. They can refuse to supply the requested information or supply partial, distorted, or inaccurate information. This type of control is often seen in a response of, "no comment."

Think of interview roles, then, not as more or less important but only different. At any given time someone is exercising directional control and someone is exercising informational control. Both roles are necessary for a successful interview. An interview will be unsuccessful if *both* participants are attempting to exercise either directional or informational control at the same time. One of them is behaving in a way that is unacceptable, unexpected, and unnatural for their role, and thus the interview is left either directionless or informationless. Either problem can be disastrous.

Alternating Roles

Both interview participants cannot play both directional and informational roles *at the same time*, but the same person can play both roles at different times and the roles can alternate between participants. In a counseling interview, for example, interviewers often allow respondents to control both interview direction and information. This is called the "nondirective" or "unstructured" approach and will be discussed later.

Although typically each participant is in either an interviewer or interviewee role, each one does not necessarily remain in the same role throughout the entire interaction. In fact, it is often recommended that roles alternate. A lawyer, for example, may start out providing direction and asking for information from a client and then end up supplying information in response to client inquiries. It is even possible to find roles and control changing from inquiry to inquiry. The amount of role alternation which is best depends upon the nature of the interview. There is usually little alternation in discipline or persuasion interviews, but a great deal in selection and counseling interviews. Role alternation is possible in all interviews, with the possible exception of the questionnaire.

Multiple Success Measures

The last characteristic of an interview relates to how success is measured. No one yardstick exists by which you can determine interview success. Interview success is closely related to the purpose of the interview, but as was pointed out earlier, an interview can have many general and specific purposes and these purposes can change. Your purpose may not be the same as the interviewee's purpose. Immediate and long-range purposes may differ. There can be attitudinal and behavioral purposes, as well as overt and covert purposes. Because of the multiple interview purposes, there are multiple measures of interview success. You must assess success from various viewpoints: interviewer and interviewee, long-range and short-term, attitudinal and behavioral, and many others.

Think of interview success as a relative concept. It is possible to label the same interview as either successful or unsuccessful depending upon your viewpoint. That is why there is no claim made in this book that you will become a *successful* interview participant. This book is designed simply to make you *skillful*. You can be skillful and yet not be successful depending on how you measure success. For the purposes of this book, skill is the best measure of interview success.

These, then, are ten basic characteristics of an interview. They give you a way of looking at and understanding what is meant by the term, "interview." Using them you could say that, for the most part, an interview is a *planned, oral, face-to-face dyadic interaction utilizing inquiries and responses to gain objective and subjective information with differentiated and alternating participant roles, a serious purpose, and multiple measures of success.*

BECOMING A SKILLFUL INTERVIEW PARTICIPANT

This book is based on the premise that there are eight skills which you must learn and practice in order to be a skillful interview participant. You must develop skill in (1) preparing to interview, (2) developing an interview guide, (3) opening an interview, (4) asking and answering questions, (5) probing, (6) listening, (7) recording, and (8) concluding the interview. These eight basic skills apply to all types of interviews. A brief overview of each skill might help you see how they interrelate and give you a bird's-eye view of Part I of this text.

Each of the following eight chapters is devoted to one of these skills. Each is an in-depth examination of the skill and contains activities and exercises to help you master each skill. The activities require that you actually do something, such as take part in a mock interview. The exercises are written, pictorial, and mental problems and tests to help you better understand the concepts. To get the most out of this book, you should read the text *and* do the exercises and activities. Examples are sometimes left out of the text on the assumption that the exercise will make the concept clear. In other words, the exercise becomes the example. Now for a preview of the eight basic interview skills.

Skill 1: Preparing to Interview

Although some interviews occur on the spur of the moment, most are scheduled well enough in advance to allow both participants time to prepare. This preparation time should be used wisely. There are two types of preparation: *general* preparation, which includes learning about human nature and yourself, and *specific* preparation, which includes learning about the other participant and the subject of the interview. Skillful interview participants are generally and specifically prepared before an interview begins.

Beyond this, the interviewer or the person exercising directional control also has some added preparation responsibilities, such as choosing the interview time, preparing the setting, and planning the opening and structure. Good interview preparation does not come easily or naturally; it must be learned and practiced before it is perfected.

Skill 2: Developing the Interview Guide

Developing an interview guide is part of preparation, but it is a separate skill as well, because in many ways it is the most crucial skill of all. There are several types of interview guides, including nondirective guides, which are little more than a blank sheet of paper, semidirective guides, which normally include only the topics to be covered, and directive guides, which include both topics and questions. All include space to record responses.

In order to develop an interview guide, you first need to determine what topics you intend to cover and in what sequence, then what types of information are necessary to cover each topic, and last what types of questions you will ask and in what sequence. These three aspects of interview guide development lie at the very heart of the interviewing process. The chapter on interview guides also includes a discussion of how to create and use transitions between topics and questions. A skillful interviewer puts a lot of time and effort into each interview guide, because without a good one, it is very easy to leave an interview directionless. Guides are especially useful for beginning interviewers—a skillfully prepared guide can be thought of as a roadmap to interview success.

Skill 3: Opening the Interview

During an interview opening, the climate is established, interviewee orientation takes place, and the first main question is asked. *Climate* refers to the mood or tone of the interview and includes icebreaking comments and other verbal and nonverbal behaviors which help establish the desired atmosphere. It is easy to say you want to establish a climate which will encourage respondents to answer questions openly and honestly, but it takes skill to establish such a climate. The interviewer must carefully "size up" each respondent without jumping to the wrong conclusions. At the same time each interviewee is trying to "size up" the interviewer. And all of this is done before a proper climate is established.

The orientation portion of an opening is designed to help interviewees understand the nature of the role(s) they are to take during the interview. Such information as the amount of prior preparation, projected interview length, when roles can alternate, and how the information will be used are all important to include in interviewee orientation. Then comes the opening question. It is usually planned ahead of time and provides a bridge or transition to the main body of the interview. If well chosen, it moves the interview smoothly into the central area of inquiry.

Skill 4: Asking and Answering Questions

The way in which a question is asked is just as important as what is asked. Such simple things as word choice, phrasing, tone of voice, and rate of delivery can make the difference between a well prepared question and a poor one. Questions serve many purposes besides information collection. These include maintaining directional control, shaping responses, encouraging participation, and reinforcing the climate. It takes skill and practice to ask questions in such a way that all these purposes are served. Depending on the way you ask them, questions can be simple or complex, clear or ambiguous, objective or subjective, direct or indirect, neutral or leading, too long, precise, sharp, or double-barreled.

In the same way, it is important to learn how to respond properly to inquiries. A skillful response can sometimes turn a bad question into a good one. Asking and answering questions is also, in part, a matter of personal style. All interviewers and interviewees develop a unique style. But, they must learn to adapt their own style to that of the other participant. This is where your skill shows and each inquiry and response either succeeds or fails.

Skill 5: Probing

A probe is a follow-up inquiry. Rarely will a single question cover an area of information completely. Probes allow you to fill in the gaps. There are hundreds of different ways to probe, each of which has both advantages and disadvantages. Probes can be either verbal or nonverbal. A nod of the head, for example, can mean the same as the statement, "Go on." Some of the best probes are nonverbal. Besides gathering further information, probes are also used to maintain directional control. The three main types of informational probes are designed to produce amplification, clarification, and confrontation. Amplification probes request greater depth and/or range of response. Clarification probes reduce response confusion. A confrontation probe requires an explanation of any inconsistency. In probing your interview finesse really shows through. Most experts agree that probing is what separates good from poor interviewers.

Skill 6: Listening

Skillful interviewers spend approximately 70 percent of their interview time listening. Interviewees are listening approximately 30 percent of the time. Listening includes not only hearing and understanding the words that are spoken, but also interpreting the other person's nonverbal cues. Listening is a commonly neglected interviewing skill. Participants take listening for granted. Skillful listening is not a passive, but an extremely active process. Listening benefits both the listener and the speaker. Such listening obstacles as physical and setting limitations, source and fact focusing, fatigue and boredom, tension, emotional blindspots, mind wandering, planning ahead, conclusion jumping, and mental arguing should be avoided. It takes both knowledge and practice to increase your listening skill, and a skillful interview participant must be a good listener.

Skill 7: Recording the Interview

Experts disagree about how best to record interview information, but there is no disagreement over the fact that most interviewers need a permanent record of the interview. Three methods are normally used to record interview interaction and impressions: memorization, pencil and paper notes, and tape (audio and video) recording. Skillful interviewers use all three and recognize the advantages and drawbacks of each. Memorization is seldom used alone any more, but it is invaluable as a supplement to both of the other techniques. Pencil and paper notetaking is still the most common recording technique. There are several ways of taking written notes. Electronic recording of interviews is the newest and fastest growing technique. Skillful use of a tape recorder involves more than just pressing the "start" button. Regardless of the technique or combination of recording techniques you use, it must be accurate, relevant, objective, uniform, and complete.

Skill 8: Concluding the Interview

Just as it is important to know how and when to open an interview, it takes skill and practice to properly conclude interviews. Among other things, you must prepare to terminate, do a final summary, set post-interview goals, relax respondents, and produce a graceful exit. In many cases, the conclusion determines the perception of interview success in the mind of an interviewee. Although a good conclusion will not save a poor interview, a poor conclusion can destroy a good interview.

An interview does not end with the departure of one of the participants. Most interviews require considerable follow-up effort. Information analysis, supplemental notes, information checking, report writing, checking on goal progress, recognizing your own good and poor behaviors, and determining purpose accomplishment are all common follow-up behaviors. They are as important to a skillful interviewer as the preparation that occurs before the interview.

Helping you develop these eight skills is the main purpose of Part I of this book. Many interview participants try to develop them on their own, but instead merely learn and reinforce poor behaviors. If you learn how to interview the right way from the very beginning, you will become skillful much more quickly. Once you have learned them, then you need to understand how they apply to various types of interviews. That is the objective of Part II of this book.

INTERVIEWING APPLICATIONS

There are a great many different types of interviews; it would be impossible to discuss them all. For our purposes, ten common types of interviews have been chosen which reflect different uses or purposes and which are used to a greater or lesser degree by people in almost all occupations. The ten types of interviews discussed in this book, along with a general introduction to each, follow.

The Information Interview

Almost all interviews include some aspect of information gathering. Some interviews, however, are devoted primarily to gathering information. These have been called "journalistic," "elite," "oral history," and "key informant" interviews. As used in this text, the information interview is an interview aimed at obtaining information from a single respondent for the sole purpose of understanding the information from the interviewee's point of view. One of the main values of using an interview for such a purpose, rather than one of the many other ways of gathering information, is that the interviewer can probe for below-the-surface information. Another value of gathering information through an interview is that the information is not necessarily available anywhere else but in a respondent's head. This type of interview is discussed first because it has so much in common with many of the other types.

The Research Interview

The research interview is the most carefully planned and conducted interview of all. It is often called a "survey" interview and is primarily designed to gather the same or similar information from a large number of respondents. It is for this reason that research interviewers have often turned to quasi-interview techniques such as questionnaires and telephone interviews. On the basis of multiple interviews, research interviewers attempt to draw conclusions and make decisions which apply to large numbers of people. Advertising campaigns, political appeals, congressional legislation, product modifications, company policy decisions, and a great many other purposes are served by these interviews. Unique features of research interviews are extensive preparation, pilot testing, rigid structure, use of sampling techniques, and statistical tabulation.

The Selection Interview

Selection interviewing is extremely common. Approximately one hundred and fifty million such interviews take place each year in the United States. The main purpose of a selection interview is to determine an individual's suitability for a particular job. It is usually more formal than an information interview, and the participants are generally of unequal status. Most of you have probably already taken part in such an interview at one time or another in your life. Some of the unique features of the selection interview are the legal restrictions which surround it, the preparation and use of job descriptions, resumés, cover letters, application forms, and the common separation of the screening interview from the actual hiring interview.

The Counseling Interview

The counseling interview has also been called a "helping" or "therapeutic" interview. It is perhaps the most sensitive of all interview types because counseling interviews commonly are used to deal with sensitive subjective information such as feelings, attitudes, and personal problems. Alcoholism, drug abuse, mental health, marital strife, and sexual inadequacies are all common topics for counseling interviews. The goal of most counseling interviewers is to get interviewees to gain insight into their own problems and attempt to solve them themselves. For this reason, most counseling interviewers try to use a more nondirective approach than diagnostic interviewers. The diagnostic interviewer is only interested in results, whereas the counseling interviewer is also concerned about the means to the end. There are a great many professional counseling interviewers such as ministers and psychiatrists, but many more amateurs get involved in such interviews every day when those around them ask for help and vice versa.

The Diagnostic Interview

The purpose of a diagnostic interview is to ascertain or analyze the nature of a problem or situation. Such an interview is in constant use by physicians, nurses, lawyers, law enforcement officers, social workers, and many others. Although the participants usually are of unequal status, they generally do not work for the same organization, and, therefore, are not in a worker/boss or superior/subordinate relationship. The interviewer wants to gain objective information and insight into the situation under study. In some cases, such as in a medical setting, respondents are very willing to divulge the information requested, whereas in other situations, such as law enforcement, interviewees may be unwilling to talk freely. In these latter cases special interviewing techniques may be necessary.

The Performance Interview

Performance interviews are almost as common as selection interviews. Most organizations use such an interview to help develop their personnel, measure employee performance, improve performance, determine compensation levels, identify worker potential, plan manpower usage, and simply improve the relationship between superiors and subordinates. The fact that performance interviews normally take place between superiors and subordinates distinguishes them from the diagnostic interview. Another unique feature is that these interviews are generally based on an organization-wide, written appraisal form which strongly influences the nature of the interview itself. Successful organizations depend heavily on well-developed performance appraisal programs.

The Persuasion Interview

Like a discipline interview, persuasion interviews are designed to get an interviewee to think, feel, or do something the interviewer wants him or her to do. In a discipline interview, however, the threat of punishment is usually the prime motivator. In a persuasion interview the promise of reward is the more common means of influence. Persuasion is used between people of more or less equal status and power, whereas discipline usually requires a superior and subordinate relationship. We persuade our spouses and discipline our children. Salespersons use a persuasion interview to sell a product. A college president uses a persuasion interview to convince members of the board of trustees to vote in a certain manner. A child uses a persuasion interview to convince a friend to share a toy.

The difference between a persuasion interview and other types of persuasive presentations, such as a speech, is the method employed. If the salesperson, college president, and child in each of the preceding examples uses inquiry and response either to gather useful information on which to base the influence attempt or as a means of influencing opinions such as a leading question, then it becomes a persuasion interview. In other words, the persuasion involves a dialogue between persuader (interviewer) and persuadee (interviewee).

The Discipline Interview

Probably the most dreaded of all interviews is the discipline interview. Neither interviewers nor interviewees feel comfortable in such interviews. At times, however, discipline interviews are necessary, and if done correctly can have a very positive effect. Society, organizations, and individuals all set standards and norms which each of us is expected to meet. When these written and unwritten rules are broken, a disciplinary interview is usually conducted to correct the situation. The purpose of this interview is to change a respondent's behavior or attitude. There should probably be more formal disciplinary interviews conducted, but because they are so distasteful, they are often overlooked or conducted very poorly.

The Termination Interview

Organizations use termination interviews to reduce turnover, better utilize personnel, update policies, improve job descriptions, design appraisal programs, change salary structures, identify managerial deficiencies, assess training and development efforts, and determine if the right people are leaving and staying. It is the last formal contact an employee usually has with an employer. If done properly, termination interviews can save organizations a great deal of money. The loss of one employee commonly costs organizations between three and five thousand dollars. For some jobs the cost can go as high as twenty to thirty thousand dollars in recruiting, selection, and training of a replacement. Although such an interview may not save that particular interviewee, the information gained can help the company save others.

The Group Interview

All of the interview types listed above usually involve a dyadic relationship with a single interviewer and a single interviewee. Group interviews can have multiple interviewers or multiple interviewees. There are, however, both advantages and disadvantages to group interviews. Very little research has been done on group interviews, and there is widespread debate over their usefulness for various purposes. Because of the growing use of group interviews, it is essential that students be aware of their values and limitations and how best to use them.

INTERVIEW TYPE AND SKILL EXERCISE

Directions: Think back to three different types of interviews in which you took part during the last twelve months. Then record the interview type (selection, performance, persuasion, etc.), the participants, the specific purpose, the outcome, and evaluate your skills and those of the other participant. Use the following format:

Interview Type: _____

Participants: Interviewer _____

                 Interviewee _____

Specific Purpose: _____

_____

Outcome: _____

Interviewer Skill Evaluation: _____

_____

_____

Interviewee Skill Evaluation: _____

_____

_____

SUMMARY

You have now had a small taste of what this book contains, as well as an extensive look at what an interview is and what it is not. An interview has ten basic characteristics: serious purpose, planned interaction, oral interaction, face-to-face interaction, dyadic interaction, inquiry and response, objective and subjective information, role differentiation, alternating role, and multiple measures of success. The premise of this book is that there are eight basic skills that must be mastered in order to become a skillful interview participant: preparing, guide developing, opening, asking and answering questions, probing, listening, recording, and concluding. These eight basic skills are then applied to ten types of interview: information, research, selection, counseling, diagnostic, performance, persuasion, discipline, termination, and group.

ACTIVITIES

Activity #1

Directions: Listen to a normal conversation of which you are not a participant or record a conversation in which you are a participant. This is *not* to be an interview. Make a record of the following information:
1. The conversation purpose.
2. The way the conversation opened and closed.
3. The nature of the information exchanged.
4. The number of turns taken by each participant.
5. The number of questions asked and answered.
Answer each of the following questions and explain your answer, if necessary.
Did this conversation have a serious purpose?
Was this conversation a planned interaction?
Was this conversation a face-to-face interaction?
Did this conversation involve inquiry and response?
Did this conversation involve objective and subjective information?
Was there role differentiation in this conversation?
Did the roles alternate in this conversation?
Was this conversation successful?
How did it differ from an "interview" as defined in this chapter?

Activity #2

Directions: Think of at least five people you know who commonly use interviewing as a part of their job. Look up their names, addresses, and telephone numbers, and record this information. Later, you will have to talk with one or more of these individuals. Try to think of people who use interviews for different purposes (i.e., selection, discipline, research, etc.).

Part one

The
Skills
of
Interviewing

Chapter 1

Skill 1
Preparing to Interview

Conducting the interview without preparation is not unlike a surgeon entering the operating room before examining the necessary x rays. Both procedures may be successful, in spite of the limited familiarity with the situation. But time will have been wasted and the inevitable groping may have caused unnecessary pain. (O'Leary, 1976, p. 15)

Preparing to interview is perhaps the most important of all the skills necessary to be an effective interviewer. Often it is neglected or slighted, however, because interviewers either do not know how to do it, or they believe it takes too much time. In fact, interview preparation is not that hard and need not take a great deal of time. And, the rewards for good preparation are boundless.

The purpose of preparation is not to impress interviewees but, instead, to talk and question them intelligently and to anticipate the inhibitors and facilitators of a successful interview. Preparation removes the guesswork from the interviewing process. It allows you to *predict* and *plan* what will occur during the course of an interview. It is better to be overprepared for an interview than to be underprepared. Some of the penalties for being underprepared are: missing important material, running out of time, long embarrassing pauses, misunderstandings, inadequate responses, and general dissatisfaction. Evidence of preparation is flattering to interviewees. They need to know that you are concerned enough to take the time to prepare.

In the preparation stage you should focus on all of the skills of interviewing. You need to plan how you will open the interview, what questions you will ask, the types of probes you will use, how you will record responses, and so on. In this chapter, basic information on general preparation will be presented. However, you will find specific details that should also be considered in the preparation process in other chapters as well, especially the following chapter on developing an interview guide.

Preparation differs depending upon the type of interview that is being employed. Therefore, in Part Two you will find more specific advice about preparing for each type of interview. There's a great deal of difference between preparation for an interviewee-initiated interview and an interviewer-initiated interview. The person who initiates the interview has the primary responsibility for preparing. The other participant has less formal preparation responsibility.

GENERAL PREPARATION

Before you can begin to consider conducting an interview, you need some general preparation on human nature and on yourself. These two general aspects of interview preparation will be discussed first.

Some Basic Principles of Human Nature

It would be impossible to discuss in one brief section all of the important aspects of human nature. Scientists and philosophers have devoted entire volumes to this subject. The following ten principles should provide the basic groundwork every interview participant should have. You must recognize, however, that human nature is very complicated. If you have not already taken a course or read in this area, it would be to your advantage to do so.

Principle #1: No Two People Are Alike.
This may seem obvious, but it is a principle that interviewers and interviewees often forget. We tend to classify people together because they wear similar clothes, come from the same neighborhood, or talk alike, but each person *is* unique. Research interviewers, for example, often begin to anticipate responses because they have already done a great many interviews with similar people. They "second guess" a response before it is given—a habit which can cause a great deal of harm to the interview results. They should instead be constantly alert to the individuality of each respondent.

Principle #2: People Are Conditioned by Their Environment and Past Experiences.
It is environment and past experiences that makes an individual unique. Each person has certain attitudes about objects, people, and ideas. One purpose of the interview is to learn those attitudes. It is up to each interview participant to learn as much as possible about the environment and past experiences of the other person and anticipate how these factors will help or hurt the interaction. Some interviewees, for example, may have had a bad experience in a previous interview, and must overcome that experience before the current interview can be successful.

Principle #3: People Behave Both Verbally and Nonverbally on the Basis of Their Needs.
Our *needs* motivate us to behave as we do. Maslow (1954) said humans have five basic types of needs: physiological, security, acceptance, self-esteem, and self-actualization. These needs are extremely important in both understanding the motivations of and in motivating people. Discipline and termination interviews, for example, can threaten the very basic physiological, security, and acceptance needs of individuals. Such interviewees will be motivated, therefore, to defend themselves in any way possible. Very often you can understand a person's needs by examining his or her environment and past experiences.

Principle #4: Needs May Be Conscious or Unconscious.

People are not always aware of their needs. One of the first jobs of a counseling or diagnostic interviewer may be to uncover the needs of a client. Such an interviewer may have to probe very deeply to discover respondents' needs and hence their motivations. Interviewers have been known to hypnotize interviewees in order to discover unconscious needs.

Principle #5: Needs Have Both Logical and Emotional Elements.

Many interviewers tend to think that people will always behave in the most logical and rational way when given a chance. This is far from the truth. Some authors, in fact, feel that in most cases the emotional elements are stronger than the logical ones:

Neglect of the truism that emotion transcends reason usually results in futile arguments with patients, clients, and students. A rise in blood pressure is often the sole outcome for both interviewer and interviewee.

(Fenlason, 1952, p. 72)

Principle #6: A Person's Needs Can Distort Their Perceptions and Recollections.

People are willing to do almost anything to protect their own self-centered universe. Confusion, distortion, and omission either to perceive or remember information are ways of protecting themselves. They will try to minimize the pain and maximize pleasure in their universe. Whatever threatens to increase their needs will be resisted, and whatever offers to reduce their needs will be accepted even if the information has to be distorted to fit their desires. A threat to one's needs is a threat to ego and self-image.

Principle #7: People Need the Recognition, Acceptance, and Approval of Others.

This principle refers to the belongingness need mentioned earlier. Humans are social animals. They enjoy talking with others and will do almost anything to please others they like. This is why people have a tendency to conform to the beliefs, values, and attitudes of those around them. Kahn and Cannell (1957) called this tendency *intrinsic motivation*. Intrinsic motivation refers to the desire on the part of interviewees to help interviewers. Often interviewers are surprised to find that many respondents simply like to express themselves with no ulterior motive to change or influence anything. It is dependent, however, upon how respondents perceive the interviewer. To achieve intrinsic motivation you must be perceived as a person who will understand, accept, and value what people are saying.

Principle #8: People Have a Need to Organize and Structure the World.

In effect this principle means that people need to know, to gain knowledge and understanding. In some ways this aspect of human nature is valuable for the interview process. It makes people want to interview and be interviewed by other people. The interview is one of the best ways to gain knowledge about the world.

However, this need to organize and structure the world also has drawbacks for the interview process. These drawbacks occur mostly in the form of stereotypes. A *stereotype* is a generalization people make about similar objects, people, or ideas. In order to understand the world we all have a tendency to simplify it. By stereotyping we can easily think about large groups of things without the need to individualize them. Hence, referring back to the first principle, interviewers have a tendency to think of different people as being alike. Stereotyping can cause problems for both interviewers and interviewees.

Principle #9: People Have a Need to Influence the World.

People can only satisfy needs by influencing either themselves or the world around them. This is why some experts suggest that all communication has an element of influence attached to it. This desire to influence the world is the basis for what Kahn and Cannell (1957) call extrinsic motivation. *Extrinsic motivation* to take part in an interview is derived from the task or subject under discussion. Very often people take part in interviews to influence the person with whom they are interacting. Interviewees only become extrinsically motivated when they see the purpose and subject of the interview as relevant to a task or change they desire, and secondly, perceive the interviewer as someone with the ability to bring about the desired goal or to handle the situation in the manner they believe most desirable. Very often, interviewees will not see these connections, and it is your responsibility, as an interviewer, to point out how answering your questions will benefit them. In a door-to-door research interview, for example, the interviewer must convince potential respondents to answer questions even though they are busy with other things. They must be told how answering your questions can help them achieve some goal they desire such as better roads, schools, or city services. In this case you must appear to have some connection with government or other authorities who can bring about the changes recommended by respondents.

Principle # 10: Constructive and Lasting Changes Usually Come from Satisfying, Successful Experiences.

This last principle suggests that people normally react better to pleasure than to pain. They are motivated more by approval than by exhortation and censure. For the most part, then, people will learn and remember something better if they discover it on their own than if someone attempts to force it on them. In order to utilize this principle many interviewers refrain from any directive comments, choosing instead to indirectly lead respondents to do something which they can then praise. This is not always possible, however, as you will discover later in this chapter, but it certainly should be tried whenever feasible.

This section on human nature has barely scratched the surface of the general information needed to adequately prepare for an interview. You will discover other basic principles of human nature as you continue to read this book. Very often those people who do the best job of interviewing use common sense based on their past experience and a firm knowledge of how and why people behave as they do.

Understanding Yourself

Once you feel you have a preliminary grasp of human nature in general, you must become more specific and examine yourself. Regardless of whether you are the interviewer or interviewee, your own needs, values, and motivations will have an important effect on the interview outcome. The difference between two computers exchanging information and two people exchanging information is that people have individual and unique personalities which can help or hurt the interview.

You can begin to understand what effect this subjective aspect of an interview has on the outcome by first examining yourself. You must be willing and able to look at yourself as the other participant will. Recognize that your own motivations and personality are based on your own inner needs and strivings and that they will have a direct effect on your presence within the interview and interview success.

Many beginning interviewers attempt to hide behind a mask and play the role of someone different from themselves. You must be totally honest with yourself. This means becoming *aware* of your own prejudices and anxieties prior to entering an interview. Such questions as "Will the interviewee/interviewer like me?" "Will I like the interviewer/interviewee?" "Will I understand the interviewer/interviewee?" and "Can I accomplish my goal?" produce anxieties which everyone faces before their initial plunge into an interview. If you are not aware of your own shortcomings and anxieties, you can easily bias other aspects of the interview, such as how you ask and respond to questions, record information, probe, summarize, and follow-up. You must be willing to give of yourself openly and honestly to the interview, if you expect the other person to do the same.

One of the most important attitudes you should look for within yourself is *tolerance*, an acceptance of all types of people. You must determine your ability to discuss and interact with individuals, even though you may not like them personally. Skillful interviewers are willing to overlook the faults and shortcomings of others in order to conduct a satisfying and productive interview. They also have a true desire to *help* interviewees. Respondents are on the lookout for those who offer false promises of help. Skillful interviewers are also *trusting* people. They trust interviewees to give them the information they want openly and honestly. Respondents will seldom trust someone they perceive as having little or no trust in them. Some types of interviews, such as counseling and diagnostic interviews, demand a great deal of trust while others require less. Interviewers must also trust their own ideas and feelings as they occur within an interview. To do this, you will need to understand yourself—both your strengths and weaknesses—and your own expectations and feelings regarding the interview. Unsure, hesitant interviewers seldom achieve high quality results.

As an interviewee, you must examine your feelings about interviews in general. Many respondents enter an interview with a great deal of fear and anxiety. You should view an interview as a place to meet new people, discover new ideas, probe your own knowledge, and improve yourself. In other words, skillful respondents enjoy interviews and see them as potential sources of reward. This positive mental attitude helps determine your interview satisfaction. People who enter a selection interview fearfully rather than confidently will often find they aren't offered the job.

Preparing Yourself

Once you have come to understand yourself—your personality, motivations, and biases—you can begin to prepare yourself to be a skillful interviewer. There are two major parts to interviewer training: learning the theory and actually practicing the various skills. You will find in this book much of the theoretical orientation you will need in order to be successful. The practice and "real life" training necessary to sharpen your interviewing skills is something you must develop within the classroom and out in the interviewing environment. An active balance of theory and practice is the best way to learn to interview.

Preparing yourself means not only recognizing your faults but also being *willing* to *correct* the shortcomings that could introduce bias into the interview. For example, if you discover that you are shy, intolerant, dogmatic, or prejudiced, you must try to either change those personality characteristics or control them while participating in an interview. This is perhaps the hardest part of personal preparation.

Selling Yourself

If you know yourself and have prepared yourself for an interview, you are ready to sell yourself to the other participant. You need to convince them that you are the type of person they'd like to interact with. Interviewees are usually only willing to give information to those people whom they like, trust, and respect. It is up to you, when an interviewer, to convince interviewees that you are that type of person. In the same fashion, interviewers such as employers, doctors, therapists, police officers, and social workers are more willing to help interviewees whom they like, trust, and respect.

One of the most important ways in which you can sell yourself is by appearing credible. *Credibility* is based on the other person's perception of your competence, trustworthiness, and dynamism. *Competence* refers to your knowledge or expertise with regard to the topic under consideration. Competence is especially important for interviewers—this is why they spend so much time preparing. Interviewees also like to appear competent. The more competent a respondent appears in selection, performance, information, and research interviews, the more likely the interviewer is to accept and trust the information given. Since the main purpose of an interview is to exchange information, the more competent each participant appears to the other, the greater the chance for a successful interview.

Trustworthiness refers to your personality or character. A person who is trustworthy is perceived as reliable, honest, and believable. Someone who is perceived as being competent must also be thought to be trustworthy. This means you not only possess the necessary information but are willing to give or request it in a straightforward, complete, and honest manner. Both participants must sell the other on their trustworthiness as well as their competence.

Dynamism is a more elusive concept to grasp and portray in an interview. It relates to your general presence. Both interviewers and interviewees like to interact with others who are enthusiastic, interested, and concerned. Persons who appear bored and indifferent, even if they are competent and trustworthy, will not necessarily be perceived as credible. Doctors lose credibility, for example, when they ask questions in a monotone without looking up from their notes. This is sometimes referred to as poor "bedside manner." Dynamism shows up in tone of voice, facial expression, eye contact, touch, and many other nonverbal behaviors. It has been shown that patients are more likely to follow the advice of doctors who appear interested and concerned (Milmoe, et al., 1967).

All three of these credibility factors must be communicated early in an interview. You must sell the other participant on your competence, trustworthiness, and dynamism. You can do so only if you are aware of the importance of credibility and prepare yourself well. All of these factors—knowing yourself, preparing yourself, and selling yourself—are essential aspects of general interview preparation.

SELF-ANALYSIS EXERCISE

Directions: Below is a series of credibility scales. Fill out the first set of scales as you see yourself. Rate yourself as you think others see you on the second set of scales. Have a friend rate you on the third set of scales. Finally, on the fourth set of scales have someone you just met rate you. At the end of this exercise you will be given further instructions.

Analysis #1

Experienced __: __: __: __: __: __: __ Inexperienced

Reliable __: __: __: __: __: __: __ Unreliable

Enthusiastic __: __: __: __: __: __: __ Unenthusiastic

Skilled __: __: __: __: __: __: __ Unskilled

Honest __: __: __: __: __: __: __ Dishonest

Interested __: __: __: __: __: __: __ Uninterested

Informed __: __: __: __: __: __: __ Uninformed

Trustworthy __: __: __: __: __: __: __ Untrustworthy

Concerned __: __: __: __: __: __: __ Unconcerned

Analysis #2

Experienced __: __: __: __: __: __: __ Inexperienced

Reliable __: __: __: __: __: __: __ Unreliable

Enthusiastic __: __: __: __: __: __: __ Unenthusiastic

Skilled __: __: __: __: __: __: __ Unskilled

Honest __: __: __: __: __: __: __ Dishonest

Interested __: __: __: __: __: __: __ Uninterested

Informed __: __: __: __: __: __: __ Uninformed

Trustworthy __: __: __: __: __: __: __ Untrustworthy

Concerned __: __: __: __: __: __: __ Unconcerned

Analysis #3

Experienced __: __: __: __: __: __: __ Inexperienced

Reliable __: __: __: __: __: __: __ Unreliable

Enthusiastic __: __: __: __: __: __: __ Unenthusiastic

Skilled __: __: __: __: __: __: __ Unskilled

Honest __: __: __: __: __: __: __ Dishonest

Interested __: __: __: __: __: __: __ Uninterested

Informed __: __: __: __: __: __: __ Uninformed

Trustworthy __: __: __: __: __: __: __ Untrustworthy

Concerned __: __: __: __: __: __: __ Unconcerned

Analysis #4

Experienced __: __: __: __: __: __: __ Inexperienced

Reliable __: __: __: __: __: __: __ Unreliable

Enthusiastic __: __: __: __: __: __: __ Unenthusiastic

Skilled __: __: __: __: __: __: __ Unskilled

Honest __: __: __: __: __: __: __ Dishonest

Interested __: __: __: __: __: __: __ Uninterested

Informed __: __: __: __: __: __: __ Uninformed

Trustworthy __: __: __: __: __: __: __ Untrustworthy

Concerned __: __: __: __: __: __: __ Unconcerned

SCORING DIRECTIONS: Number the scale positions as shown below:

Experienced _1_ : _2_ : _3_ : _4_ : _5_ : _6_ : _7_ Inexperienced

Enter your score from each analysis on the following form:

Scale	#1	#2	#3	#4	Average
Experienced					
Reliable					
Enthusiastic					
Skilled					
Honest					
Interested					
Informed					
Trustworthy					
Concerned					
TOTAL					

Now enter your average score for each scale in the appropriate place and the total for each analysis at the bottom. Now figure your total competence, trustworthiness, and dynamism scores below. You can find them in the following manner: *Competence Score* = Experienced Score + Skilled Score + Informed Score (for each analysis). *Trustworthiness Score* = Reliable Score + Honest Score + Trustworthy Score (for each analysis). *Dynamism Score* = Enthusiastic Score + Interested Score + Concerned Score (for each analysis).

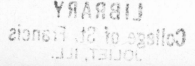

Scale	#1	#2	#3	#4	Average
Competence					
Trustworthiness					
Dynamism					

Analyze what this data means to you. Try to answer the question, "How Credible Am I?"

SPECIFIC PREPARATION

The preceding sections on understanding human nature and yourself are both general areas of preparation which can be done far in advance of an interview. The following two preparation areas—understanding the interviewer/interviewee and understanding the subject—are different for each interview.

Understand the Interviewee/Interviewer

It has already been noted that people are different, have different needs and motivations, and should be treated as unique. An interviewer will seek to gather two types of information about an individual: objective and subjective. Objective information includes demographic data such as name, age, sex, height, weight, and background. Any factual information that is a matter of public record is included here also, such as credit rating, criminal record, previous employment, and health history.

Objective information about an individual can be gathered from documents, observation, or third person interviews. *Documents* include birth certificates, school or health records, supervisor ratings, test profiles, legal contracts, military service forms, credit statements, employment applications, or any other type of written information. There is a great deal of information about each of us contained in documents which are accessible to a potential interviewer/interviewee. Good interview participants examine as many relevant documents as possible before an interview.

Objective information can also be gathered by *observing* a person in settings outside of the interview. Very often, for example, before a performance interview, it is possible for a superior to go out into the work area and observe subordinates to gather some first-hand objective information. It might be useful to see who, within the organization, the employee talks with most often. The superior could also observe the subordinate's general work routine. When feasible, observation can yield a great deal of useful information about an interviewee. For some interviews, however, it is not possible to observe the interviewee beforehand. Diagnostic and research interviews, for example, are of this type. When possible, however, interviewers should try to gather some objective information by observing the interviewee prior to the interview.

A third way in which you can obtain information about future respondents and interviewers is through *third person interviews*. You might ask for information from friends, previous employers, other interviewees/interviewers, or anyone else who knows the individual well. These individuals can often supply a great deal of objective (as well as subjective) information. The objective information to be known about each participant will differ, of course, depending upon the type of interview and the interview subject. Gathering objective information is important because it allows you to gain some insight into the other person's frame of reference and better prepare questions and responses to achieve the interview purpose.

Respondents can also get to know an interviewer ahead of time. This is not always an easy task. In many interview settings, you are never really certain who the interviewer will be. There are, however, some settings where it is possible to get to know the interviewer. Again a performance interview, where an employee is being evaluated by a superior, is one example. You should try to get to know your employers beyond the superficial information that you normally receive through the job. You should get to know something about their attitudes, beliefs, feelings, and general view of the world through observation, documents, or third person interviews. All possible ethical means should be used to gather information about an interviewer. Any information you can obtain ahead of time might be important during the course of the interview.

When you are the person about whom objective information is being gathered, you should be sure that all such information is accurate. Continually update all documents that pertain to you. Review all documents that are relevant to an interview purpose. When you know you might be observed, be on your best behavior. There is little you can do to change what people report about you except giving them nothing negative to say. In a selection interview, for example, where collecting objective information is a common occurrence, interviewees usually are asked to supply names of references and relevant documents to support objective information given in an interview.

It is usually much harder to gather subjective information. Some can be gathered from documents, observations, and/or third person interviews. It is impossible, however, to get a complete picture of the subjective aspects of an individual simply from these sources of information, which aren't always reliable. A better way to gain this information is to try to take the other person's point of view. This ability to take someone else's viewpoint and imagine how that person will think and react is one of the most important abilities of skillful interviewers and interviewees.

To see the world as another sees it requires *anticipatory empathy*. Anticipatory empathy involves trying to guess what the other person's position will feel like, what that person will be thinking about during the interview, and finally, the type of person to which that individual will best respond. The ability to practice anticipatory empathy allows you to make subjective judgments about others.

Both objective and subjective information is important for beginning an interview because each facilitates interaction. If you know as much objective information regarding other participants as possible and have made some accurate guesses as to their subjective point of view, the interview itself will generally move smoothly.

OBJECTIVE/SUBJECTIVE QUESTION EXERCISE

Directions: Identify each of the following questions as either objective or subjective. You will find the correct answers at the end of this chapter.

1. What is your name?
2. How old are you?
3. Where were you born?
4. Did you like your hometown?
5. What are your parents' names?
6. Did you get along with your parents?
7. How many brothers and sisters do you have?
8. Have you ever been in the military?
9. Have you ever been convicted of a crime?
10. Why did you apply for this job?
11. Do you have any location preferences?
12. Have you ever done this kind of work before?
13. Which of your previous jobs did you like best?
14. Why did you like that job best?
15. Why did you leave that job?
16. What kind of starting salary are you looking for?
17. What are your major strengths?
18. Who recommended us to you?
19. What are your long-range career objectives?
20. Why should I hire you?

Understand the Subject

There is one more specific preparation step before you take part in an interview; you must gather some information regarding the subject of the interview. If, for example, as a lawyer you know that a client's difficulty involves dissolving a business partnership, you must become familiar with the details of contract law. If you are a journalist who is going to be interviewing a politician on a particular issue, you must spend some time researching that issue. These respondents will also be gathering information on the interview subject. Subject information can be found in books, magazines, newspapers, various documents that exist in a city or county hall, or in any number of other sources and locations. Subject research not only saves time during the interview, but also helps you understand what the questions or answers to questions mean.

Before you begin to gather information on a subject, however, you must have at least a general interview purpose. It is even better if you have already decided on the specific interview goal. A specific purpose will help focus your information gathering, as well as help you develop an interview guide. Different purposes can lead to different areas of subject research. Gordon (1980) makes this point clearly:

> *The purpose can be viewed in terms of the central focus of the* information *and in terms of the actual* purpose *for which the information is to be used. If the purpose of the information is to test theory, then the interviewer must be intimately familiar with the theory he is testing. If the purpose is to gather information as a basis for social action, the interviewer should know to what extent the alternative actions are predetermined and to what extent the purpose of the interview is to discover categories of possible action perceived by the respondents. If the alternatives are predetermined, then the interviewer should be familiar with what the alternatives are and their relationship to the specific objectives of the interview.*
>
> *(Gordon, 1980, pp. 487–8)*

Learn to separate relevant from irrelevant information—examine all aspects of the subject and eliminate those details which are irrelevant to the specific purpose. As you research a subject, jot down various general areas or topics to be covered and possible questions that could be asked regarding each topic to achieve the interview purpose. An interview *topic* is a relevant aspect of the subject that must be questioned before you can achieve the interview purpose. How you do this will be discussed in the following chapter. Questions are then prepared to accomplish the objective of each topic. At a minimum an interview guide must consist of two or three topics relevant to the interview subject and purpose.

There is no simple formula for narrowing the interview subject. Very often, this ability to select topics and questions only comes from experience.

> *The development of specific objectives for an interview depends not upon the application of techniques but upon ingenuity, insight, and experience of the interviewer. The determination of interview objectives is primarily a matter of getting insights and hunches as to what things may be important in explaining the problem to be solved, or what factors may be related to the broad question which constitutes the purpose of the interview.*
>
> *(Kahn & Cannell, 1957, p. 98)*

A beginning journalist, for example, goes into an interview with only a general idea of the information which can be obtained from an interviewee. The more experienced journalist, on the other hand, has a much more specific idea of what kind of information interviewees possess and how willing they will be to disclose it. Because experienced interviewers usually have a much more specific purpose and have narrowly focused their research, they obtain more specific information, whereas beginning interviewers get more general and, therefore, less useful information.

Remember that *general questions get general answers*, while specific questions get specific answers. Gathering specific information on a subject usually leads to specific questions. For some it is impossible to gather a great deal of specific information ahead of time. This is especially true of interviews which are interviewee initiated. In medical interviews, for example, doctors seldom have time to do specific research for each patient. They have to depend on general information which is part of their professional training. Subject preparation is important no matter how much detail is possible. It is up to interviewers to be as knowledgeable about the subject as they can before beginning an interview.

CHOOSING AN INTERVIEW TIME ✓

When is the best time to conduct an interview? Some interviewers suggest early in the day, because interviewees are rested, more alert, and thus, better able to provide the information desired. On the other hand, there are interviewers who suggest conducting an interview later in the day allows interviewees to go home and think about the information they have given and received.

Perhaps there is no best time to conduct all types of interviews. It varies from situation to situation. If the interview is one which could potentially have a negative effect upon the interviewee (such as a performance or discipline interview), it might be better to have it late in the day, so that interviewees can absorb and react to the information received in their own homes. If the interview is one of simple information gathering, it would probably be better handled in the morning when the interviewee is fresh and rested.

Whatever the case, the time for an interview should be *mutually* acceptable to both parties. It should be a time that has been negotiated between you and the interviewee prior to scheduling the interview. If you are conducting a series of interviews, you must be sure you have time between them to collect your thoughts and record any final information or impressions about each one. Although some interviewers give little consideration to the timing of an interview, it can have a profound effect on interview success.

THE INTERVIEW SETTING ✓

Selecting a setting where an interview will take place can also have important consequences. The interview setting can either encourage or discourage open, honest, and complete information exchange. Interviews conducted inside an interviewer's office, for example, are generally more threatening, and the interviewee is likely to be more defensive than those conducted outside an interviewer's office or in the interviewee's environment. Most interview types require a nonthreatening, relaxed setting to achieve maximum results. There are only a few interview types, such as a police interrogation, where the setting is deliberately chosen to make respondents uncomfortable.

No matter where an interview takes place, there are a number of things that you can do ahead of time to prepare the setting. Interviewees generally feel more at ease and responsive if they sit in comfortable chairs facing you without barriers such as desks or tables. If a desk or table is to be used, you should sit across the corner of the table facing respondents and not across the entire expanse of the table. Providing an ashtray, coffee, or a soft drink for interviewees helps produce a pleasant, informal environment.

The interview room should be well lit. "Homey" decorations such as plants, pictures, and soft colors help create a relaxed atmosphere. If an interviewer's desk is cluttered with papers, books, computer print-out sheets, and the like, interviewees may begin to feel anxious and apprehensive.

A most important aspect of the setting is that it be *private*. Interviewees have difficulty expressing themselves when other people are present or when the interviewer is continually being interrupted by a telephone or secretary. Many professional interviewers hang a "Do Not Disturb!" sign on the door as the interviewee enters. This is done not only to keep others out, but also to provide immediate assurance to interviewees that the conversation will indeed be private. Bad places to conduct an interview are out in the middle of a busy room or in the interviewee's work area if others are within hearing distance. One of the reasons, for example, that savings and loan associations have been so successful in luring clients away from banks is because each potential borrower is interviewed in a private room instead of at a desk out in the middle of a busy bank building.

SETTING EXERCISE

Directions: Pictured below are several different settings where an interview might take place. Assess what you think is good about each setting and what you think is bad. In some cases you may have to qualify your comments depending upon the type of interview taking place.

1.

2.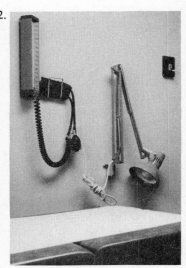

3.

PREPARE OPENING COMMENTS

The *icebreaking* portion of an interview is the opening minute or two, when you and the interviewee meet one another and begin to interact. The nature of interview icebreaking is highly dependent on whether the interview is initiated by the interviewee or interviewer. In an interviewee-initiated interview, very little icebreaking takes place. A simple "Hello, how are you?" is usually all that is needed. At that point, the interviewee will probably launch into the reason for the interview. A diagnostic interview, for example, is generally of this type. The interviewee has an objective in mind and is unwilling to spend too much time icebreaking.

On the other hand, if the interview is interviewer initiated, a greater amount of icebreaking usually is necessary to put the interviewee at ease. This can be done in a number of ways which will be discussed in the section on opening an interview. At this point, you should simply recognize that it is important to prepare icebreaking comments ahead of time. Icebreaking is usually successful if you have taken the time to gather information about the interviewee (or interviewer) beforehand. If you look for such information as hobbies, interests, or hometown, you can sometimes use these to break the ice. Questions such as, "Have you been skiing lately?" or "Did you see the Stones concert last night?" are good icebreakers.

The *orientation* portion of an interview opening lasts from icebreaking to the opening question of the interview. You should plan to inform respondents of several points before getting to the interview guide. In most cases, you will tell the interviewee (1) the purpose of the interview, (2) how the information gathered is to be used, (3) the degree of confidentiality, and (4) the nature of the roles that each participant will assume in the course of the interview. The orientation should be fully planned prior to beginning an interview.

In most cases, you should plan to be open and honest about the purpose of the interview. Even the most difficult interviews can be less threatening if you plan the purpose statement carefully. In a discipline interview, for example, you might begin by saying, "I understand you have been having some difficulties. I would like to talk with you about them and see if we can get the situation back on track." There are some cases, however, when interviewers would rather keep the true purpose of the interview hidden. This may be justified in research, counseling, and/or persuasion interviews where knowing the purpose could distort the information. In the large majority of cases, however, interviewees should be fully informed as to the purpose and nature of the interview.

Your orientation planning should also include some mention of how the information gathered will be used. If the information collected in a performance interview will be used to make promotion decisions, or the information from a research interview will be made public, the interviewee should be informed.

Confidentiality refers to whether or not the interviewee's name is to be used and how much information will be disclosed. Very often, people will answer questions differently if they know that their name is to be attached to the information they provide. If you tell an interviewee that the information you receive will be kept confidential, it is your moral responsibility to do so.

Finally, planning *roles* for both the interviewer and interviewee is an extremely important part of preparing to orient the interviewee. If you want interviewees to take some control of the interaction direction, such as in a counseling interview, then they ought to be informed. You should tell them if their questions will be allowed later in the interview or can be asked as they come to mind during the course of the interview. In selection interviews, for example, interviewers very often do the questioning during the first part of the interview and tell interviewees that they will be allowed to ask questions at the end.

Icebreaking and orientation preparation is so important that some interviewers will actually rehearse icebreaking and orientation comments in an attempt to make sure that they adequately prepare a respondent for the main body of the interview. The skill of interview opening, including icebreaking, orientation, and the opening question will be discussed in detail later.

CHOOSING THE INTERVIEW STRUCTURE

All interviews have a structure regardless of whether it is planned or develops naturally as the interview progresses. Interview structure should be determined very early in the preparation process. There are two basic types: directive and nondirective. *Directive* interview structure is highly interviewer-controlled whereas the *nondirective* structure is much more interviewee-controlled. In a directive interview, interviewers determine the purpose and develop a detailed interview guide to accomplish that purpose. In a nondirective interview, interviewers allow and sometimes even encourage interviewees to lead the interview in any direction they desire.

Each structure has advantages and disadvantages. A directive structure allows you to develop a detailed road map and timetable for the interview and can provide you with a sense of security. You have less chance of forgetting important bits of information or rambling. Generally, more material is covered in a directive interview than in a nondirective one. Directive structure is often used when you want to maintain some consistency between interviews.

On the other hand, directive interviews can become very mechanical. They often eliminate important content areas that interviewees might have brought up had they been given the opportunity. Directive interviews generally take more planning and preparation and they usually are more time consuming and harder for a novice interviewer, but they overcome many of the disadvantages of directive interviews. The nondirective structure is useful for certain types of interviews, especially those that are interviewee-initiated.

Interviews need not be totally directive or totally nondirective. A pleasant middle ground probably characterizes most good interviews. You must remember that directive and nondirective interview structures mark the two ends of a continuum. It is up to you, the interviewer, to plan where on that continuum your interview will fall. Later, in the section on the various types of interviews, some suggestions will be made as to the appropriate amount of structure for different interview types.

SUMMARY

Preparation is the first, and in many ways, the most important skill necessary for a successful interview. Often, interview participants do not spend as much time as they should in preparation. The nature and extent of interview preparation differs greatly depending upon the purpose of the interview, the interview topic, and the nature of both the respondent and the interviewer.

You should know as much general information about human nature and the interviewing process as possible. Remember, people are different; are conditioned by their environment and past experiences; behave on the basis of their conscious and unconscious, logical and emotional needs; often distort their perceptions and recollections; need recognition, knowledge, and influence; and learn best from successful experiences. Examine your own personality, motivation, and prejudices. When you find problems within yourself, they should be corrected by both personal and professional preparation on your part. The final step in general preparation is to plan how you will sell yourself.

The next step is to gather specific objective and subjective information about the other participant. Use documents, observation, third-person interviews, and then put yourself in the other person's shoes. Finally, you need to gather information on the subject of the interview. Without subject information you are not prepared to achieve the purpose of an interview. All of this specific information will help you prepare the interview guide.

The timing and setting of an interview are also important parts of preparation. The timing of an interview depends on its purpose. The interview setting can be manipulated to create the proper atmosphere. Finally, you need to plan the opening. This includes icebreaking and orientation. Both are dependent on whether the interview structure is directive or nondirective.

ACTIVITIES

Activity #1

Directions: Call one of the people you listed in the introductory exercise who commonly uses interviewing in their jobs. Make an appointment to talk about preparing for an interview. Be honest and say you are trying to improve your own interviewing skills. If possible, try to contact someone who does a lot of preparation before an interview, such as a journalist, personnel officer, researcher, or manager. When you meet, ask about the following aspects of interview preparation:

1. Basic principles of human nature such as interviewer and interviewee needs and motivation.
2. How they understand, prepare, and sell themselves to respondents, including the three aspects of credibility: competence, trustworthiness, and dynamism.

3. What objective and subjective information they try to collect regarding a respondent.
4. How they go about collecting this information, do they rely on documents, observations, or third-person interviews.
5. How they go about researching the subject of the interview.
6. How they develop interview topics.
7. What they consider to be the best time for an interview, and how to schedule one.
8. What they do to prepare the setting, including comfort and privacy.
9. How they prepare their opening and closing comments such as icebreaking and orientation.
10. When they use a directive or nondirective interview structure.

You may have to explain some of this terminology to them, but generally the terms used in this book are common to most professional interviewers. Be sure to keep a record of the responses you receive. Also, since this is your first real interview since beginning the book, try to assess how well you performed as an interviewer. Don't be discouraged if you did not do as well as you would have liked; you are just beginning—you will get better. If you are using this book as part of a class or workshop, you will be asked to share the information you received and also how you think you did as an interviewer. If you are reading this book on your own, review your notes and use them to help you prepare for your next interview.

Activity #2

Directions: Find someone who you think would be willing to talk with you in a trusting and self-disclosing manner. If you are part of a class you may be assigned to a partner. Sit face-to-face with your partner. Try to get to know one another by asking for and disclosing information in a nonevaluative atmosphere. All of the data discussed will be kept strictly confidential. Each item must be taken in order. Don't skip any statements. Each of you must respond to each statement before continuing. Either of you may decline to answer any question. Stop the activity when either of you becomes uncomfortable or anxious. This activity is an adaptation of "Dyadic Encounter" found in *A Handbook of Structured Experiences for Human Relations Training*, by J. William Pfeiffer and John E. Jones (Volume 1, University Associates Press, 1969: pp. 97–107). Remember, take each item in order and both answer before going on.

1. My name is . . .
2. My titles are . . .
3. My marital status is . . .
4. My hometown is . . .
5. The reason I'm here is . . .
6. Right now I'm feeling . . .
7. When I think about the future, I see myself . . .
8. When I am an interviewer I usually feel . . .

9. When I am an interviewee I usually feel . . .
10. When I am feeling anxious I usually . . .
11. When I am the interviewee, I feel most comfortable when the interviewer . . .
12. When I am the interviewer, I feel most comfortable when the interviewee . . .
13. In ambiguous, unstructured situations I . . .
14. I am happiest when . . .
15. The thing that turns me on the most is . . .
16. Right now I'm feeling . . .
17. The thing that concerns me most about being an interviewee is . . .
18. The thing that concerns me most about being an interviewer is . . .
19. When I am rejected I usually . . .
20. To me, belonging is . . .
21. A forceful, directive interviewer makes me feel . . .
22. Breaking rules that seem arbitrary makes me feel . . .
23. I like to be just a follower when . . .
24. The thing that turns me off the most is . . .
25. I feel most affectionate when . . .
26. Toward you right now, I feel . . .
27. In an interview I usually get most involved when . . .
28. To me, taking orders from another person . . .
29. I am rebellious when . . .
30. In an interview, having an interview guide . . .
31. The emotion I find most difficult to control is . . .
32. My weakest point is . . .
33. I love . . .
34. I feel jealous about . . .
35. Right now I'm feeling . . .
36. I am afraid of . . .
37. I believe in . . .
38. I am most ashamed of . . .
39. I am prejudiced toward . . .
40. I am prejudiced against . . .
41. Right now this experience is making me feel . . .
42. The thing I like best about you is . . .
43. You are . . .
44. To be a skillful interviewee I think you need to . . .
45. To be a skillful interviewer I think you need to . . .

Activity #3

Directions: Think of two or three people in your vicinity for whom there is information available or who have information on a topic for which there is information available. Prepare to do an information interview. Before collecting the information, however, call each individual until you find one who is willing to talk with you about themselves or a particular topic once you have gotten somewhat further along in your knowledge of interviewing. In other words, you do not want to do a great deal of research if it's not going to produce an actual interview. The person you contact should NOT be someone you know well, like your father or mother or best friend. When doing this exercise in the past, students have contacted such people as the basketball coach, the mayor, a prominent professor on campus, local business leaders, and so on. They were all willing to commit themselves to an interview even though they knew it was a class project. You will be surprised how often important people will say, "yes." Once you have gotten everything arranged, begin your research on the individual, the subject, or both. Collect as much information as you can. Later activities will tell you what to with it right up to the point where you do the interview.

Answers to the Objective/Subjective Question Exercise:
1 = O, 2 = O, 3 = O, 4 = S, 5 = O, 6 = S, 7 = O, 8 = O, 9 = O, 10 = S, 11 = S, 12 = O, 13 = S, 14 = S, 15 = O, 16 = S, 17 = S, 18 = O, 19 = S, 20 = S. (O = Objective, S = Subjective)

Chapter 2

Skill 2
Developing the Interview Guide

In a sense, the interviewer uses the interview guide as a motorist uses a road map. It reminds him of possible routes to many objectives and is a convenient way of recording where he has been and what he has missed. (Gordon, 1980, p. 60)

An interviewer's preparation skill is reflected in the interview guide. If you have prepared properly and developed a good interview guide, you need not wonder where the interview will go next. It provides direction and allows you to maintain control. A well thought out interview guide also permits an easy flow of conversation and avoids confusion. In all interviews except the totally nondirective, you will want to guarantee coverage and a record of at least basic information. This requires an interview guide.

TYPES OF INTERVIEW GUIDES

An interview guide has two main functions: to help you accomplish the interview purpose and to provide a place for you to record information and impressions. There are a number of different types of interview guides that can serve these purposes. A detailed interview guide is used when the interviewer desires a directive interview structure. When the planned structure is nondirective a less detailed guide is normally employed.

A detailed guide is especially useful for beginning interviewers. As a general rule, the more novice the interviewer, the more complete the interview guide should be. A directive interview guide specifies possible wording and sequence of topics and questions, while less directive guides consist of a brief list of possible topic areas with little or no indication of sequence or specific questions to be asked for each topic. Until you become experienced enough to know what should happen in the interview and are able to compare that to what is happening, however, too much flexibility can cause you problems. Experienced interviewers use both types of guides depending on the interview type and purpose.

Nondirective Guides

Probably the least directive interview guide is a *blank sheet of paper*. It simply provides you with a place to record information and impressions. Such a guide assumes that you have no specific purpose or topics for the interview before it starts. You are merely acting as a tape recorder. Since very few interviews fit this criteria, however, this type of guide is seldom used. The counseling interviewer is about the only one who uses such a guide with any regularity.

Even the most nondirective interviewers generally have some basic purpose to accomplish. Sometimes the purpose develops as an interview progresses, at which time they jot down some topics to be covered and/or some questions to ask. For lack of a better term, this will be called an *in-progress interview guide*. In-progress interview guides are normally used in interviewee initiated interviews, such as a diagnostic interview. Interviewees come with a purpose in mind which you must discover. You then attempt to develop a guide while the interview is in-progress which will help accomplish that purpose. Nondirective interview guides are difficult to use because they require an ability to listen, record, and plan ahead all at the same time while the interview is taking place.

IN-PROGRESS INTERVIEW GUIDE EXERCISE

Directions: You are a helping interviewer who is meeting Mrs. Garcia for the first time. She has come to you for advice on her constant conflicts with her parents and her husband. She is extremely nervous and upset. She is under 30 years of age, good-looking, mentally alert, honest, and trusting. The following is what she tells you in her own words. You are to determine four topics you think you might develop as an in-progress interview guide.

1 "There is so much trouble at home I just don't think I can stand it anymore. I fight constantly with my parents and my husband. We fight about every-thing—clothes, friends, work, food, ideas, everything. My parents and my husband think I am too advanced; I think they are too old fashioned. My
5 parents came from Mexico. They believe in the old traditions. They have never been rich. When I was a child, my mother used to make all my clothes. I had to quit school after the eighth grade. I worked in a laundry. I got paid pretty good. The first fight I can remember with my parents was when I wanted to buy a new dress. My girl friends made me feel ashamed of my
10 homemade dresses. When I came home with the dress, my mother nearly fainted. She said, "Well, what next? Aren't you ashamed of yourself? You look like a street girl." She cried and said I was putting her in her grave. I told her I would wear her dresses to church, but that I had to look good to compete with the American girls. I turned over a lot of my money to my
15 parents, and pretty soon I began resenting that. Our biggest fights came when I wanted to date American boys. They did not approve of American

boys. I was miserable. I told them I did not want to marry these boys, and if they trusted me they would let me date anybody I chose. They said I was disgracing them. I finally did marry a Mexican man. He also believes in the
20 old ways. He believes he is the boss. In an American home the woman is looked up to, and naturally Mexican girls want to get as much recognition as is due to them. My mother and husband want me to have children, but I want to work some more first. My mother keeps telling me it is a sin not to have children. One time I told her that it was a sin to have more children
25 than people could afford like she did. You should see how my brothers are growing up. They have already been in jail. They are fighting and stealing all the time, and they treat my parents like they are dirt. With my husband it's gotten so bad that I don't even want to talk to him. I think he loves me, but he is so uninteresting. I feel sorry for him. I think I have ruined his life as well as
30 mine.''

Semidirective Guides

Semidirective interview guides consist of a simple listing of the *topics* to be covered. In a selection interview, for example, such a guide might include the following topics:
1. Experience
2. Extracurricular Activities
3. Future
4. Background
5. Education
These topics may or may not be taken in that order and the range and depth of each topic is unspecified. It is simply a reminder of the topics that need to be covered. A semidirective guide gives you a great deal of leeway as to the phrasing of original and follow-up questions for each topic. Flexibility is one of the important advantages of these interview guides. You can adapt questions to fit each individual respondent.

In most cases, semidirective interviewers at least have the topics sequenced, that is, put in some logical order, such as:
1. Background
2. Education
3. Experience
4. Extracurricular Activities
5. Future
A sequenced guide usually creates a smoother flowing interview. Topic sequencing does not force you to stick to that order, but at least respondents do not feel that you are picking topics at random. In the above example a somewhat chronological sequence provides a logical pattern which can be perceived by the interviewee. Other topic sequences are presented later in this chapter.

There are a great many problems which can arise when using such an abbreviated listing of topics even if they are sequenced. You can easily run out of time. You sometimes forget to ask important questions. Beginning interviewers often find themselves formulating questions rather than listening to a reply. When you do try to listen carefully to a response, there is often a prolonged silence while you prepare to ask the next question. Added to this, you also have the task of recording the response. There is just too much for most novice interviewers to do all at the same time.

This does not mean that beginning interviewers cannot use a semidirective guide, but only that the topics should be expanded. The following are two topics and their subareas taken from a suggested topic outline for a selection interview (Hariton, 1970). Space for recording notes has been eliminated from this example but would normally be included.

Education: College   Dates

                                     Why Picked

                                     Major and Minor, Why

                                     Best Subjects, Why

                                     Poorest Subjects, Why

                                     Efforts Required   Extracurricular

                                     Grades

                                     Class Standing and Size of Class

                                     Special Awards   Jobs

                                                                 In School

                                                                  Summers

                                     Career Plans

                                     Evaluation of Accomplishments

                                     Other Schooling

Work Experience   Company—When, Where, Why, How

                                     Assignments

                                     Salary Progression

                                     Best—Least Liked Duties, Why

                                     Accomplishments and Difficulties

                                     Why Leave

(Hariton, 1970, pp. 85–87)

This interview guide with its greater detail could be used by a beginning interviewer. You will notice that this expanded guide also includes some suggested questions.

Directive Guides

Directive interview guides contain both topics and questions. The following six questions that every beginning journalist learns, might be asked regarding each topic: Who? What? When? Where? Why? and How? These are called the five "W's" and an "H." They represent the basic facts a journalist should get from any source on any topic. The following is a portion of an even more expanded directive interview guide used in a nationwide research interview project on leisure activity.

1. *First, I'd like to get a general idea about the specific kinds of things you do for recreation or to relax. I have a list of activities people sometimes do. Please think back over the past month. As I read each activity, please tell me whether or not you have done it this past month. Did you:*
   a. *Go to a movie?*
   b. *Dine at a restaurant for pleasure?*
   c. *Go window shopping?*
   d. *Go to a theater or concert?*
   e. *Go on a picnic?*
   f. *Go hunting or fishing?*
   g. *Read for pleasure?*
   h. *Take a ride in an automobile for pleasure?*
   i. *Do gardening for pleasure?*
   j. *Participate in a civic or religious organization or club?*
   k. *Go for a walk or a hike?*
   l. *Go to a professional, college, or high school sports event?*
2. *Now, I have some questions about sports. Please think back over the past year. Did you:*
   a. *Play badminton?*
   b. *Play basketball?*
   c. *Go bowling?*
   d. *Play football?*
   e. *Play golf?*
   f. *Play racketball, handball, paddleball or squash?*
   g. *Play softball or baseball?*
   h. *Swim?*
   i. *Play tennis?*
3. *In the last week, about how many hours a day did you watch television?*
4. *About how many hours a day did you listen to the radio?*
5. *And about how many hours a day did you listen to records or tapes?*
6. *In general, how important to you are the activities which you do in your leisure time or for recreation? Are they very important, moderately important, slightly important, or not at all important?*

(Bradburn, et al., 1979, 186)

Had you helped conduct this research interview, you would have been required to ask each question exactly as it is written. You would not have been allowed to paraphrase or repeat a question. Many directive interview guides do not require interviewers to read the questions verbatim from the guide. They must, however, be familiar enough with them to paraphrase each question to fit a respondent. This requires that you have a solid grasp and clear understanding of all questions so that you can reword a question and the answer can still be recorded in the proper place even if it comes earlier or later than expected.

The most directive interview guide of all is a questionnaire. It leaves nothing for an interviewer to do. In many cases respondents do not even see you; you simply mail the questionnaire to them. Questionnaires must provide their own motivation for respondents to answer the questions and there is no way to clarify confusing questions. You have all seen examples of questionnaires. People are constantly asking us to fill them out. In some ways it is not really even correct to call the questionnaire an "interview guide" because there is no actual oral interview.

A variety of interview guides are available, then, ranging from a blank piece of paper to a questionnaire which needs no interviewer. They can include topics alone, neither topics nor questions, or both topics and questions. The type of interview guide chosen should fit the interview setting, structure, purpose, and participants.

The recommended type of interview guide for your probable purposes includes six major features: topics to be covered; questions to complete each topic; possible probes (or follow-up questions); topics and question sequence; transition statements; notes relating to the opening and closing of the interview; and space to record responses.

TOPIC DEVELOPMENT

Since all interview guides grow out of the interview purpose, the first decision you need to make after determining the interview purpose is what topics need to be covered to accomplish that purpose. Several topics usually become evident during preparation. Sometimes the important topics are well known to almost all interviewers in that field, such as the selection interview guide example presented earlier. At other times, however, it is up to you, the interviewer, to discover the relevant topics through research. In every case, however, the interview purpose should always be your guide to topic development.

There is no set number of topics that need to be or can be covered in a single interview. In general, a good rule of thumb to follow is that if you need to cover more than five or six topics, you should consider scheduling two or more interviews. Most topics normally take approximately 10–12 minutes to cover adequately. Most interview participants (both interviewers and interviewees) are good for about a one hour interview. This hour long rule of thumb can change, of course, depending on the range and depth of each topic.

Preparing an interview guide is difficult and time-consuming work.

Topic Range and Depth

Topic *range* refers to how much *objective* information is to be gathered. For some topics a greater range of objective information needs to be gathered than for others. You should, however, always be alert to other information on a topic which may be brought up by an interviewee, which you had not even considered and which can increase the range. If an interview topic is too limited in terms of the objective information required, you should consider a broader topic and make each narrow information area into one or two questions within that larger topic. Respondents generally react negatively to a long list of topics and rapid topic shifts. This means covering a fairly broad range of information under each topic. In the selection interview example given previously, if you tried to cover experience or education under background, the topic would be too broad. On the other hand, if you tried to make academic subjects, grades, or special awards separate topics, the range of each would be too narrow.

Topic *depth* refers to the amount of *subjective* information required for each topic. It is possible to have a fairly narrow topic but desire a great deal of depth concerning an individual's feelings regarding that topic. Whereas a performance interviewer may want to know how employees feel about their job in general, discipline and termination interviewers may want specific and detailed information regarding employee attitudes about each individual aspect of their job.

There is no magic formula that can help you choose and develop the topics to be covered in an interview guide other than hard work. Most interviewers list all possible topics and then narrow or expand them later. Once you have some general idea of the topics you wish to cover for a particular interview you might ask yourself, "Are these the topics I need to cover to accomplish my interview purpose?" The answer to this question helps you determine what topics can be omitted and whether some important topics have been left out. Sometimes you will find that two or more topics can be merged into one. At other times you will realize you are trying to cover too much in one topic and must split it up into two or more topics.

Topic Sequence

Assuming you have selected the four or five main topics, you then need to determine how they relate to one another. Are the topics all parallel and distinct from one another? Or are there some topics that cannot be discussed until information about a previous topic is known? Sometimes you will see an obvious topic sequence, that is, an obvious order in which the topics should be discussed. At other times you will need to determine a rationale for the sequence in which you cover the topics.

There are six common topic sequences for most interviews: chronological, spatial, topical, difficulty, causal, and problem/solution. Those of you who have had some public speaking training will recognize these as common methods of organizing ideas in a speech. There is little difference in the way you order ideas to present them to an audience and the way you order topics to obtain information from an interviewee. The logic of information exchange is the same regardless of whether one is giving or collecting information. This list of topic sequences is not exhaustive; other sequences can be used, or these types can be combined, depending upon the interview purpose. However, these six methods of ordering topics are distinct and will be explained separately.

Chronological Sequence.

Topics sequenced chronologically are covered according to the *time* or *order* in which they occurred. A lawyer might use this sequence, for example, to determine what a client or witness was doing prior to, during, or after a particular event. A chronological sequence can cover years, months, weeks, days, minutes, or seconds. This usually becomes obvious once the topics are developed. A selection interviewer may question previous jobs in chronological order. A doctor may get a medical history in chronological order. A counselor may ask how a problem developed in chronological order. The chronological sequence is also useful because it is easily followed by interviewees. They see it as a natural order of questioning.

Spatial Sequence.

The spatial sequence is similar to the chronological sequence except that topics are taken according to their placement in *space*, not time. Geographical topics fit this pattern. A survey done at the University of Wyoming, for example, attempted to discover people's attitudes regarding shopping in various Wyoming communities. Each town, such as Rawlins, Laramie, Cheyenne, Casper, and Rock Springs became a major topic. Geographical areas are not the only topics that can employ a spatial sequence. Any time the spatial structure of anything is involved this sequence can be used. A doctor might use this sequence by asking first about a stomach ache, then dizziness of the head, then weakness of the knees, and so on.

Topical Sequence.

A topical sequence is useful when the interview purpose naturally falls into several *categories* or *classifications*. A pollster, for example, surveying attitudes about presidential candidates might list each candidate as one topic and ask the same questions about each. With the topical sequence it usually makes little difference which comes first, second, third, or last. Sometimes the order is altered to eliminate any bias that might occur because of topic placement. This sequence should not be thought of as a catch-all, but should be used only when a natural, but somewhat parallel, group of topics must be covered.

Difficulty Sequence.

When the purpose of an interview involves covering one or more topics that are relatively complex, the difficulty sequence should be considered. Using this sequence you cover the easiest topics first and work toward the most difficult. The difficulty need not lie in the objective information questioned, but can also relate to subjective difficulty such as marital or financial problems. This sequence allows you to relax respondents before tackling threatening or embarrassing topics. It helps develop interviewee confidence in their ability to answer the questions. The difficulty sequence is used a great deal in counseling, discipline, performance, and other interviews where interviewee anxiety is high.

Causal Sequence.

The main topics of a causal sequence deal with *cause* and *effect*. It is possible, using this sequence to move either from cause-to-effect or from effect-to-cause. An information interviewer, for example, covering some type of accident or disaster might begin by questioning the cause of the occurrence and then the effect or vice versa. The causal sequence is useful whenever you are trying to understand some event both in terms of what caused it and the effects it has or might have. Information, diagnostic, counseling, termination, and research interviewers often find themselves in this circumstance.

Problem/Solution Sequence.

The problem/solution sequence is very similar to the reflective thinking or problem-solving pattern described by John Dewey (1910). Dewey suggested that people should approach a problem by asking the following five questions:
1. What is the nature of the problem?
2. What are the causes?
3. What are the possible solutions?
4. Which is the best solution?
5. How can this solution be put into effect?
In interviewing, this sequence involves finding out the nature of a problem and then trying to help interviewees discover a solution. It is very popular in performance interviews. A supervisor first describes a job related problem, the employee responds and is probed, and then both work toward a mutually acceptable solution. The problem/solution sequence is also extremely useful for interviewee-initiated interviews where the interviewer does not understand the problem ahead of time.

Topic development is a very important part of interview guide preparation. It represents the transformation of raw information gathered from documents, observations, and third person interviews into a productive interview guide. It is not a good idea to develop questions until you have chosen, refined, and ordered the topics you wish to cover. This provides the skeleton or outline from which questions grow. A semidirective interview guide stops at this point, and the interviewer creates the questions to cover each topic during the interview. Regardless of whether you include questions in the guide or create them as the need arises during the interview, it is important that you know how to develop interview topics.

TOPIC DEVELOPMENT EXERCISE

Directions: You know the following information about Jane Hammond. Develop a semidirective interview guide which includes the topic sequence. You may make your guide as detailed as you think necessary.

Jane is an average-looking women of approximately thirty-two. Before she came to work for your company, she worked in a women's dress shop, but she became proficient at general office work very quickly. After a few months on the job, you suggested that she take the company's typing course in order to prepare herself for a higher-paying job. She did not do very well in the course, but she did qualify as a typist for the general secretarial pool, and then she came back to your office as an assistant office secretary. That's when her troubles began. A great many spelling errors turned up in her work, and you discovered she has a very limited vocabulary. You suggested she take the company's course in copy editing in hopes it would improve her spelling and vocabulary. She didn't want to do it at first, but later decided (based on your urging) to enroll in the course. You have just been told that she stopped attending the course after three lessons. She has not said anything to you about dropping the course, and you have called her into your office to discuss her performance, which has still not improved, and to ask about the course.

INFORMATION TYPES

Once you have determined what topics you will be covering in your interview guide, you must then begin to select those questions you believe will elicit the information you need on each topic. This means first identifying exactly what kind of information you desire. Dillman (1978) suggests that questions can usually be classified as requesting one or more of the following four types of information:
1. What people say they want: their *attitudes*

2. What people think is true: their *beliefs*
3. What people do: their *behavior*
4. What people are: their *attributes*   (Dillman, 1978, p. 80)

   Attitude questions will tell you how people feel about something or someone. They are basically subjective in nature. They are designed to get at information that cannot be gained any other way, that is, information that is in a respondent's head. You are asking if a respondent has a positive or negative attitude regarding the question topic or subtopic. Like all four information types, attitude questions can be asked in a variety of ways. The following are two examples of attitude questions:

   Should the military draft be continued?   Yes/No
   What do you think of the military draft?

   A *belief*, according to Dillman, (1978, p. 81) is an assessment of "what a person thinks is true or false." Beliefs differ from attitudes in so much as a belief does not imply a positive or negative judgment. Belief questions simply inquire whether an interviewee thinks something exists or does not exist. They tap a person's perceptions of the past, present, or future. If you ask them whether they think something is good or bad, you have asked an attitude question. Belief questions are more objective than attitude questions because you can often compare a respondent's perception of a thing with the actual thing as described by other sources such as documents, observations, or third person interviews. It is possible, however, to ask a belief question for which there is no objectively verifiable reality, such as, "Why did you decide to leave your husband?" You are asking the respondent why she believes she chose a particular course of action. She might respond with either a belief, "I found someone I liked better," or an attitude "He is a terrible individual." The following are two examples of belief questions:

   Is it fairly easy to obtain a divorce in this state?
   Do you think the increasing divorce rate is a sign of moral decay in
        America?   Yes/No

   Behavior questions are designed to discover "what people have done in the past, what they are currently doing, or what they plan to do in the future." (Dillman, 1978, p. 83) Whereas a belief question might ask how respondents *think* people are behaving, a behavior question asks how respondents *have* behaved, are actually behaving, or plan to behave. In this way, behavior questions are much more concrete and direct than belief questions. Past and current behavior can usually be objectively verified, and future behavior will be verifiable at some later date. A performance interviewer, for example, who receives a promise of changed behavior will be able to determine if the changes take place. The following are examples of past, present, and future-oriented behavior questions:

   Have you ever been drunk on the job?   Yes/No
   Are you currently drinking on the job?   Yes/No
   Do you think there are conditions under which you might be tempted to
        have a drink on the job?
        No
        Probably No
        Probably Yes
        Yes

Attributes are characteristics of individuals. These are sometimes referred to as personal or demographic information questions. Attributes that are important in performance interviews, for example, include leadership, initiative, cooperation, judgment, creativity, dependability, intelligence, motivation, decisiveness, responsibility, stability, self-control, maturity, loyalty, and integrity. In selection interviews there are certain attributes about which you cannot legally inquire such as age, sex, marital status, religion, and race. Some attribute information is collected in almost all types of interviews. The purpose of asking for attribute information is to more fully understand other kinds of information such as attitudes, beliefs, and behaviors. The following are two examples of attribute questions:

What is your present income level?
0–$5,000
$5,001–$10,000
$10,001–$20,000
$20,001–$30,000
$30,001–$50,000
Over $50,001
How old were you on your last birthday?

Distinguishing among the various types of information desired is important for a number of reasons. First, it helps you clarify the objective of each topic. Questions cannot be prepared until you know exactly what type of information you desire for each topic. Do you want to know how people feel, what they think is true, what they actually do, or what they are? A second reason for determining the type of information you want is that questions of each type need to be written differently. According to Dittman, attitude questions are more sensitive to wording variations than the other question types. Belief questions are the next most sensitive, while behavior and attribute questions are the least sensitive of all. Most people can respond easily about their actual behavior or attributes, although not always, especially if the information is considered embarrassing or threatening. The type of question you select must grow out of your interview purpose and each topic. Until you specify the type of information needed, however, efforts to select and write questions will be useless.

TYPES OF INFORMATION EXERCISE

Directions: Label each of the following questions using the code:
A = Attitude Question
B = Belief Question
C = Behavior Question
D = Attribute Question
The correct answers can be found at the end of this chapter.
1. Are you married?
2. How can we improve this company?

3. Who do you talk to most often in your job?
4. How well do you get along with your fellow workers?
      Very Well
      Fairly Well
      About Average
      Not Too Well
      Not At All Well
5. Why do most people resign in your department?
      Health Reasons
      Better Paying Job
      Trouble With the Supervisor
      Working Conditions
      Other
6. Why are you resigning your job?
7. Have you liked working here?
8. Do you consider yourself to be:
      A Republican
      A Democrat
      Independent
      Other
9. How satisfied are you with your present financial situation?
      Completely Satisfied
      Very Satisfied
      Moderately Satisfied
      Slightly Satisfied
      Not Satisfied at All
10. In general, would you say your health is:
      Excellent
      Good
      Fair
      Poor
11. Have you ever been convicted of a crime?
12. Is this statement true or false? "Masturbation is almost as common as kissing."
      True
      False

QUESTION STRUCTURE

Having decided on what type or types of information you want for each topic you are *almost* ready to begin writing questions. You must first consider the question structure. Question structure relates to the amount of specificity desired in a response. Some questions limit the possible responses while others place no limits on a response. You may have already noticed the differences in structure of the sample questions presented earlier in this chapter. Question structure is closely tied to interview structure; directive interviews normally contain fairly specific questions that limit responses, while nondirective interviews usually contain unrestricted questions. Unrestricted questions allow interviewees to determine the response limits. Valuable information can be gained by observing where and how respondents limit their answers.

Questions which limit or restrict possible answers are termed *closed* questions, and questions which do not limit or specify a response are called *open* questions. Open questions only restrict the content area of the answer. The following are examples of open and closed questions:

"Why don't you tell me something about yourself?"   (Open)
"Are you single, married, divorced, widowed, or separated?"   (Closed)
"How do you like school?"   (Open)
"Do you like school?"   (Closed)
"How are things going on your job?"   (Open)
"Things aren't going very well on your job, are they?"   (Closed)

Open Questions

Open questions are often used in the early stages of an interview and at the beginning of each new topic. They are valuable because they provide information regarding an interviewee's frame of reference, knowledge level, and priorities. An additional reason for using open questions at the beginning of an interview and for each new topic is that they are usually perceived as less threatening and easier to answer than closed questions. Open questions also encourage respondents to do most of the talking, and this allows you to observe their emotional state, vocabulary, prejudices, and stereotypes, as well as what they think is important regarding each topic. Open questions are also good for increasing the depth of a topic. When a preponderance of open questions is used in an interview, it is considered to be nondirective.

There are, however, a number of disadvantages to open questions—since open questions generally tend to give more control to respondents, it is more difficult to guide and control interview progress. Open questions allow interviewees to dwell on information areas with which you may not be concerned. Unrestricted questions can result in lengthy, rambling, and unorganized answers. They also require greater time and energy to record and analyze. Open questions sometimes have an unsettling effect on interviewees; many prefer to answer specific questions. With such an interviewee, you often get a brief answer to a broad question requiring many follow-up questions in order to get the desired information. Open questions are especially difficult for unsophisticated respondents since they place a heavy load on them to select and organize a response.

Closed Questions

Closed questions give you greater control. They allow you to specify answer range and depth. You can usually ask a lot of closed questions during an interview. Closed questions are valuable when a broad range of objective information is desired; you need not wait for interviewees to volunteer the information. Closed questions are easier for respondents to answer and interviewers to record and analyze. This becomes important when many comparable responses are needed such as in research interviewing. A closed question is easier for beginning interviewers to use.

But a closed question may elicit too little information, and require more follow-up questions. This is especially true of bipolar questions. A *bipolar question* is a closed question which offers only two answers, like "yes" or "no." Bipolar questions are frequently found in interviews and frequently misused. The underlying assumption of a bipolar question is that there are only two possible answers —"yes" or "no," "right" or "wrong," "happy" or "unhappy." An interviewee may not feel or believe completely one way or the other, and if you insist on a bipolar answer, you may not be getting an accurate indication of an interviewee's true feelings. You are forcing the interviewee to make a choice between two alternatives, neither of which is accurate. You should be very careful when using bipolar questions and examine each one carefully.

Bipolar questions are not the only type of closed questions. You have already seen several other types of closed questions in this chapter—closed questions with ordered answer choices, closed questions with unordered answer choices, and partially closed questions. A *closed question with ordered answer choices* offers respondents the choice of several gradations of a single dimension of some concept. These questions are almost as limited as bipolar questions. However, they lend themselves to several forms of sophisticated statistical analysis. They are useful for determining the intensity of attitudes, degrees of belief, or frequency of behavior. They are usually less demanding for respondents because the range of choices is limited. The following are two examples of such questions:

How do you feel about this statement? "Everyone should own insurance
    to protect their family."
    Strongly Agree
    Mildly Agree
    Neither Agree or Disagree
    Mildly Disagree
    Strongly Disagree
How often are you late for work?
    Once a Week or More
    Two or Three Times a Month
    About Once a Month
    Less Than Once a Month but Several Times a Year
    Once a Year or Less

Closed questions with unordered answer choices give respondents the choice of several independent alternatives, each representing a different concept. The choices do not represent gradations of a single dimension of a single concept. Each alternative must be weighed in an interviewee's mind against each other alternative. These questions are good for determining priorities or deciding among alternatives. They are more difficult for respondents than either bipolar or ordered answer choice questions, because they require a respondent to balance and evaluate various concepts. These are also very difficult questions to write because you must be sure to include all possible options. The following are two examples of closed questions with unordered answer choices:

Which of the following cities would you prefer to live in:
Philadelphia
Detroit
Chicago
New York
Los Angeles

Which of your fellow workers do you like best?
Bob Young
Mary Campagna
Carol Baker
Ed Schwartz

Partially closed questions are similar to questions with unordered answer choices except that respondents are offered the choice of rejecting all of the possible alternatives and adding one or more of their own. This is an attempt to be sure that all possible options are open to respondents and a natural compromise between an open and closed format. It allows the flexibility of an open question and still limits the response range. The following are two examples of partially closed questions:

Which of the following areas do you think is in need of the most
improvement in this company?
Salary
Working Conditions
Training and Development
Potential for Advancement
Other (Please Specify)

What is the most important attribute of a good supervisor?
Can Work Well with Anybody
Is Consistent in Relations with Others
Is a Clear Thinker
Is Unruffled in Emergencies or Crises
Please List as Many Others as You Can Think of

As you can see there are many varieties of closed questions, each of which has been designed to overcome one or more of the disadvantages of the basic closed question. Perhaps the most important disadvantage of closed questions is that they tend to be asked in rapid-fire succession. This can put interviewees on the defensive and make them anxious. Finally, the use of closed questions assumes that you already know the language level, knowledge level, and frame of reference of a respondent—a big assumption.

The type of question you use should be based upon the interview's purpose, structure, and topic range and depth, as well as your and the interviewee's personalities. In most interviews you will find that a combination of both open and closed questions allows you to get the desired scope and depth of response necessary for each topic.

QUESTION TYPES

The two general types of information which you will attempt to gain from an interviewee, objective and subjective, require different types of questions. Perhaps the best classification of both objective and subjective questions comes from Bloom (1956). Bloom's taxonomy of questions was designed to help teachers develop student understanding through questioning. This question taxonomy, however, also has value for all types of inquiry situations. Bloom divides questions into those dealing with the *cognitive domain*, those which elicit objective information, and those dealing with the *affective domain*, which elicit subjective information. In the following sections you will find, in abbreviated fashion, Bloom's classification of questions in each of these domains. By learning, understanding, and using Bloom's taxonomy in developing your interview guide, you will find you have a much better grasp of the questioning process.

Objective Questions (Cognitive Domain)

Bloom proposed six different types of objective questions to tap information in the cognitive domain: knowledge, comprehension, application, analysis, synthesis, and evaluation. Each of these question levels is a necessary prerequisite for the level which follows; that is, each succeeding level is more difficult for a respondent. It is important, therefore, that you learn the six question levels in sequence. It is useful in preparing an interview guide to develop questions about each topic following this suggested sequence. You should also note that it is possible to write questions at almost every level in either an open or closed form.

Knowledge Questions.
Knowledge questions, the first level of objective questions, are the basis of a greater understanding between you and an interviewee. They determine if respondents possess certain knowledge. Interviewees are not necessarily expected to understand the information or be able to make use of it, only be aware of it. You might ask, for example, if respondents have heard of a certain political candidate. They need not know what the candidate looks like or the candidate's philosophy—all you care about is recognition of the candidate's name. This does not mean that these are poor questions and that a stress on knowledge questions is bad. The effectiveness of all knowledge questions must be judged in relationship to the purpose of the interview. If your purpose is to determine an interviewee's data base, then knowledge questions are useful. They are also useful as a forerunner to later objective questions. If respondents do not have a certain knowledge level, it is useless to ask further objective questions. This first level of objective questions can inquire into knowledge of terminology, specific facts, conventions, trends and sequences, classifications, categories, criteria, methodology, principles and generalizations, and/or theories and structures. The following are some examples of such knowledge questions.
  1. (Terminology Knowledge) What is the meaning of the word "inflation"?

2. (Specific Facts Knowledge) The percentage of eligible voters voting in the last election was?

   About 50%
   About 90%
   About 70%
   About 40%

3. (Conventions Knowledge) What is the normal procedure for filing a grievance in this company?
4. (Trends and Sequences Knowledge) What events led up to this situation? (Consequences Knowledge) What effect do you think this decision will have on the company?
5. (Classification Knowledge) What are the major ethnic groups in this country?
6. (Categories Knowledge) How does management categorize workers in your department?
7. (Criteria Knowledge) How does the government determine if an organization is meeting the E.P.A. guidelines?
8. (Methodology Knowledge) What is the best method for determining if a person needs surgery?
9. (Principles and Generalizations Knowledge) Do you understand the principles underlying contract law?
10. (Theories and Structures Knowledge) How does the law of supply and demand operate?

Questions of knowledge are extremely important; they allow you to determine the range of interviewee knowledge. There are different levels and degrees of knowledge that can be questioned in an interview. The level of a knowledge question is not only determined by its wording, but also by the context in which it is asked and prior information presented. Knowledge questions are sometimes called *filter* questions because they filter out those people unqualified to answer further questions. That is why they usually come very early in an interview. They are easy to formulate and interviewers need very little practice to ask them.

Comprehension Questions.

Once you understand the range of interviewees' knowledge, you may begin to tap their comprehension of that knowledge. This is the lowest level of understanding, and does not imply complete understanding. Respondents are only asked to answer in such a way that you perceive some minimal grasp of the information. You test for comprehension by asking respondents to translate, interpret, or extrapolate from the knowledge they possess. The following illustrate questions of this type:

1. (Translation Question) In this company we use the phrase "equal pay for equal work"; in your own words, what does that mean to you?
2. (Interpretation Question) Explain what this graph tells us.
3. (Extrapolation Question) Estimate what you think will be the effect of this piece of legislation on inflation and unemployment rates.

Application Questions.

Once you are sure that respondents know and understand the topic area, questions may be asked which require application or abstraction of the information. Application questions allow interviewees to apply the knowledge demonstrated at the previous two levels. These questions generally require additional thinking time on the part of respondents. There are a wide variety of application questions, and they are often used to get respondents to apply information to a particular situation confronting themselves, the organization, the community, or the nation. Application questions can be either hypothetical or based on actual situations. The following are some examples of application questions.

1. Now that we have looked at your performance evaluation and discussed what it means, would you apply it to the planning of your future behavior?
2. You have said that you are in favor of bringing new industry into the community; looking at this map, show where you think would be the best possible locations for these plants?
3. You have said that there are a number of different reasons why you are leaving the company; if you were a member of management, what new policies would you develop in order to improve the situation and prevent others from leaving?

Analysis Questions.

Analysis questions are used to determine how respondents think—how they organize and structure information. Analysis questions help you and the interviewee separate fact from hypotheses, conclusions from supporting materials, relevant from irrelevant information, main from subordinate ideas, and to see how the ideas relate to one another. Analysis questions force respondents to break down statements into their various elements and to show how the various elements relate to one another. Analysis questions often help both interviewers and respondents clarify their thinking on the subject being discussed.

Logic is a very important part of analysis questions. Interviewees are asked to reach valid and accurate conclusions based upon inductive and deductive reasoning. *Inductive logic* is reasoning from specific information to broader principles and relationships. *Deductive logic* is just the reverse, and involves seeing specific conclusions in more general propositions. Inductive and deductive reasoning do not require interviewees to have a formal knowledge of logic, and in many cases, respondents operate logically without ever being aware that they are doing so. Bloom identifies three levels of analysis questions, each of which depends on and progresses from the other: elements, relationships, and organizational principles. The following are examples of questions of each type.

1. (Elements Analysis) The affirmative action recommendation which requires that the individual representing a minority should be given the first consideration when two people are equally qualified for a job, is based on which of the following assumptions?
   A. Minorities are more effective workers.
   B. Minorities have been discriminated against in the past.
   C. Minorities have a greater need for employment.
   D. People need to experience the views of minorities.
2. (Relationships Analysis) How do you think your problems at home are related to your problems on the job?
3. (Organizational Principles Analysis) What do you think was management's reason for establishing these rules?

Both interviewers and interviewees often have difficulty distinguishing between analysis and comprehension questions. According to Bloom, comprehension deals with information content, whereas analysis deals with both content and form. Much depends upon the context in which the question is asked. Some authors have suggested that a comprehension question is really asking for a "common sense" answer while an analysis question asks for a more rigorous logical response.

Synthesis Questions.

Synthesis questions represent the fifth level of Bloom's objective information taxonomy. They emphasize respondent uniqueness and originality. Whereas, previous question levels asked interviewees to answer within a framework provided by the interviewer, synthesis questions ask respondents to create the framework. Interviewees are given freedom to produce messages unanticipated by the interviewer, so interviewee responses are a product of their own unique ideas, feelings, and experiences.

It is very difficult to write a closed synthesis question. Synthesis questions normally do not take very long to ask but require a great deal of time to answer. It is not unusual for synthesis questions to produce mediocre answers, because at this level responses depend primarily upon an interviewee's ability, interest in the topic, and the time available for dealing with the question. This is the level at which respondents can really begin to test their own thinking. You should assist interviewees as much as possible, without biasing the response. Bloom divides synthesis questions into three subcategories primarily on the basis of the product: a unique communication, a plan or set of operations, or a set of abstract relations. Examples of each subcategory follow:

1. (Unique Communication Question) If we decided to hire you, where would you like to be in this company in ten years?
2. (Plan Question) Considering the social disorders and international terrorism which are taking place at the present time; can you offer a proposal which you think should be adopted by the government to handle these situations?
3. (Set of Operations Question) Can you suggest a series of steps which you think will encourage workers in the company to be more safety conscious?
4. (Abstract Relations Question) You say you have no prejudices. You advocate that minorities should be given opportunities equal to those of all others. However, a few months ago, after a black family moved into your neighborhood, you were disturbed and began to think about moving. How do you explain your behavior?

Evaluation Questions.

This is the last category of questions in the cognitive domain. Evaluation questions are a "floating" category because they can be used at each and every level of questioning. A respondent will usually be continually evaluating the interview exchanges, and in turn, you can ask about an interviewee's evaluation during the interview. Perceived threat, familiarity with the interviewer, degree of interview formality, and other factors affect a respondent's evaluation.

"Evaluations" are considered more thought-out than what we usually refer to as "opinions," although both refer to somewhat the same process. People are sometimes unaware of the reasons behind an opinion, but an evaluation reflects an appraisal based on conscious criteria. These criteria can be either internal or external. Some examples of evaluation questions requiring internal and external evidence are:

1. (Internal Evidence Question) Senator, how is your current vote against the continuation of the Department of Education consistent with your campaign promise to improve the quality of education for children in your district?
2. (External Evidence Question) All things considered, how would you compare your job efficiency to that of the other people in your office?

Evaluation is the last objective type of question, but it is an important link to the set of subjective questions too. Subjective questions deal with attitudes, values, liking and disliking, enjoying and hating, while the emphasis in evaluation questions is primarily cognitive.

It is one thing to read about questions at the several cognitive levels and to study examples; it is quite another to create such questions. In order to get a handle on questions at the various cognitive levels, you should examine the sample questions. What are the major features of questions at each level or sublevel? With what words do questions at each level start? How are the questions at various levels different? What are the situations in which certain questions might be asked?

It is easy to recognize questions when they are grouped together in cognitive levels; it is a lot harder to pick out question types when they are not labeled. The following exercise should help you learn to recognize the various types of objective questions. Remember, that questions asked in isolation may be easily misclassified. The level of a question is in part determined by the context in which it is raised as well as the intent of the question. You may find, therefore, that your answers do not always agree with those given at the end of the exercise. That is all right; if you think your judgment is sound, you have not necessarily misclassified the statement. But try to understand the context in which the question could be labeled the way it is in the exercise. Remember, the form of the question has nothing to do with its cognitive level.

OBJECTIVE QUESTION EXERCISE

Directions: Label each of the following questions using this code:

A = Knowledge Question   B = Comprehension Question
C = Application Question   D = Analysis Question
E = Synthesis Question   F = Evaluation Question

Answers can be found at the end of this chapter.
1. When employees state that they take small items purchased by the company for use at home because it is standard operating procedure (S.O.P.), these people are:
    Behaving as Mature Adults
    Experiencing a Delusion
    Acting in a Childish Manner
    Rationalizing

2. You have been telling me that a great many of your problems stem from difficulties you are having at home; how might you categorize those problems?
3. Do you understand "supply side economics"?
4. If you could, how would you change the criteria for determining promotions in our company?
5. Of the two methods of solving problems which we have discussed, which would you judge to have the best chance of succeeding?
6. How would you describe the work atmosphere in this company?
7. On the basis of what we have said here today, what do you think you will do differently in the future?
8. Do you think the information you presented earlier is in line with what you are telling me now?
9. Judging from what you have told me about the situation, what kind of case do you think the prosecuting attorney will present when you go on trial?
10. Why should I believe your story instead of the one an eyewitness told me?

Subjective Questions (Affective Domain)

Subjective questions deal with the feelings, attitudes, and values of a respondent. You will just as often be interested in subjective information as you are in knowledge, comprehension, application, analysis, synthesis, and evaluation. You shouldn't expect to make a clear-cut distinction between information in the cognitive and affective domains. It is almost impossible for interviewees to process objective data without some subjective or affective response as well. As an interviewer, you must constantly keep in mind that you are dealing with both domains at all times. This taxonomy of questions in the affective domain is once again taken from the work of Bloom and others who helped with the taxonomy project. Questions in the affective domain consist of five levels: receiving, responding, valuing, organization, and characterization. Once again the sequence is very important.

Receiving (Attending).

Receiving relates to how closely a respondent will attend to the subject under consideration. You want to know whether or not they have enough interest in the topic to pay attention. This is the first subjective determination of an interview topic. Respondents can range from being extremely passive, leaving much responsibility for question success with the interviewer, to extremely active. Each of the following levels of questions is designed to determine the degree of interviewee willingness to attend to or receive and answer questions at that level.
1. Are you aware of why we are conducting these interviews?
2. Our company is bringing in an expert on safety standards to talk to all employees. Would you be willing to listen to what she has to say?
3. Of the five topics I have just mentioned, which would you prefer to discuss first?

Receiving or attending questions are extremely important because a successful interview requires at least a minimum level of interviewee interest. People's values and emotions are reflected in what they choose for attention and reception. Receiving questions help you identify those subjective areas or topics which may cause problems later. They filter interviewees for further subjective questions, just as knowledge questions filter respondents for later objective questions.

Responding.

Responding questions also help determine if interviewees are willing to become sufficiently involved in the topic to make its discussion worthwhile. Receiving questions have already determined respondent willingness to listen. Responding questions measure how willing interviewees are to commit themselves in some measure with a response. Responding questions can go beyond the interview itself and ask if an interviewee would also be willing to comply or do something after the interview is over—with a little urging. Respondents need not volunteer, but if asked, would they agree to make the attempt? There are several levels of responding, from responses due only to interviewer pressure to response for the pleasure or enjoyment to be gained by the interviewee. The following are some examples of various levels of responding questions.

1. Hello, I am Officer Jones from the County Sheriff's office. I would like to ask you a few questions about the automobile accident in which you were involved. May I do so now?
2. I think your problem is beyond the scope of this interview; perhaps you should consult a specialist in this area. If I called and set up an appointment for you and reminded you just before the appointment, would you go and explain your problem to the specialist?
3. Mrs. Smith, you have been coming to me for counseling now for over three months. Do you think our sessions have been helping you?

The first goal of many interviews is simply to get the interviewee to provide information. Noting an interviewee's willingness to respond is an important part of the skillful interviewer's job. Responding is important not only in the interview proper, but it also predicts post-interview behavior, which can be just as important.

Valuing.

Valuing questions are used to determine interviewee attitudes, beliefs, or values. In tapping the affective domain, it is important to get some idea of what values and attitudes a respondent holds because this knowledge helps you prepare the opening, sequencing topics and questions, and interview probing.

. . . (Valuing) is employed in its usual sense: that a thing, phenomenon, or behavior has worth. . . . Behavior categorized at this level is sufficiently consistent and stable to have taken on the characteristics of a belief or an attitude. . . . An important element of behavior characterized as valuing is that it is motivated, not by desire to comply or obey, but by the individual's commitment to the underlying value guiding the behavior.

(Krathwohl, et al., 1964, p. 180–181)

If you know a respondent's values and attitudes, then it is possible to

61

anticipate potentially embarrassing and threatening topics and questions beforehand. Such knowledge can also help you predict the response of the interviewee both during the interview and after the interview is concluded. There are several subcategories of valuing questions, each of which asks for varying levels of commitment to a value from mere acceptance to value preference and, finally, value commitment. The following are examples of each:

1. There is an old saying that "honesty is the best policy." Do you accept that statement?
2. Education is worthwhile.
   Agree ____: ____: ____: ____: ____ Disagree
3. Rank order each of the following activities according to which you would do first (#1), second (#2), third (#3) and so on:
   Eat, Sleep, Party, Work, Exercise, Read.
4. You say that your religious beliefs prevent you from accepting any form of medical attention. If I said that your child will probably die without medical attention, would you be willing to allow the child to accept such treatment?

As with most subjective question categories, the distinction between the various levels of valuing questions is a matter of degree rather than kind. Questions aimed at value preference really differ from questions aimed at value commitment only from the standpoint of intent and certainty. Distinctions based on intent and degree of certainty are often unclear and difficult to separate. Valuing questions often begin by asking interviewees if they have done something or if they accept or agree with something as encountered.

Organization.

Organization questions represent an attempt on the part of interviewers to tap the underlying value *system* of interviewees. Value systems develop gradually and change slowly. You try to explore how the system is organized, the interrelationships that exist between various values, and which values seem to be the most important. In some cases, you will find a coherent and consistent value system; in other cases you will find a value system which is not well formed. You may discover that it fluctuates depending on the interviewee's state of mind and the environment. You may even find a somewhat new value system develops during the course of the interview, either with or without the conscious intent of the interviewee. The following are examples of questions designed to tap the organization of respondent value systems:

1. *You say you believe in total honesty, yet you are willing to take certain objects from your place of employment such as pens, paper clips, cellophane tape, and so forth; how do you reconcile this belief with your behavior?*
2. *In your opinion should a senator consider the opinions and concerns of individuals who represent minority views?*
   Yes
   No
   Not sure
3. *Please explain why you think people must be humane when dealing with the poor of other countries?*

4. *Directions: Each of the following situations or questions is followed by four possible attitudes or answers. Arrange these answers in the order of your personal preference by writing at the right a score of 4, 3, 2, or 1. To the statement you prefer most give 4, to the statement that is second most attractive 3, and so on.*

A. *In your opinion, a man who works in business all week can best spend Sunday in*
   a. *trying to educate himself by reading serious books.*
   b. *trying to win at golf, or racing.*
   c. *going to an orchestral concert.*
   d. *hearing a really good sermon.*

B. *Viewing Leonardo da Vinci's picture, "The Last Supper," would you tend to think of it*
   a. *as expressing the highest spiritual aspirations and emotions.*
   b. *as one of the most priceless and irreplaceable pictures ever painted.*
   c. *in relation to Leonardo's versatility and its place in history.*
   d. *the quintessence of harmony and design.*

(Allport, Vernon, and Gardner, 1960)

Organization questions often begin by asking if an individual has done something, suggested some action, developed a plan, drawn some conclusions, or made some judgment. They are parallel to analysis questions in the cognitive domain. The questions do not ask about the value system directly, but from the respondent's answers you get a pretty good idea of the value system.

Characterization.

This is the highest level of questioning in the affective domain. Bloom calls this level "Characterization by a Value or Value Complex." Such questions are similar to those at the objective levels of synthesis and evaluation. You are trying to get at the deepest levels of belief or attitude structure, the interviewee's central personality and/or world view. This is the foundation upon which a great deal of an individual's thought processes and behavior rest. You are, in effect, asking an interviewee to answer the questions, "Who are you?" "Why do you behave as you do?" and "What do you stand for?" Answers to these questions reflect the total realm of a respondent's past experiences, including a delicate balance between personal and societal values. A question can have no greater depth than that. The following are examples of characterization questions:

1. You have said your philosophy as a supervisor has always been "let each employee handle his or her own problems." How does this philosophy help you solve the problem of your subordinates constantly being late for work?

2. *Which of the following statements is a more nearly adequate expression of your main life goal?*
   Serving God, doing God's will.
   Self-discipline—overcoming my irrational emotions and sensuous desires.
   Power—gaining control of others.
   Doing my duty.
   Serving the community of which I am a part.
   Finding a place in life and accepting it.

Making a place for myself in this world; getting ahead.
Security—protecting my way of life against adverse changes.
Survival—continued existence.
Getting as many pleasures out of life as I can.
Achieving personal immortality in heaven.
Living for the pleasure of the moment.
Peace of mind, contentment.
      (*Adapted from* General Goals of Life; Inventory H-Alb—*Cooperative*
        Study in General Education, American Council on Education, 1942)

3. How would you describe yourself?

Characterization questions often begin by asking respondents what they should or would do in a particular situation. The situation can either be real or hypothetical. In that sense, these questions are existential, for they do not ask what others should do, but rather what choice they would make in a free-choice situation. These are sometimes called *magic wand* questions, because they ask interviewees what they would do if they had a magic wand and could make any changes they wished.

When asking questions in the affective domain, you must remember that subjective questions deal with emotions, interests, attitudes, beliefs, and values. They are generally more difficult for interviewees to answer, because they ask them to reveal part of themselves, sometimes a very personal part. Respondents need to be given time and support. Although the main target of many interviews is the affective domain, and one of the real values of an interview is that subjective information is revealed, this kind of questioning is easily mishandled. Some people feel no guilt about lying to protect their own ego. Their value system obviously allows them to distort information to fit their own needs. Such beliefs may directly conflict with your value system, and you may react negatively once you discover them. Once your negative opinion becomes obvious to the respondent, the interview will probably deteriorate. You must be willing to accept any information in the affective domain of respondents even if it conflicts with your beliefs. You should try to treat subjective information in the same unbiased manner you treat objective information.

Various levels of subjective questions are not as clear-cut as those dealing with the cognitive domain. The context in which a question is couched is very important in retrieving subjective information. The question, "How would you describe yourself?" will be answered very differently if it is the first question in a selection interview or the last question in a counseling interview. In the former it is a general introductory comment to be handled briefly. In the latter it may be the culmination of the interview. Both interviewers and interviewees need to become context conscious in order to effectively use and recognize subjective questions.

You will often use *both* objective and subjective questions. Many interview guides are developed with the idea of first getting the objective information and then determining a respondent's subjective feelings about that information. If handled properly, by working up the levels for both domains, combining questions is not a problem. Instead, it can be a real help in achieving interview success.

SUBJECTIVE QUESTION EXERCISE

Directions: Label each of the following questions using this code:

A = Receiving
B = Responding
C = Valuing
D = Organization
E = Characterization

Answers can be found at the end of this chapter.

1. Hello, I'm Sam Goodman from the University Survey Center. We are trying to determine citizen attitudes toward the present administration's stand on defense spending. Would you be willing to answer a few questions?
2. If you had your choice between a four-year college degree with public recognition (a diploma) upon graduation, *or* spending four years in isolation studying anything you wanted followed by no public recognition, which option would you select?
3. What would you say if I were to tell you that we are laying off employees based on seniority, not merit?
4. How do you reconcile the fact that you tell your children not to smoke or drink, and yet you do both?
5. If you are put on the witness stand and asked what you know about this matter, you will either have to tell the truth or you could be sent to jail. Are you willing to go to jail rather than tell what you know?
6. What subjects did you enjoy most in college?
7. Look at this list of names and tell me which ones you recognize.
8. What are some of the extracurricular activities in which you engaged during your college days?
9. What is your main goal in life?
10. How do you as a supervisor compare your responsibilities to the organization and your responsibilities to your employees?

But you must first be familiar with the levels and sequences for both types of questions.

This discussion of question types is far from complete. A brief review of the interviewing literature indicates twenty or thirty different question types discussed, very often given different names by different authors. Only those types which seem to be the most important in preparing the interview guide have been presented here. At this point the focus shifts to one other important aspect of question preparation: the way in which questions should be ordered within each topic.

QUESTION SEQUENCE

There are two basic types of question sequences which are discussed in almost every interviewing book, the funnel and pyramid (inverted funnel) sequences. There are also a number of other alternatives, two of which (the tunnel and quintamensional design) will also be discussed in this section. Remember that question sequence refers to the sequence of questions within each topic area.

Funnel Sequence

In the funnel sequence, general questions give way to more restricted ones as the topic is worked through. Thus, the funnel sequence generally begins with open questions and ends with closed questions. The following series of diagnostic interview questions illustrate this sequence.
1. How do you feel today?
2. Of the ailments you have mentioned, which one or ones seem to be giving you the most problem?
3. How often do you feel this way?
4. Are there any particular times when you feel worse than others?
5. When did you first begin to notice these ailments?
6. What are some of the symptoms of these ailments?
7. Are you also having headaches?
8. Are you getting enough sleep?
9. Do you get stomach pains when these ailments occur?

The decision to use the funnel sequence should be based on a number of factors including the interviewee, the interviewer, and the topic under consideration. The following suggestions should help you determine if you should consider using a funnel question sequence. Most of these follow directly from the advantages and disadvantages of open questions discussed earlier.

The funnel sequence, with open unrestricted questions at the beginning, is useful when you want to first assess interviewee priorities, frame of reference, depth of knowledge, vocabulary level, and emotional state. Because this allows interviewees to respond in their own words and in their own way, the funnel sequence can help you if you think that there may be some responses which you have not been able to anticipate. This assumes, of course, that an interviewee is motivated to supply the information you have requested. The funnel sequence also allows you to get an overall assessment of interviewees without biasing later questions. The funnel sequence can save time—interviewees will often respond with information in early questions you might have planned to ask later. Because open questions are generally easier to answer, they pose less threat at the beginning and are a way of getting an interviewee's unbiased response earlier in the interview. Closed questions are then used later to probe information not covered.

The funnel sequence is also useful in an emotional interview. Open questions allow interviewees to feel important and get things off their chest by allowing them to talk at length. Emotional interviewees want to answer questions in their own way and discuss sensitive areas in a manner of their own choosing. They often digress into areas which may not be part of the interview guide. This consumes more interview time, and you must be willing to give over a great deal of topic control to the interviewee. The funnel sequence makes it difficult for beginning interviewers to record responses because they must be familiar enough with the interview guide to place answers under the proper topics when they come up in the early open questions.

Pyramid Sequence

The pyramid sequence is also called the *inverted funnel sequence*. A pyramid or inverted funnel sequence begins with the specific questions at the beginning and introduces more open questions at the end—it utilizes inductive reasoning. The funnel sequence depends on what was earlier described as deductive logic or reasoning.

By using the pyramid sequence, you lose most of the advantages of the funnel sequence, but there are a number of advantages to the pyramid sequence given the proper circumstances. When you are dealing with an interviewee who has little motivation and no strong feeling regarding the topic, for example, the pyramid sequence should be seriously considered. A series of closed questions can relieve interviewee doubts about their ability to answer the questions. Also, by answering a series of closed questions interviewees can be motivated to discover an interest in a topic—closed questions can be used as a means of "priming the pump." For example, a survey interviewer may be interested in respondent feelings regarding an upcoming city-wide election. If asked an open question, many respondents would probably reply, "I don't know, I'm not all that interested in city politics." When closed questions are used early in the interview, they may give fairly specific and knowledgeable answers. In this case, the pyramid sequence would have worked, whereas a funnel sequence might have failed.

The pyramid sequence is also useful when respondents are extremely knowledgeable and/or biased with regard to the topic. By asking an open question, you simply receive a listing of their prejudices, rather than a judgment based upon the facts. Once allowed to express their prejudices without thinking through the facts, they may feel forced to stick with those statements, even though later questions may lead them to a contrary opinion. Once interviewees have publicly committed themselves to a stand, it is extremely hard to change their mind. Any attempt to have them change a statement is seen as an ego threat. By asking interviewees closed questions, they are forced to clarify their own thinking before arriving at a conclusion.

A word of warning is in order at this point. If you choose to use the pyramid sequence, you should be extremely careful in choosing and wording each question. If early closed questions in the pyramid sequence are not worded properly, you can easily bias responses that are given to later questions. Respondents may discover what answer you expect, and give you that answer. In the same way, under certain circumstances, a rapid series of closed questions can pose a threat to interviewees. They may get the feeling that they are being interrogated. Finally, if there is any hope of unanticipated responses from interviewees, a series of closed questions can prevent them from expressing those unanticipated responses. If there is any danger of these problems occurring as a result of using the pyramid question sequence, you should seriously consider using the funnel sequence or one of the other sequences discussed in the following paragraphs.

Other Question Sequences

The funnel and pyramid sequences are by far the most commonly used question sequences. There are, however, two other sequences which should be mentioned for possible use under certain circumstances. The first of these is called the *quintamensional design sequence*. It was developed by the pollster, Gallup. He finds this sequence useful in determining the intensity of attitudes or emotions held by individuals. It consists of five steps: awareness, uninfluenced attitudes, specific attitude, reason why, and intensity of attitude. The quintamensional design sequence closely follows the cognitive and affective questioning strategy discussed earlier in this chapter. First, respondents are asked if they are aware of the topic under discussion—"Have you ever heard of the term *merit pay*?" Second, they are asked a general attitude question—"What do you think the majority of employees think about the merit pay system?" In the third step respondents are asked for their specific attitude—"Do you approve or disapprove of a merit pay system?" Interviewees are then asked why they hold these particular attitudes—"Why do you feel that way?" Finally, the most important question in the quintamensional design sequence focuses upon the intensity of the attitude—"Is your mind made up on this matter or do you think it could be changed?" As you can see, like Bloom's approach, the quintamensional design sequence asks for deepening levels of information. In many situations, such as a persuasion interview, it is important not only to determine an interviewee's attitude regarding a particular topic but also the intensity or depth of that attitude. Persuaders must know exactly how much opposition they face prior to presenting their arguments. In such a case, the quintamensional design sequence should be considered.

The last type of question sequence should be obvious from the earlier discussion of funnel and pyramid sequences. It is called the *tunnel sequence*. The tunnel sequence is either made up completely of open questions or of closed questions. The journalistic questions of who, what, when, where, how, and why are an example of a tunnel sequence. The order of the questions is not important—none of the questions either broaden or narrow the scope of questioning. Research interviewers often use a tunnel sequence of closed questions, while counseling interviewers often use a tunnel sequence of open questions. The tunnel sequence is much simpler than the others discussed. In developing an interview guide, you should choose the question sequence which best meets your interview demands and purpose.

QUESTION SEQUENCE EXERCISE

Directions: Here is a description of a counseling situation. Read it and then write five questions each, first using the funnel sequence, then the pyramid sequence, then the quintamensional design sequence, then the tunnel sequence (questions can be open or closed).

You are a guidance counselor at a large university. Jane Johnson, age 21, has been referred to you by the university health center. She has been demanding more and more amphetamines. Last year she asked for and received low doses to help her diet. When she did not lose any weight, she stopped taking them. A month later, after her prescription ran out, she went back to the doctor for more. She said they helped her when she felt tired, blue, and out-of-sorts. She has been on them ever since, almost nine months. This would be her sixth prescription for amphetamines.

Question development is an extremely important part of interview guide preparation. Questions which are chosen and sequenced with care can make even the most novice interviewer appear much more skillful. This is why it is recommended that you include some questions along with topics as part of your interview guide. You need not use all of the questions you have chosen, but if you have as many questions as possible prepared ahead of time, you are almost guaranteed a smooth, professional appearance.

TRANSITIONS

Many interviewers like to prepare and include transition statements in their interview guide in order to facilitate smooth information flow. A transition can be thought of as a bridge between various parts or sections of an interview. It allows

After preparing an interview guide, you should check it with someone else.

interviewers and respondents to adjust and prevent the carry-over of old preconceptions to new topics or questions. Without a transition an interviewee is likely to ask, "Why are you asking me about that? I thought we were talking about X, not Y."

Transitions should serve a predetermined purpose whenever they are used in an interview. They can be used to shift topics or question reference, tie topics or questions to the interview purpose, reintroduce material mentioned earlier, increase or decrease the emotional level, shift the topic away from uncomfortable or threatening information, and much more. If the sequence of questions and topics is well planned and obvious to a respondent, very few transitions are needed. When each topic or question naturally grows or flows out of the preceding one, it is called a *natural* transition. A skillful interviewer works to develop as many natural transitions as possible.

Transitions are not the sole right of an interviewer. Interviewees will sometimes try to make a shift back to a previous topic or question or ahead to a new topic or question. Most interviewers will note the attempted shift and try to discover its cause. They will, however, eventually come back to the main topic if it has not been covered completely. Such respondent-initiated transitions can signal boredom, threat, topic exhaustion, primary areas of interest, and many other interviewee feelings. You must constantly be aware of interviewee-initiated transitions.

Rapid and frequent transitions aren't desirable. They can cause you to lose valuable information that a respondent might have volunteered had you allowed sufficient time. Be sure each topic or question has been exhausted before initiating a transition. Remember, every time a transition occurs, both the interviewee and interviewer must adjust.

Never interrupt to initiate a transition. As you become more experienced, you will become sensitive to when a transition is needed. You will notice such things as respondents repeating information, losing enthusiasm, and hesitating. Their eyes will wander, or they may begin to fidget. There are many signs when a new topic or question is needed.

As you prepare transitions for an interview guide, you might try to find something in the preceding topic or question that relates to the new topic or question. A performance interviewer, for example, might go from a discussion of an employee's good points to a problem area by saying, "You are one of the fastest and most efficient workers employed here, Bob, and that's what sometimes causes problems. You have a tendency to use your free time to disrupt other workers who are not as efficient as you and have not yet completed their jobs." You can make a smooth transition by referring back to the overall topic pattern— "Well, I think I have all the information I need about the cause of your problem, let's go on and discuss some possible solutions, if that's all you have to say too," would be such a transition.

Transitions should be as brief as possible, but still leave little doubt in a respondent's mind that the previous topic is closed. One good way to do this is to precede a transition with a summary. That is, you try to mention the highlights of previous responses before making a transition. This informs respondents that you have been listening, now possess all information necessary for that topic or question, and wish to move on to a new area. A summary ties up the loose ends.

Whether you prepare transitions ahead of time and include them in the interview guide or not, they should always help interviewees follow the logic of the interview and help both you and a respondent mentally "shift gears" when necessary to satisfy the interview purpose. As you practice interviewing, you will find yourself making smoother and more appropriate transitions without planning. Initially, however, it is a good idea to plan and include transition statements in the interview guide.

SUMMARY

The material presented in this chapter is part of what you need to know in order to prepare an interview guide. Besides knowing what type of question to ask, you must also know how to ask questions in order to receive a good response. Interview guides can include possible follow-up (probe) questions for each major question listed and notes related to the interview opening and closing. The aim of the chapter has been to introduce you to the essentials of interview guide preparation.

The first such essential was the types of interview guides that are available. They include nondirective guides such as an in-progress guide, semidirective guides in which the topics can be either sequenced or not, and directive guides which can be as detailed as you wish right up to a questionnaire (which does not even require an interview). A directive guide is recommended at least until your skills become highly developed.

The second essential of interview guide preparation is the development of topics to satisfy the interview purpose. These topics are defined in the preparation stage, but their depth, range, and sequence are determined as you create the interview guide. Topic development is essential to preparing an effective interview guide. It provides the framework for question development.

Question selection is the hardest part of creating the interview guide. It includes the consideration of what type of information you are seeking; whether the questions should be open or closed; if the questions are closed, what type of closed questions to use; and much more. You must learn to use the different types of objective and subjective questions, as well as know the order in which they should be asked. Six types of objective questions were listed and discussed and five levels of subjective questions. If you're able to select and use the various types of question levels discussed in this chapter, you are well on your way to becoming a skillful interviewer.

The final aspect of question selection you have learned is how to sequence them for best effect. The most common sequences are the funnel and pyramid types, but other sequences were mentioned for special situations.

The last essential of interview guide preparation involves creating and using transitions. Transitions communicate the structure of the interview to a respondent. They allow you to move from topic to topic and from question to question smoothly. They add polish to your interview and keep respondents informed of where you are going and why.

By the time you have finished preparing an interview guide, you are ready to begin interviewing. You will know what you expect to accomplish and how you will go about it. An interview guide is your blueprint or road map to success. Its value is found in its preparation, as well as its use. It forces you to prepare fully and plan the interview structure. You will be surprised at the feeling of accomplishment and confidence you have once you have prepared such a guide. You will actually be anxious to do the interview and see if it goes as you have planned.

ACTIVITIES

Activity #1

Directions: Select a printed interview from one of the major magazines that carry full transcripts such as the *New York Times, Nutshell, Rolling Stone,* or *Playboy.* Read the interview carefully and see if you can answer each of the following questions about the interview. What you will be trying to do is reproduce the interview guide from the transcript of the interview. This is sometimes a very difficult assignment because interviewers often allow interviewees to digress from the guide. You must look for clues as to when the interviewer is working from the guide and when the respondent has directional control.

1. Would you say the interview guide used was:
   Directive
   Semidirective
   Nondirective
2. What were the major topics covered? In sequence.
3. Which topic was covered in the greatest depth and range?
4. Which topic sequence was used?
5. What was the main type of information sought?
   Attitudes
   Beliefs
   Behaviors
   Attributes
6. What types of questions were used?
   Open
   Bipolar
   Closed with ordered answer choices
   Closed with unordered answer choices
   Partially closed
7. Give an example of the main type of question used and any other question types used.
8. Give examples of any objective and subjective questions you found and label the subcategory to which you think they belong.
9. What was the main question sequence?
   Funnel

>   Pyramid
>   Quintamensional
>   Tunnel
>
> 10. Give at least two examples of transitions that were used either to bridge between topics or questions.
> 11. See if you can reproduce the whole guide including opening notations, topics, questions, probes, transitions, closing notations, etc. These do not have to be full sentences but simply the type of outline notes that most interviewers use.
> 12. If you were the interviewer, what would you have done differently? Why?
>
> ## Activity #2
>
> Directions: Contact any of the interviewers you listed in the introductory activity and see if they have any organization prepared or individually prepared interview guides you might copy. If they do, analyze them using the same basic criteria suggested above. It is also very useful to have a file of such guides available to you when you want to create your own. If you are part of a class or workshop it is a good idea to exchange guides and make copies of as many other interview guides as you can for your files.
>
> ## Activity #3
>
> Directions: Using the information you gained doing activity #3 for the last chapter, develop an interview guide which you will use to interview that individual. Make your interview guide as detailed as possible and also include what you think will be the appropriate amount of space for recording answers. Remember, you will actually be using this guide; so be as careful and thoughtful as you can. Try to make sure you cover all pertinent information. Once you think you have everything you will need, type it. It is hard to do a good interview if you cannot read the information you have prepared. You might also mark those topics or questions which you want to make sure you cover.

Answers to the Types of Information Exercise.
1 = D, 2 = A, 3 = C, 4 = B, 5 = B, 6 = C, 7 = A, 8 = D, 9 = A, 10 = D, 11 = C, and 12 = B

Answers to the Objective Question Exercise.
1 = B, 2 = D, 3 = A, 4 = B, 5 = F, 6 = E, 7 = C, 8 = D, 9 = E, and 10 = F

Answers to the Subjective Question Exercise.
1 = B, 2 = C, 3 = E, 4 = D, 5 = C, 6 = B, 7 = A, 8 = A, 9 = E, and 10 = D

Chapter 3

Skill 3
Opening the Interview

In short, he (the interviewer) should handle the first few minutes of the interview in such a way that the applicant gets the distinct impression that the interviewer is an easy person with whom to talk. (Fear, 1978, p. 62)

A good interview opening is a product of preparation, sensitivity, and flexibility. It is similar in many respects to the opening of any communication; it sets the tone for the remainder of the interaction. In an interview the opening must facilitate the purpose, and matching the opening to the purpose doesn't just happen—it must be planned ahead of time and if necessary, adjusted. Both participants must be sensitive enough to recognize what adjustments need to be made and flexible enough to make them. Three important activities take place during the opening of an interview: establishment of the climate, interviewee briefing, and the opening question.

ESTABLISHING THE INTERVIEW CLIMATE

Climate refers to the mood or tone of the interview. It is the sum total of all the tangible and intangible forces affecting both participants. To a greater or lesser degree, everything discussed in this book has some bearing on the interview climate. Some of these forces are beyond the control of interviewers—such as the interviewee's sex and financial status, while others can be manipulated to establish a productive climate—such as planning the timing and setting of the interview.

What Is the Best Climate?

Interview climate is a continuum ranging from warm (or hot) on one end to cool (or cold) on the other end. Many experts suggest the development of a warm climate for all types of interviews, but such an all-or-nothing approach is much too simplistic. The most desirable climate is the one which helps accomplish the purpose of the interview, hence there is no one "best" interview climate. It should be determined by your personality and motivations, the motivations and personality of the interviewee, and the interview type and purpose.

Breaking the Ice

No matter what type of climate you intend to establish, the first few minutes are extremely important. This is called the icebreaking portion of the interview. Very often, beginning interviewers have trouble breaking the ice because they are poorly prepared. If you have done your homework and know human nature, yourself, the interviewee, the subject, and the purpose of the interview, you will have much less difficulty in establishing a productive climate.

Icebreaking is also influenced by who initiates the interview. If the interaction is interviewee-initiated, the respondent carries the major responsibility for breaking the ice. About all that is required of you as an interviewer, is to listen. Respondents can either begin with some small talk or go directly into their reason for scheduling the interview. In such a case, you should follow their lead and accept the climate they desire. This does not mean that you should take no notice of the climate. If it is inappropriate to the purpose you can subtly try to change it.

In an interviewer-initiated interaction, icebreaking is sometimes more difficult, and greater responsibility falls on the interviewer, who is responsible for breaking the ice. Respondents are usually quite tense during these early moments. Most interviewees experience what is called *primary tension*, that is, tension due to the uniqueness of the situation. You must allow time for them to get accustomed to this new situation.

Two aspects of an interview need to be established in the opening in order to reduce primary tension and establish a productive climate: formality and rapport. *Formality* relates to the participant status and role relationship, while *rapport* refers to the degree of harmony or empathy which exists between interviewers and respondents. These two climate factors are closely related to one another, just as they are closely related to other aspects of the interview, such as the degree of interview structure. They are, however, separate aspects of the climate and should be dealt with separately.

Formality Level

A formal climate is marked by a definite superior/subordinate relationship; but when the climate is informal, participants treat one another as equals. For some situations, such as discipline and termination interviews, a formal climate is best. On the other hand, most other interview types usually operate better with an informal climate.

Interview type is only one factor that helps determine the proper level of formality. The nature and preference of the participants is also important. Some interviewers and interviewees have trouble working in either a formal or an informal climate. It is, therefore, important to select, create, and maintain the most productive formality level, considering both interview type and participant preference.

Nonverbal Techniques.

Many of the techniques skillful interviewers use to establish a proper formality level do not involve spoken words. To establish an informal climate, they will shake hands and smile at respondents to ease primary tension. They provide a comfortable chair which is in direct eye contact with the interviewer. In formal interviews a less friendly greeting and a more status-oriented seating arrangement may be chosen, such as psychiatrists often choose—they sit while the patient reclines.

The distance between the chairs can nonverbally indicate the desired formality level. If you are trying to create an informal climate, you will establish a close interaction distance. If, on the other hand, you want to maintain a somewhat more formal climate, you can place the chairs farther apart or uncomfortably close together. Some form of barrier, such as a desk, may be used to establish a formal climate, while an informal climate is established by the removal of any physical barriers between interactants. If less formality is desired, you might offer respondents a cup of coffee or soft drink and indicate that they may smoke.

All of these and many other nonverbal formality-reducing tactics are designed to make the interviewee feel like a guest or equal in the interviewer's "home," rather than a subordinate in an interviewer's "office." Formality-increasing techniques create just the opposite effect. Prepared interviewees very often look for these nonverbal indicators of formality level either consciously or unconsciously and put a great deal of faith in them.

Verbal Techniques.

There are also a number of verbal strategies that help establish the planned formality level. One of the first things you should do, regardless of the planned climate, is to greet each interviewee by name and use it often. An informal or formal climate is signaled by whether you use the interviewee's first or last name. You encourage a warm informal climate by using the first name, and a more formal climate is established by using titles such as "Mr." and "Mrs." and the respondent's last name.

In a less formal interview, icebreaking usually includes a period of "small talk." If you have prepared properly and know something about the interviewee, it is fairly easy to develop an informal climate through small talk. You might mention a couple of interests or activities that you have in common or ask about a respondent's family. The goal at this point is to get interviewees talking. People generally feel more relaxed and less formal once they begin to talk and find that they have something in common with one another. At this point, your focus should be on the person and the climate, not on obtaining information. Perhaps the most important thing is that you, as an informal interviewer, should be at ease and relaxed yourself if you intend to create the same feeling in respondents.

A formal interview climate is created by skipping the small talk and getting right to the subject. Even in an informal climate, however, remember that too much idle chit-chat or small talk can sometimes harm the opening. Very often, the main concern in an interviewee's mind is the purpose, and the only thing that will reduce primary tension is getting on to it. For most interviews a minute or two is enough time to break the ice, regardless of formality level.

Beware of Formula Openings.

Some interviewers have tried to develop formula openings. This is especially true of formal interviewers and those who do not interview often. They try to devise some all-purpose icebreakers which they feel will work with almost anyone. Be wary of developing a formula opening. You are much better off if you research each individual and prepare an opening which will create the proper level of formality for that particular person and interview purpose. Formula openings give interviewers the appearance of being hurried, and never seem to carry the sincerity that is found in a specifically prepared opening.

FORMALITY LEVEL EXERCISE

Directions: For each of the following situations, describe the formality level you would try to establish and what you would do or say to try to reach your chosen level of formality. Use the following terms to describe the formality level: "Very Formal," "Somewhat Formal," "Neutral," "Somewhat Informal," and "Very Informal." Suggested levels can be found at the end of this chapter.

1. You are the Dean of the College of Education at a major university. As is normal procedure, you have been asked to meet with a prospective professor in the Educational Foundations Department. Your only concern is that a couple of the professor's letters of recommendation imply that she has trouble maintaining discipline in her classes.
2. You are a journalist who has finally gotten an interview with a government official accused of embezzling funds. The only way you got the interview was by promising to allow this person to "tell his side of the story."
3. You are a counselor who is meeting a new client for the first time. This person was referred to you because he has a severe drinking problem and is, therefore, absent from work quite often. When he is at work, however, he is very productive.
4. You are the Vice-Principal of a high school about to interview a student accused of smoking a controlled substance on the school grounds. The student is not disruptive in class and generally a "C" student. He was caught by one of the teachers in his car before school started that morning.
5. You are a real estate saleswoman meeting a couple who called you about buying a new home. They have just come into your office.

Although formality level is begun during icebreaking, it can, and often does, change as the interview proceeds. But don't try to make radical changes in the formality level after the opening. You are better off creating in the opening the formality level that you plan to maintain throughout the interview—radical changes are confusing and unsettling. No matter what formality climate is set, interviewees soon get used to it and resent any change. If you must change, you should begin somewhat more formally and become less formal as the discussion progresses. It is usually easier to become less formal than more formal.

Be consciously aware of and constantly work at setting a productive formality level in the opening. Rapport development must be considered at the same time. Without rapport, no level of formality will be productive.

Rapport Development

The French word "rapport" means the degree of harmony and trust that exists between people. Rapport does *not* necessarily imply friendship or liking. In a formal interview, rapport can come through respect without friendship. It is hard to have harmony and trust, however, if respect is lacking. The interview's rapport level is at least as important to the climate as the formality level. Few interviews are productive without good rapport.

Forming First Impressions.

The first thing you normally do, as part of icebreaking, is observe your interaction partner. From this observation, you gain a number of first impressions which may come from the way other individuals are dressed, their facial expression, physical build, skin color, hair length, jewelry, eye behavior, and many other features. You begin to categorize and make judgments about them based on these impressions. Categorization usually precedes rapport development.

The importance of first impressions will differ depending on whether or not an individual is a stranger or someone you have known. If the individual is a stranger, first impressions will have considerable influence on the way you classify and behave toward that person. If the individual is known to you, clothing, facial expression, body type, and so on do not have as much influence on your judgment.

You must be careful not to let first impressions mislead you. Try very hard to withhold judgment. First impressions can be very inaccurate; you should wait until you hear the other individual talk before you form lasting impressions. Develop a "wait and see" attitude. But because people are influenced by first impressions, you should make your appearance and behavior suitable for developing rapport.

Once your interaction partner begins to speak and gesture, there are a number of things that you should notice. First, notice the manner in which they speak—the loudness of their voice, voice pitch, and speech rate. One of the things that you can do which will help establish greater rapport is to match your manner of speaking to that of the other individual. Vocal synchronization helps to convey the message that you are in harmony with the other participant. Synchronization of gestures, posture, and other nonverbal and verbal behaviors will also promote harmony and trust. All of us form greater rapport with people who appear similar to ourselves.

Another factor you will notice when interview participants begin to talk is their vocabulary or language level. Some people have a fairly large vocabulary and are able to handle many ideas and concepts, while others have a more limited vocabulary. Again, you should try to harmonize or synchronize your vocabulary level, both in terms of the questions you ask, if you're the interviewer, and the vocabulary level of the responses you give, if you're the interviewee, to that of the other participant. Using an understandable vocabulary level is important not only in rapport development, but also in question wording and probing.

Determining Frame of Reference.

The impressions you form during the opening help give you some idea of the other person's frame of reference. *Frame of reference* refers to the way individuals see the world. It is very often based upon their past experiences as well as their personality, values, attitudes, and beliefs. For example, people's dress often reflects their frame of reference. People who wear the latest fashions usually have a different frame of reference from those who dress more conservatively. Conservatism in dress, in this case, can reflect a conservative frame of reference. You must, however, check to be sure your impression is accurate. By checking the frame of reference of the other participant, you will be able to determine whether or not your prior preparation and analysis is accurate. You will also be able to determine how close their frame of reference is to your own. Rapport is most often found between people with similar frames of reference.

If you find that the other participant's frame of reference is different from your own or that which you expected, you should be prepared to adjust your approach. Since an interview guide is based on prior assumptions, be flexible enough to reword a question within the interview guide to match the interviewee's frame of reference and vocabulary level. Whether you are the interviewer or the interviewee, you should use a great deal of finesse and be as subtle as possible in determining another's frame of reference. Do not hurry to judge one's frame of reference; sometimes it takes a little time. The preceding are some characteristics of rapport development which are true for both the interviewer and the interviewee.

Try to make the interviewee feel comfortable and welcome.

RAPPORT DEVELOPMENT EXERCISE

Directions: Think of two interviews you have been involved in lately. Describe the level of rapport that existed in the interview, at least from your perspective. Use the following terms to describe the rapport level: "Excellent Rapport," "Good Rapport," "Fair Rapport," "Poor Rapport," or "Terrible Rapport." Then describe your first impressions of your interview partner, your frame of reference, their frame of reference (in your opinion), how rapport was developed, and how it could have been improved.

Interviewer Perspective

As an interviewer, you will have spent some preparation time gathering information about each interviewee. During the opening you determine whether or not your information is accurate. You must check to see if your interview guide will, in fact, provide a fairly accurate map of the way you can best establish rapport and reach the interview purpose.

Some interviewers choose to take a passive role during this portion of the opening. They accept whatever attitudes and ideas are put forward until they are sure of the interviewee's frame of reference and have determined whether or not they can establish rapport and the proper formality level. Other interviewers like to step forward and take the initiative early. If they have decided that the climate should be informal, they develop rapport by encouraging interviewees to do most of the talking. When a formal climate is desired, they develop rapport by taking a very direct, no-nonsense approach.

An important and ever-present preliminary to rapport development is how you size up, categorize, or stereotype respondents. Interviewers tend to place an interviewee in one of several categories, on the basis of those people they have met, known, or interviewed in the past. Here are profiles of ten common interviewee types and how each should be handled to develop rapport:

The Apprehensive Interviewee.

All interviewees experience some primary tension during the opening. Apprehensive respondents just have more of this tension. They usually have nothing to hide and are generally good respondents once their primary tension wears off. Their early responses do not come at all, come out in a hesitant manner, or they come out with much omitted. The main cause of such apprehension is a fear of interviews in general, sometimes caused by feelings of insecurity or inferiority. Sometimes they have had a bad interview experience in the past, or this may be the first interview of a certain type they have ever experienced.

Often, nonverbal behavior such as an unsteady voice, nervous gestures, constant body shifts, and a frozen facial expression are the sign of extreme apprehension. These respondents must be made to see that their fears are unfounded; this takes constant reassurance and a calm, relaxed approach. An extended icebreaking period before any serious questioning usually helps. Apprehensive interviewees should be handled carefully and patiently until they begin to relax and talk freely. Early questions should be simple, open, and easy to answer "correctly."

The Defensive Interviewee.

At first, defensive interviewees appear to be apprehensive. Their comments are slow; they give many short or "I don't know" responses; and they leave details out of their answers. Their fear stems, however, not from the newness of the situation, but from a concern about the impression their information will create about themselves and their cause. Such fear is ego- or self-centered. They will continue being hesitant and defensive until they are certain of the rapport and confidentiality level. Defensive interviewees need to know how their information will be used and that it will be accepted uncritically.

Once again, the opening is very important when approaching defensive interviewees. They should not be hurried—rapport is developed when they are given time to weigh each answer as carefully as they feel necessary. Defensive interviewees will often repeat a question in order to gain thinking time. They are deciding what to reveal, how much to reveal, and whether to reveal the information honestly or in a distorted fashion. They may exaggerate or conceal unfavorable facts.

You should praise honest responses and, thus, subtly let defensive respondents know that mistakes and distortions will be detected and rejected. Ask simple narrow questions which they know are common knowledge or can be checked. This pyramid sequence will help focus attention on answers and away from internal fears. Once the ground rules are established, rapport can develop. Even in the face of distortion, you should not use harsh words or condemnation, but treat it as a mistake and give them a way of backing down and saving face. Remember, you are asking defensive interviewees to reveal information which they believe to be private or threatening. They are taking what they consider to be a large risk and leaving themselves vulnerable to rejection. You must help build their confidence in you.

The Stolid Interviewee.

Stolid interviewees are not easily stirred either physically or mentally. These respondents are impassive, unemotional, and/or slow-witted. This can be caused by mental deficiencies, slower reaction time, or a desire to be extremely careful with each answer. Whatever the reason, stolid interviewees seem to take forever to reply. When a response comes it is often disconnected, incomplete, or illogical.

Rapport development and questioning should again be slow and handled very patiently. At times this may seem totally exhausting and frustrating. Question vocabulary should be carefully chosen. Respondents need to be taken over each topic again and again to help dig out other facts. Sometimes missing ideas can be suggested in a follow-up probe. With patience, stolid interviewees will sometimes develop increased enthusiasm and rapport, but this task calls for ingenuity and perseverance.

The Disorganized Interviewee.

Disorganized interviewees are easily confused and distracted. You can almost see their mind slip off the track and go in some new or unrelated direction either because they're confused by the question at hand or because they're always confused. If disorganization is a general pattern of behavior, interviewees should be treated like the stolid interviewee—with patience.

If the disorganized response is a reflection of confusion over the topic, it is your responsibility to constantly focus attention on the matter at hand. Closed and directed questions in a tunnel or pyramid sequence will again be most helpful in accomplishing this task. You can also help bring clarity to answers by giving some background and order in the question preface or by summarizing frequently. Disorganized interviewees are usually grateful for such help, and this creates rapport. Be careful, however, not to bias a response by suggesting an answer to such interviewees.

The Too-Talkative Interviewee.

Too-talkative interviewees are prone to saying too much. With these people you often have a hard time getting a word in edgewise. Their overtalking can be either a digression or a long-winded response to each and every question. In either case, you should be careful not to rudely interrupt a response since this could hurt rapport and cause them to stop talking completely. Instead, you should phrase questions in a way that limits the scope of their responses.

In the case of digression, you should wait until the inappropriate response is finished and restate the question or phrase it in a more limited fashion. Too-talkative interviewees should not be allowed to move on to another question until the immediate question has been completely and properly answered. If they seem to be on the brink of digressing again, you should tactfully interject, either verbally or nonverbally, and bring the conversation back to the topic. Too-talkative interviewees are often good respondents, once they discover the response range and depth you desire. Rapport is hard to develop until these interviewees learn to respond properly. As with other interviewee types, however, the level of rapport often fluctuates.

The Overeager Interviewee.

Overeager interviewees may appear, at first, to be talkative because of their long and detailed answers. They are not motivated, however, by a desire to hear themselves talk, but instead to help or aid you as much as possible. Overeager interviewees develop a high level of rapport with interviewers almost instantly. This enthusiasm and rapport often lead to answers which they think you want to hear, regardless of whether they are accurate or not.

It is your responsibility to make clear to overeager interviewees that what you want is an accurate and complete answer. Be alert for slanted responses and then probe to discover the accurate answer. Be careful not to be too flattered by such willing respondents and then being blind to biased responses.

The Tenacious Interviewee.

Tenacious interviewees seldom, if ever, admit the possibility of error. These people believe everything they say to be the truth. They are usually bold, aggressive, ego-involved, and stubborn. They will defend a statement or action even when it reaches a point of being ridiculous, and are unwilling to engage in the normal give-and-take of an interview. These interviewees sometimes exaggerate good points and omit bad points in order not to appear wrong. They have difficulty separating their ego and opinions from the cold, hard facts.

Tenacious interviewees need polite, but inflexible, control. You can only lead them to modify their statements by small degrees. Sometimes you must confront them with obvious contradictions. Even in the face of a contradiction, some tenacious interviewees will not admit error. It is extremely hard to develop rapport with these interviewees. You cannot afford to agree with everything they say for the sake of gaining rapport. Most interviewers have all they can handle just to get the needed information. A direct assault may cause more harm than good. Indirect and tactful approaches are about all that will work until they become less rigid.

The Arrogant Interviewee.

Arrogant interviewees are determined to answer each question as concisely and sharply as possible. They like to respond with comments such as "yeah," "no," "so what?" or "no comment." Although they may be fearful and nervous inside, arrogant interviewees are determined to act insolent, cute, or in any other way give the impression that the whole interview is beneath them.

On discovering such interviewees, you must be careful not to cause embarrassment or use a "put down," although it is very tempting. Nothing ruins rapport as quickly as a "put down." You must show how answering your question will benefit them. Probing, with increasing directness, is one way to get the required information. Pauses and silences can also be used to encourage further elaboration. It is up to you to determine just how much arrogance you can tolerate in order to gain rapport and complete the interview.

The Hostile Interviewee.

Hostile interviewees won't cooperate. They withhold information or try to present it in a worthless manner. Hostility can be a product of fear, anger, impatience, or a number of other things—it is up to you to detect or get these respondents to admit the reason for their hostility and reassure them that cooperation can be rewarding.

If they are hostile to only one part of the interview, you might try to find a way to approach other topics without touching on the hostility-producing topic, or at least waiting until later to approach that topic. For example, some people who are the focus of many research interviews, such as American Indians or members of religious sects, are hostile to questions concerning any of their controversial practices, but not more general questions. As the interview progresses, rapport may develop and the hostility may be reduced to the point where the hostility-producing topic can be discussed. Hostility may also be due to the relationship between the participants, such as a perceived "personality clash." If so, these perceptions, as with the other sources of hostility, must be brought into the open and resolved before any level of rapport can be developed. If the "clash" is too serious, another interviewer should be brought in to obtain the information.

The Crafty Interviewee.

Crafty interviewees are out to deceive you. They usually have something to hide or are trying to play a "game" with you. Some crafty interviewees are extremely clever in their attempts to outwit you. In most cases you will have to be as wily and cunning as they are to establish rapport and get the interview on track. This does not mean that you have to use dishonest or unscrupulous methods, but it is often necessary to prove to crafty interviewees that two people can play the same game. You cannot let them think that their ploy is working. Faced with such interviewees, most interviewers will look for another information source. Crafty people can cause even the most skillful interviewer to become angry and impolite.

INTERVIEWEE CLASSIFICATION EXERCISE

Directions: You are the production foreman for a large furniture manufacturing company. Yesterday, while you were in the plant you noticed one of your employees using the equipment carelessly. You mentioned the problem to the employee at the time, but since getting back to your office and looking at the employee's personnel file, you notice that this is the third time that same employee has been reprimanded by managers. You decide to bring the employee in for a formal discipline interview with the possibility of imposing some more serious punishment. Before making any decision, however, you want to talk with the employee and ask him a few questions. You decide to use a fairly formal approach and start off immediately by stating: "Mr. Thompson, I asked you to come see me today to discuss the way you have been operating the equipment. I mentioned this to you yesterday, but I noticed from your personnel file that you have been warned about this same thing at least twice before. I would like you to tell me why you seem to be having trouble correcting this problem." Here are several possible responses, representing the different interviewee types just discussed. For each response, identify the interviewee type being represented and write a follow-up comment or question which you think would be appropriate for each response. Answers can be found at the end of the chapter.

1. You guys are so picky. You think the world was coming to an end every time somebody does something a little bit different than you want it done. I've never broken any machine, and I can get the work out faster if I do it my way.
2. Well . . . I don't know . . . I guess . . . I just don't know what to say.
3. Wait a minute! Nobody ever told me I was doing anything wrong until you said something yesterday. I don't know where you got your information, but somebody's lying.
4. You know I'm the fastest worker you got. I try to do things right, but sometimes I get in a hurry. It's just like when I go bowling. I'm a good bowler. You know I carry a 200 average. My wife says that with a little practice I could be a professional bowler. Do you think I should try to be a professional bowler?

5. Ah ta hell with it; I quit.
6. I'm sorry, Mr. Jones. I don't know why I keep getting in trouble. I really have tried to use the equipment the way you want. I just can't seem to remember all the time. I really like it around here. I think you are the best boss I have ever worked for. I know I can get it right if you will just give me another chance. I need this job awful bad. My wife is due to have our third baby in May, and I don't know where I can find a job as good as this one. I'm sure if you tell me again what I am doing wrong, I can get it right. I sure do like it here.

Each of the preceding respondent types has some problem which prevents easy rapport development. There are many other types of problem interviewees, but these represent a good cross section. Perhaps the last type of interviewee that should be discussed is the "perfect" respondent. Such a person has none of these characteristics. Experienced interviewers will tell you that no such type exists. Almost every interviewee has some characteristics of one or more of the preceding categories. You should be able to recognize each and every one of them. Once categorized, you can determine the proper level of formality and rapport. Sometimes this is quite easy, while at other times it can be one of the most difficult aspects of interviewing.

Interviewee Perspective

Since most interviewees enter an interview with a good deal of tension and anxiety, they are often more concerned with themselves and how they will appear than they are in trying to size up the interviewer. Successful interviewees, however, have prepared themselves and developed a state of mind which allows them to make judgments about interviewers in much the same way that interviewers judge them. They realize that it takes two people to develop rapport. They look for small details, such as the strength and intensity of the handshake, facial expression, tone of voice, and other cues to the personality of and climate desired by an interviewer.

Successful interviewees will generally try to be somewhat formal during the interview opening. They let the interviewer take the lead and responsibility for setting the climate. They respond to interviewer leads but do not overtalk or become too friendly. As an interviewee, this gives you a chance to size up an interviewer and the interview climate. In some cases, it may be necessary to take control of the interaction, but at the start, you will generally take a submissive role. It is better to hesitate and not make a mistake than to charge ahead and have to backtrack later.

Interviewees also categorize interviewers. They look for certain characteristics typical of various types. Once these characteristics have been identified, they classify the interviewer into one of several types and determine an acceptable means of developing rapport. The rapport that does develop requires effort on the part of both participants. Almost fifty years ago, Young (1935) categorized the following ten general types of interviewers. Her list still fits today. Again this is only a representative list.

The Salesman or Missionary Interviewer.

Missionaries or salesmen have an idea and try to "sell" it to the interviewee. They believe so strongly in the correctness of their own ideas that they feel justified in using any means, including artificial or faked rapport, to break down resistance and override interviewee objections. These interviewers have a great deal of difficulty considering an interviewee's frame of reference or problems. It is almost impossible for them to see any point of view except their own and, therefore, they have trouble establishing mutual trust.

The Routine Interviewer.

Routine interviewers have little imagination and even less sensitivity. These people are often called "'detailists" because they become overly concerned with the routine operations and minute details involved in interviewing. Routine interviewers focus so much attention doing an interview correctly and in the prescribed amount of time that they are rarely even aware of the interview outcome, let alone the level of rapport. Structure is more important than the outcome or the climate. Routine interviewers usually have trouble understanding why they do not conduct good interviews.

The Research Interviewer.

Researchers see all information as equally relevant and make little or no attempt to determine the relative value of each individual piece. The human needs of an interviewee are of little concern. Such interviewers are easily side-tracked from the main point into something that they find interesting from a "research point of view." They see the interview in the abstract and want to collect a great deal of data about and from interviewing without ever considering the rapport needs of each individual interviewee, let alone trying to establish rapport. Researchers may be shrewd and skillful, but like the salesman and routine interviewers, they are insensitive.

The Therapeutic-Nihilist Interviewer.

Therapeutic-nihilists are always on the lookout for problems. They often attempt to tie the specific problems in the interview to greater ills within society. When they find a pathological situation, they let it run its course with little or no interference. Therapeutic-nihilists see themselves as observers of the "evils of the world" around them, but are unwilling to attempt to correct those evils. They are generally very negative, and have trouble working harmoniously with and trusting others. Many are constantly suspicious.

The Scatterbrained Interviewer.

Scatterbrained interviewers are extremely talkative but cannot stick to the purpose of the interview. Unless the interviewee is a rambler, there is little chance for rapport. They are continually skipping all over the interview guide with no real sense of order or sequence. The mind and thoughts of such interviewers are unorganized and undisciplined and thus, they normally elicit only partial information. Very often, scatterbrained interviewers are nervous or haven't prepared. No matter what the reason, interviewees have an extremely difficult time working with interviewers whose questions are illogically organized.

The Domineering Interviewer.

Domineering interviewers often take the lead away from an interviewee. They may suffer from an inferiority complex which they attempt to hide by acting superior. Such interviewers have little patience for rapport development, for weak answers, and cannot handle "I don't know" responses. They are also brutally honest and meet interviewees head-on or attempt to belittle their ideas or proposals. This certainly does not lead to rapport. Sometimes dominators claim to be extremely sensitive to the motivations and desires of interviewees and able to classify them from a facial expression, gesture, or look in the eye. In fact, they are generally very inaccurate and therefore misjudge interviewee rapport needs.

The Moralistic Interviewer.

Moralists are quick to make judgments about interviewees, as well as their statements. They label any statement or person as "right" or "wrong" and will openly challenge interviewees' ideas, especially if they perceive them to be of the "wrong" culture, religion, or social group. Moralists are inflexible and incapable of developing rapport once they have determined that interviewees or their ideas are "wrong."

The "Paul-Pry" Interviewer.

Paul-Prys are prone to ask questions and make statements about things which are none of their business. They prefer to dwell on topics that are embarrassing or threatening. Interviewees are usually suspicious of someone who only wants to pry into their darkest secrets. Paul-Prys have difficulty establishing satisfactory levels of rapport with interviewees although their prying may be an attempt to gain rapport. Frequently, they have some serious unsolved personal problems of their own.

The Sentimental Interviewer.

Sentimentalists have no problem harmonizing with and trusting an interviewee. As a matter of fact, their problem is establishing more intimate rapport than is necessary. They have little or no control over their own emotions within the interview. Sentimental interviewers feel and express each of the emotions suggested by an interviewee. In many interviews it is important to establish a great deal of rapport, but even then it is also important for interviewers to maintain their own role so they can help the interviewee and complete a productive interview.

The Give-and-Take Interviewer.

According to Young, these are the "perfect" interviewers. This interviewer "sees situations from the client's point of view and is able to accord them proper recognition of social and personal status. He is tolerant of divergent views and practices and is able to interact wholesomely with his interviewees. He plans with them and not for them and has genuine sympathetic insight into their problems." (Young, 1935, p. 259) You seldom find the "perfect" interviewer, but this is the type that every interviewee hopes to find. It is also the type of interviewer that every student should attempt to be. The give-and-take interviewer is flexible enough to establish a rapport level that fits both the interview and the respondent. If, after sizing you up, an interviewee categorizes you as a give-and-take interviewer, you will be well on your way to achieving a productive level of rapport.

INTERVIEWER CLASSIFICATION EXERCISE

Directions: From the preceding list, identify the type of interviewer that would make each of the following comments. Suggested answers can be found at the end of this chapter.

1. I know you want to talk about your work experience, but I haven't finished asking you about your education. I always talk about education before experience.
2. I feel so bad about this thing I could just cry. I once lost my pet turtle, so I know exactly how you feel since your wife died. Let's go get a drink before we both start weeping.
3. You think you've got it made here don't you? You think you can get away with anything. Well, I'm here to tell you I don't want to hear any of your excuses. Shape up or ship out.
4. You know, I knew you were going to say that! Everyone in this neighborhood answers all these questions the same way.
5. I think I understand what you mean. I can see how you might want to drink to get away from your problems. I agree that what we need to do is figure out how you can solve your problems, not hide from them.
6. You know, the best thing I ever did was to go hear Reverend Phillips. He set my life straight. I know you're not big on religion, but I think faith is the answer to your problems.
7. Well, now, let's see. You are from New York, and you have a B.A. in Political Science. Ah, who do you think will win the basketball game on Saturday?
8. Your kind never could do an honest day's work for an honest day's pay. You're always trying to find the easy way out, and when you are caught, you try to weasel your way out of it.
9. I don't really think you want to give up drugs at all. You're just a product of your environment. You're stuck.
10. I like to know as much as I can about my employees. Tell me, do you have a steady boyfriend, or do you sleep around?

Be wary of premature classification. Very often, because they are nervous, anxious, or unprepared, interviewers or interviewees may appear to be some type they are not. If you classify and stereotype interviewees or interviewers too early, you may begin to respond to them inappropriately. You can even produce a *self-fulfilling prophecy*. This means that after sizing up and categorizing individuals, you begin to act toward them in ways which induce them to act like the kind of person you've decided they are. The development of a self-fulfilling prophecy can have disastrous consequences—most experienced interview participants withhold judgment until they have complete, firm, and verifiable evidence.

If, however, as an interviewee, you have withheld judgment and still feel you have complete, firm, and verifiable evidence that your interviewer falls into one of the less desirable categories described here, there is little you can do directly to change that interviewer's style. Unlike the interviewer, who can take steps to achieve a successful outcome with a difficult interviewee, interviewees do not have equivalent opportunities. The interviewer has directional control and the interviewee has informational control. Therefore, the only direct response available to such an interviewee is to withhold information. This is obviously a last resort. It should be used only after other indirect techniques have failed to change the interviewer's style. A number of such indirect techniques will be discussed and illustrated in the chapters on asking and answering questions and listening. You will find, however, that even with these indirect strategies, there is very often little you can do to alter interviewer style.

ORIENTING THE INTERVIEWEE

Once you have begun to establish the interview climate you feel is appropriate, the next step is to brief interviewees to the goals of the interview and how you intend to reach those goals. You need to provide them with a verbal description of how the interview will proceed. Early orientation statements are important not only to the success of the interview, but also help to further establish the climate; they help relieve primary tension. The orientation phase of an interview opening sets the groundwork for the body of the interview and gives interviewees some basic facts about the purpose of the interview.

How to Orient Interviewees

One of the worst things an interviewer can do is assume that interviewees know why a discussion is taking place. This assumption is often signalled by a statement such as, "I suppose you know why I called you here?" Such an opening comment can make respondents very anxious. Interviewees generally have some idea as to why an interaction is taking place, but they may be unclear regarding the specifics of what the interview will include, its purpose, or how it will be conducted. A much better way of briefing respondents is to simply be straightforward by using wording such as, "Let me tell you what we will be discussing." Interviewees have the right to know the purpose of an interview before answering questions. This promotes rapport and launches the interview properly.

A serious danger of the orientation phase is that it can turn into a lecture. You should provide interviewees with all of the information necessary to insure a successful interview, but your orientation need not go beyond that point. During orientation some interviewers tend to become rather authoritative. Patronizing, condescending, and aloof behavior is a poor beginning. You certainly need to maintain the initiative and indicate the direction that the interview will take, but don't let this particular portion of the interview contradict the climate that has been built earlier. The best way to prevent lecturing is to be brief. After the orientation, the interviewee should be more, rather than less, willing to accomplish the purpose of the interview.

What to Include

Different interviewers include different information in their orientation statement. At a bare minimum, however, it should contain a description of the purpose of the interview and the topics which will be covered. These are often taken directly from the interview guide. Other common orientation information includes: 1) some indication of the preparation that has been done prior to the interview, 2) the projected length of the interview, 3) when interviewees will be able to comment or ask questions, and 4) how the information will be used.

Indicating the *preparation* that went into an interview establishes the seriousness with which you perceive the interaction that will follow. It also forewarns an interviewee that any deliberate omissions, inaccuracies, or exaggeration will be noticed. An example might be the statement, "Joe, I've spent some time going over your records, and I've talked to several of your previous supervisors about your job performance and potential for advancement."

Indicating the *length of time* that an interview will be conducted is simply a matter of courtesy. It also indicates whether you want long or short responses to questions and thus helps respondents participate properly. Sometimes such a statement makes it much easier to conclude the interaction later. A brief comment such as, "This shouldn't take more than fifteen minutes of your time, Mrs. Brown," is useful in getting a person to respond.

Indicating *when respondents can comment or ask questions* helps to define your role and that of the interviewee. Very often respondents will have an inquiry or something to say during the course of an interview. If the preferred place for questions and comments has been indicated beforehand, they will be withheld until that point. If you have not indicated the appropriate place for such comments and questions, interviewees will constantly interrupt you and disrupt the flow. In a selection interview, for example, it is common to indicate that interviewees may ask any questions about the company, salary, work location, and potential for advancement at the end of the interview. This provides a degree of security for both participants throughout the interview. In other interviews, respondents may be told they can comment or question at any time during the interview.

Telling an interviewee *how the information will be used* can be vitally important. This is called the *confidentiality statement*. If you are going to be asking sensitive or somewhat threatening questions, interviewees are less likely to provide accurate information unless they have first been assured their statements will remain confidential. Also, interviewees are usually willing to provide a greater quantity of honest and accurate information if they know that the source of the information will never be disclosed; that is, if they know their name will not be linked to the information.

Some interviewers, such as doctors, lawyers, and priests, have legal protection against forced information disclosure. Other interviewers, such as journalists, are attempting to obtain such legal protection against forced disclosure of information and sources, but as of this writing, they have not achieved their goal. There are, however, a great many journalistic interviewers who have maintained the confidentiality they promised sources, even if it meant going to jail. If a confidentiality statement is made, it should be followed to the letter. Nothing can hurt your credibility and later rapport worse than disclosure of information that was given in confidence.

You can add other information to the orientation statement as you see fit and as the interview demands. When the situation requires it, the following types of information may also be included in an orientation statement: 1) a request for cooperation, 2) a statement of the importance of the interview, 3) mention of any financial reward or other benefit, 4) explanation as to why and how the respondent was selected, 5) who recommended the interview, and 6) reference to the sponsoring organization. Anything you think will help an interviewee be a better participant can be part of the orientation statement.

The orientation phase of an interview opening establishes the foundation upon which the rest of the interview will grow. It also helps establish and maintain the interview climate. If the orientation is done with subtlety and finesse, an important step will have been taken toward insuring interview success. A long-winded, dogmatic orientation or no orientation at all can doom an interview before it begins.

The orientation is the foundation upon which an interview grows.

ORIENTATION EXERCISE

Directions: Below you will find several orientation statements. What do you think should be added to or eliminated from each statement?

1. Hello, Mr. Peterson, we are taking a survey of how people feel about the local newspaper.
2. Ed, I suppose you know why you're here. I have a report that you were late for work again. We can't be too long with this interview. I have a doctor's appointment in twenty minutes. I think you know what I have to do now.
3. Well, Susan, the reason I called you here is because we need to evaluate your job performance over the last six months and plan for the next six months. First, we will discuss those areas where you have made definite improvement, and then we will look at a couple of areas where you still need to improve. Earlier I gave you a copy of your written performance appraisal. I think the areas of cooperation and time utilization will be our focus for improvement. Before we get into that, however, I would like to assure you that anything you say here is strictly confidential. I have set aside an hour for this discussion, but if it takes longer, we can schedule a continuation tomorrow. If you have any questions or comments, don't be afraid to make them at any time. I need your full cooperation if we are to help you improve and advance in this organization. I really do think you have a great deal of advancement potential.
4. Mrs. Botts, my name is Ralph Wilcox, and I'm from the *Miami Post*. I am doing a story on senior citizen opportunities in our community. I was given your name by Phil Wilson. He said you participate in a lot of the senior citizen programs. This shouldn't take more than a half hour or so. I would like to ask you about your feelings regarding some of these programs. I will not use your name in my story if you don't want me to.

THE OPENING QUESTION

The first or opening question of an interview serves as a transition from the opening to the main body of the interview itself. It should directly relate to the interview purpose. While preparing the opening question, carefully examine the information you have about the interviewee. You shouldn't use "canned" openers. With a little care and effort, you can create a good opening question for each interviewee.

The opening question should encourage interviewees to give information. It should be nonthreatening and request information which the interviewee can easily answer. Usually, the opening question is quite general because general questions are less stressful and help interviewees relax. They allow respondents to ease into the body of the interview. The opening question should assume consent on the part of the interviewee—you should use positive phrasing such as, "Suppose you tell me . . . ." rather than, "I wonder if you would tell me. . . ." You can tell a great deal about the way the interview will go from the response by an interviewee to the opening question.

OPENING QUESTION EXERCISE

Directions: Review the preceding exercise. For each of the four orientation statements in that exercise, write an opening question. Be sure to take into account any changes you made in the orientation statements.

SUMMARY

In this chapter, the three parts of an interview opening have been discussed: establishing the climate, orienting the interviewee, and the opening question. Interview climate is determined by your personality, the interviewee's personality, and type of interview to be conducted. It includes level of formality and rapport development. Formality exists on a continuum with "formal" on one end to "informal" on the other. Creating and reducing formality can be achieved verbally and nonverbally. Rapport was said to evolve from the sizing up or categorizing process, and several categories of interviewees and interviewers were listed and discussed.

The second aspect of an interview opening is orienting interviewees. A number of areas that should and could be covered during orientation were listed. The two most important of these were the statement of the objectives and the way in which those objectives will be achieved. The last part of an interview opening is the opening question, which provides a transition from the opening to the main body of the interview. The opening question should be rather general, especially prepared for each respondent, and directly related to the interview purpose.

The interview opening is important because it sets the tone and establishes the ground rules for the rest of the interview. If you are skillful at opening an interview, you are a long way toward guaranteeing success. You should not linger in the opening, but you should be sure that your opening prepares interviewees both logically and emotionally for what is to come.

ACTIVITIES

Activity #1

Directions: The way you open an interview is similar to the way you open other types of interaction. All involve icebreaking, formality level development, rapport development, categorization, and so on. Keep a record of all the interaction openings you take part in during a day. If you don't have at least ten, continue for another day or more until you have recorded ten interaction openings. Keep a record of the following information and then answer each of the questions once you have completed your task.

1. Who were you talking to? How many were relatives or *very* close friends? Regular friends or acquaintances? Strangers?
2. How did the openings differ depending on how well you knew the person with whom you were interacting?
3. Were any of these openings planned ahead of time? If so, how did this affect the opening?
4. Describe some of the typical ways in which the ice was broken in these openings and which methods you thought were best.
5. Describe the most and least formal openings you encountered and the verbal and nonverbal techniques used to establish these different levels of formality.
6. Which do you think established the best rapport and why?
7. Describe your first impressions of each of the people you talked with and how you arrived at those impressions.
8. Did any of the people you talked with fit any of the categories given for interviewers or interviewees? If so, name the category and any difficulties you had interacting with them.
9. Was there any orientation or opening question as part of any of these interactions? If so, describe them.
10. What differences did you see in the interaction openings you recorded and those which you believe occur in an interview?

Activity #2

Sit with another person and role play the openings for various types of interviews. A role play requires that you try to imagine yourself in the place of an interviewer or interviewee. Be yourself, but also try to behave as you think you really would in each situation. This will seem a little strange at first, but you will get used to it. Don't make these role plays a joke, or you will not get the full benefit out of them. They are an excellent form of practice. You will be given many more opportunities to role play throughout this book. In these opening role plays, spend no more than five minutes establishing the climate, briefing the respondent, and asking the opening question. If you are working alone, you and your volunteer partner should switch interviewer and interviewee roles each time and evaluate one another as you go along. If you are part of a workshop or class, your instructor will seat you in the double circle pattern shown below:

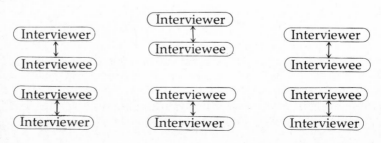

Your instructor will call out the type of opening to be role played each time. After each interaction either the inner or outer circle members will shift to the left or right and all participants will change from interviewer to interviewee or vice versa. Some very brief descriptions of interview situations that can be used follow here. Feel free to change the situation if you can think of a better one. Remember, you need not do anything more specific than open the interview.

> *Information Interview*: You want the interviewee to give you an oral history of his or her hometown.
>
> *Research Interview*: You are taking a survey of people's attitudes toward the local city government.
>
> *Selection Interview*: You are a campus recruiter hiring people in your interviewee's area of interest.
>
> *Counseling Interview*: The interviewee has come to you with a dating or marriage problem.
>
> *Diagnostic Interview*: You are a police officer talking to a witness to a hit-and-run automobile accident.
>
> *Performance Interview*: You are the interviewee's supervisor and this is your annual performance review.
>
> *Persuasion Interview*: The interviewee has just walked onto your used car lot and is looking at a 1980 Subaru.
>
> *Discipline Interview*: You have just caught this student using "cheat notes" on a test.
>
> *Termination Interview*: This interviewee has just resigned as a waiter /waitress in your restaurant.
>
> *Group Interview*: You are marketing a new laundry soap and have called ten people together to tell you what they like and dislike about their current brands.

Compare and contrast the various openings. You may use the questions listed in the previous activity as a guide. The main question you should consider, however, is how the openings to various interview types differ, and why.

Activity #3

This exercise again relates to planning to conduct an information interview. Completely prepare your opening including the climate you wish to establish, how you will go about establishing that climate through icebreaking, level of formality, and rapport development, the information you will include in your orientation, and what your first question will be. Don't write all this out, but have it clearly outlined in such a way that you can do it well.

Answers to the Formality Level Exercise.
1 = Somewhat Informal, 2 = Somewhat Formal, 3 = Neutral, 4 = Very Formal, 5 = Very Informal.

Answers to the Interviewee Classification Exercise.
Several alternatives are offered depending on the interviewee's motive. Your response

should reflect the motive or classification you have chosen.
1 = Arrogant, Tenacious, or Hostile; 2 = Apprehensive, Defensive, or Stolid; 3 = Hostile, Crafty, or Tenacious; 4 = Disorganized or Too Talkative; 5 = Tenacious, Hostile, Crafty, or Arrogant; and 6 = Overeager or Too Talkative.

Answers to the Interviewer Classification Exercise.

1 = Routine, 2 = Sentimental, 3 = Domineering, 4 = Research, 5 = Give and Take, 6 = Salesman, 7 = Scatterbrained, 8 = Moralistic, 9 = Therapeutic, and 10 = Paul Pry.

Chapter 4

Skill 4
Asking and Answering Questions

Questioning is a much abused art. It appears to be very difficult for interviewers to ask a clear, unequivocal, understandable question and then be quiet long enough to give the interviewee an unhampered, uninterrupted opportunity to answer. (Kadushin, 1972, p. 157)

Developing skill in asking and answering questions has been stressed for at least two thousand years. The Greek philosopher, Socrates, used questioning as both a teaching and information gathering device. Inquiry and response skill is as important today as it was in ancient Athens. Questions and answers lie at the very heart of the interviewing process. Earlier the various types of interview questions were described. In this chapter you will learn how to structure, phrase, and ask those questions. The way a question is asked is no less important than the type of question asked.

As important as questioning is to an interview, be careful not to spend too much time doing it. Most experts agree that no more than twenty to thirty percent of interaction time should be used by an interviewer in asking questions or making statements. The following chapters on listening and recording will emphasize this point. As you will also see in the chapter on probing, there are many other ways of getting information from an interviewee besides asking direct questions. Beginning interviewers tend to ask too many questions.

Inquiries serve many purposes besides eliciting information. First, they allow you to maintain control of the interview. By asking questions you guide the interviewee. Second, the nature of a question, in part, shapes the response. The way in which you ask a question tells interviewees what type of information you desire and how much. Third, questions encourage participation. A well-prepared question encourages interviewees to respond freely and fully. Fourth, questions help maintain the appropriate level of formality and rapport. The interview climate, which is established in the opening, can either be maintained or altered during questioning. Fifth, questions can help interviewees discover new information about themselves and the topic which they might not even know they possess.

All of these purposes are served both by the nature and wording of the questions you ask and the way in which you ask them. In this chapter you will also find information regarding appropriate responses. This chapter in conjunction with the interview guide chapter should prepare you to develop and use high quality questions and answers in the course of any interview.

FOCUS ON THE RESPONDENT

In both the preparation and asking of questions, use the respondent as a guide. Your questions should reflect the goals, attitudes, background, and problems of your interviewee. Some interviewers refer to this as a "you-focus" or "other-orientation" instead of an "I-focus" or "self-orientation." When translated into actual interview behavior, an other-orientation means adjusting your pace, vocabulary, phrasing, and general style to fit each respondent. This requires a willingness on your part to deviate from the interview guide when appropriate. Except in rare circumstances, such as police interrogation, stress tactics are a very poor way to ask questions. Balinsky and Burger (1959) provide the following advice in this regard:

The thoughtful interviewer will word his questions so as to:
Probe, not cross-examine.
Inquire, not challenge.
Suggest, not demand.
Uncover, not trap.
Draw out, not pump.
Guide, not dominate.
The test of your questions is not merely "How much information did I get?" but, equally important, "How subtly did I guide the exchange?"
(Balinsky and Burger, 1959, p. 59)

WORD CHOICE

In interviewing, word choice or vocabulary is extremely important. Our language is complex and flexible, and words can have more than one meaning both in the dictionary and in an interviewee's head. There are special vocabularies associated with different professions, occupations, social strata, and regions of the country. You can never assume that your vocabulary, as an interviewer, will be understood by interviewees in the same way as you intended. The word meanings that are important in an interview are those found inside the heads of the interviewer and the interviewee, not those in the dictionary. This warning is important in asking questions, as well as in listening for and recording information.

Complexity

It is up to you to discover and use the vocabulary of the interviewee, not attempt to impose your own words upon a respondent. You can discover if your word choice is appropriate by watching for puzzled looks, confused pauses, and responses which indicate misinterpretation. Continued requests for question clarification is perhaps the most obvious cue of incorrect vocabulary choice. On the basis of a few cues as to the vocabulary level of an interviewee, skillful interviewers are capable of adjusting their entire language level to that of a respondent. After you have adapted and begin to use words which are easily understood, the flow of interaction becomes smooth.

Some words are too abstract for most respondents. Whenever possible you should try to substitute simple words for more complex ones. The following is a sample list of complex words and their simpler substitutes:

Employment	Work	Presume	Think
Assistance	Help	Misguided	Unwise
Rectify	Correct	Virtually	Nearly
Accelerate	Speed Up	Inflexible	Strict
Objective	Goal	Inflammation	Sore
Salience	Importance	Laborious	Hard

One of the problems with using simple words is that they sometimes turn short sentences into long ones. Dillman (1978) cites the example of trying to simplify the question, "Should the sales tax on prescription drugs be reduced from 5 percent to 1 percent?" The result was the question, "Should the state sales tax on those medicines that can only be bought under a doctor's order be lowered so that people would pay 1 cent tax instead of 5 cents tax for every dollar spent on such medicine?" The question went from fifteen words to thirty-nine words.

Simple words can also increase the risk of "talking down" to respondents. That is, they may feel you are treating them like children by using overly simple words. The level of word complexity should be carefully balanced to fit each respondent, or in the case of research interviews, to be uniformly understood by all respondents.

Ambiguity

Many English words are extremely ambiguous. Indefinite and vague, they carry different meanings, references, and implications for different people. The most ambiguous words are those which are highly abstract. Words such as "freedom," "happiness," and "responsibility" are good examples of abstract words. If you ask an interviewee, "Are you given a great deal of freedom and responsibility on your job?" you are asking an ambiguous question. The question is ambiguous because respondents can interpret it in many ways. A less ambiguous question might be, "Can you come and go whenever you please on your job?"

Ambiguous questions frequently produce ambiguous answers. People interpret them differently and, therefore, answer them differently. Respondents answer based on their own interpretation and their own viewpoint. It is then up to you to search out the real meaning of the response. Whenever possible avoid ambiguity in the questions you prepare, and look for indications of ambiguity in interviewee responses.

Sometimes ambiguity can be used as a technique in questioning. Many open questions are intentionally phrased in a somewhat ambiguous manner in order to encourage interviewees to respond in any direction they please. When used for this purpose there is nothing wrong with ambiguity, but you should be aware that a question is ambiguous. Realize that you are giving respondents a great deal of response leeway. When you want specific information but phrase a question in an ambiguous manner, problems can arise.

Subjectivity

Words can carry both subjective and objective meanings, sometimes referred to as connotative and denotative meanings. *Denotative* meaning is the dictionary or common meaning for a word. The denotative meaning for the word, "therapist," for example, is "one who treats a disease as by some remedial or curative process." The *connotative* meaning of a word is the implied or associated meaning of the word. This is the meaning that is found only in people's heads. For some, the connotative meaning of the word "therapist" might be "shrink," "savior," "quack," or "friend" depending upon their previous experiences with people called "therapists."

All words have connotative meanings for people. They add subjectivity to your questions. These connotative, emotional, subjective overtones can produce biased questions and responses. Some words carry subjective meanings for almost everyone. Obscenities, for example, can produce an emotional response in anyone who hears them, especially if spoken with special emphasis. A question such as, "What the HELL is going on in this office?" is enough to cause any respondent to become defensive or hostile. Subjectivity can occur in either questions or answers. You must be constantly on the alert for the connotative meanings of the words you use in an interview.

Jargon

Doctors, lawyers, social workers, nurses, police officers, and many other people who regularly use interviews as a part of their job have special terms which are related to their profession, but which can be easily misunderstood or not understood by interviewees. This special terminology is commonly referred to as jargon. To a lawyer, for example, terms such as "plaintiff," "tort," "litigation," and "arraignment" are common words. They have little or no meaning to most non-lawyers.

It may be difficult for interviewers to adapt their normal jargon to the vocabulary of a respondent. This does not mean that you should try to imitate the poor vocabulary of some respondents, but only that you should be sure your words are understood. Questions such as, "Are you sure you ain't done that before?" would be unbecoming to most interviewers. It could also be offensive and inappropriate to the interviewee/interviewer role relationship.

Jargon also includes the use of abbreviations. The abbreviation, A.B.A., for example, would be interpreted differently if you were talking to lawyers or basketball coaches. Using abbreviations is justifiable if they are identified first and used in order to avoid repeating long titles or names many times. Whenever possible, abbreviations and jargon should be avoided in the questions you prepare or in your comments to an interviewee.

In summary, then, keep a number of factors in mind concerning word choice. First, try to use words which are familiar to interviewees. Second, be sure that the meanings of the words you use are the same for respondents as they are for you, both the denotative and connotative meanings. Third, don't make assumptions regarding word meaning. Fourth, watch for abstract or ambiguous words. Fifth, don't use jargon of any sort. Always try to use the correct word in the correct place for best understanding by respondents. Word choice affects the quality of both questions and answer categories when using closed questions. Sometimes it is useful to have a third person evaluate your word choices when you prepare questions ahead of time. This is common in research interviews. Other people can note words that may cause problems. The final test of your word choice, however, comes in the interview itself, in the form of the response you receive to your questions.

WORD CHOICE EXERCISE

Directions: Here are several examples of poorly worded questions. Rewrite each question, avoiding complexity, ambiguity, subjectivity, and jargon. If you are not sure what the question is asking, do your best to interpret it correctly.

1. Do you feel secure in your job?
2. Do you think the V.P.'s approval of merit pay will be opposed by the N.E.A.?
3. Would you be more definitive about what you mean?
4. Do you think this larceny was premeditated?
5. We've got a sweet setup here, don't we?
6. Do you think our government, the United States Government, our elected officials, should continue to help each of us after we are too old to continue working by taking money out of the pay of those people who still are working?
7. Do you feel you are making a contribution here?   Yes/No
8. For our next sale, do you think we should have our dresses:
    a. 10%–20% off
    b. 1/3rd off
    c. Half off
    d. More than half off
9. Do you think grade inflation is affecting the quality of education at this university?
10. Do you consider yourself to be a puritan when it comes to sexual experimentation?

FRAMING QUESTIONS

Every question occurs within a context. The purpose of the interview, the level of formality and rapport, and the time and location of the interview are all aspects of question context. From a narrower perspective, preceding questions and topics also establish question context. It is up to you to frame each question to fit the context. In some ways this is done through your question sequence, but even more important is the preface which leads to the question. A *preface* is a statement which immediately precedes a question and provides the frame which allows an interviewee to interpret the question correctly.

Factual Preface

Remember, interviewees come to an interview with certain basic assumptions. If those assumptions are the ones which you desire, then little or no question preface is necessary. If, on the other hand, those assumptions are inaccurate, or you suspect they may be inaccurate, then a factual preface may be necessary. A factual preface supplies needed data which help an interviewee respond to a question properly. These facts can stimulate a respondent's memory. They can also help reduce chronological confusion. Here's an example of a question with a factual preface:

I am sure you have heard that the city council must decide next month whether or not to establish a new city park. The land they are considering will cost approximately $50,000 initially and another $100,000 to make it operational. They plan to float a bond and repay it in ten years. If interest rates remain the same the park will end up costing the city approximately $300,000. How do you feel about the city park issue?

Obviously, a preface can sometimes introduce bias into questions. If the preface is slanted, omits vital facts, or is made up of distorted facts, it can cause respondents to answer the way they think they should answer rather than how they really feel. A factual preface should be worded carefully and checked to be sure that it is made up of complete and unbiased information.

Factual prefaces can help prevent response distortion. A high-school counselor who says to a student, "I have talked to a number of your teachers about your progress," may head off answers which are fabrications. It is generally a matter of etiquette to let interviewees know what you know and your sources of information. There are, however, some interviews, such as criminal suspect questioning, when this principle doesn't apply. The police sometimes feel the quest for truth and cooperation of informants requires them to withhold such information from a respondent. A factual preface should not give the impression that you have all of the facts, but that you know some of them and that obvious distortions will be detected.

Motivational Preface

Question framing can also be useful in motivating a respondent. A motivational preface can arouse interest in an interviewee—"One of the most exciting aspects of this job is its unlimited potential for advancement," is a motivational preface. Others recognize an interviewee's special efforts or qualifications. Prefacing a question with the statement, "I understand you have a lot of experience in this area," can make a respondent feel obliged to answer questions on that particular subject. You can also motivate by offering some reward in the preface. "One of the things we need to know before promoting someone in this company . . ." would be enough incentive to encourage almost any employee to answer a question.

A preface can also motivate responses by reducing the threat of the question. You can insert a possible excuse in the preface in order to give the interviewee a way of face-saving. A statement such as, "I know you have some problems at home, but . . ." or "You're not the only one I have seen doing things this way, but . . ." are examples of *face-saving prefaces*. You can also encourage interviewees to respond by using their name or the pronoun "you" as part of the question preface. People feel more involved and motivated to respond if the preface relates directly to them. This is why, for example, mail questionnaires and advertisements are often accompanied by form letters to which the respondent's name has been added in key places.

Framing is an extremely important part of good questioning. Skillful interviewers frame each question to help interviewees provide the most accurate and complete information possible. A preface is one of the most effective ways of framing. Question framing is similar to response shaping, which is discussed in the following section. The difference is that the main purpose of framing is to provide an interviewee with information and motivation to answer a question accurately, whereas the purpose of response shaping is to somehow dictate the nature of the desired response. However, framing sometimes helps shape a response as well.

QUESTION FRAMING EXERCISE

Directions: For the discipline interview situation described here, write question frames in the form of a preface designed to (1) jog the interviewee's memory, (2) prevent response distortion, (3) motivate a response by recognizing special qualifications, and (4) motivate a response by helping the respondent save face.

Mr. Clark is the chief accountant for your department store. Among his other responsibilities, he supervises the claims handlers. You have always known that he is strict, autocratic, and systematic, but he is also extremely fair with his employees and the best person you have had in that position. Recently, however, it has come to your attention that the turnover of claims handlers far exceeds that of other store personnel. You are not sure whether Clark is aware of the problem or not, but you feel you should talk to him and try to get to the bottom of this matter.

QUESTION PHRASING

Good questions should be purposeful, clear, natural, brief, thought-provoking, limited in scope, and unbiased. A question is *purposeful* if it is designed to achieve a specific goal. A question is *clear* if an interviewee understands the meaning in the same way the interviewer intended it. A question is *natural* if it is spoken in simple understandable words. A question is *brief* if it is phrased in the fewest possible words. A question is *thought-provoking* if it stimulates interviewees to consider it carefully. A question is *limited in scope* if it specifies the range and depth of response required, and it is *unbiased* if it does not suggest a preferred answer. Some of these qualities of good questions have already been mentioned, but in this section you will discover some further ways of improving questions through phrasing.

Small phrasing changes can make a great deal of difference in the responses supplied by respondents. Gorden (1980, p. 287) cites the example of two questions which obtained different responses from tornado victims:

> *What were some of the problems which arose during the rescue operations after the tornado struck?*
> *What sorts of trouble did people have trying to help folks who were hurt or trapped in the wreckage?*

Which do you think got the better response and why? If you said the second question, you were right. The phrasing of the first question, especially the word "problems," puzzled many of the interviewees. A skillful interviewer is constantly sensitive to the effect question phrasing is having on interviewee responses.

Long Questions

Perhaps the best way to study question phrasing is to look at a number of problems poorly phrased questions cause. Long questions can confuse respondents. Long questions are usually characterized by repetition, vagueness, and unnecessary preface statements. As a general rule, you should consider any question too long that is more than two sentences. In most cases you should use the first sentence to set the frame and the second sentence to ask the actual question.

Short or Precise Questions

In their desire to avoid overly long questions, some interviewers ask questions that are so short that respondents cannot answer them either because they do not understand them or the information requested is too specific to recall accurately. The question, "What's new?" for example, is too short. The respondent doesn't know what specific information you desire. Short questions often get a question in return, such as, "What's new with what?"

The question, "How many television shows have you watched in the last year?" is too precise. Few of us keep accurate count of the routine things we do each day. The use of broad categories and a reduced time perspective can make the question more effective. You might, for example, inquire as to how many hours of television respondents watch per day and make the necessary calculations to determine the number of shows they watch per year. Being too short or precise can be as bad as being too long.

Double-Barrelled Questions

A third problem in phrasing questions is the introduction of more than one idea in the same question. An example would be, "How do you feel about pollution, and what do you intend to do about it?" These are sometimes called multiple or double-barrelled questions. They are often motivated by a desire to clarify the question, but they do exactly the opposite—they make the question ambiguous. The interviewee ends up only answering part of the question—often the part you are least interested in. Each question should be phrased to contain only one, clear idea to the interviewee. The problem of multiple questions can easily be solved by breaking them into separate questions.

Negative Questions

Negative questions lead to defensiveness and endless qualifying. Questions which begin "What do you dislike about . . . ," "What is the worst . . . ," or "What problems . . ," are all negative. If at all possible, questions should be phrased positively. Instead of asking about problems, ask about successes. Instead of asking what someone dislikes, ask what they like.

Sharp Questions

A fifth question-phrasing problem which normally puts interviewees on the defensive is the overly sharp question. Examples might be questions like "Are you telling the truth?" or "Were you fired from your last job?" This usually occurs with closed questions. Good questions are phrased with qualifying words and phrases to soften their impact. Words such as "might," "perhaps," "somewhat," and "fairly" help soften the impact of a question, as do the phrases, "Is it possible that . . . ," "Would you say that . . . ," "How did you happen to . . . ," "To what extent . . . ," and "To what do you attribute . . . ." Questions can also be softened by the tone in which they are asked. This aspect will be discussed later in the section on interviewer style.

Direct Questions

Up to now, it has been assumed that an interviewee is both capable of and willing to answer your questions and that you can ask for information directly. This assumption is probably fair in most cases—if you have prepared well, established a favorable climate, and asked a clear question, most interviewees will respond with the information desired. But sometimes respondents may be unwilling to divulge information if you ask them directly. This is especially true when the information is perceived as either embarrassing or threatening. Such questions include those which ask about violations of social norms such as prejudice toward minority groups, use of drugs, sexual relationships, and personal questions about age, income, and marital status, or even something as simple as whether or not they voted in the last election. Interviewees may be offended and attempt to protect themselves by giving partial or biased information. In such situations, you need to make a series of important decisions.

The first decision is whether the information can be elicited within an interview at all. If you decide that an interviewee will probably be unwilling to give you such information, then try to gain the information in some other way, such as with documents, observations, or third-person interviews. If you feel that the information can only be gained through an interview and that it is important to receive the information even if it is only partial, then determine whether the information should be solicited through a direct question or whether an indirect phrasing should be used. Interviewing would be a much less important means of gathering information if you could not ask questions indirectly.

An indirect approach is one which tries to elicit the information without coming out and openly asking for it. Indirect methods of obtaining information are many and varied. One of the most common methods is to phrase the question in the third person. A *third person question* permits interviewees to camouflage their response by directing the focus of the question to a person or persons other than themselves. Suppose, for example, you were the department head in a college and wanted to find out how a particular teacher was doing. You might directly ask a student, "How do you think Professor Thorsen is doing in this course?" or instead you might phrase the question in a third person form such as, "How do most students perceive what is happening in Professor Thorsen's course?" The assumption is that respondents will answer the question in line with their own feelings, but by asking it in a third person form, you have allowed the student to answer honestly without fear of reprisal from the professor. By making the question less personal, you increase the chances of getting an honest response.

The third person question is only one technique interviewers have developed to get at embarrassing or threatening information indirectly. Other methods include the use of tests, drawings, and pictures, descriptions or brief anecdotes, or merely the introduction of a hypothetical person. You might, for example, show interviewees pictures of different situations and ask which they prefer, which they would like to be part of, why they made that choice, and what differences they perceive between the various situations pictured.

Psychologists have made very interesting discoveries about personality characteristics by using similar methods called *projective techniques.* The Rorschach test is one example of a projective technique. It consists of a series of cards with inkblot designs. Each design is random, that is, it has little relationship to anything in the real world. Respondents are asked to tell what they "see" in each of the cards. Since the cards are without meaning, the meaning assigned to them is the meaning that comes from within the individual responding. From the descriptions provided by a respondent, the psychologist attempts to indirectly determine certain attributes about the individual's personality. When using indirect methods such as projective techniques, you must be careful in how you interpret the meaning of the information provided. This is a difficult process and requires extensive training.

Descriptions or *anecdotes* are used in much the same way. The interviewer provides a description or anecdote which the interviewee is asked to analyze. "I had a funny situation occur a couple of months ago . . ." might be the preface to an indirect question of this sort. The interviewees' analyses of the description or anecdote are assumed to be indications of their true feelings about the subject under consideration.

This same basic approach can be used with a *hypothetical person* described by respondents. You have probably seen dramatizations of interviews where the interviewee describes a "friend" who is having a problem. The friend is actually the interviewee, but the interviewer allows the respondent to continue talking about the hypothetical person rather than confronting the interviewee with the fact that no such person exists. A good interviewer can encourage the development of such a hypothetical person to elicit information indirectly.

There are a number of other indirect means of getting information. You might, for example, ask for broad categories of information rather than specifics. Information on age and income is usually collected in this manner. Instead of directly asking a person's age or income, you can give a range, such as 35–40 years or $15,000–$20,000. Another method is to preface embarrassing or threatening questions in such a way that directness is blunted. This was mentioned earlier as a face-saving preface. Dillman (1978) provides the following example of how survey researchers indirectly find out whether a person has ever shoplifted:

As you know, there is now a great deal of discussion about shoplifting in this community, and questions as to how it should be handled. Some people feel it is a serious problem about which something should be done, others feel it is not a serious problem. How about yourself? Do you consider shoplifting to be a serious, moderate, slight, or no problem at all in our community?
   1. Serious
   2. Moderate
   3. Slight
   4. Not at all
During the past few years do you think the frequency of shoplifting has increased, stayed about the same, or decreased in this community?
   1. Increased
   2. Stayed about the same
   3. Decreased
Please try to recall the time when you were a teenager. Do you recall personally knowing anyone who took something from a store without paying for it?
   1. No
   2. Yes
How about yourself? Did you ever consider taking anything from a store without paying for it?
   1. No
   2. Yes
   (If yes)
Did you actually take it?
   1. No
   2. Yes

(Dillman, 1978, p. 107)

This is a very effective nondirective method of obtaining information you think you could not obtain by direct questioning.

The main point of all this is that while preparing questions, be alert to how direct questioning of each topic will be perceived. If a direct question is likely to elicit a less than accurate and complete answer, then you should be prepared to phrase questions in a way that will produce the information indirectly. It is sometimes the only way important information can be obtained.

DIRECT/INDIRECT QUESTION EXERCISE

Directions: Rephrase each of the following direct questions to get at the same information indirectly.
1. Would you say your marriage is completely happy?
2. Did you see who started the fight in that bar you were in last night?
3. May I tape record this interview?
4. Have you ever used marijuana or hashish?
5. Did XYZ Company try to bribe you to vote their way on this piece of legislation?

Leading Question

The final, and perhaps most significant problem in question phrasing is the introduction of bias. By far the most consistent source of interview bias is the leading question. A leading question either directly or indirectly suggests a "right" answer to an interviewee. They influence respondents to answer in a manner that does not necessarily reflect their true attitudes, beliefs, behaviors, or attributes. Why and how interviewers come to formulate leading questions and how and when they should be avoided is one of the most widely discussed issues in the interviewing literature.

Much of this debate started in the literature on legal interviewing. In 1863, Bell wrote about the use of leading questions in the courtroom.

> . . . [A question is leading] where the question assumes any fact which is in controversy so that the answer may really or apparently admit that fact. Such are the forked questions habitually put by some counsel if unchecked as, "What was the plaintiff doing when the defendant struck him?" The controversy being whether the defendant did strike. A dull or a forward witness may answer the first part of the question and neglect the last.

(Young, P., 1935)

In legal interviewing, a leading question is sometimes used to supply a false memory for the witness, that is, to suggest desired answers not in truth based upon the actual recollection of the witness. Leading questions are often allowed in the cross-examination of the other side's witness because it's assumed that a witness for the opposition is already biased in a particular direction and will be reluctant to accept a cross-examiner's suggestion, that is, leading question.

The majority of interviewing experts advise never to use a leading question. There are, however, interviewers, especially those dealing with embarrassing and threatening information, who suggest that leading questions have a definite purpose and role in interviewing. Kinsey (1948), for example, used leading questions while conducting interviews on sexual behavior.

The interviewer should not make it easy for a subject to deny his participation in any form of sexual activity. It is too easy to say no if he is simply asked whether he has engaged in a particular activity. Consequently we always begin by asking when they first engaged in such activity . . . and since it becomes apparent from the form of our question that we would not be surprised if he had had such experience, there seems to be less reason for denying it. It might be thought this approach would bias the answer, but there is no indication that we get false admissions of participations in forms of sexual behavior in which the subject was not actually involved.

(Kinsey et al., 1948, pp. 53–55)

Effects of Leading Questions.

There are three situations which must be distinguished with regard to the use of leading questions. The first is the case where the leading question helps obtain more accurate information. The second is when legitimate information is revealed, regardless of whether or not the question is leading. The third situation, perhaps the most common, is where a leading question intentionally or unintentionally influences or distorts an answer. Leading questions of the first type occur when respondents are certain about what they know but fear reporting it because an accurate answer would be embarrassing or incriminating. An example of this type of situation, where the leading question actually produces more accurate information, would be the sexual behavior interviews described by Kinsey. Interviewees may believe that they would be violating public norms if they directly told Kinsey about their sexual behaviors. In order to achieve responses contrary to public norms (that is, true responses) Kinsey and his associates had to use leading questions.

Leading questions of the second type, where accurate information is obtained despite the presence of a leading question, occur when respondents are certain about what they know and intend to report it no matter how the question is phrased. An example of this situation would be the cross-examination portion of a court trial. A witness supposedly would have the information clearly in mind, and under the rules of the court must report it accurately. The cross-examining attorney may use leading questions to test the accuracy of the information and the witness's certainty. In many cases, interviewers other than attorneys also use leading questions which do not bias information. Doctors, social workers, police officers, and journalists all use leading questions at times to test information accuracy, especially when they feel that respondents may be withholding or distorting information even though it is clear in their minds.

In many cases the use of a leading question does bias the response away from the truth. If a great deal of time has elapsed since the occurrence of a particular situation, the information may not be clear in the respondent's mind. In this case, the interviewee may be easily led. Sometimes the information requested is not very important to respondents, and therefore, they are anxious to get the interview over quickly by answering in the direction suggested, even if it means an inaccurate response. In situations where the interviewer has more status than an interviewee, such as in a selection, performance, counseling, or diagnostic interview, respondents will very often distort or omit information because they are afraid to say, "I don't know," "I don't remember," or "I'm not sure." They do not want to appear unintelligent or uncooperative.

When an interviewer is perceived as a real threat, respondents sometimes rationalize with such mental statements as, "He doesn't really want to know the truth anyway," or "He wouldn't do anything with the information if I gave it to him." It is important for you to be aware of all of the conditions in which leading questions can produce positive, neutral, and negative effects. It is an oversimplification to suggest that leading questions should never be used. It is a much more difficult decision to determine when leading questions should be used.

Types of Leading Questions.

There are a number of different types of leading questions—five will be described here. First, there are leading questions which are due to the preceding questions. Persuasive interviewers use the *yes-yes strategy*. The idea is to get respondents saying "yes" to several questions in a row and then ask for a decision. The interviewee's natural inclination is to say "yes" to the decision question as well. This is an obvious example, but there are many ways to lead respondents by your question sequence. Research interviewers often alter their question sequence to prevent this very problem from biasing the results.

The second, and probably the largest category of leading questions are those which contain leading prefaces. You probably already noticed some examples of leading prefaces earlier in this chapter. You could identify the expected response by the preface. Another example of this would be, "In our company we think employees should change locations every three to five years. Do you mind relocating?" Sometimes a leading preface associates a response with a desired goal. An example might be, "Most people want financial security for their family." Another type of leading preface associates a particular response with some person the interviewee regards highly or someone who is in a position superior to the interviewee. An example might be, "Mr. Jones, your boss, suggested that you would have time to talk with me for a few minutes. Do you have a few minutes to spare?" Leading prefaces of this type do not have to be associated with some particular individual or group, the reference can be impersonal—"Since large numbers of high-school students are graduating without being able to read, do you think we should reevaluate our educational standards?" All of these are questions which are leading because they slant the interviewee's views prior to asking the question.

The third way questions can be leading is because they use emotionally charged words. The question, "How do you feel about Mr. Smith *buying* the nomination of his party?" would probably draw a great many more negative responses than the more neutral question, "How do you feel about Mr. Smith *receiving* the nomination?" There are many English words which have either a positive or negative slant and, therefore, bias interviewees either in a positive or negative direction. Hayakawa (1964) calls these "snarl words" and "purr words." Words like "socialist," "boss," "fussy," and "aggressive" are all snarl words, whereas words such as "lovely," "equality," "honesty," and "wonderful" are all purr words. It is not humanly possible to strip all questions of emotionally charged words. The best you can hope to do is balance question phrasing in such a way that these snarl and purr words cancel each other. Look at the following illustration and decide which question presents an unbalanced and, therefore, leading use of emotionally charged words.

Who is responsible for the high inflation rate?
Laborers
Business Persons
Washington Bureaucrats
Who is responsible for the high inflation rate?
Labor
Business
Government

Fourth, a question can be leading if it omits a possible category which is an appropriate interviewee response or if it presents unequal categories. Compare the question, "Are you married or single?" with the question, "Are you married, single, divorced, widowed, or separated?" You will notice that in the first question several categories were left out which were included in the last question. The first question would obviously gain a great many more "single" responses, whereas the last question would gain a more accurate statement of each interviewee's actual marital status. The following is another example of unequal categories:

Do you think the amount of money this company spends on training and development should be:
Decreased
Stay the same
Increased a little
Increased somewhat
Increased a great deal

This question would tend to lead people to select one of the "increase" categories. The middle option is not neutral (i.e., "stay the same"), but is slanted in the direction of increasing such funds. Remember, a leading question is phrased so that it appears to the respondent that the interviewer wants or expects a particular answer.

Following are some examples of the types of questions encyclopedia salespeople are told to use when negotiating and closing a sale. You will notice all of these questions are leading. They are designed to lead the prospect to sign a contract.

1. *Can't afford excuse:* "That is quite a lot of money!"
   Smile and agree: "Mr. Dugan, I agree that it is quite a lot of money."
   Turn the excuse (pride and love): "But, then, Mary is quite a lot of future success to plan for, isn't she?"

2. *See husband excuse:* "You will have to see my husband."
Smile and agree: "Mrs. Collins, although I'm very busy, I would be delighted to see your husband."
Turn the excuse (pride): "But you and I know exactly what will happen don't we? He will turn to you when I'm halfway through and say, 'Well, honey, what do you think?' If he were sitting here right now saying this, as we both know he would, what would you say?"

3. *Buy later excuse:* "I think I'd rather wait because then we can get more up-to-date material."
Smile and agree: "Mrs. Kennedy, we always want to give our children the most modern tools, don't we?"
Turn the excuse (caution): "But, we must give them tools when they begin to need them. Children start to develop habits the minute they are born. It's the little things children do from day to day that form the habits which affect character, personality, and disposition, isn't it?"

A fifth type of leading question has come to be known as a *loaded question*. A loaded question is one which either dictates an answer or leaves interviewees wondering how they can possibly answer the question at all. Questions of the former type include: "How do you feel about these damn constant increases in natural gas?" "Isn't that the most asinine statement you've ever heard?" and "No one really believes that, do they?" Questions of the type which leave the respondent no possible answer include, "How long do you really expect us to keep you around when you perform in that manner?" "Have you stopped cheating on your income tax?" and "When was the last time you were high on marijuana?" Loaded questions are certainly not subtle. In many ways they can be considered *rhetorical* questions. A rhetorical question is one where the interviewer really does not even expect an answer. As with the encyclopedia questions and answers, very often the salesperson does not even wait for the prospect to answer.

LEADING QUESTION EXERCISE

Directions: Change each of the following leading questions to nonleading ones. Be careful, some of them are tricky.

1. You would say that you oppose dirty books, wouldn't you?
2. Doesn't it hurt here?
3. Do you like our President's suggestion that more power should be given to the state governments?
4. When was the last time you were drunk?
5. A recent newspaper poll showed most of the citizens of our city are in favor of a new library. How do you feel about it?
6. How do you think I am doing so far as your supervisor?
7. Would you say the person you saw leaving was Asian?
8. Would you say you like to work outdoors?
9. Who is responsible for the increase in burglaries in this neighborhood? The Police

> The City Government
> The Young Punks
> Your Neighbors
> 10. You do think this is the best book you have ever read, don't you?

Careful phrasing is important no matter what type of interview you are conducting. You should strive to make your questions purposeful, clear, natural, brief, thought-provoking, limited in scope, and unbiased. You can do this if you avoid all of the phrasing problems mentioned here. In phrasing questions, ask yourself whether the question is one that you would feel comfortable answering yourself.

INTERVIEWER STYLE

In Chapter 3, several different types of interviewers were described. Remember the sales or missionary interviewer, the routine interviewer, the research interviewer, the therapeutic-nihilistic interviewer, the scatterbrained interviewer, the domineering interviewer, the moralistic interviewer, the "Paul-Pry" interviewer, and the sentimental interviewer? Each of these refer directly to interviewer style. Here you will find some suggestions of ways you can become a give-and-take interviewer.

Use Your Personality

No one style is best for everyone—skillful interviewers use many different styles. They have found a style which fits their own personality, as well as the personality of their interviewees and interview purpose. Beginning interviewers

Practice interviews help you learn to ask and answer questions.

are sometimes afraid to use their personality as part of their style. They constantly attempt to maintain a "poker face." This can be a big mistake. Interviewees find it much easier to open up and talk to a person who is not afraid to be themselves. If you are normally a fairly humorous person, there is no reason why you cannot use humor in the interview. If you are not an outgoing person, then don't try to be one during the interview. At any rate, you should be as natural as possible. The only thing you might want to watch, however, is putting in too many personal opinions. Let your personality show through, but do not let your personal opinions affect interviewee responses.

Be Sincere

A second aspect of interviewer style which goes along with presentation of personality is sincerity. Sincerity means responding to interviewees openly and honestly. If respondents perceive an interviewer as dishonest, they will normally be less likely to give the information desired.

Your questions may need to be difficult but they should not be tricky or crafty. As an interviewer, you should always be as frank and straightforward with interviewees as possible. Sincerity is communicated through eye contact, a natural, relaxed, attentive posture, and a candid tone of voice. These nonverbal behaviors communicate not only sincerity, but also confidence.

Maintain Control

A troublesome question for many interviewers who act naturally and are sincere is how to maintain control of the interview. It is possible, however, to allow your personality to show through and be sincere and yet not give up the control necessary to conduct a successful interview. The question/answer process which is typical of most interviews *makes* the interviewer the authority and directional controller of interaction.

Don't be overly concerned with maintaining authority and control, but you must not allow interviews to digress. Encourage interviewees to stay on the topic with emphasis techniques. Loudness and pitch can create emphasis, as well as pauses. By properly emphasizing important parts of a question, you will focus interviewee attention on those areas which you see as important. Phrasing and framing also help you to maintain fairly strict control over interview content.

Adjust Interview Pace

Another key aspect of interviewer style is the pace of the interview. *Pace* refers to how fast or slowly questions are asked and how much time is allowed for interviewee responses. Some interview participants tend to talk either very quickly or very slowly. It is up to an interviewer to find an appropriate pace and maintain it throughout the interview. Adjust the pace to fit the needs and demands of each interviewee. Asking questions too quickly or asking too many questions can confuse interviewees.

A rapid pace can make interviewees feel as if they are being cross-examined by a prosecuting attorney. This can happen when interviewers stick too close to the interview guide and read questions. You must be flexible in using the interview guide. Be familiar enough with the guide to ask questions in a conversational tone and with a conversational pace. This means your presentation should flow at approximately the rate it would in normal conversation.

Pace also refers to the amount of response time. As a general rule, you should allow interviewees to tell their own story in their own way and at their own pace. This includes giving them time to think about a response. Beginning interviewers have a tendency to interrupt responses once they feel they have heard all they want to know. Resist this temptation. Interruption assumes that you already know or don't care about the response that will be given. Never assume anything with regard to an interviewee response.

Don't Repeat

By the same token, skillful interviewers seldom, if ever, exactly repeat a question. It encourages inattention. Respondents who know that every question is going to be asked at least twice will often neglect listening to the question when it is asked the first time. Question repetition normally occurs when interviewees take a few seconds to think about an answer. This indicates impatience and unwillingness to let them answer. There is no reason for interviewers to continue talking after asking a question, unless they are certain the question was not heard completely.

Another distracting interviewer habit is to repeat part or all of every answer given by respondents. This wastes time and changes the pace of the interview. If it is done to check a response, it should happen during a summary and not after each individual response. All of these aspects of interviewer style—personality, sincerity, control, repetition, and pace—are important for you to keep in mind as an interview progresses. But they must suit you, the interviewee, and interview purpose.

INTERVIEWER STYLE EXERCISE

Directions: Here are two versions of the same persuasive interview. A woman has just entered the High Style Shoe Store on a busy Saturday afternoon. As soon as the salesperson approaches, she says she would like to try on a pair of shoes she saw in the window. The salesperson notes the type of shoe, asks her to be seated, removes her shoe, and then measures her foot. Her foot is obviously too slender to be comfortable in the style she has selected. The salesperson brings her that style anyway to try on. Identify those things in the first interview you think the interviewer is doing right and wrong.

1 Salesperson: That doesn't feel very comfortable, does it? It must feel like you're walking in a box. (Laughing)
Customer: It sure doesn't fit very well. It gaps on the side and my heel slides up and down. I think that . . .
5 Salesperson: Yeah, I knew that would happen. Your foot requires a tailored

shoe. I brought one along with me. Put this one on and see if it doesn't fit better.

Customer: But that's not the style I want.

Salesperson: It's not the style, but the fit I want you to notice.

10 Customer: If I am going to try on a shoe, I want to try on one I like. Do you have one in that style (pointing to one on the display rack)? I want a high-heeled . . .

Salesperson: You want a high-heeled shoe? Everyone is wearing lower heels nowadays. That one is last year's fashion. Why don't you try this one on?

15 Customer: Oh, O.K. But, will you go get me one like that one on display? (She begins to put on the low-heeled shoe.)

Salesperson: I don't think we have one in your size. We only have those in a wider width. You need a narrow width. Doesn't that shoe feel good? It makes your foot look nice and dainty. How does it feel to you? Walk around

20 a little bit and see how it feels. Look at it in the mirror. I think that's the shoe for you. Doesn't it feel better than that other shoe?

Customer: (Taking off the shoe) I guess I don't need another pair of shoes anyway. Thank you for your help. I've got to be going now. (She puts on her old shoes, picks up her parcels, and leaves.)

Now Notice How This Interview Could Have Been Handled

1 Salesperson: (After putting on the shoe the woman selected before she walked into the store) How does that feel?

Customer: It doesn't seem to fit. It gaps on the side and my heel slides up and down. I think that it's too big.

5 Salesperson: It's your size. That, however, is not the best shoe for your foot. You have a slender foot which requires a tailored shoe. May I show you what I mean?

Customer: I always have trouble getting a comfortable pair of shoes that still have some style.

10 Salesperson: I'm sure that's true. Do you see anything on this tailored shoe display rack that you like?

Customer: (Looking on the rack indicated) Well, this one's kind of nice (pointing to a high-heeled shoe).

Salesperson: O.K., let me see if we have that in your size. (The salesperson

15 leaves to get the shoe while the customer continues to look at the display shoes.)

Salesperson: Let me put this on your foot. Walk around in it and see how it feels.

Customer: This is really a nice-looking shoe. It fits better than the first one,

20 but all my weight seems to be on the ball on my foot where I have arch trouble.

Salesperson: Yes, that's true. A high-heeled shoe will do that. All of your weight is on the ball of your foot. A low-heeled shoe distributes the weight more evenly on the whole foot. Would you like to see what I mean?

25 Customer: Well, O.K. Do you have any with some style?

Salesperson: Yes, I think we do. (Leaves and returns with another shoe.) Try this one on and see what you think of it.

Customer: Oh, my! I have never had so comfortable a shoe on my foot. It's snug and still has plenty of length. I never realized how comfortable this
30 type of shoe could be. But, doesn't it look old-fashioned?

Salesperson: Not really. Lower-heeled shoes are the style this year. People, like yourself, are looking for comfort.

Customer: Do you have this shoe in a different color?

Salesperson: Yes, we have it in several colors. What do you prefer?
35 Customer: Something in a lighter color, maybe a tan.

Salesperson: I think we have a tan in your size. Let me just go see. (Leaves and returns with a tan shoe of the same type.)

Customer: Yes, I like that.

Salesperson: That is very becoming on you. It makes your foot look nice and
40 dainty.

Customer: How much does this shoe cost?

Salesperson: This is our very finest shoe and sells for $59.95. This shoe never goes on sale.

Customer: My heavens! I've never paid that much for shoes.
45 Salesperson: That may be one of the reasons you have arch trouble. This shoe will last two or three times as long as our cheaper shoes and give you more satisfaction.

Customer: O.K., I'll give them a try, but you'll take them back if I'm not happy in ten or twelve years, won't you?
50 Salesperson: (Laughing) Oh, sure. By that time you will have two or three more pairs of these shoes.

(After paying, she leaves wearing her new shoes)

RESPONDING TO QUESTIONS

We've spent a great deal of time discussing how an interviewer goes about preparing and asking good questions. In this section, the emphasis shifts to the qualities of good and bad answers.

What Is a Good Answer?

To oversimplify, a good answer can be thought of as one which supplies the information requested by the interviewer and a bad answer does not. This definition does not, however, completely cover the subject of good versus bad responses. It is possible for an answer to be bad and still contain the information desired. In order to discover how this is possible, you should first examine all the ways in which an answer can be bad.

In general, answers fall into one of three categories: correct, incorrect, and partially correct. Correctness of an answer depends both on how the question is meant by the questioner and how it is interpreted by a respondent. Sometimes a respondent answers incorrectly because he or she misunderstood the question. Misunderstanding can be a product of the vocabulary used, the way in which the question is phrased, or a number of other reasons. Incorrect answers can be due to respondent hostility or resistance—when interviewees intentionally give an incorrect response. Incorrect responses can also be caused by a desire to please the interviewer.

On the whole, however, correct or incorrect responses are fairly easy to handle. The partially correct response is the most difficult to handle. Slanting, distorting, and omitting all produce partially correct responses. They are especially hard to handle if you have not prepared ahead of time and do not know exactly what type of response you wanted for each question.

Let's say you are a termination interviewer who wants to find out why an employee has resigned. You have checked some records and found that three other employees in the same department have quit in the last two months. All of those employees, as well as the one you are about to interview, are female. You also overheard in the company lunchroom some negative comments by females regarding the department supervisor. Once you are in the termination interview and ask the employee why she is leaving, her first response is that she has been offered a better job. When you ask about the new job you find out she is taking a five percent cut in pay. When you ask about working conditions in her old department, she says she was having trouble getting along with some of her co-workers. When you press, she also includes her supervisor in that same group. No matter how hard you try, she refuses to be specific. Finally, as she is about to leave, you try once more, assuring her that nothing she says will be used against her and that her name will be kept confidential. You tell her that it is your job to discover the real reasons why people are leaving in order to retain other employees. She finally breaks down and says that her boss has been making advances toward her and other female employees.

Had you not done your homework and carefully set up your final inquiry, you probably would have accepted one of her earlier responses. It would have been partially correct in that you would have known the supervisor was the problem, but you would not have known why. Other ways of handling incorrect and partially correct responses will be discussed in greater detail in the chapter on probing.

How to Improve Responses

Now, how is it possible for an answer to be correct, but still not be a good answer? Correct but poor responses are spoken too rapidly, contain too little or too much detail, are unclear, encourage premature evaluation by an interviewer, or are boring. It must be remembered that when you are an interviewee, you have a high stake in the outcome of most interviews. It is, therefore, up to you to make sure that the information is not only given correctly, but that each answer also contains qualities which will encourage an interviewer to listen, understand, and record it.

Interviewees can do a number of things to improve the quality of their answers. First, they should prepare interviewers for their answers. Very often this is done as a preface to the response. Such a preface might tell an interviewer just how certain you are about the response. "I've thought about that a lot and . . ." or "I'm not completely certain, but . . ." are examples of such prefaces. They tell an interviewer how to take a response, and help the interviewer become a better listener and notetaker. Sometimes some background information can be supplied, such as "Let me first tell you how this came about." Some respondents like to tell interviewers what the answer is not, as well as what it is. Other interviewees ask an interviewer to hear out the whole response before interrupting. There are also some less direct ways of preparing interviewers, such as speaking slowly and thoughtfully and using few, if any, dogmatic statements.

During each response, you can also do a number of things that improve the quality of each answer. For example, you should be sure that the answer is clear. Using examples, details, and presenting both sides of the issue are all ways to clarify an answer. Clarity also consists of being brief, but complete. When you are an interviewee, you should always attempt to reduce the number of inferences and guesses you include in a response. Most interviewers like to see that respondents are aware of their own biases. Finally, good interviewees allow enough time for an interviewer to take notes. Response timing is not only important in clarifying answers, but it also helps the interviewer become a better listener and notetaker.

A final quality of good answers is that they are stimulating. Try to hold the interviewer's attention. Answers are stimulating if they include some variety and novelty. Stimulating answers prevent interviewers from jumping to premature conclusions. One of the most common causes of boredom and reduced attention is too much detail. If necessary, you should ask interviewers exactly how much detail they want in response to any particular question. This not only helps in preparation of the answer, but also indicates to the interviewer that you are alert and willing to respond. All of these qualities of good answers are in addition to your attempt to answer each question as completely and honestly as possible. Although the focus has been on other aspects of good responses, remember that a good answer begins as a correct answer.

RESPONSE EXERCISE

Directions: Briefly describe what is wrong with each of the following responses to the question "Tell me a little bit about your background."
1. Well, there's not much to tell. I was born and grew up in this town. I finished high school in 1979.
2. Yeah, good question. I was born in St. Luke's Hospital in 1970. My mom wasn't working then. Before she got pregnant, she worked for the telephone company. She came from Maine, originally. I got two sisters, one 22 years old and one 14 years old. I got no dad. He died in Vietnam. He was career military. My mom has a boyfriend name Tom. (This goes on and on.)
3. Well, I was born in California. I am 19 years old. I have two sisters. Both my parents are still living in California. I finished high school two years ago and have been working as a carpenter ever since. What else do you want to know?

4. I guess I'm not sure exactly what you want to know. Could you be a little more specific?
5. I really need this job. I have been out of work ever since I graduated from high school last year. My mom and dad have been after me to get a job. They say all I do is play video games at the arcade all day. If I could get this job, I would have less time to play those games. I think I'm hooked on them.

RESPONDENT STYLE

Just as every interviewer has a unique style, so does every respondent. No one style fits every interviewee. In this section, however, you will find several aspects of respondent style which seem to be successful.

Be Natural

Respondents need to allow their personality to show in the interview. Some respondents are outgoing and dynamic; others are shy and withdrawn. Regardless of your personality, never try to fake a different one. You should be as natural as possible when answering questions. A skillful respondent answers all questions in a confident and dignified manner. There is no need to apologize or be afraid of unflattering information. Everyone has something about them that is not positive. When asked about these areas, you usually should answer as fully and honestly as possible.

Many respondents feel that they have to please or flatter an interviewer. Experienced interviewers very quickly spot flattery and distorted information, and they don't like it. It is difficult to keep up distortion over the course of an entire interview. It is best to not even try.

Let your personality show when asking or answering questions.

Answer Carefully

Good responses require careful listening and thought. Interviewers prefer that you think through your answers rather than respond immediately with one that is less than complete or accurate. This can happen when respondents let their words get ahead of their thoughts. Words must be chosen carefully in response to a question. When tentative or qualifying language is needed, it should be made part of the response. *Tentative language* includes statements such as, "I'm not quite sure, but . . . ," "I haven't really thought about it completely, but . . . ," or "I think . . ." Careful listening also involves the ability to clarify a confusing question. Never be afraid to ask, "What did you say?" Be sure you understand the question before you try to answer it.

Good responses should be framed and phrased as carefully as good questions. They should be purposeful, clear, natural, brief, thought-provoking, limited in scope, and unbiased. Carefully consider each response. Never use sarcasm or argue with an interviewer. Responses should never be delivered in a way that encourages misinterpretation.

Good Answers to Bad Questions

Some respondents are capable of turning a bad question into a good question. For example, you can give a negative question a positive response. In response to "What classes did you dislike in college?" you could respond, "I liked all my classes, especially. . . ." In the same way, you should be prepared to ask questions to clarify a question or to learn how detailed the response should be.

Respondents should let interviewers control the flow and pace of the interview. This means stopping talk when an interviewer interrupts, and reading the nonverbal messages sent by the interviewer with regard to length and direction of response desired.

Respondent style should parallel interviewer style as much as possible. In this text, much of the emphasis is on interviewer behavior, but interviewee skill is no less important, and in most cases, is not that different from interviewer behavior. It might be useful for you to go back and review the ten categories of interviewees discussed in Chapter 3. Apprehensive, defensive, stolid, disorganized, too-talkative, overeager, tenacious, arrogant, hostile, and crafty interviewee styles should all be avoided.

SUMMARY

Skill in actually asking and responding to questions is just as important as the preparation of questions and responses. Advice regarding wording and phrasing of questions should be taken into consideration in preparing the interview guide as well. Questions have many purposes besides simply eliciting information. Maintaining control of the interview, shaping responses, encouraging participation, maintaining the climate, and helping interviewees better understand themselves are all dependent on the questioning process.

Word choice and question framing were discussed and several vocabulary and question preface problems and possibilities were suggested. Different ways of motivating respondents were presented. Perhaps the most important portion of this chapter was the discussion of how questions should be phrased—the simple changing of a word or two within a question can often dramatically affect the nature of the response to that question.

Another major section of this chapter was the discussion of interviewer style. It is not only the wording of a question, but the style in which it is delivered which determines the quality of the response. Several aspects of interviewer style were mentioned, including personality, sincerity, degree of control, and interview pace.

Finally, some evaluation of the importance and quality of answers or responses to questions in the interview setting was made. A good answer is one which is accurate and conforms to the requirements of the question. Partially correct answers cause the most problems—more than incorrect answers. Response quality can be improved with preface statements, use of examples, details, and two-sided presentation, completeness with brevity, response timing, and making the answer interesting and stimulating. Good respondent style is very similar to good interviewer style. It must be both natural and careful with use of tentative language where necessary.

In both Chapters 3 and 4 the focus has been primarily upon initial questions. These questions are usually prepared before the actual interview. In the next chapter, you will find a discussion of the follow-up or probe question. Probing questions help clarify and amplify initial questions and are not usually prepared ahead of time.

ACTIVITIES

Activity #1

Directions: Obtain an audio or video tape of an actual interview. You can (1) borrow a tape from one of the interviewers you know who makes such recordings, (2) obtain permission to tape record an interview done by one of the professionals you know, (3) record one of the interviews that commonly take place on radio or television, or perhaps the easiest way, (4) have your instructor play such a tape for your workshop or class. Look over each of the following questions, and then watch and/or listen carefully to the way the questions are asked and answered. If necessary, play the recording a second or third time until you can answer each of the questions. Save this tape for an activity in Chapter 5.

1. How much talking, including both questions and statements, did the interviewer do in comparison to the interviewee? (If possible, time the interviewee's total speaking and subtract that from total interview time. If that is not possible give a rough approximation.)

2. Identify one question each which you think:
    a. helped the interviewer maintain control
    b. helped shape a response
    c. encouraged participation
    d. helped maintain the formality level
    e. helped improve rapport
    f. demonstrated an other-orientation
    g. contained a factual preface
    h. contained a motivational preface
    i. used an indirect approach
3. Give examples of any *words* used by the *interviewer* which you think were too simple, complex, ambiguous, subjective, or jargonistic.
4. Give two examples of *questions* which you think contained phrasing which was purposeful, clear, natural, brief, thought-provoking, limited in scope, and unbiased.
5. Give two examples of *responses* which you think contained phrasing which was purposeful, clear, natural, brief, thought-provoking, limited in scope, and unbiased.
6. Give one example each of questions which you think were:
    a. Overly long
    b. Overly precise
    c. Double barrelled
    d. Negative
    e. Too sharp
    f. Too direct
    g. Leading
7. Give one example each of responses which you think:
    a. Were too rapid
    b. Were too detailed
    c. Were too simple
    d. Were only partially accurate
    e. Caused premature evaluation
    f. Needed a preface
    g. Were boring
    h. Had any other problems
8. Evaluate the *interviewer's* style, including personality, sincerity, maintenance of control, pace, repetition, etc.
9. Evaluate the *interviewee's* style, including personality, sincerity, naturalness, accuracy, pace, etc.

Activity #2

Write a short paper (no more than two typewritten pages) describing how you would have conducted the taped interview differently. Be sure to mention interviewer versus interviewee talking time, any word, phrasing, or question choice you would alter, style changes, and anything else you think could have been improved.

Activity #3

Now, you are prepared to have your first interview practice. You have been preparing to do an information interview through the preceding chapter activities. Before you do it, however, you need a "dress rehearsal." Find someone who is willing to play the role of the person you are preparing to interview. Brief them thoroughly about the person you will be interviewing. As you conduct the interview, have your helper stop you anytime you do something wrong. Talk about the problem, and try to get it corrected. By the end of this exercise you should be fully prepared to conduct your interview. The only things you have not yet learned are how to listen to the respondent, how to record the responses, how to probe, and how to close the interview. You will learn how to do these things in the next four chapters. These other activities come as part of the interview itself. Call your interviewee and set the interview appointment to correspond with your completing those chapters.

Chapter 5

Skill 5
Probing

Knowing when not to inject oneself into the interview is often as important as asking questions deftly. (Fenlason, 1952, p. 134) Though probing for a bullet is pretty painful, mental probing can be far worse . . . . (Garrett, 1942, p. 38)

A single predetermined question will seldom be enough to cover an interview topic completely. In most cases the initial response will not be adequate, so you need to produce follow-up questions, or as they are usually termed, *probes*. A probe is any verbal or nonverbal interviewer message designed to motivate the interviewee to amplify, clarify, or confront; it can also be used to control or focus the interaction toward a topic, question, or purpose. The two basic probe functions are to motivate better responses and to help control interview progress.

No matter how well you prepare, there will usually be some areas of interviewee information which will need additional probing. Probes normally request 1) amplification—greater depth or range of response, 2) clarification—reduction of response confusion or ambiguity, or 3) confrontation—explanation of any inconsistency. If you do not probe, you can easily make incorrect assumptions about responses. You need to probe any time a response does not meet the objectives of the question. In many cases, interviewees may not even be aware that their response was not clear, consistent, or complete. Nondirective interviews which use many open questions require more probing than highly directive interviews which use more closed questions.

Probes also help interviewers control and focus the interaction. They allow you to bring the interview back on course when respondents wander and bring up irrelevant information. The original question should focus interviewee attention on the information desired, but if it doesn't, misunderstandings can occur, and probes are necessary to produce valid and complete responses.

At times, a probe can provoke negative interviewee reactions. Too much probing, for example, can make interviewers appear domineering and authoritarian. Respondents begin to feel interrogated. You must be careful, therefore, not to probe directly too often, but encourage the flow of relevant information through indirect means. In other words, a good probe allows you to control the interaction without *appearing* to control it. In this chapter you will find a discussion of how to probe, as well as several types of probes.

Good probes motivate respondent amplification and clarification.

PROBING TIPS

As with most interview skills, good probing begins with preparation. In general, probes cannot be planned ahead of time, but interviewers must know what type of response is required for each question. If you're prepared, you will be alert to inadequate responses. In a matter of two to three seconds, you must decide whether or not to probe, what to probe, and which probe will elicit the necessary information. If these decisions are not made fairly quickly, respondents become anxious, and the interviewer appears unsure of him or herself. Such quick decision making demands a firm grasp of the interview purpose, knowledge of what is required for each topic, active listening, and a great deal of practice.

Probing is what separates good and poor interviewers. Poor interviewers are unaware of what constitutes an adequate response and what information is necessary to completely cover each topic. Those who *do* realize that an inadequate response has been given may not be ready to probe for the necessary information.

A good probe goes beyond the surface of a response. You must be prepared to probe until all of the relevant information is revealed. An indirect advantage of probing is that it shows interviewees that you are interested in and listening to their responses. The simple fact that you are probing often encourages them to go beyond the obvious on their own.

A less positive side effect of probes is the possible introduction of bias. Since probes are usually not prepared ahead of time or part of most interview guides, their hasty structure and phrasing can lead a respondent to answers implied by the probe. "Why do you say that?" or "What do you mean by that?" for example, when spoken with a certain tone of voice and facial expression, can imply criticism and lead respondents to modify their answers. Be on guard to make sure that your probes do not lead or bias responses.

In much the same way, probe questions can sometimes alter or extend the meaning of a primary question. For example, a primary question may ask for specific objective information, but the probe may elicit subjective comments which are irrelevant to the topic. Curiosity often causes interviewers to probe for information which is none of their business. Both primary questions and probes must be guided by the overall purpose of the interview.

A good many probes deal with the affective domain and are designed to elicit subjective information. Affective interviewee words or behaviors often indicate a needed probe. If you indicate to interviewees that feelings and emotions are a normal and valuable part of the interview, then they will not hide these signals in areas that might be important. These affective probe cues are often consciously or unconsciously communicated by interviewees. You may notice, for example, that the feelings expressed nonverbally do not match the words spoken. If the discrepancy affects the purpose of the interview, you will want to probe it. In order to deal with subjective information effectively, you must be aware of your own feelings and emotions. Such an awareness will allow you to probe interviewee feelings without biasing the results.

Some interviewers suggest that you can elicit interviewee feeling and emotion statements by providing a model for interviewees. In other words, they advise you to communicate or disclose your own feelings to interviewees. This demands first, that you recognize your feelings, and second, that you are able to disclose your feelings without burdening interviewees with your own problems. Such self-disclosure will usually cause reciprocal self-disclosure by respondents. To be effective, such feeling statements must be spontaneous. It is important, however, that you do not overshadow interviewees by expressing feelings which are beyond their comprehension.

As you practice interviewing you will develop a probing technique which fits you, your interviewees, and the type of interviews you most often conduct. You will also find several useful probing tips in the following section on types of probes.

PROBE VS. PRIMARY QUESTION EXERCISE

Directions: Below you will find a condensed social work interview. Label each of the questions as either a primary question (1) or a probe (2). Answers will be found at the end of this chapter.

1. Q. Did you know anything about social agencies in the old country?
   A. They haven't got them there. In a nationality like ours they make their own living before they take charity—struggle through somehow. . . .

2. Q. Did you have any dealings with a social agency before your marriage?
   A. I didn't know anything about them until the year my husband died.

Before that we struggled along. I worked. He stayed home and watched the kids.

3. Q. What were your feelings about the questions you were asked at first (by social workers)?

A. I didn't like their questions at all. They asked too many when they didn't understand themselves. They usually think you have more than you tell them you have. That's what hurts us. It's really the opposite—you don't like to tell them you have so little.

4. Q. You mean you want to keep a front?

A. Yes.

5. Q. Did you feel that they were trying to pry into your affairs?

A. Yes. One came and said. "Let me see your pantry if you got something in it." She would not sit down and be friendly with you. She sat in the chair—spinster-looking like this (demonstrating) and looking around.

6. Q. That made you feel uncomfortable?

A. Yeh. Sometimes you feel like asking them, "Where do you think you sit?"

7. Q. Did you get over that feeling about her?

A. Yes. Later on she was very nice to me and gave me my share. She found out I had no mattresses and bought some and sent them. I told her I couldn't be handled like that—it hurts. She wanted to know why I had five children, too. She thought I was not very wise—broadminded—to have so many children and a sick husband. In one way she was right, but I said I lived the life, not her . . . . She had told me she would bring some clothes for the baby but she didn't. My husband was laying on his deathbed at the time, and I couldn't hear anything about him. I found out afterwards the neighbors came to see me but they wouldn't let them in—only nearest relatives can get in a hospital.

8. Q. Did you ever tell the social worker about the strain you had been under?

A. No, I never had a chance. She went away and dropped the trouble and another one came. Had one right after the other then. I never got very friendly with any one of them.

9. Q. Did you like being changed from one to another?

A. No, you like one because they find out more. You are always on guard with a new one and can't be natural. If you know she's good to you you lose yourself and say nothing.

10. Q. Did you ever get acquainted with a social worker right away—felt at ease at first, or do you have to go through a certain period?

A. Never right away. You never know which way they are coming. They keep things to themselves and you don't know whether they are trying to take off from you or give you.

11. Q. (Silence)

A. Most of them look down on you and that hurts you so you don't want to say any more. (Young, 1935, pp. 359–60)

TYPES OF PROBES

Hundreds of different types of probes are available to a skillful interviewer. In the following paragraphs you will find a discussion of the advantages and disadvantages of the most common probes. They fall into the three main categories: amplification, clarification, and confrontation.

Amplification Probes

Amplification probes ask interviewees to expand upon the information they've presented. They are designed to increase either the range or depth of response, and reveal justifications, circumstances, reasons, attitudes, and beliefs which underlie responses. Five types of amplification probes seem to be most common: silence, minimal encouragement, restatement, direct amplification, and reflection.

Silence.

Recently research has been done on *Reaction Time Latency* (RTL). Reaction time latency refers to the break or silence between the time one speaker stops and another speaker begins. RTL is commonly referred to as silence. Beginning interviewers normally allow very short reaction time latency, that is, very little silence. They seem to be afraid of silence and want to rush in and fill up any that occurs during interaction.

The ability to delay reaction time and accept silence must be developed before you can become a skilled interview participant. Skillful interviewers normally have a reaction time latency of from one to four seconds. Silence should not exceed ten seconds. Research evidence indicates that an RTL of five seconds causes interviewees to amplify a response approximately 25 percent of the time. This means that one out of every four five-second silences you use will act as an amplification probe, and you don't have to do a thing except not talk. Silent interviewers allow interviewees to continue in any direction they choose. Silence says "tell me more." It also allows interviewees to recover their poise at crucial points within the interview.

The use and misuse of silence is an extremely complex aspect of interviews. Silence should never be interpreted as the absence of communication. It can be just as communicative as any words or other nonverbal behaviors. Silence on the part of an interviewee may indicate confusion, lack of knowledge, or an emotional block. As an interviewer, you must be careful, because silence can sometimes be perceived as a threat or a demand for further information. Such a demand is sometimes met with hostility or repetition of old information. Both are usually counterproductive.

Even with these possible negative consequences, it is good for beginning interviewers to attempt to lengthen their reaction time latency. One of the main benefits of using silence as an amplification probe is that it carries little potential for biasing interviewee responses. You cannot lead respondents if you do not say or do anything that can be taken as a signal of what you want to hear. Increased reaction time latency on the part of an interviewer is also valuable in that it encourages interviewees to use silence. With silence comes good listening for both participants and much better interviewee responses.

Minimal Encouragement.

Minimal encouragements include nonverbal noises and gestures along with short comments which are designed to get interviewees to amplify their responses, but they do not indicate any particular response direction. Minimal encouragements include "uh huh," "um-hmm," "humm," "really," "yes," a nod of the head, an expectant facial expression, a poised pencil, and any number of other comments and behaviors. A minimal encouragement says to interviewees, "Go on. I am listening and following you." You are showing interest and involvement, but allowing respondents to direct a response.

Sometimes beginning interviewers overuse minimal encouragement. They use it to fill up every pause or natural break in the interview. Minimal encouragement can become distracting if overused. As with any probe, the cue should come from the interviewee. Look for a sentence that finishes with an inflection and shift of eye gaze. This is the interviewee's way of checking to determine whether you are still interested. Minimal encouragement will reassure the interviewee that continuation is not only acceptable, but desired. Without such signals the interviewee should remain silent.

The minimal encouragement probe has drawbacks, however. Unlike silence, some minimal encouragements can lead respondents. "Uh-huh" can be interpreted as a sign of acceptance or agreement. In such a case, interviewees may continue making the same type of statements they made prior to the "uh-huh" regardless of whether they believe them to be true or not. Comments such as, "I see," "Go on," "Tell me more," and "Please continue," do not have the same leading effect. You should be sure interviewees do not misinterpret minimal encouragement as agreement, rather than a request for amplification.

Be careful, too, that your minimal encouragements are coordinated with careful listening. Some interviewers attempt to fake listening with minimal encouragements. Such artificiality does not help interviewers maintain control or satisfy the interview purpose. When used in conjunction with listening and as a direct result of what respondents have said, minimal encouragements can be a purposeful controlling technique. Skillful interviewers have a number of minimal encouragements in their arsenal of probes and use them with care.

Restatement.

Restatement probes are an exact or nearly exact repetition of interviewee words. Some call them "echo" or "mirror" probes. Like silence and minimal encouragement probes, restatement indicates that you are paying close attention and listening carefully to what is being said, as well as requesting amplification. Restatement probes are most useful when used selectively to indicate exactly what portion of the answer you want amplified.

Very often the only change in the interviewee's wording is the pronoun. For example, the statement "I feel terrible today," may be followed with a restatement probe of "You feel terrible today?" In some cases, however, a word or two may be changed in order not to make the restatement seem too artifical. The restatement probe in the previous example may become, "Why do you feel terrible today?" In many cases, an interviewer is better off not making a restatement a question, but leaving it as a flat declarative sentence with a rising inflection at the end.

Some interviewing experts differentiate between immediate and retrospective probes. An *immediate* probe asks for amplification on the preceding response. A *retrospective* probe, on the other hand, asks for amplification upon a response or statement made earlier in the interview. Silence and minimal encouragement can only be used as immediate probes. Restatement, and most other probes, on the other hand, can be immediate or retrospective. In its retrospective form, a typical restatement would be "Let's go back to when you said . . . ."

Most experienced interviewers make a very conscious decision to use an immediate or retrospective probe. Probing immediately implies less topic control and is more nondirective. In some cases, you may want to be less directive at the beginning of an interview and more directive later on. You may want to use a retrospective rather than an immediate probe when too many amplification interruptions will inhibit answers. This is often the case in the interview opening or when dealing with embarrassing or threatening topics. Spontaneous responses with little or no interruption can elicit a great deal of unanticipated information which is suppressed if immediate probes come too early.

You should also resist making immediate probes if you know there are a number of other closely related topics to come which will encourage respondents to amplify earlier statements. In almost every interview, you will find respondents coming back to similar information when asked different primary questions. When this is true, you may want to wait to see if amplification information comes later. Practice and try to master both immediate and retrospective restatement probes. Effective restatement probes require good notes— especially *retrospective* restatement probes.

Direct Amplification.
"What happened after that?" "Tell me more about . . . ." "Explain further the point about . . . ." "What did you do after . . . ." "Then what happened?" "What else could you say about that?" "Is there anything you would like to add?" "Could you spell that out a little bit more?" "What else can you think of about this?" "When did that happen?" "How did you find that out?" These are all examples of direct amplification probes. With direct amplification probes you come out directly and ask for amplification. Obviously, it is much more authoritarian and controlling than the amplification probe discussed previously. The interviewer specifies exactly what additional information is needed, and may ask, "Where were you just before that happened?" or anything else which relates to the interviewee response.

A form of direct amplification probe, called a *mutation probe* (Merton, 1946), introduces a subject only indirectly related to the topic. A mutation probe is similar to a second question within an interview topic. For example, if you ask an interviewee what happened in a particular situation, a mutation probe might be "Why do you think that happened?" The "why?" was not implied in the original question, so the probe extends the question somewhat. It is extremely hard to separate amplification and mutation probes; mutation probes usually deal with information that was not anticipated when the interview guide was developed, but which seems important enough during the interview to follow-up. They are a sign of interview guide flexibility.

Reflection.

The probes discussed so far are used primarily for the amplification of objective information. The reflection probe deals with amplification of subjective information or information in the affective domain. It encourages interviewees to reveal the meaning or feelings behind the words spoken or expressed nonverbally through facial expression, eye movement, gestures, tone of voice, and so on.

In some cases, a reflection probe requires interviewees to bring emotions, beliefs, and attitudes which are operating below the conscious level to the surface. This probe attempts to get interviewees to specify information which has only been implied. In these cases, a reflection probe can help interviewees better understand themselves and what they are expressing. "You feel angry?" "How did you react to it?" "How did you feel?" "What do you think about it?" are all examples of reflection probes.

Effective use of reflection probes demands that you pay close attention to interviewees and establish a high level of rapport and empathy. You must attend to the *entire* message of the interviewee. This is sometimes called using your "third ear." Interviewees often, either consciously or unconsciously, hide or suppress their emotions. It is sometimes useful to imagine yourself in the position which the interviewee describes. You must constantly look for affective words as well as nonverbal signals of the respondent's true feelings. When interviewees are out of touch with their own feelings, your reflection probe may come as a shock to them.

All restatements of feelings should be clear, concise, and accurate. Be sure to identify the essence or foundation of the underlying feelings communicated. This includes recognizing that respondent feelings are often mixed. It is possible, for example, for an interviewee to feel both angry and frustrated with some problem on the job. You must be aware of both emotions underlying the problem and be able to reflect each accurately, if you want amplification of all subjective information. If your probe only reflects one of the emotions, then the interviewee may place undue attention on that single aspect of the problem.

In using reflection probes, you should try to deal with current feelings and use the present tense. Focus on the emotions that are occurring during the interview and *not* those that were felt during the situation or prior to the interview. Probes such as "How *do* you feel about that?" instead of "How *did* you feel about that?" illustrate this approach. In most cases, the same emotions are being felt while describing the situation as were felt when the situation occurred. You will find it easier to deal with emotions in the present than those in the past. It is too easy for respondents to deny, escape, or underrate past feelings.

When reflecting many subjective feelings, you should use a number of introductory phrases such as "It seems that you feel . . . ," "You believe . . . ," "It sounds like . . . ," "In other words you feel . . . ," "I gather that . . . ," and "You really are . . . ." By using a variety of introductory phrases rather than just a few, the interviewee feels more comfortable with reflection probes—they aren't repetitive and stale. Whenever possible, try for variety in all your probes.

It is important to be able to identify and reflect all types of emotions. Positive feelings can be just as important to probe as negative ones. However, you must be careful not to overinterpret interviewee feelings. Do not assume or read too much into interviewee statements. A reflection probe such as "You feel damned angry, don't you?" may threaten and irritate an interviewee and reduce rapport.

A reflection probe is appropriate at any point during an interview. They are especially useful when you feel that some information in the affective domain is blocking complete and accurate responses. In such cases, you need to bring those feelings to a conscious level so that you and the interviewee can deal with them and get on with the main purpose of the interview. Subjective information should be reflected regardless of whether it pertains to the interviewee, the interviewer, or some other individual. The interviewee may even have some negative feelings about you. If so, you still need to probe those feelings and encourage them to be expressed and dealt with before the interview continues.

The reflection probe has been discussed last because it is somewhat different from the other four amplification probes. Reflection probes deal with a different kind of information—affective, rather than a way of probing. In other words, it is possible to use silence, minimal encouragement, restatement, or direct amplification to probe for subjective information. When used for this purpose, each would also be a reflection probe.

Amplification probes are probably the most common type of probe. It takes time to master them, but once learned, they quickly become one of your most useful and used skills, especially in combination with their close relatives, clarification probes.

AMPLIFICATION PROBE EXERCISE

Directions: For each of the following interviewee statements, choose what you believe is the best amplification probe. If you think it is silence, simply write, "Silence." If you think a minimal encouragement, restatement, direct amplification, or reflection probe is called for, write out what you would say. There are no right or wrong answers for this exercise.

1. It's hard to talk about it. You are the first person I have told. See, I drink from early in the morning after my husband leaves for work until he gets home again.
2. I guess I left my last job because of the working conditions.
3. It's difficult to know where to start.
4. When I get into situations in which there are other people who expect me to talk, I'm afraid I'll faint. I become very nervous. I don't know why. Ah . . . I guess . . . humm.
5. I keep thinking about the problems my parents are having at home.
6. We don't know too much about what happened here. All we know is that this small plane crashed, and two people have been taken to the hospital.
7. After my parents separated, I felt deserted. I had nowhere to turn—just nowhere. I feel so left out. I'm not sure anyone cares whether I live or die.

8. It's my daughter, we're having trouble with her. She won't listen to us, and she stays out all night. I'm sick.
9. Do I like this community? Yeah.
10. I got it! I really got it! You said to come and tell you how it turned out. I got the job. I start on Monday.

Clarification Probes

A clarification probe is used when one or more aspects of an interviewee response is unclear, confusing, or ambiguous. Interviewers use clarification probes to make sure they understand respondents completely and accurately. In this section you will find a discussion of three common varieties of clarification probes: paraphrase, summary, and direct clarification.

Paraphrase.

The paraphrase probe is very similar to the restatement probe except that you do not try to use interviewee words; its purpose is to clarify responses rather than get interviewees to amplify them. When you simplify interviewee statements with your own words to make sure no mistake has been made, you have used a paraphrase probe. The response will either be agreement or disagreement with the new phrasing. Here's an example:

Interviewee: *"Generally the reason I'm late for work is because I have to drop my son off at the daycare center first, and he always wants to show me something he's been doing like a picture or a clay animal. I just don't feel that I would be a good mother if I didn't show some interest in the things that he is so proud of with his work at the daycare center."*

Interviewer: *"You're late then because of the demands put upon you by your family responsibilities. Is that right?"* (Clarification probe)

Interviewee: *"That's right."* (Affirmation of probe)

In order to use a paraphrase probe well, you must continually search for the essence or central idea of what has been said and find a way of restating it so that the meaning is as close as possible to that intended by the interviewee. A paraphrase probe helps you understand the interviewee's frame of reference. A good paraphrase not only clarifies the information presented, but also communicates that you are listening and understanding. Sometimes your paraphrasing will actually help respondents overcome any confusion they might have regarding their own feelings.

Good paraphrasing makes listening and notetaking much easier. Any time interviewers write down words other than those used by an interviewee, a paraphrase probe should be used to assure that the respondent would consider them accurate. Several comments relevant to paraphrase probes are included in the discussion of the summary probe.

Summary.

A summary probe is simply an expanded paraphrase. Whereas the paraphrase probe can be used after each response, a summary probe is normally used at the end of a series of responses. A summary probe normally includes several different but related thoughts expressed by an interviewee during questioning, rather than one thought expressed in response to a single question. Just as with a paraphrase, the interviewee should affirm or deny the accuracy of the summary probe. A preface such as, "Let's see if I've got all this right" normally indicates a summary probe.

Summary probes serve several functions besides clarification of lengthy, rambling, or confused interviewee responses. They allow you to pull together related ideas and wrap up loose ends. They give respondents a chance to focus on those ideas that are of most concern to them, and they are a way of checking to make sure that nothing has been left out. Many skillful interviewers make it a practice to ask a direct question such as, "Is there anything else?" at the end of each summary probe.

Summary probes also signal the end of each interview guide topic. They wrap up each topic by confirming a degree of mutual agreement and understanding on the information covered. Summary probes make good transitions from one topic to another; they give interviewees a feeling of accomplishment and motivate them to move on to the following topic.

Timely summary probes help you maintain control. They can be used to subtly cut off discussion of a particular topic once the relevant information has been gained. Although topic closure may seem premature to the interviewee, if you work in some statement about those topics that still need to be covered, interviewees can usually see why the topic must be concluded. As with most of the other probes discussed, a summary probe demonstrates to interviewees that you have been paying close attention and your notes accurately reflect their statements.

Summary probes need be neither formal nor lengthy. They should simply highlight the key ideas expressed and give nearly equal weight to each. If interviewees want to stress different topic ideas, then they can do so after the summary is completed. Like the paraphrase probe, a summary probe demands that you be able to spot the main ideas within responses. Beginning interviewers usually have a great deal of trouble discovering and then restating the main ideas without changing their meaning. The art of unbiased paraphrasing and summarizing demands a great deal of training and effort.

Once begun, summary probes become a natural part of the interview. They should be employed consistently throughout the entire interview—even if a particular topic is rushed, the summary probe should not be. Summary probes should be complete, concise, accurate, and timely. In some cases, however, you may find it better to leave certain information out of the summary, especially if it is embarrassing or threatening to the interviewee. Also, if the information was given "off the record," it should not be included in a summary probe.

Normally, at the end of an interview there is a *final summary*. This final summary will be discussed in the chapter on closing interviews. In most cases, the final summary is simply a collection of the ideas expressed in the summary probes for each topic. As you will see, there is very little difference between the qualities that make for a good summary probe and those that make for a good final summary.

Direct Clarification.

Like the direct amplification probe, a direct clarification probe is a straightforward request for clarification of a response. Whenever a vague, confusing, or ambiguous statement is made, one of the following direct clarification probes might be in order.

"I'm not sure I understand your point."
"I don't understand."
"Could you explain a little more?"
"What do you mean by that?"
"What do you mean by . . . ?"
"What did you have in mind when you said . . . ?"
"Please define . . . for me."
"Was that a million, or a billion?"

Direct clarification probes are designed to get interviewees to repeat a response in different words. It is possible to make a retrospective direct clarification probe, which asks an interviewee to go back to an earlier part of the interview and clarify something that was said. It is usually better, however, to have a response clarified right after it's given and not wait until the meaning is forgotten. A direct clarification probe suggests to an interviewee that you are immediately sensitive to ambiguity, confusion, and qualification.

Be sure that your direct clarification probes are not misinterpreted to indicate disbelief or suspected dishonesty. A direct clarification probe should reflect that you are fallible and might not be able to understand everything that is said upon first hearing. In most cases, interviewees are happy when they realize that you understand and accept your own fallibility. Once the interviewee clarifies a response, the interview can continue normally. Beginning interviewers should be aware of the difference between direct clarification probes and confrontation probes.

CLARIFICATION PROBE EXERCISE

Directions: Write a paraphrase, summary, or direct clarification probe for each of the answers listed below.

This performance interview takes place between Sam, the general manager of a large manufacturing company, and Sue, the chief engineer and Sam's immediate subordinate. Sue is recognized company-wide as an engineering genius, both intellectually and creatively. Older, more experienced people both within the company and outside of it seek her advice. She was promoted to chief engineer four years ago. After one year the department started to have problems. Productivity fell, turnover increased, and morale was low. Assuming she had been pushed along too fast, the company president made her special assistant for training and development. She was excellent—helpful, enthusiastic, and willing to help on any assignment. Last year she was returned to chief engineer and the old problems returned again. This is her first performance interview since becoming chief engineer once more. The opening has been skipped here. The interview begins with the first main weakness area.

Q. Why don't you tell me first of all about the level of turnover in your department?

A. Oh, that's a difficult situation. Several of my people feel there is not enough opportunity for advancement in this company. They want to move ahead so they leave us.
Paraphrase probe?

A. Yeah, I spend a lot of time and effort training them to make the kind of contribution they are capable of making, and they get an offer from one of our competitors, and they leave.
Direct clarification probe?

A. Take Richard Hicks, for example, my assistant. He's got talent, and he wants greater responsibilities and salary. He is now considering an offer from another company. The next step for him would be my job, and he could handle it well. I think he could be used in other areas also, where we have some pretty weak supervisors.
Direct clarification probe?

A. I don't want to mention any names, but many of the people we have in other departments sure aren't the engineer Dick is.
Paraphrase probe?

A. At least I'm not very impressed by them.
Paraphrase probe?

A. They are always late with their work. When they have a problem, they wait until the last minute to come see me. And, if I can't get at their problem right away, they get mad and stomp out of my office. Pretty soon they tell other people that I'm unwilling to help them. Maybe I ought to turn them over to Dick. Could you dig up more money for him if I gave him some added responsibilities?
Summary probe?

(This discussion goes on for awhile. Finally, you turn to the question of low morale and productivity in Sue's department.)

A. I think that comes primarily from sone of the people we have hired lately. They just don't have the engineering background necessary to do this job.
Paraphrase probe?

A. They come to me with elementary engineering problems. I guess I get pretty frustrated. They just don't do anything unless I lean on them or explain exactly how to do it to them.
Paraphrase probe?

A. Yeah, and their work never comes out the way I explained.
   Direct clarification probe?

A. They just don't listen.
   Paraphrase probe?

A. That's about it. When I picked them, they looked good, but now they don't do anything unless I tell them, and then they go and do it differently anyway. They change a little bit when I talk to them, but then they go right back to what they were doing before. Can you think of anything I should do?
   Direct amplification probe?

A. You know as you were just talking I was thinking that the only thing I haven't tried is getting off their backs and giving them more responsibility and letting them try some things on their own. That could cause us more morale and productivity problems, but I'm ready to try anything. What do you think of that idea?
   Summary probe?

Confrontation Probes

Whenever you notice some inconsistency between two interviewee statements, a statement made by an interviewee and information you know from another source, or an interviewee's words and actions, the inconsistency should be questioned with a confrontation probe. A confrontation probe is a form of challenge—it need not be strong and overt; it can be subtle and indirect. If a confrontation probe is not made, not only might the interviewee continue responding inconsistently, but your credibility and ability come into question. You appear unprepared, stupid, or gullible.

Remember that omissions, discrepancies, exaggerations, and even lies are often unintentional. People are not always consistent in what they say. In many cases, a confrontation probe is helpful to interviewees; if they are unclear or confused, it allows them to explore, identify, and resolve inaccurate statements. If a trusting, open climate has been established, confrontation probes will not threaten. To be fair, you must be sure to focus on every inconsistency, not just negative ones.

A confrontation probe also has value in promoting honesty. Respondents sometimes intentionally lie in order to hide imperfections and get respect, acceptance, and recognition. Regardless of whether a mistake is intentional or unintentional, it must be handled in the same manner. That is, it must be confronted directly, and you need to persist until it is corrected.

The key to good confrontation probing is being sensitive to the feelings and attitudes of interviewees. Begin by assuming that the inconsistency is unintended, and be willing to explore the problem with respondents. In most cases, the indirect approach works best. Go back over inconsistent responses with clarification probes. In this way, you check to make sure that there *is* a discrepancy. This also has the value of focusing attention on objective information. You may find out that you were wrong, and heard or recorded a response inaccurately. The clarification probe may encourage interviewees to change their response to become consistent. In this way you allow them to "save face" and "back down" gracefully. Be sure to accept this face-saving nonjudgmentally. In no case should you become biased or prejudiced toward interviewees because they change their responses. Many times an inconsistency can be resolved without using a confrontation probe.

In some situations interviewees will not recognize or change a discrepancy. At these times confrontation probes are necessary. Even in these difficult cases, however, remain tactful and diplomatic and continue to focus on the observed, objective, specific information. Point out problems in a descriptive, not judgmental manner. Tactful and respectful statements such as, "Could it be?", "Could you be mistaken?", "I heard it differently", and "Are you certain of that?" are all ways in which interviewees can be confronted in an open and yet tentative manner. Notice the difference between these confrontations and "You're a damn liar!"

You must learn to confront discrepancy and inconsistency without rejecting respondents personally. Some interviewers feel it is important to determine the reason for a discrepancy. They want to find out whether it is the result of a defense mechanism, due to some mental conflict, an attempt to please the interviewer, based on lack of information, or reflects confusion, a sign of memory lapse, or any number of other causes. Good interviewers are more concerned about clearing up a problem than always discovering its cause. Probing for a cause can sometimes threaten and embarrass respondents.

The timing of confrontation probes is critical. They should only be used after good rapport has developed. Before that, almost every confrontation probe will be perceived as a threat. Wait until an interview is well under way to confront problem responses. Many interviewers like to hold such probes until toward the end of the interview. That way they have already gathered most of the desired information.

Confrontation probes should only be used when you are fairly certain that they will be accepted. You need full interviewee attention, a low level of anxiety, a willingness to listen, and a desire to respond accurately and honestly. If you have been nonjudgmental and respectful throughout the entire interview, the interviewee will have no reason to lie or exaggerate. If you have accepted socially undesirable responses as well as positive ones, then interviewees will not feel a threat. In many ways, your openness, honesty, and consistency is a model for respondents. If you have consistently avoided "right" or "wrong" comments, then interviewees will feel at ease in expressing opinions.

CONFRONTATION PROBE EXERCISE

Directions: Write a confrontation statement for each of the following situations. There are no right or wrong answers for this exercise.

1. (After stating that he just bought a new expensive set of golf clubs) I really

don't know where I am going to get the money to pay this month's rent.

2. (The same respondent then states) It's really my wife's fault, she refuses to get a job until the kids are old enough to go to school.

3. (You notice on this respondent's application form that he lists holding a full-time job with ABC Corporation during the same two years he was supposedly a full-time student.)

4. (This respondent's eyes are down, she seems nervous, and she speaks in a monotone.) As far as I am concerned everything is going real good in the job. It's the best job I have ever had.

5. (This patient is obviously overweight and has high blood pressure.) I don't think I have a weight problem. I like to eat whatever I want. It doesn't hurt me; I feel as good now as I did when I weighed fifty pounds less.

6. (This student is always late for class and is failing the course.) I really enjoy your course, professor, and I study harder for this course than any other one I have.

7. (This employee is always arguing with his coworkers and telling them that they are doing everything wrong.) Actually I'm a pretty easygoing guy. I get along with everybody.

8. (You have three witnesses that saw this person pull a knife and threaten a storeowner.) I wasn't anywhere near there; besides I don't even carry a knife.

9. (This customer is wearing old clothes and generally appears to have little or no money.) I'd like to look at that $300 watch you have in the window, please.

10. (This senator continually votes for reducing income tax for large businesses and increasing taxes on those people in the lower income bracket.) I am very definitely for the little person in this country. I think we have an obligation to help those less fortunate than ourselves.

You may be wondering what happens if none of these suggestions works, and an interviewee becomes hostile and defensive when faced with a confrontation probe. There are no easy solutions. Each case is unique and must be handled as such, but here are some suggestions which might help you.

First, be absolutely certain a problem exists. This means checking plausibility, internal consistency, and any other questionable areas to be sure that the interviewee is not accurate. Sometimes this means asking for further details or checking with someone outside the interview. If you cannot be absolutely certain that falsification has taken place, then you are probably better off not confronting or pushing the issue.

When you are certain beyond a shadow of a doubt that a mistake has been made, then you must be honest and firm. Let interviewees know that you intend to resolve the problem. That in itself will make many interviewees backtrack and re-examine their earlier statements. You might also suggest other ways of looking at the material to get them to see things from your perspective.

If no resolution is forthcoming, you are probably better off summarizing and going on to the next topic. Under no circumstances should you let interviewees think they have won. A good comment to make at this point is, "Let's drop the subject, for now." This calls for delicate handling, but you should avoid, at all costs, arguing or direct accusations. Do not attempt to domineer, interrogate, or play the role of teacher or judge for interviewees. Be careful of criticism and moralizing; yet do not minimize the problem. Remember, it is much easier to face hostility that is expressed than that which remains hidden. You want interviewees to express, recognize, and summarize any hostile attitudes. Under no circumstances should you allow them to discredit you or become defensive. Defensive statements are those where interviewees attempt to blame others, find excuses, or simply forget the problem. Sometimes they may even fake acceptance in order to get off the topic.

Confrontation probes are most effective when they are used sparingly. But you must confront the first discrepancy that occurs. This sets the standard of honesty and completeness which most interviewees will recognize and follow throughout the interview. After the first confrontation, there usually is no need for further confrontation probes. If it is handled well, a confrontation probe will normally lead to self-examination and discrepancy resolution and avoid interviewee embarrassment and ego damage. The key to using confrontation probes wisely is giving interviewees the benefit of the doubt.

Why?

Before concluding this discussion of probing, some mention should be made of the most common probe of all: Why? Interviewers use "why?" by itself, as part of a probe, as well as to begin a primary question. Recently, however, using "why?" has come under considerable attack. Perhaps the most significant critic of the probe, "why?" is Benjamin (1969), a psychologist at Haifa University. Benjamin believes that "why?" has been misused and that its original meaning has been distorted. He suggests that it now connotates disapproval or displeasure. According to Benjamin, this probe forces interviewees to defend themselves, to withdraw and avoid the question, or to attack. Benjamin tells us how this probe has come to suggest blame and condemnation:

In their early years children used the word frequently—often to our distraction. For them it is a key to unlock the secrets of the world about them; it enables them to explore and discover. They ask for information without implying moral judgment, approval, or disapproval. But they learn. They learn that the adults surrounding them use the word differently—to put them on the spot, to show them they are behaving in an unacceptable manner. Slowly but surely the children stop using the word for the purpose of inquiry and begin to employ it against others the way it has been used against them. The child's ears ring with the questions: "Why did you muddy my clean floor?" "Why are you barefoot?" "Why don't you use your knife and fork properly?" "Why did you break that dish?" etc., etc. He learns to imitate his elders. Soon enough he will say to his friends, "Why did you take my bike?" to show that he disapproves of the act and not because he is interested in obtaining a bit of useful information. He will say to his mother, "Why must I go to the store?" not because he wants a reason but because he doesn't wish to go. This is his way of saying, "No, I am against it."

(Benjamin, 1974, p. 80)

According to Benjamin, children soon learn to defend themselves against the threatening "why?" At first, they treat the question as a rhetorical one. That is, they do not even bother to reply. If such withdrawal does not satisfy the questioner, children learn to defend themselves or to attack the questioner. Even when you do not use this probe in a negative way, it may be interpreted that way by interviewees. The following example illustrates this point.

Interviewer: "Jane, why have you been taking only forty-five minutes for lunch?"

Interviewee: "I'm *sorry*, Mr. Saunders, I've been running a little bit behind on my work, and I thought I could use the extra fifteen minutes to catch up."

Interviewer: "But, Jane, I wasn't finding fault. I just thought that somebody might have told you to do that. Now that you have caught up with your work, take an hour or two off to make up for the time you worked extra during the busy period."

In this case, Mr. Saunders' intentions were good, but there was a misunderstanding because of the word "why?" There was no real harm done, it just requires clearing up, and the less clearing up needed in an interview the better. There might also be some reduction of trust and respect between the two participants, because Jane still may harbor some belief that Mr. Saunders was condemning her in some way.

Benjamin also sees "why?" as a type of probing interviewers may resort to so they can express their own frustration with the interview. This can lead to a tug-of-war between you and an interviewee. Interviewees may easily view the question "why?" as asking for information which they do not want to yield. They feel, therefore, threatened, pushed, and prodded. This can make them withdraw, lie, or hit back, even if the only way possible is with silence.

Even Benjamin suggests that "why?" will continue to pop up frequently in interviews. He proposes that "why?" probably does not hurt a great deal, if an interviewee finds you unthreatening and legitimately interested in the information. Too often, however, this relationship is not established early in an interview, at least not before the word "why?" is used for the first time. "Why?" should be used as little as possible. At the very least you should be aware of its possible negative connotations and use it sparingly as part of an interview guide or as a probe.

SUMMARY PROBING EXERCISE

Directions: Since most of the exercises in this chapter have had no right or wrong answers to help you test your probing ability, this summary probing exercise is designed to allow you to see how you might have scored had the other exercises been graded. You will find several of the same situations, but this time you will be given some choices and correct answers. When you have finished, you should go back and see how close you came when you were writing the probes.

1. It's hard to talk about it. You are the first person I have told. See, I drink

from early in the morning after my husband leaves for work until he gets home again. (Choose best amplification probe.)
   a. Does your husband drink?
   b. You drink from morning till night?
   c. Humm
   d. I guess that's not an easy thing to talk about.
   e. (Silence)
2. It's difficult to know where to start. (Choose best amplification probe.)
   a. Why don't you just start at the beginning?
   b. It *is* hard starting.
   c. Oh?
   d. Why is it hard for you to start?
   e. (Silence)
3. We don't know too much about what happened here. All we know is that this small plane crashed, and two people have been taken to the hospital. (Choose best amplification probe.)
   a. Do you know the people's names?
   b. A plane crashed and two people are in the hospital.
   c. Gee
   d. How do you feel about this?
   e. (Silence)
4. After my parents separated, I felt deserted. I had nowhere to turn—just nowhere. I feel so left out. I'm not sure anyone cares whether I live or die. (Choose best amplification probe.)
   a. Tell me why your parents separated.
   b. You feel deserted and left out, don't you?
   c. Humm
   d. You sound depressed at this moment.
   e. (Silence)
5. Do I like this community? Yeah. (Choose best amplification probe.)
   a. What do you mean by "yeah"?
   b. You do like this community?
   c. OK
   d. This community makes you feel happy?
   e. (Silence)
6. (From the performance interview in the clarification probe exercise) Oh, that's a difficult situation. Several of my people feel there is not enough opportunity for advancement in this company. They want to move ahead so they leave us. (Choose best paraphrase probe.)
   a. They are frustrated here?
   b. You find it difficult to advance them?
   c. They perceive limited advancement opportunities here and go to companies where they can move ahead?
   d. Are you saying this company is cheap?
7. I don't want to mention any names, but many of the people we have in other departments sure aren't the engineer Dick is. (Choose best paraphrase probe.)
   a. We have been hiring poor engineers?

     b. Dick is better than others in higher positions?

     c. Dick is our best engineer?

     d. Our promotion procedures need changing?

8. They are always late with their work. When they have a problem, they wait until the last minute to come see me. And, if I can't get at their problem right away, they get mad and stomp out of my office. Pretty soon they tell other people that I'm unwilling to help them. Maybe I ought to turn them over to Dick. Could you dig up more money for him if I gave him some additional responsibilities? (Choose best summary probe.)

     a. You said Dick was your assistant, didn't you? He should be doing that already with no extra pay.

     b. You're saying we hire poor engineers, and they block the way for good people like Dick, right?

     c. If I understand you correctly, people like Dick are leaving your department because they have little room for advancement in this company. Less knowledgeable engineers are asking for your advice, and you don't have the time to give it to them. You think you might be able to solve both problems by giving Dick a promotion and allowing him to help train some of the engineers in other departments. Is that right?

     d. Poor advancement opportunities, unimpressive engineers in other departments, and too much work in your own department are causing turnover in your department?

9. Yeah, and their work never comes out the way I explained. (Choose the best direct clarification probe.)

     a. I'm not sure I understand what you mean?

     b. What do you mean by the "way you explained"?

     c. What?

     d. Ah, come on. What do you mean by that?

10. That's about it. When I picked them, they looked good, but now they don't do anything unless I tell them, and then they go and do it differently anyway. They change a little bit when I talk to them, but then they go right back to what they were doing before. Can you think of anything I should do? (Choose best direct clarification probe.)

     a. What do you mean they "looked good when you picked them"?

     b. How do they change when you talk to them?

     c. What do you think you should do?

     d. Yeah, why don't you stop telling them what to do.

11. (After stating that he just bought a new expensive set of golf clubs) I really don't know where I am going to get the money to pay this month's rent. (Choose best confrontation probe.)

     a. Should have thought of that before you bought the new golf clubs.

     b. I'm a bit confused. Earlier you said you bought some new golf clubs and now you're worried about the rent. It seems hard for you to manage your money.

     c. Maybe the bank will loan you the money.

     d. (Silence—let it go by.)

12. (This respondent's eyes are down, she seems nervous, and she speaks in a

monotone.) As far as I am concerned everything is going real good in the job. It's the best job I ever had. (Choose best confrontation probe.)
   a. You say you are happy, but your expression and tone of voice suggest otherwise.
   b. Don't tell me that. I can see something's bothering you.
   c. You look like you just lost your best friend.
   d. (Silence—just let it go.)
13. (This customer is wearing old clothes and generally appears to have little or no money.) I'd like to look at that $300 watch you have in the window, please. (Choose best confrontation probe.)
   a. Are you sure you can afford that watch?
   b. No way, you probably want to steal it.
   c. How can you dress like that and afford a $300 watch?
   d. (Silence—get the watch.)

HANDLING RESISTANCE

Resistance is very common in interview opening and questioning. This can be overcome by using a probe. One of the first obstacles to interviewing is a reluctance to take part. The comment, "I'm too busy" is often used, for example, to put off a research interviewer at the door. The best way to meet this is to make an appointment—you can offer to return at another time—and in the same breath describe the length and topic of the interview. If interviewees insist that they are still too busy, you should not force the point, but try to make the appointment and return as promised. Sometimes, however, your description of the length and topic of the interview, as well as an attempt to get in the first question, will overcome this initial resistance.

Another potential problem area is the notetaking or recording issue. Some people do not like to be recorded on tape or are fearful when they see you take out a pad and pencil. The best way to overcome this form of resistance is to explain the reason for it ("to be as accurate as possible") and suggest that the note pad or tape

Initial resistance can be overcome without arguing.

recorder can be put away if they don't like it. Sometimes you can offer to show your notes to the interviewee to make sure that they are accurate. Both the "I'm too busy" and "I don't want to be recorded" resistance are usually encountered early in the interview. In most cases, they can be overcome if you explain carefully and do not push too hard.

Other forms of response resistance may occur over the topics or questions within the interview. The first of these is the "I don't know anything about that" comment. Again, avoid challenging or persuading interviewees to answer a question. It is quite possible that the respondent does not know anything about that particular topic. A single probe question will usually determine whether or not an interviewee is qualified to answer the question. If you discover that the interviewee can't answer the question, you should ask who can. On the other hand, if you find that an interviewee simply used this excuse to avoid answering the question, then you should go right on. Sometimes a series of closed probe questions will help get the necessary information and convince interviewees that they can answer the questions.

Another type of resistance along the same line as "I don't know anything about that" is "I don't remember," and it should be handled in much the same way. Again, remember that interviewees may not remember or know the information. It is up to you to supply the necessary cues to help them remember and answer the question. Sometimes a silence probe will encourage respondents to remember or discuss the information. You should not press, but allow time to think and remember the answer. Suggest to interviewees that they can take a guess at the answer, if they choose. It is also possible to reword questions and come at the information from a slightly different angle which may help. As a last resort, you may have to skip the question or come back to it later.

Superficial answers are another form of resistance. A simple cursory, "Yes, I think so" is a superficial answer to a detailed question. Superficial answers can usually be overcome once an interviewee is made to see that you are not going to give up until the entire range of information desired is collected. If a superficial answer is accepted, an interviewee will be motivated to give more and more superficial answers. Use closed questions and dig out the necessary information.

A slightly different form of resistance is presented by interviewees who answer a question with a question. The first of these is the "What do you mean by that?" response. This can be a legitimate interviewee response, and at first, should be treated as a simple attempt to clarify the question. It should be treated as legitimate, even if you think it isn't. When said with a certain inflection, "What do you mean by *that*?" can be accusing and hostile and indicate definite interviewee resistance. You should resist the temptation to respond with an immediate "put down." Instead, try to find out the source of the hostility by approaching the question from several different angles and using more closed questions. In most cases, such resistance will stop as soon as an interviewee discovers that you are going to persist until the information is obtained.

Interviewees will often ask, "What do *you* think about that?" You must attempt to satisfy the interviewee's curiosity without biasing the interview. Sometimes this can be done by offering, "I'm not sure," but such a response will probably not satisfy the respondent. Realize that hardly any response, other than one which biases the interview, will be satifactory to the interviewee. Some experts suggest that you should be as honest as possible and state your own feelings. In doing so, however, you run the risk of interviewees patterning their responses to match yours. Perhaps the best response is to offer several legitimate reasons why you cannot answer the question and prejudice the interview. Interviewees will usually see the wisdom of this answer and offer their feelings first. You might plan to tell them your attitude at the end of the interview when there is no longer any chance of affecting their answers.

Interviewees may ask you about your background, family, friends, or hobbies. It is up to you to determine the reason for such personal questions. It may be motivated by curiosity or politeness. It may also be an attempt to establish rapport. As with most questions asked by interviewees, it is usually best to be as open and honest as possible and then return the focus to your question. Under no circumstances should you either ignore or argue with an interviewee when faced with resistance. How you handle resistance can affect the climate and success of the interview.

RESISTANCE EXERCISE

Directions: Below you will find a series of responses for each resistance situation. Choose the response you think is best for each situation. Answers will be found at the end of this chapter.

1. You are a research interviewer taking a poll. You give your opening statement, to which the homeowner replies, "I'm busy right now, I can't talk to you." Your best response is:
   a. This won't take very much time.
   b. When can I come back and talk to you?
   c. You sure don't look like you're doing anything important.
   d. Please, I will be fired if you don't talk to me.
2. You are an information interviewer. You have gotten an interview with a very important person, but when you take out your tape recorder, you hear, "Don't do that; I don't want to be recorded!" You should reply:
   a. Can I use a pencil and paper instead?
   b. Heck, I do this all the time and nobody minds.
   c. O.K. I'll put it away.
   d. I want to quote you as accurately as possible, and a tape recorder will let me do that.
3. You are the vice principal of a high school and have just asked a student who you think should know, "Where is the 'kegger' on Friday night being held?" The student replies, "Why are you asking me? I don't know anything about a 'kegger' on Friday night!" You should respond:
   a. Did you go the "kegger" last Friday?
   b. Oh, the hell you don't.
   c. All right, go back to class.
   d. I will repeat the question one more time.
4. To the same question as #3, the student responds, "Gee, someone told me, but I forgot. I'd sure tell you if I could remember." To this you should say,

     a. Who told you?

     b. I bet you forgot on purpose and will remember later.

     c. Was it someplace where they've had a "kegger" before?

     d. (Silence)

5. When you ask this same student, "Is it going to be held west of town?" you receive the response, "Yeah, I think so." You should then say:

     a. O.K. go back to class.

     b. What do you mean, "you think so"?

     c. Is it on Cooper's Ridge?

     d. (Silence)

6. You are a performance interviewer who has just asked a supervisor whom you are appraising why the work from her department is usually slower than from other departments, to which she replies, "What do you mean by *that*?" Your best response is:

     a. I have the reports right here and your department is the slowest of all; why is that?

     b. Don't you hear well?

     c. You know what I mean.

     d. I mean, why are you goofing off?

7. You are a counseling interviewer who has just asked a female client how she feels about putting her elderly mother in a senior citizens' home. She replies, "I don't know what to do. What would you do?" You ought to answer:

     a. Well, frankly I'd go ahead and admit her.

     b. I'd take her there and let her decide.

     c. I won't be responsible for that decision.

     d. I'm not sure; I've never faced that question.

8. The same client asks you, "Is your mother still living?" Your best response would be:

     a. Yes, she is.

     b. That's none of your business.

     c. Yes, she is. Now how do you think you will decide what to do with your mother?

     d. (Silence)

SUMMARY

This chapter has focused on the very difficult and important skill of probing. Three types of probes were discussed: amplification, clarification, and confrontation. An amplification probe is a follow-up question which requests an interviewee to go beyond and expand upon information given in response to a primary question. Amplification probes include silence, minimal encouragement, restatement, direct amplification, and reflection. Clarification probes are follow-up questions designed to reduce response confusion and ambiguity. Paraphrase, summary, and direct clarification are the three types of clarification probes discussed. A confrontation probe requests explanation of some inconsistency. Most of these probes can apply to the immediately preceding question or be retro-spective to some earlier question.

This chapter also provided a great many tips regarding how you can improve your interviewing skill. Some analysis was made of the question, "Why?" which has been challenged for being too negative. The final section in this chapter involved ways of meeting different forms of interviewee resistance. Ways of meeting resistance to the interview itself, ways of meeting resistance to particular topics or questions, and ways of meeting the form of resistance where an inter-viewee asks a question in response to an interviewer question or probe were described. You should practice your probing skill until you are confident you can handle it properly.

ACTIVITIES

Activity #1

Directions: As a part of the activities for the preceding chapter, you obtained a tape of an actual interview. That tape probably contains examples of both primary and probe questions. If it does not contain these kinds of questions, then obtain a tape which does include primary and probe questions. Listen carefully to the tape and write down every inquiry including silence and minimal encouragements. Be sure each is an inquiry in your opinion. Don't write down every pause. Once you think you have every inquiry on paper, go back and listen to the tape again to be sure. You are to then label each inquiry:

P = Primary Question
A = Amplification Probe
C = Clarification Probe
X = Confrontation Probe

Once you have each inquiry labeled, answer the following questions and record your answers.
1. Who were the participants?
2. What was the purpose of the interaction?
3. Was the interaction directive or nondirective?
4. How many primary questions did you find?
5. How did you determine which were primary questions?
6. How many probes did you discover?
7. Did any of the probes introduce bias? If "yes" give an example.
8. Did any of the probes alter or extend the meaning of a primary question? If "yes" give an example.
9. Did any of the probes include self-disclosure on the part of the interviewer? If "yes" give an example.
10. How many amplification probes were there in the interaction? Give examples of each of the following amplification probes if they occurred in the interaction and the circumstances surrounding them: Silence, Minimal Encouragement, Restatement, Direct Amplification.
11. How many of the probes asked for reflection of subjective information?

How many of these were silence? How many were minimal encouragement? How many were restatement? How many were direct amplification?
12. How many clarification probes did you find? Give examples of each of the following clarification probes if they occurred in the interaction and the circumstances surrounding them: Paraphrase, Summary, Direct Clarification.
13. How many confrontation probes occurred in the interaction? Give an example of a confrontation probe and how it affected the interaction.
14. If there were any "Why?" probes or questions, did they have a connotation of blame or condemnation? Give an example and explain.
15. Give any example of resistance you found and how it was handled.

Activity #2

Try conducting an interview or interaction without using any probe questions. In other words, you cannot follow-up any of your primary questions. Continue this interaction as long as you or the other participant is willing. After the interaction ask your partner if he or she noticed anything different about the interview. Now ask yourself the following questions and record your answers.
1. Were you frustrated? If your answer is "yes," why were you frustrated?
2. How did the limitation on the type of question you could ask affect the type and amount of information you gained?
3. Did you feel you lost control of the interview? If your answer is "yes," give an example of when you feel you lost control.
4. What other comments do you have about this activity?

Activity #3

The third activity at the end of the preceding chapter said that you were almost fully prepared to conduct your actual information interview. What you are to do now is re-examine your prepared interview guide and anticipate any amplification, clarification, or confrontation probes you may need in the interview. Try to anticipate how your respondent will answer the questions. If you can anticipate any needed probes or possible resistance, jot down some ideas regarding how you will handle them.

Answers to the Probe Vs Primary Question Exercise.
1 = 1, 2 = 1, 3 = 1, 4 = 2, 5 = 2, 6 = 2, 7 = 1, 8 = 1, 9 = 2, 10 = 1, and 11 = 2.

Answers to the Summary Probing Exercise.
1 = D, 2 = E, 3 = A, 4 = D, 5 = B, 6 = C, 7 = B, 8 = C, 9 = A, 10 = B, 11 = B, 12 = A, and 13 = D.

Answers to the Resistance Exercise.
1 = B, 2 = D, 3 = A, 4 = C or D, 5 = C, 6 = A, 7 = D, and 8 = C.

Chapter 6

Skill 6
Listening

Interviewers must learn to listen. Clearly no interviewer can hope to succeed in his task if he fails to notice the significant remark and explore it, or observe the silence and probe its implications. (Beveridge, 1975, p. 98)

Interviewers can learn nothing while talking. In almost every type of interview, you should be doing at least twice as much listening as talking. The problem is, however, that very often interviewers and interviewees are neither talking nor listening. They are daydreaming, planning ahead, or doing any one of many other things. And, when they are listening, they do so half-heartedly. It is estimated that most people listen effectively to only about 25% of what is said to them.

In this chapter you will find a discussion of several aspects of listening which are important for both respondents and interviewers. The first section illustrates the nature of listening and differentiates it from merely receiving or hearing. Next the value of listening within an interview is discussed, and a number of obstacles to effective listening are listed. The final section deals with improving your listening skills. Since listening is an important part of an interview for both interviewers and interviewees, this chapter is written with both participants in mind.

LISTENING DEFINED

A most confusing distinction for many people is between hearing and listening. *Hearing* is simply the reception of sound—in order to listen, you must pay attention to, interpret, and remember the sound stimuli. There are many stimuli that occur around you to which you seldom, if ever, listen. You consider them unimportant and do not bother to interpret or remember them. Hirsch (1979) divides verbal listening into the following nine steps:

1. *Hearing the sound stimuli from another person*
2. *Identifying the sound stimuli as symbols*
3. *Assigning importance to the symbols*
4. *Relating the symbols to past experiences*
5. *Evaluating the symbols*

6. *Interpreting the symbols*
7. *Expanding the meaning of the symbols*
8. *Integrating the meaning of the symbols*
9. *Remembering the integrated meaning on both the short- and long-term basis*

(Hirsch, 1979, p. 7)

Hearing is necessary for listening, but listening does not always occur along with hearing. It is important for interviewers to learn to listen, not just hear, what an interviewee is saying.

Listening Beyond Words

You listen not only with your ears, but also with your eyes and your mind. There are basically three channels by which information travels between you and an interviewee: verbal, other vocal, and nonverbal. The *verbal* channel contains the words that are spoken. The *other vocal* channel refers to all of the sounds which come out of a person's mouth which are not words. Such qualities as loudness, pitch, and rate of speaking are all part of the vocal channel of communication. The *nonverbal* channel, as defined earlier, consists of a great many other ways by which you communicate information. It includes such things as posture, angle and set of the head, body movement, eye gaze, arm and hand movement (often called gestures), facial expression and coloration, as well as many, many other stimuli which can be received and interpreted to have meaning. Although listening was originally defined to include only the perception and assimilation of the sound stimuli, in this book listening refers to *all* stimuli which have meaning to either an interviewee or interviewer.

Information Listening

There are different types of information to which you can be sensitive during an interview. Two information types have already been discussed—subjective and objective. Objective information is the factual information in a message. Subjective information deals with the speaker's feelings and emotions. Objective information comes mostly through the verbal channel, while subjective information is found in the vocal and nonverbal channels as well. Subjective information is based on beliefs and values; objective information is based on verifiable facts, or at least facts as they are perceived by the receiver.

In different interview settings, an interviewer often listens for different types of information. A lawyer cross-examining a witness may listen for factual inconsistencies, omissions, distortions, or contradictions. A counseling interviewer may listen for clues to emotions and anxieties underlying interviewee problems. Research interviewers may listen only for the objective facts as they are presented. In each interview setting, both participants have different listening goals.

Active Listening

Good listening is not a passive process. It is an extremely active process and takes a great deal of effort. You cannot sit back and expect information to flow into your eyes, ears, and brain with no effort on your part. In order to completely understand what is being communicated, you must get to the meaning which underlies the words and other stimuli. A common axiom of listening is that "meaning is in people, not in words." The active listener must work to discover what each person's meaning is and not assume the obvious meaning.

Most people *listen selectively*; they filter out certain sound and visual stimuli. This selectivity isn't always conscious. For example, you unconsciously filter out the sound of cars going by outside your window, the color of the room in which you are sitting, and irrelevant noises and mistakes in messages you are receiving. What you filter out is determined in part by your own mental set, previous experiences, and personal and physical needs. You must remember that no one listens perfectly; everyone listens selectively. The difference between good and poor listeners is what they choose to perceive and assimilate, and what they choose to neglect and filter out.

ACTIVE LISTENING EXERCISE

Directions: This exercise simulates a listening situation. It is a test of your ability to follow instructions accurately and rapidly. You are to pretend that someone is giving you these instructions orally. Take out a piece of blank paper and time yourself; if you are really an active listener, you should be able to complete it in less than one minute. When you are ready, you may begin.

1. Read all items before doing anything.
2. True or false: There are three channels by which information travels between speaker and listener: verbal, vocal, and nonverbal.
3. Write down your name, address, and phone number.
4. Fill in the blank: "Meaning is in _____ not in words." (If you forgot, make a guess and go on quickly.)
5. Draw a circle around this page number and write it here.
6. True or false: Most people listen selectively.
7. Describe the last time you think you were an active listener.
8. Reread the first instruction.
9. Do only items number one and ten.
10. Do you still think you are an active listener (and reader)?

THE VALUE OF INTERVIEW LISTENING

There are two main values to interview listening. First, good listening helps interviewees, it makes them feel part of the process, gives them a feeling of worth and acceptance, and therefore, encourages more open and honest communication. The second, and more obvious benefit, is that good listening enables you to accurately interpret and record the information provided by a speaker.

153

Interviewee Benefits

Interviewees are complimented when they think an interviewer has genuine interest in what they say. They feel that what they have to say is important. This enhances the interview climate by reducing anxiety and defensiveness. Whether the interview is formal or informal, respondents are more willing to talk to someone who shows an active interest in them and their information.

When respondents feel valued and accepted, they are motivated to provide more high quality information. They try to be as open and completely honest as possible, which is precisely what you want. Good listening does not necessarily mean agreement. For most interviews, it is enough that you show a willingness to listen. Interviewees are willing to share fairly intimate information about themselves and their ideas, as long as they know that the information will be given a fair hearing. Few expect everything they say to be completely accepted. In the same way, most interviewers do not expect every question to be answered, only given a fair hearing.

A side benefit of good listening is what is commonly called the *modeling effect*. When you practice good listening, it becomes apparent to respondents that they can and should listen carefully too. Interviewees who see that there is no threat or risk involved in responding to both the content and the feeling of questions will follow the lead of the interviewer and be less defensive. This generally improves response quality. You should be totally sincere and not fake interest or listening. Interviewees will sense this behavior and use it as a model. Good listening then not only motivates good responses on the part of the interviewee, but also encourages better respondent listening as well.

Interviewer Benefits

Active listening helps interviewers obtain the information they desire. If you are listening well, you are always prepared to hear something you did not expect. If a response calls for a follow-up question or a question calls for an extended answer, it is important that it come at the appropriate point. This means listening not only for what you expect to hear, but also for what you do not expect to hear.

Good interviewer responses, questioning, and probing are all dependent on good listening. Without good listening it is impossible to get an accurate record of what is said and complete the interview guide. In the preceding chapter on probing, you learned how listening can control the messages of respondents and keep them in line with what you see as the interview's purpose. In many ways the terms "skillful listener" and "skillful interviewer/interviewee" are almost synonymous.

OBSTACLES TO LISTENING

Perhaps the biggest obstacle to effective listening is the temptation to take it for granted. It is natural to follow the "line-of-least-effort." It takes less effort to consider the listening process passive. If you don't think about it, you don't have to work at it. It takes self-discipline and mental effort to listen actively. It takes much less effort to listen to a speaker's first few words and anticipate the rest of the question or response. It takes effort not to "turn off" or "tune out" repeated information. It takes effort to give more of your thought time to listening. It is much easier to let your mind wander. The first, and perhaps most important obstacle to listening, then, is laziness. You can think of most of the following specific obstacles as subcategories of laziness.

Listening is one of the most widely discussed, yet misunderstood, aspects of the communication process. This is not only true for listening in an interview, but all forms of listening. An examination of the listening literature reveals the following fifteen major barriers to effective interview listening:

a. *Physical Limitations*
b. *Setting Limitations*
c. *Primary and Secondary Tension*
d. *Source Focusing*
e. *Fact Focusing*
f. *Emotional Blindspots*
g. *Mind Wandering*
h. *Planning Ahead*
i. *Conclusion Jumping*
j. *Mental Arguing*
k. *Overtalking*
l. *Fatigue and Boredom*
m. *Uncritical Acceptance*
n. *Faking Attention*
o. *Poor Response or Question*

Physical Limitations

Physical limitations prevent you from being able to fully receive all of the stimuli coming your way. You may have some trouble hearing or seeing, which will prevent you from becoming an effective listener. You should probably have your hearing and sight tested. Very often these tests are given at no charge by clinics in your community.

A great many tests have been developed to assess reading ability but there are only a few which measure listening ability directly. Perhaps the best known listening test is the *Brown-Carlson Listening Comprehension Test* (1955). It was originally designed to test high-school students and first-year college students, but it has been found useful in all levels of college, as well as in measuring on-the-job listening ability. It measures the assimilation of spoken symbols in a face-to-face situation, with both vocal and visual cues. All interviewing students should take this or some other listening test in order to determine their listening ability. The source for this test is in the bibliography.

Listening tests have two basic uses. They let people know if they have a deficiency in some listening area so they can focus attention on it and upgrade their skills in that area. A second, and equally important use of such a test, is to create a recognition of the importance of listening skills. It helps people understand that listening skills vary greatly within the population, just as people vary greatly in other attributes.

Physical barriers can hurt listening efficiency.

Just as some people are more sensitive than others to reception of verbal information, some people are more sensitive to nonverbal communication. The *Profile of Nonverbal Sensitivity* (Rosenthal, 1979) has been developed to test nonverbal listening ability. It consists of 220 individual scenes and measures 11 different aspects of nonverbal communication sensitivity. The test is designed to alert you to whether you are focusing more on the vocalic, postural, facial, or other nonverbal cue areas, as well as how sensitive you are to positive/negative and dominant/submissive cues. Like the Brown-Carlson Listening Test, the Profile of Nonverbal Sensitivity has been the subject of much research and testing. It also alerts you to weak spots in your nonverbal receiving ability and helps you recognize the importance and variability of nonverbal communication sensitivity within listeners. The source for this test is also in the bibliography of this book.

Setting Limitations

The setting is not only important in relaxing interview participants and establishing the climate for the interview, it also promotes productive listening. The presence of distractions and the seating position of the interviewee vis-à-vis the interviewer are important setting variables.

Distractions include noises such as ringing telephones, people talking, and outside street noises; visual stimuli within the setting, such as posters on the wall or papers and notes on a desk; and such things as the temperature, size, and color of a room. It is hard to listen effectively in a setting filled with visual and vocal distractions. Interviewers should reduce these distractions as much as possible. Sometimes this is as easy as closing a door or window or moving away from a cluttered desk. If a distraction cannot be eliminated, it is up to the listener to use added listening concentration to overcome it.

Seating position is another extremely important aspect of the interview setting. Find a seating position which allows easy reception of all available information. This means removing barriers, such as desks, which prevent you from receiving information coming from the lower half of a respondent's body, such as a jiggling foot, bouncing leg, and so on. If a barrier must be present in order to take notes or for any other reason, then participants should sit across the corner of the desk or table rather than in front and behind it.

As mentioned earlier, many skillful interviewers intentionally move away from barriers and have what they call an "interviewing area." This area normally consists of two soft chairs with a coffee table or end table for ashtrays, soft drinks, relevant papers, and notes if necessary. Most of these aspects of the interview setting should be prepared ahead of time and need not concern you during the course of the interview.

Primary and Secondary Tension

Primary tension (tension which occurs because of the newness of the situation) is important in determining the interview climate. It can also be a major barrier in interview listening. Secondary tension grows out of unresolved frustration and stress during an interview. This tension occurs because of what is being discussed and not the newness of the situation. Both kinds of tension limit your ability to listen effectively—they make you focus more upon yourself and your tension than upon the message. Until primary and secondary tension are reduced, it is difficult for a listener to function effectively. The interview opening should reduce primary tension. Secondary tension must be recognized and dealt with as it occurs.

Source Focusing

Source focusing is the tendency for some listeners to evaluate the source of the message and not the message itself. There is no doubt that in some cases you should evaluate interviewers' or interviewees' emotional level, credibility, and degree of involvement with the message. On the other hand, source focusing can disrupt listening if you are overly concerned with the source's physical appearance, ethnic origins, unusual mannerisms, clothing, accent or dialect, or vocabulary. They become barriers and distractions to listening in the same way as outside noise and visual distractions. A good listener will notice these things but not let them be a distraction to message reception.

A recent article by Stephen (1981) illustrates how a source distraction can reduce listening efficiency. She is writing about women who undo the third or "modesty" button on their blouse.

> *The effect is ever so subtle—nothing tacky like a frankly plunging neckline or a see-through blouse. No, the effect is almost accidental. A quality silk shirt ripples discreetly. Now it's open. Now it's closed. Now you see it. Now you don't . . . . When one is interviewing a best-selling author or a psychologist who gives assertiveness training workshops, it hardly seems appropriate to inquire if she has forgotten to button her blouse. Instead, one is slightly embarrassed and pretends not to notice. Your eyes meet her eyes and lock right there. The button is as powerful a way of commanding attention as talking in a whisper can be.*

The preceding is the way such a distraction affects a female interviewer. Stephen then quotes the third button reaction of a male job interviewer.

> *As a guy, I don't know what I am supposed to do. Am I supposed to look or not look? Is it an invitation or is it just something everybody is doing? One woman's clothes seemed to convey a double message—take me seriously, but check me out. I didn't trust her. I felt she was being manipulative and I don't like women to manipulate me sexually—at least not in a job interview.*

Obviously, both of these interviewers were source focusing and reduced listening was probably the result.

Fact Focusing

You are probably saying, "Well, isn't my purpose as an interviewer to get the facts? How can fact focusing be a barrier to listening?" The answer is that the facts should be secondary to the *ideas* presented in the message. When you are just trying to "get the facts," you become bogged down in details and do not listen to how all of the details relate to one another. It is not easy to pick out the main ideas in interviewee comments and responses. They rarely give you any signals that a main idea is coming. They don't say, "Now, here is the main idea of what I'm saying." What they may do, however, is give you some vocal signals, such as a pause before a main idea, speak slower, or speak louder. You must be alert to catch these vocal signals. Yates (1979) suggests three other ways you can identify main ideas:

1. *Identify the details, examples, digressions, and any further supplementary information so that you will not mistake these for the main ideas. (Process of elimination.)*
2. *Identify the order in which information is presented, so that the order can help you identify the main idea.*
3. *Make a tentative guess by seeing how this idea is supported by the examples and details presented.*

(Yates, 1979, pp. 16–17)

Yates' suggestions are self-explanatory except for the one on order. What Yates means by order is how the examples and main ideas are sequenced. Some people like to give the main idea first and then follow up with examples. This is similar to the deductive approach discussed earlier. Yates calls this the MI-EX or main idea-example order. On the other hand, some people like to present the examples first and then follow up with the main idea (EX-MI approach). This is similar to the inductive approach: Yates suggests that this order is used less frequently and makes a listener do more work. You should discover what the examples have in common and what conclusion can be drawn from them. Sometimes, with this order, the main idea is introduced by a signal such as, "I conclude from this . . . ," "All of these examples suggest to me . . . ," or "In summary . . . " Once you discover which order is preferred by an interviewee, you will usually find the same order occurring for each response. Discovering the main idea in either a question that is being asked of you or a response given by an interviewee is sometimes a very difficult task. If you focus only on the facts, it is impossible.

MAIN IDEA EXERCISE

Directions: Below are some interviewee responses. Select the main idea in each response.

1. That's why his complaining and calling me names bothers me. I know husbands and wives fight and call each other names all the time. Everybody does it. But, it bothers me because what he says is just true enough to mean something. When I first met him he was so nice to me. He hadn't been in town too long, and one of my friends told me she thought he had a wife. I asked him about it, but he said, "No." Naturally I believed him. He was the perfect man for me. I was pretty dumb about the world. I was only eighteen years old. We kept going together. I asked him if we could get married, but he always had some excuse. By that time, I knew I was pregnant, and I was scared.

2. Well, I'll tell you. That was one of the most difficult jobs I ever had. It wasn't difficult physically; it was just difficult in terms of doing the same thing over and over again. I had to put the same screws in the same place hour after hour. I don't think I ever want a job like that again. I'd start daydreaming and forget what I was doing. I almost hurt myself several times.

3. That particular compressor has had its packing replaced twelve times in the last three years. Most of the time, the packing was worn but not totally destroyed. We have had to replace the rings about once a year. We got an engineer from the manufacturer to look at it, and he said the machine was still in pretty good shape and that we should plan for regular maintenance to prevent down time. I think we should take his advice.

4. I guess I've spent less time in the field with my men than my predecessor. He used to go out with the men all the time. I have sent my assistant to do most of that; besides it helps him get experience. I think I should be setting policy and working with some of our bigger clients. I have called on them without a salesman along, but I have always given the salesman a report on what happened. I guess I have been less friendly with the sales staff than I

was when I was a salesman too. One of them even calls me by my last name when she used to call me by my first name. I think everyone does that when they become a manager. This job calls for more formality. I have to make decisions on them now and tell them what to do. That's deliberate on my part. You said I should increase sales and profit, and I can't do that if I am away from my desk all the time. I'm perfectly willing to be more friendly, but I won't do it at the expense of the business.

5. "Young people are looking for people who not only teach but who live the example. That is one reason why the cults have grown so rapidly. I oppose the cults, but you cannot question the success of the hundreds of cults in this country attracting young people. They demand more. Mainline churches— and the Baptists are part of the mainline—decided a generation ago not to demand much, and that's where they lost the young people. Churches like ours that are very strongly committed to the Fundamentalist doctrine and to separatist lifestyles are attracting young people. That's what young people are looking for." (Jerry Falwell, president of Moral Majority Inc., in *Nutshell*, 1981/82, p. 38)

A second aspect of the fact-focusing barrier is that listeners need to understand the attitudes and feelings behind words. Words and facts represent objective information, while attitudes and feelings represent the subjective information which is an equally important part of interview listening. Listeners who try to determine the main ideas in a comment are more likely to comprehend and remember the whole message. It is also easier to write up an interview when focusing on ideas and not words or facts. If you are interested in only words or facts, you should probably use a tape recorder. Main ideas can occur at the beginning, middle, or end of a response, and you must be constantly alert to pick them up.

Emotional Blindspots

Everyone has biases, prejudices, or emotional blindspots to certain types of information. It is up to you to recognize and control your biases and blindspots. If your attention is focused on emotional blindspots, less energy will be devoted to the task of listening. Emotional blindspots may occur because of the subject or content of the interview or because of certain words that are used by the speaker. They normally involve areas of great sensitivity, such as your deepest beliefs and values. Everyone has certain convictions and prejudices which they protect very carefully and react strongly to when they are questioned.

Good listeners know their own emotional blindspots. When such topics as race, religion, politics, or nationalism come up, you should work especially hard because most people have emotional blindspots in those areas. In the same way, certain words or phrases can trigger emotional blindspots. Ethnic words such as "pollock," "wop," and "nigger," are especially good examples of emotion-laden words. Many other similar words can also trigger emotional blindspots. Once an emotional blindspot is triggered, it prevents accurate reception.

Mind Wandering

Everyone is capable of thinking and listening almost four times as fast as a normal person talks. This is called the *thought/speech speed differential*. This extra thinking time allows for a great deal of mind wandering. Mind wandering becomes a listening barrier when you spend more of your thinking time on other subjects than you spend concentrating on the message being presented. Mind wandering or daydreaming may take many forms. You may think back to some problem you are having at home or on your job. Your mind may wander to an upcoming interview or the interview which preceded the one which is currently taking place. When listeners let their mind wander, productive listening drops. Mind wandering is one of the most seductive of listening barriers.

Planning Ahead

This barrier, like mind wandering is caused by the thought/speech speed differential. While some listeners are letting their mind wander, others are planning ahead to the next question or the next answer. This is especially true of beginning interviewers and respondents who are uncertain about their next question, probe, or answer. Planning ahead during interchanges is usually a sign of poor preparation.

A sure sign of planning ahead is looking at the interview guide while an interviewee is answering a question. This becomes a barrier not only to listening, but also to a good response. Respondents do not answer easily and completely when an interviewer is obviously not listening. Interviewees plan ahead when they feel threatened or defensive. If a good climate is not developed, they feel they must plan ahead to protect themselves. They are also mentally looking backwards to make sure they do not contradict themselves.

Conclusion Jumping

Conclusion jumping is a third way in which poor listeners let the thought/speech speed differential hurt their listening. After a few minutes, listeners may stereotype the other participant or anticipate their questions or answers. They jump to conclusions and hear what they expect to hear; they begin to filter and selectively perceive messages. This difficulty often occurs when an interviewer has done many interviews on the same subject and begins to see a pattern developing in responses. Instead of probing an unclear response, the interviewer merely assumes that the respondent means the same thing as the others. A sure sign of conclusion jumping is when you see responses appear in your notes before they are actually spoken. It is not your responsibility to fill in the gaps or anticipate the responses or questions of the respondent.

FACT/INFERENCE EXERCISE

Directions: Below is a description given by a respondent and observations by an interviewer based on that description. Indicate whether you think the interviewer's observations are true (T), false (F), or inferences (?), that is, conclusions based on conclusion jumping. Read the description as often as you like before looking at the observations, but do not reread it once you have begun judging the observations. Answers will be found at the end of this chapter.

Well, I had just closed up the store and walked outside when a dark figure appeared in the alley and demanded money. I took out my wallet, handed it over, and the individual left.

1. The thief appeared in the alley.
2. The owner closed up the store.
3. A dark figure demanded money.
4. Money was stolen by somebody.
5. The interviewee was beaten up.
6. The interviewee took out his wallet.
7. The dark figure took the wallet.
8. The interviewee handed over a wallet.
9. The store manager did not take out his wallet.
10. No one demanded money.
11. The mugger left on foot.
12. The interviewee's husband demanded money.
13. This incident took place at night.
14. The interviewee walked out the back door of the store into the alley.
15. In this description three people are referred to.

Mental Arguing

And finally, poor listeners resolve the thought/speech speed differential by mental arguing, a tendency closely related to emotional blindspots. These people listen with an open mind only until they find a problem with a question or response and then they mentally argue with it. Unless participants see things exactly the same way, there will always be some basis on which a listener can argue with a speaker. It is the responsibility of both parties not to argue mentally or verbally with each other. Listeners should remain open-minded. Those who are easily threatened, insulted, or become resistant to messages that contradict their own beliefs, attitudes, ideas, or values are especially susceptible to mental arguing. Interviewers who interrupt interviewee responses are frequently practicing mental arguing.

Overtalking

Many people like to talk. They have extremely strong verbal skills and talking is much more natural than listening. Talking makes interviewers feel in control of an interview. Such people should cultivate the ability to listen as skillfully as they talk and to feel comfortable with the silences which often occur as part of good listening. Short probes and requests for further information are useful and evidence of active listening. Overtalking, however, is a definite sign of poor listening, and interrupting is usually a sign of overtalking. Interrupting during a pause is a sure way of limiting or stopping further response.

Overtalking can become a serious interviewer problem. Once this habit has developed, it is extremely hard to adopt a productive listening attitude. Remember our earlier formula of approximately 70% interviewee talk and 30% interviewer talk. A greater percentage of talk is usually a sign of overtalking. Skillful interviewers never forget that the interviewee is the most important part of the interview and has the information needed to make the interview a success.

Fatigue and Boredom

In every interview there are times when the participants are concentrating and there are other times when attention is at a low level. It is almost impossible for listeners to be interested all of the time. Most people are attentive at the beginning of a message, but attentiveness wanes as the end approaches. Reduced attention can be due to boredom or fatigue. Some interviewers and interviewees rationalize poor listening by convincing themselves that an answer, question, or topic is uninteresting. The value of a response or question should not be judged by how interesting it is. Sometimes it is extremely difficult to maintain a high level of interest after the third or fourth time you have received or given the same information during a series of interviews. If you do not maintain interest, it is easy to neglect relevant probes, or responses, and jump to conclusions. A number of research studies have pointed out that the effectiveness of your listening is directly related to the interest you find in the message. Boredom always leads to reduced listening.

Whereas boredom refers to the lack of interest in an answer or subject, fatigue relates to the listener's energy level. Long interviews or repeated interviewing can be tiring and reduce listening accuracy. When fatigue begins to set in, you might suggest that the interview be continued at a later time. There are a number of signs of interview fatigue: mind wandering, an overly relaxed posture, wandering eyes, or a reduced level of notetaking. Interviewee fatigue can be seen in short, disorganized answers and longer pauses. You should be alert to any decline in listening based upon fatigue or boredom.

Uncritical Acceptance

Uncritical acceptance is simply absorbing information like a sponge. A good listener is more than a tape recorder. Some participants fall into the habit of accepting everything the other person says. It is hard to become a good listener if you aren't willing to listen to and analyze all types of information. This does not mean that you should mentally argue with questions and responses, but merely try to understand them.

People who listen uncritically are unwilling to pass judgment on the assumptions, arguments, evidence, and logic behind messages. As an interviewer, you can't accept information that is not based on fact and not developed logically. You must continually encourage listener responses with probes and requests for further clarification. A brief comment or probe tells speakers that you are interested, attentive, and wish them to continue. A good probe does not interfere with a speaker's train of thought. You must also be prepared to confront speakers when you recognize omissions, fabrications, or exaggerations. The barrier of uncritical acceptance is extremely difficult to overcome, once you get in the habit of being a passive listener.

Faking Attention

Some listeners look like those little dolls whose heads are on a spring and bounce up and down with every movement. These listeners are usually faking attention. They think that if they look like they are listening, the speaker will be pleased and respond better. They constantly smile and nod their heads in agreement, but are actually never fully aware of what is being said. It is extremely hard to fake attention and actually listen at the same time. The loser in such a situation is the listener. It takes a great deal of effort to fake attention, effort which must be drained from the true listening effort. Sometimes faked attention is detected with a cleverly inserted question, probe, or response. Often, however, this embarrasses the listener and jeopardizes the interview climate.

Poor Response or Question

Almost all of the barriers discussed up to this point relate to some problem on the part of the listener. This last barrier, poor response or question, shows that poor listening might also come from some weakness on the part of a speaker. Unorganized, unclear, overly broad, and other poor questions and responses may have a direct effect upon your ability to receive the message. In these situations it is up to you to make sure the message is presented so that you can understand it.

Using inappropriate language often confuses interviewees. If an interviewer and interviewee speak different languages, then a bilingual interviewer should be brought in to conduct the interview. In most cases, however, the problem doesn't center on a difference in the language spoken, but on differences in vocabulary level. Listeners who are continually trying to define words used by the other participant have a difficult time listening to the entire message. They find themselves focusing on words and facts instead of the ideas discussed. You should work to increase and expand your vocabulary if you intend to interview with many different types of respondents and interviewers.

This is not meant to be an exhaustive list of the barriers to listening, but it reflects the major ones identified by listening experts. There is one other barrier that is often mentioned: notetaking. Since notetaking is such an important part of the interview process, however, it will be discussed in detail in the following chapter.

LISTENING BARRIERS EXERCISE

Directions: You are listening in an interview while an interviewer/interviewee is asking/answering a question. Below are several thoughts that might be running through your head. Each thought represents one of the fifteen listening barriers just discussed. Identify the kind of listening barrier you are experiencing. Answers can be found at the end of this chapter.

1. I wonder if I forgot to turn off the coffee pot before I left home this morning.
2. If I hear the word, "ya-all" again, I'm going to go crazy.
3. I can see his lips moving, but I can barely hear the words he is saying.
4. Boy, I sure like that painting she has got hanging on the wall.
5. This client hardly says anything; I had better keep giving her information or we'll never get anywhere.
6. I'd better figure out what I am going to ask next; he is almost finished with this answer.
7. I asked if she liked the east coast or the west coast and she said, "yes." What does that mean?
8. I guess I had better agree with him; I don't have time to check out his information.
9. This is my first interview, and I'm sure nervous.
10. Why did she use the word "boss," and not "supervisor"?
11. Oh no, Ralph is a homosexual.
12. I can just see it now. This guy is going to throw the book at me.
13. How can any rational person believe what she's saying?
14. This is about the fifth time she's said the same thing.
15. If I just keep nodding my head, he will think I'm listening.
16. I can't let that go by. I'd better interrupt her right here and straighten her out.
17. He should have phrased that question differently.
18. I don't even understand half the words in that question.
19. Just keep smiling.
20. That last applicant sure answered this question well.
21. He just said there are "communists" in this company.
22. I like sitting behind my desk. It gives me a feeling of power.
23. Everything is blurred.
24. I remember he said he got in at "8:05" on "Thursday," but I did not catch the reason.
25. The interviewer is challenging me. What do I do now? I can't even think straight.
26. He's answering this question positively; so he will probably answer the next question positively as well.
27. When he asks me how I feel about that, I will say, "I don't like it."

28. She's the boss. I'd better do what she says.
29. Boy, is that a fancy sportcoat he's wearing.
30. This interview has gone on for two hours; when will it ever end?

IMPROVING LISTENING SKILLS

You can improve your listening ability by becoming aware of each of the fifteen barriers to listening and working to overcome them. The following are some suggestions for improving your listening skills.

1. Test your verbal and nonverbal receiving abilities to make sure you do not have any physical limitations which would prevent you from listening effectively.
2. Eliminate all distractions and be sure to choose a seating arrangement that allows you to pick up all of the information coming from a speaker.
3. Be aware of primary and secondary tension when it occurs in you or the other participant, and force yourself to listen in spite of this tension until it recedes.
4. Do not be distracted by the dress, behavior, or other aspects of the source, but focus on the message itself.
5. Discover the ideas and emotions underlying the words and facts being spoken by the message sender.
6. Be aware of your own emotional blindspots and do not let sensitive words or concepts distract you from hearing the entire message in an unbiased manner.
7. Force yourself to keep your entire mind focused upon the speaker's message and not upon your own daydreams and fantasies.
8. Do your planning prior to the interview and keep your attention upon the current question or response, not what is to come.
9. Treat each question or response as unique and worthy of a full and unbiased hearing, rather than jumping to conclusions.
10. Refrain from arguing, interrupting, or debating with speakers simply because you disagree with what they have to say.
11. Be sure to limit the amount of talking you do to approximately one-third if you are the interviewer or two-thirds if you are the interviewee.
12. Force yourself to be interested and energetic and concentrate on everything the speaker has to say.
13. Be continually evaluating, analyzing, probing, and clarifying information rather than uncritically accepting every message.
14. Don't ever try to play games with a speaker and fake listening.
15. Be aware of poor responses and questions and how they may impair your listening.

But effective listening is more than correcting bad habits as shown in the following description of an ideal listener:

The ideal listener primarily keeps an open, curious mind. He listens for new ideas everywhere, integrating what he hears with what he already knows. He's also self-perceptive and thus listens to others with his total being or self. Thus, he becomes personally involved with what he hears. Being this aware, he is not willing to blindly follow the listening crowd. He maintains conscious perspectives in what is going on instead. He looks for ideas, organization and arguments but always listens to the essence of things. Knowing that no two people listen the same, he stays mentally alert by outlining, objecting, approving, adding illustrations of his own. He is introspective but he has the capacity and desire to critically examine, understand, and attempt to transform some of his values, attitudes, and relationships within himself and with others. He focuses his mind on the listening and listens to the speaker's ideas, but he also listens with feeling and intuition.

(Pflaumer, in Duker, 1971, pp. 46–47)

Improved listening is basically a product of the proper frame of mind. It requires a willingness and desire to listen. You must convince yourself that you enjoy listening to what other people have to say. Work to achieve a level of rapport that promotes mutual respect and allows each participant to listen and appreciate the other's beliefs and uniqueness.

Look for Verbal and Nonverbal Signals

A number of verbal and nonverbal signals also identify a skillful listener and suggest guidelines for listening improvement. To improve your listening, you must monitor all three of the information channels: verbal, other vocal, and nonverbal. Be alert to not only how these channels are used by the other participant, but also the way you are attending to them as a listener. Smiling and nodding are ways of indicating you are listening. Good listeners normally maintain a relaxed posture. They lean toward the speaker to indicate that they have an interest in what is going on. Be aware not only of the words that are spoken but also the pauses that occur during the message. Pauses and silences can be very useful if interpreted correctly. Inflection, angle of the head, eye direction, body posture, facial expression, and gestures are all ways in which interviewees and

Good eye contact is a sign of a good listener.

interviewers communicate information. As a listener, you must use your eyes as well as your ears. Sensitivity to nonverbal and vocal channels can help you understand what is meant even though it may be said very poorly.

In the verbal area, you must train yourself to look not only for the words and ideas presented, but also the association between those ideas. Shifts in topic and emphasis, opening and closing statements, and themes that recur throughout a message should be noticed. Inconsistencies and gaps may indicate a number of things about a speaker and the information communicated. That is, note what is *not* said as well as what is said. This was earlier referred to as listening with the "inner" or "third ear."

You Are More Than a Recording Machine

Productive listeners are able to note everything and filter out the irrelevant. They use the thought/speech speed differential in a productive, rather than a disruptive, manner. You should continually weigh the information presented, reviewing what has come before, and searching for meaning between the lines. Perhaps this focus is best illustrated by Benjamin (1974) when asked by novice counseling interviewers what they should seek to understand from an interviewee.

1. *How the interviewee thinks and feels about himself; how he perceives himself.*
2. *What he thinks and feels about others in his world, especially significant others; what he thinks and feels about people in general.*
3. *How he perceives others relating to him; how in his eyes others think and feel about him, especially significant others in his life.*
4. *How he perceives the material that he, the interviewer, or both wish to discuss; what he thinks and how he feels about what is involved.*
5. *What his aspirations, ambitions, and goals are.*
6. *What defense mechanisms he employs.*
7. *What coping mechanisms he uses or may use or may be able to use.*
8. *What values he holds; what his philosophy of life is.*

(Benjamin, 1974, p. 46)

These may be somewhat idealistic goals for the beginning interviewer, but you should strive for them. A skillful interviewer will not only get the objective information presented, but all of the subjective information suggested by Benjamin. The skillful listener is an active participant in the interviewing process, as active as the speaker.

SUMMARY

In this chapter you found a definition of listening, its value, fifteen barriers to listening, and ways to improve your listening ability. Listening is more than hearing. It means focusing, perceiving, and assimilating. Listening includes monitoring the verbal, other vocal, and nonverbal channels of information. The value of listening is not only in its objective information-obtaining potential; it also has motivational potential. Good listening produces higher quality information and motivates speakers to ask or answer questions openly and honestly. It is up to you to improve your own listening abilities. This can be done by under-standing the obstacles to listening, formal training, and conscious effort.

ACTIVITIES

Activity #1

Directions: This activity is a role play. Two roles are described below: one for the Chief Purchasing Agent and a second for the General Manager. Do *not* read either of these roles until you decide who will play which role. If you are reading this book on your own, you will have to find someone to help you. If you are a part of a larger interviewing study group, the roles can be assigned by your instructor. Once you know which role you will play (it makes no dif-ference), read only that role before beginning to interact. The purchasing agent is a persuasion interviewer and the general manager is the interviewee. The interview takes place in the general manager's office. Once you have studied your role and feel you understand it completely, you may begin. Be sure to set the role aside once you begin. If you need to make notes on anything, do it on a separate sheet of paper. Do not look at the role while doing the activity. Be sure to play your role as strongly as it is written. Once you have finished the activity, discuss the nature and quality of the listening that took place. This exercise is adapted from "Not Listening" in *A Handbook of Structured Experiences for Human Relations Training,* by J. William Pfieffer and John E. Jones (Volume III, Univer-sity Associates Press, 1971, pp. 12–15).

    CHIEF PURCHASING AGENT: You have just been hired as the Chief Pur-chasing Agent of a large, multi-faceted corporation. You have a Ph.D. in economics from Harvard, have headed a presidential advisory board, and published two books in the field. You are actually vice-president in charge of purchasing. You see that the one best way to bring order out of chaos is to centralize the purchasing operations, but this must be done quickly! You have decided that any purchase over $10,000 must be approved by the head office. You realize that the independent purchasing power of each plant has been jealously guarded. Also, you are aware that the peak buying season starts in three weeks. You have decided that the only way to get this policy instituted in time is to visit each plant and inform the general manager that this new policy *will be* followed. You know that you are going to meet some stiff opposition; however, *you are* the expert, and you *do have* the power. Therefore, you have decided that the best approach is to make sure that the general manager is fully aware of your plan, that he/she understands why it is necessary, and that you will not let him/her sidetrack you with minor objections. You are the only one who knows the total picture. (Do *not* read any further.)

    GENERAL MANAGER: You are the General Manager of the second largest plant in the corporation. You have been employed at this plant for 27 years, starting out as an office clerk and working your way up through sales, purchas-ing, and production until you took over the top position three years ago. No one knows more about the inner workings of this plant than you. Last year the home office even gave a testimonial dinner for you to show its appreciation of the fine job you have done and are doing. You have just received a memo from the home office that a new chief purchasing agent has been hired, and the word is that he may try to centralize the purchasing operation. You know that, while this might look good on paper, in reality, the strength of the corporation's position has always been in the fact that it is flexible and can initiate change quickly. The key to this flexibility has been that the corporation always stressed management development and then let the plants make their own decisions. You are aware that if this new policy takes effect, not only will it reduce the plant's flexibility, but it could signal the beginning of a power shift away from plant managers. You are determined that the chief purchasing agent will not enforce his/her policy if you can help it. Sure, he/she probably means well, but he/she just doesn't understand the situation at your plant. After all, you have 27 years experience and are more competent to make any decisions affecting this plant than anyone else. Because of the time factor, you will have to make your points *quickly* and *decisively* when he/she comes to see you today. He/she has got to know who is boss at this location, since your prestige with your subordinate managers also rests on the outcome of this interview.

Activity #2

In the preceding activity you should have learned how and why people often don't listen to one another. This activity is designed to help you learn to listen better. It requires three people, two interview participants and one referee. One of the participants will act as a *nondirective* interviewer and the other will be the interviewee. The interviewer may choose any contemporary issue. The following are some examples that have been used in the past:

Coeducational dormitories	Premarital sex
Interracial marriages	Military draft
Stiffer grading policy	Vietnam veterans
Child pornography	Gun control
Drug usage	Sexual assault

The only catch in this activity is that before each participant speaks, he or she must first summarize, in his or her own words and without notes, what the previous speaker has said. If the summary is judged incorrect by either the listener or the referee, they may interrupt and clear up the misunderstanding. After approximately ten minutes, each of the participants will change roles and the new interviewer can pick a new topic. Once everyone has played every role, discuss the following questions:

1. What gave you difficulty in listening during this exercise? Why?
2. Which of the following barriers caused you the most problems: physical limitations, setting limitations, primary or secondary tension, source focusing, fact focusing, emotional blindspots, mind wandering, planning ahead, conclusion jumping, mental arguing, overtalking, fatigue or

boredom, uncritical acceptance, faking attention, or poor response or question?
3. How did the paraphrasing help your listening?
4. Was the paraphrase normally longer or shorter than the original statement? Why?
5. When did you find you were not getting across what you wanted to say?
6. Was there a difference between hearing and listening?
7. Did you use information coming from verbal, vocal, and nonverbal channels?
8. Did you listen for objective and subjective information?
9. When did you have to be an active listener?
10. How did interviewer listening benefit the interviewee?
11. How did interviewer listening benefit the interviewer?
12. Were you more than a recording machine?

Activity #3

Spend one entire day listening as carefully as you can to everything that goes on around you. Remember, this means using both your ears and your eyes. This may sound like a silly activity, but it isn't. It's easy to tell people that they don't listen as well as they should, but they really don't understand what you mean until they actively concentrate on listening. As you go through this day, constantly tell yourself, "I am going to listen as closely as I can to everything—the noises on the street, people talking two chairs away, the color of rooms, the movements of co-workers, and especially people talking to me. I will block out everything from my mind except listening. I will even listen to myself talking and be aware of my own behaviors." If you really make a conscious attempt to do this exercise right and be an active listener, you will be surprised just how much you learn about yourself and your listening ability. To make the activity even more interesting, see if you can find examples of where each of the barriers to listening discussed in this chapter caused you to be a less than perfect listener. List those examples.

Answers to the Fact/Inference Exercise.
1 = ?, 2 = ?, 3 = T, 4 = ?, 5 = ?, 6 = ?, 7 = ?, 8 = T, 9 =?, 10 = F, 11 = ?, 12 = ?, 13 = ?, 14 = ?, and 15 = ?

Answers to the Listening Barriers Exercise.
1 = Mind Wandering, 2 = Source Focusing, 3 = Physical Limitations, 4 = Setting Limitations, 5 = Overtalking, 6 = Planning Ahead, 7 = Poor Response, 8 = Uncritical Acceptance, 9 = Primary Tension, 10 = Fact Focusing, 11 = Emotional Blindspots, 12 = Conclusion Jumping, 13 = Mental Arguing, 14 = Boredom, 15 = Faking Attention, 16 = Overtalking, 17 = Mental Arguing, 18 = Poor Question, 19 = Faking Attention, 20 = Mind Wandering, 21 = Emotional Blindspots, 22 = Setting Limitations, 23 = Physical Limitations, 24 = Fact Focusing, 25 = Secondary Tension, 26 = Conclusion Jumping, 27 = Planning Ahead, 28 = Uncritical Acceptance, 29 = Source Focusing, 30 = Fatigue.

Chapter 7

Skill 7
Recording the Interview

In recording an interview, use the tool—tape recorder or pencil—that works best for you. But know how to use both. You never know when it will be wise—or necessary—to employ the tool you don't habitually rely on. (Sherwood 1969, p. 62)

To some of you, the process of taking notes may seem simple and unworthy of an entire chapter. You say to yourself, "I learned how to take notes when I began school, and I've been taking them ever since." But notetaking in a classroom or at a business meeting is very different from recording an interview. In a classroom, you are one of many people taking notes and your notetaking rarely disrupts the instructor's flow of communication. In an interview, however, you are face-to-face, one-on-one, with an interviewee, and the quality and quantity of your notetaking can decidedly affect the information flow. You must, therefore, break some of the old notetaking habits that you learned in school in order to be a good interview recorder.

Interviewers take notes to establish a permanent record of the interaction. Interview records also help you determine the success of interviews once they're over, and help you chart your growth as an interviewer. It allows you to see what you did and did not do, how you behave in different interviews, and your success with different interviewees under different circumstances. Notes taken early in an interview can be used later for probing, confronting, summarizing, and concluding. Interview recording is important, then, both during and after the interview.

The three main interview recording techniques are memorization, notetaking, and electronic recording. You should choose a recording technique that works best for you and best fits the type of interview you are conducting. You should, however, have all three recording techniques as part of your interviewing repertoire. In many interviews it is useful to combine two or more interview recording methods. Your criteria for choosing a particular method for an interview should be which one gives you the most accurate, relevant, appropriate, objective, uniform, and complete record.

MEMORIZING

Most skillful interviewers have a highly developed capacity to remember information. A good memory is not only useful as a recording method, but it is also helpful for recalling such things as an interviewee's name, hobbies, family member's names, and all sorts of information which can be used to create a pleasant climate during the opening.

Memorization can be especially useful when a pencil and paper or tape recorder are inappropriate. Truman Capote, author of the book, *In Cold Blood,* for example, found it almost impossible to interview criminals and persons closely involved with murders while taking notes or using a tape recorder. According to Capote, "If you write down or tape what people say, it makes them feel inhibited and self-conscious. It makes them say what they think you *expect* them to say." Capote, therefore, trained himself to memorize information and record it later after an interview was over. When asked how he managed to train himself to memorize so much information, Capote responded:

It wasn't as hard as it might sound. What I'd do was have a friend talk or read for a set length of time, tape what he was saying, and meanwhile listen to him as intently as I could. Then I'd go write down what he had said as I remembered it, and later compare what I had with the tape . . . . Finally, when I got to be about 97 percent accurate, I felt ready to take on this book.

(Brady, 1977, p. 123)

There are many books devoted to helping you improve your memory. Several are listed in the bibliography. Anyone can improve their memory if they work at it. It takes a conscious effort to remember information over short and long periods of time. If you start with little bits of information, you will be surprised how soon you can remember an entire interview—if you do not wait too long to record it. The secret to taking good memorized notes is to write down the information as soon as possible. Some interviewers even make the excuse of going to the restroom in the middle of an interview when they find that there's so much information being presented that they don't think they can remember it all until the end of the interview. They write down what they have memorized while in the restroom and begin memorizing again once the interview reconvenes.

MEMORY EXERCISE

Directions: Read each of the following lists or statements to yourself aloud one at a time. After carefully reading each list aloud, cover it up and try to reproduce each item exactly. They need not be in sequence. At the end of the exercise, count the number of items or words you missed and record your score. If you missed less than ten, including spelling and punctuation, you have a pretty good memory.

1. 4, 9, 8, 2, 5

2. 16, 10, 38, 92, 157, 87, 45
3. Hat, Shoes, Gloves, Pants, Jacket, Socks, Shirt, Tie, Shirt
4. orh, rumt, hagt, juf, magh, wagdt
5. "Language," wrote George Santayana, "is the door to knowledge."
6. The woman explained sadly that her marriage was breaking up because her husband, "Drank like a fish out of water" and would soon end up in the "expensive care unit."

Advantages of Memorization

The biggest advantage of memorizing as an interview recording tool is that it can be used on occasions when you cannot easily take notes or electronically record interview information. A journalist trying to interview someone "on the run" cannot easily whip out a note pad and pencil while walking or continually hold a microphone in front of the face of an interviewee. The same problem occurs when a respondent is in a crowd. A luncheon or dinner interview also presents problems, as does an interview in a dimly lighted environment.

A second advantage of memorization comes when you are dealing with tense, inhibited, or self-conscious interviewees. Such people are normally very reticent in the first place, and the sight of a pencil and pad or tape recorder can make them clam up completely. If you can memorize information, such respondents will feel they are simply having a conversation with you.

The third advantage of memorization is that it helps prevent the *interviewer effect*. The interviewer effect is similar to what researchers call the "experimenter effect." It has been found that subjects tend to behave and respond in ways they think an experimenter wants them to. The same is true in interviews where a pencil and paper or electronic recorder is visible. When respondents know they are being recorded or quoted, many will say what they think is appropriate and not necessarily what is accurate.

A final advantage of using memorization is that it can be a supplementary tool to both a tape recorder and notetaking. Obviously, with a pencil and paper every word cannot be noted. Interviewers who have a good memory can expand upon brief notes after the interview is over and, therefore, obtain a more accurate record.

Disadvantages of Memorization

The disadvantages of using memorization are 1) it takes a great deal of time that could be better spent in other ways; 2) it distracts from good listening; 3) it is easy to forget important facts; 4) you cannot get direct quotes; and 5) it is sometimes not possible to record memorized notes immediately. These are very formidable disadvantages. It is for these reasons, and probably some others, that most interviewers do not use memorization as the main form of interview recording. Let's, however, look at these disadvantages in greater detail.

The *time* disadvantage occurs not only in the interview itself, but also in the time it takes to train yourself to be a good memorizer. To achieve the kind of accuracy described by Truman Capote, it would probably take you at least a month or two of continuous practice. Most interviewers do not have this kind of time to devote to the practice of memorization. Within the interview, memorization does not take much time at all. The added time comes in making a written record of memorized notes at the end of the interview. A memorizer must sit and try to remember specific information that was said, and it usually takes time to dredge these up from memory. Sometimes it takes as long as the interview took in the first place. Again, most professionals do not have this kind of time, especially if they are doing a great many interviews. For both of these reasons, this technique is not recommended for beginners.

A serious drawback of memorization during an interview is that it is *distracting*. You are constantly thinking about what has happened, instead of what is happening or what is going to happen. Beginners normally have enough trouble trying to sort out relevant from irrelevant information, plan probes, and maintain the interview climate. If their mind is also busy trying to remember facts during the interview, they cannot do either very well.

A less than perfect memorizer is also likely to *forget* important facts or opinions. This is probably the main reason most advanced interviewers do not use only the memorization technique. In some interviews it could be disastrous to forget small bits of information. Even the shortest of written notes help jog your memory. Individuals who do make extensive use of the memorization technique usually also take short notes regarding spellings, figures, names, and addresses. Even Truman Capote only claimed a 97 percent accuracy rate; that means he forgot 3 percent of what was said. There is no way to know how important that 3 percent might have been later on.

In many interviews it is important to have direct *quotes*, that is, to have information from respondents in their own words. Information interviewers, for example, often use direct quotes as part of the stories or articles they prepare based on interviews. It is almost impossible to remember direct quotes—they demand the use of some immediate recording technique.

The last disadvantage to memorization is that other matters can come up which prevent the *immediate recording* of memorized notes. Telephone calls, interruptions by a secretary, or unexpected messages are all common occurrences in an interviewer's life. Memorized notes usually need to be recorded within an hour after an interview takes place, and interruptions can make this almost impossible. Interruptions also tend to shake loose memorized material. This is especially true if the interruption is important enough to divert your mind from the information memorized.

The first technique for recording interview information, memorization, has both advantages and disadvantages which should be taken into account before considering it as the prime mode of recording the interview. Memorization is extremely useful as a secondary or additional means of recording interview content. For this reason alone, you should attempt to develop your memory.

NOTETAKING

Taking notes with a pencil and paper is probably the most widely used means of recording interview information. In most cases, notetaking is used in conjunction with memorization. Taking good notes is a skill that demands a great deal of effort and concentration. There is much more to notetaking than simply writing down responses. Notetaking serves many purposes within an interview. In this section some of those purposes will be described, as well as how to improve your interview notetaking ability.

The presence of a pencil and paper can make some people extremely tense and reduce the quantity and quality of information obtained. On the other hand, for some other people, the presence of a note pad and pencil can be quite flattering. These people feel important and are more willing to give you accurate information if they see that you are recording the information. Notetaking, therefore, can help or hurt information gathering and rapport development. It can also affect the formality level of an interview. In most cases, notes increase the level of formality. Respondents tend to be more careful and precise when they see a note pad.

Notetaking can help you control information flow. Writing down a comment indicates to respondents that you want the interview to continue in the same direction, whereas lifting your pencil off the paper or putting in down on a table informs them that a response is not going in the proper direction or that the topic is completed. In this same manner, you can indicate to interviewees what is "on the record" and what is "off the record."

The phrase, "off the record," comes from journalistic interviews. When respondents are being interviewed for a possible newspaper or magazine article, there are times when they don't want to be quoted or cited. They then ask that the information be given off the record (i.e., not for publication). In press clubs throughout the country, some type of symbol is commonly used by speakers to indicate when information is off the record. In the San Francisco Press Club, for example, this symbol is a ceramic cat. When the cat is facing the audience, the information can be quoted, and when the cat is turned backward, the information is not for publication.

Notetaking can also be used as a means of preventing interviewer interruption. You are more likely to interrupt when using a tape recorder where less concentration is needed to record the interview. Notetaking helps in probing and summarizing. By looking at what has been recorded, you can often see what is missing and what needs to be probed further. Good notes help you discover inconsistencies and inaccuracies. If you find you have one answer in one part of your notes and a different answer in another part, you realize that another question is needed for clarification.

Finally, in the follow-up phase of an interview, notes are also useful. Notes help remind you of promises that you made to interviewees and promises that interviewees have made to you. Notes can remind you of the next interview time or any formal correspondence that needs to be sent after the interview. All of these notetaking functions will be discussed in detail later. Obviously, this is not an exhaustive list of the functions that notetaking performs aside from the simple recording function, but it does give you some indication of how important it can be to the progress of an interview as well as its success.

Notetaking Techniques

The first and often the most difficult part of taking notes is trying to get them accepted by respondents. There is some disagreement among interviewers as to whether or not permission should be requested. Some suggest that you should not apologize for or ask permission to take notes. They believe that notetaking is an implied part of interviewing and that anyone who agrees to be interviewed naturally also agrees to have notes taken on their responses. Other interviewers feel that you should seek approval before beginning to take notes and recommend several ways of doing it effectively. Some suggest that the best way to approach notetaking is to make reference to your "bad memory." Others advise you to simply tell respondents that you are taking notes in order to get "complete and accurate information." In either case, you should be positive in asking to take notes. Once permission is given either explicitly or implicitly, you take out your paper and pencil and begin to record the interview. If permission is not given, you memorize.

Many interviewers also encourage interviewees to take notes and even offer pencil and paper. This is especially important in performance, discipline, selection, or any type of interviewing where the interviewee will be required to do or remember something after the interaction is completed. Interviewee notetaking can help establish the acceptability of interviewer notetaking. There are two important aspects of notetaking that should be learned by a beginning interviewer. The first of these is how to behave while taking notes and the second relates to ways to take notes. Both are important for interview success. In the following paragraphs, each will be discussed separately even though they are closely related.

Notetaking Behavior

The first decision a notetaker needs to make is where to position the notepad. It should be as unobtrusive as possible; yet you should not try to hide the fact that notes are being taken. There is a matter of ethics regarding the concealment of notes. Although this ethical code is not always followed by all interviewers, most professionals feel that the risk of being caught and losing their credibility is not worth the potential gain. They suggest that you cross your legs, put the notepad on your knee, and have a pencil in hand from the very beginning. This way the pad and pencil are below eye level, but the interviewee is aware that notes are being taken.

Skillful interviewers learn to take notes without looking at the notepad or by looking at it only briefly. If you write notes fairly constantly, the fact that they are being taken is soon forgotten. When you stop writing, you can sometimes confuse respondents and make them feel their answer is not proper. The main point is to not divert your eyes from interviewees for more than a few seconds. Try to take your notes by looking down only during pauses. Don't worry if there is a slight lull in conversation. These pauses during notetaking can be an effective means of encouraging interviewees to continue a statement.

Be sure to observe reactions to your notetaking. If you see that an interviewee is not upset or tense because you are recording information, then continue what you are doing. If a respondent does become upset and your notetaking seems to be disrupting the flow of interaction, you need to alter your notetaking technique until you find one that is comfortable for the interviewee and yourself. After doing several interviews, you will settle on a technique which seems to work fairly well for you.

Remember, your behavior during notetaking can be a signal to interviewees. If these signals are done on purpose, they can be quite useful, but if done unintentionally, they can reduce interview efficiency. A poised pencil, for example, can mean "Tell me more." Dropping your pencil or drumming the eraser can tell interviewees that they are "off the track." Putting away a pencil and pad suggests that the interview is over. Your pencil and paper are another nonverbal control device.

Forms of Notetaking

Most interviewers use one or more of the following four forms of notetaking: verbatim notes, central idea notes, checking predetermined categories, or probe notes. You should be able to use all of these techniques or any combination. Obviously, verbatim notes do not mean recording the entire interview word for word. This is impossible unless you know shorthand or use a stenographic machine such as one found in a courtroom. If you are going to do this, you might as well use a tape recorder.

Verbatim notes do not refer to recording the entire interview, word for word. The term means recording important ideas with the words used by the interviewee. Quotation marks are usually used to indicate a verbatim quote. When taking verbatim notes, do not paraphrase or summarize a respondent's ideas. Don't put words into an interviewee's mouth. When extensive verbatim notes are needed, it is common to have a second person present to record notes while the interviewer asks questions and talks with the interviewee. It takes a great deal more of an interviewer's attention to take verbatim notes than any of the other three types, so they can be very distracting for interviewees and interviewers. The following are examples of verbatim notes:

Mother "always complaining"

Claims to be "practical," "down-to-earth," "nuts-and-bolts man."

"I'm satisfied we do have a foreign policy."—Ronald Reagan

"Only an ostrich could have missed the contradictions in Reagonomics."—Walter Heller, economist.

"For myself, it (abortion) is simply offensive, but I'm over the hill. I'm not going to be pregnant again. It is easy for me to say now."—Sandra Day O'Connor in her confirmation hearing interview.

"First the Shah, now Sadat—it is fatal to be America's friend."—A Saudi diplomat.

"Hitler and Nazism only have a bad name because they lost."—Col. Muammar Gaddafi, Libya.

Sometimes verbatim notes can catch humorous or colorful information.

"They were delicious."—Chinese Vice-Premier Deng Xiaoping when asked how he liked the rare musk oxen presented to his country by President Nixon.

"We're looking into all kinds of schemes, starting with banana peels in the parking lot."—State Department official when asked about improving U.S. embassy security.

"But the game was much closer than the score indicated."—A coach after a scoreless tie.

Perhaps the most common form of interview notetaking is the *central idea* format. With this technique, you listen for the main idea of an entire response and then jot down a word or two which represents that central idea. After the interview, you can expand your central idea notes. You must be careful not to make notes on digressions, examples, and details. Look for main or key ideas contained in the message. Central idea notes are only designed to be memory joggers for later elaboration, so you must be choosy in what you note. Beginning interviewers using this technique normally end up with too many notes. As you become more proficient, you will find that you can get along with fewer and fewer central idea notes and depend more on your memory to translate those notes into full statements after the interview is completed.

Interviewers using both verbatim and central idea notes normally learn to abbreviate. Here's a list of abbreviations that are commonly used in notetaking. They should become familiar to you.

@	at	lk	like
#	number	°	degree
/	per	%	percent
→	increase—continue	$	dollar
		¢	cent
←	decrease—discontinue	Yr.	year
W/	with	oz.	ounce
W/O	without	>	larger than
W/i	within	<	smaller than
app.	approximate	Ch.	chapter

M/PH	miles per hour	Ex.	example
'	feet	Lr.	learn
"	inches	Q	question
∴	therefore	Vz	versus-opposed
&	and	ref.	reference
Dept.	department	diff.	difference
Intro.	introduction	B/4	before
Max.	maximum	B/c	because
Gvt.	government	ie	that is
Wrt.	write	etc	and so on
rt.	right	pg.	page
- -	there is	Lk.	like
2	to–two–too	wd.	word

(Yates, 1979, pp. 48–49)

The following are some notes made by Merriman Smith after a press conference with Franklin D. Roosevelt. Can you figure them out?

tnk be gud tng sy smtg re ILO NA 20 Apl—34 cntrs—vry impt mtg bcs undbtly whn we cme to devise UNs org, ILO will be ind but afltd cum new org of UNs.

(Brady, 1977, p. 130)

Almost every good interviewer has a unique form of shorthand which is often puzzling for others. You will develop your own as well. This is the translation of the notes above.

I think it would be a good thing to say something today about the meeting of the International Labor Organization in Philadelphia on the twentieth of April. Thirty-four countries will be represented. It will be a very important meeting because when we come to devise the United Nations Organization, the I.L.O. will be independent, but affiliated with the new organization of the United Nations.

(Brady, 1977, p. 131)

In using central idea notes, be aware of and note subjective aspects of the interview, as well as objective information. Your notes will contain observations and hypotheses along with facts. Terms such as "friendly," "aggressive," or "expresses ideas freely" are all examples of noting subjective information. You must be careful, however, in the kinds of notes you take regarding subjective information. This is especially true if a respondent has access to your notes.

Interviewees sometimes ask that you share your notes with them, and this can be very embarrassing if you have negative comments. Some interviewers develop a code which allows them to note subjective information in a way which would not be understandable to the interviewee. Switching from script to printing, for example, can be used to note questionable information.

Be careful, too, about *when* you write negative comments on the interview guide. If interviewees see you writing only after they present negative information, they may become defensive and limited in their responses, or they may begin to give you more and more negative information because they think that is what you want to record. The best way to record negative information is to wait until something positive has been said and then note both positive and negative comments at the same time. This takes some practice and requires memorization. And finally, do not take down only those ideas which agree with your own. It is very easy for inexperienced interviewers to note central ideas which *they* think are "correct." This can lead to a distorted and invalid analysis of the interview. In the previous chapter you did an exercise on locating central ideas. Go back and see if you can write central idea notes from the responses given in that exercise.

Some interviews involve the checking of *predetermined answer categories.* Predetermined categories are very convenient and reduce the amount of time devoted to notetaking. In many cases, however, a single category may not be a full representation of the answer. If it is not, then space for notes should be included. Predetermined category systems are commonly used by research and diagnostic interviewers because they prefer closed rather than open questions. When an interview involves only closed questions, the predetermined category system is very efficient. If, however, the interview also contains a series of open questions, more space is needed, and the verbatim or central idea approaches are more effective. Earlier, you were introduced to various types of closed questions employing ordered, unordered, and partial predetermined answer categories.

Verbatim notes, central idea notes, and predetermined categories are all useful for storing information and analyzing it after an interview has terminated. *Probe notes,* on the other hand, are designed to be used during an interview. In answer to a question, for example, you may see some subtle change in the interviewee or some remark which you want to probe later. At this point, you would take a probe note—mark it in some way, such as circling it, for later reference. This separates it from your other notes for quick reference. Probe notes are often written in respondent's words. Before each topic is completed, you go back and look for your probe notes. Probe notes allow you to remain silent while an interviewee is talking and yet not lose sight of important points which need to be covered in detail. This prevents you from continually interrupting to probe in the middle of a response. Probe notes are used in combination with the other notational forms.

Keep Notes Brief

Skillful interviewers take no more notes than are absolutely necessary. Important information such as names, addresses, dates, ages, spellings, and place of previous employment or residence should be noted and checked when they are first mentioned. Many beginning interviewers feel compelled to fill in all of the note space on an interview guide during the interview. Experienced interviewers leave much space empty on the guide and fill it in after the interview has been conducted and the respondent has left.

A couple of other useful notetaking techniques are also worth mentioning. Make some kind of mark in the border of the interview guide to indicate especially important responses. These are used for summarizing, concluding, and focusing during the analysis phase. Some interviewers like to use a separate page for each new topic covered. They find single pages easier to edit, especially when they are combining the results of one interview with the results of several others. Regardless of the form you use in notetaking or the techniques you employ or develop on your own, be sure to always aim for accuracy, objectivity, uniformity, and completeness in the notes you do take.

NOTETAKING EXERCISE

Directions: For *each* of the following interviewee statements, *write* one central idea, verbatim, and probe note which you think would be the most important to record on your interview guide. Each statement also includes a predetermined category note. Identify the category that best represents the statement made. Recommended answers are found at the end of this chapter.

1. (In response to the question, "How do you feel about the XYZ bleachery dumping waste in Silver stream?") "Well, I hear that the bleachery is one of the worst polluters in the area. No one can fish any more within the mile or so below the plant."

    Predetermined Category Note:
    Strongly Oppose
    Mildly Oppose
    Neither Oppose nor Favor
    Mildly Favor
    Strongly Favor

2. As part of the annual performance evaluation, each supervisor has been asked to inquire about the new office-position (salary) evaluation plan installed a few months ago. You are interviewing Roberta (a billing clerk), and when you bring up this question she responds with the following: "I'm almost always backlogged with work. It is also getting increasingly complicated. And I've been watching Sharon's work (a key-punch operator). She has plenty of time to spend in the lounge. And the stuff she does is all routine. If she's worth $5 more a week, so am I."

    Predetermined Category Note:
    Very Satisfied
    Quite Satisfied
    Somewhat Satisfied
    Slightly Satisfied
    Neither Satisfied nor Dissatisfied

Slightly Dissatisfied
Somewhat Dissatisfied
Quite Dissatisfied
Very Dissatisfied

3. Q. "Why have you resigned your position in this company?"
   A. "I have decided to enter business with my father-in-law."
   Q. "Were you satisfied with your position here?"
   A. "I have no complaints about my supervision, working conditions, or salary. I do believe I had a lot more to offer than the company recognized."
   Q. "Didn't you attend the management training program?"
   A. "Oh, yes. That was the biggest waste of time I have ever seen. And when I got back I was still given some very poor assignments, and I was never even considered for promotion. This company sure didn't turn out to be what the college recruiter promised it would be. Well, that's about all I have to say."

   Predetermined Category Note:
   Other Job
   Illness
   Return to School
   Pregnancy
   Relocation of Family
   Retirement
   Other—Specify

4. As a school counselor, you have just asked one of your advisees why she is having trouble with grades. "There's just too much competition. I feel the other students are better than I am. I've thought about changing my program, but I don't know what I want to go to. I don't like making decisions anyway. I've been cutting my physics class. It's the worst anyway. My parents keep putting pressure on me to get good grades. My physics class is really the worst. I get nervous whenever I go to class. I sit by myself. I don't talk or volunteer answers. I have trouble concentrating, and I keep thinking how much I wish I were someplace else. I guess I just don't do as well in physics."

   Predetermined Category Note:
   1. Needs more effort on assignments
   2. Has too many demands on time
   3. Does poorly on exams and tests
   4. Apparently wastes study time
   5. Fails to hand in assignments
   6. Is absent too often
   7. Submits illegible and disorganized work
   8. Excessive tardiness
   9. Is a disturbing influence in class
   10. Is inconsiderate in class
   11. Is inattentive in class
   12. Aims just to get by

13. Gives up too easily
14. Experiences difficulty in expressing ideas
15. Needs to go in for additional help
16. Other—Specify

Advantages of Notetaking

A first advantage of notetaking is that it can prevent you from continually interrupting interviewers. Notetaking interviewers must put some of their concentration into writing their notes and, therefore, do not have much mental time to be arguing, interrupting, and overtalking. A second advantage of notes is that taking them makes interviewees feel important. If respondents feel important and that their information is valuable, they are more likely to provide open and honest responses. Third, pencils and paper are cheaper than electronic recording devices and tapes. This may seem to be a trivial matter with regard to audio tape recorders, but it is certainly an important one when compared to video recording costs.

Also in comparison to electronic recording, notetaking generally takes less time in the analysis stage. When an interview has been tape recorded, you normally need to sit and listen to the entire interview again, and take notes. Some interviewers have the tape transcribed and then read the information, circling those points they want to be sure to remember. It is normally faster to edit notes as you listen to a respondent. Also, you need not complete your notes as quickly as a person who tries to memorize the information. A further advantage of notetaking is that it is universally accepted by almost all interviewees, whereas a tape recorder meets more resistance.

When notetaking you can record probe notes and jot down visual messages, personal feelings, and hypotheses. This is not possible with electronic recording. Many interviewers who use electronic recording devices also take notes to retain

Notetaking can be a distraction.

these advantages. Otherwise, this visual information—gestures, facial expressions, and other nonverbal cues—may be lost. The most obvious advantage of notetaking over memorization is the greater detail and accuracy that can be gained. This added detail and accuracy explains why few interviewers attempt to use memorization alone. Since notetaking is so well accepted, there is seldom any need to lose accuracy and detail through memorization.

Disadvantages of Notetaking

An often-cited disadvantage of notetaking is the tension it can create, tension which may inhibit high quality responses. Even though the initial tension that is sometimes part of a tape recorded interview may be great, the presence of a tape recorder is more easily forgotten. Notetaking, if poorly done, is continually distracting. Good interviewers can take extensive notes without ever influencing the climate or biasing a respondent. If you keep the notepad out of sight, maintain good eye contact, and keep your writing unobtrusive, then few tension problems occur. The anxiety is usually only in the mind of the interviewer.

A more serious disadvantage of notetaking is its potential to break the flow of conversation and lead interviewees to biased responses. Respondents automatically hesitate when you are taking notes. They think—often correctly—that you are not listening when you are writing. If you are not skillful enough to take notes and still maintain interview flow, you should choose some other form of recording.

By watching what the interviewer writes down, interviewees may be led to discuss more of that particular kind of material. To prevent this problem, do not always record material the minute it is presented, but wait until other information or a pause allows a better chance for recording. In this way you do not unintentionally bias or lead interviewees.

Interviewers cannot possibly record every response with pencil and paper. Some interviewees speak much too rapidly for efficient notetaking. When an interviewee is excited and speaking quickly, a great deal of important information is often presented. This is when you have the least amount of time for taking notes. You may find your best notes are on the least significant part of the interview—when the interviewee was speaking slowly. You must be sure all important information is noted, even if you need to ask interviewees to repeat an answer.

It is hard to pay attention and take notes at the same time. By its very nature, notetaking reduces your comprehension, concentration, and listening ability. In some interview situations, like a counseling interview, where listening and attention is especially important, you should probably use an electronic recording device.

A final disadvantage of notetaking is that notes must be expanded soon after an interview is completed. Although you can generally wait longer to complete written notes than memorized notes, it is still less than the time necessary for tape recorder analysis and note expansion. These then are the major disadvantages of notetaking. In spite of them, however, most interviewers would agree that the advantages of notetaking far outweigh its disadvantages.

ELECTRONIC INTERVIEW RECORDING

Electronic recording involves the use of an audio or video tape recorder to note what is being said. Audio tape machines are of three types: reel-to-reel, cassette, and microcassette. Some audio recorders require an outside microphone, while others have a built-in microphone. Audio tape machines have become smaller and less expensive, some now selling for as little as $20–$25. Cost should no longer be a reason to neglect the possible use of audio tape in interview recording. Cassette and microcassette tape recorders seem to be best for interviews because they are small and not too distracting. Cassette and microcassette tapes are available which will tape 120 minutes' worth of interview (60 minutes per side). No serious interviewer should be without an audio tape recorder.

Video tape recorders, on the other hand, are quite expensive. It is hard to find a good one for less than $1,000. The advantages of a video tape recorder, however, are so great that many interviewers are beginning to use them in spite of the cost. There are a number of obvious advantages to recording the full range of participant behavior. Video tape recording machines are available that will record up to six hours of interview. Many organizations that do a lot of interviewing are investing in videotape equipment.

Equipment Purchase and Preparation

Whether you choose audio or video equipment, be sure to buy an electronic recording device with a counter. A counter allows you to take notes in conjunction with the recording. You do this by writing down the number on the counter corresponding to the point in the interview which relates to a note. You should set the counter at zero when beginning each interview.

You should check the equipment prior to the interview. For video recording, this means checking the recorder, the cameras, and the microphones. For an audio tape recorder, only the microphone and the machine need to be checked. Checking means being sure you know how it works, having enough of the right kind of recording tape, testing the tape before the interview (giving name, title, and affiliation of the interviewee at the beginning of the tape), checking the power source to be sure you have batteries or a wall plug, and marking the tape in order to avoid later confusion.

Using Electronic Equipment

There are also a number of things you should remember about operating a tape machine during interviews. You can easily learn to work the buttons and change the tape on your recording machine without looking at it. Never hide electronic recording equipment, but do not place it directly in front of interviewees, either. If possible, put it slightly to the side but between you and a respondent.

Because electronic recording of interviews is not as well accepted as notetaking, you should ask permission to use it. You should also offer to shut it off if the interviewee desires, or let the interviewee hear the tape and make corrections. Be sure to tell respondents what you will be doing with the tape in order to assure them confidentiality. Once the tape is turned on, it will create some primary tension in respondents, but as the conversation continues the equipment is usually forgotten.

You might also take brief notes along with the electronic recording. Notes provide a degree of insurance against breakdowns and help you conduct the interview. It is up to you to glance at the tape occasionally to be sure it is still running. During an interview, however, it is impossible for you to be sure that responses and questions are in fact being recorded. By taking at least brief notes, you have some record of the interview content. Notes are also useful as an aid for further probes, summaries, or the conclusion. They are useful in recording promises, appointments, and future actions, especially if you are not able to get back to the tape for some time.

Advantages of Electronic Recording

Probably the biggest advantage of the use of electronic interview recording is that it helps beginning interviewers become seasoned professionals. Beginners can not only go back over the tape time and time again until all relevant information is extracted from it, but electronic recordings can also help improve their interviewing skills. This is especially true of video tape. There is probably no better way to improve your interviewing skills than to watch yourself on video tape. Even audio tape, however, can be an invaluable teaching device for beginners. Both new and professional interviewers are beginning to move more and more to electronic recording. Benjamin reflects this movement when he says:

To me, the most exciting and, I admit, the most threatening aspect of video tape is

Electronic recording encourages better listening, questioning, and probing.

that it enables us to study simultaneously both our verbal and nonverbal communication. We can judge for ourselves to what extent our words match our actions. The mouth speaks and so does the rest of the body. Now we can compare and contrast the two. We can see ourselves as the interviewee may see us. Does our behavior, there on the screen, form a whole? Are we in fact the words and feelings we express or do we notice a clash somewhere, a slight descrepancy perhaps, between word and gesture, which may well arouse doubt in the interviewee as to our sincerity? Most important of all, do we only sound genuine or do we look genuine as well?

(Benjamin, 1974, p. 63)

Another advantage of electronic recording is its *versatility*. Audio recording, especially, allows you to conduct an interview almost anywhere—over lunch, while walking down a street, or almost any place without arousing curiosity. You can even interview in the dark. The interview can also be evaluated later by someone other than the interviewer. In many cases the person asking questions and the person responsible for doing the analysis are different. In a selection interview on campus, for example, the campus recruiter can easily take an audio or video tape back to the parent organization for review by other managers or personnel administrators or submit it for evaluation by trained psychologists. There are even professional selection groups which make decisions based on tape recorded interviews. You ask a set of predetermined questions of potential employees and send the tape to these people. They then tell you who to hire based on various psychological indicators.

A third advantage of electronic recording is its *permanence*. You can come back to the interview tape after a long period of time if necessary. This is especially helpful if a respondent needs to be interviewed again or reminded of what was said during the original interview. The ability to delay the analysis portion of an interview and not lose information is valuable if you have to do a great many interviews in a short period or if you cannot get to the analysis quickly.

A fourth advantage of electronic recording is *accuracy*. This is important for long, controversial, and detailed interviews, especially where legal action may arise as a result of the interview. It allows you to take more accurate notes upon second hearing. You can listen to rapid parts of the interaction two or three times. You can turn the machine off and take notes and, thus, not record the irrelevant material that was covered during the interview. You can be much more selective upon second interview listening or viewing. This accuracy is very useful when verbatim comments are required. It allows a journalistic interviewer, for example, to capture colorful speech and quote an interviewee accurately. Verbatim comments from an electronically recorded interview always have the ring of truth.

Electronic recording also has some definite advantages during an interview. You can ask many more questions in less time, and need not take the time to memorize or note responses. It allows you to relax and concentrate on listening to the interviewee, note questions to ask, and discover areas to probe. You need not divide your attention between a notepad and a respondent. Electronic recording reduces the amount of interviewer fatigue, so you can be more alert.

Finally, a tape recorder can be used as a cue much the same way as a pencil and notepad. If interviewees are digressing, you can turn off the machine to indicate that the response is off target. Turning off a tape recorder at the end of the interview will signal its conclusion. Sometimes changing the tape or turning it off can be used as a time to ask an "off the record" question.

Disadvantages of Electronic Recording

Probably the most significant disadvantage of electronic interview recording is the possibility of inhibiting responses. Although, as with notetaking, there is often much more anxiety in the interviewer's mind than in the interviewee's, more respondent anxiety is usually aroused with a tape recorder than with notes. Respondents know that every word they utter will be recorded. This is sometimes a frightening prospect and can harm interview climate, especially if that climate is based on informality and rapport.

Many people do not like to have their answers recorded verbatim. They are afraid that direct quotes may show them to be inarticulate. Few interviewees speak so fluently that every word they say can be quoted directly and sound good. Allowing interviewees to listen to the tape or read the interview transcript may reduce this kind of anxiety. Even when a respondent allows electronic recording, it can inhibit complete and honest responses. Interviewees are more guarded and reluctant to divulge certain kinds of information if they know it is being recorded.

If you sense that a respondent is holding back information, you should turn off the electronic recording device to obtain a better response. There are, however, some people who like to perform before a microphone. They may exaggerate and add details to the point where the information becomes almost useless. Always be alert to any unnatural behavior, regardless of whether it be inhibition or exhibition.

A second disadvantage of electronic recording is the cost of analysis. Transcribing an electronically recorded interview is costly in both time and money. When interview analysis is needed quickly, electronic recording may not be as efficient as notetaking or memorizing. If you do not transcribe the interview, you have to watch or listen to the entire interview for a second time. It is like holding two interviews. Many interviewers feel they cannot justify such cost to analyze a single interview.

Another complaint about electronic recording, especially videotaping, is that it captures *too* much information. Electronic recording can bog you down in trivia. Sometimes it is better to concentrate on the main points or ideas during the interview itself, rather than try to go back over an interview and pull out each tiny detail. A tape recorder can give you so much information that you can't see the forest for the trees.

Other disadvantages of electronic recording concern the equipment itself. Both audio and video tape are prone to pick up outside noises. Some super-sensitive machines pick up outside sounds so well that it is difficult to distinguish what is being said from the background noise. In a group interview, you may not be able to tell who says what. Unless the voices of the group participants are so different that they can be easily identified, a great deal of time may be taken up in attributing each response or question to the correct individual.

Many interviewers combine recording techniques.

A final problem with the equipment is that it sometimes fails. It is possible for the batteries to die, the machine to record improperly, or to run out of tape unnoticed. Any of these problems can leave an interviewer without any record of the interview. This is why it was suggested earlier that notetaking be combined with electronic recording.

Electronic recording is becoming more and more important in interviewing. It probably should not be used by itself. It can, however, be used very well in conjunction with notetaking and/or memorizing. In the final analysis, a combination of all three of the techniques discussed in this chapter probably provides the best means of recording an interview.

SUMMARY

The best recording technique is that which provides you with the most accurate, relevant, objective, uniform, and complete record of interview content. Three main recording techniques were discussed: memorizing, notetaking, and electronic recording. Memorization is probably the least used recording technique. It takes a great deal of practice and skill to use as the only means of interview recording. In certain situations, however, when neither of the other two recording methods are available or desirable, memorization may be the only alternative. It is most important, however, when used in conjunction with notetaking and/or electronic recording.

Notetaking is still the most common method of recording an interview. It is simple, direct, and well received by most interviewees. Like memorizing, however, it takes practice and skill in order to take good notes. Notetaking can inhibit interviewee responsiveness and, thus, must be used carefully. Four notetaking types were discussed: verbatim notes, central idea notes, predetermined categories, and probe notes. Most interviewers use all four types to some degree. Every interviewer should know how to take written notes.

The last method of interview recording is electronic recording. It is by far the newest and fastest growing method. There are many types of electronic recording equipment available and methods for using them. Almost every beginning interviewer ought to make use of video or audio tape, both as a recording and training tool. The major disadvantage of electronic recording is that it can inhibit respondents, but its values in terms of versatility, permanence, and accuracy, in many cases, outweigh the disadvantages mentioned. Audio and video tape should not be the only record of the interview. Notetaking, memorizing, and electronic recording can all be used in almost any interview.

ACTIVITIES

Activity #1

Directions: Try Truman Capote's method of testing and improving your memory. Have someone read or talk to you for a set length of time, tape what he or she is saying, and listen as intently as you can. When the person is finished, go write down what was said as best you can remember and then compare your notes with the tape or script. Try doing it for two minutes at first and determine your accuracy percentage. You need not have everything word for word, but be sure you have every point. If ten points were made by the speaker and you got eight of them, your percentage is 80. Keep extending the amount of time you listen until you can take about a half hour's worth of memorization. Even though you may never run into a situation similar to that of Mr. Capote, this activity will help you remember important information even when you are taking written notes or electronically recording an interview.

Activity #2

Carry a *small* notepad and pencil and take notes on everything that is said to you during a single day. When someone asks you what you are doing, just tell them you are practicing your notetaking skills. If someone objects, handle it as you think you might in an interview. Don't try to hide the fact that you are taking notes or apologize. Practice taking verbatim, central idea, and probe notes. Use as many abbreviations as you can, and keep them as brief as possible. See if you can take your notes as unobtrusively as possible. In other words, try to maintain eye contact as much as possible while still taking notes.

You will discover how difficult this is and how brief your notes have to be. If you can master this art of interview notetaking, you are well on your way to being a skillful interviewer. Once you have finished taking notes on one or two conversations, rewrite them and expand them based on what you remember from the interactions. Evaluate yourself. How close did you come to getting everything that was said? This will give you a good idea of how you will do in an actual interview. Keep going until you think you are efficient.

Activity #3

This last activity concerns the use of electronic recording equipment. If you do not already own a cassette or microcassette tape recorder, borrow one or purchase one. You will be surprised how valuable it will be to you in all kinds of situations. Practice using it as if you are in an interview. Memorize what each button does, so that you can operate it without looking. Experiment to see how far away from a person the recorder can be and still get a good recording. Get used to setting the counter at "0" each time you use the machine. Note what it looks like in the window when you are about to run out of tape and when the machine is operating correctly. Practice recording the name, title, and affiliation of the person you are recording. Try turning the tape over with a minimum of effort and time until you can do it smoothly. Finally, try recording an actual conversation or interview using your tape and also taking written notes. Look at the counter when taking an important note and record that number on your notes for quick reference. A tape recorder is like any other tool; it is only as good as the person who uses it. If you have access to video tape equipment, you should also become familiar with it. Don't try to use any electronic recording equipment without help until you are thoroughly proficient with it.

Answers to the Notetaking Exercise.

Statement # 1—(Main Idea Note) Doesn't like it; hurts fishing. (Verbatim Note) "Worst polluters" "No one can fish" (Probe Note) Where heard? Other polluters? How bad? etc . . . . (Predetermined Category Note) Mildly Oppose.

Statement #2—(Main Idea Note) Billing clerk equal to key-punch operator. (Verbatim Note) "Backlogged" "Increasingly complicated" "Worth $5 more per week" (Probe Note) Why backlogged? How more complicated? How do you know key-punch is routine? etc . . . . (Predetermined Category Note) Quite Dissatisfied.

Statement #3—(Main Idea Note) Supervision, working conditions & salary—OK. Training a waste, Poor assignments. No promotion. Recruiter lied. Work w/ father-in-law. (Verbatim Note) "Enter business with my father-in-law" "No complaints . . . supervision, working conditions, or salary" "More to offer" Management training—"waste of time" "Poor assignments" "Didn't turn out to be what college recruiter promised" (Probe Notes) Why not recognized? Why training waste of time? Poor assignments? Did you ask for promotion? What did recruiter promise? (Predetermined Category Note) Other Job, Other—Poor assignments, No promotion.

Statement #4—(Main Idea Note) Feels inadequate. Parental pressure. Physics worst. Nervous, quiet, and distracted. Cutting class. (Verbatim Note) "Too much competition" "Don't like making decisions" "Trouble concentrating" etc . . . . (Predetermined Category Note) first, sixth, eleventh, thirteenth, fourteenth, sixteenth—Parent pressure, insecure.

Chapter 8

Skill 8
Concluding the Interview

The success of an interview can often be measured by the attitude of the interviewee at the close. Too often, the interviewer is inclined to let his own feelings be the guide. Nothing could be more misleading. Absorbed in his own feeling of accomplishment, he may in fact be guilty of communicating a note of triumph. The important thing is to express satisfaction with the person being interviewed.

(Balinsky/Burger, 1979, p. 180)

There are probably as many different styles of closing interviews as there are interviewers. Without a doubt, the way an interview terminates has a clear and direct effect upon its perceived success. Both interviewers and interviewees will review the interview discussion in their heads after they have separated: what was said, what they should have said, and how well the session went.

The perceived success of an interview often depends on participants having something to point to and remember. This is usually the information discussed in the conclusion, so it determines a participant's perception of the entire interview. In the following discussion of interview concluding, you will learn when and how to terminate an interview, problems that can arise, and the four stages of interview conclusions: conclusion preparation, final summary, goal setting, and post-interview discussion.

WHEN TO CONCLUDE

Interview termination is forecast during the opening. At that time, you should have informed the respondent of the amount of time the interview would take, as well as the topics to be covered. If this is done properly, the conclusion should not come as a surprise.

The decision to end the interview should be mutual. Both participants should perceive a natural stopping point and be prepared to conclude. Neither participant should see the conclusion as hasty or rushed, but at the same time neither should feel that the interview is dragging on and that termination is long overdue. An interview should not just peter out and end with a sigh of relief. Once all the issues are covered, the conclusion should occur—not before nor after.

The interview conclusion should be a pleasant, mutual decision.

Early Conclusions

At times, however, an interview ends early. Either participant may choose to end an interview before the natural ending point arrives. In most cases, when an interview ends early, it is not *concluded,* but simply *interrupted.* True termination only comes when all of the planned topics and questions have been covered.

In most cases it is the interviewer who sees reasons to end an interview early. First, an interviewee may not possess the information you want. Second, something may come up which you need to check before continuing the interview. If this occurs, you should try to locate the information quickly, during the interview if possible, by telephone or some other means. There are times, however, when such information is not readily available and you will need to interrupt the interview to check something, or gather some further information.

A third reason for early interview termination is that you simply run out of available time before you complete the interview guide. When this happens, you should indicate a desire to continue, but honestly state you've run out of time. A continuation time and place should be designated.

In the latter two cases, you must realize that interruptions can cause a great many problems. If the continuation does not come soon after the initial interview, the information or the climate may change. If at all possible, it is inadvisable to interrupt a productive interview.

Interviewee Concludes Interview

The interviewee may wish to conclude an interview early for several reasons. First, they may become disenchanted and threatened, embarrassed, hostile, or inadequate. Second, they may have run out of time. This may be the interviewer's fault for taking more time than was planned for. In this case, interviewees are justified in asking for termination. It is an interviewer responsibility to keep within the stated interview time. If you see that the stated time is not going to be enough, you should ask for more time or schedule a continuation interview. Whenever interviewees ask for an early conclusion, you should find out why and persuade them to remain, if at all possible.

Early conclusions can have detrimental effects, regardless of who initiates them. If an interview must be interrupted, try to make the last few minutes as positive as possible. In other words, it should be handled like a "normal" interview conclusion discussed in the following sections.

HOW TO CLOSE AN INTERVIEW

The way interviewers close depends upon the type and purpose of the interview as well as the personalities involved. Some interviews (like research interviews) end very quickly with a simple "Thank you" or "That's all the questions I have for now." For most other interviews, however, the conclusion is less abrupt. It involves at least four stages: conclusion preparation, final summary, goal setting, and post-interview discussion.

Preparing to Terminate

Whether an interview ends quickly or is prolonged, you should be conscious of the climate when moving toward the conclusion. The climate should reflect what has gone before—during the opening and the body of the interview. The closing should end as pleasantly as possible.

The interviewer is responsible for preparing to conclude the interaction. In most cases, you should begin to look toward the conclusion at least five to ten minutes before time is due to run out. Many interviewers save an easy topic for last. The purpose of this technique is to neutralize any strong emotions or

Subtle cues can help prepare a respondent to terminate.

negative feelings which have developed earlier. Easy concluding questions make interviewees comfortable and help them feel confident and pleased with their performance.

There are a number of other ways in which you can signal an upcoming conclusion. Your voice inflection, more frequent postural shifts, arranging your notes, putting away your pencil, and, even less subtly, glancing at your watch can all serve as signals that the conclusion is near. A skillful interviewer is conscious of these nonverbal behaviors and uses them intentionally to prepare interviewees for termination. Sometimes a wall clock, for example, is placed in the interview room in such a position that it can be easily seen by both participants.

There are also a number of verbal cues which prepare respondents for the conclusion. Statements such as, "In the short time we have left, . . ." or "Before we conclude, . . ." are both helpful signals of the beginning of the end. As you become more experienced, you will develop ending comments of your own. Regardless of the techniques used, this winding-down period should be friendly and cooperative, but definite. It should lead directly to the next formal stage of the closing, the final summary.

CONCLUSION PREPARATION EXERCISE

Directions: For each of the following situations, choose what you think would be the proper response, either verbal or nonverbal. Correct answers are found at the end of this chapter.

1. You realize you are coming to the end of your time, but you see that the respondent is still talking a mile a minute and isn't aware of the time or doesn't care. You should:
   a. Let the interviewee talk.
   b. Interrupt and say, "We will have to stop soon."
   c. Stop recording and look at your watch.
   d. Say, "I think I've got everything I need now."
2. You discover that the respondent does not possess the information that you need. You should:
   a. Go on with the interview anyway, but rush through.
   b. Say, "This is a waste of both our times, so long."
   c. Close your notes, get up, and leave.
   d. Say, "Thank you for your time, but I better see if I can find someone who might be able to give me a little more information on this, do you know of anyone who might be able to help me?"
3. The respondent begins making noises which indicate an attempt to end the interview early such as saying, "Well, I think you have everything I know about that, I don't think there's anything more I can tell you." You should:
   a. Say, "Well, I still have several more topics I would like to cover, let's go on to those."
   b. Close your notebook, say "So long, thank you," and leave.

c. Say, "Now wait a minute, you said you would answer all of my questions, and I'm not through."

d. Say, "Oh please, I need to complete all of this; won't you answer just a few more questions?"

4. You notice that the interviewee is running out of enthusiasm, and you have collected all the information you need. You should prepare to close by:

a. Putting away your recording materials.

b. Say, "In the short time we have left . . . ."

c. Say, "That's all I need to know for now."

d. Doing any or all of the above.

5. You are out of time, but you still have some things you want to ask the respondent. You should:

a. Continue the interview and pretend you don't know about the time.

b. Stop the interview and figure you can guess the rest.

c. Ask, "I wonder if you would be willing to come back tomorrow about this same time, so we can finish this interview?"

d. Say, "I want to see you back here in the near future so we can finish this."

The Final Summary

As noted earlier, a summary probe generally comes at the end of each interview topic. At the end of an interview there should be an overall or final summary as well. The purpose of the final summary is to pull together all of the main ideas agreed to in each of the summary probes and provide an overall picture of everything that has taken place. As with the verbal and nonverbal conclusion preparation cues, the final summary helps interviewees make the transition from the body of the interview to the conclusion. Like summary probes, the final summary is a good test of listening and notetaking. It helps both interviewers and interviewees organize their thoughts and tie loose ends together. The final summary is a consolidation of the entire interview. If done properly, it should give both participants a feeling of accomplishment and satisfaction.

Many interviewers prepare for the final summary by placing an asterisk or some other identifying mark next to ideas in their notes that they intend to include. The final summary should not be a listing of every comment that has been made—it must be somewhat more selective. It's boring to hear all of the same ideas repeated again in the same words. You should pull together and relate ideas from the various topics and show that you have been listening to the interviewers' explanations and clarifications. The final summary is an opportunity to highlight the key aspects and overall conclusions. In some cases, when your summary brings diverse elements together into a meaningful whole, interviewees see for the first time the full implications of the statements made. The summary can provide not only feedback to interviewees but also a fresh outlook.

The final summary should point out both the areas of agreement and disagreement. It would certainly be nice if every interview ended with complete agreement, but most often, this is not the case. By the time the conclusion is reached, both participants should be well aware of each other's views. Areas where there is perceived disagreement should not be avoided in the summary. The only points that might be left out are those which are not directly relevant to the purpose of the interview. Sometimes these include personal or "off the record" statements which do not have a direct bearing on the interview purpose. The final summary is not just a means of highlighting and emphasizing an interviewer's perceptions of the interview, but also should reflect the interviewee's perceptions. In this way it is a consolidation of *all* of the discussion that has taken place.

At the end of the final summary, respondents should be asked if anything has been left out or if anything has been summarized inaccurately. Even if you have used the final summary properly, and the sources for inferences drawn are obvious to the respondent, there will probably be some questions or comments. These usually relate to what happens after the interview. You should not respond directly to these inquiries until its agreed that the final summary is accurate and acceptable.

Some interviewers like to ask interviewees to summarize interview information in their own words. This may be done as a substitute for the interviewer summary, or after it in response to it. When interviewees do a final summary it helps them collect their thoughts and review the interview in their own minds. A further advantage of interviewee summaries is that the interviewee often becomes more committed to the agreements reached. In all but the pure information interview, the final summary will lead directly to post-interview goal setting.

FINAL SUMMARY EXERCISE

Directions: Write a final summary for the selection interview which follows. Since you do not have an interview guide to work from, mark what you consider important comments in the script as you read it. Once you have marked the script, only look at the marked comments and write a summary as you think you would present it to the applicant in the conclusion.

1 You: I have your application and resume and have had a chance to go over it briefly. I'd like now to ask you to fill me in a little bit more on your background, education, previous work experience, and interest in this sales position. After that I will answer any questions you have. O.K.?

5 App: Sounds good to me.
  You: I see you were born in Colorado and went to school there. Is there anything in your background that you think might help me evaluate your potential for this job?
  App: Well, I have always been interested in selling. Like most kids, I sold
10 raffle tickets, Christmas cards, and other things for clubs I belonged to. I never had any problem selling and usually did better than most of the others. I really enjoyed selling. I got a thrill when somebody bought something from me. I guess I'm kind of an extrovert. I also held some other selling

jobs, as you can see from my resume. I have spent my entire life, so far, in
15 Colorado. I like it here, but I'm also interested in seeing more of the world.
My Dad is a salesman, but he doesn't travel very much anymore. He used to
travel a lot, and he tells me its a great way to see things. My Mom is a school
teacher. I can't think of anything else.
You: Good. Tell me about your communication and business majors. What
20 are some of the courses and work you have done which you think will help
you in sales?
App: The reason I got into communication and business is because I wanted
to go into sales. I mentioned the travel. I also like the money you can make if
you're a good salesman. I tried to take as many courses as I could that related
25 to sales, management, and business in general. I took public speaking,
argumentation, persuasion, advertising, marketing, organizational communication, management, accounting, and others. Humm . . . let's see,
what were the names of those others?
You: That's okay. Do you think communication and business are a good
30 combination?
App: Oh, yeah. I think it's the best combination for sales. You get practical
stuff in combination with theory. I even did some projects out of class, like
the internship I had with an insurance company. I got to go out in the field
with insurance salesmen as well as see how things were processed in the
35 main office. I really liked that. When you're working for a salary, you don't
get to see all that.
You: Good, well, why don't you tell me about your previous jobs now? Did
any of them involve a lot of selling?
App: Yeah, one did. That was the one I had in the clothing store. I sold men's
40 clothes on a part-time basis for a year and a half. I also worked in the
dormitory for a while. Most of my college career, I didn't work, however,
because I was on scholarship, and I thought I better study. My parents
didn't have to pay anything for my college education . . .
You: That's very good. Were you active in any clubs or organizations or in
45 sports?
App: Some sports and clubs. I joined a fraternity and played intermurals for
awhile. That was okay. Like I said I worked on my homework mostly.
You: What is your grade point average?
App: Oh, about a 2.5 overall, and 2.8 in my major.
50 You: Humm . . . why did you choose this company?
App: You were having interviews for a sales position, and that's what I want
to do, so I applied. Can you tell me what the position is all about?
You: O.K., but let me see if I can summarize all this first.

Post-Interview Goal Setting

Goal setting is an extremely important part of many interviews; it involves
the determination of actions to be taken or ends to be achieved by both participants once the interaction is over. Although goal setting can occur at the end of

each topic, it most often comes either directly before or as part of the conclusion.

Goal-setting purpose and method depend on the general purpose of the interview. In a persuasion or discipline interview, interviewers normally have some idea of the goals even before the interview begins. Most other interviewers prefer to delay goal setting until they have heard and considered interviewee responses. This means any post-interview plan is tentative until the final summary is complete. Because of the wide variation in goal-setting methods used by interviewers, a specific discussion of different techniques is included in the chapters on uses and types of interviews. Some general comments on goal setting follow.

Setting Clear and Realistic Goals.

If the goal setting is to be successful, the objectives and actions to be taken should be both clear and realistic. It is important that both participants know exactly what actions are to be taken to reach the goal, how goal achievement will be measured, and when progress will be checked. It is a good idea to make a written record of all this. Participants need to remember the what, when, where, how, and why of every goal set, so you must be very specific. Many professional interviewers ask interviewees to repeat the goals set or actions to be taken to be sure that they are understood and then follow-up with a memo.

No matter how clear a goal is to both the interviewer and interviewee, it won't be achieved if it is unrealistic. For example, planning to make major changes in a very short period of time is unrealistic. A realistic goal must have the full commitment of both participants and be achievable. It is the interviewer's responsibility to be sure that the objectives and actions planned are a product of mutual and honest agreement.

There are a number of ways in which goals can be unrealistic. Goals are unrealistic when they 1) are set too far in the future, 2) based on unwarranted reassurances from either participant, 3) require unobtainable resources, or 4) require complete personality or behavioral changes. During the course of the interview the interviewer should assess how realistic each goal is for each interviewee.

Sometimes goal setting requires homework or decision-making. For example, you may ask interviewees to go home and think something over and report their decision to you within a day or two. In a selection interview, it is the interviewer or some representative of the company who makes the decision after some thought. In this case, interviewees should be told what will determine the decision, when the decision can be expected, and how they will receive word. In other cases, a decision can only be made once interviewers have received test results, investigated further, or relayed evaluation data to someone in greater authority. It is important that neither interviewers nor interviewees make promises which cannot be kept. A diagnostic interviewer, for example, should not tell interviewees that they will receive word in a day or two, when in fact, it may take several weeks to get test results.

Follow-up Interviews.

In some situations, goal or action decisions require a follow-up interview. When this is the case, let interviewees know when and where the follow-up interview will take place, and what is to be expected from it. The initiative for follow-up always falls on the interviewer's shoulders. In most cases, follow-up interviews which are designed to set goals or check progress are briefer and more direct than the original interview. If no future interview is planned, make sure to leave the "door open" for contacts between interviews.

Handling Goal Disagreement.

It is always possible that there will be some disagreement when interview participants try to set goals. When agreement on future goals and actions cannot be reached, it is your job to be certain that interviewees clearly understand the possible goals. If they still disagree, don't try to force agreement. Planned goals and actions are usually unsuccessful if agreement is forced.

A skillful interviewer will normally allow interviewees to express dissent and try to discover the source of the disagreement. At all times, you should continue to indicate respect for respondents. Remember, goal setting is a mutual activity which will be successful only when the decisions are acceptable to both parties.

In some cases interviewers have to compromise to reach agreement. Compromising is not a loss of face, but a legitimate and important part of the entire interviewing process. If a compromise cannot be reached, close the interview and schedule a follow-up or some other means of change. Planned actions and goal setting will be successful only when respondents leave the interview with an honest desire to effect change.

GOAL SETTING EXERCISE

Directions: List three goals you think might be the outcome for each of the following two situations. Be sure your goals are clear and realistic, and mention any special circumstances you think might surround either situation such as any homework, follow-up interviews, or disagreement.

1. You have just finished the main portion of a performance interview with Susan Baker. She has been with the company for five years. She is an intelligent, efficient, and capable employee. Her problem is that she gives other employees the impression that she is better than they are. A good example is that she generally delivers work to others by tossing it on their desks. When she answers a question, she sometimes looks at the other person like they should have known the answer. She doesn't do this all the time, but enough to be troublesome. She does have some friends on the job and is very friendly when she wants to be. She is married and works only because she wants to. In the past when you have confronted her, she says she didn't mean to offend anybody. If she could correct this one problem, you feel she would be an excellent employee.

2. You have just finished the main portion of a counseling interview with Mr. Clark. Mrs. Clark called and made the appointment for her husband, whom she said was drinking to excess. He isn't sure he has a problem, even though he has lost his job, been jailed for drunk driving, and most recently broke an

arm when he fell down some stairs while drunk. When he arrived you could smell liquor on his breath. He was obviously not drunk, however, and admitted he had been drinking "a little." He attributes his recent difficulties to "hard luck." He said he had had too much to drink in the past but that was all over. He admitted that his marriage was now in jeopardy, but wasn't sure why. After some prodding, he says that he is willing to work with you in setting some goals to help him quit or "cut down" his drinking.

Post-Interview Discussion

The setting and acceptance of goals signals the end of the formal part of an interview. Once this is done, however, there is normally a little time before the interviewee actually leaves the interview setting. This can be anywhere from a few seconds to several minutes and is called the post-interview discussion. If used productively, this can be a very important part of the closing. Like the icebreaking portion of the opening, no formal notes are taken and interviewers and interviewees just chit-chat. It can also be a time, however, when many important points can be made and enlightening observations revealed.

The Value of Post-Interview Discussion.

From the interviewer's viewpoint, the post-interview discussion is a time to reassure interviewees, reduce the emotional level, build confidence, and allow respondents to regain their composure. You can reassure interviewees by pointing out the value and significance of the interview. Many interviewers use this as a time to restate the confidential nature, purpose, and use of the information discussed. After the goal-setting period, you may notice some continued emotional distress on the part of interviewees, and often this can be relieved by simply talking for a while. Such conversation allows interviewees to regain their composure.

The post-interview discussion is initiated when you turn off the tape recorder or close your notebook. Sometimes a comment such as, "Well are you glad it's over?" begins this particular stage of the interview. No new information should be introduced at this point by the interviewer, but often important comments are made by interviewees during the post-interview discussion. They tend to relax once their comments seem to be "off the record." They may open up and state any inhibiting effects they feel. When you feel that the interviewee is reluctant to say something during the actual interview, you might allow extra time for the post-interview discussion and hope that informality produces the desired information. There is little to be lost in a post-interview discussion and possibly much to be gained.

Handling Reluctance to Leave.

In some cases interview termination may be perceived as rejection. If the interview was a fairly satisfying experience, respondents may be reluctant to leave. Counseling interviewers often find this to be the case. If allowed, some interviewees would prolong the experience as much as possible. This feeling of rejection can be alleviated if you set up another interview or leave the door open for further contact. It is important, however, not to yield to attempts to prolong an interview beyond its scheduled time. In some cases this is difficult because interviewees become hostile or remorseful. Regardless of what ploys are used, you must be friendly but firm. On the other hand, reluctance on the part of an interviewee to leave can be a sign that there is more information to be covered. When you sense this is the case, you should either continue the discussion or schedule a follow-up.

The Farewell.

The end of the post-interview discussion is marked by the actual departure or farewell. There are several parts to the farewell process: preparing to stand, standing, moving to the door, opening the door, preparing to shake hands, shaking hands, and saying the final farewell. Beginning interviewers sometimes become frustrated when an interviewee does not offer to shake hands. A handshake is not an absolute necessity. The interviewee may be bewildered and confused and still thinking about what went on in the interview. Simply assume their gratitude and thanks—do not demand it. In most cases, however, the whole parting process takes very few seconds and goes quite smoothly. Make it as quick, pleasant, and efficient as possible.

THE FOLLOW-UP

Just as an interview does not begin with the opening, but with preparation, so an interview does not conclude with a farewell, but with follow-up. The first, and perhaps most important, aspect of follow-up is interpretation of the information provided by the interviewee. As noted earlier, you should write down your reactions and analysis within ten minutes after the interview has concluded. This is the time to expand upon notes before the details become blurred. As most of you know, notes you take in classes are hard to understand once you have let them sit for a couple of days. After a month you may not be able to understand them at all. With the briefer, more abbreviated notes that are taken in interviews, this problem is compounded. The longer you wait, the greater chance of error.

Interview success can be measured in many ways and is determined primarily in terms of the interview purpose. The purpose can be either immediate or long-range. Therefore, you must be wary of drawing conclusions at this point. Conclusions drawn right after the interview has concluded can be premature if the goals set involve long-range actions. You can only assess your short-range success immediately.

The follow-up to an interview may also involve checking the information gathered. You cannot be sure you have been successful until you check out information or see if the interview goals are realized. Most often it is better to leave the evaluation until later when you can review and analyze the interview and

The interview follow up often includes checking the information gathered.

absorb some of the less immediately obvious aspects of the interview. In this respect, Kadushin (1971), suggests several questions you should ask yourself in order to determine the success of any interview.

1. *In retrospect, what were the purposes of this interview—for the interviewee, for the agency?*
2. *To what extent were the purposes achieved?*
3. *What interventions helped to achieve the purposes? What intervention hindered the achievement?*
4. *What was my feeling about the interviewee?*
5. *At what point was my feeling most positive? Most negative?*
6. *How might these feelings have been manifested in what I said or did?*
7. *If I now empathize with the interviewee, how did he seem to see me? What seemed to be the reaction of the interviewee to the interview?*
8. *When did the interview seem to falter? When was it going smoothly?*
9. *At what point did the interviewee show signs of resistance, irritation? What had I said or done just prior to that?*
10. *At what point did it cease to be an interview and become conversation, a discussion, or argument?*
11. *If I had the opportunity of doing the interview over again, what changes would I make? What justifies such changes?*
12. *What, in general, did this interview teach me about myself as an interviewer?*

(Kadushin, 1971, p. 214)

After most interviews, a number of documents must be completed. Sometimes you need to give a report to a superior. This is especially true if certain decisions have been or need to be reached that will involve the superior. Some interviewers have their written or tape recorded notes transcribed to provide documentation of the interview and record any decisions made within the interview. You should make it a practice to give copies of the goals and plans for future action to the interviewee and to the appropriate superior, keeping at least one copy for yourself. There are a number of other written documents which are important as follow-up to different types of interviews, such as forms, letters, memos, and reports.

A final aspect of the follow-up for many interviews is checking goal progress. In some cases, an interviewee is responsible for giving an interviewer progress reports. In other cases, it will be your responsibility to make certain the goals are being accomplished. In still other cases, a follow-up interview is used to check on goal progress. No matter what technique is selected, you need to be sure the decisions reached and the goals set during the interview are put into practice after the interview is completed. Only when the follow-up is completed will you be able to determine whether or not you have been a skillful and successful interviewer.

FOLLOW-UP EXERCISE

Directions: Describe what you would do as a follow-up for each of the situations described in earlier exercises in this chapter: the selection interview for the sales job, the performance interview with Susan Baker, and the counseling interview with Mr. Clark. List three follow-up behaviors you might try for each.

SUMMARY

This chapter discussed interview conclusions and related subjects. You learned that an interview should conclude when all of the information has been covered. The major part of this chapter discussed how to conclude interviews. This involved an examination of the major stages of interview termination: preparing to conclude, final summary (which involves an overview and restatement of all the major points made within the interview), and goal setting. Then comes the informal post-interview discussion where any difficulties that may have developed during the interview are eased. The conclusion of an interview is actual departure. Most interviews do not end here, however, but with the follow-up. This is when interviewers and interviewees complete all of the details necessary in order to determine the success of the interview and their future actions.

ACTIVITIES

Activity #1

Directions: Interview closings are very similar to other kinds of interaction closings. You want to leave the other participant with a good impression of you and the interaction. You want them to feel the interaction has been a success and that further interactions would not be unpleasant. The differences between interview closings and other types of interaction closings are goal setting and follow-up. For this activity, keep a record of the terminations of various interactions in which you take part during a day. Then answer each of the following questions and make any comments.

1. Were the conclusions perceived as a natural stopping point?
2. Were the conclusions a mutual decision?
3. Were there any early conclusions, and who caused the terminations?
4. What verbal or nonverbal signals were given that it was time to conclude?
5. Was a final summary part of any of these interactions?
6. Was there any post-interview goal setting during the conclusions?
7. If there was, were the goals clear and realistic?
8. Was there any goal disagreement? If so, how was it handled?
9. What occurred during the post-interaction discussion?
10. Did either you or the other participant have to do any post-interaction follow-up after the termination?
11. What were the principal differences between the conclusions you took part in and those which should occur as part of an interview?

Activity #2

Examine the conclusions of the written and electronically recorded interviews you have collected for previous exercises. Which of those conclusions do you think were effective and which were less effective? Use the questions in the preceding activity as your guide. Be sure to listen to or read each of these conclusions from the viewpoint of both the interviewer and the interviewee. In your opinion, would the success of the interview differ according to which participant role you were playing? What would you have done differently in each case to improve the interview conclusions?

Activity #3

Well, the time has finally come. Throughout most of the preceding exercises you have been preparing to conduct an information interview. You have contacted the individual and guaranteed his or her participation. You gathered as much information as you could on the person and the subject of the interview. You planned and prepared the interview guide, including opening comments, topics, questions, and so on. You have even practiced the interview and tried to anticipate necessary probes. You cannot put it off any longer. *Go conduct the interview*. If possible, make an electronic recording as well as taking written notes. This will help you improve your interviewing skills as well as writing up the interview as you will be asked to do in the next chapter. When you get to the conclusion, be sure to prepare the respondent to stop, do a final summary, and use the post-interview discussion productively. Goal setting or follow-up other than your write-up of the interview probably won't be necessary. You are now well prepared, so you should expect to do very well. Good luck and make it an enjoyable experience.

Answers to the Conclusion Preparation Exercise.
1 = C, 2 = D, 3 = A, 4 = D, and 5 = C

Part two

The Applications of Interviewing

Chapter 9

The Information Interview

In interviewing, you will have a modest feeling of power. Not the power of manipulation, but the power of knowledge—of holding a handmade key to a secret room of the subject's mind. The feeling is ephemeral, but sturdy and true. (Brady, 1977, p. 4)

The word, "information," means any knowledge sent or received concerning a particular fact(s) or circumstance(s). An information interview, then, is one where an interviewer attempts to get facts or circumstances from an interviewee, and an interviewee attempts to give facts or circumstances to an interviewer. This use of the interview process is discussed first because it is the most pure and genuine type of interviewing. Your purpose is to elicit and understand something the interviewee knows with no other motive such as determining qualifications for a job, diagnosing a problem, appraising work performance, disciplining, persuading, or any of the other motives discussed in Chapters 10–18. You are simply trying to see the world, or some particular part of it, from the interviewee's perspective.

The most common label for an information interview is "journalistic." Journalistic interviews are used by reporters to prepare news and feature stories. A recent text (Downs, 1980) also uses the terms "broadcast" and "news conference" along with "journalistic" to refer to information interviews used in the mass media. Dexter (1970, p. 5) uses the term, "elite," to refer to a similar type of information interview, that is, interviews conducted with "*any* interviewee—and stress should be placed on the word 'any'—who in terms of the current purposes of the interviewer is given special, nonstandardized treatment," including defining, structuring, and controlling the interview direction and content. Elite interviewees are prominent people such as world leaders, film or television stars, or sports heroes.

Another term currently in vogue is "oral history" interviewing. Oral history involves finding people with unique historical knowledge and asking them to retrieve that knowledge. For example, the John F. Kennedy oral history project involved interviewing over three hundred persons having some special knowledge about the late president. A number of colleges, libraries, and historical societies are collecting oral histories on many different topics. Anthropologists and sociologists call such information gathering "key informant" interviews. Key informants are people who are knowledgeable about and well-connected with a social or cultural group and are willing to share that information. Whyte (1955) described this kind of interview as follows:

As I sat and listened, I learned answers to questions that I would not even have had the sense to ask if I had been getting information solely on an interviewing basis. I did not abandon questioning all together of course. I simply learned to judge how and when to question.

(Whyte, 1955, pp. 29–30)

These are only a few of the many terms used to refer to various forms of information interviews. It is a wide-ranging and extremely important type of interview on its own, but it also forms the basis of many of the other types of interviews discussed later in this book. Some time is devoted to information gathering in almost all interviews, so you should learn how to conduct an information interview before you tackle other types of interviews.

INFORMATION INTERVIEW PREPARATION

The first obstacle faced by an information interviewer is *locating* the right people and *getting* interviews with them—be they elite respondents, key informants, persons with historical knowledge, those with newsworthy information, or anyone else who possesses the information you wish to obtain. Barbara Walters, for example, prides herself on being able to obtain interviews from "elite" interviewees who do not ordinarily give them. Her success is evidenced in her interviews with former Secretary of State Dean Rusk, Fidel Castro, Menachem Begin, and many, many others. To her and other information interviewers the "thrill of the chase" is one of the most important parts of information interviewing.

Sometimes obtaining an information interview is as simple as looking up a name in the telephone book and making a call. In other cases you have to work like *Washington Post* reporters Carl Bernstein and Bob Woodward did—twelve to eighteen hours a day, seven days a week, knocking on doors, making phone calls, and getting one person to lead you to another. Even when they found the right people, nine times out of ten they would not let the reporters in the door or refused to speak to them on the telephone.

You will be surprised, however, that in many cases even very important people are willing to give an interview if you write or phone them, tell them who you are, with whom you're affiliated, what you want to talk about, the length of the interview, and where it is to be held. In most cases you will want to make an appointment at least *one week* in advance. Only in rare circumstances should you waive the one week rule—it gives interviewees a chance to collect their thoughts and prepare for the interview. Many interviewees are irritated if they do not have at least a week's advance notice. In some cases interviewees will ask to see a list of the questions you want answered. If it does not affect your purpose, you should be willing to provide such a list. Interviewee preparation very often makes the interview flow more smoothly.

Professional information interviewers have developed many techniques for obtaining interviews. Some of these include calling at lunch time to get past secretaries, asking for "constructive criticism" instead of "an interview," obtaining a letter of introduction from someone the desired interviewee already knows, sending a telegram, wining and dining the potential interviewee's secretary, and many, many others. In most cases, you will get your interview if you are honest, polite, precise, and punctual. And, if at first you don't succeed, don't give up. Many information interviews are only achieved after a great deal of hard work, persistence, and enterprise.

A second major aspect of information interview preparation is doing the research necessary to ask intelligent questions and probes. Perhaps in no other kind of interview is research as important as in an information interview. If people have granted you an interview on a particular subject which they know well, they do not want to be providing basic information which could have been easily gained elsewhere if you had done your homework. Nothing is more infuriating to a busy person than engaging in an interview with an unprepared interviewer.

Most professional information interviewers advise you to spend approximately ten minutes on research for every minute spent in the actual interview. It is better to be over prepared than under prepared. Very often you will find that interviewees will also have researched you, the interviewer. Potential respondents frequently will delay granting you an interview until they have had a chance to check your credentials. Journalistic interviewers, for example, often find that an interviewee has read almost everything they have written prior to their arriving at the interview.

In most cases your research begins in the library. Some interviewers find using a library as tough as getting the potential interviewee to agree to the interview in the first place. You must, however, learn to effectively use a library. Your research should focus on both the interviewee and the subject of the interview. Some information can be gathered simply by consulting an encyclopedia, almanac, atlas, and other such general interest references. You must also be able to use an index. The *Readers' Guide to Periodical Literature* is an index to articles appearing in general interest magazines. There are indexes to newspapers such as the *Wall Street Journal, Christian Science Monitor, New York Times, National*

A good information interviewer plans on ten minutes of research for every one minute of interview time.

Observer, Washington Post, and many others. For more scholarly sources of information, look to indexes such as the *Social Sciences Index, Humanities Index, Business Periodicals Index, Applied Science and Technology Index, Drama Index,* and *Music Index.* Biographical information can be found in the *Biography Index* and *Current Biography* as well as the many Who's Who books. Before you can truly be a good information interviewer, you have to become familiar with the library. You should know about previous interviews with your respondent, other people's thoughts on the subject of your interview, anything the interviewee has written, and any other known facts about the subject or respondent. You can also receive much useful research information from friends and relatives of the individual whom you are interviewing. In some cases these third person interviews may be as hard to get as those with a primary respondent. However you get the information, you always attempt to learn everything possible before the interview.

THE INFORMATION INTERVIEW GUIDE

Information interviewers often use a nondirective guide. Since their purpose is to see the world through the eyes of respondents, why not allow an interviewee to guide the progress of the interview? They notify the interviewee of the subject they are interested in, and simply say, "As I told you on the telephone, I am interested in discussing . . . , why don't you tell me what you know about . . . ?" This is a very common approach in oral history interviewing. When you allow interviewees to structure the interview you can usually assume that the topics that come up first are those which they see as most important. You not only get the information, but some idea of the value of the information to the interviewee. Hence one type of information interview guide is really no guide at all.

Although most information interviewers use very broad, open nondirective questions, only a few allow their participation to be so limited. Through their research they have identified a number of topics and specific areas which they feel are important enough to ask about if the subject does not freely provide the information. Such a semidirective guide guarantees that you cover all areas your research indicates are important. In some cases, simply mentioning a topic will jog an interviewee's memory and start the information flowing. Aside from this memory-jogging function, an information interview guide has all of the other values mentioned in Chapter 2, such as keeping the interview on track, preventing long silences, providing interviewer security, and presenting proof to respondents that you have given some thought, time, and effort to preparing for the interview.

In an information interview, perhaps more than any other, the interview guide must be tailored to each interviewee and subject. This entails not only a lot of work but also a great deal of flexibility. You must be willing to alter your predetermined topic and question sequence to fit earlier responses. If you have no predetermined goal (other than gathering information) information interviews allow you to maintain flexibility. You can adapt to the respondent's structure rather than force each respondent to fit your predetermined guide. An information interview guide functions more as a reminder than a road map.

INFORMATION INTERVIEW OPENING

There are several aspects of an information interview opening which are somewhat different from other interview openings. You should still make ice-breaking comments, establish a productive climate, and orient respondents, but the nature of this type of interview makes some techniques inappropriate. The role of an information interviewer is very different from the role played by other interviewers. You are not the interviewee's boss; nor do you hold the key to future employment for the interviewee. The interviewee has *granted* you an interview. You have had to seek him or her out and request the interview. This gives the interviewee a certain amount of power and status which is not possessed by other respondents. Very often the people you are interviewing are busy and important. They do not have time for the chit-chat and small talk that often accompany an interview opening. In other words, they are doing you a favor and not vice versa. This has a profound effect on the nature of the interview opening as well as the conduct and closing of information interviews.

The best way to open an information interview is to be reasonably cordial but watch interviewees' cues for how much icebreaking they are willing to accept. Be willing to engage in small talk and other rapport development techniques, but be prepared to go quickly into the orientation when interviewees give signs of becoming impatient or disturbed. This does not mean that climate development is any less important than in other types of interviews, but only that the interviewee has much more control.

In many cases, you are in the interviewee's environment. That makes you the guest and puts the respondent in the superior, host position. It is you who is told where to sit and whether to smoke or not. It is you who must be on your best behavior. It is you who must call the interviewee by title, first, and last name unless given permission. It is you who must dress appropriately, be punctual, knock before entering, and introduce yourself. And, it is very often you who is experiencing the greater primary tension. All of this means that in many ways the opening of an information interview is just the reverse of that discussed earlier.

Still, you must attempt to establish a productive climate. You do this not by taking the lead, but by overtly accepting the climate set by the interviewee, and at the same time using subtle methods to change it if you do not feel it will be productive. Some interviewees, for example, like to be very formal when granting information interviews. You need to take advantage of every opportunity to establish the degree of rapport and trust which will eventually get you the information you desire. The best way to accomplish that is to show a warm and friendly interest in respondents. Make them feel you are impressed by them. This does not mean that you have to be dishonest or take an artificial approach. Just allow yourself to empathize with each person. See if you can find something that you and each interviewee have in common, such as hobbies, sports, books, etc. This is where prior research comes in handy. If interviewees sense that you have empathy with them, they will open up to you. Just don't try to bluff your way through the opening as did a reporter described in Hunter Thompson's *Hells Angels* who tried to interview a gang leader.

He came into El Adobe and immediately asked to buy some marijuana. Then, before they could decide if he was a poison toad or narco agent he pulled out some grass of his own and offered it around. This didn't work either, although it might have broken the ice if he'd rolled a joint for himself. Then he offered to buy a round of beers, talking constantly in bop jargon. The angels tolerated him for awhile but after several beers he began asking questions of Hitler and gang rapes and sodomy. Finally Sonny told him he had thirty seconds to get his ass out of sight and if he showed up again they would work on his head with a chain.

(Brady, 1976, p. 55)

INFORMATION INTERVIEW QUESTIONING AND RESPONDING

Keep in mind that in most cases respondents are doing you a favor by granting you an interview and answering your questions. Hard nosed, overly direct, or insulting questions will receive a response of "no comment." Phrase questions so respondents will want to answer them and, therefore, *will* answer them. This means wording questions so respondents feel you really want to know the answer.

One way you can show you are interested is to be sure you never interrupt. If your question is unclear or for some other reason a respondent does not provide all of the information you desire, wait until the end of the response to ask for clarification or amplification. By interrupting you communicate that you are more concerned about yourself than the respondent. This may allow long and sometimes irrelevant answers, but that is one of the hazards you face in an information interview.

Another way you can show interest and keep the focus on respondents is to preface and frame questions to indicate you have prepared thoroughly, recognize respondent expertise, or desire a complete accounting of all pertinent facts. Overly long, ambiguous, double-barreled, and negative questions should be avoided. They tend to confuse respondents. A good information interviewer tries to ask as few questions as possible and still get as much information as possible from each respondent.

Information interview respondents often claim that they have been "misquoted." Although they sometimes are right, it is equally common that such misinterpretation was caused by poor responses. An information interviewee has the responsibility to make answers clear, complete, accurate, and stimulating. It is also the respondent's responsibility to allow time for the interviewer to take good notes. Interviewees who tend to wander off the subject, speak too rapidly, give too many or too few details, or speak in a monotone are much more likely to be misquoted. As noted earlier, respondents must be natural, answer carefully, and sometimes be willing and able to turn a bad question into a good answer. Perhaps the biggest mistake of an information interviewee is assuming too much prior knowledge on the part of an interviewer.

INFORMATION INTERVIEW PROBING

Since most information interviewers use a fairly unstructured guide of many open questions, probing becomes especially important. All three types of probes discussed earlier—amplification, clarification, and confrontation—are used. The ways in which these three types of probes are used, however, differ greatly and account for the varying degrees of success obtained by information interviewers.

Amplification probes are used primarily to obtain quotes. Many interviewees are most comfortable presenting only very general statements. It is up to you to ask respondents for specifics. Specifics allow you and a reader to see what a respondent really means. Quotes are especially important to journalistic interviewers since they help enliven a story. They call this *"adding color."* Sherwood (1969) speaks of the importance of such amplification material:

> For it is anecdotes, examples, facts, and illustrations that bring most written material to life and that render any general observations an interviewee may make interesting and believable. If the interviewee does not offer these in support of his observations, it is the duty of the interviewer to ask for, even to press, for them. It is not necessary, of course, that every statement an interviewee makes be supported by an example, but enough should be to make the result seem meaningful.
>
> *(Sherwood, 1969, p. 71)*

Very often amplification can be gained by using silence, minimal encouragement, and restatement. Mike Wallace, for example, speaks of reaction time latency when he says "the single most interesting thing that you can do in television, I find, is to ask a good question and then let the answer hang there for two or three or four seconds as though you're expecting more. You know what? They get a little embarrassed and give you more." Brady (1976), talks about the "sympathetic noise."

> One of the most potent follow-up questions is a nonquestion: the Sympathetic Noise. 'You feel very strongly about that, don't you?' 'Sounds like you had a tough time of it, cleaning bar rooms.' On its face, the sympathetic noise may seem to do little but stall the subject until the interviewer can think up a real question. Actually, it takes account of the fact that subjects, like human beings at large, are cautious soul-bearers; they are reluctant to confess until they have proof positive that their interviewer is sympathetic. (Then they are all too willing.) The sympathetic noise— which is often simply reinforcement, or a gentle rephrasing of what the subject has just said—can unlatch a torrent of anecdotes and naked quotes.
>
> *(Brady, 1976, p. 82)*

Good information interviewers are masters of all forms of amplification probes.

There are also many times in an information interview when material either given by the interviewee or asked by the interviewer is confusing. Confusing or unclear messages require clarification probes by either an interviewer or respondent. If you are the respondent, you should not be afraid to ask the interviewer to repeat or rephrase a question. In the same way, as an interviewer, you should be aware of such things as puzzled looks and then ask "Was that question clear to you?" When respondent answers ramble or are unclear, a useful technique for drawing them out is to lay the problem on yourself: "Gosh, I guess I'm just thick-headed today, I didn't understand that answer" or "That's not quite clear to me, could you give me an example?" Sometimes it is a good idea to appear to be "dumb." As some authors suggest, "dumb is smart" in an information interview. Playing "dumb" will very often bring you a great deal of clarification. If the rambling continues, you should probably leave the question and come back to it later. Never make respondents feel they are totally unable to get their point across. You can also use the technique of paraphrasing or summarizing what you think interviewees said and have them either confirm or deny your interpretation.

Confrontation probes can also be used in an information interview. Sooner or later you will run into someone who lies, either intentionally or unintentionally. You must be diplomatic, but you should not be afraid to get tough. Getting tough does not mean getting hostile, however, it means being frank but also sincere. Often respondents do not blatantly lie but simply shade the truth or utter self-serving statements that make them appear better than they really are. If you feel it is absolutely essential to correct the inaccuracy, you must be careful to do it with finesse and delicacy. If you do it too directly, the person will become defensive and clam up completely. In many cases, you are better off disregarding the inconsistency or at least waiting to clear it up until toward the end of the interview. Remember, you have asked respondents for their perceptions, usually of the past, and it is very easy for hindsight to be distorted. That is still their perception.

There is one other aspect of information interview probing that needs to be discussed. That is the "off the record" comment. Sometimes interviewees are willing to amplify or clarify a comment only if their response is "off the record." They give you the information for "background only," and they do not want to have their name attached to it. It is up to you to either agree or disagree to accept an "off the record" statement. Most interviewers will agree to accept some material as "off the record." It depends, however, on the importance of the material to the entire interview. Close your notepad or turn off the tape recorder if you agree to allow respondents to give you information "off the record."

INFORMATION INTERVIEW LISTENING

The secret of good information interviewing is to keep the interviewee talking. This requires that you remain in the listener role. Although your research will probably suggest plenty of questions that you want to ask, you must withhold them until you are sure the information will not come voluntarily. In information interviewing, interviewers very often do not know what will be said until it actually comes out of an interviewee's mouth. What may seem like a routine interview may turn out to be the most exciting and important one you have ever conducted, if you are willing to listen for and then probe new and unexpected ideas. The only way you can pick up new and unexpected information is by allowing respondents to tell their own story in their own way and listening to them.

Information interview listening also requires that you notice the respondents' nonverbal behaviors. You must look for and catch the meanings and feelings which may not be expressed verbally. A nod of the head, wink of the eye, or a simple gesture with the hand may give you more information than what is being put into words. To see the world from the interviewee's perspective means more than simply knowing what the interviewee knows; it means feeling what the interviewee feels. This can be accomplished only by listening and watching very carefully.

INFORMATION INTERVIEW RECORDING

There has probably been more written about recording techniques by information interviewers than any other type of interview expert. This is because accurate notes are so very important to them. They are concerned not only with the central ideas expressed by respondents, but very often also need verbatim notes. This is especially valuable for journalistic interviewers who often use quoted material as part of a story. A well-trained information interviewer is adept at all three of the basic methods of interview recording. Even memorization is important in order to record information when it is dark, during a meal, or whenever a pad and pencil or tape recorder are inappropriate.

Still, pencil and paper is probably the most commonly used recording technique. Members of the Washington press corps, for example, must know how to take pencil and paper notes, because tape recorders are commonly outlawed at so-called "background" conferences held by the president, cabinet officers, and other high ranking federal officials. These officials do not always want to be identified with their statements. Reporters who attend background conferences realize they may not use a tape recorder and that they are not allowed to identify sources other than statements such as "a high state department official" or "parties close to the president."

Almost every journalist will tell you they depend primarily on their notepad even though they may use a tape recorder as well. They find that a paper and pencil gives them the speed they need in order to transform their notes into a story before they must meet a deadline. The journalist that uses a tape recorder alone must listen to the tape and take notes or try to work from thirty to forty pages of interview transcript. Many professionals simply find it easier to write from their hand-written notes. In journalism, speed is often important when a story is timely.

Although pencil and paper is still the most common recording method, these interviewers have been in the forefront of using electronic recording techniques. Oral history interviewers, for example, use electronic recording almost exclusively, except to take probe notes. In journalism as well, the use of the tape recorder is growing. Brady (1977) lists the following seven advantages of a tape recorder for the journalist:

First, the interviewer can ask more questions in less time than the notetaker.

Second, taped interviews tend to have that crisp ring of truth.

Third, the interviewer can concentrate on the interview.

Fourth, a taped interview is reassuring to an editor or publisher if the subject matter is at all controversial.

Fifth, a tape recorder frees the writer on the road.

Sixth, when the interviewer's hands are tied, a tape recorder is of real assistance.

Seventh, tape recorders can be used to record lengthy documents.

(Brady, 1977, pp. 140–141)

It is for these reasons as well as the development of new, smaller, and more efficient electronic recording equipment that information interviewers are either switching to electronic recording or combining it with the more traditional methods of memorization and written notes.

Journalists often check information while writing the story.

INFORMATION INTERVIEW CONCLUDING

How you conclude information interviews is especially important since you may have to interview the individual again or check back to fill in gaps. You should, therefore, thank respondents and if at all possible tell them the interview was valuable. Many respondents have had little experience and need reassurance that they have been helpful. Even the most hard-nosed respondents will give a smile of appreciation when told they provided a good interview. Try to keep information interviews no more than five or ten minutes beyond the time requested. The departure should then be fairly prompt but not hurried.

As you are leaving, you must be alert to any post-interview comments. Respondents may suddenly remember something they should have told you. You do not want to take notes, but listen very carefully. If interviewees are willing to give you such comments then you know they feel you deserve their help. You have established good rapport. Once you have left you should write down those post-interview comments as quickly as possible.

Many information interviewers allow respondents to review the interview transcript before it reaches final form. This reassures interviewees and also is a way of picking up any crucial mistakes. You should not, however, let respondents make major changes in the transcript. In some cases you will need a release before you can use the material. A *release* is a simple signed form which says that the respondent has reviewed the interview and confirms that it is accurate. Journalists often do this and send one copy of the release to the respondent, one to the editor, and keep one for their own files. This gives them legal protection.

Following up an information interview sometimes involves *verification*. That is, you make sure that the information you gathered is accurate. You can do this in a number of ways—check back with the library, talk with people mentioned by a respondent, or do anything else that will help you determine the accuracy of a manuscript. Once the manuscript is in final form, a copy should be sent to the respondent. Respondents should also be kept posted on reactions to the interview. You might even send them information or new developments you find which you think might interest them. In this way you "court him shrewdly, with an eye toward your next article; like wine, a good source improves with age and occasional care." (Brady, 1976, p. 184)

SUMMARY

The information interview was presented first because of its relevance to all other forms of interviewing. The interviewer has no other motive than to collect as much pertinent information as possible. Preparation for this interview includes contacting potential respondents, researching the topic and interviewee, and preparing an interview guide. Information interview openings are difficult because respondents often have greater status than the interviewer. As during the whole interview, in the opening you should be cordial, nondirective, and accepting. Nondirective amplification, clarification, and confrontation probes are used to be sure all relevant information is covered. Careful verbal and nonverbal listening is necessary to gather unbiased and complete information. Many information interviewers use electronic recording to get accurate details, quotes, and anecdotes. The conclusion should be brief, but unhurried, with positive reinforcement and an offer to see the final transcript. Follow-up often involves verification before preparing the final product, which is usually an article, book, or news story. If you master the techniques of the information interview, you are well on your way to becoming skillful in all of the following types of interviews.

ACTIVITIES

Activity #1

Directions: If you have been doing the exercises through Part I, you know that emphasis has been placed on preparing for and conducting an information interview. By now, you should have conducted the interview. You should have your notes on your interview guide or some type of electronic recording of the interview. Organize your notes and prepare a human interest or information story based on your interview. It should be no more than five pages long and should contain the essence of the interview. *Do not write the story in interview style*. Use quotes, anecdotes, and anything else from the interview you think will make the story interesting. Once you have written your first draft, look it over and see where you can improve. This is not a book on writing, but the following are some things you should look for once you have developed your first draft:

1. Does the lead seem adequate? Do you feel that the story follows naturally from this lead?
2. Can you trace your line of thought from the lead to the conclusion?
3. Do the various parts of the story seem to stand in proper relationship to one another and to be in proportion?
4. Read your story aloud. Does it "sound right"?
5. Are allusions, illustrations, and the like well chosen?
6. Check all important words to see that you have the exact word in the right place.
7. Have you dramatized your story where possible?
8. Have you appealed to the reader's senses as fully as seems suitable for this story? That is, have you given him something to see, to hear, to feel, to smell, to taste?
9. Check your phrasing; sentence structure; noun, verb, and modifer choice, spelling and punctuation, and transitions and connectives to be sure they reflect your best efforts.

(Taken in part from Presson, 1967, pp. 148–149)

Now write your final draft.

Activity #2

Directions: Select one of the following hypothetical cases and role-play it, being sure to use the concepts and skills discussed in this and previous chapters. These cases merely describe a common information interview situation. You are free to add any other information you like to make the role-play better. Try to make the interview as realistic as possible.

ORAL HISTORY INTERVIEW: The interviewer, *Susan Jones*, is planning to prepare a short history of this region for the Chamber of Commerce. After asking around, she has located *Abner Tallcott*, a long time resident of the area. Abner is somewhere over 90 years of age and still remembers many occurrences quite clearly. The only problem is that Abner is not much of a talker. Others who have tried to interview him say he keeps making up excuses not to meet with them. His friends, however, say that once you get him started, you can't shut him up. Susan is determined to get the interview and learn as much colorful information as she can about the region.

KEY INFORMANT INTERVIEW: *Halldór Thorsteinsson* is a senior in high school in Iceland. He would like very much to go to college in the United States, but isn't sure he will like it or the country. He has heard many unflattering stories about what goes on in America. He has decided to talk with *Emma Todd*, an American student attending his high school while her father serves his tour of duty on a nearby military base. Halldór decides to meet Emma and find out as much as he can about the United States before deciding if he wants to apply for college there. He is especially concerned about the way he has heard foreign students are treated, the crime rate, costs, and the quality of education.

NEWS CONFERENCE: (This role play can be done by an entire class) The interviewers, Washington, D.C. reporters, are attending the President of the United States' semi-monthly news conference. They have been told to prepare whatever questions they would like to ask the president about either foreign or domestic affairs and that the president would call on them individually during the interview. Each reporter has prepared at least three questions concerning recent events. Since each reporter knows he or she will probably only have one chance, each has prepared a primary question very carefully including whatever preface is necessary to be sure the question is understood and answered directly by the president. Government officials are notorious for trying to give vague or partial answers to novice newspersons.

Activity #3

Directions: On the basis of what you have just learned in this chapter and Part I, analyze the following interview between Gore Vidal, a candidate for U.S. Senator from California in 1982, and Fred Epstein. This interview appeared in the May 27, 1982 issue of *Rolling Stone* Magazine.

I was trained from childhood to be a politician, but I was born a writer.
—GORE VIDAL

Gore Vidal is dead serious about becoming a United States senator. But on this particular spring afternoon, as he walks sluggishly onto the patio of his Hollywood Hills villa wearing a tattered maroon velour pullover and rumpled charcoal-gray slacks, his appearance masks his political training almost as much as it caricatures his literary birthright. Vidal hasn't shaved, combed his hair, or eaten since the day before. Settling awkwardly into a redwood chaise lounge, he has to use one hand to keep his shirt from riding up above his belly. With the other hand, he holds two hard-boiled eggs in a small glass bowl. He announces that these eggs are all he will eat today.

This is not the normal way candidates for high office meet the press; but then, Gore Vidal is not a normal candidate—even by California standards. Born in 1925, he grew up around his maternal grandfather, United States Senator Thomas Pryor Gore. His father served in Franklin Roosevelt's first administration, and his stepfather was wealthy investment banker Hugh Auchincloss, who later became the stepfather of Jacqueline Bouvier, who later married a Massachusetts senator named Kennedy. Vidal wrote his first novel when he was nineteen and has since published seventeen more novels, five collections of essays and one collection of short stories, and written numerous successful stage, screen, and television plays. In 1960, already a public figure in his own right, Vidal ran for Congress as a Democrat from primarily Republican upstate New York. He lost, but he's quick to point out that in his district he picked up 20,000 more votes than did the Kennedy-Johnson presidential ticket.

Vidal sees himself as a man of letters in the old-world tradition, but it is his wickedly amusing persona on the television talk show that has positioned him for the senatorial race. While Jerry Brown's nine other challengers scramble for snips of news coverage and money for commercials, a simple announcement of candidacy was all Vidal needed to put him in second place—albeit far from the lead. His message is either outrageous or refreshing, depending on your point of view, but the messenger is undeniably formidable.

1 *E:* Several times since you ran for Congress, in 1960, you've said that you had no interest in seeking elective office again. Could you trace the events that led to your change of mind?
V: It all came out of a hunch that between a major depression and a major
5 war there is a very narrow valley, and that in a very serious time we might need a serious candidate. There are some things I do that no one else does: I can dramatize things on television, and I have an overview of the country and the world. But there's a point at which you get absolutely frustrated. Yes, I can go on television any time I want. I can write anything I want. And
10 yet there isn't anything I can do. I was going to write an exposé of the CIA; I've got stacks of material upstairs. But wouldn't it be better to schedule a secret session of the Senate to examine the CIA budget?
    Now whether you can be elected on this, I don't know. I think you can. It may well be that I'll never have a chance to find out, since at a certain point
15 these things are ninety percent money, and that's where I'm weakest.
E: Is there something short of victory, then, that you would accept as a measure of success?
V: You don't really accept anything other than election. At the moment, the best I can say is that I'm beautifully positioned. I have thirty-eight percent
20 name recognition and not much negative. (These figures are based on polls conducted by Vidal.) That's the highest recognition of anyone except Brown, and he's got fifty-seven percent negative. I have passed in the polls His Honor, the mayor of Fresno—whom I refer to as the Lion of Fresno— and the state senator from Cypress, and they hold office and have organiza-
25 tions.
    I must say, the Lion of Fresno roared the other day. Someone told me they read in the paper where he called me a "New York socialite." "Oh, my God," I said. "They fight dirty out there in Fresno." Then I picked up the paper and saw that he called me a "New York socialist." Well, I can live with
30 that.
E: Can the voters? Your comments favoring socialism, opposing Christianity, supporting legalized drugs, calling for a constitutional convention— these aren't things the people of Orange County are used to hearing.
V: You've got to be on the same wavelength as your constituents, though
35 nobody with ideas is ever going to be a perfect match. I think on certain major issues, like war and peace and taxation, there is an affinity. In Sacramento the other day, I spoke before a large crowd at the Comstock Club. All conservatives. And I'm talking about turning back the American empire, bringing home the troops from Europe, a freeze on nuclear weap-
40 ons—everything they're not supposed to like—and yet they were an enormously friendly crowd. They're not stupid.

E: Some political observers suggest that your campaign can only contribute to the election of another Goldwater or Reagan—a more conservative Republican.

45 *V:* I can't contribute because the polls show Brown can't win it. He's finished.

E: Two years ago, talking about the field of presidential candidates, you said, "Brown is the most interesting of the lot. He understands the world we're living in . . . ."

50 *V:* Brown had absolutely the right pitch. It's like a singer losing his voice; at a certain point, Brown just lost his nerve. I think the second presidential race was such a fiasco that he ended up looking silly. And that's one thing about politics: you can look like a monster—Nixon got away with it for a long time—but you cannot look like a fool.

55 *E:* Whatever his faults, Brown has impressed many people because he seems far more intelligent and thoughtful than most politicians.

V: From what I've seen of him, I would now say no to that. But I should have picked up on him sooner, because, when he was a groupie for McCarthy in Chicago in 1968, he was always trying to think of something to say that

60 would impress me. He would talk so rapidly, watching my eyes to make sure he'd scored. And I would torture him a bit, you know, by never acknowledging that anything had registered.

E: And now you're torturing him again.

V: Yes, yet again. I don't mind twitting him a bit. It's very bad for one's

65 character to run for office five times in eight years. All he does, really, is go around asking for money and making buzzwords, trying to stay ahead of the pack.

E: You talked before about scheduling a hearing to examine the CIA budget. Do you see yourself working successfully with archconservatives like Strom

70 Thurmond and Jeremiah Denton?

V: First of all, the Senate isn't really like that. In my grandfather's day, there was a lot of interaction; senators did control, threaten, and lobby one another. Now it's mostly enormous staffs that carry senators like little icons, as they march about with a life of their own.

75 *E:* But we're talking about getting a hearing scheduled on a subject that has resisted a thorough investigation for a long time. Staffs don't make those decisions.

V: There are many parliamentary tricks you can resort to. The best example of someone who is rather comparable to me, in a way, is Bella Abzug. Bella

80 studied parliamentary procedure, and she was invoking cloture rules from 1847. She had the place tied up in knots because she did her homework and was serious about the things she wanted to do.

E: Two years ago you said that while the United States was fast turning into Paraguay, it wasn't happening fast enough to make Ronald Reagan presi-

85 dent.

V: It happened fast enough. Welcome to Asunción.

E: Let's go through a few issues. What about the tax initiative that Californians passed in 1978—Proposition 13?

V: I like the notion of it. I was sitting right here in this house when the tax bill
90 came. It was dramatically different—the first time I'd ever seen democracy
in action in the United States. I'm all for tax revolt. I might lead one myself
one day against the Pentagon.

E: What, in your mind, would be an adequate level of defense spending?

V: It's impossible to really make sense of it, other than cutting back on new
95 systems we'll never be able to afford. The idea of a large land army is a very
sinister notion. There's no place to deploy one, except to conquer Latin
America and seize the Mexican oil fields, or to keep the turbulent cities of the
United States quiet when the bad times come. That's what they're thinking
about when they talk about the draft.

100 *E:* What about busing?

V: I think Brown versus the Board of Education [of Topeka, 1954] was one of
the great moments in American history, and I would say, by and large, it
turned out well. I don't believe absolutely in busing. I've never really been
against it, but one thing has always fascinated me. I remember talking with
105 Eleanor Roosevelt in the late Fifties about segregation. We agreed that there
was a real hatred between the races and that the only way you could get
around it was to start with babies in kindergarten. If you did it at that level, it
would work perfectly; but you're not going to get a bunch of fourteen-year-
olds, who are blazing through puberty and whose minds are already set and
110 filled with rage and adolescent paranoia, and put them together. It isn't
going to work.

E: What about the gun issue?

V: I have a notion that anyone who buys a handgun—regardless of whatever restrictions are put on them by federal, state, or municipal law—should
115 be obliged to take out liability insurance at a reasonably high premium. If
you hear that Hartford is in my corner, you'll know I've done it through
guns.

E: Poland?

V: I think the Soviet Union is going to be tied down for the next two
120 generations with a major uprising on its hands. This is very bad for the Poles
and excellent for the U.S. Between Poland and Afghanistan and a crumbling
economy, the Soviets are in worse trouble than we are. The danger, however, is that some lunatic like Caspar Weinberger will think it's a good idea to
give them a push, and they'll snap back with nuclear weapons. Then we're
125 all gone. God know they're villainous, but they're no direct threat to us at all
now.

E: Not even in El Salvador? Why are Caspar Weinberger and Alexander Haig
so upset, then?

V: They live in a world of false syllogisms. People of limited intelligence
130 who, through luck or by hook or by crook, get themselves into positions of
power can't really think. They can't even understand the consequence of
what they're saying. They're just inventing, inventing, inventing, desper-
ately trying to justify $1600 billion for the Pentagon over the next five years.
You've got to have an enemy to justify this waste, so they invent enemies.
135 It's demented. The moment I heard Nixon announce that American troops

had just entered Cambodia, but that it was not an invasion—and he wasn't even called on that sentence—I said, this is a country that is going mad.

E: You've talked about a constitutional convention. Are you among those who foresee a grave danger to the Bill of Rights?

140 V: There's a danger, but I don't think it's very grave. Put it this way: if the majority of people are going to work militantly against the Bill of Rights, then it's a very good thing to know right now, rather than let Warren Burger remove our liberties one by one—by stealth.

E: What about drugs?

145 V: I would, in order to remove crime—in order to promote better law and order, let's put it that way—I would decriminalize all victimless crimes: prostitution, gambling, and drugs. With hard drugs, I would use something on the order of the British system, wherein you get a doctor's prescription and buy them at cost. If these were poor people, I would get them off
150 [heroin] with methadone, or whatever is used. If the fix didn't cost anything, or if it cost twenty-five cents or whatever, there would be no more crime, there would be no more mafia because there would be no more profit, and there would be no more playground pushers. And, God forbid, there would be no more Bureau of Narcotics. The Bureau of Narcotics never goes
155 after the mafia, and the mafia never goes after the Bureau of Narcotics. The only victims are the people who get addicted and need money and create more victims. I say, turn it over to the doctors.

E: Are you looking forward to all of this, to campaigning, to being a senator?

V: I don't want to be a senator; I want to go to the Senate for six years. I love
160 campaigning, getting around, seeing people. Raising money is a nightmare; I don't look forward to having to ring people for money. What's enjoyable is knowing I'm going to fly to Fresno and speak to a thousand people, mill around, listen and find out things. That part is fascinating. It's very strange: either you like it or you don't. Not many people do, and those who do can't
165 get enough of it. It's like a narcotic.

E: Might you have preferred, if only for the sake of irony, to seek California's other Senate seat—the one that once belonged to Richard Nixon?

V: No. It would be thrilling, though. Ah, how I miss him.

Chapter 10

The Research Interview

The field of public opinion measurement is comparatively new. Its purpose is to find out what the public thinks on given subjects. The area selected in which to measure the attitude of the people may be as large as the United States, as small as a single town. (Williams, 1942, p. 634)

The research interview goes by many names including "public opinion polls," "organizational audits," "consumer surveys," and "market analysis." The purpose of these interviews is to gather information about a particular group of people by obtaining information from selected representatives of that group. In addition to the face-to-face interview, a number of techniques, such as questionnaires and telephone surveys, have been developed by research interviewers to gain information. All of these techniques will be discussed in this chapter.

The information interview is designed to collect information from single individuals about their own unique experiences. Research interviews, on the other hand, focus not so much on individual interviewee's responses, but the aggregate or sum of responses from many interviewees. Because of this broader emphasis and the requirement that information gathered from each individual interviewee be comparable to the information gathered from other respondents, research interviews must be very carefully planned and conducted. If they are not, the result is unsystematic information collection which is useless to the researcher.

There has been a great deal written about how to most effectively collect systematic information through interviews, questionnaires, and telephone surveys. In this chapter you will find a brief outline of how to use these techniques, the problems that can occur when doing research interviews, and some possible solutions.

RESEARCH INTERVIEW PREPARATION

In research interviewing the preparation stage is by far the most important of all. Besides all of the normal preparation that precedes most every other interview, research interviewers must carefully select respondents, prepare a detailed directive interview guide, choose and train interviewers, analyze the target community, publicize the interview project, and determine whether the interview should be face-to-face or utilize some alternative data collection method. The following section will cover these unique preparation features.

Selecting Respondents

Assuming that all the necessary background research has been done, the next preparation step is selecting respondents. In research interviewing, the individuals selected as respondents are called a *sample*. To be useful, the sample must be truly representative of the larger group to which the results will be generalized. This larger group is known as the *population*. The population may be a city, state, organization, or any large group of people. If the sample is not representative of the population, then the collected data is useless. It is your goal, as a research interviewer, to select a "population in miniature, drawn to scale." To achieve a representative sample, you must choose respondents very carefully and scientifically. The most common and long-standing approach to scientific respondent selection is found in the "Basic Instructions for Interviewers" used by the National Opinion Research Center:

> *On the assignments which you receive, the quota which you are to complete will be divided into so many men and so many women, so many people in different age groups, so many in different economic levels, etc. Within these groups, however, you select your respondents at random—in the home, on the street, in the office, in a store, etc. In order to insure that yours is a random selection of respondents, most—if possible all—of the people in your cross-section should be strangers. It is the objectivity of this method that ensures our results being representative of the country as a whole. This procedure, and the size and characteristics of our sample, are statistically sound, and have been proven so.*　　　　(Williams, 1942, p. 634)

Research interviews normally take place in the field.

This approach combines "stratified" and "random" respondent selection procedures. A *stratified* sample is one in which each characteristic considered important in the population is represented in the same proportion in the sample. If your population is the inhabitants of the U.S., and 10 percent of all people in the United States live in the Rocky Mountain Region, then 10 percent of your interviews must take place in the Rocky Mountain area. Some of the most frequent stratification characteristics are age, education, occupation, income, sex, marital status, family composition, home ownership, race, politics, and religion.

A *random* sample means that each member of the population has an equal chance of being interviewed. If it were possible, for example, to put the names of every person in the population in a hat and draw respondent names, this would be a random sample. Other ways of getting random samples are using a table of random numbers (found in most statistics books), choosing cities or blocks within cities, or blindly dialing telephone numbers (called random digit dialing–RDD). The purpose of both stratified and random respondent selection is to increase the generalizability and value of the interview results by being sure that the sample truly represents the population.

Selecting and Training Interviewers

In most types of interviews one individual is responsible for doing all the interviewing. Because of the large sample size needed, research interviewing very often requires more than one interviewer. It then becomes the responsibility of the chief researcher, often called the *project director,* to select and train additional interviewers. The way these interviewers are selected and trained very often has a great deal to do with the success or failure of the research project.

Probably the most extensive study of how much interviewer selection and training affect accurate data collection was done by Hyman and his associates at the National Opinion Research Center (1954). They found that a number of personality and situational factors can create an *interviewer effect:* the systematic introduction of error into data collection. Every project director tries to minimize the interviewer effect.

Perhaps the best way to reduce interviewer effects is to understand those qualities and attitudes which make a successful research interviewer. Although somewhat dated (Hyman, 1954), the table (figure 10.1) gives you some idea of how important various qualities and attitudes are to the success of any research project.

Other characteristics that should be taken into account when selecting interviewers are sex, age, race, ethnic background, social class, ability to follow instructions, and responsiveness to training. All of these have been found to affect the quality of information collection. It would be difficult, for example, to have women conducting interviews concerning men's shaving habits. In the same way, it would be difficult for high school students to interview retired couples concerning social security benefits. Respondents will generally be more open and honest when being interviewed by someone of their own sex, age, race, ethnic background, and social class. The ability to follow instructions and respond to training are obvious qualifications in terms of reducing preparation time. These are only a few of the many considerations which must be taken into account when

10.1 The Qualities and Attitudes of a Successful Interviewer Suggested by Thirty-eight Different Investigators

	No. of Times Mentioned
Expert knowledge in the field of investigation	5
Broad general knowledge	2
Previous knowledge of the interviewee	1
Poise, interviewer should be organized emotionally, should understand himself	5
Good personal appearance, pleasant manner, well-dressed	5
Attitude toward interviewee:	
Respect interviewee, understand his point of view, do not ridicule or talk down to him	19
Helpfulness, "here is a friend"	13
Non-moralistic or noncritical attitude, without emphasis on misdeeds of interviewee	13
Impersonal, detached, unsentimental, unsympathetic	11
Sympathetic	10
Unemotional, never feel surprise or shock	8
Responsiveness to interviewee, never bored	6
Impartial, unprejudiced	5
Be a good listener, give interviewee complete attention	4

General qualities, mentioned by only one or two persons:
Health, drive, perseverance, humor, patience, jollying, cheerfulness, punctuality, courage, business-likeness, ease in talking

"The Qualities and Attitudes of a Successful Interview, etc." From Herbert H. Hyman, *Interviewing in Social Research*, p. 287. Copyright 1954 by The University of Chicago.

selecting research interviewers. Entire volumes have been devoted to this important subject.

The number of interviewers needed will depend upon the length of each interview, the number of interviews to be conducted, the location of respondents, and the total time alloted for completion of the study. On the average, interviewers have trouble doing more than ten to fifteen thirty-minute interviews per day. Beyond that point fatigue and boredom can cause error.

Regardless of whether beginners or seasoned veterans are chosen, some training is necessary for almost any research interview project. Very elaborate systems of interviewer training have been developed. The Survey Research Center, part of the Institute for Social Research at Ann Arbor, Michigan, for example, uses a training program based on coded audiotape recordings of interviewer behavior.

Overall, the coding system indicates whether questions were asked correctly or incorrectly, whether probes were non-directive or directive, whether responses were summarized accurately or inaccurately, and whether various other behaviors were appropriate or inappropriate. The coded results reflect the degree to which the interviewer employs the methods in which he has been trained. That is, an "incorrect" or "inappropriate" behavior is defined as one which the interviewer has been trained to avoid.

This system is useful in three ways:

1. *In initial training, it teaches the novice interviewer which interviewing techniques are acceptable and which are not.*
2. *It serves as a basis for interviewers and supervisors to review work in the field by coding interviews and discussing the problems which the coding reveals.*
3. *It provides an assessment of an interviewer's performance, which can be compared both with the performances of other interviewers and with the individual's own performances during other interviews. In order to make such comparisons, the distribution of good and poor behavior for each interviewer is compared with the distribution for all interviewers.*

(Cannell, Lawson, and Hausser, 1975, p. 3)

The purpose of interviewer training is not only to provide practice interviews and insure common behaviors for all interviewers but also to motivate. Each member of the interview research team should feel they are doing something important. Interviewers who aren't motivated will often fabricate results. Motivation is provided by explaining the entire purpose and method of the project. If all people involved know how their part fits into the entire research scheme, they are prone to uphold their part of the process. They feel that others depend on them for overall success and are more likely to conduct interviews in the prescribed manner. Once the training is completed each successful trainee is certified for work as a member of the interview research team. Training does not necessarily stop at this point, however, since continual observation and analysis of interviewer performance is usually a part of most successful research interview projects.

Community Analysis and Publicity

Just as it is important for interviewers to analyze potential interviewees, it is necessary for research interviewers to understand the community where potential interviewees live. Research is conducted within the limitations of the neighborhood, community, or culture of the study population. Some communities are hostile to research interviews while others are more receptive to such projects. Interviews conducted in a prison or ghetto will generally encounter less cooperation, for example, than those conducted with members of service organizations or in suburban neighborhoods. When interviews must take place in a hostile environment, interviewers must be trained to handle various forms of resistance.

The research project director and the interviewers should be familiar with the community in which the interviews will take place and the reasons for resistance.

A community can be prepared for research interviews and thus increase cooperation by using *pre-interview publicity*. Articles in local newspapers, radio spots, and television advertisements can publicize upcoming research interviews and increase credibility. Another way of publicizing a research interview is to send each potential respondent a notice or to telephone perspective respondents and ask their permission ahead of time. Studies of telephone pre-notification, for example, show that the return rate for mailed questionnaires increased from 26.2% to 46.3% in one study and from 20.5% to 68.2% in another. (Jolson, 1977, p. 78). Any reasonable means that can be used to increase respondent cooperation should be employed in preparing for research interviews.

Face-to-Face Versus Other Information-Gathering Techniques

Much has been written on the advantages and disadvantages of face-to-face research interviews. They are on the decline for several reasons. First, it is becoming more expensive to conduct large-scale face-to-face research interviews. Second, researchers are finding it more and more difficult to find cooperative respondents. This is due not only to the fact that respondents are becoming less cooperative in general, but also because of the increasing number of households where both adults are employed. Sometimes interviewers must call back several times before the selected respondent can be contacted. Third, the number of willing, competent, and inexpensive interviewers is decreasing. Interviewing is a highly skilled and difficult activity, especially when done in a climate of increasing hostility. Interviewers must be willing to work at night and on weekends to contact working respondents. In some neighborhoods this can be dangerous. In many cases the low pay for such work is not considered worth the risk.

These difficulties have caused face-to-face research interview project directors to compromise in both the design and execution of their studies. Smaller sample sizes, "safe" but unrepresentative communities, and the switch to alternative means of information gathering are a few of the changes they have made. When combined with the increasing sophistication of data collection techniques, as well as evidence that the results are not that much different from those obtained through face-to-face interviews, it is no wonder that they are being used more often. The following is a comparison of telephone and face-to-face interview findings:

1. *The quality of data gained on complex attitudinal and knowledge items is the same with both interviewing methods.*
2. *The quality of data on personal items is about the same, with some respondents preferring the anonymity of the telephone.*
3. *Respondents are somewhat more likely to give socially acceptable answers in face-to-face interviews.*
4. *The interviewee rate of refusal to take part in or to complete interviews running forty-five minutes or longer is about the same with either method.*
5. *Interviewees in certain neighborhoods prefer telephone interviews because they do not want to open their doors to strangers.*

6. *Potential interviewees without telephones can be interviewed face-to-face without distorting data because of mixture of methods.*
7. *Telephone interviews remove dress, appearance, and nonverbal communications as potential biasing factors.*
8. *Interviewer preference for telephone and face-to-face interviews is nearly the same.*

(Stewart and Cash, 1982, p. 120)

It may not be too long before the face-to-face research interview is a thing of the past. Its use may be limited to captive populations such as employees within organizations.

The choosing of respondents, selection and training of interviewers, community analysis and publicity, and the decison of whether to use face-to-face or other means of information collection are all important aspects of research interview preparation. But they are only a small part of what must be taken into account in preparing for research interviews. Other aspects of research interview preparation will be discussed in the following section on the research interview guide.

THE RESEARCH INTERVIEW GUIDE

The primary concerns in research interview guide preparation are reliability and validity. *Reliability* refers to the consistency or stability of interview guide questions. A reliable interview guide is one where each question is interpreted in the same way by different interviewees, by the same interviewee seeing or hearing a question at different times, or by different interviewers asking the same question. A reliable interview guide will elicit comparable information from each interview. Interview guide *validity* refers to whether or not the questions elicit accurate information. Questions are valid if the information collected is a true and honest reflection of the respondent's attitudes, beliefs, behavior, or attributes.

In order to achieve both reliability and validity, researchers tend to develop highly structured interview guides. All of the questions and their sequence are carefully prepared. This is done to assure that each respondent gets every question in exactly the same manner as every other respondent. This is important whether the interview is face-to-face, over the telephone, or presented on a questionnaire. This means that much time and effort must go into research interview guide construction. There is little or no difference between the interview guides that are used in face-to-face, telephone, or written interviews. With minor modifications, the guide marked figure 10.2 could be used for any research information gathering approach.

RESEARCH INTERVIEW GUIDE EXERCISE

Directions: Note the changes you would make in this guide.

10.2 Sample Research Interview Guide

(Space for recording information has been omitted)

Hello, I'm _____ , from _____ .
We are conducting a survey to obtain homeowners' opinions about solar energy—if you have a few minutes, I'd like to ask you some questions, such as:

Do you own or rent your home?   Own . . . . . (continue)

Rent . . . . (terminate)

Do you currently own any solar energy systems?   Yes . . . . (terminate)

No . . . . (continue)

Can you name the ways that solar energy can be used in the home?

_____ Heating swimming pools

_____ Heating hot tubs or spas

_____ Heating your home

_____ Heating hot water for domestic use

_____ Solar greenhouse

_____ Solariums

_____ Cooling the home/air conditioning

_____ Electricity for lights and cooking

_____ Passive dehydration

What other ways have you heard of for using solar energy?

Have you seen any solar equipment in operation? (If so, what?)

How do you personally feel about solar energy, on a scale of 1 to 5 with one being very favorable, 3 neutral, and 5 completely unfavorable?

How do you think most of your friends and coworkers feel about solar energy using the same scale of 1 to 5?

At present, most people don't own solar energy systems. What do you think are the most important reasons that people have not purchased solar equipment for their homes? Can you think of any other reasons?

What are the most important reasons that you can think of *for* installing a solar energy system? Can you think of any other reasons?

Have you personally ever considered purchasing or building solar energy equipment? Yes _____ No _____ (Why or why not?)

What is your occupation?

What is your spouse's occupation?

Would you describe your combined income as:

_____ lower class

_____ lower middle class

_____ middle class

_____ upper middle class

_____ upper class

Thank you very much for your cooperation!

Respondent identification number: _____

Respondent address: _____

You will note in this example, more use is made of closed questions than most other types of interviews. This is done so the same information is gained from all interviewees. The questions must also be asked in the same order for each respondent. Question sequence can influence responses. In order to insure that the guide gets valid and consistent responses from all interviewees, it is a common practice to pre-test or pilot test them. A *pilot test* involves interviewing people similar to those included in the sample, but who will not be part of the sample. Pilot testing helps researchers determine if interviewees understand what information is wanted from each question, if any questions are perceived negatively, if some questions overlap, if the questions are clear, if the response categories are complete, and if anything else can be done to help improve the validity or reliability of the guide. After pilot testing, the guide is refined and put in final form.

The preceding comments and example make research interview guide preparation seem easy. In fact, it is a very difficult and time-consuming aspect of research interview preparation. There has been more research done on how to prepare a research guide, especially questionnaires, than any other type of interview guide. Some of the specific suggestions made have been: making the guide appealing to the eye and easy to complete; numbering items and pages; putting titles and headings in bold type; using clear instructions and examples where possible; grouping similar items and topics together; putting easy items at the beginning and end; avoiding words like "questionnaire" or "checklist"; specifying the type of information desired; skipping lines or marking the guide for easy reading; including "other," "don't know," and "comments" sections where useful; checking to see if response options are complete, exclusive, and independent; and carefully checking wording to be sure it is purposeful, clear, natural, brief, thoughtprovoking, limited in scope, and unbiased. Before developing an actual research interview guide, you should consult one of the many references listed in the bibliography.

At this point, some comment should be made regarding how to stimulate interviewee responses. Low response rate is one of the biggest obstacles that must be overcome by research interviewers using face-to-face, telephone, or questionnaire formats. In many projects, a response rate of 50 percent or one-half of the chosen sample is considered a "good" response. There are some researchers, especially those using questionnaires, that consider response rates as low as 30 percent as adequate. You must, therefore, do everything possible to improve response rate. If the response rate is too low you cannot be certain that the entire population is accurately represented.

A low response rate cannot be counteracted by increasing the sample size. The people who do respond must be truly representative of the population. To increase responses to all forms of research interviews you can 1) personalize the interview in some way, such as addressing cover letters personally or using a hand written signature; 2) assure anonymity and confidentiality by mentioning you will not release respondent names or asking respondents not to sign the questionnaire; and 3) offer some form of "incentive" such as money or a gift with the questionnaire or promise something for completing the interview. All of these techniques have been used with varying degrees of success. The tactics chosen will depend a great deal upon the nature of the respondents selected as well as the purpose, length, and difficulty of the interview. It is important, however, that some consideration be given to increasing research interview response rate.

RESEARCH INTERVIEW OPENING

In the past, many researchers have depended upon a "canned" introduction. In the case of questionnaire cover letters, the introduction must be canned. For telephone and face-to-face research interviews, however, a canned introduction often sounds stilted and awkward. The main purpose of the opening is to gain respondent cooperation. The best way to accomplish that purpose is to make the opening as short and positive as possible. In this way you get to the first interview question as quickly as possible and give respondents little chance to resist. Two or three sentences which identify the sponsor, interviewer, and purpose of the interview are usually sufficient. The following is an example of such an introduction:

> Good morning, my name is Bob Brown, and I'm conducting an interview for radio station WXYZ on listener preferences. I'd like to get your response to a few questions such as, "Where do you get most of your news, from the radio, from television, or in the newspapers?"

In most cases such an opening will elicit a response to the question rather than some form of resistance. Your voice should indicate that you are doing something you find interesting and that the respondent will enjoy. If you do encounter resistance you may have to explain that you are not "selling something," convince respondents that they are qualified to answer your questions, or mention that the interview will not take too much of their time. Do whatever you feel is necessary to convince respondents to take part in the interview.

Climate setting is not as important in research interviewing as in other forms of interviewing. There is no question that rapport influences whether or not interviewees agree to respond to your questions, but this is not something you develop through idle chit-chat. Rapport comes as an initial impression from your dress, manner of speaking, personality, and attitude. Spending too much time trying to develop rapport only gives respondents time to resist. So the research interview opening is short and to the point.

RESEARCH INTERVIEW QUESTIONING AND RESPONDING

Even though research questions are usually totally prepared before conducting the interview, the way they are asked can also affect the responses. Interviewers must ask questions in the same manner every time. The following table (10.3) used to train interviewers at the Institute for Social Research, will give you some idea of appropriate and inappropriate ways of asking research interview questions. You must be as neutral as possible, asking each question exactly as it is worded in the interview guide without any verbal or nonverbal changes whatsoever.

10.3 Survey Research Center Reduced Code

Code	Definition
1—Correct Question Asking	Interviewer reads question either exactly as printed on the questionnaire or with minor modifications which do not alter the frame of reference
2—Incorrect Question Asking	Interviewer either significantly alters part of question, or omits part of question, or replaces question with own statement, or reads question which should have been skipped
3—Probes or Clarifies Non-directively	Interviewer either makes up in own words a probe which is non-directive, repeats all or part of either question or respondent's answer in a non-directive manner, or confirms a frame of reference for respondent correctly
4—Probes or Clarifies Directively	Interviewer either makes up probe which is directive, repeats question or respondent's answer incorrectly, gives a directive introduction, or confirms a frame of reference incorrectly
5—Other Appropriate Behavior	Interviewer gives either acceptable task-oriented clarification or other appropriate feedback
6—Other Inappropriate Behavior	Interviewer either interrupts respondent, or gives personal opinion, or records responses incorrectly on questionnaire
7—Non-recorded Activity	Interviewer either omits a question, or there is missing data
8—Pace	Interviewer conducts interview either too slowly or too rapidly
9—Background of Study	Interviewer mentions own name, study sponsorship, respondent selection, anonymity, purpose of study

From Charles F. Cannell, et al., *A Technique for Evaluating Interviewer Performance*, p. 18. © 1975 Institute for Social Research of The University of Michigan.

If respondents ask for an explanation of a question, you simply repeat the question exactly as it is worded. Rephrasing, changing, or omitting questions is taboo. Even the simplest question change could affect the reliability and validity of the interview guide. Slight changes in tone of voice, facial expression, posture, or manner can lead to bias and error.

This is not meant to suggest that research interview questioning should be mechanical and "dead pan" serious. Questioning should be friendly and conversational, but the same for each interviewee. There are some research projects which give interviewers more leeway in questioning, but all research directors attempt to maintain as much uniformity as possible.

Responding to a research interview is usually straightforward. The main determination is whether you, the potential interviewee, want to answer the questions or not. You always have the right to decline. If you think you could not be completely honest in your answers, you should decline. If you do accept, you should be as accurate and complete as the interviewer desires. Remember, the results of such research interviews are usually designed to help you and others like you. You represent many people in the population.

RESEARCH INTERVIEW PROBING

As was mentioned earlier, the amount of probing allowed depends on the design and purpose of the interview. Very strict research projects allow little or no probing. These directors feel that probes are likely to introduce error into the data collection. In other research interviews, a certain amount of leeway is allowed. Some guides have acceptable probes actually written into them. Others use the word "Why?" to indicate that probes are acceptable. The interviewer must use an appropriate probe whenever the question "Why?" appears on the guide. Examples of such probes are "What is your main reason for giving that response?" "May I ask you why you think that way?" or "Could you explain your answer?" Few, if any, research interviews allow unlimited probing. For most, the number and types of probes are severely limited in both the interview guide and interviewer training.

The one time when probing is allowed in almost all research interviews is when respondents reply, "No opinion" or "Don't know." It is the interviewer's responsibility to determine whether or not they really do have "no opinion" or whether that response is being used to avoid threatening or embarrassing information. Sometimes interviewees respond with, "Well, I—I—I, I don't know . . . ." They may be "buying time" in order to collect their thoughts. If you think this is the case, use a silent probe, and do not record the "Don't know" answer immediately. In other cases, a more direct probe such as "You really haven't made up your mind?" is useful in determining the intent of a "Don't know" comment. Novices record a great many "Don't know" answers, whereas more experienced research interviewers probe to determine if a "No opinion" or "Don't know" response is really an accurate reflection of a respondent's feelings.

RESEARCH INTERVIEW LISTENING AND RECORDING

After preparation, the most crucial element of good research interviewing is the ability to listen and record responses accurately. Most research interview guides require the checking of an appropriate response category. Although this sounds easy, it is sometimes extremely difficult. Unless the list of possible answers is included as part of the question, respondents are likely to give extended answers which you must carefully analyze to check the proper response category. Often, a respondent answer fits into more than one category. Careful listening is required to determine which is the most appropriate category.

When open questions are used, it is your responsibility to record the main idea contained in each interviewee answer. Open questions often accompany closed questions to determine why respondents answered in the way they did.

Sometimes you will record respondent answers verbatim. In most cases this does not mean that you include every word and phrase used, but you must try to include as much of a respondent's language as possible. Sometimes even the way an interviewee answers a question can change the meaning and must be recorded. Many project directors warn against trying to paraphrase or interpret a response. They demand careful listening, short memorization, and accurate recording. Any special information is noted in the space labeled "comments" on the interview guide. The shades of meaning that appear on an interview guide very often make the difference between a good and poor research interviewer. The information that appears in the "comments" section can be more illuminating than that which appears in the predetermined categories. This extra information can only be gained if you are listening and recording carefully. The key to good research interview listening and recording is constantly focusing your attention on the respondent and not letting your mind wander or become fatigued.

RESEARCH INTERVIEW CONCLUDING

Closing a research interview is similar to its opening. It should be fairly brief and friendly. You should express appreciation for cooperation, and if time permits and a respondent asks, explain the purpose of the interview in detail. Closings must be positive and predispose interviewees to welcome and be just as cooperative with future research interviewers. The general climate for research interviewing is often hostile, and a great deal of that hostility is the result of previous research interviewers leaving respondents bitter and nonreceptive.

As each interview is completed, the project director should check it to be sure the initials of the interviewer appear in the indicated space and that all of the questions have been answered properly. A few omissions or problems can throw off the results. Both the interviewer and supervisor must be sure that the guide— be it a questionnaire, telephone survey, or interview—is completed properly before it is returned to the central office for tabulation and analysis.

Another aspect of closing a research interview involves checking to make sure that the interviewers have been honest, accurate, and conscientious in their work. The last questions on most research interview guides ask for the respondent's name and address. If an interviewee asks why the name and address is necessary, you should explain that the sponsoring group will check the accuracy of responses by sending out postcards or making telephone calls. Such checks are done not only to make sure that the questions were asked, but also to be sure the interviewer was courteous and professional. Follow-up phone calls or postcards are absolutely necessary to ensure the validity and reliability of interviews. This, in conjunction with close supervision, make for more professional research projects.

The next step is the tabulation and analysis of results. Tabulation and analysis are fairly easy if the project director has spent some time planning how to tabulate and analyze the data during the preparation stage. Very often the people responsible for tabulation and analysis are brought into the planning process very early. This eliminates many problems—without their early involvement much information may be lost.

Research interviews usually require computer-assisted tabulation and analysis of results.

Many times analysis requires the use of a computer. Depending upon the computer program which will be used for the analysis, various types of data coding systems can be used. In some cases, data tabulation can be done directly from the interview guide. This is especially true when only closed questions are used. When open questions are used, some content analysis may be needed to code the information. One way of doing content analysis is to establish *ad hoc categories;* that is, categories developed after reading a great many interviewee responses and grouping those that are similar. Once the content categories are developed, researchers go back and determine where each open response fits best. The reliability of categories should be checked to be sure that each answer is properly analyzed and coded. Once the coding has been done and the information fed into the computer, totals and percentages are available very rapidly.

Once the statistics are available, someone should determine what they actually mean with regard to the project purpose. This analysis may be done by the project director or by the sponsoring group. Some researchers prefer not to draw conclusions but simply turn over the information to the agency or person which commissioned and paid for it. In other cases the project director is asked to analyze the data and turn in a report of the final conclusions. If such is the case, the final report must be as unbiased as possible. It is very easy for research interviewers to either intentionally or unintentionally distort results in order to confirm their own point of view. Sometimes such distortion occurs in order to please the sponsoring group. Regardless of the reason, this is unethical.

If respondents have been promised anonymity and confidentiality, it is your responsibility to be sure that all interviewee-specific information has been destroyed and does not appear on the research report. Once the report has been completed and checked for accuracy it should be distributed as soon as possible. This signals the end of the research interview.

SUMMARY

The term research interview has been used in this chapter to refer to all forms of systematic data collection. Its main purpose is to collect information from a sample of respondents representative of a larger population. In these interviews, the preparation, interview guide development, and listening/recording stages take on special importance. Preparation involves selecting respondents, selecting and training interviewers, analyzing and preparing the environment, and determining which information gathering technique to use. Reliability and validity are the goals in interview guide preparation. This is assured with careful topic and question construction, pilot testing, and working to increase response rate. Careful and accurate listening and recording are also necessary to obtain reliable and valid results.

Research interview opening, questioning, probing, and closing are all predetermined and prescribed before the first interview begins. Each should be friendly but to the point and standardized. This approach is designed to eliminate the interviewer effect. Although somewhat specialized, the research interview, in all of its forms, will continue to be used to gather information about all of us. In fact, this information is becoming more important to politicians, factory owners, marketing executives, educators, and many others as modern society becomes more complex and human behavior more difficult to understand.

ACTIVITIES

Activity #1

Directions: Perhaps the most carefully prepared, distributed, and analyzed research interview of all is the U.S. census. Congress directed Secretary of State Thomas Jefferson to conduct the first census in 1790. United States marshals and their assistants were the first census takers and were paid between one-third cent and two cents for every inhabitant counted in the sixteen states. The first census consisted of five questions: number of free white males 16 years of age or older, number of free white males under 16 years, number of free white females, number of other free persons, and number of slaves. The count took 18 months and showed a population of less than four million. The Bureau of the Census now does both the decennial census and interim censuses and surveys to maintain current information. The 1980 census, illustrated and annotated on pages 242–243, was expected to count approximately 222 million people and 86 million housing units. Its purpose is still the same: to provide a basis for fair apportionment of seats in the House of Representatives. However, now it also does more; it helps government assess the people's needs and influences economic, educational, employment, military, human welfare, business, energy, and international relations decisions. The census could be taken over the telephone or face-to-face, and sometimes it is with people who cannot read. Carefully examine the census information provided. Why do you think the changes discussed in this report were made? Are there any ways to improve the questions asked or the response options? What are some of the good points about this research interview?

Here are the **QUESTIONS** ↓	These are the columns for **ANSWERS** ➡ *Please fill one column for each person listed in Question 1.*	**PERSON in column 1**
		Last name

2. How is this person related to the person in column 1?

Fill one circle.

If "Other relative" of person in column 1, give exact relationship, such as mother-in-law, niece, grandson, etc.

<u>START</u> *in this column with the household member (or one of the members) in whose name the home is owned or rented. If there is no such person, start in this column with any adult household member.*

---

3. Sex *Fill one circle.*

○ Male ■ ○ Female

---

4. Is this person —

Fill one circle.

○ White ○ Asian Indian
○ Black or Negro ○ Hawaiian
○ Japanese ○ Guamanian
○ Chinese ○ Samoan
○ Filipino ○ Eskimo
○ Korean ○ Aleut
○ Vietnamese ○ Other — *Specify*
○ Indian (Amer.)
Print
tribe ➡ _ _ _ _ _ _ _ _ _ _ _

---

5. Age, and month and year of birth

a. Print age at last birthday.

b. Print month and fill one circle.

c. Print year in the spaces, and fill one circle below each number.

a. Age at last birthday

b. Month of birth

○ Jan.—Mar.
○ Apr.—June
○ July—Sept.
○ Oct.—Dec.

c. Year of birth

1

1 ● 8 ○ Ø ○ Ø ○
9 ○ 1 ○ 1 ○
2 ○ 2 ○
3 ○ 3 ○
4 ○ 4 ○
5 ○ 5 ○
6 ○ 6 ○
7 ○ 7 ○
8 ○ 8 ○
9 ○ 9 ○

---

6. Marital status

Fill one circle.

○ Now married ○ Separated
○ Widowed ○ Never married
○ Divorced

---

7. Is this person of Spanish/Hispanic origin or descent?

Fill one circle.

○ No (not Spanish/Hispanic)
○ Yes, Mexican, Mexican-Amer., Chicano
○ Yes, Puerto Rican ■
○ Yes, Cuban
○ Yes, other Spanish/Hispanic

---

8. <u>Since February 1, 1980</u>, has this person attended regular school or college at any time? *Fill one circle. Count nursery school, kindergarten, elementary school and schooling which leads to a high school diploma or college degree.*

○ No, has not attended since February 1
○ Yes, public school, public college
○ Yes, private, church-related
○ Yes, private, not church-related

Commentary on U.S. Census Questions

2.   provides information on type of household (husband/wife, other type of family, or single person households) and the number of persons in the household. Because of changes in society since 1970, the concept of household "head" has been replaced with that of a reference person in whose name the dwelling unit is owned or rented. This key change means data will not be exactly comparable to "male-headed" or "female-headed" household data from the 1970 Census, but it will be easy to identify families and other types of households. In many tabulations characteristics will be shown for both husband and wife where they were shown previously only for the head of family households.

The questionnaire has space for up to seven household members to provide answers. We show only column 1. In question 2, columns 2 through 7 have the following language instead of the "Start in this column" language: "If relative of person in column 1: Husband/wife; Son/daughter; Brother/sister; Father/mother; Other relative (specify). If not related to person in column 1: Roomer, boarder; Partner, roommate; Paid employee; Other nonrelative (specify)."

Two of the categories are new: "Partner, roommate" and "Paid employee." The first was added to obtain statistics on the growing number of people who live together without being married.

3.   same as in 1970.

4.   expands the possible answers about race from nine in 1970 to 15. As a result we can expect a few Samoans to turn up in places like Kansas City, just because that alternative is listed. The expansion is the result of growing ethnic awareness, but note that the word "race" does not appear.

5.   same as in 1970.

6.   same as in 1970.

7.   for the first time asks all Americans a single question about Spanish origin. These data will not be comparable with previous censuses. In 1970, this question was asked of a maximum of 15 percent of the population, and the data were tabulated differently for different regions of the country. This question ends the population questions asked of all Americans. The next three questions appear on the long form questionnaire only.

8.   similar to 1970, but what was previously called "parochial" schools is now called "church related."

Activity #2

Directions: Arrange an interview with one of the local organizations in your community who commonly do research interviews. Various departments in a college, the local chamber of commerce, radio and television stations, newspapers, businesses, and your state and local governments all do such interviews. Ask the person you visit how they go about preparing for, conducting, and analyzing their information gathering projects. See if you can obtain copies of recent research interview guides as well as the results. Analyze the information and write a paper detailing what you consider to be the strengths and weaknesses of their efforts. Be sure to critically analyze the questions asked and the response categories provided.

Activity #3

Directions: Select one of the following hypothetical cases and role-play it, being sure to use the concepts and skills discussed in this and previous chapters. These cases merely describe a common research interview situation. You are free to add any other information you like to make the role-play better. Try to make the interview as realistic as possible.

PUBLIC OPINION POLL: *Robert Saxton* is planning to run for city council. First, however, he decides to find out what issues are foremost on the voter's minds. He has some ideas already such as sales taxes, street maintenance, garbage collection, and zoning, but he wants more specific information. He decides to randomly select neighborhoods and go door-to-door and talk with the voters. He makes up a very brief guide listing some specific areas he'd like information on, but hopes to use a lot of nondirective questions as well. Bob is approaching his first house.

ORGANIZATIONAL AUDIT: *Sara Sharpe* is the Personnel Director for a large manufacturing company. Recently she has been hearing reports that morale is low in various parts of the organization. She decides to do a formal audit. She plans to develop an interview guide which asks people how they see their role in the organization, how that role fits with management's objectives, their personal objectives, the overall communication climate in the organization, the sources of conflict, and what they would suggest to improve morale. She must complete a draft of the questionnaire and pilot test it on several employees.

CONSUMER SURVEY: *Tom Richards* works for The Consumer Laboratory. He has just been given an assignment: determine why increasing numbers of grocery shoppers are buying generic products rather than name brands. He decides that a telephone survey would probably be the most efficient way to collect the information. He plans on getting at the information quickly, no more than five minutes on the phone and using a nationwide sample. He develops a five-question interview guide and set of instructions for the interviewers he will hire to do the phoning. He must now go about selecting interviewers and training them. Once that is done, he will monitor calls by various interviewers to see how things are going. He hopes to have an answer for his superiors within the month.

Chapter 11

The Selection Interview

Ten applications for a well-paying job lie on my desk. They represent the best candidates of some one hundred persons who threw their hats in the ring. Each of these finalists is qualified for the position. Which one of the ten will get the job? The one who is most effective in the interview. (Komar, 1979, p. 11)

There has probably been more written about the selection interview than almost any other type of interview discussed in this book. Several terms have been used to designate it, including "employment," "recruitment," "screening," "placement," "assessment," "hiring," "job," and "evaluation" interviews. No matter what they are called, however, the primary purpose of a selection interview remains fairly constant—to determine the appropriateness of a candidate for a particular job.

Selection interviewing is a process of mutual assessment on the part of *both* interviewers and interviewees. Not only are employers selecting employees, but candidates are also selecting an employer. These interviews are heavily stressed in interviewing books because they are of such immediate concern to students, many of whom will be looking for their first permanent job after leaving college. On the whole, however, selection interviewing plays a much less important role throughout a person's lifetime than do many of the other types of interviews. Once an applicant has found a job, performance, counseling, and discipline interviews become much more important, usually taking place at least a few times per year.

The entire selection process normally includes more than just an interview. Various kinds of tests—personality, aptitude, achievement, and performance— as well as application forms and reference checks are usually included as part of the total selection procedure. Even the selection interview itself can include as many as three or four different types of interviews. An initial *screening* interview determines whether applicants meet the minimum qualifications for a job. If they do, a more comprehensive *assessment* interview is usually conducted. These first two steps may be individual or group interviews and are usually conducted by individuals directly involved in the hiring decision. Figure 11.1 is a summary of the selection procedures used by a major organization.

Many hiring organizations are moving toward a more structured process

11.1 Employment Flow Chart Kendall Mills, Division of the Kendall Company

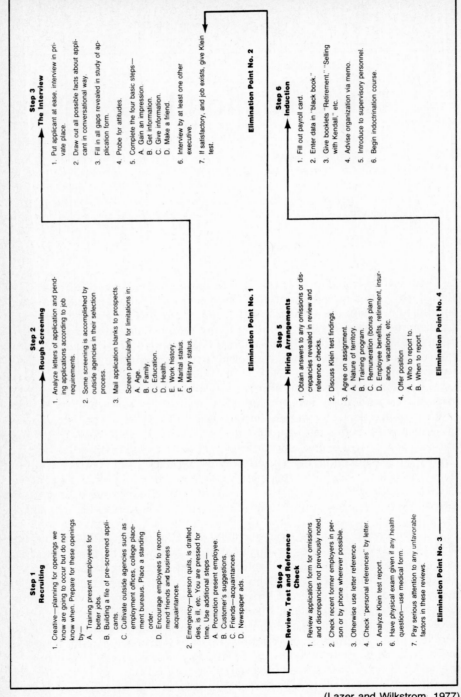

Step 1
Recruiting

1. Creative—planning for openings we know are going to occur but do not know when. Prepare for these openings by—
   A. Training present employees for better jobs.
   B. Building a file of pre-screened applicants.
   C. Cultivate outside agencies such as employment offices, college placement bureaus. Place a standing order.
   D. Encourage employees to recommend friends and business acquaintances.
2. Emergency—person quits, is drafted, dies, is ill, etc. You are pressed for time. Use additional steps—
   A. Promotion present employee.
   B. Customer's suggestions.
   C. Friends—acquaintances.
   D. Newspaper ads.

Step 2
Rough Screening

1. Analyze letters of application and pending applications according to job requirements.
2. Some screening is accomplished by outside agencies in their selection process.
3. Mail application blanks to prospects.

   Screen particularly for limitations in:
   A. Age.
   B. Family.
   C. Education.
   D. Health.
   E. Work history.
   F. Marital status.
   G. Military status.

Elimination Point No. 1

Step 3
The Interview

1. Put applicant at ease, interview in private place.
2. Draw out all possible facts about applicant in conversational way.
3. Fill in all gaps revealed in study of application form.
4. Probe for attitudes.
5. Complete the four basic steps—
   A. Gain an impression.
   B. Get information.
   C. Give information.
   D. Make a friend.
6. Interview by at least one other executive.
7. If satisfactory, and job exists, give Klein test.

Elimination Point No. 2

Step 4
Review, Test and Reference Check

1. Review application form for omissions and discrepancies not previously noted.
2. Check recent former employers in person or by phone wherever possible.
3. Otherwise use letter reference.
4. Check "personal references" by letter.
5. Analyze Klein test report.
6. Have physical exam given if any health question—use medical form.
7. Pay serious attention to any unfavorable factors in these reviews.

Elimination Point No. 3

Step 5
Hiring Arrangements

1. Obtain answers to any omissions or discrepancies revealed in review and reference checks.
2. Discuss Klein test findings.
3. Agree on assignment.
   A. Nature of territory.
   B. Training program.
   C. Remuneration (bonus plan)
   D. Employee benefits, retirement, insurance, vacations, etc.
4. Offer position
   A. Who to report to.
   B. When to report.

Elimination Point No. 4

Step 6
Induction

1. Fill out payroll card.
2. Enter data in "black book."
3. Give booklets "Retirement," "Selling with Kendall," etc.
4. Advise organization via memo.
5. Introduce to supervisory personnel.
6. Begin indoctrination course.

(Lazer and Wilkstrom, 1977)

called the *assessment center,* a place where employees and potential employees are given standardized exercises and tests designed to determine their skill and knowledge. Assessment centers are treated in a number of good books and articles which discuss their advantages and disadvantages as well as the ways and means of using them effectively. Many of these references can be found in the bibliography. Briefly, the strengths of an assessment center lie in its ability to measure administrative and organizational skills, identify emerging leaders, help individuals identify their weaknesses, aid in correcting these weaknesses, help evaluate existing training and development programs, improve group participation and problem solving techniques, and assess an individual's interpersonal behavior. Probably the biggest reason many companies are using assessment centers is that they have been identified by the Equal Employment Opportunity Commission (EEOC) as an *aid* in demonstrating affirmative action. On the other hand, there are also some drawbacks in assessment centers, such as the cost ($50–$1,000 per participant), the need to customize them for particular positions and organizations, the effect they have on people who have to take the tests, and their lack of demonstrated reliability and validity. The assessment center approach to employee selection is still in the testing stage.

Why have many organizations decided to use other procedures in conjunction with or as an alternative to selection interviews? In most cases they have done so because of some inherent weaknesses in the nature of interviews. Often, selection interviewers do not seek the information which distinguishes successful and unsuccessful employees. While questioning, they sometimes overlap some areas and miss others completely. When they do receive necessary information, they often misinterpret it. There is solid evidence that bias and stereotypes strongly affect interviewer judgments, and they seem more alert to negative rather than positive information. This is due, in part, to the fact that they are often judged not on the good people they pass over, but on the poor people they hire. Their judgments are often based on the quality of other candidates interviewed and not on the qualifications of each individual candidate for the job. These are only a few of the problems and weaknesses of the selection interview. You will discover others as you continue to read this chapter.

There is no question that the interview is not a perfect method of selecting employees. But if it is conducted properly, most of the problems and limitations can be overcome, and the interview's ability to determine the applicant's background and competence, ability to fit in, compatibility with other employees, and growth potential, and the ability of the company to satisfy the applicant far outweigh the limitations of the process. In this chapter you will learn some ways of conducting and responding in high-quality selection interviews.

SELECTION INTERVIEW PREPARATION

Just as with the research interview, the selection interview involves a great deal of preparation. Unlike the research interview, however, selection interviews demand preparation on the part of both participants. In this section the preparation requirements for selection interviewers and interviewees will be discussed separately.

Interviewer Preparation

The first thing to do, as a selection interviewer, is become fully acquainted with all aspects of your own organization which may interest a respondent. This includes knowing the organization's philosophy, corporate structure, history, financial standing, operations, products, benefits, and anything else of a general nature which can help you sell the company to an applicant or answer an applicant's questions. A good interviewee will have gathered some of this information and will be prepared to question many of these areas. Nothing makes interviewers look more inept than to be unable to answer simple questions regarding the organization which they represent.

The second preparation step is to do an intensive *job analysis*—obtain a detailed job description, observe job performance first hand, and talk with various people regarding the job. Once you have done that, your information should be checked for accuracy by competent individuals who know the job. Figure 11.2 is an example of a typical job analysis form.

11.2 Sample Job Analysis Form

POSITION TITLE:
REQUIREMENTS:
  Education:
  Experience:
    1. Essential:
    2. Desirable:
POSITION DESCRIPTION:
    1. What does the employee do?
    2. What is the employee's schedule?
    3. How closely is the employee supervised?
    4. Nature and amount of contact with other departments, customers/clients, etc.
    5. What is the nature of the surrounding environment? (high/low pressure, fast/slow pace, etc.)
    6. Is the employee required to make decisions or set policy?
PERSONAL REQUIREMENTS:
    1. What personal characteristics or attributes does an employee need to fill this position? (initiative, cooperation, responsibility, self-control, self-expression, integrity, maturity, etc.)
    2. Is growth potential important for this position?
COMPENSATION FACTORS:
    1. Salary
    2. Fringe benefits
MISCELLANEOUS:

It is usually impossible to question respondents fully in one or even several interviews. What you need to do is determine the critical requirements of the job. The *critical requirements* of any job are those skills or personality factors which seem to differentiate between people who succeed or fail at it. There are usually five or six critical requirements for any position. This is where the advice of individuals more knowledgeable about the job is extremely useful. One approach is to go through each of the factors isolated through job analysis and ask the source, "Without this factor or requirement, can people succeed in this job?" Once determined, the critical requirements become the main focus or topics of the interview guide.

A third aspect of selection interview preparation is the development and use of an *application form*. An application form is the interviewer's equivalent of a resume. Since resumes are often biased toward the applicant or because some jobs do not demand a resume, most interviewers also administer their own application form. Application forms can be standardized for use throughout a company, or specialized for different job types. The purpose of an application form is to check for *minimum qualifications* and at the same time provide applicants with some preliminary information regarding the organization and job. The form should be clear, easy to complete, and leave applicants with a positive feeling toward the organization. Figure 11.3 is a typical application form.

Application forms are normally filled out at least two or three days, and usually a week or more, ahead of the actual interview. This is an interviewee's first direct contact with the organization other than a brief visit, letter, or telephone call to solicit the application form. Application forms often contain personal data such as date of birth, citizenship, residence, telephone number, and position desired; educational information such as name and address of schools attended, degrees, major courses, and class standing; work experience such as names and addresses of present and past employers, dates of employment, positions held, salary earned, name and title of supervisors, brief description of duties, and reason for leaving each position; and special skills and avocations such as hobbies, interests, licenses possessed, equipment operated, membership in organizations, and so on.

Some questions are prohibited by law on an application form, such as those regarding sex, age, race, religion, national origin, and arrest record. Other information you will probably not be asked for are personal references which are of little value since they generally contain the names of only those people who will give positive information regarding the applicant; and information which will be requested in the interview. A good application form can be extremely valuable in helping you prepare for the interview. Very often both participants save time by discovering from the application form that an individual does not meet the minimum qualifications for a job.

Interviewers should check the written information provided by applicants. Information checking includes consulting public records such as credit information, driving history, workmen's compensation claims, and criminal history. A second means of checking applicant information is called the *reference check*. Reference checking normally involves telephoning or writing an applicant's previous employers. You should ask the applicant if it is ok to contact his or her present employer.

Recently, some legal restrictions have been placed upon pre-employment information and reference checking. Public Law 93–579, The Privacy Act of 1974,

11.3 Sample Application Form

APPLICATION FOR EMPLOYMENT

Personal Information

Date _____   S.S. # _____

Name _____   Age _____   Sex _____
     Last   First   Middle

Address _____
     Street   City   State   Zip

Phone # _____ Height _____ Weight _____

Date of Birth _____ U.S. Citizen?   Yes ☐   No ☐

If Related to Anyone in Our Employ,
State Name and Department _____

Employment Desired

Position _____ Date You   Salary
                   Can Start _____ Desired _____

Are You Employed Now? _____ Present Employer: _____

Ever Applied to this Company Before? _____ When _____

Education	School Name & Location	Years Attended	Date Graduated
High School			
College			
Trade, Business or Correspondence School			

Special Subjects Studied _____

What Foreign Languages Do You Speak or Write Fluently? _____

U.S. Military or
Naval Service _____ Rank _____

Former Employers (List Last Two Employers, Starting With Last One First)

Date, Month and Year	Name and Address	Salary	Position	Reason For Leaving

PHYSICAL RECORD

List Any Physical Defects _____

Were You Ever Injured?   Give Details _____

In Case of
Emergency Notify
             Name   Address   Phone #
_____

I authorize investigation of all statements contained in this application. I understand that misrepresentation or omission of facts called for is cause for dismissal. Further, I understand and agree that my employment is for no definite period and may, regardless of the date of payment of my wages and salary, be terminated at any time without previous notice.

Signature _____ Date _____

Almost every job requires a completed application form.

safeguards an individual against invasion of personal privacy. It allows individuals to determine what records can be collected, maintained, used, or disseminated about them; to review and correct their records; to prevent the use of such records for purposes other than those for which they were collected; and to bring suit for damages sustained by an incorrect usage of such records. The Fair Credit and Reporting Act allows individuals access to information obtained about them through credit checking. The Family Education Right and Privacy Act (Buckley Amendment) allows students to review their own education records as well as prevent universities from disclosing certain types of information pertaining to students without their consent. Finally, the Freedom of Information Act permits individuals to see information that federal agencies use in making hiring and similar decisions.

Along with these federal laws there is much state legislation which applies to reference and information checking. Even in light of this privacy legislation, however, organizations can still collect and check written information if they adhere to the following guidelines:

1. *Request job related information only.*
2. *Obtain written releases from job candidates prior to checking references.*
3. *Stay away from subjective areas.*
4. *Continue to use reference checks.*
5. *Evaluate who provides any subjective reference material received.*

(Rice, 1978, p. 49–50)

There are also guidelines for people who provide such information. The following guidelines come directly from current legislation, expected legislation, and current practices.

1. *Do not black list former employees.*
2. *Fully document all released information.*
3. *Make no subjective statements.*

4. *Obtain written consent from employees prior to providing reference data.*
5. *Use a telephone "call back" procedure when verifying application blank data.*
6. *Do not offer reference data over the telephone.*
7. *Release only the following acceptable general types of information (subject to written consent of the employee):*
   Dates of employment
   Job titles during employment; time in position
   Promotions, demotions
   Attendance record and salary
   Reason for termination (no details, just reason)
8. *Do not answer the rehire questions.*

(Rice, 1978, pp. 50–51)

Even with these limitations, information and reference checking continue to be an important part of your preparation for conducting selection interviews. It is necessary to collect objective, quantifiable, job-relevant facts about applicants. The vice-president of a major executive recruiting company has the following to say about the importance of reference checking:

Reference auditing is the key to balancing an individual's strengths and weaknesses and projecting how they will apply to company objectives. It permits in-depth probing of day to day professional skills, personal relationships and work patterns. It allows an interviewer to evaluate the accuracy of the candidate's self-view in relation to the perceptions of his or her peer group and superiors. The overriding purpose of reference audits is to examine candidates from several valuable perspectives. It is the only technique available for presenting a complete picture.

(Rabinowitz, 1979, p. 35)

Once you have become familiar with the organization, done a complete job analysis, prepared and administered an application form, and checked the information obtained from the applicant, you are ready to plan the time and place for the interview and develop an interview guide. The timing and setting for a selection interview should meet all of the requirements discussed in Part I. It should be informal, private, and comfortable. Many selection interviews take place on campus at the college placement service. In this case the setting is arranged ahead of time by the academic institution. There are some things a campus interviewer can still control, however, such as where respondents sit, the nature and amount of information which is available ahead of time to each respondent, as well as the possibility of interviewing outside of the placement office, such as over lunch or dinner.

When the setting for a selection interview is at the job site, you have much greater control over the setting. Interviews may take place in a personnel office, at the job site, in a company cafeteria, or any one of a number of other locations. Sometimes dinner or cocktail parties are planned as part of the interviewing process for upper-level personnel. Very often these informal interviews are designed to determine the personality and social characteristics of both the potential applicant and the applicant's spouse. No matter what type of setting is chosen for a selection interview, it should be one which is acceptable to both participants.

Interviewee Preparation

Effective applicants spend at least as much time in preparation as interviewers do. There are six basic steps that you as a job applicant, should do in preparation for a selection interview: 1) analyze yourself, 2) develop a resume, 3) research the organization, 4) make initial contact, 5) study the job description, and 6) prepare for the interview. If each step is done carefully and efficiently your chances for success are good.

The first step, self analysis, is sometimes the most difficult of all. Self analysis means making a very careful evaluation of yourself. Based on your education, training, and experience, what are you qualified to do? What do you want to do? What are your main strengths and weaknesses? What type of employer would you like to work for? What type of people do you like to work with? What in your background has made you what you are today? These and many other questions help you analyze yourself. The more you know about yourself, the better able you will be to answer questions about yourself in the interview and determine whether or not to accept certain jobs if they are offered.

SELF ANALYSIS EXERCISE

Directions: Follow the instructions for each section. This exercise is adapted from "Life Planning" in *A Handbook of Structured Experiences for Human Relations Training*, by J. William Pfeiffer and John E. Jones (Volume II, University Associates Press, 1970), pp. 113–127.

1. Where am I Now?   Envision a business progress chart as you draw a line that depicts the past, present, and future of your career. On this line mark an "X" to show where you are now.
2. Who am I?   Write down twenty adjectives which describe yourself most accurately in regard to your career.
3. Regroup your career list of adjectives into the following categories: positive, neutral, and negative.
4. What would be ideal attainments in your career? Be as free as possible in selecting these goals. Summarize your career fantasies. Example: I want to become president of my own company.
5. Assign a priority value to each of your career goals. Using the following four-point scale, write the appropriate value next to each goal. (See #4 above)
   1—of *little* importance.
   2—of *moderate* importance.
   3—of *great* importance.
   4—of *very great* importance.
6. Now summarize what this exercise tells you about yourself. Also try to answer the questions in the paragraph immediately preceding this exercise. This is not a complete self analysis but it will get you started.

7. On a separate sheet of paper select the five goals you rated highest in question #4 and plan a program with component steps and deadlines for attaining each of these objectives. Be as realistic as you can and yet don't underestimate yourself.

Once you feel confident you have done a thorough self analysis, it is time to develop your resume. A *resume* is a formal written summary of your background and qualifications. Many books and hundreds of articles have been devoted to resume preparation and construction, and many companies can help you prepare a resume. Their services, however, are very expensive and, at least for your first job, are not that much more effective than what you can do for yourself.

There is no "perfect" resume that fits every job seeker. Your resume is a reflection of you to representatives of organizations in which you are interested, so it must be the best possible representation of you. You should not necessarily copy any particular resume format, but look at many different ones and pick or create one which you think will best help you get the type of job you seek.

You do not, however, need to start from scratch. Five basic pieces of information should be included in a resume:

Personal Data
Education
Experience
General Information
References

In the *Personal Data* category you should include current and/or permanent address, telephone number(s), date and place of birth, and physical make up such as height, weight, and general health, although some people are omitting various personal items as irrelevant to job performance. In *Education* you should include institutions attended, degrees obtained, major and minor courses of study, years attended, and grade point average. *Experience* should include names of previous employers, dates of employment, positions held, nature of employment (full-time, part-time, or summer), and a general description of your duties and responsibilities. *General Information* that should be included in your resume are extracurricular activities (memberships in clubs and organizations), special honors, achievements, awards, hobbies, interests, and anything else you think will help you get the job you want. The *References* section can either list the names of various people who can be contacted for references or how a potential employer can obtain reference information. Although almost every suggested resume format contains this basic information, the way in which the information is put together differs widely. The following are a few examples of resume formats.

These examples should give you some ideas. Select those features which appeal to you, but you should keep some guidelines in mind when developing your resume. You will notice that some of this advice is not followed in some of the sample resumes. Again, the final decision as to how to structure your resume is up to you. The following guidelines should be taken as suggestions, not absolute requirements.

11.4 Sample Resume

NAME:	Robert G. Brown 274 G. Street Pinta, Ohio 54321
TELEPHONE:	Home: 987–654–3210
PERSONAL:	Married, 5′ 11″, 185 pounds. Born: July 4, 1961.
PROFESSIONAL OBJECTIVE:	To acquire skills in various aspects of business which will help qualify me for management.
EDUCATION:	Ohio State University, B.S. in Business Administration, May, 1983. Major: Management; GPA = 3.12 Support Areas: 1) Economics 2) Accounting Cumulative GPA = 2.97
EXPERIENCE:	
8–82 to 5–83	Full-time student (working 15 hours per week in school dormitory).
5–82 to 8–82	Summer: Tennis instructor and counselor at Williams County Scout Camp.
8–81 to 5–82	Full-time student (working 15 hours per week in school dormitory).
5–81 to 8–81	Summer: Worked full time as kitchen helper for McDonald's Restaurant, Pinta, Ohio.
8–80 to 5–81	Full-time student (working 20 hours per week for Alpha Beta Sorority).
5–80 to 8–80	Summer: Worked full time as kitchen helper for McDonald's Restaurant, Pinta, Ohio.
8–79 to 5–80	Full-time student (working 10 hours per week for Alpha Beta Sorority).
PROFESSIONAL AND SOCIAL ACTIVITIES:	1. President Young Explorer's Club (two years) 2. Vice-President Omega Delta Fraternity 3. Future Business Administrators Club 4. Varsity Swimming Team
LOCATION PREFERENCE:	Midwest
SALARY:	Open

The maximum length of a resume is two pages. For most new college graduates, one page is sufficient. Effective resumes are neat and error-free. This means professional printing or careful typing with no misspelled words or erasures.

BACKGROUND:	I was born and raised in Pinta, Ohio, the youngest of three children. My father is Vice-President of the First Pinta Bank; my mother is a secretary. I graduated from Pinta High School where I participated in varsity swimming. I was a member of the Drama Club and student council. I was also involved in church youth activities.
REFERENCES:	Dr. Francis Drake, Chairman Business Administration Department Ohio State University 624 State St. Columbus, Ohio 54361 Phone: 987-321-6540 Susan Haskins, Manager McDonald's Restaurant 1250 Baker Rd. Pinta, Ohio 54321 Phone: 987-749-6399

PROFESSIONAL PREPARATION:

	Semester Hours
Accounting	
Accounting I	3
Accounting II	3
Advanced Accounting	3
Cost Accounting	3
	12 hours
Business Administration	
Business Administration I	3
Business Administration II	3
Small Business Administration	3
Business Administration Theory	3
Advanced Business Administration	3
Business Administration Seminar	3
	18 hours
Economics	
Economics I	3
Economics II	3
Advanced Economics	3
	9 hours

11.5 Sample Resume

BROWN, ROBERT L.

PRESENT ADDRESS: 321 Hayes Hall   Home Address: 274 G. St.
                   Ohio State University   Pinta, OH 54321
                   Columbus, Ohio 54361   (987) 654-3210
                   (987) 321-8502

PERSONAL   Married, Born July 4, 1961, 5' 11", 185 lbs., U.S. Citizen,
                   Excellent Health

OBJECTIVE   Entry level position with opportunity for training and ad-
                   vancement. Willing to relocate and travel.

EDUCATION   Ohio State University—B.S. Business Administration,
                   May, 1983. Special emphasis in small business admin-
                   istration. Overall G.P.A. 2.97/ A= 4. G.P.A. in major
                   3.12/ A= 4. Support: Working—50%, Scholarship—20%,
                   Family—30%. Selected for membership in Future Busi-
                   ness Administrators Club.

EXPERIENCE   WILLIAMS COUNTY SCOUT CAMP, Williams County,
Summer '82   Ohio, Tennis Instructor and Counselor, Worked in all
                   areas of the camp. Responsible for cash receipts, se-
                   curity, supervised two other counselors.

Summers '80-'81   MCDONALD'S RESTAURANT, Pinta, Ohio, Kitchen
                   Helper, Bussed dishes, cooked, and helped with cash
                   accounting.

EXTRACURRICULAR   Participated in varsity swimming. President of Young Ex-
ACTIVITIES   plorer's Club. Vice-President of the Omega Delta
                   Fraternity.

SUPPLEMENTAL   Worked part-time during junior and senior years in the
INFORMATION   school dormitory and for Alpha Beta Sorority during
                   freshman and sophomore years. Active in scouts and
                   church activities.

REFERENCES   Letters of recommendation available from Placement
                   Service, Ohio State University, P.O. Box 564, Columbus,
                   OH. 54361

11.6 Sample Resume

ROBERT G. BROWN

Address:

274 G. Street
Pinta, Ohio 54321
(987) 654-3210

Personal:

5' 11"
185 lbs
Married

Education

Presently finishing a B.S. degree in Business Administration at Ohio State University. Course of study included basic economics and accounting. Graduation date is May, 1983. Overall G.P.A. is 2.97 and G.P.A. in major is 3.12, both on a 4-point scale. Special area of emphasis is small business administration.

College Activities

Future Business Administrators Club, 1981–present. President of Young Explorer's Club, 1980–82. Vice-President Omega Delta Fraternity, 1982. Member of varsity swim team.

Work Experience

Part-time (School year)
School Dormitory
August 1981 to
present.

Fifteen hours per week. Duties include counseling and security.

Tennis Instructor,
Counselor
May 1982 to August 1982.

Full-time. Worked in all areas of the camp. Responsible for cash receipts, security, and supervised two counselors. Williams County Scout Camp, Williams County, Ohio.

Kitchen Helper,
Summers 1980 and 1981.

Bussed dishes, cooked and helped with cash accounting. McDonald's Restaurant, Pinta, Ohio.

Part-time (School year)
Alpha Beta Sorority
August 1979 to May 1981.

20 hours per week (1980–81) and 10 hours per week (1979–80). Duties included general maintenance and repair.

References

Available upon request.

A photograph may be included as part of the resume, but it is not necessary. You should carefully consider the inclusion of a "professional objective." If you know exactly what kind of job you are seeking, a professional objective statement can help you, but if you are going to apply for a number of different types of jobs, you are probably better off without it. You can make it part of your cover letter, along with such things as location preference, availability, salary, and preparation for a particular position. This will help you make greater use of your resume, especially if you have two or three hundred printed copies. Your resume should be brief, to the point, and worded in the past tense. Omit pronouns such as "I" and "me" or any other personal references. As was mentioned earlier, individual reference listings are normally ignored by interviewers. They are much more likely to check references with previous employers and others of their own choosing who can testify to your character and abilities. Your experience should be listed in reverse chronological order. You need not include a list of the courses you have taken or individual grades since this information is easily obtained through a registrar's office. Do not outdate your resume by including a preparation date or your current age. Use your birthdate instead. Finally, be sure to have your final resume examined by someone for clarity, impressiveness, spelling, and punctuation. These are only a few suggestions: check with other sources or your instructor for further aid.

Resume construction is difficult and time consuming, but once it is done, you can keep it forever, making only minor changes when necessary. Most organizations ask for a resume as part of the selection process, but it is useful even for those organizations which do not require it, since it helps you fill out job application forms.

Having completed your self analysis and resume preparation, you are ready to start looking for a job. This means checking the want ads, registering with your college placement service and checking their literature and interview schedule, and consulting various listings of corporations and agencies. There are many directories of organizations in libraries and placement centers. Your placement service will be more than willing to provide you with all the information you will need; you should make extensive use of them in all facets of your selection interview preparation.

Private employment agencies can also help you obtain interviews. Some of these agencies are more helpful than others. Their fee is normally a certain percentage of your first year's salary. In some cases it is possible to get employers to pay the employment agency fee. Be sure you carefully consider hiring a private employment agency.

One of your best sources of potential employers is the yellow pages of a telephone book; it is full of company names and addresses in your preferred location. Libraries carry a large selection of telephone books from different cities. You should make use of all of these sources and any others you can think of, such as friends and relatives. You never know where you're going to find the organization which best suits your needs and has an opening for which you qualify.

Once you have found one or more organizations which seem "right," do some research on them. Sometimes this research is relatively easy because infor-

Job openings can be found in many different ways.

mation regarding location, net sales, profit, employment opportunities, company history, product line, and other general reference data can be found in sources such as the *Dunn and Bradstreet Million Dollar Directory*, *Moody's Manuals* (industrial, municipal and government, and public utility), and the *Standard and Poor's Register of Corporations, Directors, and Executives*. Your local librarian will help you find the information you need. This research not only helps you choose the right organization, but you can impress interviewers by mentioning or asking about something in their organization which you have discovered in your research. This lets them know you have done your "homework" and normally makes a good impression. Careful and thorough research can pay off in your job search and final job selection.

You are now ready to make initial contact with potential employers and arrange for an interview. The normal methods for making an initial contact are telephone and letter. In either case your approach is very similar. You should call or address your letter to a specific person. This may be the personnel manager or the head of the particular section where you would like to work. Initial contact should be businesslike and brief. Tell the individual how you learned about the organization or position, why you feel the company should consider you for employment, and when you are available for an interview. Be confident and enthusiastic, but avoid being too personal. Remember, you are trying to attract a prospective employer's interest. Your main pitch will come in the interview.

If you are making a telephone contact, have a pencil and paper ready to take down any relevant information. The most important information is the time and place of the selection interview, if your contact is successful. When making initial contact by letter you should include a copy of your resume. Figure 11.7 is an example of a letter of inquiry, or as it is sometimes called, a *cover letter*.

11.7 Sample Cover Letter

Mary F. Alexander
1242 Riverside Ave.
San Francisco, CA 94321

Mr. James L. Berger, Director
Personnel Office
Flintstone Tire & Rubber Company
Los Angeles, CA 94678

Dear Mr. Berger:

Ms. Allen, my advisor, recently informed me that the Flintstone Tire and Rubber Company is adding employees to its salesforce. I have since done some research, and believe that your company is the type of organization I would like to work for. Your reputation for top quality and service along with the continued growth in sales makes me believe it would be an honor to represent such a company.

As my enclosed resume indicates, I will be graduating from San Francisco University in May. My entire education has been aimed toward a career in sales. I believe my sales experience and knowledge of your major sales region, the eleven western states, makes me an ideal candidate for the openings you have available.

I would like an opportunity to meet with you or one of your staff to discuss further my background and find out more about the opportunities available with the Flintstone Tire and Rubber Company. I will be in Los Angeles the week of March 17th. If I haven't heard from you by the 15th, I will call you when I get into town.

Thank you for your consideration.

Sincerely,

Mary F. Alexander

Mary F. Alexander

As was mentioned earlier, a cover letter can be used to amplify the information contained in your resume. You can also use it to explain any special circumstances. Remain brief and simply state how you learned about the organization, why you are contacting them, and what kind of position you are looking for. As with the resume, your cover letter should be neat and clear and, if possible, original and creative. You must remember that many selection interviewers receive two or three hundred applications per day. "Canned" and "run of the mill" inquiries probably won't get you an interview and, therefore, the job.

If an organization sends you descriptions of various available jobs, try to determine which job best fits your qualifications. Match your capabilities and desires to job descriptions. Do not apply for jobs for which you are not qualified, but at the same time, don't bypass jobs for which you have the minimum qualifications. Remember, your purpose is to get an interview. Once you are in the interview, you can amplify on your qualifications. Almost every hiring decision involves some form of compromise. Employers seldom get the "ideal" candidate, and applicants seldom get the "ideal" job. Your interview purpose is to convince interviewers that you are the best available applicant.

Once you have a selection interview appointment, start preparing for it. Try to anticipate questions which you may be asked; prepare questions to ask about the organization; and decide what you will wear, what approach you'll take, and the way in which you will respond to questions. Most selection interviewers ask the same general questions. The following is a list of likely questions. Go through them and plan your responses. If possible, have someone ask you each question, answer the question out loud, and evaluate your response. You would not think of presenting a speech without practicing, and yet many interviewees walk into a selection interview never having practiced their answers to even the most obvious questions. This results in prolonged pauses, stumbling on answers, and sometimes even giving inaccurate information. As you practice answering these questions try to work in additional information about your willingness to learn, desire to excel, and any other qualities you feel would make you a good employee.

Typical Selection Interview Questions

1. Why did you pick the major and minor you chose in college?
2. What were some of the courses you liked best in college? Why?
3. If you were starting again would you pick the same major?
4. Do you think you have done the best work you can in college?
5. Do you think grades are a good indicator of your training?
6. Were your extracurricular activities worth the time spent on them?
7. Would you be willing to give up your education and start again?
8. How does your education prepare you for this job?
9. Of your previous jobs, which did you like most? Least? Why?
10. How did you obtain the jobs you have held?
11. What was your most rewarding work experience?
12. Have you ever had problems working with other employees?
13. Which of your bosses did you like best? Least? Why?
14. What did you learn from each of your previous jobs?
15. What have you done in previous jobs that demonstrates your willingness to work, creativity, leadership, etc.?
16. How did your previous work experiences prepare you for this job?
17. What are your goals for the future?
18. What personal characteristics do you possess that especially prepare you for this job?
19. Why do you think you want to work for our company?
20. What environment do you prefer to live in? Location?
21. Do you prefer to work with others or by yourself?
22. What characteristics do you look for in friends?
23. What are your greatest strengths and weaknesses?
24. Where would you like to be in ten (twenty) years?
25. Why should I hire you?

Once you are prepared to respond to interview inquiries you must plan the questions which you will ask. In most selection interviews, some time is set aside for interviewee questions. If you use this time wisely, you can create a very positive impression about yourself, as well as gain some extremely valuable information. In most cases your questions should address various conditions of employment which concern you. The following is a list of employment conditions about which you might want to inquire. From this list you should select those questions which are most important to you for each particular job. Do not ask about all of these areas. Once you have selected six or eight areas, prepare questions for each. These questions can then be typed out and taken with you to the interview. There is nothing wrong with having some notes.

1. Initial salary and raise schedule
2. Sick leave payment
3. Separation allowance (severance pay)
4. Old-age, survivors, disability and health insurance
5. Travel and per diem compensation
6. Worker's compensation
7. Bonuses, commissions, and similar compensations
8. Credit union
9. Union affiliation
10. Service awards
11. Chances for advancement
12. Company-paid education programs
13. Paid holidays
14. Unemployment compensation
15. Management incentives
16. Special clothing allowance
17. Necessity to relocate
18. Reimbursement for moving
19. Special company training programs
20. Paid vacations
21. Pension plan
22. Potential for advancement within company
23. Job safety record
24. Travel requirements
25. Purchasing discounts for employees
26. Suggestion bonuses
27. Size of organization
28. Major health plans available
29. Tax-sheltered annuities
30. Number of supervisors
31. Overtime requirements and pay
32. Degree of privacy
33. Profit-sharing programs
34. Employee thrift plans
35. Degree of independence
36. Retirement plan

37. *Job security*
38. *Geographic location*
39. *Patent or publication rights*   *(Figgins, 1978, p. 692)*

You must plan your appearance and behavior. Your clothes should reflect your own good taste. You should always be neat and clean and dressed for the job you want. If you are interviewing with a conservative bank, you do not wear a pair of jeans, or a slit skirt. Most interviewees have little trouble in choosing proper attire.

Think about how you'll conduct yourself during the interview. Professional interviewers often list the following as major interviewee behavior problems: lack of interest, belligerent attitude, lacking sincerity, evasive, unable to concentrate, lack of initiative, arrogant manner, cynical, intolerant, unclear in responding, poor career planning, no company research, immature, low moral standard, impolite, wants to start at top, and oversells case. You should avoid all of these problems. This is the last preparation stage before the interview. Once all of these tasks are taken care of, you are ready to go to the interview and your chances of succeeding are excellent.

THE SELECTION INTERVIEW GUIDE

Selection techniques other than tests . . . may be improperly used so as to have the effect of discriminating against minority groups. Such techniques include, but are not restricted to, unscored or casual interviews and unscored application forms. Where there are data suggesting employment discrimination, a person may be called upon to deliver evidence concerning the validity of his unscored procedures.
                                   (EEOC Guidelines, Section 1607.13)

Because of the preceding and other similar legislation, selection interviewers use more scheduled interview guides than they used to. Most major organizations can no longer afford to make selections based upon rambling, unstructured interviews. The EEOC guidelines specifically state that all questions, measures, or criteria must be "relevant to the extent that they represent critical or important job duties, work behaviors, or work outcomes as developed from the review of job information." In other words, all questions contained within the interview guide must represent *Bona Fide Occupational Qualifications* (BFOQ).

In most cases, questions relating to marital and family status, age, race, religion, sex, ethnic background, credit rating, and arrest record are all illegal (not BFOQ) unless employers can prove they are in some way directly related to the job under consideration. For example, questions to determine if a man or woman can meet specified work schedules; obtaining proof of age from a minor; asking applicants if they read, write, or speak a foreign language fluently; or inquiries into actual criminal convictions are BFOQ's if they relate directly to the job (such as a security guard). In each case, it is the responsibility of an employer to prove that any borderline inquiry relates to the job. In most cases, good common sense is a reliable guide in question selection. As a measure of your common sense, take the pre-employment inquiry quiz, figure 11.8 (Minter, 1972). Check one space for each inquiry.

11.8 Pre-Employment Inquiry Quiz

Pre-Employment Inquiry	Lawful	Unlawful
A. Asking the applicant if he has ever worked under another name.	_____	_____
B. Asking the applicant to name his birthplace.	_____	_____
C. Asking the birthplace of the applicant's parents, spouse, or other close relative.	_____	_____
D. Asking the applicant to submit proof of age by supplying birth certificate or baptismal record.	_____	_____
E. Asking the applicant for his religious affiliation, name of church, parish, or religious holidays observed.	_____	_____
F. Asking the applicant if he is a citizen of the United States.	_____	_____
G. Asking the applicant if he is a naturalized citizen.	_____	_____
H. Asking the applicant for the date when he acquired his citizenship.	_____	_____
I. Asking the applicant if he has ever been arrested for any crime, and to indicate when and where.	_____	_____
J. Asking the applicant to indicate what foreign languages he can read, write, or speak fluently.	_____	_____
K. Asking the applicant how he acquired his ability to read, write, or speak a foreign language.	_____	_____

If you did fairly well on this quiz, you are ready to develop a selection interview guide. If you did not do so well, you should check further into federal restrictions on selection interviews. The essential point is that all questions must relate directly to skill and knowledge relevant to performing job tasks. Any form of question can be used. Hypothetical questions, for example, are appropriate if they pertain directly to the job and are asked of all respondents. It is acceptable, for example, to ask the hypothetical question, "What would you do if someone got very vulgar and abusive when talking to you on the telephone?"

These same restrictions also apply to interview probes—they are permissible if related to job performance. But it is easy to probe into forbidden areas; that is why most selection interviewers use structured guides. If you use an unstructured informal interview guide and ad-lib your questions and probes, the information you obtain from applicants is not comparable, and all applicants are not given an equal chance for selection. Federal authorities consider asking different

Pre-Employment Inquiry	Lawful	Unlawful
L. Asking the applicant about his past work experience.	_____	_____
M. Requesting the applicant to provide names of three relatives other than one's father, husband or wife, or minor-age dependent children.	_____	_____
N. Asking the applicant for his wife's maiden name.	_____	_____
O. Asking the maiden name of applicant's mother.	_____	_____
P. Asking the full names of applicant's brothers and sisters.	_____	_____
Q. Asking the applicant for a list of names of all clubs, societies, and lodges to which he belongs.	_____	_____
R. Asking the applicant to include a photograph with his application for employment.	_____	_____
S. Asking the applicant to supply addresses of relatives such as cousins, uncles, aunts, nephews, grandparents, who can be contacted for references.	_____	_____

You should have marked all unlawful except F, J, and L

From Minter, R. L. "Human Rights Laws and Pre-Employment Inquiries," *Personnel Journal*, 52 (June, 1972): 431–433.

questions to different applicants the same as giving different applicants different tests or exercises.

Even if you have a structured interview guide with specific job-related questions, you can still be challenged in court if you base your decision on feelings or subjective information rather than objective qualifications. Some companies have tried to solve the objectivity problem by adopting some form of numerical rating scheme. They then try to combine the ratings on specific items to arrive at an overall decision. This can be useful if the appropriate job attributes have been selected. If the attributes are subjective, the ratings may still be unlawful. Some selection interviewers say that getting a "feel" for an interviewee is the main advantage of using an interview. This advantage can be a disadvantage in court. If your "feeling" for a respondent involves making a decision on subjective impressions, you are open to challenge. If you are planning to conduct selection interviews, spend part of your preparation time reviewing the various guidelines and articles relating to what is legal and illegal.

You can question personality characteristics which are job relevant such as decisiveness, initiative, innovativeness, and flexibility. This is one of the real values of a face-to-face interview if handled carefully and within legal requirements. Management functions such as planning, leading, organizing, controlling, and communicating are often an important part of an upper-level selection or promotion interview. Questions regarding education and job knowledge or work experience are usually follow-ups to information found in an applicant's resume or job application form. Other legal selection interview topic areas often mentioned are responsibilities and duties of the job; salary and benefits; working conditions; supervisor's style; candidate's personality, attitude, ability, potential, success in previous positions, ability to fit in with current department employees, ability to perform the job, interests, dependability and future opportunities within the organization; and finally, the stability and security of the position.

Once you have selected the major topic areas and familiarized yourself with current legal restrictions, you are ready to write the interview guide. In preparing and structuring questions, you should follow the general rules presented in Chapter 2 regarding question vocabulary, phrasing, style, structure, and sequence. You may use either open or closed questions, although open questions are generally preferred in selection interviews because they allow respondents to expand upon answers and give clues to their enthusiasm, communication ability, and interest.

QUESTION PREPARATION EXERCISE

Directions: Without going back and looking at the typical questions listed earlier, try to write one good open question to cover each of the following common selection interview topics.

Education:
1. Choice of college
2. Choice of major
3. Preferred courses
4. Educational financing
5. Extracurricular activities

Experience:
1. Jobs preferred
2. Knowledge and skills acquired
3. Application to current position
4. Supervisor preferences
5. Termination reasons

Career Goals:
1. Salary
2. Position

3. Organization
4. Relocation, travel, overtime, weekends, etc.

Miscellaneous:
1. Personality
2. Personal characteristics

Once you have selected the critical topic areas and prepared questions, you have completed approximately 75 percent of the interview guide. All you need to do at this point is decide what you will tell the candidate about your organization and the job. You must prepare to sell the position to the respondent. You should prepare both a brief and a detailed list of the responsibilities and duties necessary for the job. The brief description will be used during the orientation—if it is too specific, you can inadvertently coach interviewees as to how they should respond and behave during the interview to qualify for the job.

The detailed description is used after you've assessed the applicant and all pertinent questions have been answered. Then you try to sell an applicant on accepting the job if it is offered. As a part of your influence attempt, applicants are normally offered the opportunity to ask any questions about either the organization or the position. Try to make your answers as positive as possible in order to attract the applicant. Giving the interviewee information normally takes the other 25 percent of a selection interview guide. It should, however, be planned and consistently presented to all interviewees. Some selection interviewers intentionally do a weak selling job because they have mentally eliminated a respondent from consideration. This is a mistake, because other hiring authorities may not see things the same way you do; and even if they do, you want to leave every applicant with a good impression of your organization. This information-giving portion of the selection interview guide should, therefore, be prepared and presented in exactly the same manner to all applicants. Figure 11.9 is an example of a typical selection interview guide once both the assessment and selling portions have been completed.

SELECTION INTERVIEW OPENING

Most job applicants are rather tense. It is your job, as an interviewer, to do whatever you can in the opening to put them at ease and establish a permissive climate of rapport and informality. This is somewhat difficult, however, since there is a definite power imbalance between an organization representative and a job applicant. The interviewer controls a job which the respondent wants. Selection interviewers can afford to be relaxed and comfortable, perhaps even blasé, but the interview is much too important to interviewees to assume a similar attitude, unless encouraged to do so. You can create a relaxed climate by greeting applicants in a friendly manner and introducing yourself using your first name. You can make some small talk regarding the weather, activities earlier in the day, or common interests. Some early icebreaking possibilities can be gained from a respondent's resume or job application.

11.9 Sample Selection Interview Guide
(Space for information recording has been omitted)

ICEBREAKING:
  Interests:
  Other:
ORIENTATION:
  Brief position description:
  Interview structure: (Applicant questions at end)
  Length, confidentiality, etc. . . .
OPENING QUESTION:
  Why applied?
EDUCATION:
  Major (and minor)?
  Subjects?
  Application to position?
  Special achievements?
  Grades?
  Effort?
  Financing?
  Extracurricular activities?
EXPERIENCE:
  Position descriptions?
  Position preferences?
  Achievements?
  Leadership experience?
  Knowledge and skills acquired?
  Supervisor preferences?
  Termination reasons?
  Application to current position?

CAREER GOALS:
  Long/Short Range?
  Organization?
  Position?
  Relocation, travel, overtime, weekends, etc.?
  Salary?
MISCELLANEOUS:
  Military service?
  Health status?
  Relocation?
  Strengths/Weaknesses?
  Temperament? Creativity? Leadership etc.?
  Why should I hire you?
  Organization and position knowledge?
ORGANIZATION DESCRIPTION:
POSITION DESCRIPTION:
RESPONDENT QUESTIONS:
CONCLUSION:
  Who makes decision:
  When decision made:
  How applicant will be informed:
    (Check address & phone #)
  Words of encouragement:

If your manner and approach are relaxed and open then respondents will generally assume a similar attitude. You might want to use your brief comments regarding the job and organization to give a respondent time to relax. Sometimes this takes only a minute or two, while in other cases it may mean ten or fifteen minutes of icebreaking. Nothing productive can be accomplished until each interviewee is relaxed and the proper degree of rapport, informality, and openness has been achieved.

Once respondents are fairly relaxed, a brief orientation is necessary. If you have not done so yet, you can briefly describe the organization and job. You should preview what topics will be discussed, how long the interview will take, and when the respondent may ask questions. Basically the orientation is a simple overview or roadmap of what will follow. It should be brief and to the point. The following is an example of an effective selection interview orientation.

In the next half hour we need to accomplish several things. First, I'll be asking you several questions about yourself such as your education, work experience, and general capabilities. Then I will explain our job position in greater detail and describe our organization to you. I'll then be happy to answer any questions you might have. If at any time you feel there is anything I should know about you, please fill me in. All of the information you give me in this interview is strictly confidential and will be disclosed only to those individuals responsible for making the job decision, so please be as open and honest as possible in responding to my questions.

After such an orientation statement you ask the opening question which will usually be one you think the respondent can answer fairly easily. Then move directly into the body of the interview.

As a respondent, your sole objective in the opening is to become relaxed and natural as quickly as possible. Follow the lead of the interviewer. Remember, most skillful interviewers will discount a certain amount of nervousness. Try to avoid those mannerisms which make your nervousness more obvious. If you don't know where to put your hands, for example, leave them in your lap and keep them still. As you greet the interviewer be sure you get the correct name and its pronunciation. Don't sit until you are offered a chair or smoke unless you are invited to do so. Listen carefully during the orientation. Remember, you are trying to sell yourself. Don't try to "put on an act" or be phony. Make the interviewer's job as easy as possible. Most interviewers are impressed with respondents with whom they feel comfortable and at ease.

The selection interview opening is extremely important because selection interviewers tend to make decisions very early in an interview. Simple first impression behaviors such as how you are dressed, your tone of voice, handshake, and facial expression can all help or hurt you. A bad first impression can make interviewers misperceive later information. Keep the line of communication open by meeting the interviewer's opening expectations.

SELECTION INTERVIEW QUESTIONING AND RESPONDING

The art of selection interview questioning involves keeping the focus on respondents while maintaining control. Perhaps the biggest problem with most selection interviewers is that they talk too much. Since they often use a fairly

A job applicant must make a good first impression.

structured guide, they focus more on the guide than the applicant. They ask questions exactly in the order listed on the guide and become mechanical. Once you adopt this rigid approach, it manifests itself in many ways. First, you tend to become very "stone" or "poker" faced. You take on an attitude which is much too serious for the informal climate set in the opening. Second, you are too quick to ask new questions and end up cutting off interviewee responses. Very often this happens when your eyes drop to the interview guide rather than remaining upon the respondent. Third, you fail to fully probe respondent answers. You don't get the depth and range of coverage necessary to make an informed decision. Fourth, you fail to use summaries and transitions in order to warn applicants that one topic is finished and another is about to begin. Finally, you forget to use a clearinghouse question. A *clearinghouse question* is one where you ask interviewees if there is anything else which should be covered regarding a particular topic which will help you make the final job decision. It is essential that you let applicants add any supplemental information which may be relevant in determining their qualifications for the job. All of these problems stem from over-dependence on the interview guide. The interview guide should not be a straight-jacket which inhibits questioning and keeps you from gaining the necessary information to make a good job decision.

You want to encourage respondents to give you complete, open, and honest information. One of the best ways to do this is to "pat applicants on the back" to encourage them. Comments such as "Very good!" or "You deserve a lot of credit for that!" or "That's really interesting!" are all examples of encouraging comments. Extra effort, high grades, honors, promotions, and other accomplishments should be rewarded. When such encouragement is given, interviewees will visibly relax and become more spontaneous and expansive in their comments. Your encouragement should, however, be genuine. If interviewees feel that an interviewer recognizes their achievements, they will be much more willing to discuss their shortcomings.

When applicants present unfavorable information, you should "play it down" with a casual and understanding remark. You may probe the information, but don't make a big deal out of it. Some interviewers like to use an example of some failure in their own background to help reduce the anxiety involved with a similar interviewee self-disclosure. It is not your place to condone unfavorable past behavior, but you should reduce the negative effect of its disclosure on the interview climate. If you give the slightest indication of moral judgment or being adversely influenced by such information, no further information of that sort will be offered. You must remain neutral and accepting. The following are ten other questioning behaviors of skillful selection interviewers.

1. *He doesn't ask questions which can be answered by "Yes" or "No." Most of them are worded so that the candidate must expand his answers. The interviewer also repeatedly asks questions on this order:*
   "How did you get interested in that?" and "How did you feel about that?"
2. *He pauses for at least a few seconds after the applicant appears to have finished an answer. This gives the applicant the chance to further talk. On this point, it has been suggested that "knowing when not to inject onself into the interview is often as important as asking questions deftly. . . . The interviewer who feels he must fill every minute of silence should know that his eagerness to talk is usually*

caused by concern about his own comfort rather than concern for the applicant.''

3. *He tries several different subjects at the beginning, to determine which is most provocative in encouraging the applicant to talk. He returns to those topics on which the candidate froze, nevertheless, in order to determine if the lack of response is significant.*
4. *He repeats part of the key sentences of the applicant, in a questioning tone, to indicate that he wants elaboration.*
5. *He asks one question at a time.*
6. *He makes his questions clear, without indicating what he thinks the correct answer is.*
7. *His manner is interested; his attention is uninterrupted; and by neither manner nor word does he imply impatience or a critical attitude toward what is being said by the candidate.*
8. *He doesn't ask highly personal questions until rapport has been established.*
9. *When the applicant digresses, the interviewer does not bring him abruptly back to the point.*
10. *He uses language appropriate to the applicant.* *

Just as selection interviewers must be careful about the way they ask questions, interviewees must be just as careful about their responses. Extremely short answers to open questions aren't impressive—most interviewers prefer respondents who are enthusiastic and elaborate upon their responses. A good response is one which shows thought and maturity. If it is possible to answer a question quickly yet still intelligently, you should do so. Quickwittedness can impress interviewers. If, however, you feel a quick answer may be confused or inconsistent, you should take your time and think before responding.

Your best guard against presenting inconsistent or contradictory information is to tell the plain and simple truth at all times. A good honest answer, even if it is a little unfavorable to you, is better than being caught in a lie. You will be able to provide good, honest, and extended answers if you have taken the time to practice answering the typical interview questions presented earlier. Whenever possible, tie your education, experience, and other qualifications directly to the job for which you are applying. Remember, you are trying to sell yourself. Know your own worth, be confident, and volunteer information if there are any gaps which you think need to be filled in order to better qualify you for a job.

SELECTION INTERVIEW PROBING

Selection interviewers make extensive use of nondirective probes such as silence, restatement, and minimal encouragements in order to obtain elaboration and clarification. Fear (1978) calls this the *calculated pause.*

Inexperienced interviewers have a tendency to become uncomfortable whenever a slight pause occurs. Hence, they are likely to break in prematurely with unnecessary comments or questions. Experienced interviewers, on the other hand, tend to wait the applicant out, purposely permitting a pause to occur from time to time. They do this as a conscious technique, knowing full well that the applicant will frequently elaborate on a previous point rather than allow the discussion to come to a standstill. The latter often senses that the interviewer by his very silence expects a fuller treatment of the topic under consideration. The calculated pause is one of the most powerful techniques that the interviewer can draw upon in terms of developing spontaneous information. Such pauses are not only remarkably effective in drawing out the applicant but they also enable the interviewer to do less talking himself and help him to perfect the art of becoming a good listener.

(Fear, 1978, pp. 77–78)

It is your responsibility to probe each topic area carefully and thoroughly. If, for example, interviewees suggest that they are "good at working with people," try to find out what that means and where they demonstrated evidence of that characteristic. Be aware that applicants have a tendency to give socially acceptable responses regardless of whether or not they are true. This won't happen if they know you will probe for evidence of characteristics claimed as well as names of people who can verify their claims.

Moffatt (1979) discusses what he calls the *cone system* of interview questioning and probing. The cone system involves using open-focus questions followed by moderate-focus questions, and finally closed-focus questions to achieve your objective. It is really a type of funnel sequence. Figure 11.10 is an illustration of a general cone sequence. According to Moffatt, cones can be used to examine any topic, such as previous employment, educational background, special training, outside activities and interests, or attitudes and motivations. A significant feature of the cone sequence is what Moffatt calls *flags*. A flag is a statement, word, or nonverbal behavior picked up by interviewers which indicates areas needing probes. Through careful listening, flags can be identified. Flags may show up not only in an interview but also in a resume, job application, or reference check. It is your responsibility to probe all flags.

Interviewers are not the only ones who should watch for flags. Interviewees should also be alert for flags as to areas where an interviewer may be withholding information and probe those areas.

Probably the most difficult aspect of selection interview probing involves sensitive, threatening, or embarrassing information. Don't be afraid to deal with sensitive content but do so with finesse and subtlety. This generally means avoiding such content areas early in an interview, overly direct questions in sensitive areas, moral judgment, or direct challenge. If, for example, you notice a large gap in an interviewee's employment record, it should be probed. The probing, however, ought to be done so respondents can save face and put their explanation in the best possible light. Moffatt (1979) gives examples of ways in which sensitive questions can be modified to maintain a positive climate in figure 11.11.

Sensitive and subtle probing allows interviewers to get at information which interviewees may not be willing to offer. There is no problem with selection interview probing if, like initial questions, it relates directly to the Bona Fide Occupational Qualifications of a respondent. The same guidelines as those dis-

11.10 The Cone

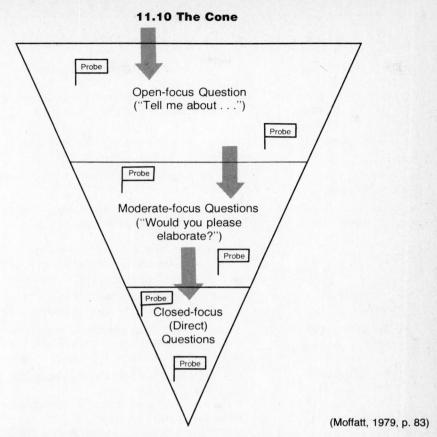

Probe

Open-focus Question
("Tell me about . . .")

Probe

Probe

Moderate-focus Questions
("Would you please
elaborate?")

Probe

Probe

Closed-focus
(Direct)
Questions

Probe

(Moffatt, 1979, p. 83)

cussed for interview guide preparation should be followed for probing. The ability to use follow-up probing is one definite advantage of the selection interview over other written means of employee selection.

SELECTION INTERVIEW LISTENING

In a selection interview, you must listen not only to what is said, but also to what is not said. Applicants naturally downplay weak points and stress their good points. Interviewers also tend to downplay the weak points of a job or their organization. Skillful selection interview participants look for both verbal and nonverbal clues as to the meaning and significance of any particular utterance. Very often, the difference between hiring a successful and unsuccessful job applicant or choosing the right company is the information sent nonverbally. It is from nonverbal information that many interviewers judge not whether applicants have the technical competence to perform a job satisfactorily, but whether they have the stamina to continue to produce at a high level when the going gets rough, if they have personal integrity, or whether they can fit in with current

11.11 Sensitive Questions and Their Alternatives

Too Direct or Sensitive	*Less Direct or Sensitive*
Why were you fired from your last job? *or* Why are you looking for another job?	What are some of your reasons for considering other employment at this time?
Did you have trouble with your boss?	How would you describe your boss?
Why did you leave school before you got your degree?	Was there any particular reason that you decided to leave school when you did?
To what do you attribute your poor employment record?	I see you have changed jobs several times. What were some of your reasons for seeking new opportunities? *or* Everyone has problems with some aspects of their jobs. Could you describe some of the things that posed problems for you on previous jobs?
Did you get along with your co-workers?	Could you describe your relationship with a co-worker or colleague whom you were particularly close to?
What didn't you like about your last job?	Most situations have some aspects that are not as pleasant as others. Were there any less pleasant aspects of your last job?
Are you free to move?	How would you feel about moving to another city at the present time? *or* If you were relocated to another area, what problems would this present for you? (*Note:* The relocation question usually takes more time and should not be approached so directly. The whole topic can become a separate area of nondirective inquiry.)
Your sales record must have been poor last year, since you didn't get a bonus.	How would you describe your sales success during the past year? *or* We all realize that sales often reflect various conditions of the economy. Could you comment on some factors that might have precluded your meeting last year's quotas?
You mean to say you're unemployed?	At present you're not employed, then, is that correct?
I suppose you're on unemployment, huh?	Were you eligible to receive unemployment compensation after you were laid off?
Why would you think you are qualified to go into research and development, with your background?	Would you comment on how you feel you could use your background in our research and development area?

(Moffatt, 1979, pp. 24–25)

employees. These intangible factors often make the difference between interview success and failure.

A major problem in selection interview listening is the halo effect. The *halo effect* is a tendency on the part of some interviewers to allow one applicant characteristic to overshadow all others. If, for example, an interviewer is impressed with the college from which an applicant graduated, this may overshadow work experience, job qualifications, and other relevant information. The interviewer has allowed educational background to cast a halo around the applicant making all other information appear better. The halo effect can also work in the opposite direction. If, for example, you find a low grade-point average, this may negatively affect the way you listen to other information. It is your responsibility to listen to all information carefully and consider each on its own merits. There is no doubt that initial impressions will color and influence future information, but you should be sure that each statement is given careful consideration. The halo effect can cause a poor hiring decision and hurt both the organization and applicants. The halo effect can also cause interviewees to make a poor career decision.

Finally, you must be careful not to encourage or listen to illegal information. Organizations are liable when illegal information is transmitted, even if it is not solicited. It is your responsibility to cut it off as soon as it is recognized and explain that your organization is not interested in such information. A simple explanation that you are following federal guidelines is usually sufficient. Do not be rude or condescending, but merely indicate that you know the law and your job. Listen to and record only that information which is directly relevant to the Bona Fide Occupational Qualifications of respondents.

SELECTION INTERVIEW RECORDING

Interviewers are often required to fill out a detailed and highly structured evaluation form during or after the interview. Here is an example of such a form (figure 11.12), but be careful, a couple of these areas may not meet the EEOC guidelines if not handled properly.

Other interviewers take pencil and paper or tape-recorded notes and turn in an unstructured analysis of each interview. Regardless of how you take notes, it is most important that you do not confuse applicants or divert their attention. You must take notes unobtrusively. This can be done by either jotting down comments while looking at interviewees or making brief central idea notes after each response. In many cases, some of the information needed to complete the written evaluation can be found on the applicant's resume.

When taking pencil and paper notes, be certain that interviewees can't read what you are writing. Also be sure not to write down only negative information; your notes should be brief enough to capture only the key points of a response and yet long enough to help you remember the entire response after the interview concludes. Skilled interviewers depend a great deal on their memories when taking notes. Most of your time should be spent looking at applicants rather than writing.

11.12 Sample Selection Interview Recording Form
(Space for information recording has been omitted.)

INTERVIEW RATING FORM

Date _____

Interviewer _____

Name _____ Age _____ Position _____

1. WORK HISTORY

                                Above avg.   Avg.   Below avg.

2. EDUCATION AND TRAINING

                                Above avg.   Avg.   Below avg.

3. EARLY HOME BACKGROUND

                                Above avg.   Avg.   Below avg.

4. PRESENT SOCIAL ADJUSTMENT

                                Above avg.   Avg.   Below avg.

5. PERSONALITY, MOTIVATION,
   AND CHARACTER
   $(+, A+, A, A-, -)$

                                Above avg.   Avg.   Below avg.

( ) a. Maturity   ( ) f. Tough-mindedness   ( ) l. Conscientiousness

( ) b. Emotional   ( ) g. Self-discipline   ( ) m. Hard worker

        adjustment   ( ) h. Initiative   ( ) n. Honesty and

( ) c. Teamworker   ( ) i. Follow-through   sincerity

( ) d. Tact   ( ) j. Self-confident

( ) e. Adaptability   ( ) k. Personal forcefulness

6. SUMMARY OF ASSETS   SUMMARY OF SHORTCOMINGS

7. OVERALL SUMMARY

8. OVERALL RATING _____

                Excellent Above Average Average Below Average Poor

(Fear, 1978, pp. 307–308)

Many selection interviewers are now using electronic means to record interviewee responses. They take written notes, then, basically for probing rather than record keeping. Interview recording, like interview questioning, has come under the scrutiny of the government. A number of selection interviewers have lost their jobs because they take notes which appear to be some kind of "secret code." For example, interviewers have been challenged for filling the circles of p's, o's, and other letters which could be taken as a code. This is another reason electronic recording is used—it provides evidence of what took place in each interview. You must be extremely careful when you record selection interviews for both legality and accuracy.

SELECTION INTERVIEW CONCLUDING

Closing a selection interview generally involves a detailed description of the organization and job as well as answering interviewee questions. As was mentioned earlier, most of this information is planned and included in your interview guide. Your description should contain as much information as seems necessary for all applicants to know at that particular point. It should be presented simply, honestly, and completely. Unless you have final decision-making authority, you should not oversell the organization and position. This can be done later, once a decision has been made. Responses to interviewee questions should also be as open and honest as possible. Remember, interviewees as well as interviewers are making an important decision.

Since most selection interviews are not concluded with a hiring decision, it is your responsibility to inform interviewees of how and when the decision will be made and when they will be notified. There is a difference of opinion among professionals as to whether respondents should be given any indication of their possible success in the closing. Some believe that all selection interviews should be concluded with no indication given as to the probable result. They feel that an interviewer should neither encourage nor discourage candidates. The interviewee learns the decision through a letter or telephone call.

Others feel that it is only fair to give respondents some indication of how they have done before they leave. They feel that applicants have a right to know about where they stand. The arguments on both sides of this question are very strong. Perhaps the best compromise suggestion is that you tell interviewees who have little or no chance they will probably not be selected, but do not encourage those individuals who have a chance of obtaining the position. This decision, however, is yours to make when you conduct a selection interview. Regardless of your choice, you should always leave the respondent in a positive frame of mind.

The follow-up portion of a selection interview closing includes completing the organization's standard rating form or a nonstructured applicant analysis. Regardless of the form used, your applicant analysis should be based upon information gathered prior to the interview, during the interview, and discovered after the interview is completed. In most cases, the employment decision depends upon the job requirements and the qualifications of other applicants. In completing an applicant analysis, you must evaluate the whole person in relation to the total job description. Be as careful, honest, unbiased, and broad-minded as possible. It is your responsibility not only to obtain the necessary information regarding each applicant, but also to interpret that information correctly.

The results of selection interview decisions are important to your organization in terms of both time and money, and they are extremely important to job applicants. Making the right hiring decision, therefore, should be of utmost importance to you. This means a careful and accurate analysis of each interviewee. Your written analysis is often all that will be seen of applicants by the individual or individuals responsible for making the final decision or selecting people for further interviews.

Once the decision has been made, both successful and unsuccessful applicants should be notified. All records of interviews with both successful and unsuccessful applicants should be filed to meet both federal and state regulations. The reasons for disqualification of unsuccessful applicants should be carefully noted. These reasons must be as specific and job-related as possible. The term "better qualified applicant" is not a sufficient reason. You must be prepared to compare the qualifications of various applicants. As federal and state regulations become more strict, it will become even more important to keep complete and accurate records of all selection interviews and decisions.

SUMMARY

This is one of the longest chapters in this book because of its importance to most students. Although this chapter is not guaranteed to make you successful every time, it does provide a starting point for both selection interviewers and interviewees. Some of the pre-interview topics of special interest discussed in this chapter were assessment centers; interviewer preparation, including organizational knowledge, critical job requirements, the application form, and information/reference checking; interview preparation such as self analysis, resume development, organizational research, initial contact, analyzing the job description, and planning appearance and behavior; and methods of preparing a legal and successful interview guide.

The selection interview itself should be relaxed and informal with a brief but thorough orientation, subtle and complete questioning and probing, good honest responses, unbiased listening and recording, and a pleasant but fairly noncommittal closing. A successful selection interview is one where both participants feel the information given and received is sufficient to make the correct employment decision. Anything less than this can be costly for both participants.

ACTIVITIES

Activity #1

Directions: On the basis of what you have learned in this chapter and in Part I, analyze this selection interview. Look for both good and bad points of both the interviewer and interviewee. Use the line number to refer to comments.

R = Interviewer   E = Interviewee

1 R: Hello, Bob. I'm glad you had a chance to stop by today. I read your resume and application form, and we have positions for people with your background. You look a little chilly; is it cold outside?

E: Yeah, it sure is. I just walked over here from class, and the snow is getting
5 worse. I appreciate your talking with me.

R: Well, we are always on the lookout for new talented people. We have doubled our sales in the last five years and a great deal of credit goes to our public relations department. That's why we always need new people and new ideas to keep us growing. These interviews usually take about a half
10 hour. I like to talk with applicants about their background and ideas for a while and then talk a little about the organization and position. Once that is done feel free to ask any questions you may have. How does that sound to you?

E: That sounds fine.

15 R: Why don't you just consider the next fifteen minutes or so a version of "This is your life." Perhaps you could start off by telling me a little about your last four years in college, your major, courses, or anything else you think important.

E: Well, let me start at the beginning. I was born in Dearborn, Michigan. I
20 lived there till I went to college. I have one brother and two sisters.

R: Where do you fit in?

E: What? Where do I fit in?

R: Yes, are you the youngest or oldest?

E: Oh, I see, I am the next to oldest. My older sister is 24 and works for the
25 telephone company.

R: I see. Go on.

E: I guess it was my dad that talked me into going to college. He was sold on education. He never went to college himself, and he wanted to be sure I went. He would check all our report cards and wouldn't let us watch TV if
30 they weren't high enough.

R: How did you feel about that?

E: I guess I wasn't too happy then, but he was right. I was always happier working in the summer than going to school. I did OK in high school though; at least I did well enough to get into college. I started out trying to be
35 an engineer like my dad wanted, but after a year I decided all that math and science wasn't for me. I took some general education classes in the social sciences and liked those much better. I decided to go into business and combine that with social science. Accounting and economics also took more math than I liked, so I went into marketing, advertising, journalism, com-
40 munication, and things like that and finally decided on public relations. Since that's been my major, I have really started liking school.

R: Found your niche, huh?

E: You bet; this is really what I want to do. My grades came up. My outlook got better. I am happy right now. I love my marketing and advertising and
45 communication classes. I go home and start studying before dinner. I have even had time to do some of the other things I want to do, like play

raquetball and go out on the town. Before I had to work so hard studying I didn't want to do anything else.

R: Well, it sounds like you have the education for this job. Let's look at your
50 experience. I have some information about your previous jobs on your resume. Could you tell me which of these jobs you liked the best and which you think helped you most in your public relations career, that is, will help you most in your public relations career?

E: Well, the thing that helped me most for public relations was not any of my
55 jobs, but the internship program I am in this year. I am working in an advertising company, well, not really working, but observing. I am spending five hours a week in the advertising firm and writing a paper about my experiences. I am learning more there than I ever thought I could. They have even let me work on a small campaign myself. Most of my jobs were just to
60 help me earn money for school. I learned about getting along with people in those jobs but not too much about public relations other than meeting the public. I guess from that point, the job I had checking groceries in a store was the biggest help. I got to learn how wacky and yet good-hearted people can be. I really like working with people.

65 *R:* Tell me a little more about that "campaign" you are working on.

E: It's just for a local hot stove company, you know, one of those stoves people use to heat their house rather than use oil.

R: Yeah.

E: I have been writing some local radio spots for them. Two of my spots have
70 already been run.

R: What did you do to prepare those spots?

E: I had to talk with the customer, that is, the owner of the company, read all of their literature, write the spots, and then get the radio people to record them. I guess I spent a whole lot more time on that project than my five
75 hours a week, but I thought it was a good experience, and I wanted to do it right. I was really proud when I heard them played.

R: Yeah, that's something you should be proud of. It's nice when you see your efforts pay off, isn't it?

E: Yeah, I've always been that way. I don't mind working hard when I know
80 something will come of it.

R: You also said earlier that you liked "working with people." How do you mean that?

E: I guess, I'm just naturally outgoing. I like to talk with people and help them when I can. One time, for example, I noticed that a lady had a box of
85 cereal that had a cut in it and some of the cereal had fallen out. She was really happy when I told her about it, and that made me happy all day.

R: Were you ever fired from any of your jobs?

E: No. I quit a couple because I didn't like them.

R: Which were those?

90 *E:* Let's see. I quit that kitchen helper job. The boss wanted me to clean the grease off the stove every day, and it kept getting all over my clothes. He wouldn't give me any old clothes to wear, and my mom said I had to quit because she was getting tired of buying clothes and my ruining them. I also quit the wood splitting job. I almost hit myself with an axe one day, and I

95 decided it just wasn't worth it.

R: I see. Why are you interested in a job with our company?

E: I don't know too much about your company, but I do know I want to get a public relations job. Could you tell me a little about your company?

R: Yes. We are the Titan Power Tool Company, and our main line is the
100 production and sales of power tools for home use. We are in a very competitive business, and therefore, public relations means a lot to us. We advertise in all of the mass media as well as in hardware stores and lumber companies, any place where they sell power tools. We use pamphlets, posters, and any other way we can think of to get our message across that we sell the best for
105 less.

E: I see.

R: Whenever we bring someone new into the public relations department, we try to have them work closely with one of the senior staff members until they get the hang of the job. Kind of on-the-spot training, as it were.

110 *E:* That's good, kind of like my internship.

R: That's right. What we really look for is someone we think we can train to do the job. Someone with ambition, energy, and a willingness to learn. We like for our new people to have some background in public relations, so we don't have to go over the very basics, but on the whole we like to train our
115 employees ourselves. Do you have any questions?

E: No. I think you have covered everything I need to know.

R: Oh, well alright. I will be talking to several other applicants before I have a chance to sit down and make some decisions. I should be getting back to you in a couple of weeks, one way or the other. It's been interesting talking
120 with you. I wish you success in your public relations career.

E: Thank you, I'll be waiting to hear from you.

R: Well, don't put all your hopes on this job. As I said I have several more people to talk with before I make my decision. You know most people interview several times before finding a company and position that is right
125 for both parties. Like I said, I will let you know one way or the other in a couple of weeks. Good bye.

E: Good bye. Thanks again.

Will this applicant get the job? Probably not! The interviewee made a great many of the common basic interview mistakes. Can you identify them? The interviewer also made some mistakes. Can you identify them? Your list should be quite long. Keep this list. It will be used in the next activity.

Activity #2

Directions: This activity involves the use of audio or video tape recording. What you try to do is simulate a selection interview using your own resume, application, cover letter, etc. The way we usually set this activity up in classes is to sign up students to come in pairs to our video facility. Each student is assigned as either the interviewer or interviewee for each time period. The schedule is organized so that no two students ever interview one another twice. There is always one person who stays and switches roles as a new student arrives. Before doing the interview, however, the people who are interviewing one another sit and talk about what type of job interview will take place. It is the interviewee's responsibility to develop the company, either real or hypothetical, and all of the organization and position information necessary for the interview. This can be done by gathering literature on real companies from the library, placement service, or actual local organizations. Once all interviewers are prepared with organization and position information by their interviewee, they must develop a selection interview guide. The interviewees prepare as they normally would for a selection interview. Remember, each student is both an interviewer and an interviewee, so each student does everything. Everything about the interview is to be as realistic as possible right down to the way the participants dress. As each interview takes place, it is videotaped (an audio tape recorder would also work, but not as well). No one is allowed to see the recording at that time. Each participant must prepare a critical evaluation of his or her performance as both the interviewer and interviewee. This is where the notes taken regarding the first activity come in handy. They can be used as a basis for comparison in writing the critical analysis. Once the analysis is prepared, each pair of participants discuss their strengths and weaknesses in the interview with the instructor and one another, view the videotape, and then make a summary analysis. Students find this activity to be one of the most valuable learning experiences they have in the entire course. This is because that first career job interview is so important to them. For those of you who are not part of a class, many placement centers are beginning to offer a similar service for persons preparing for their first selection interview.

Activity #3

Directions: Select one of the following hypothetical cases and role-play it, being sure to use the concepts and skills discussed in this and previous chapters. These cases merely describe a common selection interview situation. You are free to add any other information you like to make the role-play better. Try to make the interview as realistic as possible.

CASE A: *Ray Clark* has a B.A. degree from Texas Polytech in mechanical engineering and an M.B.A. in industrial management. He has been working for the last two years as a project engineer for U.S. Conveyor Company. He started as an industrial engineer and was promoted after three years to project engineer. His salary, however, has not kept up with his promotions. U.S. Conveyor is not noted for its generosity. He has been looking for a better paying position for several months now and has an appointment to talk with a major competitor, the Jones Manufacturing Company. He knows he must be careful about what he says regarding his reasons for wanting to leave U.S. Conveyor and also be sure he has this new job before anyone at U.S. Conveyor finds out he is job hunting. He has not even asked for any letters of recommendation yet, but he knows he can get good ones when he leaves. He is not sure about the salary at Jones Company, but he has heard they pay much better than U.S. Conveyor. His current salary is $21,500 per year.

Arthur Haskins, the personnel manager for Jones Manufacturing Company, has a position to fill in the engineering department. The job requires someone with experience and leadership ability, since this person must supervise the work of other engineers. None of the current engineers are yet ready for the position so he has decided to go outside of the organization. The position pays $20,000 for the six-month probation period, then jumps to $25,000 per year. Arthur knows little about Ray Clark other than the information on his application which says that he currently works for U.S. Conveyor Company as a project engineer. Clark left the reason-for-leaving question blank. It would be a relief to get someone to fill the position quickly, but Arthur generally does not approve of hiring people away from competitors. That can get to be a dangerous practice and can cost both organizations a great deal of money.

CASE B: *Amy Tate,* the interviewee, is applying to the Nationwide Airline Corporation to become a flight attendant. She meets all of the basic requirements such as vision, hearing, etc. Becoming a flight attendant has always been her ambition. She applied with another airline earlier but was turned down because they said she was indecisive and not outgoing enough. She worked as a secretary for the last year in the Sherahilt Hotel. She was fired from that job last week because, as her boss said, "You don't answer the phone or treat our guests in a friendly and helpful manner." That's when Amy decided to try to be a flight attendant again. She is determined to be outgoing, friendly, and all of the other things she knows will make the interviewer choose her, even though that's not her basic nature. *Wanda Harper,* the interviewer, has worked for Nationwide Airline Corporation for fifteen years. For the first thirteen years she worked as a flight attendant, and when this chance to stay in the home office and interview applicants came along, she took it. The main things she looks for in applicants is a desire to travel, enthusiasm, dependability, initiative, ability to inspire confidence, calmness, self-discipline, good appearance, sense of humor, decisiveness, and breadth of outlook. All of the applicants are screened for the physical requirements before she sees them. She sees five or six applicants a day and can only select about a tenth of the people who apply. It's a tough job, but she prefers it to her old job. Between the interviews and reference checks she must make on each applicant, she keeps busy. The reference check on Amy Tate produced the information that she had recently left the Sherahilt Hotel rather abruptly. They would not say why, but Wanda got the feeling something was wrong.

CASE C: *Bob Thomas* recently dropped out of high school. He just couldn't hack the studying anymore. He decided to work for a while. He has applied for a job at the ABC Grocery Store as a take-out boy. *Rachel Fiske* is the manager of ABC Grocery Store. Whenever she hires employees, she looks for a desire to work and a pleasant personality. The job only pays minimum wage, but in this day and age you can get a lot of good people at that rate if you are careful. The only information she has on Bob Thomas is that he is a high-school dropout.

Chapter 12

The Counseling Interview

Most clients believe that the counselor will have words of wisdom and specific solutions for their problems. This is true even of sophisticated individuals who have had wide exposure to theories of treatment through books and through reports of their friends' experiences. The person who is hurt or troubled, anxious or depressed, wants a prescription that will take away the pain. Whereas the counselor knows beforehand he has no special answers, the client is disappointed when the counselor offers few, if any, suggestions as to what the client should do to solve his problem. And it takes time in the treatment for the client to recognize that his hopes to be "cured" are themselves items to be worked on. (Edinburg, Zinberg, and Kelman, 1975, pp. 1–2)

The counseling interview is what is commonly called a *helping* interview. You are trying to help someone solve a problem. There are basically two approaches to helping interviews. The traditional, diagnostic approach is highly directive and involves a great deal of interviewer input. The interviewee explains the problem and the interviewer suggests a proper course of action. This approach will be discussed in Chapter 13. The second approach is often called the *client-centered* or *nondirective* approach to helping. The counselor acts as a facilitator rather than an advisor. The goal of a counseling interview is to help interviewees (usually called clients) identify and solve their own problems. Both helping approaches are valuable, and you should know how to handle each. In some helping interviews it is possible or necessary to combine both the counseling and diagnostic approaches.

Counseling interviews are very sensitive and nondirective. They are commonly interviewee-initiated and usually involve stressful and emotional problems. Thwarted ambitions, retirement, alcoholism, drug abuse, marital difficulties, and many other similar problems are common topics. It seems that the more difficult, stressful, and complicated our world becomes, the more important and frequent counseling interviews become.

These interviews are often conducted by professionals such as religious leaders, marital advisors, mental health experts, psychologists, and psychiatrists. They are also conducted by lay persons such as business managers, school teachers, parents, and friends. Sometimes interviewees consciously seek counseling, while at other times both professional and amateur counselors volunteer their services. Such a volunteer might be a manager or supervisor who feels that some type of personal problem is affecting a subordinate's work. Although not wholly qualified to offer professional help, the superior feels obligated to at least offer some assistance. Wise managers will seek professional help if the problem exceeds their capabilities. Regardless of whether you are a professional or an amateur faced with a situation which calls for a counseling approach, the necessary basic skills are the same.

COUNSELING INTERVIEW PREPARATION

A great deal of general preparation goes into effective counseling, but little specific preparation, because in most cases you are not aware of the problem until the interview begins. This is true of most interviewee-initiated interviews. Preparation, therefore, usually consists of deciding whether to counsel or to refer the respondent to someone better prepared to handle the problem. Even this decision must sometimes be delayed until the respondent begins discussing the problem.

In terms of general preparation, however, there are a number of things you can do to mentally prepare for a counseling interview. Stewart and Cash (1978) suggest that potential counselors ask themselves six essential questions regarding their abilities, capabilities, and perceptions of the situation before attempting to conduct such an interview:

1. *Are you a good listener?*
2. *Do you have the patience necessary for dealing with trying, time-consuming situations?*
3. *Are you involved with the client or the client's problem?*
4. *Do you have a realistic view of your counseling skills, training, and experiences?*
5. *Do you have a realistic view of what can and cannot be accomplished in a particular situation?*
6. *Do you have a sincere desire to help people without trying to play God?*

(Stewart and Cash, 1978, p. 184)

If you answer all of those questions "yes," except number three, then you have the proper mental disposition to handle a counseling interview.

Once you have decided you are willing, you need to get in the proper frame of mind. The proper frame of mind includes a strong desire to help, a willingness to listen, and the ability to give something of yourself. You must be aware of your own strengths and weaknesses, biases and prejudices, and ego defenses. Once aware of them, be willing to discard them for the sake of helping the respondent. The following is an eloquent statement of what can be accomplished in a counseling interview if you have your own problems squared away and are willing to adopt a truly helping attitude.

The less defensive we as interviewers can become, the more we shall help our interviewees discard their defenses. Communication between us will improve as a consequence. The more we become aware of what our values are and the less we need to impose them on the interviewee, the more we may help him become aware of his own values and retain, adapt, or reject them as he sees fit. Knowing my own values, I can state them. If I can accept them as a changing part of my changing self, I may be able to accept his as a changing part of his changing self. Some of these values of mine may remain constant for me, and some may for him; but I shall not be afraid to expose mine, nor shall I fear being exposed to his. He, in turn, may learn not to fear exposing his values or being exposed to mine because he will know that he is not being threatened. In such an atmosphere he may learn to describe his values without fear of being judged. He will not need to defend because he will not feel attacked. Perceiving no necessity to adjust to the interviewer's values, he may discover those he really believes in.

(Benjamin, 1969, p. 92).

Once the proper mental attitude is established and whatever needed background information has been gathered, you are ready to prepare the time and place for the interview. In professional counseling interviews, timing is extremely important. Professional counselors make appointments and stick to the scheduled time period very closely. This may necessitate scheduling a continuation interview at a later time. Professional counseling interviews, such as psychiatric therapy sessions, may continue over a period of several months or even years. It is probably better to hold nonprofessional counseling interviews toward the end of the day because of the sensitive nature of the subject matter involved. This cannot always be done, however, and counseling interviews can take place at almost any time.

When most of you think of a counseling interview setting, you probably think of a psychiatrist sitting in a chair and the interviewee lying down on a couch. This stereotype is not accurate in modern counseling interviews. It does, however, demonstrate the need for choosing a setting which allows the respondent to be as comfortable and relaxed as possible. Soft chairs and pleasant surroundings encourage the conversational, informal atmosphere that is desired. It is absolutely essential that there be no interruptions or distractions throughout the entire interview. Nothing disrupts a counseling interview more than to have ringing telephones, intruders, or outside noises. Privacy and comfort are absolutely essential.

Even though the stereotype of the counselor sitting in a chair behind the client's head is outmoded, it illustrates another important point about counseling interviews. The reason therapists used to sit out-of-sight was to keep from unconsciously leading the respondent. These interviewers were well aware that the slightest cue, such as a head nod, jotting of a note, or smile could direct respondents to a particular response. Such directive behavior, be it conscious or unconscious, must be avoided. Careful preparation of the setting as well as all other parts of the interview can help you keep the interview nondirective and allow respondents to come to grips with and solve their own problems.

THE COUNSELING INTERVIEW GUIDE

Since few specifics are generally known ahead of time about the topic in a counseling interview, it is difficult to prepare a detailed guide. At most you can briefly outline some potential topics, questions, and probes. Because most counseling interviews are nondirective, the interviewee will control progress and direction as well as supply information. The direction is not determined ahead of time: this is a major difference between counseling and diagnostic interviews. Almost all interviewer questions and statements come as probes in a counseling interview.

There are, however, a number of what Cormier and Cormier (1979) call *treatment strategies* which should be familiar to all counseling interviewers and form a kind of unstructured interview guide. These strategies include symbolic modeling, self-as-a-model, participant modeling, emotive imagery, covert modeling, cognitive modeling, thought-stopping, cognitive restructuring, stress inoculation, mediation, muscle relaxation, systematic desensitization, self-monitoring, stimulus control, self-reward, self-punishment, and self-contracting. They are all useful counseling strategies and deserve some brief discussion.

Symbolic modeling consists of presenting written materials, audio tape, films, or slide tapes to interviewees and encouraging them to copy or "model" their own behavior after the behavior presented. In the *self-as-a-model* strategy, interviewees serve as their own models. This can be done with recorders and is sometimes extremely useful because it provides personalized feedback. With the help of the tape, you can point out both desirable and undesirable behaviors. *Participant modeling* is somewhat more involved and requires respondents to learn specific behaviors in the interview and then transfer them to their usual environments. First you demonstrate the desired behavior, then the respondent practices it with you, and finally the interviewee practices the behavior with others in their regular environments. Various forms of modeling can be useful in counseling interviews. It requires, however, respondent action.

In some cases, you can't provide models or have interviewees engage in overt behavior practice. It may be more useful to employ strategies that utilize the respondent's imagination, such as emotive imagery and covert modeling. *Emotive imagery* requires the interviewee to think positive thoughts or imagine pleasant images when faced with a problem situation. A respondent who is having problems adjusting to routine work, for example, might be encouraged to make a game of the job or think of a sunset to counteract feelings of worthlessness. *Covert modeling* is a strategy whereby the interviewee imagines some other individual or "model" performing the necessary behaviors. Cormier and Cormier (1979) point out the advantages of covert modeling:

> There are several advantages of covert modeling: the procedure does not require elaborate therapeutic or induction aids; scenes can be developed to deal with a variety of problems; the scenes can be individualized to fit the unique concerns of the client; the client can practice imagery scenes alone; the client can use the imagery scenes as a self-control procedure in problem situations; and covert modeling may be a good alternative when live or filmed models cannot be used or when it is difficult to use overt rehearsal in the interview.

> (Cormier and Cormier, 1979, p. 308)

The preceding five techniques are designed to help interviewees correct problem behaviors. The next two, cognitive modeling and thought-stopping, are designed to help interviewees modify problem thoughts, attitudes, and beliefs. *Cognitive modeling* is a strategy whereby you, the counselor, serve as a model by first performing a task while talking aloud to yourself; the clients then perform the task while you instruct; next, the respondents perform the task again while doing their own instructing; they then whisper instructions to themselves while performing the task; and finally the clients perform the task while silently producing their own instructions.

Thought-stopping helps interviewees control unproductive or self-defeating thoughts. Before using this strategy, however, interviewees must be aware that they do have self-defeating thoughts. Thought-stopping is accomplished by first allowing an interviewee to let any thoughts or images come to mind. When a self-defeating thought or image occurs, you interrupt with a loud "stop!" As with cognitive modeling, interviewees learn how to identify and stop such self-defeating thoughts on their own and are then taught how to shift to more positive thoughts, such as a beautiful painting, some pleasant thing that happened during the day, or an interesting object in the room.

Cognitive restructuring and *stress inoculation* are designed to help clients determine the relationship between their beliefs, values, or attitudes and the resulting emotions and behaviors which are causing problems. *Cognitive restructuring* is simply a matter of getting interviewees to change the way they see problem situations. Poor mental attitudes and thoughts are first identified and then "coping" thoughts, statements, and self-instructions are learned. For example, the self-defeating thought of "failing" at some task is replaced by the coping thought of "doing my best." Other coping thoughts include "Focus on the task," "What is it I want to accomplish now?" "Relax so I can focus on the situation," "Slow down, take my time, don't rush," and "OK, don't get out of control. It's a signal to cope." *Stress inoculation* teaches interviewees both physical and cognitive skills. It involves educating them about the nature of stressful reactions, having them rehearse various coping behaviors, and helping them apply these skills during controlled exposure to stressful situations. Coping thoughts are often combined with relaxation techniques so that clients relax both physically and mentally.

Counseling interviewers find that stress and anxiety account for a great many of interviewees' problems. Meditation and muscle relaxation are used to treat both cognitive and physiological stress, including anxiety, anger, and pain. *Meditation* is primarily a cognitive relaxation procedure, whereas muscle relaxation focuses on physical sensations. Meditation must be conducted in a quiet, calm environment. You give the interviewee instructions on body comfort, breathing, passive attitude, and a mental device such as a single syllable sound or word like "in," "out," "one," or "zun." The respondent repeats the word silently for each inhalation and exhalation. This frees them from focusing on their logical or externally-oriented problems. *Muscle relaxation* consists of teaching clients how to tense and relax major muscle groups. They are then encouraged to tense and relax each muscle group at least twice to relieve stress and anxiety. This is first done under your guidance and then by the interviewee alone.

Systematic desensitization requires identifying problem situations for the client and then exposing the interviewee to weak doses of the troublesome situation until the stimulus progressively loses its ability to cause problems. Desensitization is one of the most traditional of all counseling strategies. The anxiety produced by the situation is replaced by something else, like relaxation.

Self-monitoring helps interviewees observe and record specific aspects of their feelings and behaviors in problem situations. It helps interviewees define their own problems and collect evaluative data about a problem. It is less useful as a self-change strategy, so it is often used in conjunction with other self management procedures such as stimulus control, self-reward, self-punishment, and self-contracting. Self-monitoring is a very useful strategy for amateur counselors since it does not involve any complex procedures. You simply help respondents perceive their own problems objectively.

Stimulus control requires that interviewees rearrange environmental cues or conditions to modify certain behaviors. For example, an interviewee who is having drinking problems when a certain person is around arranges to be with that person as little as possible. *Self-reward* allows interviewees to reward themselves following a desired response, such as turning down a drink at a bar. The reward can be verbal, material, or imaginary. *Self-punishment* requires that, following an undesired response, interviewees remove a positive stimulus, such as a pleasant activity, or present themselves with an unpleasant stimulus, such as paying a fine. *Self-contracting* is a self-management strategy which involves determining the consequences that will follow either desired or undesired behaviors in advance. In other words, interviewees make a "contract" with themselves. For example, the interviewee determines not to take a lunch break until a job is finished.

All of these basic strategies suggested by Cormier and Cormier (1979) should be kept in mind when preparing for a counseling interview. They are tested procedures which can help interviewees cope with various problems. They all depend, however, on your ability to guide interviewees to a recognition of the problems that motivated the interview. In most cases, they cannot be planned ahead of time, but become a means of guiding the interview once the problems are recognized.

COUNSELING INTERVIEW OPENING

The success or failure of a counseling interview is often determined by the climate set at the very beginning. Interviewees usually come to a counseling interview with a great deal of anxiety and fear. In most cases, they already know they have a problem, even though they may not be able to identify it accurately. The idea of "going to a shrink," however, makes them extremely tense. They want you to "tell them" what they should do about their problem—they want a direction. The nondirective counseling interviewer will, however, refuse to provide "an answer." This often increases interviewee anxiety.

The opening is the place to set the nondirective, nonjudgmental tone for the entire interview. As an interviewee walks into the office, for example, and asks where to sit, you should respond, "wherever you like." This starts them making their own choices from the very beginning. If clients choose to be called by their first name, you should request that they call you by your first name. Such simple, seemingly unimportant details can have a tremendous impact on the opening climate. The point to be made in the opening is that the climate will be informal, permissive, accepting, and nonevaluative. You want to give the interviewee the impression that you can be trusted, are approachable, and can maintain confidentiality.

You can create a productive climate in many different ways. One way is with your appearance. Extremely sloppy clothes, make up, or hair style may make interviewees question your maturity. Your clothing should be as similar as possible to the respondent's. More important, however, is the way in which you interact and behave. You must be empathetic, neutral, objective, and conversational. This can be extremely difficult. The temptation is to give respondents advice. If at all possible, you must try to get interviewees to do most, if not all, of the talking. Use silence and minimal encouragements from the very beginning.

The opening often takes quite a long time in a counseling interview. You must be absolutely certain that a proper climate has been established. One of the biggest mistakes counseling interviewers can make is to proceed into the body before establishing the proper climate. No matter how long it takes, respondents must realize they will be responsible for identifying and solving their own problems. Once you have the climate set, the next step is to ask the opening question. It is also very open and nondirective. Questions such as "What brings you here?" "What do you want to talk about?" or "How did your problems begin?" are typical examples of opening counseling interview questions. They should reinforce the nondirective nature of the interview.

COUNSELING INTERVIEW QUESTIONING AND RESPONDING

Most experts suggest that the fewer questions asked in a counseling interview the better. You should be concerned with listening and probing rather than questioning. Asking questions encourages interviewees to be dependent on an interviewer. By refusing to ask direct questions, you reject interviewee dependency. Even an open question can encourage dependency because it is followed by a question mark, and implies that the interviewer has greater status and power.

To avoid dependency and still obtain the necessary information, learn how to inquire indirectly. This is an art which takes years of practice to perfect. It is the ability to question without seeming to do so. Below are some examples of direct questions followed by their indirect counterparts:

You've had this job a month now, how do you like it?
You've had this job a month, you must have some feelings about it by now.

It's hard to get back into the 'dating scene' after a divorce, isn't it?
It must be hard dating again after your divorce.

What do you think of your teachers this semester?
I'd sure like to hear about your teachers this semester.

No one could lie without knowing it, could they?
I wonder if someone could lie without knowing it.

You may say that some of these examples are not inquiries at all. But they are good indirect questions, because they do get responses from clients. That is the art of counseling questioning—to get a response without asking a question. You appear to be talking with clients, not at them. You become their peer, not a superior or authority. In this way they will open up to you and yet not expect you to solve their problems for them.

This type of questioning is difficult. We all are inclined, when we see what we think is the proper course of action, to lead respondents to that alternative, often by the way we ask questions. Until you try to be completely nondirective and use indirect questions, you will not realize how hard it is. You work harder trying not to cue the client than you ever work as a directive interviewer.

Since the counseling interview is interviewee-initiated, a great deal of responsibility for its success lies with the respondent. If you are the counseling respondent, you must be willing to tell the counselor everything that is bothering you or could account for your problem(s). This is often difficult because very often you think this type of information is threatening or embarrassing. You must remember, however, that your counselor has probably heard such sensitive information before and is willing to listen without making a judgment. You must place your complete trust in the counselor—do not expect to get immediate solutions, but allow counselors to help you in whatever way they believe to be appropriate. When asked a question, be completely open and honest. Do not hold anything back, or you will be hurting your own chances of being helped. If the counselor suggests any of the treatment strategies discussed earlier, give them your full attention and effort, even though they may seem useless to you at first. Both the questioner and responder must be trusting and sensitive for a counseling interview to succeed.

COUNSELING INTERVIEW PROBING

In a counseling interview, probes are the primary means of interviewer communication with clients. As with questioning, it is important that probes be as unbiased and nondirective as possible. They must offer little or no threat to a respondent. Therefore, probes such as silence, minimal encouragement, restatement, reflection, paraphrase, and summary are normally preferred to direct amplification, direct clarification, and confrontation. Probes offering advice, moralizing, disapproval, disbelief, ridicule, contradiction, commands, punishment, or even humor should all be avoided.

The probe should help interviewees identify problems and solutions. It should not, however, suggest or hint at the desired response. Probes merely help you explore a client's perception of a situation and encourage the client to explore it too. This means in-depth probing for both subjective and objective information. Comments such as "You sound irritated," "You seem depressed," and "Waiting makes you feel impatient" are examples of how counseling interviewers reflect feelings. Notice that these probes, like questions, are indirect. They not only encourage continued exploration and increase client self-awareness, but they also demonstrate your understanding of the interviewee's perceptions and feelings. Objective aspects of interviewee statements can be probed with paraphrase and summary. They check your understanding of responses and indirectly stimulate exploration. These clarification probes also help you organize your own thoughts.

In some counseling interviews, confrontation probing is necessary. It can help you and interviewees recognize and resolve contradictions and inconsistencies. Confrontation should only be used once a solid, trusting, warm climate has been established. It will destroy the climate of a counseling interview if not handled carefully and tentatively. It should never be used as a means of punishment or revenge, but can often help overcome unrealistic interviewee evaluations and goals.

Another common probing technique is self-disclosure. *Self-disclosure* involves sharing personal information about yourself. An example of a good self-disclosing probe in response to an interviewee statement regarding a relative's leukemia might be something like, "I understand what you're saying. It was really difficult for me when a friend of mine was dying of cancer." A good self-disclosure should be spontaneous and in no way overshadow or deny what a client has already said; it should be relevant to what interviewees have stated and the topic under discussion. Interviewer self-disclosure is designed to encourage self-disclosing on the part of interviewees. It helps them focus more clearly and accurately upon the problem and also establishes greater trust and openness between participants. Self-disclosure is appropriate during the early stages of a counseling interview to build rapport and can be an extremely useful probe device during later interview stages.

Careful probing is the key which can unlock a great deal of information—it takes the place of direct questions used in other types of interviews. Remember, good counseling interviews contain few, if any, real questions. When done well and in an unbiased manner, probes encourage interviewees to examine their own problems and arrive at realistic solutions. This, in essence, is the purpose of a counseling interview.

COUNSELING INTERVIEW LISTENING

The term *attending behavior* is used by Ivey and Authier (1978) to refer to counseling interview listening. In their well-known attending behavior workshops, they suggest that three basic observable behaviors are essential for good listening:

1. *Using varied eye contact to communicate with the helpee.*
2. *Using a natural,* relaxed *posture and gestures. No need to sit rigid and "professional." Use your body to communicate your involvement.*
3. *Staying on the topic. Don't topic jump or interrupt. Simply note what the helpee has said and take your cues from him/her. There is no need to go into your own head to think of what to say. The helpee has already told you. If you get lost and can't think of anything to say, simply hesitate a moment and think of something said earlier that interested you. Go back and make a comment or ask a question about that topic. You are still attending! This simple point has been a life saver to many helpers.* (*Ivey and Authier, 1978, p. 438*)

Unlike other interview types where the ratio of interviewee to interviewer talk is approximately 70/30, in a counseling interview you should be attending to the client from 90 to 95 percent of the time and only talking 5 to 10 percent of the time. One key to being a good listener is to practice good attending behaviors.

Another key is the ability to "read between the lines." This means attending to the nonverbal behaviors of clients as well as the verbal responses. Much of the valuable information in a counseling interview is subjective. It consists of feelings, values, beliefs, and attitudes. It is very often communicated through lowered eyes, a furrow of the brow, tears, smiles, quivering lips, rigid mouth, nodding head, shrugging shoulders, forward leaning, slouching, trembling fingers, clenched fists, foot tapping, rocking back and forth, whispering, stuttering, clammy hands, shallow breathing, and blushing. Nonverbal behaviors allow a counseling interviewer to understand the meaning underlying the respondent's words. As a matter of fact, professional counseling interviewers are responsible for much of the research which has been done on nonverbal behavior.

According to Benjamin (1969), there are three ways to understand another human being. The first way is to understand them through the eyes of other people. The second way is through your own eyes. The third and most important way, is through their own eyes. You must discover how respondents think, feel, and see the world *through their own eyes*. This is extremely hard work and requires well-developed listening skills. Because so much time is devoted to listening, if you perfect your listening skills in a counseling interview, you will find listening in almost every other type of interview easy.

COUNSELING INTERVIEW RECORDING

As with most other types of interviews, the most common method of counseling interview recording is with pencil and paper. Written notes can interfere with conversational flow. Comments such as "Could you slow down, I'm having trouble keeping up," can distract and disturb interviewees. In a counseling interview, recording should always be subordinate to the interviewing process. You should never allow notes to be an interpersonal barrier. Banjamin (1969, p. 59) cites the example of a counseling interviewee who once complained "He uses his notes the way my husband uses his newspaper. I can't get through to either one."

Counseling notes should never be taken secretively, and as an interviewer, you should never write down anything you do not want an interviewee to see. Because of the informal climate and rapport established in counseling, interviewers are often asked what they are writing. The entire climate of the interview can be destroyed if you are unwilling to show an interviewee your notes. Once counseling interview notes are taken, they should be kept confidential—even locked up. Remember, you are taking notes on extremely sensitive material. You have a responsibility to your client not to reveal what has been said.

More and more counseling interviewers are moving to electronic recording techniques. In most cases, such recordings are used for teaching and research. They can be extremely useful, however, in showing interviewees things about their own behavior. Various modeling strategies, for example, use audio and videotape for this purpose. Because of the anxiety-producing nature of electronic recording, it usually isn't used until the third or fourth interview, when trust and confidence have been developed. In the future, it is likely that electronic recording will be used more because it frees an interviewer to concentrate on the respondent.

COUNSELING INTERVIEW CONCLUDING

In a counseling interview, the conclusion should flow naturally from the interaction. Never rush it. Since most counseling interviews are scheduled for a specific period of time, it is not always possible to arrive at a satisfactory overall conclusion in one or two sessions. If no action plan emerges in the first session, you should set another appointment or encourage the respondent to return as soon as possible.

Besides the uncompleted interview, there are other problems that arise in the concluding phase of a counseling interview. Interviewees may try to prolong the interview. This may be a sign that they are anxious. They may begin long, complicated statements when the interview is due to conclude. You should not allow them to prolong the session, and, therefore, prolong the anxiety. In most cases, you are obviously not going to reach a final conclusion during that appointment. The client's reasons for prolonging the session must be made conscious, and they are a potential topic for future discussion. All counseling interviews should stay within the predetermined time limits. Statements such as "Our time is up" or "Do you find it hard to leave?" are common at this point. You must be friendly, but firm.

A second problem involves clients who want to leave early. They may be anxious, uncomfortable, or angry. Very often it is a form of escape or flight reaction. You should encourage such interviewees to remain and discuss the problem. You might point out that no problem can be solved if they continually escape or hide from it.

Counseling interviews should conclude only through mutual agreement. You might wrap it up with encouragement for the client's new capacity for perceiving and handling problems. This promotes respondent self-respect and confidence. It says that from your perspective the session has been successful. Good counseling interviewers avoid sermons at this point although it is tempting.

You should remind interviewees that your "door is always open." Even if another session is scheduled, encourage them to make contact either in person, by telephone, or by letter if problems occur prior to the following session. After the final counseling is completed, you should follow up and check with respondents to be sure they are still identifying and solving their own problems. If similar problems and conflicts have reappeared, you can either schedule another interview or refer the interviewee to a more specialized professional.

SUMMARY

The counseling interview is one type of helping interview. It employs a nondirective approach to help clients identify and solve their own problems. It is a useful approach for professional and amateur counselors alike. Little specific preparation is normally done before a counseling interview. There are, however, several treatment strategies that should be used as part of such interviews. The opening, questioning, probing, and concluding portions of these interviews must develop and maintain the informal, and nondirective approach which typifies a counseling interview. This means reducing anxiety and stress, using indirect questions and probes, carefully monitoring and recording both verbal and non-verbal communication, and concluding with an expression of confidence in the respondent's ability to meet and overcome similar problems in the future. The underlying assumption is that you can help respondents best by nondirectively encouraging and teaching them to stand on their own two feet.

ACTIVITIES

Activity #1

Directions: On the basis of what you have learned in this chapter and in Part I, analyze the following counseling interview. Look for both good and bad points of both the interviewer and interviewee. This is the last portion of an actual interview between Dr. Benjamin Sachs (1966, pp. 237–240) and a sixteen-year-old boy who has extreme guilt and anxiety from living in a home and school environment where grades are the mark of success. Use the line number to refer to comments. R = Interviewer (Sachs) E = Interviewee (the boy)

1 R: Tell me, is the family happy? Your family?

E: Yeah, yeah. I think they're happy.

R: But you're not.

E: Well, I'm happy. Yeah, I'm not unhappy. This is just the way I'd like to see

5 things done. Sure, I'm not happy when I have to do things rush, rush, rush, but I'm not so unhappy that I'm gonna leave.

R: Leave. What do you mean "leave"?

E: I don't get so unhappy I say I'm going to run away or commit suicide or anything like that. I'm not that unhappy. There's lots of good moments.

10 There's lots of good times. We sit down, listen to records. We talk. We have lots of fine times. But that's just the way I think things should be. Just take it easy. Like in school, there's only an hour in which you can do so much. I'd like to have somebody—say give me the assignment—then take my own time. I'm sure I'll get them all done because I've done it before. That's the

15 way I think things ought to be done. I can't see this rush, rush, rush. Just calmly take your time. Relax and you think better. And I know I definitely want to get good grades this next semester, and I'm gonna try. I'm gonna have to sit down. I'm gonna have to *force* myself to do it the way that is expected of me. Instead of calmly going off some place, maybe taking a book

20 with me. Maybe going up into the hills. The atmosphere is better up there. I can read. Instead of four walls around me.

R: The atmosphere is better?

E: Yeah, it's calm. It's peaceful.

R: You mean it isn't calm and peaceful at home?

25 E: Oh, the kids are yelling upstairs or something, or the sewing machine is going upstairs. Or my brother's in there cussing at himself because he made a mistake or something like that. You see what I mean?

R: Yes, I see this. But then you said you wanted some friends. [earlier in the interview before this excerpt]

30 *E:* Sure I like to have friends. But I'm not particularly unhappy because I haven't got a best friend here or something. I have a girl friend. Things are going rather slow with her, but she likes me. Now, I've told this to my parents before, and they don't say it's impossible. They just think I'm dreaming.

35 *R:* Just what?

E: Dreaming.

R: Dreaming?

E: That's the way I am.

R: What do you mean, dreaming?

40 *E:* Oh, well, I just think that this is a better way. Really, it's not. They just think I'm trying to lollygag. Trying to get out of studying or something. But I've done it before. I've calmly sat down. Calmly separated everything. Not in a rush. Calmly just sat down. But usually now they want me to stay in my room and do nothing but study. I like to get up if I feel tired or something, go

45 out and walk around.

R: Well, what do you do when you're lying in bed?

E: I just think. Think of what a glorious thing it could be. How glorious I could be.

R: Do you think of how bad you are?

50 *E:* Sometimes. Sometimes I think of the horrible mess I made of my life. That's another thing.

R: (Sadly) Go ahead.

E: People—somehow or another, it always comes up. You better do something fast 'cuz your life's just going to dwindle away, if you don't change.

55 Sure it's going to dwindle away. But now I don't much care. I don't know what's coming up. Things just don't seem to work right. Things seem to be coming in pressing. That's why I like to go off by myself. So I can think. I've got the trees that I can talk to. But as I say, my parents, they say, well, this is wrong. I don't tell them this 'cuz I know what they'll say. "Ah baloney, now

60 you go down and do your studying. Why can't you be normal?" But what's wrong with this other way? And that's what I told them. When I do a job, I like to do it slow. I like to relax. Like weeding. I like to sit there and just calmly pick out the weeds. I get the weeds out. To them it's got to be fast, 'cuz there's another job to be done. As soon as you're done, you got to go

65 over and do that job.

R: The tape's running out. Did you enjoy this discussion?

E: I'm glad to get it off my chest and tell somebody. I hope they hear this tape. I hope they know how I feel.

R: You found this important?

70 *E:* (With relief) Yeah. I feel a lot better. I got somebody to talk to. That's what was so good about camp. Me and Don, he'd call me to sit down to saw on some wood. And I just sat there sawing back and forth. Maybe not fast. I just sat there, and I told him. Remember the time I blew my stack. You remember?

75 *R:* Yeah.

E: No. You weren't there. But I blew my stack. Oh, this camp is all messed

up, and everything like that. I was having a mood. Oh, I'm moody. Moody, terribly moody. So I took off up the road, and turned around and here came Don, walking up after me. He says, "I feel the same way." He says, "Can
80 you suggest anything?" So I did. We sat there, and we had a conversation by ourselves. I could walk around. I could—I was looking at the map then _____ Country, all the wonderful places. I had to go down to the corral. I talk to myself. I admit I talk to myself.
R: Everybody does.
85 E: And I tell myself how wonderful things could be. I was relaxed. I had nobody to shout, "You gotta do this. You gotta do this right away, so you can do this, so you can do that." I just sat there very cool and calm.

Activity #2

Directions: Arrange an interview with someone who commonly does counseling interviews, such as a trained psychologist or psychiatrist. Very often they make tapes of their interviews, just as Dr. Sachs did for the preceding activity, and they might let you hear one which is not considered confidential. You do not really get a feel for the counseling interview until you actually see or hear it. Even if the interviewer you visit with will not let you hear a tape, you can still talk with him or her and find out how they go about doing a counseling interview and how success is measured. Once you have done this, write a short paper describing what you found out which goes beyond this chapter. Because of space, there is much omitted in this chapter regarding the very difficult task of doing a successful counseling interview.

Activity #3

Directions: Select one of the following hypothetical cases and role-play it, being sure to use the concepts and skills discussed in this and previous chapters. These cases merely describe common counseling interview situations. You are free to add any other information you like to make the role-play better. Try to make the interview as realistic as possible.

CASE A: Bruce Patterson works in the blending department of a large midwestern pharmaceutical company. He works hard but cannot seem to keep his mind on his work recently. His mind is continually wandering to the debts he owes. With easy credit, he has become a chronic borrower. His borrowing is not due to illness, rent payments, or any of the other common and accepted reasons people go into debt. He borrows for luxuries like the new car he just bought or the water skiing boat he bought last year or the diamond necklace he gave his wife recently. Bruce is forty-five years old. He divorced his wife of fifteen years, just three years ago, and six months later married a twenty-three-year-old telephone operator (Jane). In the last five years, he has twice bid for a higher-paying job elsewhere in the company. In both cases he was advised that he did not have the necessary educational qualifications for advancement into a skilled trade. Bruce realizes that his work is falling off somewhat but is absolutely convinced he will get it straightened out soon.

Steven Pollard, Bruce's supervisor, has noticed his work beginning to deteriorate. The number of batches he mixes per shift fell from 15 to 11 in the last six months, and on several occasions he has "scorched" a batch. The last time Steve talked to Bruce about this slump, he said, "Everything is all right, I'm just a little untracked right now, I'll get it going again." Despite this assurance, however, Bruce's work has continued to be poor. Steve knows about Bruce's bids for other jobs in the company and suspects his problems may be financial. Bruce has always been a good worker up to this point, and Steve wants to keep him if possible. He feels that Bruce is not going to get over his problems, however, without some help. He decided to call Bruce in and see if he can help.

CASE B: Peggy Johnson is a senior in geology. Her grades have been borderline throughout her college career. This semester she has been especially rushed since she is taking an extra course in order to graduate on time in the spring; she is the pledge trainer for her sorority; and she is working part-time (15 hours per week) in a local dress shop to supplement what her parents send her to live on. Her toughest course is the senior geology seminar. It requires two major papers, a great deal of reading, and several examinations. She received a "D" on the first examination and a "D+" on the second. Her first paper is due at midterm. She has not had time to work on the paper and has instead decided to check out a somewhat obscure geology journal and copy most of the information for her paper from an article. She was able to go through one of the articles in only one night, change a couple of dozen words, and complete the paper. At the time, this seemed like a reasonable way out for Peggy. She would get the paper done, probably get a good grade and help her standing in the class, and the professor would never know the difference. She completed typing the paper over the weekend, and it is due this coming Friday. But now her conscience is bothering her; she can't seem to get the damn paper off her mind. She has even been dreaming about the professor catching her cheating. She has decided to talk with her best friend and sorority sister, *Myrna Foster*, about the problem. Myrna is a biology senior and knows what the pressures are this semester. It is probably too late to write a new paper, and the professor has already said he will not accept any late papers. If she fails this paper, she will probably fail the course and not graduate in May.

CASE C: Linda Gates is a 24-year-old high school counselor. This is her first job since completing a Psychology/Guidance and Counseling degree. Her most difficult case so far has been *Rebecca*, a girl of 15 years of age. In their first meeting Linda discovered that "Becky" is obsessed with her own inferiority, somewhat retarded in her mental processes, given to daydreaming, antagonistic toward her family who call her "dumb and crazy," and in serious conflict over her inability to understand or completely repress sexual ideas and impulses. She has recently begun seeing a boy whom she likes very much, but he wants her to "prove her love for him." The first session went very well and Becky seems to have gained much trust in Linda. Today is Linda's second interview with Becky.

Chapter 13

The Diagnostic Interview

The real skills of the diagnostic interviewer lie in his ability to raise significant, nonthreatening questions, to leave them open-ended so the interviewee can state his own position, and follow them to the point of reaching some insights concerning the subject at hand. (Sachs, 1966, p. 27)

Like the counseling interview, the diagnostic interview is a helping interview. The methods used, however, are quite different. As you have learned in Chapter 12, counseling interviewers play the role of facilitator rather than advisor and, therefore, adopt a nondirective, client-centered approach so interviewees achieve insights into their *own* problems and develop their *own* solutions. On the other hand, diagnostic interviewers are sought out by interviewees as advisors, and they are expected to play that role. To fulfill that function, interviewers utilize a directive approach.

Diagnostic interviews most commonly take place between lawyers and clients, doctors and patients, social workers and clients, high school counselors and students, lawyers and witnesses, police officers and witnesses, police officers and suspects, and many other professionals and lay people. The term "professional" in this instance is best defined in the following quotation:

When the conversation is aimed at furnishing insight and gaining information, or furthering understanding, or arriving at some form of help and counsel, its purpose is usually a professional one, and the interviewer is likely to be working in some field of human adjustment. The word professional *implies that the interviewer has had special preparation for his work; that his training, based on transmittable knowledge and skills, has been acquired formally.*

(Fenlason, 1952, p. 3)

The diagnostic interview, then, refers to an interview between an interviewer who possesses special knowledge and skills and a respondent who provides information so that the interviewer can analyze a specific situation or problem. Although the techniques discussed here focus on recognized diagnostic professionals, they apply equally well to any situation demanding a direct interview approach. In many cases, such as interviews between doctors, lawyers, and social workers and their clients, the exchange is interviewee-initiated and respondents are willing to divulge all relevant information. In other cases, such as interviews between police officers and suspects, prosecutors and defendants, and vice-principals and problem students, it is interviewer-initiated, and respondents are less willing to answer questions openly and honestly. In both cases, the interview is a "helping" one, but the respondent is not always the one helped. For many reasons—lack of time, respondent inability to indentify the problem, lack of knowledge, or the seriousness of the situation—helping interviewers choose to use a directive approach.

DIAGNOSTIC INTERVIEW PREPARATION

In an interviewee-initiated diagnostic interview, interviewers usually don't prepare much. Like the counseling interview, interviewers often have little or no information regarding a respondent's problem until it is presented at the interview. When information is available ahead of time, it usually comes in the form of a brief memorandum, such as the example provided for law students preparing for client counseling competition, figure 13.1. The lawyer in this situation might do some background research on the law relating to landlord/tenant relationships. In general, however, diagnostic interview professionals depend on their experience and training rather than specific preparation for each interview.

On the other hand, when a diagnostic interview is interviewer-initiated, considerable preparation may be done. A law enforcement officer may (with the help of specialists) gather as much evidence as possible regarding a crime before confronting a suspect. In the same manner, attorneys will often spend many weeks gathering evidence before confronting witnesses in the courtroom. Evidence in such cases normally consists of eyewitness identification, real evidence,

13.1 Consultation Problem for Attorneys

MEMORANDUM

TO:	LAWYER	DATE:	April 1, 1970
FROM:	SECRETARY	RE:	Harold Raymond

Mr. Harold Raymond phoned. Wants to sue landlord for $1250 in damage to furniture and clothing caused by leak from apartment roof during heavy rainstorm in March. Landlord admitted he suspected roof was in need of repairs and is fixing up the apartment and roof, but he says it's not his responsibility to pay for the damage to furniture and clothing. Landlord also claims his insurance does not cover such damage. Landlord, after threat of suit by client, offered 1 month's free rent.

Made appointment for April 4, 1970.

Copy of lease attached. Raymond will bring in list of items damaged and approximate value.

(Brown, 1979, p. 33)

or circumstantial evidence. *Eyewitness identification* or first hand evidence is a statement by an individual who observed the situation. *Real evidence* is physical evidence such as fingerprints and blood stains. *Circumstantial evidence* is an inference such as the fact that an individual knew the combination to a safe or was present when a crime took place. The gathering and evaluation of evidence is an extremely important and difficult aspect of preparation for an interviewer-initiated diagnostic interview. The following is a description of such preparation for a police interrogation interview.

> Each piece of evidence is carefully examined, thoroughly weighed, evaluated, and analyzed; indications and implications of guilt are evaluated, explained to the subject, and discussed with him if necessary. Each piece of evidence is linked to all other evidence; each piece is hand-crafted, expertly trimmed and polished, carefully and meticulously fitted as an integral part into the finished picture that the interrogator is trying to paint—and in exactly the same manner as each individually shaped piece of a jig-saw puzzle is matched up with a few other pieces at a time, until eventually all the pieces fit together, and the final picture emerges clearly.
>
> (Aubry and Caputo, 1965, pp. 94–95)

This same type of preparation precedes all interviewer-initiated diagnostic interviews.

THE DIAGNOSTIC INTERVIEW GUIDE

Since preparation in general is not an extremely important part of an interviewee-initiated diagnostic interview, preparation of an interview guide is also not crucial. When interview guides are used, they are normally fairly general and apply to a variety of situations. Legal interview guides, such as figure 13.2 (pages 304–5), are examples of such all-purpose guides.

General, all-purpose guides are normally part of the professional's training. They are useful, in that they prevent you from forgetting to ask relevant questions. They normally require that you check predetermined categories.

Interviewer-initiated guides, on the other hand, are often developed in great detail and meet the needs of each individual situation. A police officer will prepare a guide to question a particular suspect. A lawyer will prepare an interview guide (often with the help of a law clerk) to question each witness during a trial. Because respondents in these situations are often unwilling to give information freely, the interview guide usually consists of many closed questions. Questions are sometimes asked in a direct and leading manner. In a courtroom, leading questions are sometimes allowed to get to the truth when other means have failed. Leading questions are also used in interrogation; questions such as "You shot him, you killed him, anything else is a lie, isn't it?" or "You're lying about this whole rotten mess, aren't you?" are examples of such interrogation techniques. With hostile witnesses, leading questions may be the only way to get accurate responses. The assumption is that the respondent will deny the lead if it is inaccurate.

In the same way, direct, objective, closed questions are part of interviewer-initiated diagnostic interview guides. The rationale for such an approach is expressed in the following advice for people conducting criminal interrogation.

13.2 Sample Legal Interview Guide

DIVORCE

Date _____

Client Name _____ Age_____ # Marriage _____

Address _____ Phone: Bus. _____

_____ Res. _____

Business _____ Birthplace _____

Salary/Income _____ Date of Birth _____

Adverse Party Name _____ Age _____ # Marriage _____

Address _____ Phone: Bus. _____

_____ Res. _____

Adverse Party Attorney _____

Address _____ Phone: _____

Adverse Party Business _____ Birthplace _____

Salary/Income _____ Date of Birth _____

PLACE &/OR DATE OF SERVICE _____

Maiden Name _____ Restore: _____ Years Resident _____

Married _____ Date _____

Children	Age	Children	Age
_____		_____	
_____		_____	

Good questioning techniques preclude the asking of questions which call for the expression of an opinion on the part of the subject. If an accessory after the fact knows the reason for certain actions on the part of one of the principals, it will be far more effective to inquire directly into the reasons for the action, than to present the question in a manner asking for or inviting an opinion. This type question is easy to avoid, and even in its strongest form, is essentially a weak technique and to be excluded from the interrogation process. "Why did Pete Rogers call you last night?" is a far more effective way to ask the question than to say, "Why do you think Pete Rogers called you last night?" The opinion type question works to the advantage of someone who is attempting to avoid telling the truth; and in fact makes it relatively simple to give an untruthful answer. What more natural response to the question, "Why do you think Pete Rogers called you last night?" than a reply, "I haven't the slightest idea."

(Aubry and Caputo, 1965, p. 103)

Desires Custody? _____ Support (Give/Take) _____ Amount? _____

Visitation: (Weekly, Semi-Monthly, Holidays, Vacations) _____

Real Property/Address	Value	Encumbrance	Payments
_____	_____	_____	_____
_____	_____	_____	_____

Personal Property	Value	Encumbrance	Pmt's	Clients/Adverse
Furniture/Fixtures/				
Appliances	_____	_____	_____	_____
Car _____	_____	_____	_____	_____
_____	_____	_____	_____	_____
_____	_____	_____	_____	_____

Other Debts _____ : _____ :

_____ : _____ : Total: _____

Alimony: (Give/Take) _____ Lump _____ Show Cause _____ Costs _____

Fees _____ Restraining Order _____

Client Instructions _____

_____

Grounds _____

_____

_____

_____

As you can see, the nature of questions in diagnostic interview guides can be very different from those recommended for many other interviews. An interview guide containing such direct and specific questions can be as detailed as those for a research interview. Four common types of questions found in interviewer-initiated diagnostic interview guides are direct, indirect, emotional, and subterfuge.

A *direct question* or approach was discussed in Part I. You calmly and matter-of-factly preface the question with all known evidence and urge the subject to tell the truth with no lies, no excuses, and no holding back. You must be careful to avoid threats or insinuations and may instead be sympathetic and point out that anyone else might have easily acted in a similar manner. You should only use this approach when there is little or no doubt concerning the facts of the case.

Indirect questions work better when information is not so certain. Inquiries such as "Where were you at 2 p.m.?" "Did you notice any strange noises last night?'' and ''What were you doing in that part of town?'' are indirect. They are still fairly closed, but they do not specifically refer to the incident or problem about which information is being sought. The interviewee is asked to relate any information which may have a bearing on the incident. The assumption is that if a respondent is lying, discrepancies, distortions, and omissions will be revealed under indirect questioning. The interviewee should be made to feel that only with complete and honest cooperation will the interview be successful for both participants.

The *emotional approach* is designed to play upon a respondent's emotions. Questions such as ''What will your wife and children think when the facts come to light?'' ''How will you be able to live with yourself?'' or ''Why do you think your employer is so upset?'' are examples of the emotional approach. Once emotional questions get interviewees upset, nervous, and tense they may either intentionally or unintentionally let the truth slip out. Again, the point is to get at the truth in any possible manner.

The use of *subterfuge* can be very effective. Again, you should be reasonably certain of the facts before using it. Use subterfuge only after all other standard approaches have been tried and have failed. Subterfuge is essentially a bluff or lie on your part, and if it does not work you will probably be unable to obtain truthful information in the interview anyway. The interviewee and the information will, in most cases, be lost if subterfuge fails. Examples of subterfuge include a hypothetical story attributed to ''eyewitnesses,'' playing one interviewee against another by showing one an alleged confession or sworn statement by the other, or pretending to possess information which you do not know for sure. According to Aubry and Caputo (1965):

> There are many types and varieties of these approaches and they include Indifference, Sympathy or Sympathetic, ''Too Great a Temptation,'' ''Only Human to Have Acted That Way,'' Kindness, Helpful, Friendly, Extenuation, Mitigation, Shifting the Blame, ''Hot and Cold,'' Lessening the Degree of Guilt, Magnifying the Degree of Guilt, Minimizing The Consequences, The ''Fait Accompli,'' Bluffing (with advantages and disadvantages), The Stern, Business-like Approach, Compounding Falsehoods, Pretense of Physical Evidence, Repetition of One Theme, Mental Relief Through Having Told The Truth, Perseverance, Appeals to Decency and Honor, ''What's Your Side of The Story?,'' Tearing Down and Building Up, and ''Just Tell The Truth.''

(Aubry and Caputo, 1965, p. 75)

Most of the approaches mentioned by Aubry and Caputo are fairly descriptive. The only one that might not be clear is the one they labelled the *hot and cold approach*. Normally, a pair of interviewers, one using direct, hard-hitting questions, and the other using sympathy and understanding, alternate questioning the respondent or one interviewer leaves the room as the other interviewer begins. When done well, the hot and cold approach can be extremely productive. Respondents will sometimes open up to the sympathetic interviewer after being grilled by the aggressive, hard-nosed one.

Many of these question types appear to be rather unfair or unethical. In some diagnostic interviews, however, it is deemed necessary to resort to such quasi-ethical methods to gain needed information. This is especially true when the respondent perceives the information as harmful, threatening, or embarrassing.

Social work interviews can be either interviewer or interviewee initiated.

In these cases, information could probably not be gained except through the use of such special interview techniques. It is up to you to weigh the importance of the information against the morality of using these means to gain the information. There are many who would argue that using these sorts of questions make the information gained worthless. That is up to each individual interviewer to determine for themselves. Are diagnostic interviewers really doing their job if they don't use whatever means possible to get at the facts? This is an extremely difficult, and often debated, ethical question.

Before leaving the question of ethics in an interviewer-initiated diagnostic interview, one more point must be made: the respondent has certain rights and protections against unlawful questioning. Under the U.S. Constitution and state constitutions, careful and exact legal procedures have been developed to guide interviews. All responses must be made freely and voluntarily. Statements may not be induced by violence, fear, threats, coercion, or promises of any benefit. Interviewees must be told that they have the right to remain silent and have an advisor with them during questioning. No one can be forced to incriminate or degrade themselves. The observance of these rights is carefully monitored by the courts. Interviewers should have a witness available to testify that these rights were explained and understood by the respondent before questioning. This reduces the danger of quasi-ethical interview guide techniques.

DIAGNOSTIC INTERVIEW OPENING

The opening of a diagnostic interview is generally formal with little or no exchange of pleasantries such as those which characterize other types of interviews. The interviewee has either asked for the interview to obtain a diagnosis, or the interviewer has asked for the interview to collect specific information to make a diagnosis. In neither case are the participants interested in spending time in small talk—both want to get directly to the topic. This does not mean the climate is unimportant, but only that neither is willing to take the time to establish it. During the opening, one participant explains the purpose of the interview to the other, and then they move quickly to information exchange.

There is no doubt that both participants spend some of this opening time sizing each other up. The status of the participants has a lot to do with the lack of an extended opening. Professional interviewers, such as doctors, lawyers, or police officers, are either trusted or not trusted because of their status without intentional climate development. The sizing-up and climate-setting process, then, takes very little time during the opening, but continues throughout the course of the discussion. Because time is often at a premium, both participants are anxious to get to the main purpose as quickly as possible. A simple "I'd like to talk to you about . . ." is usually sufficient to begin a diagnostic interview. A simple, straightforward orientation is usually followed almost immediately by the opening question which leads directly into the body of the interview.

DIAGNOSTIC INTERVIEW QUESTIONING AND RESPONDING

Diagnostic interview questioning usually follows the pattern set in the opening—it is fairly formal, straightforward, and direct. In most cases, interviewers try to appear business-like and professional. This is what most interviewees expect. This "no nonsense" approach engenders trust, confidence, credibility, and admiration for the interviewer. It can serve your purpose whether the interview is interviewee or interviewer initiated. The respondent who says, "All right, doctor, I'm convinced I need an operation, when should I check into the hospital?" or "You're the attorney, what should I do about this problem?" is not much different from the truant high school student who says to the vice principal, "You caught me, what's going to happen now?"

Formal questioning is extremely effective when working with upset, emotional, and nervous interviewees. It works equally well for arrogant, hostile, or crafty respondents. You must be prepared to accept any statement an interviewee makes, regardless of whether it is related to a legal problem, a medical problem, or an extremely vicious crime. In some cases, it will take all of your strength and self-control to maintain a neutral attitude.

A second questioning technique is to simply invite interviewees to explain the situation in their own words. Many respondents don't expect to do much talking during a diagnostic interview. They come with the expectation of answering questions in a simple "yes"/"no" fashion. In an interviewer-initiated interview especially, they will hesitate for a moment in order to collect their thoughts. Their first statements may often include frequent hesitations and relatively long pauses. Skillful interviewers remain silent during such pauses. On the other hand, in some interviews such as interrogation, you may want to prod at such points with comments such as "Stop stalling for time and get on with your story," "You don't need all that time if you're telling the truth," or "Don't worry about how the truth sounds, just get on with it." In this case your purpose is to increase tension in order to elicit information that interviewees may be trying to hide. In an interviewee-initiated diagnostic interview, you may actually encourage respondents to take all the time necessary in order to make their final responses as accurate as possible.

In all diagnostic interviews, it is important that question vocabulary be as unambiguous and free from jargon as possible. Professional diagnostic interviewers sometimes introduce specialized jargon into their interviews, but the temptation to do this should be resisted whenever possible. In the same way overly long, double-barrelled, and negative questions must also be avoided. It is usually desirable to get all of the necessary information as quickly and efficiently as possible. This is the reason for the no-nonsense questioning approach in the first place.

In interviewer-initiated diagnostic interviews, interviewers try to give the impression that they intend to get at the truth no matter how long they have to wait and what it takes. This type of persistence may, in the long run, break down interviewee resistance so the truth comes out. There are a number of questioning techniques designed to get truthful, accurate responses often without worrying too much about how they affect the interviewee. In one such technique, the interviewer says to the respondent, "I'd hate to be in your shoes, things look awfully bad for you." This encourages respondents to find ways they can lessen the penalty. Doubt and fear is planted in the mind of an interviewee. The respondent begins to think "Maybe if I tell this person all about the situation, he or she may give me a break." Confession or coming forth with the complete truth becomes a way for the interviewees to reduce doubt and anxiety. It is an extremely useful questioning technique for interviewer-initiated diagnostic interviews with crafty or hostile respondents.

Another common interrogation technique creates anxiety nonverbally. This is done by intentionally crowding or invading the respondents personal space. The interviewer either sits or stands almost nose-to-nose or chest-to-chest with the respondent. Nonverbally this says "I dare you to lie to me!" Again, the tension is created in order to force out the truth. This technique is especially effective when combined with a loud, demanding voice.

Interviewees responding to questions in a diagnostic interview should be as natural and careful as possible. You do not want to say things which "can be used against you." You do, however, want to be direct and honest. This is especially true if you are innocent and being questioned by a police officer. You must realize in either an interviewer or interviewee-initiated interview, diagnostic interviewers cannot help you if you do not tell them the truth. Since this book is not written for people who are guilty of crimes, specific lying and deceiving techniques are not outlined. It is assumed that you will be unafraid to be completely honest as interviewees in a diagnostic interview. Open, honest, and direct methods of asking and answering questions are generally the best possible way to behave in a diagnostic interview.

DIAGNOSTIC INTERVIEW PROBING

Regardless of whether an interview is interviewer or interviewee initiated, skillful probing is necessary to accurately diagnose a problem or situation. Carefully trained diagnostic interviewers listen carefully and probe relevant areas. Very often, interviewees are unaware of what is relevant in their responses and what is not. So clarification and amplification probes are important.

Of more importance, however, is the use of confrontation probes, which should correct any error in interviewee statements. Perhaps the best confrontation probers are legal interviewers. They generally confront inferences, complex issues, emotional situations, secondary information, reports of occurrences distant in time, and free narrative reports, that is, those not solicited by direct questioning. They believe that the "facts most often correctly reported are 1) those which have been most vividly presented, 2) those which concern most directly the reporter, and 3) those which fall readily into some scheme or organization and can be presented in the form of generalizations. The facts reported with the greatest number of errors are those which the reporter habitually treats in a standardized manner" (Bingham, et al., 1931, p. 197). Confrontation probes should be used whenever you suspect that an interviewee is giving an inaccurate report, whether consciously or unconsciously. It is your responsibility to probe and confront all questionable responses.

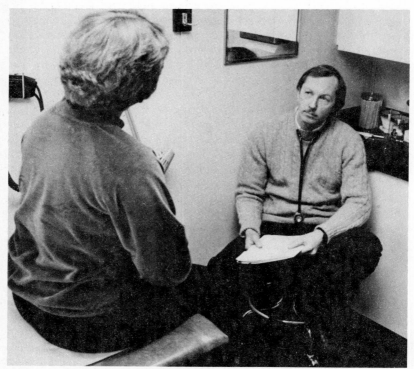

Careful listening and probing are essential elements of a diagnostic interview.

DIAGNOSTIC INTERVIEW LISTENING AND RECORDING

As with all other types of interviews, an important part of any diagnostic interview, be it interviewer or interviewee initiated, is careful active listening. There is no way to diagnose a situation or problem without listening. Professional diagnostic interviewers, with their wide experience in dealing with all kinds of problems, sometimes jump to conclusions before completely hearing out interviewees. However, a good physician knows that the same general symptoms may occur for many different diseases. The skillful medical interviewer will, therefore, listen for specific symptoms which differentiate one disease from another. The beginner will very often jump to an inaccurate conclusion and inaccurately diagnose the problem. Every criminal suspect is "innocent until proven guilty" on the basis of the facts, not hasty conclusions. It is only after all relevant interviewee responses have been heard and evaluated that you should draw conclusions.

A second major problem in diagnostic interview listening is uncritical acceptance. Very often interviewees are unclear or confused about their own problems. Therefore, it is common for interviewees to give inaccurate or distorted information without even being aware they are doing so. It is your responsibility to listen to what each interviewee has to say, but be careful not to accept information without clarifying and checking responses whenever possible. Check or challenge important interviewee comments both mentally and verbally. This is done as part of the interview and also as a follow-up procedure.

In order to know what to challenge or check, you must listen for signs of deception. Deception is usually signalled by several symptoms which manifest themselves both verbally and nonverbally. Physical symptoms include increased perspiration, flushing or paleness of the skin, enlarged veins in the head, neck, and throat, increased or irregular breathing, muscle spasms or tension, lip licking, rapid eye movements, facial tics, stuttering, and thickened or blurred speech. Other indicators include the inability to look you in the eye, clenched fists, rapid hand or body movements, shoulder shrugging, rapid foot movement, and hesitations or long pauses. Be careful in labelling these as deception signs. Such behaviors can also indicate anxiety and stress without deception. You must differentiate between those symptoms which are a natural part of a diagnostic interview and those which are unusual. Very often it is the increasing frequency or magnitude of such behaviors which is your best indicator of deception. In any case, it takes careful attention and much practice to detect. Diagnostic interviewers must develop this aspect of listening.

Diagnostic interviewers normally take pencil and paper notes. Doctors, lawyers, nurses, and social workers usually carry writing materials with them. In many cases, it is a matter of weeks or months before they need to reexamine their notes. For this reason, notes are recorded very carefully. Doctors, nurses, lawyers, and social workers get in the habit of writing down all important information immediately after it is uttered. Usually such notes are kept on a chart or as part of a client file on interview guides.

In interviewer-initiated diagnostic interviews, notes are just as important. Police officers, for example, are seldom without their notebook. For these individuals, notes often become a form of evidence. They are required to testify in court regarding respondents' statements. The proper conduct of their jobs requires that they be able to listen and take notes efficiently. Reviewing notes, such as those taken from an eyewitness, can lead a law enforcement officer to the solution of a crime. In very few cases are memorization or electronic recording used because memorization cannot be trusted, and electronic recording is too anxiety producing for spontaneous diagnostic interviews. It is only when verbatim notes are needed such as a confession or testimony in a law court that electronic or stenographic techniques are used.

DIAGNOSTIC INTERVIEW CONCLUDING

Diagnostic interview conclusions generally consist of problem analysis based upon the information provided by the respondent. In a medical interview, for example, such a conclusion might be a medical prescription, a certain type of therapy, or admittance to a hospital. In a legal interview, a lawyer might suggest certain steps for the respondent to take, possible legal remedies, or simply dropping the matter. In a diagnostic interview, it is you, the interviewer, who normally has the last word. In interviewee-initiated interviews your advice has been sought by the respondent. In interviewer-initiated interviews, interviewers have the last word because of their power, status, and position.

The follow-up to a diagnostic interview is important. Medical and legal interviewers, for example, are extremely careful to make post-interview notes regarding each diagnostic interview. In most cases you have no way of knowing when and how such information may be needed in the future. You may forward information to other individuals or simply make it a part of your records. In interviewer-initiated interviews, some kind of formal report is usually written for a superior regarding the outcome of the interview. In many cases, follow-up, as the entire interview, may have important legal implications. The conclusion—both diagnosis and follow-up—is extremely important in a diagnostic interview.

SUMMARY

The conduct of an interviewee-initiated diagnostic interview is very different from an interviewer-initiated interview. The former entails less preparation, a more standardized interview guide, and a somewhat more accepting climate. The latter consists of much more preparation in the form of evidence gathering; special (sometimes questionable) interview guide, questioning, and probing techniques; and a more judgmental climate. In the former, the respondents are being helped; whereas in the latter, they aren't necessarily being helped.

Both types of diagnostic interviews are rather formal, utilize highly directive closed questions and probes, require careful verbal and nonverbal listening and recording, and allow the interviewer to have the final decision and concluding words. It is not always possible to help people through a nondirective approach, but when it is possible you should choose it over the more directive diagnostic approach. People are helped more when they are allowed to help themselves.

ACTIVITIES

Activity #1

Directions: On the basis of what you have learned in this chapter and in Part I, analyze the following diagnostic interview. Look for both good and bad points of both the interviewer's and interviewee's behavior. This is another interview by Dr. Benjamin Sachs (1966, pp. 103ff) and a sixteen-year-old girl. She is considered to be one of the "happiest girls in school." She is a straight "A" student. This interview took place for no other reason than that Dr. Sachs felt uneasy and thought she might be putting up a "front." Notice the difference between this interview and the one in the preceding chapter. They should clarify the difference between a counseling and diagnostic interview. Use the line number to refer to your comments. R = Interviewer (Sachs) E = Interviewee (the girl)

1 *R:* How old are you?
   E: I'm sixteen.
   R: And you're a very good student, aren't you?
   E: Fairly good.
5 *R:* You mean real good.
   E: I do all right.
   R: What do you get? What are your grades?
   E: Uh—mostly "A's."
   R: Get any "B's"?
10 *E:* Well, I didn't last quarter, last semester.
   R: So you got all "A's"?
   E: Yes.
   R: And why are you so hesitant in saying this?
   E: Well, the first impression people get when you say you have straight
15 "A's" is that you're very proud of these "A's," and develop a sort of hostility toward you.
   R: Hostility toward you?
   E: Well, you're sort of put into a category when they think that you have straight "A's."
20 *R:* Who puts you into a category?
   E: The person who would ask what kind of grades you got.
   R: Does the teacher?
   E: My teachers usually know what grades I get.
   R: Do you think they put you into a category?
25 *E:* Yes. They have a different opinion of me.
   R: Than the other kids?
   E: Oh, yes.
   R: Do you like that?
   E: Yes. I enjoy being put in that category—by my teachers, that is.

30 *R:* But you don't enjoy being put in it by kids.
E: That depends upon who the kids are. With some kids, it really doesn't matter to me what they think. But with other kids, I do care (fading but audible).
R: When do you care?
35 *E:* It matters to me what some of the other kids think, but—and then again, with some of the other kids, it doesn't matter.
R: Well, with what kids does it matter to you?
E: Well, the people that I see at school usually get the same grades as I do. And it matters to me what they think. But the other kids that I don't see and
40 take classes with like the ones that take woodshop and typing, I don't see too often, and I don't care what they think.
R: You don't really care?
E: Well, I really know what they think, and there's nothing much I can do about it. So it doesn't bother me.
45 *R:* It doesn't bother you at all?
E: To a certain extent.
R: What do you mean?
E: It means that I'll have to know people like that after I get out of school, and I'll have to cope with the same opinions.
50 *R:* Does that sound pleasant? Are you a little afraid of them, in other words?
E: Yes. I would rather be among people who consider me an equal than consider me superior.
R: Why do others consider you superior?
E: Mostly because of the grades.
55 *R:* Does that make you superior?
E: I suppose they—*they* would rather think it doesn't, but I like to think that grades are important.
R: How important are grades?
E: To me, they're very important. They're my whole life.
60 *R:* Your whole life?
E: Yes. It's all I have to do.
R: What do you mean, that's all you have to do?
E: Day after day all I do is go to school and do my homework. So it has to become my whole life, going to school.
65 *R:* Do you like it to be your whole life? (Pause) Try to tell me how you feel rather than what you think I want to hear, you know, because that's one of the problems adults have. You see, if you ask any group of kids, "What shall we do about the tardy kid?" the teacher wants to hear, "Throw him out," so the kids say, "Throw him out." And so kids are always fooling adults, just as
70 adults are fooling kids, by telling them what they want to hear. I want to hear who you are. I don't need to know in name, but unless the teachers hear a real person, not one who pretends, they will just hear the pretense, you see. What I'm asking you really is, "Do you enjoy this being your whole life?"
75 *E:* (Pause) Well, I think I do. I can't think of anything else I'd rather do.
R: Nothing?

E: Uh—no. I like doing my homework. It gives me something to do. If I weren't doing my homework, I wouldn't be doing anything constructive.
R: What might you be doing instead?
80 *E:* I would most probably be watching TV, and that's about all.
R: Do you feel lonely?
E: No. As long as I have homework or something to keep me busy.
R: Suppose you don't have it?
E: Then I usually find something to read or something to keep me busy.
85 *R:* Are you happy?
E: No. I can't say I've ever been really.
R: What do you mean?
E: Happiness is a difficult term, but I don't believe I've ever been happy— ever been able to say I'm happy except a few times. Grades make me happy.
90 After report cards I'm happy.
R: For how long?
E: For a few days.
R: And then what?
E: And then back to school again for the next report card.
95 *R:* Why are you unhappy?
E: I don't know. I suppose I should be happy, content with what I'm doing.
R: Why should you be content?
E: Anyone, I suppose, should be happy to get straight "A's," and—(fades out).
100 *R:* But you're not. Why not?
E: I don't know.
R: Lonesome?
E: Uh—(Pause). I don't think so. As long as I have school and my home-work, I have something to do.
105 *R:* What would make you happy?
E: I don't know that either. If I did know, I would be happy.

Activity #2

Directions: Talk with a lawyer, doctor, police officer, or someone who fre-quently conducts diagnostic interviews. Ask them how they do their interviews and measure their success. Compare their answers to those you have received from the other interviewers you have contacted. Write a paper describing the differences.

Activity #3

Directions: Select one of the following hypothetical cases and role-play it, being sure to use the concepts and skills discussed in this and previous chapters. These cases merely describe common diagnostic interview situa-tions. Add any other information you like to make the role-play better. Try to make the interview as realistic as possible.

   LAW ENFORCEMENT INTERVIEW: Victor Reid, the suspect, is twenty-one years old. He left school when he was sixteen. He has a history of truancy and is currently out on probation after serving four months in jail for breaking into a liquor store and stealing a dozen cases of whiskey. Victor is married, and his wife, a girl of nineteen, is pregnant and expects to give birth in two months. He was working at a cannery, but was laid off when the work slowed down. The night of the liquor store robbery, he was seen with two friends who have admitted to the crime. They say Vic had gone home by the time the robbery took place. *Sara Johnson,* the investigating officer, feels that Victor may have been involved because her investigation turned up his financial problems and recent robbery conviction. She has gone to his home, where he lives with his wife's parents, to talk with him.

SOCIAL WORK INTERVIEW: Mrs. Ruth Hoffman was seventeen years old when she married Mr. Hoffman, fifteen years older than she and able to give her the comforts of life. When they had been married for twelve years, he was arrested and imprisoned for stealing from his company. Soon after his release, she discovered he had been living with another woman. When she confronted him, he disappeared with the woman and all efforts to locate him proved futile. She went to work but could not earn enough money to support herself and her three children. Her relatives and friends refused to help saying it was her husband's responsibility. She applied for assistance and a weekly allowance was arranged for her. After a time the case worker, *Ed Bass,* noticed an increasing resentment and antagonism toward him. Still later he noticed her wearing expensive clothing and jewelry which could not have been purchased out of her income. During one visit Ed saw Mrs. Hoffman whisk a man's coat from the living room. Ruth knew Ed had seen these but offered no explanation. After hearing reports that Mr. Hoffman was back in town, Ed decided to visit Mrs. Hoffman and find out if she was still eligible for aid.

CASE C: Ed Hamilton, A geology professor, has just finished reading the midterm papers from students in his senior geology seminar. One paper in particular, from a *Ms. Peggy Johnson,* struck him as familiar. (See Case B in the last chapter. Yes, she decided to turn in the paper after all.) He had the strange feeling he had read that information someplace before, but after looking through his references, he could not locate it. The paper was on the Planetesimal Hypothesis which proposes that the earth was formed by small pieces of the sun which broke off and collided and adhered to one another. This paper offered arguments opposing the hypothesis but was written in a professional style beyond what he considered the capabilities of Ms. Johnson, a "D" student up to this point. He decides to call her in and talk with her about the paper.

Chapter 14

The Performance Interview

The objective of performance appraisal is clear—to let the guy know how he is doing. Some supervisors behave as if they believe the purpose is to conduct an uncomfortable ritual, required by higher management just to keep the supervisor "on his toes." Others use performance appraisal reviews as a legitimate excuse to unload their own feelings. They expect the subordinate to sit there and take it, and assume he will react positively by displaying improved performance. (Steinmetz, 1971, p. 5)

Every day of our lives, we evaluate the performance or behaviors of others, and we are evaluated by others. Based on such evaluations we make judgments which affect our behavior toward others. These informal evaluations usually do not require an interview. But in most organizations not only is employee performance formally evaluated, but interviews are conducted to appraise and improve performance.

According to a nationwide survey (Lazer and Wilkstrom, 1977, p. 9) almost 90 percent of all major organizations use some form of performance evaluation and improvement program. According to the same survey, the objectives of these programs are remarkably similar. In order of frequency mentioned, the following eight program objectives appear consistently:

1. Personnel development—*identifying and preparing individuals for increased responsibilities or training.*
2. Performance measurement—*citing individual accomplishment and value to the organization.*
3. Performance improvement—*encouraging continued successful performance and strengthening weaknesses.*
4. Compensation—*determining salary and bonus incentives based on merit or results.*
5. Identifying potential—*finding those that are candidates for promotion.*
6. Feedback—*what is expected versus actual performance.*
7. Manpower planning—*preparing for future hiring needs.*
8. Communication—*improve understanding of individual goals and concerns through dialogue.*

Can an organization accomplish all of these objectives with a single appraisal done once a year? Probably not! The same survey shows that the actual use made of performance evaluation systems in order of importance is 1) performance feedback, 2) compensation decisions, 3) promotion decisions, 4) personnel development, 5) manpower planning, and 6) validation of selection procedures. This discrepancy between the professed objectives and actual use causes considerable dissatisfaction among subordinates and superiors.

If you examine these objectives carefully, you will notice that in some cases they are incompatible. Some, such as performance measurement and compensation, are oriented toward the past. Others, such as personnel development and performance improvement, are oriented toward the future. This is only one of many difficulties in many employee performance measurement and improvement systems. The following is a list of problems most often identified by personnel executives:

Conflicting Multiple Uses
Ratings Based by Pay Considerations
Unclear Goals of System
No Conceptual Justification for the System
Lack of Clear Performance Criteria
No Validation of Appraisal System
Absolute Versus Relative Standards of Performance
Personality Versus Performance Ratings
Separating Potential from Performance on the Appraisal
"Halo" Persistance in Ratings
Managers Dislike to Give Feedback
One-Way Communication Between Superior and Subordinate
Rater Biases
Nonfunctional Forms
No Developmental or Performance Follow-Up
Susceptible to Manipulation by Managers
No Built-In Reinforcement for Doing the Appraisal
Managers are not Trained to Administer
Conflicting Coach and Evaluator Roles
Punishing Process for All Concerned
Not Used for Top Management
No Credibility in the Organization
Administrative Chore not Related to Business Goals
No Impact on Performance

(Lazer and Wilkstrom, 1977, p. 17)

This is a damaging list of indictments. What is even worse is that these problems are almost all supported by research findings. Surveys show that over 80 percent of superiors using performance evaluation systems are dissatisfied. Yet, almost every one of them admits that some form of performance appraisal is important and almost all continue to use them. In this chapter you will find suggestions as to how performance can be improved as well as some of the reasons traditional performance evaluation programs are failing.

PERFORMANCE INTERVIEW PREPARATION

Performance appraisal and improvement should begin the day an employee is hired. Each employee needs a job description, all company documents pertaining to it, and a copy of the written evaluation form. All of these documents ought to be reviewed with new employees, usually within the first two weeks of work. That is when employees are most enthusiastic and receptive. This not only helps guarantee that employees know what is expected of them but also allows you to get to know one another. You are gathering both subjective and objective information about both work potential and one another. You begin to size up employees at that point as well as allowing employees to size you up.

As employees become established in the job and begin to perform assigned duties, it is your responsibility to keep some kind of record of their performance. Good supervisors make notes on each employee at least once a month. In order to make such a record, you must continually observe employee behavior. When problems are noted, it is also your responsibility, as their supervisor, to provide immediate feedback. Criticism must be immediate to be effective. Good superiors provide timely praise on such things as improved performance, special effort, creative suggestions, and so on. Such praise or criticism should also be direct, honest, and detailed. With criticism, it is especially important that you ask for employee ideas, listen to those ideas, and develop plans which will solve any problems. For legal purposes, it is also important that you document such discussions. This preparation requires that you be sensitive to what is going on at all times and willing to correct minor problems before they grow into major ones. A continuing dialogue and effective record-keeping system is the best possible preparation for a performance interview.

Written Performance Evaluation Forms

Performance measurement and improvement programs in most organizations include a written appraisal as well as an interview. The written appraisal normally precedes the interview and has a great deal of influence on the interview structure. There are basically six types of written evaluation techniques used throughout the United States: essay or open-ended questions, critical incidents methods, rating forms, comparison or ranking, checklists, and the management-by-objectives approach.

The *essay* or *open-ended* question technique normally consists of four or five areas of appraisal which the organization considers important. These performance areas are listed on the form and a space is given for supervisors to evaluate each employee on each questioned area. Figure 14.1 on the next page is an example of an essay form.

The essay approach has several drawbacks. First, it is impractical for large groups of employees. Second, the evaluation sometimes becomes a function of the superior's writing skill. Third, such forms are usually highly subjective which makes for a highly subjective interview. Fourth, the essay or open ended ap-

14.1 Sample Essay Performance Evaluation Form

Employee's Name: _____ Date of Hire _____

Job Title: _____ Job Grade and Code _____

Evaluation for period from _____ to _____
                            (Date)   (Date)

Please be as specific as possible in answering the following:

1. What is your evaluation of this employee's ability to perform the technical aspects of his/her position as distinct from the factors which follow?

   _____

   _____

   _____

   _____

2. What is your evaluation of his/her position effectiveness? (Initiative, Follow Through, Creativity, Dependability, Judgment, Cooperation, Responsibility, Maturity, etc.)

   _____

   _____

   _____

   _____

Supervisor's Signature: _____ Date _____

Employee's Signature: _____ Date _____

proach is very time consuming, not in its development, but in its administration and analysis. Therefore, it is seldom used as the exclusive written method of evaluating employee performance. Essay or open ended questions are often included as part of a more objective performance appraisal method. Supervisors are allowed to describe the strengths and weaknesses of employees in their own words, along with standardized objective criteria.

The *critical incident* technique is a simple variation of the essay or open ended form. It is used in approximately one out of seven organizations. To use it, employees describe specific examples of good and bad performance on their job. These must be examples or "critical incidents" rather than descriptions of general problem areas. Supervisors are also asked to provide a list of "critical incidents." In some companies, supervisors and employees are asked to maintain a log or record of such incidents as they occur throughout the year. This is done so they

14.2 Sample Critical Incident Performance Evaluation Form

Name _____Job Title _____

Division _____Unit # _____ Employment Date _____

Give specific examples of good and poor employee performance in each of the following areas. These examples should illustrate typical performance by the employee since the last performance evaluation.

JOB KNOWLEDGE: (Understanding all phases of work and related matters)

_____

_____

_____

QUALITY OF WORK: (Thoroughness, acceptability, accuracy, etc.)

_____

_____

_____

VOLUME OF WORK: (Quantity of acceptable work)

_____

_____

_____

DEPENDABILITY: (Completing responsibilities, assignments, etc.)

_____

_____

_____

COMMENTS: (Any other incidents you think important)

_____

_____

_____

will not be swayed by the most recent events. The problem, of course, is that managers and workers often fail to keep accurate logs. Once collected, the critical incidents are then developed into a performance evaluation form, such as figure 14.2.

The critical incident form is designed to keep performance reports more specific and job oriented. Its problems, however, are similar to those with the essay or open ended method. There is a great deal of emphasis on writing ability,

14.3 Sample Conventional Rating Form

Name _____ Location & Dept. _____

Position Title _____ Date _____

Instructions: (1) The employee should be reviewed on each of the factors below in relation to the present position. For each of these factors, check the box which reflects most typically the employee's performance. (2) Some factors are particularly significant in certain positions, circle the three factors which are <u>particularly</u> <u>important</u> <u>in reviewing an employee in this position</u>.

	Factor Number	Factor	Low 1	2	3	4	High 5
Position Performance	1	Position knowledge	☐	☐	☐	☐	☐
	2	Analytical ability and judgment	☐	☐	☐	☐	☐
	3	Planning and execution	☐	☐	☐	☐	☐
	4	Acceptance of responsibility	☐	☐	☐	☐	☐
	5	Dependability	☐	☐	☐	☐	☐
	6	Creative thinking	☐	☐	☐	☐	☐
Personal Performance	7	Relationship with others	☐	☐	☐	☐	☐
	8	Attitude	☐	☐	☐	☐	☐
	9	Emotional stability	☐	☐	☐	☐	☐
	10	Health	☐	☐	☐	☐	☐

and it takes a lot of time to prepare and review such forms. Separate incidents must be collected and verified for each specific job. This is a difficulty with the form, but also one of its major advantages. Employees are judged on the basis of their own job specifications rather than some general criteria. This method is a step in the direction of making performance appraisal more valid and reliable. It gives interviewers and interviewees more specific, job-related information to discuss during the performance interview.

Rating forms are the most traditional approach to performance measurement. They are now used by less than one sixth of all major organizations. There are basically two types: the conventional form and the Behaviorally Anchored Rating Scale (BARS). *Conventional rating forms* generally consist of a series of multiple-step scales to measure some employee characteristic or job behavior. The forms vary with the types of factors analyzed, the number of factors analyzed, and the number of discriminate or scale points employed. Figure 14.3 is an example of a partial conventional rating form.

Many rating forms focus on personality characteristics. Very often these characteristics are only vaguely defined. Here is a partial list of the most commonly included characteristics:

1. Knowledge of work
2. Leadership, influence
3. Initiative
4. Quality of work, accuracy
5. Quantity of work
6. Cooperation
7. Judgment
8. Creativity, resourcefulness, innovativeness
9. Dependability
10. Evaluation and development of personnel
11. Planning and organization
12. Communications
13. Mental alertness, intelligence, adaptability
14. Analytical ability, problem solving
15. Delegation
16. Attitude, personality
17. Motivation, commitment, industry, effort
18. Organization
19. Human relations, interpersonal relations, tact, courtesy
20. Planning
21. Follow-up
22. Decisiveness
23. Control
24. Grooming
25. Responsibility
26. Attendance
27. Objectivity, openness to criticism
28. Stability
29. Self-control
30. Self-expression

(Lazer and Wilkstrom, 1977, p. 21)

As you can see many of these characteristics are subjective. The ranking scales are often vaguely defined too. A bigger problem, however, is that the scales are usually added together to get an over-all rating, which assumes that all characteristics are equally important. These problems make most rating scales unreliable. Different raters will assign different scores to the same employee. Other problems with such a form are the *halo effect* (one factor influencing the overall rating), *central tendency* (little use made of the extremes), and *leniency* (too many employees rated above average). Organizations have moved away from the conventional rating approach because of these problems.

One attempt to overcome some of the drawbacks of conventional ratings forms has been the development of *Behaviorally Anchored Rating Scales* (BARS). The BARS form utilizes the critical incident method. Each BARS is unique for a particular job and its development consists of five steps: 1) collecting critical incidents from managers and subordinates, 2) collapsing these incidents into general categories or "dimensions," 3) "retranslating" the incidents or rewording

14.4 Sample Behaviorally Anchored Rating Scale

POSITION: Custodial Zone Supervisor   Date: _____

NAME: _____   Unit # _____

On each of the following pages:

1. Read the description of each task/objective and the examples of job behavior.
2. Then, as you review and discuss the employee's performance in relation to each task/objective, *circle* the number on the rating scale which indicates your evaluation of the employee. Always circle a number (1, 2, 3, 4, or 5.) Do not place a "x" or "✔" between numbers.
3. If you wish to rate an employee on an important task/objective of his/her job not included on this form, please develop the blank rating scales provided. If possible, assign mutually agreed upon examples of behavior to a point on the rating scale and then rate the employee's performance in relation to these examples.

Task/Objective #1: Receive oral and written reports from subordinates employees and occupants of buildings regarding damaged facilities, fixtures and equipment and process work orders through proper channels.

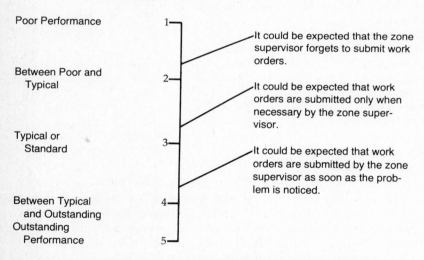

Poor Performance — 1 — It could be expected that the zone supervisor forgets to submit work orders.

Between Poor and Typical — 2 — It could be expected that work orders are submitted only when necessary by the zone supervisor.

Typical or Standard — 3 — It could be expected that work orders are submitted by the zone supervisor as soon as the problem is noticed.

Between Typical and Outstanding — 4

Outstanding Performance — 5

(Note: This BARS form would go on with similar scales until all known Task/Objectives are completed, with blank scales at the end.)

them to improve their clarity and remove ambiguity by individuals who know the position well, 4) having "experts" independently assign the incidents to the dimensions and only those with the highest degree of agreement on first and second ratings are kept, and 5) scaling incidents along a performance-dimension continuum. Figure 14.4 is an example of such a BARS development process.

As you can see, developing such a scale involves a great deal of time and effort. Organizations use this scale because they believe that if the people who use it have a hand in developing it, they will be more committed to it. They believe that such a scale is based upon very specific job behaviors and, therefore, is more reliable than other employee rating forms. Like the critical incident method, BARS gives interviewers much more specific, objective, and job-related information. Since this is a relatively new technique, only time and testing will tell if it achieves the objectives for which it was developed.

The *comparison* or *ranking approach* allows supervisors to compare employees to one another. It is believed that this is a natural evaluation process for managers and, therefore, an easier way to do performance ratings. Good supervisors should know who is the best worker and who is worst and be able to rank or compare employees in this fashion. In most cases, such rankings are relative and do not indicate the degree of difference between employees. Most ranking forms also force supervisors to make a choice; they don't allow any two employees to be ranked as equal. There are basically four types of ranking in use: *straight ranking*, where the rater considers the entire group and rates all; *alternation ranking*, where the supervisor picks the best and then the worst, second best and then second worst until all are ranked; *paired comparison*, where the rater compares each employee to each other employee one at a time with the final ranking determined by the number of choices received; and *forced distribution*, where so many people are assigned to each category, such as 10 percent high performance, 20 percent better than average performance, 40 percent average performance, 20 percent below average performance, and 10 percent poor performance. Figure 14.5 on page 326 is an example of alternation ranking.

Ranking methods are good administrative tools. They are not very useful for coaching employees during the performance interview, because there is no indication as to *why* workers rank where they do. Therefore, this technique is often used in organizations where performance appraisal is oriented toward the past rather than the future. So the performance interview is oriented less toward personnel development and more toward performance measurement and compensation.

A *checklist* consists of various traits, behaviors, or characteristics, and an appraiser checks those items which best describe each employee. On some checklists, the rater is asked to check both the "least" and "most" descriptive items for each subordinate. Checklists are used in only one out of every eight organizations. There are three basic types: simple, weighted, and forced choice (figure 14.6, p. 328).

A *simple checklist* allows the appraiser to check as many items as accurately fit the employee. Each item is taken at face value. A *weighted checklist* is more difficult and time consuming to create. After the items are determined, people in personnel assign values or "weights." If little agreement can be reached on an item, it is excluded. The rater checks the items, as with the simple checklist, but does not know the weights assigned to the various items. The checklist is then scored by someone else, usually in the personnel department.

The *forced choice checklist* consists of groups of items or statements. Figure 14.6 is a forced choice checklist. There are normally between two and five items per group. A rater must choose the best description for each subordinate from each group. The form is scored by someone other than the rater who tries to determine

14.5 Sample Performance Evaluation Ranking Form

INSTRUCTIONS FOR ALTERNATION RANKING ON PRESENT PERFORMANCE

Following the instructions is a list of employees. All of them may be performing satisfactorily, but some are almost certain to be doing a better job in their own assignment than are others in their assignment. You may use your own judgment as to what makes one employee better than another. Many factors may be considered: dependability, ability to do the work, willingness to work, cooperation, ability to get along with people, and many others which you think are important. On making your decision, use your own personal knowledge of the individuals and their work. Do not depend on the opinions of others.

NOW PROCEED AS FOLLOWS:

A. First, eliminate those you cannot rank:
   1. Look over the list of names on the other side of this page and draw a line through the name of any person whose work you do not know well.
   2. Look over the list again and draw a line through the name of any person whose work in your opinion is so different from most of the others that you do not think he (or she) can be compared with them.

B. Second, proceed with your ranking:
   1. Look over the list of the remaining names and decide which one person you think is the best on the list. Draw a line through his or her name and write it in the blank space marked "1-Highest" at the top of the page.
   2. Look over the remaining names and decide which one person is not as good as the others on the list. Draw a line through his or her name and write it in the blank space marked "1-Lowest" at the bottom of the page. Remember, you are not saying that he is unsatisfactory; you are merely saying that you consider the others better.
   3. Next, select the person you think is the best of those remaining on the list, draw a line through his or her name and write it in the blank space marked "2-Next Highest."
   4. Next, select the person you think is not as good as the others remaining on the list, draw a line through his or her name and write it in the blank space marked "2-Next Lowest."
   5. Continue this ranking procedure (selecting next highest, then next lowest) until you have drawn a line through each name on the list.

ALTERNATION RANKING REPORT (Present Performance)   CONFIDENTIAL

IMPORTANT: Before you begin read the instructions carefully.

CLASSIFICATION OF GROUP BEING RANKED

_____

DEPARTMENT   RANKER: Date:

_____

EMPLOYEES TO BE RANKED	RANKING
Akers, Barbara	1–HIGHEST *Parker, Roy*
Boyer, Frank	2–NEXT HIGHEST
DeLama, Daniel	3–NEXT HIGHEST
Fowler, Susan	4–NEXT HIGHEST
Hill, Patricia	5–NEXT HIGHEST
Lawson, Heidi	6–NEXT HIGHEST
Parker, Roy	7–NEXT HIGHEST
Perini, David	8–NEXT HIGHEST
Salazar, Gilbert	9–NEXT HIGHEST
Schmidt, Thomas	9–NEXT LOWEST
Spatuzzi, Anthony	8–NEXT LOWEST
Thompson, Bonnie	7–NEXT LOWEST
Towne, Scott	6–NEXT LOWEST
Wisnowski, Kathrine	5–NEXT LOWEST
Young, Steven	4–NEXT LOWEST
	3–NEXT LOWEST
	2–NEXT LOWEST
	1–LOWEST *Towne, Scott*

(Adapted from Lazer and Wilkstrom, 1977, pp. 118–119)

14.6 Sample Performance Evaluation Checklist

INSTRUCTIONS: Statements descriptive of employee performance are grouped below in blocks of four. For each *block* of statements indicate which statement is most like and least like the employee being described. Place an "X" in the appropriate column bracket.

Most   Least

( )   ( )   Does not get the facts necessary to do the job
( )   ( )   Receives constructive criticism well
( )   ( )   Can be promoted when the opportunity is present
( )   ( )   Gives credit to others for work well done

( )   ( )   Accepts the opinions of subordinates and superiors
( )   ( )   Quickly analyzes a situation
( )   ( )   Coordinates work flow well
( )   ( )   Has minimal knowledge of other employees' jobs

( )   ( )   Follows through even when the going gets rough
( )   ( )   Expresses himself or herself clearly
( )   ( )   Is willing to make decisions
( )   ( )   Knows how to make a convincing report

( )   ( )   Always follows company policies and procedures
( )   ( )   Has a well-organized approach to any problem
( )   ( )   Can put ideas across to others effectively
( )   ( )   Can take constructive criticism without anger

( )   ( )   Meddles into other persons' affairs
( )   ( )   Likes to make decisions
( )   ( )   Is physically unable to meet demands of job
( )   ( )   Gets along well with other employees

( )   ( )   Irritated if job has to be redone
( )   ( )   Self-confident
( )   ( )   Plans ahead carefully
( )   ( )   One of the team

( )   ( )   Does not work to limit of ability
( )   ( )   Reads and follows instructions well
( )   ( )   Always complaining
( )   ( )   Rarely needs prodding

( )   ( )   Aggressive without causing resentment
( )   ( )   Work is rarely interrupted by personal business
( )   ( )   A very clear thinker
( )   ( )   Not always punctual

NAME _____RATER _____

(Adapted from Lazer and Wilkstrom, 1977, p. 117)

which characteristics differentiate between good and bad employees, which items appear to be more favorable than others, and so on. Users of the forced choice checklist claim that it is more reliable, central tendency is reduced, and leniency is removed because the evaluator simply reports behavior rather than evaluating it. The forced choice checklist must be specialized for each position. Its biggest problem is that raters don't like to use it because they do not know how the ratings will be scored. So most organizations use other appraisal forms. Since the raters are usually the interviewers, they want to be able to control the effects of their ratings and for the most part, checklists make for past-oriented interviews.

Probably the most popular performance measurement technique is called the *Management by Objectives* (MBO) system. Recent surveys indicate that it is now being used by almost 50 percent of organizations, and almost three quarters of the managers using it find it effective. Its rationale is very simple. A person is evaluated according to a predetermined set of objectives. Such a form includes two phases: 1) establishment of goals and objectives, usually by the superior and subordinate together, and 2) performance appraisal based on the pre-established objectives (see figure 14.7).

People who use the MBO method find it has several advantages over every other performance evaluation technique. 1) It helps clarify the superior's written and oral appraisal duties. 2) Superiors and subordinates work together to develop and set priorities for performance objectives. 3) Superiors and subordinates can anticipate obstacles ahead of time. 4) The performance factors appraised are usually job related. 5) The objectives listed provide a job description if all important aspects are covered. 6) The judgment criteria are unambiguous, that is, the objectives were either accomplished or not. 7) The results of the appraisal do not come as a surprise to subordinates. 8) Such an approach encourages employees to discuss the reasons for success or failure and to plan for continued or improved

The evaluation form is an important part of a performance interview.

14.7 Sample Management by Objectives Form

INSTRUCTIONS:

Section A—LIST THE MAJOR JOB DUTIES AND RESPONSIBILITIES OF THE POSITION. At the beginning of each evaluation period the supervisor and employee meet to identify the employee's specific duties and responsibilities. Both the supervisor and employee initial the agreed-upon duties and responsibilities. The supervisor has ultimate responsibility for developing this section.

Section B—EVALUATION OF THE PERFORMANCE OF EACH MAJOR JOB DUTY/RESPONSIBILITY. Supervisors should meet with employees at regular intervals over the course of the evaluation period to discuss the employee's performance level and to identify mutual concerns. The supervisor briefly describes the employee's performance in each area and evaluates how the responsibilities and duties of the position were met.

Section C—SUPERVISOR'S COMMENTS/RECOMMENDATIONS. Provide additional documentation or comments on the employee's performance over the course of the rating period. This information should support or clarify the evaluation. The supervisor should note any training that would help the employee perform more effectively.

Section D—EMPLOYEE'S COMMENTS. The employee comments on the performance rating and the performance interview. The employee should note training that would help attain the desired performance level and provide opportunity for individual growth and development.

Section E—MANAGER REVIEW. The performance appraisal will be reviewed by the appropriate manager to note the performance level of the employee, to evaluate the performance appraisal process in an organizational context, and to comment about the rating.

Employee   Position

Department   Period Covered   Supervisor
or Division

---

performance. This is one of the few techniques that definitely has a future, rather than a past, orientation. Most people who use MBO make the appraisal phase of one evaluation period the objective-setting phase for the next period. The performance interview is one of planning as well as appraisal. This is a fairly impressive list of benefits.

MBO is very good in theory but has some problems in practice. It has been referred to as a "do it yourself hangman's kit." Both superiors and subordinates tend to set unrealistic goals. Another major problem is that the objectives set

A. List Major Job Duties & Responsibilities	Initials	B. Evaluation of the Performance of each Major Duty/Responsibility

C. Supervisor's Comments/Recommendations:

Training Recommended:

_____
Supervisor's Signature/Date

D. Employee's Comments:

Training Requested:

_____
Employee's Signature/Date

_____ I agree with this evaluation   _____ I disagree with this evaluation

E. Manager Review:

_____
Manager's Signature/Date

won't necessarily help the company reach its goals. That is, the objectives are not in line with the overall organizational objectives. For example, if the objectives for salespeople are to increase sales 10 percent, it is important to know ahead of time that production and other departments in the organization can keep up with increased sales. This is why most MBO appraisal forms must be reviewed by others in the organization.

Even with all of its problems, the Management by Objectives approach is in many ways the most successful technique now being used. Its success is due in large part to its heavy reliance on the face-to-face interview in both the objective-setting and evaluation phases. For that reason, this chapter is focused toward MBO-type performance interviews.

Other Interview Preparation

Preparing for a performance interview with a subordinate requires that you review the appraisal form, job description, employee file, and any other pertinent information. Some interviewers like to assign some "homework" to the employee as well. You can have each employee evaluate themselves, prepare changes in job objectives, review the completed written form, complete written appraisal of themselves, or collect information relevant to their evaluation. All of this is designed to get interviewees in the proper state of mind for a productive performance interview. Many people aren't aware of how they perform. It is natural to blind ourselves to our own weak spots. This is called *selective perception*. Interviewee "homework" is an attempt to get them to make a fair assessment of their own performance before the interview.

The last phase of preparation is to set the time and place for the interview and inform the interviewee of the meeting. As with most interview settings, it should be private and comfortable. Some superiors like to conduct performance interviews in their office, while others prefer to go to some neutral climate which reduces distractions for both participants. Since most performance interviews are more effective when they are informal, it is important to have a comfortable setting which helps relax participants and avoids the stress which commonly accompanies such interviews. Most interviewers like to hold performance interviews at the end of the day, so employees can go home and think about the improvement suggestions. The employee is then informed of the time and place of the meeting with some stress placed on the meeting's importance. This information should be given to employees at least two to three days in advance.

THE PERFORMANCE INTERVIEW GUIDE

The performance interview guide reflects the strategy that will be used, the performance areas which will be appraised, and possible ways to achieve better performance. Each guide must be tailored to the nature of the problem(s) and the interviewee involved. However, there are some general principles of performance interview guide preparation.

In his classic book, *The Appraisal Interview*, Maier (1958) suggests three basic approaches to performance interviews. A general summary of these approaches appears in figure 14.8.

As you can see, two of the approaches, *tell and sell* and *tell and listen*, are oriented toward evaluation of past behavior and put the interviewer in the role of a judge. Only the *problem-solving* approach is performance improvement or future oriented. It is the problem-solving approach which seems to be most successful in the performance interview.

14.8 Comparisons Among Three Types of Appraisal Interviews

Method	Tell and Sell	Tell and Listen	Problem Solving
Objectives	To communicate evaluation To persuade E to improve	To communicate evaluation To release defensive feelings	To stimulate growth and development in E
Psychological Assumptions	E desires to correct weaknesses if he knows them Any person can improve if he so chooses A superior is qualified to evaluate a subordinate	People will change if defensive feelings are removed	Growth can occur without correcting faults Discussing job problems leads to improved performance

Role of Interviewer	Judge	Judge	Helper
Attitude of Interviewer	People profit from criticism and appreciate help	One can respect the feelings of others if one understands them	Discussion develops new ideas and mutual interests
Skills of Interviewer	Salesmanship Patience	Listening and reflecting feelings Summarizing	Listening and reflecting feelings Reflecting ideas Using exploratory questions Summarizing
Reactions of Employee	Supresses defensive behavior Attempts to cover hostility	Expresses defensive behavior Feels accepted	Problem-solving behavior
Employee's Motivation for Change	Use of positive or negative incentives or both Extrinsic: motivation added to job itself	Resistance to change reduced Positive incentive Extrinsic and some intrinsic motivation	Increased freedom Increased responsibility Intrinsic motivation: interest is inherent in the task
Possible Gains	Success most probable when E respects interviewer	Develops favorable attitude toward superior which increases probability of success	Almost assured of improvement in some respect
Risks of Interviewer	Loss of loyalty Inhibition of independent judgment Face-saving problems created	Need for change may not be developed	E may lack ideas Change may be other than what superior had in mind
Probable Results	Perpetuates existing practices and values	Permits interviewer to change his views in the light of E's responses Some upward communication	Both learn since experience and views are pooled Change is facilitated

Reprinted from: Norman R. F. Maier, The Appraisal Interview: Three Basic Approaches, San Diego, CA: University Associates, Inc., 1976. Used with permission.

A future-oriented guide requires separation between the written and interview portions. Maier characterized this as an *independent relationship:* the written appraisal form precedes the post-appraisal interview. This approach is contrasted to a *dependent relationship.* The difference between the two is illustrated in the diagram marked 14.9.

The dependent post-appraisal interview has three major goals and two minor goals. Such interviewers try to accomplish all five goals in the interview. This makes the interview both past and future oriented. With the independent relationship, however, the major goal of inventory and minor goal of promotion and transfer data are part of the written appraisal and not included in the interview itself. The interview is only concerned with future-oriented topics such as personnel development and improving communication. This is not to say that information contained in the written appraisal is not considered during the interview, but only that such information is used to help determine what should be done in the future. The guide, then, is not one which says, "Here's what you did wrong" but instead one which says, "Here's what you can do in the future to improve."

To develop such an independent interview guide you need to ascertain an employee's strengths and weaknesses. With the aid of the written performance evaluation form, you can determine where problems exist and center interview topics around those problems. Noncritical areas mentioned in the written appraisal need not be discussed in the interview. In some cases, several minor problems can be combined into one general improvement topic. The point is that you should select those two or three most crucial problem areas and focus the entire interview on trying to improve those. If too many problems are tackled, the interviewee may simply "give up."

Once the two or three most important areas have been isolated, you then develop a strategy for approaching each. Flowchart 14.10, adapted from Lopez (1975, p. 240) and Schneider, Donaghy, and Newman (1975, p. 82), offers a general outline which has been useful for many performance appraisal interviewers.

The most important part of this diagram begins with the third box from the top. For each topic you begin with a question such as "What do you see as the problem?" The interviewee's response can either reflect a correct perception of the problem (far right hand column), an incorrect perception of the problem (far left hand column), or something that you have not considered (center column). If the response is one which you have not considered, then give the interviewee a *rain check,* that is, you say "I will have to look into that, I'll get back to you later on this point."

If the interviewee responds in a way that is agreeable to you, then move directly into a diagnosis of the problem, try to find solutions, and go on to the next topic once a mutually acceptable solution is reached. If the interviewee obviously does not perceive the problem, or perceives it incorrectly, then, following down the left hand column, you state the problem as you see it, get a reaction from the interviewee, explore interviewee feelings, and try to reach agreement on the problem before moving on to diagnosis and solution. This general approach has been used in developing many performance interviews. Supervisors have found

14.9 Two Types of Relationships Between the Appraisal and the Interview

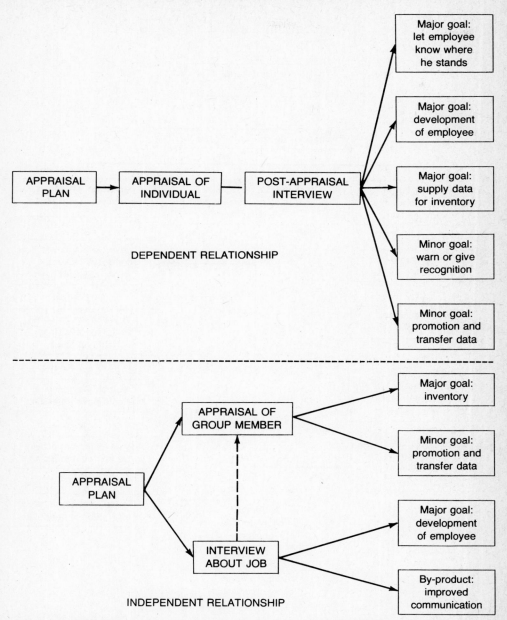

Reprinted from: Norman R. F. Maier, *The Appraisal Interview: Three Basic Approaches*, San Diego, CA: University Associates, Inc., 1976. Used with permission.

14.10 Performance Interview Flowchart

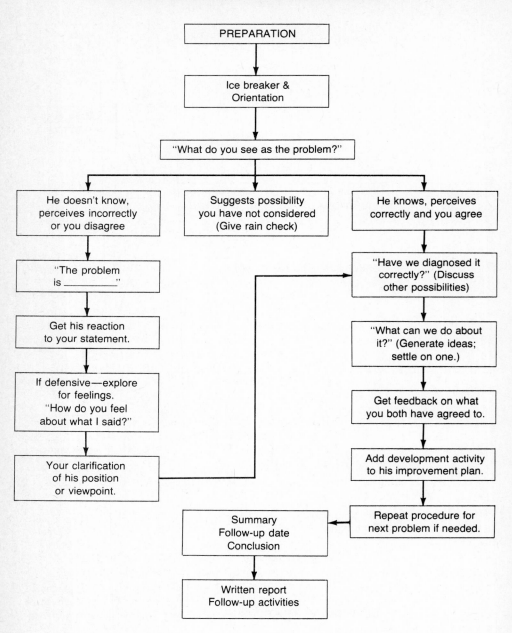

it to be a successful way to structure a performance interview guide. It allows you to see various problems from the employee's perspective, maintain interview control, and focus on specific methods of performance improvement. It works especially well in companies which have adopted a Management by Objectives approach.

PERFORMANCE INTERVIEW OPENING

Icebreaking in a performance interview normally takes no more than ninety seconds. Its purpose is to reduce respondent anxiety, reestablish interviewer credibility, and develop the climate of rapport and formality which best fits the interview purpose. Icebreaking is brief because participants usually have already established a climate of trust and rapport prior to opening the interview. You simply want to point out that this is not a fault-finding session, but instead an open and honest dialogue designed to improve future performance.

During the opening orientation you want to stress a future, rather than a past, focus for the interview. A discussion of how the information will be used, how long the interview will take, and what it will cover should also be included. You want to express a willingness to listen and a desire to guide rather than judge. The interviewee should know you want to develop a performance improvement plan and a means to monitor that plan. Under no circumstances should you allow the orientation to turn into a lecture. When it is over, interviewees should feel that the interview is a chance to have an open and honest, yet confidential, discussion with their supervisor. Research indicates that employees appreciate and want such discussions. They want to know how they are doing, and with the proper orientation, they will be not only willing but eager participants in the entire performance interview process.

PERFORMANCE INTERVIEW QUESTIONING AND RESPONDING

The nature of the interview questions to be asked was noted earlier. The manner in which these inquiries are made, however, is extremely important in assuring their success. Employees must be allowed to maintain their self-esteem. This is one of the reasons it is future oriented rather than past oriented. Under each topic, always get interviewee ideas first. In this way respondents feel that they are being treated as mature, rational, and intelligent individuals who are appreciated.

This does not imply that you should not make comments or suggestions. An open, candid, and honest evaluation of interviewee performance is the primary focus of such interviews. If respondents are unable to appraise themselves, it is your responsibility to do so. Your praise and criticism should be based upon fact, expressed impersonally, and as specific as possible. Be firm, yet supportive. Your tone and behavior must reflect concern for the employee's interests. Keep comments job relevant, and do not deal with personalities or employee characteristics which are unrelated to the job. Biased judgments and arguments are always out of place in a performance interview. Remember, your purpose is to see things from the interviewee's perspective and to arrive at mutually acceptable methods of improving performance. If the employee is too far out of line or personal problems are involved, you need to hold a discipline or counseling interview rather than a performance interview.

The pace should be geared to interviewee responses. Give employees time to think and explain their viewpoints in their own words. This may mean allowing them to save face. It is even possible, at times, to preface a question to suggests ways to avoid embarrassment. This requires careful phrasing so as not to lead the respondent. Introductions such as "Is it possible that . . ." are useful. As in all interviews, the question "Why?" should be avoided. "Why?" implies punishment and criticism, when, in fact, you are looking for improvement. Whatever you can do to maintain the upbeat, positive, and future-oriented focus of this interview will generally prove to be the proper choice.

When you are the respondent in a performance interview, you are usually very anxious. You want to know how you are doing, but you don't want to hear too many bad things about yourself. You much prefer to hear how well you are doing, and so you have a tendency to respond in ways that will put you in the best possible light. But you must be willing to admit your own mistakes and problems. If possible, you should try to beat the interviewer to identifying your strong and weak points. Also, be sure to mention what you have been doing to improve your own performance. If and when the interviewer makes a statement which you think is wrong, be calm and respond carefully. You should present your side of the issue, but don't argue or let your temper get the best of you. Keep in mind that the interviewer, in most cases, is trying to help you. The more defensive you become, the harder it will be for the interviewer to keep an open mind and evaluate you fairly.

PERFORMANCE INTERVIEW PROBING

Almost every major organization has an instruction and suggestions manual for superiors conducting performance interviews. A major portion of these manuals is usually devoted to handling and probing respondent reactions and suggestions. If you examine the various possible responses discussed and the ways in which each reaction is to be handled, you find a great deal of similarity. The following examples represent a composite of suggestions taken from many different manuals.

The first possible reaction is one where an interviewee disagrees on some point but is constructive and unemotional. You should not push or probe too hard to reach agreement but, instead, listen carefully and encourage a mutual exploration of the problem or suggestion under consideration. Performance interviewers must expect some disagreements based upon differences in participant personalities and roles within the organization. Full agreement is often impossible and not necessary. You should listen carefully, probe for amplification and clarification, and be willing to check out any new information. This type of probe leads to understanding and compromise, and should be used whenever both parties are cooperative and willing to explore alternative methods of performance improvement. Such probes encourage further positive and friendly interaction rather than defensiveness and antagonism.

A second respondent reaction is subordinate "too easy" complete agreement. The interviewee probably does not understand or his holding back objections to your suggestions. The respondent may be agreeing in order to avoid discomfort or a discussion of realistic improvement methods. In this situation, ask subordinates to repeat what you have just said. If the repetition is accurate, you know they understand, and you should then encourage them to accept your performance improvement recommendations. Try to get the respondent to make verbal commitment to undertake such improvement. You then follow up with methods to check performance improvement. If through all of this a subordinate still does not express objections, then you must assume that the point has been understood and accepted.

A third common reaction is subordinate avoidance of responsibility for poor performance. Such interviewees attempt to shift blame to others—subordinates, associates, superiors, or the company as a whole. The appropriate probe approach is to simply "hear them out" before probing to discover why they feel the problems are not their own. Encourage such respondents to talk about ways in which they might help solve the problems even though they belong to "somebody else." If possible, let these respondents know that you look more favorably on people who accept responsibility for their own behavior. At no point should you start an argument regarding who is responsible for particular behaviors or who needs improvement. Some manuals suggest that these interviewees be brought into direct face-to-face confrontation with the individuals being blamed for performance problems. This is generally not recommended; you are usually better off listening and encouraging full acceptance of responsibility. If this does not work, however, a confrontation may be your only alternative.

A fourth reaction is when individuals want to quit the organization, and you feel they are worth keeping. You should probe to find out why they want to leave. This may be a form of emotional release or an attempt to find out how you really feel about them. Stress the fact that the interview is designed to improve performance and that you would not be doing it if it did not have merit. You should reinforce your confidence in them but not allow this ploy to distract you from accomplishing the interview purpose. If respondents are serious about quitting, you should get them in touch with a member of the personnel department who does retention interviews. These interviews will be discussed in detail in the termination interview chapter.

A fifth possible subordinate reaction is to become emotional, angry, and argumentative. Again, you must not let yourself get emotionally involved. Listen and let such individuals "get it off their chest." Try to understand what they are saying and probe to bring the discussion back to the facts. Eventually, most respondents will calm down. If not, the discussion should be rescheduled. A warning is in order at this point; do not retreat and be sure such respondents understand your purpose and point of view. They must realize that the interview will be continued and that you intend to talk about performance improvement. By maintaining your own self-control, you encourage interviewees to follow suit, and they usually do.

A final common reaction is passive and unresponsive behavior. Be sure you allow respondents plenty of time to answer, and don't be too quick to judge the meaning of silence. Careful probing will often get these respondents talking about what they want to achieve, and soon you can discover the cause of the passive attitude. All employees want to grow and improve no matter what they say or do not say. Only by providing standards to measure growth and methods by which growth can be achieved will both participants be satisfied with a performance interview. Silence is often a sign of tension and nervousness. You can overcome this by moving slowly, probing the most important and familiar points first, and only going on to more difficult areas after the tension is reduced.

As you can see, meeting these reactions requires that you master all of the types of probes discussed earlier. As a performance interviewer, you must learn to use amplification probes (such as silence, minimal encouragement, and restatement), clarification probes (such as paraphrasing, summarizing, and direct amplification requests), and also be able to confront interviewees in a way that encourages growth and doesn't produce hostility and resentment. A widely used probe technique is to encourage subordinates to summarize points covered as well as goals. One of the main purposes of evaluation interviews is to get employees to undertake analyses of their problems and create performance improvement goals on their own, outside of the interview. Summary probes help accomplish that objective. They also help you determine the level of agreement and control the interview's progress and direction.

PERFORMANCE INTERVIEW LISTENING AND RECORDING

The performance interview approach described in this chapter requires active listening. Active listening does not imply agreement but simply paying enough attention to perceive problems and possible solutions from the respondent's perspective. Many times, you will have to "read between the lines" or listen with your "third ear" in order to fully understand what the respondent is trying to say. As was pointed out earlier, interviewees may not be totally aware of what they are doing or why they are doing it. Only through careful listening can you fully understand their viewpoint. Obstacles to effective listening in performance interviews include primary and secondary tension, conclusion jumping, overtalking, planning ahead, and mental arguing. All of these should be avoided whenever possible.

Performance interview recording is very difficult for many managers. They feel that electronically recording performance interviews may constitute an invasion of interviewee privacy. Respondents also tend to become very nervous and defensive when an electronic recorder is used. Therefore, most interviewers use a pencil and paper. This can also be difficult because it tends to inhibit respondents and distract interviewers. In order to overcome these problems, you must learn to take very brief notes, take notes during pauses only, and avoid writing down only negative information.

When done correctly, notetaking can be flattering to employees. Under all circumstances the notes must be accurate, relevant, objective, uniform, and complete. This is necessary for legal documentation as well as for record keeping.

One way to reduce notetaking tension is to encourage employees to take notes. If they are truly interested in improving performance, they will find notetaking extremely valuable and many arrive with a pencil and paper. This justifies notetaking on the part of the interviewer as well. It is essential that you set aside time directly after the interview to transcribe and expand upon notes. Small points can be extremely important in creating a fully accurate record of a performance interview.

PERFORMANCE INTERVIEW CONCLUDING

The conclusion of a performance interview includes a summary of points of agreement and disagreement; discussion of action plans; and termination on a friendly, collaborative, and positive note. Both participants should leave the interview with a feeling of accomplishment. Interviewees should feel that they have been able to say everything that concerns them in an open and straightforward manner. Interviewers should feel that all major problem areas have been covered and that the performance of the employee will improve once the interview is completed.

In performance interviewing, it is especially important that an accurate record be kept of all topics discussed and actions to be taken. In some cases this may mean checking employee explanations, identifying needed resources, setting times to check progress, and scheduling follow-up interviews. All of this information should be put in writing. After the interview, copies of this report are sent to the interviewee and appropriate organization officials, with a single copy being kept in your file. The follow-up consists, then, of documentation by employee and superior to show that the standards have been met.

SUMMARY

When you think that almost every employee in the world goes through a performance interview at least once a year, it is no wonder that these interviews have received so much attention. A major problem with many performance interviews is that too many conflicting objectives are covered. This chapter has focused on the future-oriented or independent performance appraisal approach. Six basic types of written performance appraisal forms were examined and the effects each has on the performance interview were noted. The MBO technique is most closely aligned with the approach found in this chapter. A suggested performance interview guide was presented which has proven useful in many interviews. In performance interviewing, the opening, questioning, and probing phases must reflect a friendly, open, honest, and nonevaluative climate until all pertinent information has been gathered. This is accomplished through careful listening and recording. Once the performance information is complete, both participants strive to reach mutually acceptable performance objectives and methods of reaching those goals. Ways of meeting various forms of employee resistance must be mastered in order to accomplish this purpose. Finally, good performance interviews end on a positive note and are followed by written documentation. When performance interviews are conducted properly, they are of benefit to employees, superiors, and the organization as a whole.

ACTIVITIES

Activity #1

Directions: On the basis of what you have learned in this chapter and in Part I, analyze the following two performance interview excerpts. Compare and contrast the two approaches. Look for both good points and bad points for both the interviewers and interviewees. Both excerpts are done with a recently hired sales manager. After taking over the Sales Department, which includes some individuals who have been with the company for almost twenty years, the new manager observed that three secretaries were employed to complete any work the sales force had to do. One of the secretaries was assigned to the sales manager and the others worked primarily with the salespersons. The new manager thought it would be more efficient to transfer the two salesperson secretaries to the company typing pool and give the salespersons dictating equipment instead. This the sales manager did and felt proud of the increased company-wide efficiency created. There seemed to be some increased resentment, but the sales manager thought it was just bad feelings over the fact that none of the sales staff had been promoted to sales manager rather than the loss of what they believed to be "their secretaries." As a matter of fact, one of the sales staff quit and took a similar job with another company. The division manager heard about the problem and decided to make it a topic of the six-month performance review. The following excerpts represent two ways the interview might have occurred. They represent the tell and sell and problem-solving approaches discussed in this chapter. Introductory and concluding materials have been omitted from these examples. R = Interviewer, E = Interviewee.

Example A:

1 R: I guess the main problem you have had since we last talked is the hostility between you and your staff. I heard about the secretary and dictaphone thing.
   E: The what?
5 R: You know, firing or transferring the secretaries and giving the sales staff dictaphones instead. You know you're never going to make it in this job if you don't work with your people.
   E: We get our work done. I've heard nothing about a problem regarding the dictaphones. I do know there is some hostility toward me because I was
10 hired instead of one of them, and . . .
   R: Listen, it's common knowledge that one of your staff has already quit over this and others are considering quitting.
   E: I expected that there would be some "settling down" time after I took over. I don't see it as anything to get upset about. We filled the position
15 quickly.
   R: I'm not upset. I'm just trying to help you improve, and I know from long years of experience that a good manager needs to have the support of

subordinates. Right now you don't have that support, and you're going to have to adjust that.

20 E: I still don't see the problem with the dictaphones. I thought I was doing the company a favor.

R: You just don't make radical changes without talking with your personnel. You don't take their secretaries away while keeping yours and expect them to be happy about it. Especially when it's making your staff mad

25 enough to quit. You have got a problem.

E: I don't think it's as big a problem as you're making it out to be . . .

R: You don't? I sure do. No more snap decisions, OK?

E: I don't think this is anything I can't handle. I did think through my decision on the secretaries. I thought it was best, and I still do.

30 R: OK. You handle it, but it better be soon. You have got to get those people on your side, or you'll be out of a job.

E: If you say so . . .

R: I certainly do.

E: All right, but I still think it's blown out of proportion. I do get along

35 with . . .

R: Let's go on to the next subject.

Example B:

1 R: Lets talk a little about staff relations. How are you getting along with your personnel? Are things settling down?

E: Yeah, I think so. We're getting used to each other.

R: Everything's OK then?

5 E: I think so . . . there is still some resentment about my being hired over one of them. Every once in a while I notice it. I told you one of the staff quit. I think it was because she thought she would become sales manager. I don't know, though.

R: Has she been replaced?

10 E: Yeah, got a good replacement too.

R: You think the resentment is settling down then?

E: Oh, yeah . . . more or less.

R: "More or less?"

E: Yeah, well, . . . I told you about my moving the secretaries to the com-

15 pany typist pool. Some of them, the staff I mean, didn't like that at first, but that's calmed down, and it did help the company as a whole.

R: Yeah, it sure did. Do you think there is any resentment remaining over that?

E: Oh, perhaps.

20 R: How might you do that differently next time?

E: I guess I rushed the change too much. I didn't realize just how much those secretaries meant to them. I should have talked more with them before making a decision. I have thought about that a lot.

R: I can see you have.

25 E: I think I hurt their feelings.

R: How so?

E: They felt more important with a secretary than a dictaphone. But, I'm still

30 sure I did the right thing. I think it improved efficiency in the whole
company.
R: Yes, but you appreciate their feelings.
E: Yes. I do. Perhaps what I can do is make my secretary a department-wide
secretary. Do you think that would help?
R: I don't know. Do you think it would?
E: Yeah, that's just what I'm going to do. I also think I am going to hold more
35 frequent meetings where we can talk things out. It would give me a chance
to try out my ideas on them and get their feelings. It would also help me get
to know them better and vice versa.
R: That sounds pretty good to me. When do you think you might start those
things?
40 E: No sense waiting too long. I'll try the first one next week.
R: You'll let me know how it goes?
E: I sure will. It will take about a month to see how these things are working.
R: Good, how about a month from today, and that will be our main topic of
conversation. I think you are on the right track.
45 E: I do too.
R: Are you read to go on to the next topic?
E: Yeah.

Activity #2

Directions: Arrange an interview with one or more people who regularly do
performance interviews. Almost any manager or supervisor of a large organization generally fits this requirement. See if you can talk with people who
appraise middle and upper managers as well as entry-level employees. Try to
get a copy of any written appraisal form they may use as well. Ask them about
their performance interviews in terms of preparation, conduct, and follow-up.
Once you have gathered this information, prepare a short paper comparing
this interview to the others you have studied thus far.

Activity #3

Directions: Select one of the following hypothetical cases and role-play it,
being sure to use the concepts and skills discussed in this and previous
chapters. These cases merely describe common performance evaluation situations. You are free to add any other information you like to make the role-play
as realistic as possible.

CASE A: Mark Thompson, the interviewee, is an estimator for a contracting
firm. He is competent and knowledgeable, but not exceptional. He totally
dislikes the details and calculations necessary to make a final estimate. Lately,
some of his estimates have been way off target, either too high so that the
company loses business or too low so the company loses money. He says he
needs an assistant to help with the "detail work." No other estimator has an
assistant. His desire to "cut through the red tape" and "get the job done" has
also sometimes come across as tactless to the other estimators. They feel he is

bucking for a promotion or a punch in the nose. He continually tells them he likes to look at the "big picture." He says that he is a professional and shouldn't have to do all of the petty work which they all have to do. *Francis Parker*, Mark's supervisor, is about to do a performance review with all of the estimators and decides to start with Mark since he is the senior member of the estimator group.

CASE B: Patricia Miles is a first year professor at a small southern college. She teaches computer science and is completing her Ph.D. degree in that field. Because of her degree work, she has not been putting in too many office hours. *Dr. Arthur Palmer,* her department head has also had some complaints that she is having trouble getting through to many of her students. This, combined with her lack of time to give individual attention to her students, has caused much frustration, especially among those who have never had a computer science course before. Patricia's student evaluations have reflected these deficiencies and her students' grade point averages are among the lowest in the computer science department. Ms. Miles feels that it is not her responsibility to be constantly available to students who simply do not want to read the textbook. She learned computer science without having somebody show her every simple step, and she feels others have the responsibility to learn on their own as well. She likes what she is doing in her job and wants to remain. Dr. Palmer has decided to talk to her on the brink of her merit evaluation.

CASE C: William Stacks works on the road crew of the city of Alcott. The members of the road crew have no assigned jobs and report to the crew chief each morning to see what they will be doing during the day. The crew chief, *Greg Webb,* sometimes assigns workers to a continuing project, at other times pulls a more experienced worker off a job for a special assignment, or simply takes assignments and personnel in the order they come on the work list. When the load is light, he sometimes even lets workers choose their assignment. When the workers are assigned an especially tough, messy job they are paid a "dirty work" bonus. Because Greg knows that Bill is an extra-hard worker and that his wife has been ill lately and has many expenses, he has been giving him more of the jobs that carry a salary premium. He did not bother to tell Bill why he was doing this. Bill, who is generally good-natured, has recently been brooding about the fact that he rarely gets to stay on one job and make friends with the people with whom he is working. Bill has been thinking about this problem all weekend and when Greg assigns him an especially dirty job on Monday, he says, "I won't take that job until every other person on the crew pulls as many dirty jobs as I have." When Greg reminds him of the money and tells him to "get going," Bill says, "NO." Greg tells Bill to wait in his office and finishes giving out the assignments. As he walks back to his office, he decides to do a formal performance evaluation with Bill, since it is almost time for them to be done anyway. Bill's refusal to take an assignment will be the first major topic.

Chapter 15

The Persuasion Interview

We are and we encounter persuasive interviewers in a variety of settings nearly everyday: the "sales rep" who wants to sell a product or service, the "recruiter" who wants people to join an organization, the "activist" who urges people to vote, to protest, or to write in behalf of a person or cause, the "PR" person who seeks to enhance the image of a person or organization, the "true believer" who wants to alter beliefs, the "campaigner" who wants support for a candidate or a referendum, and the "socializer" who urges people to go to a particular movie, game, or restaurant. (Stewart and Cash, 1982, p. 273)

The term persuasion has a somewhat negative image for many people. They think of the old-fashioned, arrogant, cigar-smoking, fast-talking super salesperson. Research interviewers often need to convince respondents that they "are not selling something." The fact of the matter is, however, that salespersons who attempt to use outdated high-pressure coercion techniques are usually unsuccessful. *Persuasion*, as it is most commonly defined, simply means assessing another person's beliefs, needs, attitudes, and behavior and then determining the best means to influence them. Since we all try to influence other people everyday—get members of the opposite sex to like us, persuade our children to hang up their clothes, or ask a friend to mail a letter for us—we are all persuaders.

The persuasion interview as it is discussed here refers to any interview which has some form of influence as its primary purpose. Obviously, this definition is broad enough to cover several of the other types of interviews discussed in this book such as performance, diagnostic, and discipline. For our purposes in this chapter, several limitations will be added to this definition to differentiate this interview from the others.

First, this discussion focuses on persuasion which occurs as part of a face-to-face dyadic relationship. Persuasion can also occur in many other situations, such as televised advertisements, classroom instruction, small groups, and public speeches. According to Stewart and Cash (1978), the face-to-face, two-person situation has several unique characteristics and advantages over other means of persuasion. The interviewer can tailor a message to fit one person, demonstrate interest in interviewees and their needs, receive immediate verbal and nonverbal feedback, adapt the message to fit the situation and the interviewee, hear and see without difficulty, select the best time and place, and alternate roles in the face of counter-arguments and evidence. These characteristics and advantages make the persuasion interview a very powerful tool in comparison with other means of persuasion.

Second, our discussion will be limited to persuasion interviews where interviewees have some choice as to whether they accept or reject the attitude or behavior advocated. This rules out coercion. *Coercion* is the use of force to influence attitudes or behaviors. Coercion usually requires that the interviewer have some power or status over the respondent such as an employer/employee relationship in a business organization. Performance and discipline interviews are more closely aligned with the methods of coercion than is a persuasion interview. Persuasion interviews usually take place between equals or peers and a respondent voluntarily accepts the influence attempt.

Many interviewing "experts" and practitioners tend to overlook or neglect the persuasion interview. Often these people do not even think of persuasion in an interview context. The fact is, however, that for an interviewer, information giving is very often just as important a part of an interview as information gathering. The chief difference between a persuasion interview and a counseling or diagnostic interview, for example, is that in the former the interviewer's primary aim is information giving, whereas in the latter the interviewer begins with some form of information gathering. The persuasion interviewer's influence goal is planned in advance. Inquiries are designed to discover how best to accomplish that goal, not what the goal should be. As you will see in the following sections, however, there is a great deal of similarity in the processes involved in skillful persuasion interviewing and other interview applications.

PERSUASION INTERVIEW PREPARATION

Getting ready for a persuasion interview begins with both general and specific preparation. You must learn about human nature, and particularly why people think and behave as they do. Most contemporary theories suggest that people think and behave in accordance with their needs. You need to discover and appeal to the most salient needs within them to influence their beliefs, attitudes, or behavior.

Very early in this book, you learned about the importance and types of needs. *Physical needs* are such things as the need for food, sex, shelter, sleep, and physical security. *Social needs* involve our relationships with other people. Our desire for love, affection, and inclusion are all part of our social needs. *Ego needs* are based on how we think about ourself. Pride, reputation, achievement, power, appearance, and creativity are ego needs. Each person's ideas and behaviors are a product of these needs and, therefore, can only be influenced through appeals to them.

Early in each persuasion interview, it is your responsibility to identify what needs are determining a respondent's current ideas and behaviors. You do this by asking questions. Different degrees of physical, social, and ego needs predominate in different individuals. If you can correctly identify respondents' most salient needs and create a persuasive presentation which will satisfy them, you will probably be able to influence them. This means gathering as much information about the subject as possible ahead of time. In some cases, as with a retail store clerk and a customer, this is impossible. In other cases, it is possible to learn a lot about each interviewee's needs before the interview. Very often the amount of information persuasion interviewers collect before the interview is proportional to the importance of the idea or cost of the product advocated. An aircraft salesperson, for example, would not think of calling on potential customers without first finding out as much as possible about them and their aircraft needs. What information cannot be gathered before the interview is collected once the interview begins.

Next, you must learn as much as possible about the product or idea you will be advocating. Automobile salespersons, for example, must learn everything possible about an automobile before interviewing prospective buyers. Teachers must learn as much about their subject as possible before tutoring students. This general preparation lets you adapt your message to the needs of interviewees.

In a sales interview, most customers base their purchasing decisions on one or more of the following five factors: price, financing, service, appearance, and quality. For some people, price is the most important factor; for others, appearance may be most important. The skillful salesperson knows about all five factors and structures each interview to the needs most important to each interviewee. This involves a great deal of preparation which may or may not be used in any particular interview.

Aside from these aspects of persuasive interview preparation, skillful persuasion interviewers carefully select the time and setting for their interviews. Just before or directly after a meal is a poor time to conduct an interview—people are more concerned about their physical needs than about social or ego needs you might want to appeal to. But if you are selling ice cream, sandwiches, or soft drinks, just before a meal might be the most effective time to persuade an interviewee. Timing, therefore, is dependent upon the nature of what is being discussed as well as the needs of the interviewee.

Settings for persuasive interviews are varied. Some, such as orientation and coaching interviews, take place in an interviewer's office. Others, such as a door-to-door sales, take place in the interviewee's environment. Neutral environments, such as restaurants, golf courses, and bars are also common locations for persuasive interviews. The proper setting again depends upon the nature of the idea or behavior under consideration as well as the participants.

All of this preparation is vital to the success of a persuasion interview. As with the diagnostic interview, it is usually impossible for persuasive interviewers to do much more than prepare generally because very often the interviewer and interviewee are strangers until the interview takes place. Therefore, a great deal of questioning, probing, and analysis occurs during the early stages of the interview.

THE PERSUASION INTERVIEW GUIDE

As you might guess, persuasion interview guides are usually very general. They include sales manuals and various kinds of checklists. Some guides are nothing more than an order form which the interviewer fills out when talking with a client. Others run to forty or fifty illustrated pages.

Persuasion interviewers usually memorize the information contained in the guide to fit each respondent. In many guides the key questions are spaced at appropriate places in the explanatory text to get a response on the part of a respondent. This is commonly referred to as the *need-satisfaction* approach; it is the primary approach used in this book. You first determine an interviewee's needs by asking questions and then try to show how the idea or behavior suggested will satisfy those needs.

The need-satisfaction persuasion interview usually involves three phases. In the first phase you get interviewees to discuss their needs. This is where the successful salesperson determines whether price, financing, service, appearance, or quality are most important to a respondent. Once you have determined as much as possible about their needs, you then get them to recognize those needs. Very often respondents do not recognize their own needs. The purpose in this phase is to try to get both you and the interviewee to agree upon the most salient needs. If you don't agree, respondents may become resentful and hostile. In the final stage, you show respondents how your idea or product will meet the needs upon which you both agree. This is called the *need fulfillment stage.* This approach is in direct contrast to persuasive interview guides where the interviewer begins by pointing out all of the important features of the idea or behavior advocated at the very beginning of the interview.

Two other aspects of a persuasion interview guide are important to mention here. The first is that it incorporates both objective and subjective questions. Objective questions allow you to determine the range of interviewee knowledge. You begin by asking knowledge questions and then progress through comprehension, application, analysis, synthesis, and finally, evaluation questions. This gives you an overall view of just how much objective information the interviewee has before you make your persuasive attempt. It would be a crucial mistake to present objective information that interviewees already possess.

With subjective questions, you can assess the depth of current attitudes and determine what types of emotional appeals will motivate respondents. What are the interviewee's feelings about your proposal? What needs are most salient for the interviewee? How can your message be tailored to meet those feelings and needs? All of this information is usually obtained in the early stages of a persuasion interview for those using a need-satisfaction guide.

A second aspect of persuasion interview guides revolves around the use of leading questions. Persuasive interviewers often feel they will be more successful if they lead respondents to their predetermined conclusion with loaded words, appeals to prejudice, raising questions in a tricky manner, or in one way or another trying to make one answer easier and more tempting for a respondent than another.

The need-satisfaction approach de-emphasizes the use of leading questions, because such questions often create more problems than they solve. Generally, need-satisfaction interviewers use them only in the second phase, when trying to reach agreement on needs. Phase one, determining needs, should only include neutral questions, whereas phase three, satisfying needs, includes very few questions. In the third stage interviewers describe how the idea or behavior recommended will fulfill the need.

PERSUASION INTERVIEW OPENING

A persuasion interviewer must establish *credibility*. In a persuasion interview, this is especially important because most people resist being influenced by people they do not perceive as credible. Respondents are more likely to accept appeals from someone who seems knowledgeable and informed about the subject under discussion. This is the competence dimension. If persuasion interviewers are not perceived as competent, interviewees are not willing to accept their proposals. Trustworthiness refers to an interviewee's perception of the persuader's honesty and character. Respondents want to be sure, not only that they can trust the things the interviewer says, but also that the interviewer will follow through with any promises made as part of the influence attempt. Finally, interviewees prefer interacting with interviewers who are active and responsive to their needs. This is the dynamism component. If you look bored, fatigued, or overbearing, you are less likely to persuade respondents. In the opening, then, it is your responsibility to appear competent, trustworthy, and dynamic. Credibility can be accomplished through both verbal and nonverbal communication techniques. Clothing, facial expression, vocabulary, use of evidence, facts, logic, and other techniques suggest credibility.

Another goal of the opening is to establish rapport. Rapport develops if you show a willingness to listen and respond positively to what interviewees have to say. This is why the opening should be a two-way process involving both interviewer and respondent comments. The principal shortcoming of the "hard-sell" or total information giving approach is that very little rapport is generated. Interviewees are often unwilling to make statements unless encouraged to do so. During the opening, then, you should treat interviewees as thinking people whose comments and questions you welcome. Demonstrate that you find them credible, and they will find you credible too. This is absolutely essential for the needs-satisfaction approach, since it will be necessary for both participants to reach agreement as to the basis on which any decision will be made. Rapport— mutual respect—leads to agreement.

PERSUASION INTERVIEW QUESTIONING AND RESPONDING

Getting people to embrace an idea or behavior you recommend is a delicate and tricky process. Almost every salesperson will tell you that they can make a fortune or go broke depending upon the way they handle the questioning. The "high pressure" or "hard-sell" approach used by some persuasive interviewers involves a very direct, aggressive, and rapidly paced sales "pitch." These people have a "grab bag" of techniques and gimmicks which they use to persuade, almost coerce, customers to accept their idea or product. They try to intimidate and interrogate to such an extent that the respondent is afraid to say anything but "yes." These people refuse to think of repondents as anything other than dumb, naive, and gullible. These are not interviewers; they are con artists. When they do use questions, they are normally leading and unethical.

The need-satisfaction approach advocated in this chapter is commonly referred to as a "soft-sell." Interviewees are treated as intelligent, rational individuals. There is little, if any, pressure put on them to make a decision. Interviewees are questioned and shown the rationale for making the desired decision, but they are not threatened or bombarded. The questioning has a definite information-gathering purpose.

Another noticeable difference between the hard-sell and soft-sell method is the pace at which the interview is conducted. Soft-sell interviews generally take longer than hard-sell interviews, since the pace is normally adjusted to that of the interviewee. When using this approach, you must take the time to perceive and understand interviewee needs, reach agreement upon those needs, and encourage interviewees to reach a mutually satisfactory decision. In order to do this you must be patient and wait for respondents to consider all information before making their decision. One of the techniques of the hard-sell is to get respondents to make quick, unthinking, and rash decisions. Some of the profitability has been taken out of such techniques since government regulations force salespeople to give respondents a "waiting period" during which they can change their decisions. Slower-paced interviews allow interviewees to reach their own decisions and so they are much less likely to change their minds later.

As an interviewee in a persuasion interview, you should control the pace. You should not be afraid to ask for repetition of any information and for time to weigh the pros and cons of the decision. If interviewers are unwilling to give you this added time or adjust the pace for you, you are fully justified in refusing to participate any further. You don't have to give the persuader your time or attention—skillful persuasion interviewers are willing to respect your freedom of choice.

This does not mean that when you are the interviewer you should not be confident and persistent. If you do not demonstrate a certain degree of confidence in yourself and the idea or behavior you propose, interviewees aren't likely to decide in your favor. Confidence, however, should not be confused with pompousness. Pompous people are so convinced of their own importance that they try to make everyone else feel insignificant. They quesion with a "better-than-thou" tone of voice and facial expression. Confident interviewers, on the other hand, ask questions in such a way that interviewees feel they are competent and trustworthy. Like confidence, persistence also involves a fine line between being "pushy" and "encouraging." You must make every effort to persuade respondents, but you must be willing to accept "no" for an answer. Pushy questioning only increases the chance of a "no." This fine line will be discussed again in the section on persuasive interview concluding. Ask questions and make comments with confidence and persistence, but always be civil to and respectful of respondents.

PERSUASION INTERVIEW PROBING

In persuasion interviews both participants probe. Interviewers probe to amplify and clarify the respondent's needs. Interviewees probe to amplify, clarify, and confront questionable aspects of interviewer facts, evidence, and logic. Clarification probes are especially useful to persuasion interviewers when moving into the second phase of need-satisfaction. By paraphrasing and summarizing interviewee statements and responses, it is possible to get respondents to see and understand their needs, maybe for the first time. In this stage you act very much like a counseling or diagnostic interviewer. The respondent has problems and you help solve those problems. The telephone company's slogan, "Let our experts help you solve your communication needs" is a good example. Such an approach allows the "experts" (i.e., persuasion interviewers) to define needs in a way which will make it easier for them to satisfy those needs by selling an idea or product.

Interviewees do much of the probing in persuasion interviews. They ask for amplification and clarification of each and every piece of information they don't understand. Those who do not demand amplification and clarification open themselves up to the hard-sell interviewer. You have probably been told that you should never sign anything until you have read and understand it completely. It's amazing, however, how many people accept new ideas, buy new products, and in other ways change their attitudes or behavior without ever being totally clear about why they are making certain decisions and the implications of those decisions. The old adage, "Let the buyer beware," applies to persuasive interviews just as it applies to any other type of persuasive communication encounter. Amplification and clarification probes help interviewees determine whether or not an interviewer's proposal is best for them.

At times during a persuasion interview you must confront interviewers about inconsistencies in the information they've presented. This is especially true when inconsistencies are noted between what an interviewer has said and a written contract you are requested to sign. Some persuasion interviewers will say, "Don't bother to read all that stuff, I told you everything that is in this contract." They may very well have told you about everything in the contract, but what they told you and what the contract says may be two different things.

PERSUASION INTERVIEW LISTENING AND RECORDING

When using the soft-sell approach, it is crucial that you listen for and understand the relevant needs as respondents express them. Careful listening determines whether or not the influence attempt will be successful. The biggest obstacles to efficient listening are overtalking, planning ahead, conclusion jumping, arguing, and uncritical acceptance. Persuaders are sometimes so convinced of the correctness of their proposal and so full of data, logic, and evidence to support it that they don't let interviewees express their thoughts. When dealing with such interviewers, respondents often experience *information overload*. Information overload means that they receive so much information that they cannot process it all. The interviewer has not bothered to find out what information is needed and piles on as much information as time will allow. Respondents do not have a chance to consider or weigh the information or even to sort it out. Information overload is almost guaranteed to make respondents delay decision-making until all of the information can be considered.

Those persuasion interviewers who are not busy overtalking are often planning ahead. They may have listened to the first response or two made by an interviewee, but they are no longer listening. They have jumped to a conclusion as to their best approach and are mentally preparing their strategy. Conclusion jumping and planning ahead can both cause real problems; they keep you from truly understanding a respondent's needs.

The opposite reaction is mental arguing. Here the interviewer listens to respondent comments, but won't accept them. This interviewer wants to change the interviewee's needs rather than design a strategy to accommodate them. Interviewers who mentally and verbally argue are generally unprepared. They have only one persuasive strategy which they use on every respondent.

Why is uncritical acceptance a listening obstacle if interviewers are supposed to accept respondent needs and design a strategy to meet them? The answer is that many times interviewees are unaware of their real needs. If they are, then no amount of mental or verbal arguing will change them. On the other hand, it is your responsibility to be sure both you and they understand their real needs. Clothing customers, for example, who say they want top quality but look first at the price tag should be tactfully led to the clothing rack which best fits their true needs. If you respond only to what people say they want, you will lose many sales. On the other hand, if a customer does want top quality and you lead them to the low-price clothing, you are just as likely to lose the sale. This is the difference between mentally arguing and uncritical acceptance. Both can be obstacles to persuasion interview listening. You must listen for the real needs of respondents and tailor your message to those needs. You cannot do this if you overtalk, plan ahead, jump to conclusions, mentally argue, accept all comments uncritically, or practice any of the other poor listening behaviors mentioned in the chapter on listening.

Very little written recording takes place in a persuasion interview. Electronic recording is usually out-of-the-question. Even when pencil and paper is used, it most often is some type of predetermined category checklist. Recording, then, normally involves memorization. An interviewer listens for and memorizes the needs of a respondent and then tries to select those arguments which are most likely to be successful. During a persuasion interview it is distracting to try to write down even central idea notes. Effective persuasion requires constant and focused attention. There is little or no time to make written notes, and electronic recording may suggest some type of devious intent. This is one of the very few cases where memorization is used as the primary means of interview recording.

PERSUASION INTERVIEW CONCLUDING

Most persuaders will tell you that the "close" is probably the most important, difficult, and demanding stage of the interview. Sales manuals usually devote many pages to the closing. This is the point when you, the interviewer, must meet interviewee objections and bring the interview to a mutually satisfactory conclusion.

Once you have probed for interviewee needs and interviewees agree that you have identified them, it is time to close the interview. Never conclude a persuasion interview until you are completely convinced that the respondent is fully

Used correctly, a need-satisfaction persuasive interview usually results in a friendly conclusion.

prepared to make a reasoned decision. There are usually a number of points during each interview when respondents are psychologically prepared to accept your influence attempt. Some interviewers suggest that you should move to close at the earliest possible point. If you are truly interested in the welfare of respondents, however, you will not try to close until you are convinced they have the information and the time to make a reasoned decision. In other words, you want them to make the right decision for them, not just for you.

Interviewees may raise many objections at the end of an influence attempt, and you must satisfy them if possible. If, for example, interviewees say they have tried the idea or behavior before and it "didn't work," you must go back and probe to discover why it didn't work, and if possible, show them that your proposal is somehow different and overcomes the problems experienced earlier. If your proposal is really sound and benefits interviewees, you will be able to handle any resistance encountered.

Probably the most difficult form of resistance to handle is an interviewee who seeks to delay the decision until after the interview is over. You might try to avoid the delay by answering any questions and responding to all objections the interviewee has. If interviewees still want to delay the decision, you are well advised to allow them time to think. As the following quotation suggests, a delay does not necessarily mean failure.

Allowing a customer to delay his decision does not necessarily signify sales-worker failure. It is the prospect's privilege to postpone. A salesman who has provided the customer with information which satisfies the customers needs can be assured that the customer will be at least favorably inclined towards a positive purchasing decision.

(Hatfield, in Huseman, Logue and Freshley, 1973, p. 405)

Once all interviewee needs have been satisfied and all objections and resistance overcome, it is time to ask for the decision. This is a traumatic moment for both interviewee and interviewer. Some interviewers put off directly asking for a decision by summarizing, asking if the interviewee needs any further information, or once again going over the important features of the proposal and showing how they satisfy the interviewee needs. This gives interviewees warning that the interview has reached the decision-making stage. If they do not take the hint, you should simply ask for a decision. If the groundwork has been prepared properly, a positive decision should be forthcoming. Even when the decision is negative, there are normally one or more reasons given. This gives you one more chance to respond to those reasons and perhaps change the decision. At this point, you can seek a delay yourself by asking the respondent to "think it over" before making an absolute, final decision.

Like most other interviews, the conclusion does not end with the decision or the separation of the participants. In all of these interviews there is a follow-up procedure, although in persuasion interviews there is no written follow-up except perhaps for an order form or a client contact report. Persuasion interview follow-up is designed to do two things: reinforce the decision if it is positive and prevent any future decision change, and second, to recruit, through word-of-mouth, future interviewees. Reinforcement normally starts as an interviewee leaves the interview setting. Comments such as "I think you've made a wise decision," "That's a fine automobile you just bought," and "If you have any problems just bring it back and we'll take care of them" reinforce decisions. After interviewees have left, most successful interviewers follow up with a letter or telephone call to handle any minor problems, restate appreciation, or inquire about satisfaction with the decision.

Persuasion interviewers are always interested in finding other interviewees. One of the best ways is word-of-mouth. If you have carefully focused on interviewee needs and made a conscious and honest attempt to satisfy those needs, you will normally receive positive recommendations. This is another benefit of the need-satisfaction approach. Hard-sell interviewers seldom receive word-of-mouth referrals.

SUMMARY

Some persuasion takes place in almost all interviews. No matter what type of interview you undertake, you can benefit from the proven techniques used by persuasion interviewers. There are many benefits to face-to-face dyad persuasion over other persuasive approaches. The amount of preparation necessary in a persuasion interview can vary from developing general background knowledge to undertaking intense interviewee analysis.

The need-satisfaction approach to interview guide preparation was recommended. It consists of identifying perceived respondent needs, agreeing upon the salient needs, and creating a strategy to meet those needs. This is done by gathering both objective and subjective information and steering clear of leading questions. Developing credibility and rapport are the main goals of the opening. Questioning follows a soft-sell approach. This requires careful and complete listening and probing by both participants for a mutually successful outcome. The final payoff comes in the closing. If everything has been done properly, the conclusion is usually positive. Reinforcement through follow-up then cements the decision. Knowledge of persuasion interview principles is especially useful for the next two applications—discipline and termination interviews.

ACTIVITIES

Activity #1

Directions: On the basis of what you have learned in this chapter and in Part I, analyze the following persuasion interview. Look for both good and bad points of both the interviewer and interviewee. Use the line number to refer to your comments.

1 R: Hello, I'm George Rhoads from the Northwest Money Management Services, Inc. I called you on the phone, and we made an appointment for this evening.

E: Yes, I've been expecting you.

5 R: Good, may I come in?

E: Certainly, come on in to the living room.

R: All right. (Sitting) I sure do like your furniture. Did you get it here in town?

E: Yes. At a custom wood furniture place on Prospect Ave.

10 R: It certainly is comfortable.

E: Thank you.

R: Well, Mr. Williams, as I told you on the phone, I think we have some information which you will find interesting regarding the development of a personal money management program for you and your family. Do you

15 know anything about Northwest Money Management Services, Inc.?

E: Nothing more than what you told me on the phone—that it would help me protect my savings against inflation.

R: Oh, yes. Well let me tell you a little about our company. We manage assets of over nine *billion* dollars. Here's a picture of our company headquar-

20 ters in Madison, Wisconsin. (Hands over picture) That's our office in the background, the tallest one. We started out in 1903 with less than $2000. Not one of our investors has ever lost a penny. Even during the crash of 1929 and through the depression, assets under our management almost doubled. We have brought peace of mind to millions of American families. We believe

25 that a sound personal money management program should rest on a balanced financial plan consisting of cash reserves, insurance protection, fixed assets, and equity assets. Does that make sense to you?

E: Well, yes . . . I guess so.

R: With the life expectancy of the average family going up and inflation

30 eating away at your family's dollars—almost 60 percent since 1945—a balanced plan is necessary to protect yourself and your earnings in the future. Don't you agree?

E: Yes.

R: The three main questions you need to ask yourself are "How much
35 money will I need to meet my financial goals?" "How much time do I have?"
and "Where do I stand right now?" Once I know that information, I can
develop a financial program to fit your particular needs. Shall we get
started?

E: All right, but let me ask you a question first. How much will this cost me?

40 R: You can invest as little or as much as you want. You don't pay me
anything. After I have determined your needs and proposed a plan for you,
you can take it, take any part of it, or leave it. It all depends on you. I make
my salary after you invest, if you decide to do so. If you don't, I don't make
anything. I think, however, you'll find that working with Northwest Money
45 Management Services to guarantee your financial future makes a lot of
sense. Then, again, maybe you already have a balanced financial plan. Let's
see. (Takes out a "client worksheet" and begins filling it out.) Theodore
Williams . . . 785 N St.—Right?

E: Yes, that's correct.

50 R: What is your age, Mr. Williams? May I call you Ted?

E: Yes, that's fine. I am twenty-eight years old.

R: (After getting social security number, spouse and dependents' names,
occupation, years employed, employer, etc.) Now, Ted, all of this information is strictly confidential. What is your approximate family income?

55 E: About $30,000.

R: That includes both your income and your wife's income?

E: Yes.

R: (Continues through the form getting information regarding cash reserve,
fixed assets, equity assets, residence value, automobile value, furniture
60 value, charge accounts, bank loans, equity loans, mortgage remaining, auto
loans, personal loans, monthly expenses, etc.) Now, Ted, let's determine
your financial objectives. How much money would you like to have at
retirement?

E: I don't know, maybe $2000 per month.

65 R: In today's dollars?

E: Yeah.

R: OK. Now, it will take me a couple of days to get all this put together and
make some recommendations. Can we get together again next Monday at
this time?

70 E: All right.

R: Good, I think you will find the time you have spent tonight to be some of
the most valuable time you have ever invested.

E: I hope so.

(On Monday, when the persuasion interviewer returns, he has a person-
75 alized folder completely listing Mr. Williams' net worth as well as various
annuity and growth funds to recommend. He is still very low-key and
simply answers questions about each recommendation. He does not push to
close but instead lets the programs sell themselves, which in most cases they
do.)

Activity #2

Directions: Almost everyone uses the persuasion interview at one time or another, but the people who are most interesting to talk with about this interviewing approach are professional persuaders, that is, people who do it for a living. Every community has a large number of professional persuaders—insurance agents, new or used automobile salespersons, appliance dealers, military recruiters, politicians, publisher's representatives, realtors, and many, many others. Arrange an interview with one or more of these people and discuss their techniques with them. Once you have gathered as much information as you can about the persuasion interview, write a short paper comparing this interview type with the others you have studied so far.

Activity #3

Directions: Select one of the following hypothetical cases and role-play it, being sure to use the concepts and skills discussed in this and previous chapters. These cases merely describe common persuasion interview situations. You are free to add any other information you like to make the role-play as realistic as possible.

CASE A: Robert Todd is a freshman history major. During his first year in college he wasted a great deal of time partying. He thought that college was going to be as easy for him as high school. He received a 1.5 GPA his first semester and was put on stage I probation. His second semester he received a 1.7 GPA and graduated to stage II probation. There is no stage III probation. Each time the Dean told him that he had to get at least a 2.0 GPA to remain in college. This third semester, so far, he has done a little better. He is currently standing around a "C" in all his classes except English composition, where he is around a "D+." His last chance to bring up the grade was on the final composition which he handed in last week. The instructor, Barbara Stevens, has just handed back the final compositions, and Bob's carried a grade of "D+" with only one comment, "Lacks effort." He is angry. He put more work into that composition than almost anything he has ever done. He even let a friend of his, who is an English major, look at it and was told that it is a good paper. Bob decides to see Ms. Stevens and try to convince her to look at the paper again and reconsider his grade.

CASE B: Betty Andrews is a sales representative for the Ponderosa Lakes Development Corporation. She is 28 years old and has been working for the company for over two years. She is firmly convinced of the value of her product—property in the Ponderosa Development. The development is situated in the mountains of California, at an elevation of 5,600 feet. It sits in a beautiful mountain valley surrounded by lakes, streams, and forest. The guiding philosophy of the development has always been to make the wonder of nature accessible and useable for people with outdoor interests. Water, sewage disposal, electricity, road maintenance, and all of the other amenities are provided by the developers. They have also provided a restaurant and lounge, community room, swimming pool, and 75 miles of cross-country ski trails.

There is something for every member of the family. Although some public presentations regarding the development are given, each prospective customer must come to the development before purchasing land, and that is where Betty works—at the development. Full acre lots range from $13,000 to $30,000 depending on the location. Twenty percent is the usual downpayment with terms up to seven years. The land is also a good investment, as prices for the land have been rising about 12 percent a year for the last five years. Approximately 60 percent of the land has already been sold. Today, Betty is scheduled to talk with *Stanley Thomas,* a vice president of a bank in a large town 150 miles away. He is looking at the land for both recreational and investment purposes. As she always does, Betty will walk him around the development showing him the different locations that are available and telling him the advantages of purchasing land at Ponderosa Lakes.

CASE C: June Webb is a local fourth grade teacher. Today is Saturday, and June, as she has done every Saturday for the last month, is manning the shopping center booth for the "Build a New Library Committee." The committee is circulating a petition to get the city to put a library bond proposal on the ballot during the next election. The current library is getting very old and probably will be condemned in the next two or three years. The town has grown rapidly, and there is no longer enough room for the necessary books. The fire marshal already calls it a "firetrap." The new library would also serve as a community center. It would have both recreational and educational programs for children and adults. She is currently talking with *Jack Patton,* a 50-year-old local businessman. Jack is more or less opposed to the library bond issue. He feels his property and other taxes are already too high. He sees no value in a new library for him. He mostly watches television, since his children have all grown and moved out. He never used the old library and doesn't see where he will use this one. The only reason he stopped is that June is a regular customer of his.

Chapter 16

The Discipline Interview

Fortunately a discipline interview does not necessarily culminate in eventual dismissal. Such a discussion can be very constructive. An employee usually is grateful for helpful criticism, particularly if he realizes that his superior's reason for giving it is based on genuine interest in his progress. Talk to almost any successful executive, and he will tell you of some instance in his past when a boss who he respected spoke to him frankly and set him straight. (Black, 1970, p. 140)

The word discipline often has distasteful connotations for both interviewers and interviewees. For this reason, many interviewers use a more positive term such as "problem-employee," "educational," or "problem-solving" interviews. In this book "discipline" is used because it most appropriately fits the interview's purpose. Discipline interviews can occur in almost any setting—home, business, military, recreation, etc.—but in this text the focus in on the employment setting. The principles discussed here, however, apply equally well to discipline interviews in all settings.

A discipline interview is conducted only when all other corrective methods have failed. By the time you decide that a disciplinary interview is needed, you have determined that one of the following four traditional disciplinary actions is necessary:

1. *Verbal reprimand*—a severe, formal, verbal expression of disapproval
2. *Written reprimand*—a formal written warning which becomes part of the employee's permanent record
3. *Forfeiture of privileges*—salary reduction, restrictions of various sorts, or loss of work for a specified period of time
4. *Dismissal*—discharge from employment

These punishments obviously differ in severity; very often they are taken in sequence, beginning with a verbal reprimand and, if necessary, ending with dismissal.

Problems which normally require a discipline interview are neglect of duties, disruptive behavior, insubordination, disregarding rules and regulations, theft, excessive absenteeism, and property damage. Disciplinary action is usually necessary not only to correct these problems, but also to maintain discipline with other employees and fulfill your responsibility as a supervisor. It is absolutely essential that superiors discipline individuals when they are "out of line." Unpunished infractions encourage future wrongdoing. Discipline must be swift, just, and equal for all.

People are normally disciplined for two reasons: incompetence or improper conduct. *Incompetence* is the inability to perform a job or task as specified. *Improper conduct* is defined as not adhering to the rules, regulations, or other policies of an organization. Almost all dismissals occur because of improper conduct, and more discipline interviews are done for improper conduct than incompetence. They are simply easier to document. No matter what the cause of a discipline interview, it requires a great deal of effort, skill, diplomacy, and intestinal fortitude.

DISCIPLINE INTERVIEW PREPARATION

Preparation begins long before any rule or regulation is violated. It is a superior's responsibility to set all organizational policies and procedures as well as the punishment for breaking them. It is an organization's responsibility to be sure that these guidelines are clear-cut and easily understood. Ambiguity and inconsistency cannot be tolerated. Discipline only works if respondents know the standards and punishments ahead of time.

Even with well-defined standards and punishments, there are still times in every organization when one or more individuals will break the rules. When violations are noticed, the first reaction should be to inform subordinates that they are in violation of the rules. This can be a very short informal exchange, some-times called a *warning interview*. It is friendly, direct, on-the-spot, and usually takes no more than a minute or two. You will want to make a brief note of the warning to remember when it took place and what it concerned, but nothing formal. There is no mention of punishment and, in the great majority of cases, this is sufficient to correct a problem.

When one or more warnings do not correct a problem, formal discipline interviews are necessary. The preparation for such an interview involves a review of the interviewee's record, a full investigation and documentation of the specifics of the violation, an examination of your own motives, scheduling a time and place for the interview, and preparing yourself to conduct it. In some cases, there is not enough time for all of this preparation. If employees come to work drunk, for example, it may be necessary to take immediate discipline action such as sending them home and docking them a day's pay. But whenever possible, you should delay a discipline interview until you have had time to fully prepare for it.

The most important part of discipline interview preparation is being abso-lutely certain you have all of the relevant facts and proper documentation. This is necessary not only so that you do not appear foolish if your claims turn out to be untrue, but also so you can present the specific evidence to the employee at the beginning of the interview. You must know the circumstances surrounding each violation as well as their nature, when and where they occurred, how they occurred, and what effects they had. Be very certain you are not operating on hearsay or jumping to conclusions. Nothing is more embarrassing or harder on morale than finding out in the middle of the interview that you have made a mistake.

You should not rush into a discipline interview, but you should also not put it off too long. Some interviewers make the mistake of conducting discipline inter-views when they are angry or upset, while others, because they are distasteful, keep postponing them until it is difficult for both participants to remember exactly what happened. Discipline interviews should be scheduled as soon as you have hold of your emotions, the facts, and the respondent. It is best to schedule them at the end of the working day so that interviewees do not return to the work site troubled, upset, or in a mood to disturb other employees. Be sure to schedule enough time to get the full interview completed in one sitting—formal discipline interviews can take an hour to an hour and a half.

Next, prepare the setting. Be sure it is as private as possible. Discipline interviewees are usually very emotional and disturbing, having others within hearing distance only serves to increase anxiety. A private location allows both interviewers and the respondents to discuss matters openly and honestly. Neither feels that they must save face in front of others.

There are some circumstances, however, when a third party should be present. A *witness* may be necessary to substantiate what went on. This is done for legal purposes and only when a severe punishment is contemplated. The witness may be a member of the organization's legal staff, a fellow supervisor, a member of the employee's union, or some other appropriate person. In cases of dismissal, organizational regulations often require the presence of a witness.

The last thing in preparation for a discipline interview is getting yourself in the proper state of mind. This means examining your own motivations. If you dislike a subordinate, be honest with yourself and admit it. Then, ask yourself if you would be taking the same action if another employee were involved. If you can truthfully say "yes", then go on with the interview.

Mentally preparing yourself also means checking precedents to be sure that the discipline you have chosen is appropriate. There is nothing wrong with "tempering justice with mercy" if the circumstances call for it. Once you are certain you are taking the proper action then grit your teeth and prepare for the difficult task. Plan to listen to what the respondent has to say, but be firm, and do what you have to do. Reprimand, criticism, punishment, and dismissal hurt both you and the employee, but neglecting this duty will only cause problems for both of you in the future.

THE DISCIPLINE INTERVIEW GUIDE

The nature of discipline interviews requires that you do most of the talking. Therefore, the interview guide is made up of specific information you plan to say. The guide is similar in many ways to an outline or notes you might make if you were going to give a speech or lecture. You should have all of the facts including dates, times, circumstances, names of witnesses, and so on written down and organized in such a way that the respondent will get a clear and accurate understanding of exactly what you see as the problem. If at all possible, present not just one specific incident, but an entire pattern of improper behavior. Your comments should be stated reasonably and objectively. Your interview guide should reflect that you are trying to be as constructive and positive as possible—you are trying to help the employee. In this respect a discipline interview is not much different from performance, counseling, or diagnostic interviews.

Whenever possible, try to tailor these early problem description statements to the personality and attitude of each respondent. Some employees can be told in a straightforward and direct manner what you see as the problem, whereas others whom you know are more sensitive should be treated in a more indirect fashion. Different forms of leadership are necessary to handle different subordinates. Your description of the problem, then, must be a carefully prepared part of the interview guide.

The inquiry portion of the guide consists of information you want from the interviewee about the problem. Downs (1980) lists four questions discipline interviewers normally ask respondents:

1. *What actually happened from the subordinate's point of view?*
2. *Why did it happen?*
3. *What was his or her perception of the rules, regulations, or circumstances?*
4. *What is the subordinate's response to the discipline?*

(Downs, 1980, pp. 223–224)

These four topic areas, along with any other questions you feel are necessary, should be planned and included in the interview guide.

By allowing respondents to explain their side of the story you reduce the feeling that they are being "railroaded." In most cases you will find their explanations insufficient from your point of view; however, it is always possible their reasons and explanations may require further examination and possible delay, reduction, or elimination of the punishment. If you have done your homework carefully and properly, and have still gone as far as to schedule and conduct a discipline interview, you should already know most, if not all, of the pertinent facts. If nothing else, a respondent's rationale and justification can be eye-opening and give you considerable insight into his or her personality and character.

The final part of the guide includes the anticipated outcome of the interview, that is, the discipline. In some cases, the punishment is already determined by the rules and regulations of the organization. In other cases, however, you will have some leeway. You may choose a verbal or written reprimand, forfeiture of privileges, or dismissal. A verbal or written reprimand is the usual outcome of the first formal discipline interview. Your list of alternatives should be clearly spelled out, because very often, your decision as to the most appropriate punishment will be determined during the interview itself, after you have heard and seen the respondent's reaction.

As you can see, discipline interview guides are fairly directive. You should know well in advance what you want to accomplish and develop a guide which gets at that purpose in a straight-forward manner. Both open and closed questions are used and usually require some type of funnel sequence. That is, you may begin by asking why the violation occurred or some similar open question and then, using closed questions, ask for specifics. Some specific closed questions will come from the interview guide while others will come up as probes. Another reason discipline interview guides are directive is that you must maintain firm and total control throughout. Directive interview guides also provide support for interviewers who are probably fairly tense and anxious about the outcome. People are always more relaxed when they know exactly what they are going to do.

DISCIPLINE INTERVIEW OPENING

There is seldom any need for small talk at the beginning of discipline inter-views. An interviewee is likely to be upset and apprehensive over the very fact that such an interview is being conducted; if they are not, they probably have not guessed the purpose of the interview. Most, however, not only know the pur-pose, but have some idea about the punishment which will probably be imposed and have prepared arguments to justify their behavior.

Even if a respondent enters the interview with no planned defense, sincerely regretting the offense, and hoping to get another chance, there is still no need for the usual pleasantries that accompany an interview opening. Both participants realize that the climate will be fairly formal with little need of friendly rapport. What interviewers need to develop is rapport based on a respect and understand-ing of their position and a feeling of trust that interviewees will receive fair treatment. You can do this by reducing as many of their fears and helping them relax as much as possible. Be calm, objective, and reasonable—do not attempt to joke, be light-hearted, or in any other way indicate that the interview is anything but very serious.

Next comes the orientation, which focuses respondent attention on the violation. Indicate that you have documentation for your accusations. Try to be as specific and exact as possible. After you detail the reasons for the interview, tell interviewees that you are willing to give them every opportunity to explain their position and will give serious consideration to what they say. The orientation is the time to set down any ground rules you have. The discipline interview is one of the only interviews where you are both judge and jury. In order to be effective, however, you must demonstrate that you are fair, impartial, and willing to listen to any valid defense.

The opening question, then, usually is a request for any comments re-spondents may have on the charges you have just stated. At that point you shift from being the speaker to the listener. During all phases of the opening, you should be assessing the employee's mood, by observing nonverbal behaviors. If interviewees are angry, hostile, or unresponsive, you can adjust your comments and questions to fit that mood. You should do nothing, however, which may cause you to lose control of the interview. Do not allow the interview to turn into a debate or in any other way give the impression that the respondent will be able to "get away with anything."

DISCIPLINE INTERVIEW QUESTIONING AND RESPONDING

Throughout the body of the interview your questioning should continue to be neutral, objective, and firm. Under no circumstances should you allow your-self to lose your temper either about the violation or what a respondent says. This very often means prefacing your questions with statements such as "From what I understand . . . ," "According to this report . . . ," "Mr. X has stated . . . ," "I have a document here which suggests . . . ." By qualifying your statements you leave room for explanation, but at the same time you notify respondents that you have done your homework.

You will often find that interviewees try to interrupt you. When this occurs you should be tactful but insist that the respondent hear you out completely. What you find, of course, is that interviewees are mentally preparing arguments and not listening to you completely. If you allow such interruptions, they will continue and become more and more disruptive. Both your manner and presence should convey your firm, but rational and objective approach to the situation.

Reactions and responses by interviewees vary widely, from the totally unresponsive to the crafty, hostile, or angry to those in tears. Be prepared to handle each of these reactions. Silence can signal acceptance and willingness to take the consequences, but it can also be a form of hostility. You can only discover which by encouraging respondents to open up. Assure them that nothing truthful they say will be held against them. Try to explain that you really want to hear their side of the story. Under no conditions, however, should you force respondents to reply. If they are unwilling to say anything, move directly into determining the appropriate punishment.

Open hostility is much easier to deal with than silence. Try to control yourself, listen to what interviewees have to say, and let them get it off their chest. Recognize that very often discipline interviewees need to release their feeling and frustrations before they can objectively view the situation and accept their punishment. Do not let them avoid responsibility for their own mistakes by denying them or placing the blame on someone else. Encourage them to face up to their problems. When distress, despair, depression, or tears are part of a response, allow them time to regain self control. Do not, however, attempt to console or in any other way reduce the seriousness of the violation. If you respond properly they will soon face up to their mistakes, and this makes it much easier for you to listen, probe, and determine the proper outcome.

Reactions to a discipline interview may vary widely.

DISCIPLINE INTERVIEW PROBING

Discipline interview probes are designed primarily to explore respondent feelings and confirm previous information. Most interviewers feel responsible to probe for the cause of interviewee problems. The punishment is often determined not only by the infraction but also the reasons given for committing the infraction. Sometimes interviewees are unwilling to talk about the problem. You should once again explain that anything they have to say will help determine an appropriate punishment. If this does not help, you may have to probe for the cause of their reluctance to talk.

Try to avoid cross-examination and interrogation techniques whenever possible. Think of yourself as an impartial judge, not a prosecuting attorney. Listen and consider the evidence and rationale and don't simply accuse. Explore the feelings, attitudes, and motivations behind behaviors, and do not automatically condemn. Use many reflective probes to bring attitudes, emotions, and feelings to the surface. Examples of such reflective probes are "How do you feel about what you did?" "Do you feel you are being discriminated against?" and "How have you changed since the incident?" These sorts of exchanges will help you choose disciplinary actions which will be most constructive and positive.

Confrontation is also important because frequently you will find inconsistencies in interviewee remarks. In disciplinary interviews, these inconsistencies must be pointed out and resolved as quickly as possible. Probes such as "Could you be mistaken?" "I heard it somewhat differently," and "Are you certain that's the way it happened?" confront respondents without putting them on the defensive. The point is not to threaten or embarrass respondents but to make sure you and they understand the situation accurately. Confrontation probes also demonstrate to respondents that you have done your homework and are not willing to let respondents "put anything over" on you. Respondents will try to defend themselves with inaccuracies, omissions, and fabrications, especially when they feel "trapped." This is why the interrogation approach often fails. The inconsistencies may not be conscious. Many of the details of any negative situation are often unconsciously distorted or repressed. Although it may be painful for a respondent, you must demand and receive complete and honest information. This is achieved through skillful use of confrontation probes.

You must be careful not to allow the interview to become a shouting match. If you, the discipline interviewer, lose your self-control to the point of engaging in loud debate with respondents, the potential constructive and positive value of the interview is lost. You must maintain objectivity and concern. You are trying to help the respondent. Once you engage in argument, your image is destroyed. A discipline interview must be a discussion and not a debate. This demands objective, careful clarification, amplification, and confrontation probing.

DISCIPLINE INTERVIEW LISTENING

Careful, accurate listening is essential for both participants in a discipline interview. The most common obstacles to overcome are primary and secondary tension, emotional blindspots, planning ahead, conclusion jumping, mental arguing, and overtalking. The fact that both participants are apprehensive when beginning (primary tension) explains why many interviewees have trouble listening to an interviewer's opening orientation. They are so nervous and upset that they are focusing on themselves rather than listening to your explanation of the situation. This is why it is necessary to get interviewees to relax during the opening—at least enough to listen carefully to what is being charged.

Secondary tension also creates problems within the interview. Tension arises whenever sensitive aspects of the situation are discussed. It is important to listen especially hard when embarrassing or threatening subjects come up. Some interviewers try to relax interviewees during these exchanges as well. It is hard for either participant to listen effectively when they are extremely tense.

Emotional blindspots occur because of something the interviewee or interviewer says or because of the feelings one of the participants has toward the other. Realize that it is natural for interviewees to object to many of the statements made in discipline interviews. This resistance and release of feelings should not only be allowed but encouraged. Respondents may say things which trigger your emotional blindspots in the same way you may say things which trigger their emotional blindspots. In either case, listeners must not allow these emotional triggers to distort effective listening. Steinmetz (1971) calls these emotional reactions "halo" and "horns" effects.

> Bias can work for or against the other person. If an interviewer is biased in favor of someone, that person benefits from the "halo" effect, that is, he will be evaluated higher than he should be. By contrast, if the interviewer is biased against someone, that person will suffer from the "horns" effect and be rated lower than he should be. This bias works both ways, of course, and affects the way the interviewee perceives and responds to the interviewer.
>
> (Steinmetz, 1971, p. 39)

An emotional blindspot may be triggered by something that is said or simply by the presence of the other participant. Skillful listeners overcome these blindspots and other obstacles to listening.

Planning ahead distracts both participants. As interviewers are describing the situation, respondents often begin to mentally plan their defense. They listen only for points they can refute. Interviewees should make sure they understand all of the charges before planning a defense. In the same way discipline interviewers must not be planning ahead to determine an appropriate punishment while an interviewee is responding to the charges. Each must listen as actively as possible while the other is speaking.

Conclusion jumping is an expansion of planning ahead. Very often interviewees assume that the interviewer has already found them guilty, the punishment has already been determined, and that the interviewer is unwilling to listen to their side of the story. Interviewers also jump to conclusions regarding a respondent, but interviewees deserve their "day in court." Presuming guilt without hearing explanations is conclusion jumping.

It is also hard not to mentally argue during a discipline interview. Interviewees mentally argue during the orientation, interviewers mentally argue during respondent defense, especially when the interviewee is resisting or venting feelings. By its very nature, a discipline interview is more or less an argument. Both participants must not allow mental arguing to distort what each has to say.

Some people feel that the way to win an argument is to out-talk the other person. Interviewers have a tendency to make the same accusations over and over again without allowing interviewees to respond. In the same way, respondents tend to keep on defending their behavior in the belief that the more they talk, the more likely they are to reduce the penalty. Sometimes this has the opposite effect. Both participants should allow the other to speak when they see signs that the other has something to say.

Some interviewers try to restrict all respondent comments until near the end of the interview. This practice is not advised because it encourages mental arguing and the attitude of "Nothing I can say will change the result of this interview." Even in the orientation, interviewees should be allowed to make comments. It is better for respondents to verbalize arguments and get them off their chests than to mentally hold them and reduce listening accuracy. Possible punishments shouldn't be brought up until interviewees have had a chance to respond to the charges. As you have probably noticed, good listening becomes progressively more difficult with each type of interview discussed. This is because the number of other things that must be done in the interview has increased, and the likelihood of conflict has also increased. Skillful discipline interview listening is perhaps the most difficult of all.

DISCIPLINE INTERVIEW RECORDING

Recording a discipline interview not only helps you evaluate the success of the interview, but may be crucial if litigation follows from these interviews. This is why witnesses are often present, and why both the witness and interviewee are often asked to examine notes taken during a discipline interview and confirm that they are accurate by initialing them. This protects both interviewees and interviewers. Many discipline interviewers now use electronic recording techniques to substantiate the accuracy of the transcript. When a formal record of disciplinary proceedings is essential (such as in a dismissal interview) electronic recording is especially useful. Protests and legal action regarding disciplinary procedures are becoming more and more common.

Sometimes witnesses are also asked to make a record of the interview. If both participants bring their own witness, two sets of notes may be made. This is often helpful because it allows you to concentrate on the interaction. The result is better listening. Courts are more willing to accept notes if they were recorded by a less-involved person. The aim in all discipline interview recording is completeness and accuracy.

DISCIPLINE INTERVIEW CONCLUDING

Once you are satisfied you have heard all of the relevant information, it is time to conclude the interview. The conclusion includes assigning of appropriate discipline as well as making sure the punishment will have a constructive and positive effect. This is possible if you are firm, impose a reasonable, consistent, and just penalty, and accept full responsibility for your actions. The need to be firm but fair is echoed by almost every successful discipline interviewer. Steinmetz (1971) offers the following advice:

> It sometimes helps supervisors in being firm to recognize that there does exist a need for criticism. Nothing, for example, is worse for morale than to have members of the employee group turning in less than a satisfactory job and getting away with it. Such a situation undermines the morale of the good workers. Yet some managers, under the misguided goal of being a "nice guy," strive to maintain a friendly and solicitous atmosphere even with subordinates whose output is less than satisfactory. The result is equivalent to bestowing privileges on the lazy or inept workers. The boss who is reluctant to criticize is accused of running a happiness school. Effective management requires that the boss level with subordinates, making clear his feelings or dissatisfaction. Obviously, this must be done in a tactful and diplomatic way. The supervisor should keep in mind that "a boss who tries to become well liked by doing favors will not only not be well liked but will also be unsuccessful as a boss."
>
> (Steinmetz, 1971, p. 51).

The penalty or punishment chosen must be *reasonable,* in that it "matches the crime;" *consistent,* in that it is the same for all employees committing the same violation; and *just,* in that it is based on all relevant information. Regardless of whether the punishment is a verbal or written reprimand, loss of privileges, or dismissal, it must meet these criteria. Don't be overly harsh or attempt to make an employee the example for others. On the other hand, don't be too lenient and encourage the respondent or others to commit the same infraction again. Your purpose is to make your unit operate smoothly and efficiently within the rules and regulations of the organization.

Accepting responsibility for a punishment means that you acknowledge that you have a degree of choice in the matter. You are the interviewer; you have heard the evidence; and you are making the decision. If you have no power to decide on the punishment or someone else has already made the decision, you were probably wrong to conduct the interview. You should have either assigned the discipline without an interview or asked the person making the decision to conduct it. Respondents will respect you more if you accept full responsibility than if you attempt to "take the easy way out" or "pass the buck" to somebody else.

After the discipline has been determined and communicated to a respondent, you should take steps to see that the punishment accomplishes its purpose. Explain to interviewees how they can correct the problem in the future and offer to help in any way possible. If anything came up during the question and answer process which you think might prevent the same violation in the future, offer to make the necessary changes. Assure respondents that there are "no hard feelings" and that once the punishment is over, everything will return to normal. Respondents must leave the interview knowing that once they have paid for their mistake, they will not continue to suffer for it. Upon making this commitment you are obligated to follow through with it. Obviously this advice does not apply if the punishment is dismissal. In that case there is no second chance.

Also plan on some form of follow-up once the disciplinary action is taken. This may mean checking on respondent behavior, making sure things are done properly in the future, and encouraging respondents when problems are corrected. Thorough follow-up is essential—you must be sure that the discipline accomplishes its purpose, to change interviewee behavior.

SUMMARY

Participating in a discipline interview is a difficult and often distasteful task. It is, however, essential to the smooth operation of an organization. It should only be undertaken when all other corrective methods have failed. Preparation for this interview includes informing employees of the rules and regulations, conducting warning interviews, collecting all relevant information, preparing yourself, and scheduling the time and place for the interview. The interview guide should include all relevant information collected, areas of objective and subjective information still needed, and possible punishments. The facts are described in the opening. The body of the interview is concerned with verifying the facts and determining motivation, attitudes, and feelings. This interview is generally somewhat formal. You must be firm but fair. Respondents must be urged to open up and tell their side of the story. Although amplification and clarification probes are helpful, it is the careful use of confrontation probes that seem to elicit the most information. Because so much is at stake in these interviews, both participants find it difficult to tell their side of the story, to listen, and to concentrate. Punishments, such as reprimand, loss of privileges, or dismissal are assigned during the conclusion. They must be reasonable, consistent, and just. If done properly, employees will respond constructively and the interview can end on a friendly note. The follow-up will tell you if your primary purpose for the interview has been accomplished: to reestablish the discipline necessary to make your unit run smoothly.

ACTIVITIES

Activity #1

Directions: On the basis of what you have learned in this chapter and in Part I, analyze the following discipline interview. Look for both good and bad points by both the interviewer and interviewee. This interview concerns a machine operator working on "piece rate," that is, getting paid according to how much he produces. The rules call for turning off the machine every time before a new unit is to be assembled. The employee very often would not do this because it cut down the amount he could produce during a work shift. The first time the interviewer caught him, he was given a brief warning and told of the dangers. He turned off the machine between units for about two weeks, but when his paycheck was down, he started letting the machine run again. This time the company safety engineer saw him doing it and told the interviewer. An hour before the end of the shift, the interviewer called in the employee, and the following interview took place. Use the line number to refer to your comments.

1   *R:* Bob, I just had a visit from the company safety engineer. He was out in the plant and saw you loading a new unit without first turning off your machine.

    E: Oh, no, I've been turning it off.

5   *R:* I don't think the safety engineer lied.

    E: Well, maybe I forgot that once.

    R: Once is all it takes to have a safety hazard. It really doesn't matter to me if it was once or a hundred times. The fact of the matter is that you broke a safety regulation that you have been warned about before.

10   *E:* I know, I just can't make enough money to live on if I turn off the machine every time I load a new unit.

    R: That's just not accurate, Bob. The pay scale was set following the regulations. The others seem to be able to make a living wage and still follow the regulations. As a matter of fact, our pay is considerably better than our

15 nearest competitor. Now, I will have to take some form of discipline. Is there anything more you would like to say about this first?

    E: Yeah, there are several things I would like to say. First of all, I am one of your best employees, and you know it. Even when I turn off the machine each time, I usually outproduce most of the others.

20   *R:* Yes, I know that, Bob. That's why this interview is so difficult. If it were one of the other workers, I probably would have fired them on the spot, but I am making allowances for your efficiency and time on the job.

    E: I don't think that's important enough to fire somebody over.

    R: I do. I've done it, and I'll do it again.

25   *E:* Are you going to fire me?

    R: I'm not sure yet.

    E: I was hoping to get a promotion. This "black mark" on my record is not going to make it any easier. Damn. I really didn't know how serious you were about this thing. Now I see how you feel. I will start turning off the

30 machine every time. I sure don't want to be fired, and I would like to get a promotion.

    R: Well, I think you will have to forget about the promotion for a while, Bob. I can't let this go with just another warning. It's too important. I don't know where you got the idea that I wasn't serious about safety.

35   *E:* In case you might want to know, the reason I need a little more money is because my wife and I are buying a home of our own and are paying double until we get the down payment loan finished.

    R: I didn't know that. Perhaps we can work out some overtime or something for you. I wish you had told me that earlier, before you decided to get the

40 money by breaking the rules. Is there anything else you would like to add?

    E: No, I guess not.

    R: Well, Bob, I don't think I will fire you. I promise you, however, that if it ever, even once, happens again I will fire you. Let's see, this is Wednesday. I am going to lay you off temporarily until next Monday.

45   *E:* Oh you can't do that! I told you why I need the money.

R: Yes I can do that, and that is exactly what I am going to do. When you come in Monday, we will talk about some overtime.

E: I'm going to appeal that decision.

R: That is your privilege. I will also have to turn in a formal report explaining
50 why I am suspending you for two days. That will become part of your record, and I will note that the next time this happens, which I hope it never does, I will dismiss you. When you come back on Monday we will wipe the slate clean and start again except for that notation of warning in your file. Is that clear?

55 *E:* Oh, very clear. I am still going to appeal. I think your decision is too harsh for such a small offense.

R: Bob, until you stop thinking about this as a "small" offense, there is going to be trouble. That is exactly why I am suspending you, so you will think about it and hopefully realize that breaking safety regulations is *not* a small
60 offense. They are designed for your safety. I would rather take this discipline than have to file a disability form for you. I have had to do that before, and I don't ever want to do it again.

E: I still intend to appeal.

R: Ok, Bob, I think you know the appeal procedures. If not I will explain
65 them to you.

E: Oh, I know them all right.

R: Fine, then I will see you on Monday or earlier if you do decide to appeal. Good bye, Bob.

E: Good bye, and thanks a lot.

Activity #2

Directions: Arrange to interview a supervisor or manager who commonly does discipline interviews. Find out what basic principles are used to guide the interviews and punishment selection. Compare the information you obtain with that found in this and previous chapters and the information you have gathered from other types of interviewers. Write a short paper on how to best conduct a discipline interview based on the information you have gathered.

Activity #3

Directions: Select one of the following hypothetical cases and role-play it, being sure to use the concepts and skills discussed in this and previous chapters. These cases describe common discipline interview situations. You are free to add any other information you like to make the role-play as realistic as possible.

CASE A: *Joseph Simpsa* is the manager of the Mid-Valley Milk Company. One of his employees, *Linda D'Amico*, delivers milk and solicits new customers in her area. Joe has recently received a letter from a Mrs. Edna Dubcek complaining about Linda's conduct. He has received minor complaints about Linda in the past such as parking her truck illegally, leaving the wrong amount of milk, or incorrect billing. But this is the first major complaint. Mrs. Dubcek says that

Linda came up to her door, apparently to solicit an order for milk from her. She told Linda that she lives alone and does not use milk. When she started to tell Mrs. Dubcek about her other products, she said she didn't want anything, at which point Linda made some derogatory remarks and gestures. She then went to her truck and made some more remarks and gestures as she drove away. Joe is not quite sure if Linda did exactly what Mrs. Dubcek says, but he feels that some disciplinary action should be taken. He is waiting, however, to decide the type of punishment until he hears Linda's side of the story.

CASE B: Peter Leach is a prelaw student majoring in political science. He is student body president and third baseman on the baseball team. Last night, as he was looking through his notes after a student council meeting, he realized that he had a test today in his international relations course. It had completely slipped his mind. When he looked at the material to be covered on the test, he realized that he could not get prepared in time. He decided instead to make a set of "crib" notes to use while taking the test. Most of the test covered terminology, and he could get that from the glossary. *Kim Vance* is a third-year political science professor. She prides herself on her reputation among students as being "firm but fair." She is close enough in age, 29 years, to them to understand their problems. She feels that students will generally respond if treated fairly. As her international relations students are taking her test, she notices that Peter Leach is constantly looking down as if he is sick. When she walks back to find out the problem, she notices him kick a piece of paper under his desk. She retrieves it and discovers the "cheat notes." She takes his test, and tells Peter to wait in her office. While the rest of the class is finishing the test, she reviews the possible punishments in her mind. She can do nothing and allow Peter to retake the test; she can flunk him on the test; or she can flunk him for the whole coures. The latter two punishments require a formal letter of explanation to the department chairperson and the Dean. Currently she is leaning toward an "F" for the course.

CASE C: At fifty years old, *Richard Trotter* considered himself a valuable asset to Acme Computer Company. So did Richard's supervisor and associates. He had been with the company 17 years and had performed well on many different assignments. He was always good natured and everyone liked him. Just a month ago, however, the computer line he specialized on was sold to another company, but Dick's services were not offered as part of the deal. Acme felt his experience would be valuable on other product lines. It soon became clear, however, that his knowledge was very specific and could not be transferred easily. Everyone kept telling him to "stick with it," but things didn't change. He made several mistakes that cost the company time and money. Something had to be done. Both Richard and the company knew it. Richard was determined not to quit, however, because he would lose his pension, but there was just no place for him to go at Acme.

Chapter 17

The Termination Interview

To determine how effectively an organization is managing its human assets, you need to stand at "the gate" and note the number, the occupations, and the behavior of those employees who are leaving it for the last time. It is at this hypothetical gate that management's mistakes, from the selection to the performance-evaluation program, are added up and the bill paid. (Lopez, 1975, p. 318)

Almost 80 percent of all organizations throughout the United States have what is called a *termination control program*. It begins at the first hint that an employee is considering leaving. It provides for organized collection of relevant information concerning the separation. Termination or exit interviews are normally an important part of such a program. These interviews are not, however, limited to business situations; they can take place when a child is leaving home, a couple is considering divorce, and any number of situations where a relationship is about to end. In this chapter, the focus will be primarily upon formal business termination interviews, but all such interviews follow a similar pattern.

A termination interview costs very little in time or money. It is normally an employee's last formal contact with the organization. If done properly, it can be one of the most important and useful methods of organizational data collection. One of the major benefits is a reduction of employee turnover. Turnover is costly in terms of recruiting, selecting, and training replacement employees. A second benefit of termination interviews is that they guarantee fairness and consistency in the treatment of all employees who are departing. To maintain such consistency, normally only a few individuals are responsible for conducting these interviews.

Termination interviews also improve morale. Morale is high if employees perceive that good workers are staying and poor workers are leaving. In addition, termination interviews help organizations evaluate the quality of their job descriptions, performance appraisal programs, job grading, salary structure, personnel policies, employment procedures, and training and development programs. In other words, they are an important means of feedback most organizations cannot afford to overlook.

Organizations which do not have a termination control program usually have never tried it or have tried it but conducted it improperly. They may regard termination interviews as unproductive and prefer to spend their time filling vacancies instead. Other common reasons for termination interview failure are 1) the organization used unskilled interviewers, 2) they conducted the interview in a perfunctory manner, and 3) they did not make the program mandatory. Any one of these problems can lead to the downfall of a termination control and interview program.

What is commonly called the termination interview is really a set of interviews. The first is a *retention* or *salvage* interview. They are conducted as soon as anyone has an indication that an employee may be considering leaving. The purpose of the interview is to try to get the employee to stay. The second type of termination interview is conducted with people who are being dismissed, an *involuntary termination* interview. Its purpose is to minimize the stressful consequences of a dismissal for both the employee and the organization. Third is the *voluntary termination* interview with employees who have resigned. This is the most important type from a data collection standpoint. Its purpose is to discover the *real* purpose behind a resignation. As you will see, there are some significant differences in the conduct of these three types of termination interviews.

TERMINATION INTERVIEW PREPARATION

The first step is to decide who is going to be responsible for termination interviews. In most organizations, they are handled by the personnel office. It is not a good idea for supervisors to conduct termination interviews, because the supervisor may be the reason for the employee's departure. Further, interviewers in the personnel department are generally better informed, more professional, more neutral, and have a better opportunity to tie the data from these interviews to other aspects of the organization, such as selection interviews. There are times, however, when it is not possible or desirable to have a specialized person interview departing employees.

Many organizations employ at least two people trained to conduct termination interviews. Sometimes these interviewers specialize in working with interviewees at different job levels. One, for example, may interview employees below the rank of supervisor; the other would talk with departing employees of supervisory or higher rank. Termination interviewers should be personable, approachable, trusted by employees, and able to draw out employee opinions and problems. A skillful termination interviewer helps guarantee the success of data collection.

A second important aspect of preparation is timing. Obviously, retention interviews normally precede voluntary termination interviews. They must also precede the actual resignation. All individuals within the organization, especially managers and supervisors, must spot and report potential job hunters so they can be interviewed. This is, however, one of the main bottlenecks in most termination control programs. Supervisors and managers are often too busy, insensitive, or harassed to effectively spot employees who are considering leaving. It is management's responsibility to put as much pressure as possible on supervisors to get them to report these individuals.

Once a job hunter is identified, a retention interview should be conducted as soon as possible. It is important to catch employees while they are still wavering. Once they are committed to resignation, it is too late. The retention interviewee must still be debating the decision. If possible it should be done the same day the possible resignation is recognized.

Neither voluntary nor involuntary termination interviews should be conducted on an employee's last working day. They can be scheduled, however, sometime during the last week of employment. Most organizations conduct them a day or two before the last working day, normally a Wednesday or Thursday. The best time is usually toward the end of the day so that the employee leaves after the interview is over. This allows the interviewee to discuss the job, organization, supervision, and so on openly and honestly without having to go back and face what may be a bad situation immediately afterwards.

It is a commonly assumed that because employees are leaving, they will be willing to express their true feelings. This is far from the truth. Employees will dodge a termination interview if given the opportunity. It must be fully supported by top level management, and be mandatory. Supervisors must be forced to turn in a termination report on each departing employee. In many organizations the supervisor is also responsible for getting employees to the termination interview.

It is impossible to overemphasize the importance of supervisors in the success of termination interviews. They usually know their employees best and have been doing performance interviews all along. Figure 17.1 is an example of a typical supervisor termination report. Supervisor reports include the stated reasons for terminating, supervisor comments, final performance appraisal, reemployment possibilities, documentation of retention efforts, property check, final salary amount, and much more. This information is absolutely essential.

Besides this written information, most interviewers also check the circumstances surrounding the termination for themselves. Few interviewers accept a supervisor's report at face value. They want to be sure employee rights were respected. Interviewers will conduct information gathering interviews with supervisors, other employees, other knowledgeable persons, and even the departing employee before the actual termination interview. With all of the legal requirements surrounding terminations, it is extremely important that you do your homework and you need to be thoroughly acquainted with all of the information employees may request during a termination interview, such as insurance coverage, appeal procedure, pension rights, reference policy, and rehire possibilities. Supervisors are normally not as familiar with these areas as personnel people whose job is to conduct termination interviews.

Involuntary termination interviews are perhaps the hardest type of exit interview to prepare for and conduct. Even professionals dread and avoid this interview. This may be one of the reasons few organizations fire employees anymore. As you learned in the last chapter, dismissals must take place, however, if an organization is to continue to be effective. To keep ineffective and insubordinate employees is costly and bad for morale.

The only way to avoid involuntary termination interviews is to take proactive measures early. These include developing objective performance standards and goals, communicating them to every employee, keeping performance records,

17.1 Sample Termination Report

Employee's Name_____ Date_____

Position_____ Dept. or Plant_____

INSTRUCTIONS TO SUPERVISOR: Rate the employee on the basis of actual work done during the past year before filling out this report. Then complete this form comparing the terminating individual with other employees who have worked under you and have done similar work. Place a (✔) check in the box below the term which best describes the employee's standing on the quality rated. Forward completed form to the Personnel Director, attached to Separation payroll notice.

			Promotes	
Interest in Job and Company	Enthusiastic ☐	Gets Along ☐	Team Effort ☐	Indifferent ☐
Position Knowledge	Meager ☐	Fairly Complete ☐	Unusually Detailed ☐	Well Informed ☐
Quality of Work	Rather Careless ☐	Error Free ☐	Many Errors ☐	Frequently Corrected ☐
Initiative	Occasional Effort ☐	Resourceful ☐	Needs Urging ☐	Exceptionally Resourceful ☐
Judgment	Lacks Judgment ☐	Good Common Sense ☐	Immature Decisions ☐	Mature Judgment ☐
Reliability	Always Dependable ☐	Needs Close Supervision ☐	Needs Little Supervision ☐	Follow-ups Required ☐
Personal Habits	Good ☐	Discredit Company ☐	Ordinary ☐	Above Criticism ☐
Health	Frequently Ill ☐	Frail ☐	Seldom Ill ☐	Never Ill ☐

Length of Notice Given: _____ Reemploy? ( ) Yes   ( ) No

(Note: On the back of this form would be a place for a detailed statement of reasons for termination and a place for the supervisor's signature)

communicating deficiencies to employees in performance and discipline interviews, conducting effective training and development programs, relocating problem employees when possible, and anything else which helps match employee and organizational goals. If these steps are taken and an employee still must be dismissed, there is no way to avoid it.

In preparing for an involuntary termination interview you must be absolutely certain that there is sufficient documentation for the dismissal. If proactive measures have been taken, then the documentation will probably be available. It is still important, however, that you check the circumstances surrounding the discharge to prevent a wrongful dismissal and to make sure that the employee's rights were respected every step of the way. This type of thorough research and documentation can improve morale among workers as much as dismissing a bad employee or retaining a good one. In some cases, proper preparation may also mean consulting with the organization's affirmative action officer, equal opportunity specialist, union representative, ombudsman, or other individuals who get involved with exiting employees.

THE TERMINATION INTERVIEW GUIDE

Two of the biggest problems of termination interviews are: 1) getting interviewees to the scene of the interview and 2) persuading them to open up and state the real reason for leaving. These two goals influence the structure of a termination interview guide a great deal. Many companies have standardized termination interview guides such as figure 17.2.

In order to get departing interviewees to show up for an interview, it must be viewed as the final clearance point before separation. This means all necessary papers can only be signed during the interview, no benefit explanations are given before the interview, it is the final property check point, and it is often where employees receive their final paycheck. If all of this is made a part of a termination interview, then it is impossible for any employee to avoid it. Discussion of these matters then becomes the first order of business in conducting a termination interview. As you will notice in the sample interview guide, there is a checklist of the items to discuss with employees. This checklist guides the information-giving portion of the interview. When an employee walks in, you should tell him or her about rehire eligibility, reference policy, insurance coverage, property check, appeal rights and procedures, official forms to be signed, and their final paycheck. Once this information is discussed the interview shifts to an information-gathering format.

The information-gathering portion of the interview leads to the main termination interview question which is, "Why are you leaving?" Usually, this question cannot be approached directly, because interviewees are afraid to say anything that can be used against them or "rock the boat." They are concerned about the references they will receive from the company. So this question is approached indirectly. Different interviewers have slightly different methods, but a common one is to begin by discussing some general job factors such as those suggested by Embrey, Mondy, and Noe (1979):

17.2 Sample Termination Interview Guide
(Space for recording information has been omitted)

Employee's Name   Job Title   Social Security Number
Supervisor   Start Date   Department
Interview Date   Termination Date   Last Performance Interview

Note any promotion, training or reclassification the employee has received within the previous 12 months:

Reason for separation: (Check one or more)

Voluntary Resignation
   Other job (note employer, position, and salary)
   Illness
   Return to school
   Pregnancy
   Relocation of family
   Retirement (voluntary)
   Other—Specify

Involuntary Resignation
   Absenteeism/tardiness
   Alcohol/drugs
   Theft/dishonesty
   Misconduct
   Insubordination
   Retirement (mandatory)
   Reduction in force
   Other—Specify

Separation Checklist:
   Property check completed.
   Eligibility for rehire:
      Eligible, employee notified
      Ineligible, employee notified
      Reasons

   Final check issued.
   Appeal Rights explained.
   Resignation notice filed.
   Separation completed.
   Date: Initials:

Explain Circumstances:
1. Employee's reason(s) for resignation. If dismissal, what are the employee's perceptions of reason for discharge?
2. What did you like about working with our company?
3. Comment on supervision you received.
   a. Were you given sufficient and consistent instructions on how to perform your job?
   b. Were your questions answered satisfactorily?
   c. Were general policies and procedures defined clearly for you?
4. Were you satisfied with the following: salary, benefits, and working conditions.
5. How were your chances for training and promotion as you saw them?
6. What types of problems or complaints have you had about working here?
7. Would you consider returning to work here?
8. Additional comments.
9. Information for employees: rehire, references, insurance coverage.

Interviewer Comments:

Date:

Interviewer Signature:

(Adapted from Garrison and Ferguson, 1977, p. 442)

1. *Let's begin by your outlining briefly some of the duties of your job.*
2. *Of the duties you just outlined, tell me three or four which are crucial to the performance of your job.*
3. *Tell me about some of the duties you like the most and what you liked about performing those duties.*
4. *Now, tell me about some of the duties you liked least and what you did not like about performing those duties.*
5. *Suppose you describe the amount of variety in your job.*
6. *Let's talk a little bit about the amount of work assigned to you. For example, was the amount assigned not enough at times, perhaps too much at times, or was it fairly stable and even overall?*
7. *Suppose you give me an example of an incident which occurred on your job which was especially satisfying to you. What about an incident which was a little less satisfying.*
8. *Let's talk now about the extent to which you feel you were given the opportunity to use your educational background, skills, and abilities on your job.*
9. *Tell me how you would assess the quality of training on your job.*
10. *Suppose you describe the promotional opportunities open to you in your job.*

(Embrey, Mondy, and Noe, 1979, p. 46)

Other areas that are often examined during this portion of the interview are supervision, compensation and working conditions, suggestions for organizational improvement, comparison of the interviewee's new job with the old one, and general complaints about the organization. These questions will often provide some clues to the real reason the employee is leaving. You are now ready to ask the main question; it usually is the last main question on a termination interview guide.

The general termination interview guide just discussed is usually used in voluntary termination interviews. Retention interview guides are somewhat different; they are usually very general and begin with information seeking. Interviewers want to see the position from the employee's perspective, so they may ask the same types of general job factor questions listed above *at the beginning* of the interview rather than after giving information. The questions are generally very open ended, and interviewee leads are followed until you are convinced you have an understanding of all pro and con forces affecting the respondent's potential resignation.

Once you have the whole picture, you will try to "buy some time." That is, you will ask interviewees to delay making a decision until you have had a chance to check out the situation and perhaps make some changes to keep the employee. In no case should you make any rash promises or try to argue employees out of their feelings. Be neutral and nonjudgmental. Promises and appeals to company loyalty seldom do any good. The only things that will keep most employees from leaving are visible changes. In this way, a retention interview is very similar to a counseling interview. It is one of listening and information seeking, not persuasion or decision making. So retention interview guides, like counseling interview guides, are very unstructured. In some cases, retention interviewers don't even use a guide.

The involuntary termination interview guide is just the opposite of that used in a retention interview. It is highly structured and stresses information giving rather than information seeking. The purpose is not to find out why employees are leaving; you already know why. You are simply trying to make their exit as pleasant and dignified as possible by giving them the information they will need to make a clean break.

People are normally disciplined or fired for two basic reasons: incompetency and improper conduct. Most involuntary termination interviews occur because of improper conduct. It is much easier to document improper conduct than incompetency and documentation is absolutely necessary before firing an employee. Since there are varying degrees of employee competency, it is extremely hard to determine at what point incompetency requires dismissal. People who are incompetent in one job are often simply transferred to another job which requires fewer or a different type of skills. Improper conduct termination interviews are generally fairly formal. You simply give respondents information regarding rehire eligibility, reference policy, insurance coverage, property check, official termination forms, and final payroll check. Some interviewers like to stop there. Others feel that employees should be allowed to "blow off steam." In either case, you usually have very few questions prepared ahead of time. Termination interviews for improper conduct are very brief, honest, and formal.

Termination interviews for incompetency can be more positive, empathetic, and constructive. You provide not only general termination information, but also often offer some career development information. Your goal is to encourage employees to search for a job on their own. Kravetz (1978), an industrial psychologist, suggests that interviewers should try to handle some of the emotional reactions employees normally have after involuntary termination. He identifies six basic psychological stages that most employees go through after being informed of their dismissal. The first stage is *shock and disbelief*. They tell others that they just cannot believe that they have been terminated. The second stage is one of *rage and anger*. Employees psychologically strike back at what they perceive as being the source of their problem, usually their supervisor. In the third stage employees resort to *defense mechanisms*. Defense mechanisms include escape or avoidance, where individuals refuse to talk about the termination; denial, where they are unwilling to accept the fact that they have been terminated; displacement, where they try to place the blame for the dismissal on somebody or something else; and repression, where individuals underreact and simply say "I don't care." In many ways defense mechanisms are good; they provide a period of temporary relief. The fourth stage consists of *distress, despair,* or *depression*. They become withdrawn in order to avoid embarrassment. They can also experience insomnia, loss of appetite, and other symptoms of depression. The fifth stage is one of *reflective grief*. The individual begins to think back to things as they were in the past and wishes events could be changed or would have taken a different course. Reflective grief is a constructive behavior in that an employee has finally come to grips with the situation and is putting the termination in its proper perspective. The sixth, and last, stage is *positive behavior*. This is when employees begin to make a realistic assessment of their strengths and weaknesses, make some career decisions, look at job ads, and establish potential employment contacts.

Kravetz suggests that an involuntary termination interviewer ought to help interviewees go through these stages. They can encourage them to establish

Employee terminations are never pleasant.

objective goals and standards, review job performance data with these individuals, help them recognize which psychological stage they are in, and guide them through the various stages. Kravetz (1978) sums up his argument for such an approach:

> *The employee relations counselor has a very important role with regard to involuntary terminations. Failure to take any counselor action can lead to psychological or physiological problems for the terminated employee, create anxiety for the remaining workforce (who will fear that similar events may happen to them), increase the number of lawsuits resulting from insufficient performance documentation, and be detrimental to the corporate image in the community. Though involuntary termination counseling is not the most enjoyable of activities for personnel professionals, it is nonetheless a necessity for all effective organizations.*

(Kravetz, 1978, p. 54)

Although not all termination interviewers would agree with Kravetz's suggestions, he is one of the few professionals who advocates treating incompetency terminations differently than improper conduct terminations.

TERMINATION INTERVIEW OPENING

The opening of a termination interview usually takes approximately ten minutes. You should explain the purpose—giving and receiving information; what you will be covering; and what kind of information you would like to receive from the respondent. The opening is designed to win an interviewee's confidence. It is extremely important that you assure respondents of the confidentiality of the interview. Interviewees will not open up or be honest if they feel they cannot trust you. This approach will develop rapport.

Voluntary and retention termination interviews are generally fairly informal, whereas involuntary termination interviews are much more formal. As with all interviews, climate development begins during the opening. To establish an informal climate, interviewees must perceive you as being uncritical, neutral, understanding, and nonjudgmental. It is only in this climate that you can learn the real reasons an employee is considering leaving or is actually leaving.

TERMINATION INTERVIEW QUESTIONING AND RESPONDING

You should maintain the spirit of trust and cooperation established in the opening. Your questions should be neutral and nonjudgmental, and shouldn't imply either condemnation or approval of interviewee statements or behavior. Because employees are keyed up during termination interviews, any bias or negative interviewer attitudes will be recognized. You should never interrupt a response. In general, questioning in a termination interview is very similar to the questioning described in Chapter 4.

Interviewee responses are often very guarded during termination interviews. Some employees feel that by telling the truth they will be a "stool pigeon." You must acknowledge the first response, but question carefully to discover the real reasons. You will find that employee responses in termination interviews are often discontinuous and illogical. It is up to you to look for a pattern which explains why they want to leave. Don't be over eager. If interviewees feel they are being interrogated, you have very little chance of receiving truthful information. Respondents are almost always on guard during termination interviews.

On the other hand, you will also find respondents who want to "expose the organization" and tell the "truth" about what goes on—loafing, cheating, and so on. These are usually the people who are involuntarily terminated. Be noncommittal and investigate the accusations later. Also beware of the braggart. Braggarts are usually showing frustration. They may be going to a worse job but are covering it up by bragging about all of its benefits. The respondents to whom you want to listen most carefully are those who are impatient or unusually quiet. These people are often difficult to start talking, but once you get them answering your questions, you usually find they have a lot of information which can help you.

Responding in a termination interview is extremely difficult. As the preceding discussion implies, you do not want to "rat" on anyone, but you do want to make your feelings known. Sometimes it is impossible to do one without doing the other. Termination interviewees should be natural, honest, complete, and accurate. Realize that the interviewer is going to try to determine your "real" reason for leaving and be prepared to give the reason. Even in retention and involuntary termination interviews, your responsibilities as a respondent remain the same.

TERMINATION INTERVIEW PROBING

As we have stressed, there are usually two reasons for an employee leaving: the *stated* reason and the *real* reason. Only about 25 percent of the time is the stated reason the same as the real reason. Stated reasons include such things as "I'm getting more money," "I just felt like changing jobs," "I'd like to move to a warmer climate," and "Family obligations." You must probe carefully for the real reason behind a voluntary termination. It requires a great deal of patience. The value of termination *interviews* as opposed to questionnaires is that an interviewer can probe for the facts. Questionnaires only elicit the stated reasons—in face-to-face interviews you can probe and get below the surface. There is no better test of your probing ability than to discover the real reason behind voluntary terminations.

Because employees are reluctant to disclose the real reason for leaving and they know that you have little recourse if they refuse to tell you, termination interviewing probing is especially difficult. Most interviewers, therefore, prefer indirect probes to the more directive forms. Silence, minimal encouragement, and restatement are the most common amplification and clarification probes. If you listen carefully when respondents are describing their work environment, you will often discover the best areas to probe. You must still be patient and tactful in order to finally get respondents to admit their true feelings.

TERMINATION INTERVIEW LISTENING AND RECORDING

During a termination interview, you must listen to what is *not* said, as well as to what *is* said by respondents. When employees are asked what they like best about a job, comments about the supervisor, salary, training and development possibilities, and so on may be conspicuously absent. You must carefully notice not only those forces which seem to be promoting resignation, but also those which are encouraging the employee to stay. Factors such as interest in work, friendship with co-workers, convenience, familiarity, money, work conditions, responsibilities, promotion opportunities, and management may or may not be listed. In order to retain an employee, you must reinforce the positive factors and reduce the negative factors. You cannot do this if you have not listened carefully enough to understand what is going on in the employee's mind. In a retention interview, you mustn't decide on your course of action until you are sure you completely understand the employee's point of view.

Listening is also important in involuntary exit interviews. Although interviewees are often bitter, antagonistic, defensive, or sullen, most still want to present their side of the story. Listen carefully to be sure that the employee's rights were respected, and record and check out anything that is in conflict with organizational policy. Even after the most thorough preparation, you will sometimes hear legitimate complaints or gripes. You must listen and probe carefully to determine if an employee is right or wrong.

Recording is normally done on a preplanned interview guide such as figure 17.1. Many guides contain predetermined categories that only need to be checked. Most, however, also allow space for interviewer comments. This pyramid or inverted funnel sequence—with closed questions at first and open questions to get at the real reason for termination—is typical. The closed questions encourage the respondent to open up and talk about the job.

In recording notes during the interview, be sure not to cue respondents. If you take notes on only negative bits of information, you will soon find interviewees providing only negative information. Your job is to learn what the organization is doing right as well as what it is doing wrong. Whenever possible, you should try to keep your notes, both good and bad, out of sight.

In most cases, you are better off taking written or memorized notes than tape-recorded notes. Because of the delicate nature of the interview and the need for confidentiality, most employees strongly react to a tape recorder. Under no circumstances should you tape the interview without the interviewee's knowledge. This information would soon get to other employees and your credibility would be jeopardized.

Notetaking is more natural if you begin the interview by filling out forms which must be completed before the respondent can leave the organization. This process gets a pencil and paper into your hands, and it is then an easy transition to taking notes on the reason why an employee is leaving. Both listening and notetaking are important in all types of termination interviews, but they are critical in retention and voluntary termination interviews.

TERMINATION INTERVIEW CONCLUDING

Once you feel you have as much information as you need, it is time to move on to the conclusion. To conclude a termination, you must determine that all information has been received and understood, and then summarize what has been said. Check to be sure that all of the necessary papers have been signed, the property check completed, the final paycheck received, and everything else noted earlier has been accomplished. End the interview by thanking employees for taking part, wishing them luck, and assuring them of the organization's continued interest.

In a retention interview, the goal in the conclusion is to buy the time to check out information provided and make any possible changes that might keep a productive employee. Your conclusion should not include rash promises. The follow-up will be an attempt to do whatever is necessary to keep the employee.

In involuntary termination interviews the goal is to make the employee exit as pleasant as possible for both the employee and the organization. Firing someone is never easy on an organization and being dismissed is never easy on an employee. You should, therefore, not look for many smiles and pleasant conversation during the conclusion. The best you can hope for is respect. Involuntary termination interview conclusions are generally very brief and formal, as the entire interview has been. You should still, however, wish respondents luck and be totally honest with them about the references they will receive. Do not be overly optimistic when optimism is not called for. As with any less-than-pleasant interview, diplomacy is what makes a conclusion succeed.

Most termination interviews call for completing follow-up forms which can only be done after careful evaluation of the answers given. The required follow-up includes not only the formal papers necessary to process the termination, but also an evaluation of how the information gained can be useful to the organization. Very often it is not so much what one employee says that affects organizational policy, but the overall comments of many departing employees. These data are absolutely essential for effective organizations, and can only be acquired through skillful termination interviewing.

SUMMARY

Although necessary, termination interviews are never pleasant. The information that may be gained can, however, be very useful to an organization. Of the three types of termination interviews, the retention interview is the most unstructured. It is done as soon as possible, with little or no preparation or guide and a great deal of questioning, probing, and listening. Its goal is to keep valuable employees. The involuntary termination interview usually involves much preparation and little questioning, probing, and listening. It is usually rather direct and to the point. It is the voluntary termination interview upon which most organizations focus. Although they cannot save that particular employee, they can gather the information necessary to save many others. Its main purpose is to discover why an employee is leaving. This question cannot be addressed directly, but must be approached tactfully. When done properly, termination interviews are a vital and necessary part of any termination control program.

ACTIVITIES

Activity #1

Directions: On the basis of what you have learned in this chapter and in Part I, analyze the following termination interview. Look for both good and bad points by both the interviewer and interviewee. *Carol Harper*, the terminating employee, works in the typing pool for a state government. About half the time the employees are under heavy pressure, but there is almost always one day a week when the work is so slack that the staff has to work hard to find something to do. When merit time came around, Carol was not given a raise. Her supervisor, *Gary Hamilton*, said she "wastes too much time." She appealed to *Carmella Daley*, the chief clerk, who agreed with Mr. Hamilton's decision. She was so upset, she submitted her resignation. During the retention interview, she told the interviewer that she was tired of working and wanted to stay home with her children more. She is due to leave on Friday. This voluntary termination interview takes place on Wednesday. The preliminaries of property check, explanation of benefits, and so forth have been omitted here. Use the line number to refer to your comments.

   R: Carol, please tell me a little about your job duties with us.
   E: Well, it isn't a bad job. We simply type whatever we are assigned by Mr. Hamilton.
   R: It doesn't sound like there is too much variety in the job.
5 *E:* No, not too much. Sometimes the stuff we type is kind of interesting.
   R: What about your work load? Was it too much at times or about even.
   E: Well . . . (Pause) sometimes it's heavier than others.
   R: Oh?
   E: Monday through Wednesday or Thursday we are usually real busy.
10 *R:* And Friday?

E: It can get pretty hard to find something to do.

R: What do the employees do to keep busy?

E: Some of them go to the lounge a lot. Most of them keep a piece of paper in their typewriter and type on it when Mr. Hamilton comes around. Some can
15 even look busy while reading a magazine in their desk drawer.

R: Is that what you do?

E: Sometimes.

R: What about the other times?

E: My desk is by the window, I just look outside.

20 *R:* I see. On your resignation you say that you are terminating because you want to stay home with your children.

E: Yes. That's right.

R: How old are your children?

E: They are twelve and fifteen.

25 *R:* Then they are both in school?

E: Yes, but I like to be there when they come home.

R: I see. What did you like about working for the government?

E: The salary is good, and the fringe benefits are great.

R: I notice that you did not receive a raise during the last merit review and
30 appealed that decision to Carmella Daley. Did that have anything to do with your decision to resign?

E: A little bit I guess, but I was ready to quit anyway . . . (Pause)

R: (Silence)

E: Because of my children.

35 *R:* Can you tell me a little about the supervision you received in your job? Was Mr. Hamilton fair? Did he answer your questions? Were you given enough instruction?

E: Yeah, he was OK.

R: Just OK?

40 *E:* He's like everybody else. He has some shortcomings, but he's OK. He tries hard.

R: Carol, it's my job to find out what we are doing right and what we are doing wrong. As I said in the beginning, everything you say here is strictly confidential. It will not reflect on your recommendations or on you in any
45 other way. This is one of the few places we can look at our operation from the employee's perspective. I have the feeling that for one reason or another you are not telling me everything. I know wanting to spend more time with your children is one reason why you are quitting, but I think there are some other reasons as well. Would you mind telling me what those reasons are? Do they
50 have anything to do with your merit raise?

E: All I want to do is leave here with good feelings. I don't want to get anybody in trouble.

R: I don't want you to name people specifically. I just want to know what is going on. Other people who have left that section tell us that the work load is
55 too uneven. That is why I asked you that question before. Is that true?

E: Yes, it is.

R: Suppose you tell me the basis for your appeal to Mrs. Daley.

E: Well, OK, this is confidential?

R: Definitely.

60 *E:* I simply told her that I did as much work as the others in my section, but that I could not fake working when there was nothing to do. I believe that my pay should be based on my work and not my ability to fool Mr. Hamilton. I guess they both believe we are all working on Thursday and Friday.

65 *R:* Who is they?

E: My supervisor and the chief clerk.

R: Would you have resigned if you had gotten the raise?

E: I don't know.

R: Would you consider returning to work here if the work load were more 70 even.

E: I guess so. But I don't think things would be the same.

R: I would like to check into this matter further. Would you be willing to delay your resignation until I can check further? I hate to see a hard-working employee resign if in fact the only problem is that you can't pretend to work 75 when there is no work to be done. Is that all right with you?

E: You said this was confidential. How can you do those things without bringing my name up or getting anyone in trouble? I think I just better resign before I am fired. (Pause) Yes, I just better resign. Even if you could change things in that section, I don't think I could be happy there again.

80 *R:* Carol, I really do want to help you and the organization.

E: I know you do, but for me, I think I would be better off getting another job.

R: Perhaps a transfer to another section would be possible. Would you consider that?

E: I don't know. Let me think about it.

85 *R:* OK, let me hold up your resignation until Friday. I will see what we have open. Can you come in Friday morning? I will either have your final paycheck or some other position for you.

E: Yeah, but I won't work for Mr. Hamilton or Mrs. Daley.

R: I know, and I appreciate your feelings. I'm just sorry we did not know 90 about this before.

E: So am I.

R: Is there anything else I should know?

E: I can't think of anything.

R: OK, I will see you on Friday then?

95 *E:* Yes, on Friday, and I'm glad someone here listens.

R: I can't promise anything, but I'll check and see what I can do.

E: Thank you.

Activity #2

Directions: Most termination interviews are the responsibility of a personnel office. Arrange an interview with one or more personnel officers who commonly do the termination interviews for an organization. Have them tell you about their best and worst termination interview experiences as well as how they prepare for, conduct, and follow up the information received. See if you can find any instances where the organization was improved because of a termination interview. Write a short paper discussing the information you obtain and how it compares to the information in this chapter and the other types of interviews discussed in this book so far.

Activity #3

Directions: Select one of the following hypothetical cases and role-play it, being sure to use the skills and concepts discussed in this and previous chapters. These cases merely describe common discipline interview situations. Add any other information you like to make the role-play as realistic as possible.

RETENTION INTERVIEW: Julie Thomas was divorced two years ago and returned to work as a media specialist for a large public relations firm. She had been in broadcasting and media technology for several years before getting married. She, along with six other men and three women, work for *Anthony Romsa.* Mr. Romsa soon recognized Julie's maturity and capabilities and began rotating her from one difficult assignment to another. She liked variety, so this pleased her, and she gloried in the attention she received from her superiors. Anthony called her his "jewel" and a "once-in-a-lifetime find" and was, therefore, surprised when she came to him one day and said she was going to quit. She said the problem was that the "other employees resented the attention he was giving her and were snubbing her." She gave him two weeks' notice. Mr. Romsa quickly called the firm's retention interviewer, *Mr. Harry Johns,* who arranged to meet with Julie that afternoon.

VOLUNTARY TERMINATION INTERVIEW: Ethel Wagner is the third grade teacher in Roosevelt Elementary School. She has been teaching there for eight years. Recently a new principal, *Gordon Novak,* was hired after the old principal retired. He brought a lot of new ideas with him which Ethel did not agree with. He emphasized the "three R's" to the exclusion of everything else. Ethel felt that her job included developing a child's personality as well as the ability to do "readin', 'ritin', and 'rithmetic." He told her to keep the children at their desks working on the "essentials." He was especially critical of the time she spent each day allowing the children to talk about what they did outside of school and how they felt about things like honesty, sportsmanship, and love. Ethel tried to get along, but toward the end of the semester she asked for a transfer. Her request was denied, mostly on the basis of Mr. Novak's comments. She finally turned in her resignation effective at the end of the year. She is now going to see *Ruth Griffith,* the termination interviewer for the school district.

INVOLUNTARY TERMINATION INTERVIEW: Larry Hardy is a custodian for the Brenner Insurance Company. His job is to clean up the offices after work each day. The job pays well. He is constantly going off somewhere in his new Porsche so that his area supervisor has to hunt to find him. He has also found Larry reading magazines in the offices. The last straw came one night when *Don Jackson,* his supervisor, found him asleep in one of the offices. Don told him to pick up his paycheck, that he was fired. He has just entered the personnel office for the termination interview and final paycheck.

Chapter 18

The Group Interview

The group interview has diagnostic, therapeutic, strategic, and administrative advantages which make it preferable to an individual interview in some circumstances. Such an interview, however, requires a change of primary worker focus from the individual to the group; a readiness and ability to share interview control with participants; a greater complexity of reactions and a greater heterogeneity of participants to which the interviewer has to respond; greater hazards to confidentiality and to the establishment and achievement of a common purpose; and the necessity of dealing with participants who assume problematic roles. (Kadushin, 1972, p. 307)

Because interviewing is primarily a two-person activity, the focus of this book has been on dyadic interviews. However, interviews can also take place with more than two people. A group interview is one in which there are two or more interviewers or interviewees. When the interviewees outnumber the interviewers, it is most commonly called a *panel* interview. When the interviewers outnumber the interviewees, it is labeled a *board* interview. In this chapter, both panel and board types of group interviews will be discussed.

Group interviewing probably began around 1925 in the German Army, when panel interviews were part of the officer selection process. The panel interview is still used chiefly for selection purposes, although it has been adapted for research interviewing as well. When a panel interview is used for research purposes it is called a *focus group* interview. Recently a great deal of attention has been devoted to the use of focus group interviews for research purposes. Researchers bring people together to discuss a topic and in this way, get a lot of information on a subject in a very short period of time. According to one advertiser, focus group interviews provide "A chance to 'experience' a 'flesh and blood' consumer . . . to go into her life and relive with her all of the satisfactions, dissatisfactions, rewards, and frustrations she experiences when she takes the product into her home" (Bellenger, Bernhardt, and Goldstucker, 1976, p. 7).

Panel group interview techniques are also gaining popularity in counseling and diagnostic situations as well. Social workers, for example, have developed what they call *family interviews* for diagnostic purposes. The following illustrates the theory behind the use of such group interviewing techniques:

Rather than seeing the disturbed child, for instance, as an isolated entity requiring treatment, the supposition is that a disturbed child implies a disturbed family, and that help for the child requires help for the family. The child is what he is because the family is what it is, and since the child does not get sick alone, he will not get well alone. The very act of assembling the family members and having them participate together in the discussion is symbolic confirmation and reinforcement of the idea that the problem belongs to the family as a unit and not to any one member.

(Kadushin, 1972, p. 288)

In the helping context, the group interview is a direct outgrowth of group psychotherapy. In group psychotherapy, however, the therapist takes an important role in the group's interaction. Although they are not necessarily directive, they do intervene to clarify, summarize, and generalize upon statements made by various group members. Out of this original group therapeutic approach has grown the "human relations approach." It requires that a leader or interviewer remain more or less detached from the group's interaction. The basic goal of human relations training is for participants to discuss their perceptions of themselves and their relationships with others in a small, face-to-face, group interview. The primary focus of human relations training is on emotional or subjective information exchange rather than objective facts. Learning takes place mostly in the affective domain and not in the cognitive domain.

Human relations training has been applied to educational problems, community involvement programmes, motivation of industrial supervisors, and various facets of personal development. It is an exciting new use for the old group interview.

(Shouksmith, 1978, p. 130)

As you can see, there are a great many uses of a panel interview—soon perhaps, panel group interviewing techniques will be applied to information interviews, persuasion interviews, and perhaps even performance, discipline, and termination interviews. Since interviewers play a more or less passive or observer role in many one-to-one interviewing situations, it is only natural that they apply the same approach with a group of interviewees. Panel group interviewing offers new and exciting horizons for the entire interview process. There are, however, several drawbacks to this approach, as you will see later in this chapter.

In board interviews, there are more interviewers than interviewees. Examples of board interviews include senate hearings, graduate student oral examinations, and site visits by potential employees who are taken to lunch or dinner and questioned by several members of the organization. Perhaps no other type of interviewing is as controversial as board interviews. Those opposed to it often say something like:

It is, in fact, my opinion that most of the evils of interviewing are to be found mainly in the Board interview. Board interviews seem to bring out the worst in every interviewer and many an interview has been used by a member of the Board merely to display his own knowledge or as a means of scoring off the candidate. This is, I realize a criticism of particular Boards, but it is my experience that this so often happens that I feel a closer, critical look at Board interviewing is required.

(Shouksmith, 1978, pp. 63–64)

Others are just as certain of the values of board interviewing, especially as part of the employee selection process. Most of the advocates of board interviews cite the low reliability and validity of dyadic selection interviews as the reason they have turned to the group interview. They feel that the traditional selection interview is based upon the whims of a single interviewer. They believe that with the proper controls and interviewer training, board interviews can be a more reliable and valid means of employee selection. In the following sections, the nature of those controls and training will be discussed.

As you begin to learn the ways in which group interviews should be handled, you must keep in mind certain inherent characteristics of all group interviews. Because more people are taking part in the interview, all concerned will perceive the interaction as much more public. Because of this, participants are likely to withdraw and become somewhat defensive. They are more inhibited than they would be in the traditional two-person interview. It is, therefore, more difficult to develop rapport between participants.

The public nature of group interviews also has some advantages. Because participants feel they are being critically observed by other members of the group, both questions and answers tend to be crisper and more to the point. Long rambling questions are unusual so the amount of information that can be collected is usually greater in a group interview.

A second characteristic of group interviews is that the purposes and desires of the various participants may differ. In a board selection interview, for example, interviewers may have different ideas as to what constitutes the criteria for hiring an employee. In order to meet these differing purposes, individuals may consciously and unconsciously develop norms and roles. *Norms* are patterns or rules of behavior which all participants must follow. Interviewer norms such as the ratio of interviewer to respondent talk, what type of information should be sought and given, and the interview climate must be worked out ahead of time. Interviewee norms are usually worked out during the course of a group interview. *Roles* are patterns of behavior for specific individuals within the group. Roles such as chairperson, recorder, prober, elaborator, clarifier, and listener are all developed either before or during the interview. It generally takes some time for norms and roles to evolve. This is especially true, for example, in focus group interviews where the participants are strangers and the client or sponsor is often an unidentified member of the group.

Norms and roles can also have positive advantages for group interviews. One of the greatest advantages is what is called the *assembly effect*. An assembly effect occurs when the questions and responses by one of the group participants elicits unique questions and responses from other participants which would not have occurred without the "triggering" or "assembly" effect. Because of the assembly effect, groups can often come up with more and better information than individuals interviewed in a dyadic situation. The assembly effect is the main idea behind *brainstorming*. Brainstorming is designed to produce a great many ideas in a short period of time. Participants are presented with a problem and are asked to throw out ideas as to its solution as quickly as possible. The key to the success of brainstorming is that no evaluation takes place until all possible suggestions have been made. The assembly effect occurs when the ideas of one participant trigger a new and often better idea from another participant. The nonevaluative nature of brainstorming encourages highly creative and unorthodox suggestions. The interviewer acts mainly as the recorder, rule enforcer, and nondirective facilitator.

The public nature of the interaction and the presence of varying purposes are two principal ways in which group interviews differ from traditional dyad interviews. You will notice other differences as you learn how to prepare, open, question, probe, listen, record, and conclude group interviews.

GROUP INTERVIEW PREPARATION

Group interviews require the same types of preparation as dyad interviews such as understanding human nature, yourself, the other participants, and the topic. In a group interview, however, other types of preparation also must be done. In a focus group, for example, you must determine what types of information the client desires. Very often, the focus group leader develops the interview guide in conjunction with a client.

It is also necessary to determine the size and membership of the group to be interviewed. Focus group interviews are normally larger than other types of group interviews; sometimes there are as many as twenty to twenty-five people. More often, however, the size of a focus group is about twelve. Because you are interested in forming a group or sample whose attitudes and feelings are truly representative of the larger population, sampling methods, like those discussed in the chapter on research interviews, are often used. In most cases it is best to select the group members at random. In some cases, however, a client may provide a list of people to be interviewed based on certain qualifications. Determining who will be a participant is one of the most important elements of focus group interview preparation. Other preparation tasks include choosing a location, determining the seating pattern, and providing name tags. The same type of preparation is necessary for almost all group interviews.

Board interviews require a few more preparation tasks: selecting a chairperson, conducting a strategy session before the interview, and assigning topics to the various interviewers. Chairpersons should be fairly passive; they do not necessarily ask any more or any different types of questions than the other members of the board. In most cases, decisions as to what and how questions will be asked are determined at a strategy session before the interview. If the interviewers do not know each other beforehand, this is when they are assigned a topic area. Such a division of labor usually makes it easier for all board interviewers. Figure 18.1 reflects a suggested group interview structure for selecting engineering craft apprentices.

Obviously, all of this preparation is based on a thorough job analysis such as that discussed in Chapter 11. As you can see, the preparation for both board and panel group interviews requires coordination rather than the information collecting that precedes dyad interviewers. Presumably, the same types of questions will be asked in a group interview as in a traditional interview, but coordinating the asking and answering must be planned ahead of time if the group interview is to be effective.

18.1 Sample Group Selection Structure

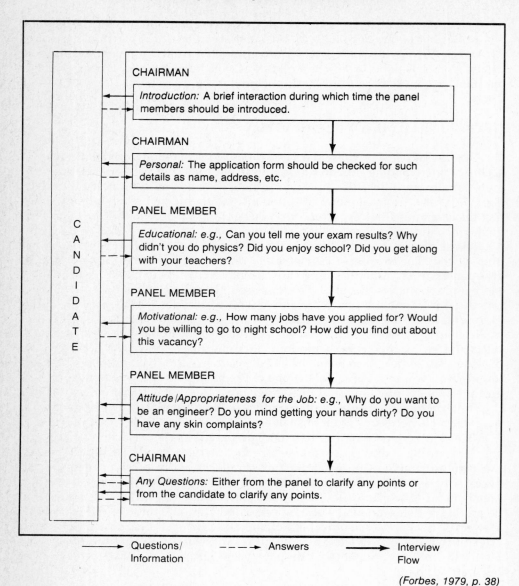

CHAIRMAN

Introduction: A brief interaction during which time the panel members should be introduced.

CHAIRMAN

Personal: The application form should be checked for such details as name, address, etc.

PANEL MEMBER

Educational: e.g., Can you tell me your exam results? Why didn't you do physics? Did you enjoy school? Did you get along with your teachers?

PANEL MEMBER

Motivational: e.g., How many jobs have you applied for? Would you be willing to go to night school? How did you find out about this vacancy?

PANEL MEMBER

Attitude/Appropriateness for the Job: e.g., Why do you want to be an engineer? Do you mind getting your hands dirty? Do you have any skin complaints?

CHAIRMAN

Any Questions: Either from the panel to clarify any points or from the candidate to clarify any points.

CANDIDATE

Questions/Information ———→   Answers ---→   Interview Flow ———→

(Forbes, 1979, p. 38)

THE GROUP INTERVIEW GUIDE

No interview guide is necessary when the interviewer intends to be merely an observer. This happens in leaderless group selection and group counseling interviews. If you are conducting a brainstorming focus group interview, you will want to do some more preparation in terms of a guide, but you are still using an unstructured approach. Focus group interview guides normally consist of a listing of the major topic areas that interest a client. These areas might include price, convenience, dependability, and other factors related to a product, service, or other purpose of the interview.

In brainstorming and focus group interviews little more than a brief mention of the topic or a broad open question is usually needed to start discussion of a particular topic area. It becomes your purpose, then, to be sure that all of the topics are covered so the client gets the desired information. This means including transitions and probes to gain the information. There are, however, some focus group interviewers who like to have a more structured interview guide. They prepare an entire series of questions for which they want very short and to-the-point answers. In this case, a highly developed interview guide is necessary. The interview becomes more directive and the interviewer much more domineering in such a group interview. Most expert opinion regarding focus groups, however, suggests that you use a less structured, nondirective approach. This allows you to get both objective and subjective information from respondents.

On the other hand, board interviews are generally highly structured:

. . . it was found that only structured interviews generated information that enabled interviewers to agree with each other. Under the structured conditions, the interviewer knew which questions to ask and what to do with the information he received. Moreover, the interviewers applied the same frame of reference to each applicant, since they covered the same areas for each. In unstructured interviews the managers received additional information, but it seemed to be disorganised [sic] and made their evaluation task more difficult. Carlson [the researcher] concluded that highly structured interviews have the greatest potential for valid selection.

(Forbes, 1979, p. 37–38)

In many ways the guide for a board selection interview looks like guides for any other selection interview. It covers interviewee background, education, experience, future plans, and so on. Because each interviewer asks specific questions about a specific topic area in board selection interviews, it is almost essential that it be highly structured with a fairly specific guide. Otherwise, interviewees may end up answering questions on only one topic area. Group interview guides come in all sizes and shapes. There are no definitive rules concerning their development.

GROUP INTERVIEW OPENING

Perhaps the most difficult aspect of group interview conduct is a proper opening. In a one-on-one interview it is fairly easy to establish the proper climate of rapport and formality, because only two people need to adjust to one another.

In a group interview, all of the participants, both interviewers and interviewees, need to adjust to one another. Good rapport and informality is difficult to achieve. Most group interviews open with a brief introduction of the participants. Sometimes participants are encouraged to engage in chit-chat before beginning the interview itself. To some extent, this can be accomplished by supplying refreshments and letting everyone mingle before sitting down for the interview. However, it is almost impossible to develop the rapport and informality of a dyad interview. This is one of the major drawbacks of group interviewing.

During the opening, groups usually develop the norms and procedures which continue throughout the interview. It is your responsibility to educate interviewees as to any special norms that must be followed. The following is a sample of productive group interview norms:

1. *To allow everyone to participate without undue interruption.*
2. *To listen carefully and attentively to what others are saying.*
3. *To respond to what others have said.*
4. *To keep one's contribution and response reasonably relevant to the focus of what is being discussed.*
5. *To share, for discussion, meaningful and significant material without regard to the usual social taboos. In fact, the more likely it is to be off limits for ordinary social interaction, the greater the obligation to share this material in the group interview.*
6. *To be willing to forego the usual social norms of self-defense and accept open discussion and group criticism of one's own problems and feelings.*
7. *To accept limitations on verbal and nonverbal acting out which might seriously threaten to break up the group.*
8. *To encourage emotional expressiveness.*

(Kadushin, 1972, p. 295)

In interviews where you are going to take a role other than observer, it is necessary to establish credibility and demonstrate tolerance and acceptance of all interviewee comments. You can do this by providing a thorough orientation for respondents. You must explain the general purpose of the interview, how the information will be used, what is expected of each participant, how the interview is being recorded, and anything else which might help establish a good climate. It is a good idea to inform interviewees that there are no "correct" answers and that all observations will be accepted. In some cases, it might also be necessary to point out that subjective observations are as important as objective information. Once the orientation is over you should go directly into the opening question which, as with other types of interviews, is normally a fairly easy question to get the interview rolling.

Do not expect the opening to go as smoothly or be as successful as the opening of a dyad interview. Each group will eventually establish its own climate and norms. In very few groups will all of the participants establish good rapport with one another. Most group interviews are fairly formal, if for no other reason than because of the public nature of the discussion and the realization that confidentiality is much more difficult to guarantee. It takes more time for primary tension and defensiveness to dissipate in a group interview. If you are careful in the opening, however, you can develop some degree of cohesiveness among the group members. But this usually occurs only after the interview is well under way.

GROUP INTERVIEW QUESTIONING AND RESPONDING

Questioning differs according to the type and purpose of a group. In an unstructured group interview, few, if any, questions are asked other than those which come from the interviewees. In a focus group interview, questioning is done by the interviewer, but only to maintain control of direction, encourage all members to participate, obtain full coverage of the various topics, and in some cases to spark controversy when the group becomes too dull. Most focus group theorists suggest that interviewers should remain as neutral as possible, in no case interrupting or inserting their own ideas. It is important, however, to deal with problem respondents. Downs (1980) suggests five types of group problem respondents: "hogs," who are dominant and overly verbal; "wallflowers," who remain silent or merely voice agreement; "axe bearers," who have a one-track mind and try to push a specific point continuously; "eager beavers," who try to get in the first word on every topic; and "compromisers," who are constantly changing their opinions. It is your responsibility to make sure none of these problem respondents destroys the group's productivity. Comments such as "How do others feel?" or "Do all of you agree?" are typical questions used by focus group interviewers.

In a more highly structured board interview, where the questioning sequence is planned, interviewees have trouble adjusting. Just when an interviewee gets used to one interviewer a new one takes over. This can break the flow and cause a great deal of interviewee stress. It is also difficult to maintain a proper interview pace when using several interviewers. Another problem is that various interviewers sometimes interrupt one another and the respondent during the asking and answering of questions. No interruption should be tolerated. You must be on guard for the interviewee who tries to manipulate the interviewers or play them against one another. All interviewers must remain totally neutral to one another and to the respondent. If interview questioning is planned well ahead of time, these problems will not occur. If unplanned, board interviews can degenerate into a shouting match. Group interview planning must also take into account question vocabulary, framing, and phrasing as well as interviewer style in order not to confuse or disorient respondents.

Responding in a panel interview is generally quite easy. Interviewees do not feel "on the spot," as if they have to respond to each and every question. As a matter of fact, panel interviewers do not want everyone to respond to every question. As a panel interviewee, you should plan to respond to those questions where you think you have something useful to add. As long as you do not become a "hog," "wallflower," "axe bearer," "eager beaver," or "compromiser" you will probably be a good respondent.

On the other hand, responding in a board interview is generally very difficult. Very often interviewees feel "overpowered" in such interviews. They think they have all kinds of questions coming at them from all different directions.

When you are in such a situation, you should try to take your time and handle each question in turn. Do not answer only those questions coming from the person you perceive to be the high-status board member; you will alienate the others. Take each question in order, no matter who it comes from. In general, you should follow the same advice given in the section on selection interviewing. Remember, by the time you have reached a board interview, you are probably one of the finalists for a job.

GROUP INTERVIEW PROBING

In a group interview, amplification and clarification probes are most common. In many cases, however, it is not the interviewer who does the probing. In panel interviews, interviewees often probe other interviewee comments. This should be allowed unless the probes become disruptive and produce nonproductive conflict. If this occurs, it is up to you to step in. There is nothing wrong with disagreement in a group interview, but nonproductive conflict should be avoided. Constructive conflict often produces the best information. It can be encouraged by presenting extreme positions and challenging statements. In the totally unstructured panel interview, you will do little or no probing at all.

When probes are used by group interviewers, they should be nondirective. The use of silence, minimal encouragement, and restatement are the most commonly used. You will also use reflection probes when looking for subjective or affective information. Questions such as "How do the rest of you feel about that?" or "It sounds like most of you feel positively toward this product, is that correct?" are common forms of group reflection probes. The paraphrase and summary are the clarification probes used most often by panel interviewers. You should periodically summarize and paraphrase statements made by one or more respondents and then see if there is general agreement. This helps groups understand where they have been and where they are going. Such nondirective amplification and clarification are also useful to participants. Another technique often used by group interviewers is self-disclosure. Self-disclosure means that you tell the group something about your own experiences in order to induce group members to do the same. This helps get at the feelings of participants in the same way as a reflection probe.

In board interviews, interviewers probe at the end of the interview. Each interviewer can ask questions regarding their specific assigned topic and then time is set aside at the end for further clarification and amplification of various points made by a respondent. If too many probes are allowed during the initial question period, it is very easy for the discussion to run overtime. Few, if any, probes are allowed during each interviewer's question period.

GROUP INTERVIEW LISTENING AND RECORDING

Most group interviews are either audio or video taped. This is because there is usually more interaction and information than memorization or notetaking could record. In interviews where a video or audio tape recorder is not used, one

In the voir dire *process, probing and listening become very important.*

individual is usually designated as note taker. This person may be a stenographer or one of the interviewers who is not assigned any particular topic area. Otherwise, it is the responsibility of each interviewer or interviewee to take their own probe notes. In some board interviews, each of the interviewers is required to listen and take notes on interviewee responses while others are asking questions. The difficulty with this arrangement is that those individuals who are not asking questions have a tendency to become distracted and let their minds wander because someone else is doing the questioning. Electronic recording solves these problems; it also allows interviewers to go back and reexamine the entire interview before making any decisions.

There are also some problems with electronic recording of group interviews. With audio tape, it is very difficult to identify who is saying what. This is not such a problem with a board interview where there is only one interviewee, but it does become a problem when the source of a comment is important. One of the ways in which some interviewers have tried to identify speakers is to have them give their name prior to each comment they make. However, this technique tends to break the flow and continuity of the interaction, especially if you must continually remind participants to identify themselves. Another problem with audio or video tape is the anxiety that it causes participants. A group interview is a fairly public process in the first place, and use of an audio or video recorder simply increases the amount of respondent tension and anxiety. But you must be totally open and honest with respondents about the fact that their comments are being recorded.

Listening is essential if groups are to achieve the "assembly effect." Each participant must listen to the comments made by other participants which can trigger their own ideas. All participants must practice active listening. It is only through such listening and direct comment that group interviews will achieve their greatest potential.

GROUP INTERVIEW CONCLUDING

When concluding a group interview, make sure that all pertinent topics have been covered and that all group members have had a chance to say everything they feel is important. Whenever possible, the discussion should be kept within the predetermined time limits. Try to end the interview on a positive note by telling all participants how valuable the session has been. Do not try to answer questions regarding any conclusions drawn from the session. Simply say that conclusions cannot be drawn until the audio or video tape has been carefully reviewed.

For a board selection interview, the conclusion is very similar to that used in a dyad selection interview. Thank interviewees and tell them when they will be informed of the decision. This is usually done by the chairperson. After an interviewee has left, the interviewers generally hold a brief discussion and then make independent assessments since this prevents any one interviewer from unduly influencing the others. Multiple and independent assessments are what make board interviews valuable: they eliminate the bias and subjectivity of a single evaluator; hence, they increase the validity and reliability of selection judgments.

The follow-up to both panel and board interviews usually consists of a written report. This written report often comes after extensive review and analysis of the audio or video tape. In focus group interviews, the nature of the report depends on what is required by the client. In some cases, the client only requires a very brief and impressionistic summary of the principal findings. This is especially true if the client was present. In other cases, the client may want a very extensive report documenting not only the major comments made but also some type of interpretation of what all of the comments mean. After a board selection interview, either a group report or individual reports may be required. In most cases, the written report is very similar to that used for a dyadic interview.

SUMMARY

Perhaps the fastest growing of all interview types is the group interview. There are two types of group interviews: panel interviews, where interviewees outnumber interviewers, and board interviews, where interviewers outnumber interviewees. It is hard to develop rapport in a panel group interview. Sometimes it is hard to even get a word in edgewise. Panel interviews are used for selection, research, and counseling. Board interviews usually have more structure and are primarily used for selections or information gathering. Board interviews take a great deal of preparation and coordination. Dyad interviews may well be replaced someday by group structures. They are not only more economical, but are also sometimes a more efficient means of information collection.

ACTIVITIES

Activity #1

Directions: On the basis of what you have learned in this chapter and in Part I, analyze the following group interview. Look for both good and bad points by the interviewer and interviewees. This focus group interview was conducted by Tony Wainwright of Wainwright, Spaeth & Wright, a Chicago-based agency specializing in new product development. The client was *Advertising Age* magazine; the purpose was to learn what a "typical" consumer thought about products and prices in today's supermarket. This is only the first portion of the interview dealing with meat. The entire interview can be found in the March 3, 1975 issue of *Advertising Age* (pp. 37–40). Use the line number to refer to your comments.

Wainwright: What's going on in the grocery store today?

Alma: I find myself no longer buying meat in the grocery store. I started this about a month ago. I feel that, for those prices, I might as well go to a butcher, pay a few pennies more and get premium meat or prime. I find that
5 whereas just going into the store with no meat used to cost me $30 or $40, now it costs me $60 to $75.

Linda: I bought half a cow a month ago. And I'm still spending the same amount of money in the grocery store every week that I did before I bought the half a cow.

10 *Wainwright:* Eileen, how are you making it today? What are you cutting back on and what are you buying more of?

Eileen: I have completely done away with Fritos, potato chips, snacks—we were big on that type of stuff. I'm going back to some of the things my grandmother did. I'm baking. We weren't really taught all that much.

15 *Rose:* I sat down with my husband the other night. I do not use that much sugar in baking. Most of my cookies are without sugar. Or they take half a cup of sugar.

Marvella: People during the holidays were complaining because of Christmas baking. They do use a tremendous amount.

20 *Linda:* I use a little brown sugar and powdered sugar. I sat down and really thought about it, and normally my consumption of sugar, if it came down to it, even with holiday baking, is 15 lbs a year.

Wainwright: Are you doing anything different, Sandra?

Sandra: I think so. You know, before I would make a lot of roasts. Now you
25 don't even think about that, except maybe once a week. Now we have more ground meat recipes.

Wainwright: You add anything to it?

Eileen: No.

Wainwright: What's a box mix?

30 *Eileen:* Hamburger Helper!

Linda: You can do a lot more yourself. You pay 79¢ for noodles.

Alma: Where I shop, they've been giving us a new cook book each week. So

I've been trying some of the things in there. It's nothing you'd buy a mix for. You make it all yourself.

35 *Kathy:* Like a meatloaf.

Wainwright: How about side dishes? Anybody serving them?

Rose: Oh, yes.

Wainwright: More or about the same?

Rose: I'm serving less. Of course, they are very expensive so you don't save

40 much.

Wainwright: What is there today?

Linda: Well, the only thing I can say is we're just eating cheaper cuts of meat. I haven't had steak since I can't remember when. But I have two teenage sons, and it's hard to tell them: You eat this piece of meat—you don't get any

45 more. You just can't say this to kids.

Kathy: All of a sudden you don't have the cookies and snacks in the house. Buy pop once a week instead of every time it runs out. All of these things are changing.

Linda: I've found what I've done—we get paid twice a month. So my big

50 shopping is twice a month, and I really go in for nothing else but milk and eggs. After they have gone through what I have bought, that's it.

Sandra: I also find I buy things on sale. If it's something I use, I will buy two, because I know when I run out it's going to be up in price.

Marvella: And then, too, don't you shop the specials of the week?

55 *Sandra:* If it's something I use, yes.

Wainwright: What about private labels?

Alma: A lot of them are a lot better.

Linda: Oh, I got some Del Monte string beans the other day, and they were about half full of string beans and were about the worst tasting stuff, so I just

60 swore off Del Monte right there.

Rose: The only way you can beat it—is to do comparison shopping. I would suggest you look at the ads on Thursday nights and go to the A&P, go to the Jewel. You have to hit all the stores.

Eileen: By that time, you've wasted a day.

65 *Sandra:* That's the only way you can beat the game. Like I work. I don't have that kind of time for it. I'm better off sticking to one store.

Alma: They say that dried beans give you the same amount of protein. Supposedly, I've heard that.

Rose: There's no way my husband is going to sit down and eat a plate full of

70 beans—unless he's at a campfire. He's strictly meat. I have to serve him that.

Wainwright: What can you do to meat? If you serve a lot of hamburger, what do you do to vary it?

Marvella: Make chili, Sloppy Joes. And then the macaroni.

Linda: You can jazz up anything—a meatloaf, even.

75 *Eileen:* I think you get tired of it, though.

Sandra: I've been buying ground turkey because that's cheap, but I'm getting tired of that too. I'd like a good roast.

Wainwright: How about that soy protein?

Kathy: I've used that. You know my husband couldn't tell the difference.

80 *Marvella:* I'll tell you what I've done. I make my spaghetti sauce, but when I cook the soy beans I use the packaged spaghetti flavoring in the water. Then I add that into my spaghetti sauce with maybe ½ lb. of ground meat or my chili sauce and this just extends it.
Alma: I had my sister over to dinner one day and made a hamburger out of it.
85 Plain. It was sort of bland, but it wasn't terrible. It tasted like ground beef.
Wainwright: What about sauces? Are any of you ladies using more sauces today?
Eileen: I marinate once in a while.
Rose: I use barbecue sauce mostly in the summer.
90 *Wainwright:* How about meat tenderizers? Or marinades?
Kathy: Marinades, yes, I use them. I use A.1., Worcestershire, something like that in spaghetti, but I don't use French's or stuff like that—you know, packaged stuff.
Wainwright: Let's switch to other areas. One item . . . .

Activity #2

Directions: Prepare a paper suggesting how you might go about doing other types of interviews, such as information, diagnostic, performance, counseling, discipline, termination, and persuasion interviews using a group approach. How would you structure it, and what advantages or disadvantages do you think it would have in comparison to a dyadic interview? Think about it carefully. Perhaps you can use some past experience you have had in a group interview or talk to someone you know who has taken part in a group interview to help with this paper.

Activity #3

Directions: The following role-plays can only be done if you are part of a class or workshop. The minimum number to do either role-play is four people, but six or eight is better. Select one of the following group interview cases and role-play it, being sure to use the skills and concepts discussed in this and previous chapters. These cases merely describe common panel and board interview situations. You are free to add any other information or change the topic to make it as realistic as possible.

PANEL INTERVIEW: Melissa Harris, the assistant superintendent for the county school district, has come to your college to talk with students about their feelings regarding primary and secondary education in the district. She feels that students who are now in college can give her some recommendations that could help improve things. She is especially interested in such things as the required subjects, the grading system, discipline, textbooks, and anything else she can learn. She has decided to use a focus group approach to get as much information as possible in a short period of time. She is also interested in the ideas of students who come from other districts that might be incorporated into her district.

BOARD INTERVIEW: Brian Haynes received a letter last week from station

WOOM in Detroit, Michigan. He interviewed with one of the station executives, a *Mr. Floyd Ward*, who spoke to his broadcasting class and said they were looking for some new disc jockeys. The letter asked if Brian could come to the station and talk with some of the other personnel and look around the facilities. Mr. Ward said that they were very interested in him. He has just driven over from his college in Illinois for the interview.

Since getting back to the station, Floyd Ward has been talking with *Harold Soloman,* the station manager; *Dick Hebreic,* sales manager; and *Louise Owen,* news director, about Brian and how impressed he was. Floyd is the station's program director. The group felt that *Sharon Johnson,* the senior disc jockey, should also be involved in interviewing Brian. Each of the interviewers was assigned the task of developing questions in the areas of education, experience, motivation, and attitude. Floyd Ward would act as the chairperson. This is the first time they have attempted to select a new employee in this manner, so all are somewhat nervous and unsure about what they should ask. They decided that they had nothing to lose and thought it might work out very well. They also decided to have a meeting after Brian had gone to talk about his qualifications and how well they thought the process had gone.

Bibliography

Books

Adams, J. S. *Interviewing Procedures: A Manual for Survey Interviews*. Chapel Hill: University of North Carolina Press, 1958.

Allport, G. W., P. E. Vernon and L. Gardner. *Study of Values,* 3rd Ed. Boston: Houghton Mifflin, 1960.

American Association of Social Workers (Committee of Chicago Chapter). *Interviews: A Study of the Methods of Analyzing and Recording Social Case Work Interviews*. Chicago: A.A.S.W., 1931.

Amesden, F. M. and N. D. White. *How to Be Successful in the Employment Interview*. Self Published, 1974.

Andersen, K. E. *Persuasion Theory and Practice*. Boston: Allyn & Bacon, 1971.

Anderson, D. and P. Benjaminson. *Investigative Reporting*. Bloomington: Indiana University Press, 1976.

Argyle, M. *Social Encounters: Readings in Social Interaction*. Chicago: Aldine, 1973.

Argyle, M. *Bodily Communication*. New York: International Universities Press, 1975.

Aubry, A. S., Jr. and R. R. Caputo. *Criminal Interrogation*. Springfield, IL: C. C. Thomas, 1965.

Backstrom, C. H. and G. D. Hursh. *Survey Research*. Evanston, IL: Northwestern University Press, 1963.

Baer, W. *Discipline and Discharge Under the Labor Agreement*. New York: American Management Association, 1972.

Baker, R. M., Jr., and G. Phifer. *Salesmanship: Communication, Persuasion, Perception*. Boston: Allyn and Bacon, 1966.

Balinsky, B. and R. Burger. *The Executive Interview: A Bridge to People*. New York: Harper, 1959.

Banaka, W. *Training in Depth Interviewing*. New York: Harper & Row, 1971.

Barbara, D. A. *Art of Listening*. Springfield, IL: C. C. Thomas, 1974.

Barker, L. L. *Communication*. Englewood Cliffs, NJ: Prentice-Hall, 1978.

Barrett, R. S. *Performance Rating*. Chicago: Science Research Associates, 1966.

Bassett, G. A. *Practical Interviewing: A Handbook for Managers*. New York: American Management Association, 1965.

Bellenger, D. N., K. L. Bernhardt and J. L. Goldstucker. *Qualitative Research in Marketing*. Chicago: American Marketing Association, 1976.

Benjamin, A. *The Helping Interview*, 2nd Ed. Boston: Houghton Mifflin, 1974.

Berdie, D. R. and J. F. Anderson. *Questionnaires: Design and Use*. Metuchen, NJ: Scarecrow, 1974.

Berenson, B. and R. Carkuff. *Sources of Gain in Counseling and Psychotherapy*. New York: Holt, Rinehart and Winston, 1967.

Berg, C. *The First Interview with a Psychiatrist*. London: Allen & Unwin, 1955.

Bermask, L. and M. I. Mordan. *Interviewing in Nursing*. New York: Macmillan, 1964.

Berne, E. *What Do You Say After You Say Hello?* New York: Grove Press, 1972.

Bernstein, L., R. S. Bernstein and R. H. Dana. *Interviewing: A Guide for Health Professionals*. New York: Appleton-Century-Crofts, 1974.

Besset, G. A. *Practical Interviewing, A Handbook for Managers*. New York: American Management Association, 1965.

Bettinghaus, E. P. *Persuasive Communication*, 3rd. Ed. New York: Holt, Rinehart and Winston, 1980.

Beveridge, W. E. *Problem Solving Interviews*. London: Allen & Unwin, 1968.

Beveridge, W. E. *The Interview in Staff Appraisal*. London: Allen & Unwin, 1975.

Bingham, W. V. D. and J. Gustad. *How to Interview*, Rev. Ed. New York: Harper, 1959.

Bird, B. *Talking with Patients*, 2nd. Ed. Philadelphia: Lippincott, 1973.

Bittel, L. R. *Performance Portfolio for What Every Supervisor Should Know*. New York: McGraw-Hill, 1974.

Black, J. M. *How to Get Results from Interviewing: A Practical Guide for Operating Management*. New York: McGraw-Hill, 1970.

Blankenship, A. B. *How to Conduct Consumer and Opinion Research*. New York: Harper, 1946.

Bloom, B. S. (Ed.). M. D. Englehart, E. J. Furst, W. H. Hill and D. R. Kratwohl. *A Taxonomy of Educational Objectives: Handbook I, The Cognitive Domain*. London: Longmans, Green, 1956.

Blum, L. H. *Reading Between the Lines: Doctor-Patient Communication*. New York: International Universities Press, 1972.

Bolles, R. N. *The Quick Job Hunting Map: A Fast Way to Help*. Berkeley: Ten Speed Press, 1979.

Bolles, R. N. *Tea Leaves: A New Look at Resumes*. Berkeley: Ten Speed Press, 1976.

Bolles, R. N. *What Color Is Your Parachute?* Berkeley: Ten Speed Press, 1972.

Bradburn, N. M. and S. Sudman. *Improving Interview Method and Questionnaire Design*. San Francisco: Jossey-Bass, 1979.

Brady, J. *The Craft of Interviewing*. New York: Vintage Books, 1977.

Brammer, L. M. *The Helping Relationship: Process and Skills*, 2nd. Ed. Englewood Cliffs, NJ: Prentice-Hall, 1979.

Brian, D. *Murderers and Other Friendly People: The Public and Private Worlds of Interviewers*. New York: McGraw-Hill, 1973.

Brooks, W. D. and P. Emmert. *Interpersonal Communication*, 2nd. Ed. Dubuque, IA: Wm. C. Brown, 1980.

Brown-Carlsen Listening Comprehension Test. New York: Harcourt Brace Jovanovich, 1955.

Brown, L. M. *Client Counseling Competition: Explanation and Consultation Situations*. Chicago: American Bar Association, Law Student Division, 1979.

Browne, M. N. and Keeley, S. M. *Asking the Right Questions*. Englewood Cliffs, NJ: Prentice-Hall, 1981.

Burtt, H. *Principles of Employment Psychology*. Boston: Houghton, 1926.

Cannell, C. F., S. A. Lawson and D. L. Hausser. *A Technique for Evaluating Interviewer Performance: A Manual for Coding and Analyzing Interviewer Behavior from Tape Recordings of Household Interviews*. Ann Arbor, MI: Survey Research Center, Institute for Social Research, 1975.

Cannell, C. F., F. J. Fowler and K. H. Marquis. *The Influence of Interviewer and Respondent: Psychological and Behavioral Variables on the Reporting in Household Interviews*. Washington, D.C.: U. S. Government Printing Office, Public Health Service Publication, Series 2, No. 26, 1968.

Cantril, H. *Gauging Public Opinion*. Princeton, NJ: Princeton University Press, 1944.

Carin. *Creative Questioning and Sensitivity: Listening Techniques*, 2nd. Ed. Columbus, OH: Merrill, 1978.

Carkhuff, R. R. and W. A. Anthony. *The Skills of Helping*. Amherst, MA: Human Resource Development Press, 1979.

Carroll, S. J. and H. Tosi, *Management by Objective*. New York: Macmillan, 1973.

Cicourel, A. *Method and Measurement in Sociology*, New York: Free Press, 1964.

Cohen, W. A. *The Executive's Guide to Finding a Superior Job*. New York: American Management Association, 1978.

Collins, M. *Communication in Health Care*. St. Louis: C. V. Mosby, 1977.

Conducting the Lawful Employment Interview. New York: Executive Enterprises, 1974.

Converse, J. M. and H. Schuman. *Conversations at Random: Survey Research as Interviewers See It*. New York: Wiley, 1974.

Cooper, J. *How to Communicate Policy and Procedure*. New London, CT: National Foremen's Institute, 1956.

Corey, G. *Theory and Practice of Counseling and Psychotherapy*. Monterey, CA: Brooks/Cole, 1977.

Cormier, W. H. and L. S. Cormier. *Interviewing Strategies for Helpers: A Guide to Assessment, Treatment and Evaluation*. Monterey, CA: Brooks/Cole, 1979.

Cornelius, Jr., E. T. *Interview: Listening Comprehension for Advanced Students*. New York: Longman, 1980.

Cottle, T. J. *Private Lives and Public Accounts*. Amherst: University of Mass. Press, 1977.

Couch, E. H. *Joint and Family Interviews in the Treatment of Marital Problems*. New York: Family Service Association of America, 1969.

Cronkite, G. *Public Speaking and Critical Listening*. Redding, MA: Benjamin/Cummings, 1978.

Cross, C. P. (Ed.). *Interviewing and Communication in Social Work*. London: Routledge & Kegan, 1974.

Crystal, J. C. and R. N. Bolles. *Where Do I Go from Here with My Life?* Berkeley: Ten Speed Press, 1978.

Cummings, L. L. and D. P. Schwab. *Performance in Organization*. Glenview, IL: Scott, Foresman, 1973.

Cundiff, M. *Kinesics: The Power of Silent Command*. West Nyack, NY: Parker Publishing, 1972.

Dailey, C. A. and A. M. Madsen. *How to Evaluate People in Business*. New York: McGraw-Hill, 1980.

Darley, J. *The Interview in Counseling, Retraining and Re-Employment Administration*. Washington, D.C.: Department of Labor, 1946.

Davis, J. A. *Elementary Survey Analysis*. Englewood Cliffs, NJ: Prentice-Hall, 1971.

Davis, J. A. *The Interview as Arena: Strategies in Standardized Interviews and Psychotherapy*. Stanford, CA: Stanford University Press, 1971.

Davitz, J. R. *The Language of Emotion*. New York: Academic Press, 1969.

De Schweinitz, E. and K. De Schweinitz. *Interviewing in the Social Services*. London: The Council on Social Work Education, 1962.

Dewey, J. *How We Think*. Lexington, MA: D. C. Heath, 1910.

Dexter, L. A. *Elite and Specialized Interviewing: Handbooks for Research in Political Behavior*. Evanston, IL: Northwestern University Press, 1970.

Dillman, D. A. *Mail and Telephone Surveys: The Total Design Method*. New York: John Wiley & Sons, 1978.

Dittman, A. T. *Interpersonal Messages of Emotion*. New York: Springer, 1973.

Donaghy, W. C. *Beyond Words: An Introduction to Nonverbal Communication*. Dubuque, IA: Gorsuch Scarisbrick, 1980.

Donaho, M. W. and J. L. Meyer. *How to Get the Job You Want: A Guide to Resumes, Interviews, and Job-Hunting Strategy*. Englewood Cliffs, NJ: Prentice-Hall, 1976.

Dorn, E. *Interviews*. San Francisco: Four Seasons Foundation, 1979.

Downs, C., D. Berg and W. A. Linkugel. *The Organizational Communicator*. New York: Harper and Row, 1977.

Downs, C. W., G. P. Smeyak and E. Martin. *Professional Interviewing*. New York: Harper and Row, 1980.

Drake, F. *Manual for Employment Interviewing*. New York: American Management Association, Research Report No. 9, 1946.

Drake, J. D. *Interviewing for Managers: Sizing Up People*. New York: American Management Association, 1972.

Duker, S. *Listening: Readings*. Vol. 1 and 2. New York: The Scarecrow Press, 1966, 1971.

Duncan, Jr., S. and D. W. Fiske *Face-To-Face Interaction: Research, Methods, and Theory*. Hillsdale, NJ: Lawrence Erlbaum Associates, 1977.

Dunnette, M. D. *Personnel Selection and Placement*. Belmont, CA: Wadsworth, 1966.

Edinburg, G. M., N. E. Zinberg, and W. Kelman. *Clinical Interviewing and Counseling*. Englewood Cliffs, NJ: Prentice-Hall, 1975.

Effective Interviewing for the Supervisor. New York: American Management Association, 1965.

Einhorn, L. J., P. H. Bradley and J. E.

Baird, Jr. *Effective Employment Interviewing* Glenview, IL: Scott, Foresman, 1982.

Ekman, P. and W. V. Friesen. *Unmasking the Face*. Englewood Cliffs, NJ: Prentice-Hall, 1975.

Emmert, P. and W. C. Donaghy. *An Introduction to Human Communication*. Reading, MA: Addison-Wesley, 1981.

Enelow, A. J. and S. N. Swisher. *Interviewing and Patient Care*. Oxford: Oxford University Press, 1972.

Equal Employment Opportunity Commission. *Guidelines on Employment Testing Procedures*. Washington, D.C.: U.S. Government Printing Office, 1966.

Erdos, P. L. *Professional Mail Surveys*. New York: McGraw-Hill, 1970.

Erickson, C. E. *The Counseling Interview*. Englewood Cliffs, N.J.: Prentice-Hall, 1950.

Evans, D. R., M. T. Hearn, M. R. Uhlemann and A. E. Ivey. *Essential Interviewing: A Programmed Approach to Effective Communication*. Monterey, CA: Brooks/Cole, 1979.

Family Welfare Association of America. *Interviews, Interviewers and Interviewing*. New York: F.W.A.A., 1931.

Fear, R. A. and B. Jordan. *Employee Evaluation Manual for Interviewers*. New York: The Psychological Corp., 1943.

Fear, R. A., *McGraw-Hill Course in Effective Interviewing*. New York: McGraw-Hill, 1973.

Fear, R. A. *The Evaluation Interview*, Rev. 2nd Ed. New York: McGraw-Hill, 1978.

Fenlason, A. *Essentials in Interviewing: For The Interviewer Offering Professional Services*, Rev. Ed. New York: Harper, 1952.

Fenton, N. *A Guide to the Personal Interview with a Child*. Sacramento: California Bureau of Juvenile Research, Bulletin 10, 1934.

Ferber, R. (Ed.). *Readings in Survey Research*. Chicago: American Marketing Association, 1978.

Figler, H. *Path: A Career Workbook for Liberal Arts Students*, 2nd. Ed. Cranston, RI: Carroll Press, 1979.

Figler, H. *The Complete Job-Search Handbook*. New York: Holt, Rinehart and Winston, 1980.

Fregly, B. *How to Get a Job*. Homewood, IL: ETC Publications, 1974.

Friberg, J. C. *Survey Research and Field Techniques: A Bibliography for the Fieldworker*. Monticello, IL: Council of Planning Librarians, Exchange Bibliography No. 513, 1974.

Frost, D. *I Gave Them a Sword*. New York: William Morrow, 1978.

Gainer, H. N. and S. L. Stark. *Choice or Chance: A Guidebook to Career Planning*. New York: McGraw-Hill, 1978.

Gallup, G. *The Gallup Poll*. Princeton, NJ: The Gallup Organization, 1977.

Garrett, A. M. *Interviewing: Its Principles and Methods*, 2nd Ed. New York: Family Service Association of America, 1972.

Geeting, B. and C. Baxter. *How to Listen Assertively*. New York: Monarch Press, 1978.

Gellerman, S. W. *The Management of Human Resources*. New York: Dryden, 1976.

Genua, R. L. *The Employer's Guide to Interviewing, Strategies & Tactics for Picking a Winner*. Englewood Cliffs, NJ: Prentice-Hall, 1979.

Gibson, J. T. *Experiencing the Inner City*. New York: Harper and Row, 1973.

Gill, M., R. Newman and F. C. Redlich. *The Initial Interview in Psychiatric Practice*. New York: International Universities Press, 1954.

Goffman, E. *Frame Analysis*. New York: Harper and Row, 1974.

Goffman, E. *The Presentation of Self in Everyday Life*. New York: Doubleday, 1959.

Gootnick, D. *Getting a Better Job*. New York: McGraw-Hill, 1978.

Gordon, R. *Interviewing: Strategy, Techniques and Tactics*, Rev. Ed. Homewood, IL: Dorsey Press, 1980.

Gordon, T. *Leader Effectiveness Training*. New York: Bantam Books, 1977.

Gottschalk, L. A. (Ed.). *Comparative Psycholinguistic Analysis of Two Psycho-*

therapeutic Interviews. New York: International Universities Press, 1961.

Goyer, R. S. and M. Z. Sincoff. *Interviewing Methods*. Dubuque, IA: Kendall/Hunt, 1977.

Goyer, R. S., W. C. Redding and J. T. Rickey. *Interviewing Principles and Techniques: A Project Text*. Dubuque, IA: Wm. C. Brown, 1968.

Greico, W. *O-My-God an Interview*. Geneva, IL: Paladin House, 1978.

Groisser, P. *How to Use the Fine Art of Questioning*. Englewood Cliffs, NJ: Prentice-Hall, 1964.

Group for the Advancement of Psychiatry. *Reports in Psychotherapy: Initial Interviews*. New York: Group for the Advancement of Psychiatry, Report 49, 1961.

Groves, R. M. and R. L. Kahn. *Comparing Telephone and Personal Interview Surveys*. New York: Academic Press, 1979.

Groves, R. M. and R. L. Kahn. *Surveys by Telephone: A National Comparison with Personal Interviews*. New York: Academic Press, 1979.

Guion, R. M. *Personnel Testing*. New York: McGraw-Hill, 1965.

Hansen, M. H., W. N. Hurwitz and W. G. Madow. *Sample Survey Methods and Theory*. Vol. 1. New York: Wiley, 1953.

Hariton, T. *Interview!: The Executive's Guide to Selecting the Right Personnel*. New York: Hastings House, 1970.

Harral, S. *Keys to Successful Interviewing*. Norman, OK: University of Oklahoma Press, 1954.

Harrington, H. F. and T. T. Frankenberg. *Essentials in Journalism*. Boston: Ginn and Co., 1912.

Harrison, R. P. *Beyond Words: An Introduction to Nonverbal Communication*. Englewood Cliffs, NJ: Prentice-Hall, 1974.

Hayakawa, S. I. *Language in Thought and Action*, 2nd Ed. New York: Harcourt, Brace and World, 1964.

Hazen, D. W. *Interviewing Sinners and Saints*. Portland, OR: Binsfords & Mort, 1942.

Headington, B. J. *Communication in the Counseling Relationship*. Cranston, RI: Carroll Press, 1979.

Hein, E. C. *Communication in Nursing Practice*. Boston: Little Brown, 1973.

Henley, N. M. *Body Politics: Power, Sex, and Nonverbal Communication*. Englewood Cliffs, NJ: Prentice-Hall, 1977.

Herbert, H. et al. *Interviewing in Social Research*. Chicago: University of Chicago Press, 1954.

Herzel, C. *Appraising Executive Performance*. New York: American Management Association, 1958.

Higginbotham, J. and K. K. Cox (Eds.). *Focus Group Interviews: A Reader*. Chicago: American Marketing Association, 1979.

Hirsch, R. O. *Listening: A Way to Process Information Aurally*. Dubuque, IA: Gorsuch Scarisbrick, 1979.

Hopkins, D. S. *Marketing Performance Evaluation*. New York: The Conference Board, 1979.

Hovland, C. I., I. Janis and H. H. Kelley. *Communication and Persuasion*. New Haven: Yale University Press, 1953.

How to Conduct a Selection Interview. New York: Preston, 1975.

How to Conduct an Appraisal Interview. New York: Preston, 1975.

Hunkins, F. P. *Questioning Strategies and Techniques*. Boston: Allyn and Bacon, 1972.

Hunkins, F. P. *Involving Students in Questioning*. Boston: Allyn and Bacon, 1976.

Hutchinson, M. A. and S. E. Spooner. *Job Search Preparedness Barometer*. Bethlehem, PA: College Placement Council, 1975.

Hyman, H. H. et al. *Interviewing in Social Research*. Chicago: University of Chicago Press, 1954.

Hyman, H. H. *Survey Design and Analysis*. Glencoe, IL: Free Press, 1955.

Hyman, R. T. *Strategic Questioning*. Englewood Cliffs, NJ: Prentice-Hall, 1979.

Ilyin, D. *Ilyin Oral Interview*. Rowley, MA: Newbury House, 1976.

Inbau, F. E. and J. E. Reid. *Criminal Inter-*

rogation and Confessions 2nd Ed., Baltimore, MD: Williams & Wilkins, 1967.

Interviews, Interviewers and Interviewing in Social Case Work. New York: Family Welfare Association of America, 1931.

Ivey, A. and J. Authier. *Microcounseling: Innovations in Interviewing, Counseling, Psychotherapy & Psychoeducation*, 2nd Ed. Springfield, IL: C. C. Thomas, 1978.

Jackson, M. *Recruiting, Interviewing, and Selecting: A Manual for Line Managers*. New York: McGraw-Hill, 1972.

Jackson, T. *Twenty-Eight Days to a Better Job*. New York: Hawthorn, 1977.

Jacoby, J. *Handbook of Questionnaire Construction*. Cambridge: Ballinger, 1979.

Janis, I. L. and C. I. Hovland (Eds.). *Personality and Persuasibility*. New Haven: Yale University Press, 1959.

Jourard, S. M. *Self-Disclosure: An Experimental Analysis of The 'Transparent Self'* New York: Wiley-Interscience, 1971.

Kadushin, A. *The Social Work Interview*. New York: Columbia University Press, 1972.

Kahn, R. L. and C. F. Cannell. *The Dynamics of Interviewing: Theory Techniques and Cases*. New York: John Wiley & Sons, 1957.

Karlins, M. and H. I. Abelson. *Persuasion: How Opinions and Attitudes Are Changed*, 2nd Ed. New York: Springer, 1970.

Keller, H. T., R. Simons, G. Wildman and R. Zahn. *Questions! Questions! Questions!* Glassboro, NJ: The Curriculum Development Council for Southern New Jersey, 1967.

Kellogg, M. S. *What to Do About Performance Appraisal*. New York: American Management Association, 1965.

Kenagy, H. and C. Yoakum. *The Selection and Training of Salesmen*. New York: McGraw-Hill, 1925.

Kendon, A., R. M. Harris and K. M. Ritchie. *Organization of Behavior in Face-To-Face Interaction*. The Hague: Mouton, 1975.

Kephart, N. C. *The Employment Interview in Industry*. New York: McGraw-Hill, 1952.

Kinsey, A. C. et al. *Sexual Behavior in the Human Male*. Philadelphia: W. B. Saunders, 1948.

Kirkpatrick, C. A. *Salesmanship: Helping Prospects Buy*. Cincinnati, OH: South-Western, 1956.

Kish, L. *Survey Sampling*. New York: John Wiley, 1965.

Kleinke, C. L. *First Impressions: The Psychology of Encountering Others*. Englewood Cliffs, NJ: Prentice-Hall, 1975.

Knapp, M. L. *Nonverbal Communication in Human Interaction*, 2nd. Ed. New York: Holt, Rinehart and Winston, 1978.

Knapp, M. *Social Intercourse: From Greetings to Goodbye*. Boston: Allyn and Bacon, 1978.

Komar, J. J. *The Interview Game: Winning Strategies for the Job Seeker*. Chicago: Follett, 1979.

Koontz, H. *Appraising Managers as Managers*. New York: McGraw-Hill, 1971.

Koos, L. V. *The Questionnaire in Education*. New York: Macmillan, 1928.

Korda, M. *Power: How to Get It, How to Use It*. New York: Random House, 1975.

Krathwohl, D. R., B. S. Bloom and B. A. Masia. *A Taxonomy of Educational Objectives: Handbook II, the Affective Domain*. New York: David MacKay, 1964.

Kron, T. *Communication in Nursing*. Philadelphia: W. B. Saunders, 1972.

Laird, D. *Psychology of Selecting Employees*. New York: McGraw-Hill, 1937.

Langdon, G. and I. W. Stout. *Teacher-Parent Interviews*. Englewood Cliffs, NJ: Prentice-Hall, 1954.

Lansing, J. B. and J. N. Morgan. *Economic Survey Methods*. Ann Arbor, MI: Survey Research Center, Institute for Social Research, 1971.

Lasswell, H. D. *Psychopathology and Politics*. Chicago: University of Chicago Press, 1930.

Lathrop, R. *Who's Hiring Who?*, 3rd Ed. Berkeley: Ten Speed Press, 1977.

Lathrop, R. *Don't Use a Resume*. Berkeley: Ten Speed Press, 1980.

Lauzar, G. *The Job Interview*. New York: State Mutual Books, 1976.

Law, S. G. *Therapy Through Interview*. New York: McGraw-Hill, 1948.

Lazer, R. I. and W. S. Wilkstrom. *Appraising Managerial Performance: Current Practices and Future Directions*. New York: The Conference Board, Inc., 1977.

Leathers, D. G. *Nonverbal Communication Systems*. Boston: Allyn and Bacon, 1976.

Lefton, R. E. and M. Sherberg. *Effective Selling Through Psychology*. New York: Wiley Interscience, 1972.

Levin, A. *Talk Back to Your Doctor: How to Demand (& Recognize) High Quality Health Care*. New York: Doubleday, 1975.

Lockerby, F. K. *Communication for Nurses*, 3rd Ed. St. Louis: C. V. Mosby, 1968.

Long, L. et al. *Questioning Skills for the Helping Process*. Monterey, CA: Brooks/Cole, in press.

Lopez, F. M. *Evaluating Employee Performance*. Chicago: Public Personnel Association, 1968.

Lopez, F. M. *Personnel Interviewing: The Working Woman's Resource Book*, 2nd Ed. New York: McGraw-Hill, 1975.

Lundberg, G. A. *Social Research: A Study in Methods of Gathering Data*. London: Longmans, Green, 1929.

Mace, A. E. *Sample-Size Determination*. Stamford, CT: Reinhold, 1964.

MacKinnon, R. A. and R. Michels. *Psychiatric Interview in Clinical Practice*. Philadelphia: Saunders, 1971.

Mahler, W. *How Effective Executives Interview*. Homewood, IL: Dow Jones-Richard D. Irwin, 1976.

Maier, N. R. F., et al. *Superior-Subordinate Communication in Management*. New York: American Management Association, 1961.

Maier, N. R. F. *The Appraisal Interview: Objectives, Methods, and Skills*. New York: John Wiley & Sons, 1965.

Maier, N. R. F. *The Appraisal Interview: Three Basic Approaches*. Iowa City, IA: University Associates, 1976.

Management Performance Appraisal Programs. Washington, D.C.: The Bureau of National Affairs, 1974.

Mandell, M. M. *Employment Interviewing*. Washington, D.C.: U. S. Civil Service Commission, Personnel Methods Series No. 5, 1956.

Mandell, M. M. *The Employment Interview*. New York: American Management Association, 1961.

Mandell, M. M. *The Selection Process*. New York: American Management Association, 1965.

Marcosson, I. F. *Adventures in Interviewing*. New York: Dodd, Mead & Co., 1923.

Martin, D. *The Executive's Guide to Handling a Press Interview*. Philadelphia: Pilot Books, 1977.

Maslow, A. *Motivation and Personality*. New York: McGraw-Hill, 1970.

Matarazzo, J. D. and A. N. Weins. *The Interview: Research on Its Anatomy and Structure*. Chicago: Aldine Publishing Co., 1972.

McCombs, M., D. L. Shaw and D. Grey. *Handbook of Reporting Methods*. Boston: Houghton-Mifflin, 1976.

McGregor, D. *The Professional Manager*. New York: McGraw-Hill, 1967.

McGregor, D. *The Human Side of Enterprise*. New York: McGraw-Hill, 1960.

Meares, A. *The Medical Interview*. Springfield, IL: C. C. Thomas, 1957.

Mehrabian, A. *Nonverbal Communication*. Chicago: Aldine Publishing Co., 1972.

Merrihue, W. V. *Managing by Communication*. New York: McGraw-Hill Book Company, 1960.

Merton, R. K., M. Fiske and P. Kendall. *The Focused Interview*. New York: Free Press, 1961.

Metzler, K. *Creative Interviewing: The Writer's Guide to Gathering Information by Asking Questions*. Englewood Cliffs, NJ: Prentice-Hall, 1977.

Meyer, J. L. and M. W. Donahue *Get the Right Person for the Right Job: Managing Interviews and Selecting Employees*. Englewood Cliffs, NJ: Prentice-Hall, 1979.

Meyer, P. *Precision Journalism*. Bloomington: Indiana University Press, 1973.

Mills, E. P. *Listening: Key to Communication*. New York: Van Nostrand Reinhold, 1974.

Moffat, T. L. *Selection Interviewing for Managers*. New York: Harper & Row, 1979.

Molyneaux, D. and V. W. Lane *Effective Interviewing: Techniques and Analysis*. Boston: Allyn and Bacon, 1982.

Moore, B. V. *The Personal Interview*. New York: Personal Research Federation, 1928.

Morgan, H. H. *The Interviewer's Manual*. New York: Harcourt Brace Jovanovich, 1973.

Moser, C. A. and G. Kalton *Survey Methods in Social Investigation*. New York: Heinemann Educational Books, 1971.

Muehl, D. (Ed.). *A Manual for Coders*. Ann Arbor, MI: Survey Research Center, 1961.

Nash, K. *Get the Best of Yourself: How to Discover Your Success Pattern and Make It Pay Off*. New York: Grosset & Dunlap, 1976.

National Opinion Research Center. *Interviewing for NORC*. Denver: N.O.R.C., 1947.

Neely, T. E. *A Study of Error in the Interview*. New York: Columbia University Press, 1937.

Nichols, R. and L. A. Stevens *Are You Listening?* New York: McGraw-Hill, 1957.

Noer, D. *How to Beat the Employment Game*. Radnor, PA: Chilton, 1975.

O'Brien, M. J. *Communications and Relationships in Nursing*. St. Louis: C. V. Mosby, 1974.

OFCC Affirmative Action Guidelines. Washington, D.C.: Bureau of National Affairs, 1972.

Oldfield, R. C. *The Psychology of the Interview*. London: Methuen and Co., Ltd., 1951.

O'Leary, L. R. *Interviewing for the Decisionmaker*. Chicago: Nelson-Hall, 1976.

Olson, R. F. *Managing the Interview*. New York: John Wiley & Sons, 1980.

Oppenheim, A. N. *Questionnaire Design and Attitude Measurement*. New York: Basic Books, 1966.

Orlando, I. J. *The Dynamic Nurse-Patient Relationship*. New York: G. P. Putnam's Sons, 1961.

Parten, M. *Surveys, Polls, and Samples: Practical Procedures*. New York: Harper, 1950.

Patterson, C. H. *Theories of Counseling and Psychotherapy*. New York: Harper, 1966.

Payne, S. L. *The Art of Asking Questions*. Princeton, NJ: Princeton University Press, 1951.

Peplau, H. *Interpersonal Relations in Nursing*. New York: G. P. Putnam's Sons, 1952.

Perls, F. S. *Gestalt Therapy Verbatim*. Lafayette, CA: Real People Press, 1969.

Personnel Policies Forum No. 104. *Management Performance Appraisal Programs*. Washington, D.C.: The Bureau of National Affairs, 1974.

Peskin, D. B. *The Art of Job Hunting*. Cleveland: World Publishing, 1967.

Peskin, D. B. *Human Behavior and Employment Interviewing*. New York: American Management Association, 1971.

Pfiffner, J. M. *Supervision of Personnel*, 2nd. Ed. Englewood Cliffs, NJ: Prentice-Hall, 1958.

Phillips, B. S. *Social Research, Strategy and Tactics*. New York: Macmillan, 1966.

Pluckhan, M. L. *Human Communication: The Matrix of Nursing*. New York: McGraw-Hill, 1978.

Polansky, N. A. *Ego Psychology and Communication: Theory for the Interview*. Chicago: Aldine, 1971.

Pope, B. *The Mental Health Interview: Research and Application*. New York: Pergamon, 1979.

Powell, C. R. *Career Planning & Placement Today*, 2nd Ed. Dubuque, IA: Kendall-Hunt, 1978.

Presson, H. *The Student Journalist and Interviewing*, Rev. Ed. New York: Richards Rosen Press, 1979.

Privacy Protection Study Commission, *Personal Privacy in an Information Society*. Washington, D.C.: U.S. Government Printing Office, 1977.

Raia, A. P. *Managing by Objectives*. Glenview, IL: Scott, Foresman, 1974.

Redding, W. C., and G. A. Sanborn, (Eds.) *Business and Industrial Communication —A Source Book*. New York: Harper, 1964.

Reik, T. *Listening with the Third Ear*. New York: Farrar, Straus & Girous, 1972.

Reynolds, B. C. *An Experiment in Short-Contact Interviewing*. Northampton, MA:

The Smith College School for Social Work, 1932.

Rich, J. *Interviewing Children and Adolescents*. New York: Macmillan, 1968.

Richardson, S. A., B. S. Dohrenwend and D. Klein. *Interviewing: Its Forms and Functions*. New York: Basic Books, 1965.

Richetto, G. M. and J. P. Zima. *Fundamentals of Interviewing*. Chicago: Science Research Associates, 1976.

Riesman, D. *Abundance for What? And Other Essays*. New York: Doubleday, 1964.

Rioch, M. W., R. Coulter and D. M. Weinberger, *Dialogues with Therapists*. San Francisco: Jossey-Bass, 1976.

Rivers, W. L. *Finding Facts*. Englewood Cliffs, NJ: Prentice-Hall, 1975.

Robertson, J. *How To Win in an Interview*. Englewood Cliffs, NJ: Prentice-Hall, 1978.

Robinson, W. P. and S. J. Rackstraw *A Question of Answers*. Boston: Routledge and Kegan, 1972.

Roethlisberger, F. J. and W. J. Dickson *Management and the Worker*. Cambridge: Harvard University Press, 1946.

Rogers, C. R. *Counseling and Psychotherapy*. Boston: Houghton Mifflin, 1942.

Rogers, C. R. *On Becoming a Person*. Boston: Houghton Mifflin, 1961.

Rogers, J. L. and W. L. Fortson *Fair Employment Interviewing*. Reading, MA: Addison-Wesley, 1976.

Rokeach, M. *Beliefs, Attitudes and Values*. San Francisco: Jossey-Bass, 1968.

Rosenberg, M. *The Logic of Survey Analysis*. New York: Basic Books, 1968.

Rosenfeld, L. B. and J. M. Civikly *With Words Unspoken*. New York: Holt, Rinehart and Winston, 1976.

Rosenthal, R., J. Hall, D. Archer, R. Matteo and P. Rogers *Sensitivity to Non-Verbal Communication*. Baltimore: Johns-Hopkins University Press, 1979.

Rosnow, R. L. and E. J. Robinson *Experiments in Persuasion*. New York: Academic Press, 1967.

Royal, R. F. and S. R. Schutt *The Gentle Art of Interviewing and Interrogation: A Professional Manual and Guide*. Englewood Cliffs, NJ: Prentice-Hall, 1976.

Rubin, I. and E. Rose *The Power of Listening*. New York: McGraw-Hill, 1978.

Ruesch, J. *Therapeutic Communication*. New York: Norton, 1961.

Sachs, B. *The Student, the Interview and the Curriculum*. New York: Houghton Mifflin, 1966.

Samovar, L. A. and S. A. Hellweg *Interviewing: A Communicative Approach*. Dubuque, IA: Gorsuch Scarisbrick, 1982.

Sartain, A. Q. and A. W. Baker *The Supervisor and His Job*. New York: McGraw-Hill, 1965.

Schachter, S. *The Psychology of Affiliation*. Stanford, CA: Stanford University Press, 1959.

Scheflen, A. E. *Communicational Structure: Analysis of a Psychotherapy Transaction*. Bloomington: Indiana University Press, 1973.

Scheflen, A. E. *How Behavior Means*. New York: Anchor Books, 1974.

Scheflen, A. E. *Human Territories: How We Behave in Space-Time*. Englewood Cliffs, NJ: Prentice-Hall, 1976.

Scheflen, A. E. and A. Scheflen *Body Language and Social Order: Communication as Behavioral Control*. Englewood Cliffs, NJ: Prentice-Hall, 1972.

Scheidel, T. M. *Persuasive Speaking*. Glenview, IL: Scott, Foresman, 1967.

Schneider, A. E., W. C. Donaghy and P. J. Newman *Organizational Communication*. New York: McGraw-Hill, 1975.

Schubert, M. *Interviewing in Social Work Practice: An Introduction*. New York: Council on Social Work Education, 1971.

Schulman, E. D. *Intervention in Human Services*, 2nd Ed. St. Louis: Mosby, 1978.

Seeman, J. *The Case of Jim*. Circle Pines, MN: American Guidance Service, 1957.

Sereno, K. K. and E. M. Bodaken. TRANS-PER: *Understanding Human Communication*. Boston: Houghton Mifflin, 1975.

Sevareid, A. E. *Conversations with Eric Sevareid*. Washington, D.C.: Public Affairs Press, 1977.

Shaeffer, R. G. *Nondiscrimination in Em-

ployment: 1973–1975. New York: The Conference Board, 1975.

Sharnia, P. C. *Interview and Techniques of Interviewing: A Selected Research Bibliography* (1930–1966). Monticello, IL.: Council of Planning Librarians, Exchange Bibliography, No. 715, 1974.

Sherwood, H. *The Journalistic Interview*, Rev. Ed. New York: Harper & Row, 1972.

Shore, N. A. *How to Test and Hire for the Professional Office*. Philadelphia: Lippincott, 1967.

Shouksmith, G. *Assessment Through Interviewing: A Handbook for Individual Interviewing and Group Selection Techniques*, 2nd Ed. New York: Pergamon, 1977.

Sidney, E. and M. Brown *The Skills of Interviewing*. London: Tavistock Publishing, 1961.

Siegman, A. W. and B. Pope *Studies in Dyadic Communication: Proceedings of a Research Conference on the Interview*. Elmsford, NY: Pergamon, 1972.

Sigal, L. V. *Reporters and Officials*. Lexington, MA: D. C. Heath, 1973.

Simons, H. W. *Persuasion: Understanding, Practice, and Analysis*. Reading, MA: Addison-Wesley, 1976.

Sitzmann, M. and R. Garcia *Successful Interviewing: A Practical Guide for the Applicant and Interviewer*. Skokie, IL: National Textbook Company, 1978.

Sjoberg, G. and R. Nett *A Methodology for Social Research*. New York: Harper, 1968.

Slavens, T. P., *Informational Interviews and Questions*. Metuchen, NJ: Scarecrow Press, 1978.

Small, I. F. *Introduction to the Clinical History*. New York: Medical Examination Publishing, 1970.

Smith, G. H. *Motivation Research in Advertising and Marketing*. New York: McGraw-Hill, 1954.

Smith, H. P. and P. J. Brouwer *Performance Appraisal and Human Development: A Practical Guide to Effective Management*. Reading, MA: Addison-Wesley, 1977.

Smith, J. M. *Interviewing in Market and Social Research*. London: Routledge & Kegan, 1972.

Speier, M. *How to Observe Face-to-Face Communication: A Sociological Introduction*. Pacific Palisades: Goodyear Publishing, 1973.

Staff of the University of Michigan. *Interviewer's Manual*. Rev. Ed. Ann Arbor, MI: Survey Research Center, Institute for Social Research, 1976.

Stano, M. E. and N. L. Reinsch, Jr. *Communication in Interviews*. Englewood Cliffs, NJ: Prentice-Hall, 1982.

Steinmetz, L. *Interviewing Skills for Supervisory Personnel*. Reading, MA: Addison-Wesley, 1971.

Stephen, F. F. and P. J. McCarthy. *Sampling Opinions: An Analysis of Survey Procedure*. New York: John Wiley & Sons, 1958.

Stermbach, J. *Group Interviewing*. Madison, WI: University of Wisconsin School of Social Work, 1965.

Stevenson, I. *The Diagnostic Interview*, 2nd Ed. New York: Harper and Row, 1971.

Stewart, C. *Interviewing Principles and Practices: A Project Text*. Dubuque, IA: Kendall-Hunt, 1980.

Stewart, C. J. and W. B. Cash, Jr. *Interviewing: Principles and Practices*, 2nd Ed. Dubuque, IA: Wm. C. Brown, 1978.

Stewart, C. J. and W. B. Cash, Jr. *Interviewing: Principles and Practices*, 3rd Ed. Dubuque, IA: Wm. C. Brown, 1982.

Still, R. R., E. W. Cundiff and N. A. P. Govoni *Sales Management*, 3rd Ed. Englewood Cliffs, NJ: Prentice-Hall, 1976.

Stone, C. H. and W. E. Kendall *Effective Personnel Selection*. Englewood Cliffs, NJ: Prentice-Hall, 1956.

Strong, Jr., E. K. *Psychology of Selling and Advertising*. New York: McGraw-Hill, 1925.

Sudman, S. *Reducing the Costs of Surveys*. Chicago: Aldine, 1967.

Sudman, S. *Applied Sampling*. New York: Academic Press, 1976.

Sudman, S. and N. M. Bradburn *Response Effects in Surveys: A Review and Synthesis*. Chicago: Aldine, 1974.

Sullivan, H. S. *The Psychiatric Interview* (Helen S. Perry and Mary L. Gawel Eds.). New York: W. W. Norton, 1970.

Sund, R. B. and A. Carin *Creative Questioning and Sensitive Listening Techniques: A Self Concept Approach*, 2nd Ed. Columbus, OH: Merrill, 1978.

The Equal Opportunity Employment Act of 1972. Washington, D.C.: Government Printing Office, 1972.

Thompson, J. M. and A. C. Bowers *Clinical Manual of Health Assessment*. St. Louis: Mosby, 1980.

Thompson, L. *Interview Aids and Trade Questions for Employment Offices*. New York: Harper, 1936.

Thompson, M. R. *Why Should I Hire You? How to Get the Job You Really Want!* New York: Harcourt Brace Jovanovich, 1977.

Thorndike, R. *Personnel Selection*. New York: John Wiley, 1949.

Torgerson, W. S. *Theory and Methods of Scaling*, 2nd Ed. New York: John Wiley, 1965.

Truax, C. B. and R. R. Carkhuff *Toward Effective Counseling and Psychotherapy*. Chicago: Aldine, 1967.

Turner, D. R. *Employment Interviewer*, 6th Ed. New York: Arco, 1968.

Udow, A. B. *The "Interviewer-Effect" in Public Opinion and Market Research Surveys*. New York: Archives of Psychology, 1942.

Ujhely, G. B. *Determinants of the Nurse-Patient Relationship*. New York: Springer, 1968.

U.S. National Center for Health Services Research *Experiments in Interviewing Techniques*. NCHSR Research Report, 78–7. Hyattsville, MD: U.S. National Center for Health Service Research, 1977.

Van Meter, C. H. *Principles of Police Interrogation*. Springfield, IL: C. C. Thomas, 1973.

Von Cranach, M. *Nonverbal Social Communication*. New York: Academic Press, 1974.

Warwick, D. P. and C. A. Lininger *The Sample Survey: Theory and Practice*. New York: McGraw-Hill, 1975.

Weaver, C. *Human Listening*. Indianapolis: The Bobbs-Merrill Co., 1972.

Weber, G. H. et al. *Notetaking and Study Skills*, Ridgewood, NJ: Forkner, 1977.

Webster, E. C. *Decision Making in the Employment Interview*. Montreal: Montreal Industrial Relations Center, 1964.

Weinberg, E. *Community Surveys with Local Talent: A Handbook*. Denver: NORC, 1971.

Weinland, J. D., and M. V. Gross *Personnel Interviewing*. New York: Ronald Press, 1952.

Weiss, C. H. *Validity of Interview Responses of Welfare Mothers: Final Report*. Bureau of Applied Social Research, New York: Columbia University, 1968.

Wellman, F. L. *The Art of Cross Examination*. New York: Macmillan, 1924.

Whisler, T. L. and S. F. Harper *Performance Appraisal: Research and Practice*. New York: Holt, Rinehart & Winston, 1962.

White, P. *Market Analysis*. New York: McGraw-Hill, 1925.

Whyte, W. F. *Street Corner Society*. Chicago: University of Chicago Press, 1955.

Whyte, W. H. *Is Anybody Listening?* New York: Simon & Schuster, 1952.

Wicks, R. J. and E. H. Josephs, Jr. *Techniques in Interviewing for Law Enforcement and Corrections Personnel: A Programmed Text*. Springfield, IL: C. C. Thomas, 1977.

Wiener, M. and A. Mehrabian *Language Within Language: Immediacy, a Channel in Verbal Communication*. New York: Appleton-Century-Crofts, 1968.

Wikstrom, W. S. *Managing by — and With — Objectives*. New York: The Conference Board, 1968.

Wolseley, R. E. *The Professional Job Hunting System*. Englewood Cliffs, NJ: Performance Dynamics, 1970.

Woody, R. H. *Psychobehavioral Counseling and Therapy: Integrating Behavioral and Insight Techniques*. New York: Appleton-Century-Crofts, 1971.

Woody, R. H. and J. D. Woody (Eds.). *Clinical Assessment in Counseling and Psy-*

chotherapy. New York: Appleton-Century-Crofts, 1972.

Wundt, W. *The Language of Gestures*. The Hague: Mouton, 1973.

Yates, F. *Sampling Methods for Censuses and Surveys*, 3rd Ed. New York: Hafner, 1960.

Yates, V. *Listening and Note-Taking*, 2nd Ed. New York: McGraw-Hill, 1979.

Young, P. V. *Interviewing in Social Work: A Sociological Analysis*. New York: McGraw-Hill, 1935.

Young, P. V. *Scientific Social Surveys and Research*. Englewood Cliffs, NJ: Prentice-Hall, 1949.

Zelko, H. P. and H. J. O'Brien *Management-Employee Communication in Action*. Cleveland: Harold Allen, 1957.

Zelko, H. P. and F. E. X. Dance *Business and Professional Speech Communication*. New York: Holt, Rinehart and Winston, 1965.

Zimbardo, P. and E. B. Ebbensen. *Influencing Attitudes and Changing Behavior*. Reading, MA: Addison-Wesley, 1969.

Zunin, L. and N. Zunin, *Contact: The First Four Minutes*. Los Angeles: Nash Publishing.

Articles

Abbate, C. A. "Security Interviewing in Business." *Office*, 88 (1978): 50–51.

Aguilera, D. C. "Relationship Between Physical Contact and Verbal Interaction Between Nurses and Patients." *Journal of Psychiatric Nursing*. 5 (1967): 5–21.

Allan, P. and S. Rosenberg "Formulating Usable Objectives for Manager Performance Appraisal." *Personnel Journal*, 57 (1978): 626–629.

Allen, B. V., A. N. Weins, W. Weitman and G. Saslow "Effects of Warm-Cold Set on Interviewee Speech." *Journal of Consulting Psychology*, 29 (1965): 480–482.

Allen, I. L. "Detecting Respondents Who Fake and Confuse Information about Question Areas on Surveys." *Journal of Applied Psychology*, 50 (1968): 523–528.

Alexander, D. C., D. F. Faules and D. M. Jabusch "Special Reports: The Effects of Basic Speech Course Training on Ability to Role-Play an Employment Interview," *Central States Speech Journal*, 25 (1974): 303–306.

Alpander, G. G. "Training First-Line Supervisors to Criticize Constructively." *Personnel Journal*, 59 (1980): 216–221.

Andler, E. C. "Pre-planned Questions for Efficient Interviewing." *Personnel Journal*, 55 (1976): 8–10.

Apfelbaum, S. "The Lawyer in Conference with His Client." *Communication Quarterly*, 2 (November, 1954): 15–16.

Bahn, C. "Expanding Use of the Exit Interview." *Personnel Journal*, 44 (1965): 620.

Bailer, B., L. Bailey and J. Stevens "Measures of Interviewer Bias and Variance." *Journal of Marketing Research*, 14 (1977): 337–343.

Baird, J. E. and G. K. Wieting "Nonverbal Communication Can Be a Motivational Tool." *Personnel Journal*, 58 (Sept., 1979): 607–610.

Ball, R. R. "What's the Answer to Performance Appraisal?" *The Personnel Administrator*, 23 (1978): 43–46.

Barath, A. and C. F. Cannell "Effect of Interviewer's Voice Intonation." *Public Opinion Quarterly*, 40 (1976): 370–373.

Baxter, J. C., E. P. Winters and R. E. Hammer "Gestural Behavior During a Brief Interview as a Function of Cognitive Variables." *Journal of Personality and Social Psychology*, 8 (1968): 303–307.

Bell, E. P. "The Interview." *Journalism Quarterly*, 1 (1924): 13–18.

Belt, J. A. "Polygraph Usage Among Major U.S. Corporations." *Personnel Journal*, 57 (1978): 80–86.

Benson, P. G. and P. S. Krois "The Polygraph in Employment: Some Unresolved Issues." *Personnel Journal*, 24 (1979): 616–621.

Berlo, D. K. "A Question of Style." *The*

Personnel Administrator, 24 (Dec., 1979): 33–37.

Blair, E. "More on the Effects of Interviewer's Voice Intonation." *Public Opinion Quarterly*, 41 (1977–78): 544–548.

Boekelheide, P. D. "Diagnostic/Therapeutic Preabortion Interview." *Journal of the American Coll. Health Association*, 27 (1978): 157–160.

Bogert, J. "Learning the Applicant's Background Through Confidential Investigations." *Personnel Journal*, 55 (1976): 272.

Boncarosky, L. D. "Guidelines to Corrective Discipline." *Personnel Journal*, 58 (1979): 698–702.

Boomer, D. S. "Speech Dysfluencies and Body Movement in Interviews." *Journal of Nervous and Mental Disease*, 136 (1963): 263–266.

Boomer, D. S. and A. T. Dittmann "Speech Rate, Filled Pause, and Body Movement in Interviews," *Journal of Nervous and Mental Disease*, 139 (1964): 324–327.

Boucher, M. L. "Effect of Seating Distance on Interpersonal Attraction in an Interview Situation." *Journal of Consulting and Clinical Psychology*, 38 (1972): 15–19.

Bowman, J. T. and G. T. Roberts "Counselor Trainee Anxiety During Counseling." *Journal of Consulting Psychology*, 26 (1979): 85–88.

Bramson, R. and N. Parlette "Methods of Data Collection for Decision Making." *Personnel Journal*, 57 (May, 1978): 243–246.

Bridge, R. G., et al. "Interviewing Changes Attitudes—Sometimes." *Public Opinion Quarterly*, 41 (1977): 56–64.

Brown, L. D. and R. Tandon "Interviews as Catalysts in a Community Setting." *Journal of Applied Psychology*, 63 (1978): 197–205.

Bruneau, T. J. "Communicative Silences: Forms and Functions." *Journal of Communication*, 23 (1973): 17–46.

Bucalo, J. "The Balanced Approach to Successful Screening Interviews." *Personnel Journal*, 57 (1978): 420–426.

Buck, R. "A Test of Nonverbal Receiving Ability: Preliminary Studies." *Human Communication Research*, 2 (1976): 162–171.

Burger, C. "How to Meet the Press." *Harvard Business Review*, 53 (1975): 62–70.

Burke, R. J. et al. "Characteristics of Effective Employee Performance Review and Development Interviews: Replication and Extension." *Personnel Psychology*, 31 (1978): 903–919.

Burke, R. J. and D. S. Wilcox "Characteristics of Effective Employee Performance Review and Development Interviews." *Personnel Psychology*, 22 (1969): 291–305.

Burton, G. E. "101 Ways to Discriminate Against Equal Employment Opportunity." *The Personnel Administrator*, 22 (1977): 42–48.

Butterfield, G. "Interjudge Reliability for Formal Aspects of Interviewee Communication." *Perceptual and Motor Skills*, 31 (1970) 311–316.

Buzzotta, V. R. and R. E. Lefton "How Healthy is Your Performance Appraisal System?" *The Personnel Administrator*, 23 (1978): 48–51.

Byham, W. C. "Common Selection Problems Can Be Overcome." *The Personnel Administrator*, 23 (1978): 42–47.

Cameron, P. and J. Anderson "Effects of Introductory Phrases and Tonal-Facial Suggestion Upon Question-Elicited Responses." *Psychological Reports*, 22 (1968): 233–234.

Campbell, J. P., M. D. Dunnette, R. D. Arvey and H. V. Hellervick "The Development and Evaluation of Behaviorally Based Rating Scales." *Journal of Applied Psychology*, 57 (1973): 15–22.

Cangemi, J. P. and J. C. Claypool "Complimentary Interviews: A System for Rewarding Outstanding Employees." *Personnel Journal*, 57 (1978): 87–90.

Cannell, C. F. and R. L. Kahn. "Interviewing." in G. Lindzey and E. Aronson (eds.). *Handbook of Social Psychology* (Vol. 2). Reading, MA: Addison-Wesley, (1966): 526–595.

Cantril, H. "Experiments in the Wording

of Questions." *Public Opinion Quarterly*, 4 (1940): 330–332.

Carlson, R. E. "Effect of Interview Information on Altering Valid Impressions." *Journal of Applied Psychology*, 55 (1971): 66–72.

Carlson, R. E. "The Relative Influence of Appearance and Factual Written Information on an Interviewer's Final Rating." *Journal of Applied Psychology*, 51 (1967): 461–468.

Carlson, R. E., P. W. Thayer, E. Mayfield and D. A. Peterson "Improvements in the Selection Interview." *Personnel Journal*, 50 (1971): 268–275.

Carter, G. H. "History Taking and Interviewing Technique." *Journal of Medical Education*, 30 (1955): 315.

Casciani, J. M. "Influence of Model's Race and Sex on Interviewee's Self Disclosure." *Journal of Consulting Psychology*, 25 (1978): 435–440.

Cataldo, E. F. et al. "Cardsorting as a Technique for Survey Interviews." *Public Opinion Quarterly* (Summer, 1971): 202–215.

Chapple, E. D. "The Standard Experimental (Stress) Interview as Used in Interaction Chronograph Investigations." *Human Organizations*, 12 (1953): 23–32.

Cheatham, T. R. and M. L. McLaughlin "A Comparison of Co-participant Perceptions of Self and Others in Placement Center Interviews." *Communication Quarterly*, 24 (Summer, 1976): 9–13.

Cocanougher, A. B. and J. M. Ivancevich "BARS Performance Rating for Sales Force Personnel." *Journal of Marketing*, 42 (1978): 87–95.

Cohen, A. A. and R. P. Harrison. "Intentionality in the Use of Hand Illustrators in Face-to-Face Communication Situations." *Journal of Personality and Social Psychology*, 28 (1973): 276–279.

Cohen, H. S. "Public Records as a Source of Employment Information." *Personnel Journal*, 57 (1978): 313, 334 & 336.

Cohen, S. L. "How Well Standardized Is Your Organization's Assessment Center?" *The Personnel Administrator*, 23 (1978): 41–51.

Cohen, S. L. and K. A. Bunker "Subtle Effects of Sex Role Stereotypes on Recruiter's Hiring Decision." *Journal of Applied Psychology*, 60 (1975): 566–572.

Colby, J. D. and R. L. Wallace "Performance Appraisal: Help or Hindrance to Employee Productivity?" *The Personnel Administrator*, 20, (1975): 37–39.

Coleman, R., M. Greenblatt and H. C. Solomon "Physiological Evidence of Rapport During Psychotherapeutic Interviews." *Disorders of the Nervous System*, 17 (1956): 2–8.

Collard, A. F. "Sharpening Interviewing Skills." *Journal of Systems Management*, 26 (1975): 6–10.

Collins, M. "Interviewer Variability: A Review of the Problem," *Journal of the Market Research Society*, 22: 77–95.

Colombotos, J. "Personal Versus Telephone Interviews: Effect on Responses." *Public Health Reports*, 84 (1969): 773–782.

"Comment on the Proposed Uniform Guidelines on Employee Selection Procedures," *The Personnel Administrator*, 23 (1978): 41–46.

Conant, J. C. "The Performance Appraisal: A Critique and an Alternative." *Business Horizons*, 16 (1973): 73–78.

Cook, J. J. "Silence in Psychotherapy." *Journal of Consulting Psychology*, 11 (1964): 42–46.

Cook, S. H. "The EEO Interview: Turning a Gamble into a Good Bet." *Management World*, (1978): 19–22.

Cox, K. K. et al. "Applications of Focus Group Interview in Marketing." *Journal of Marketing*, 40 (1976): 77–80.

Cozby, P. C. "Self-Disclosure: A Literature Review," *Psychological Bulletin*, 79 (1973): 73–91.

Creth, S. "Conducting an Effective Employment Interview." *Journal of Academic Librarianship*, 4 (1978): 355–360.

Curley, D. G. "The Other Half of Employee Communication." *The Personnel Administrator*, 24 (July, 1979): 29–32.

Daly, J. A., V. P. Richmond and S. Leth "Social Communicative Anxiety and the Personnel Selection Process: Testing the Similarity Effect in Selection Decisions."

Human Communication Research, 6 (1979): 18–32.

Daniell, R. J. and P. Lewis "Stability of Eye Contact and Physical Distance Across a Series of Structured Interviews." *Journal of Consulting and Clinical Psychology*, 39 (1972): 172.

Dapra, R. A. and W. C. Byham "Consultants' Showcase: Applying the Assessment Center Method to Selection Interviewing." *Training and Development Journal*, 32 (1978): 44–49.

D'Augelli, A. R. "Nonverbal Behavior of Helpers in Initial Helping Interactions," *Journal of Consulting Psychology*, 21 (1974): 360–363.

de la Zerda, N. and R. Hopper "Employment Interviewers' Reactions to Mexican-American Speech." *Communication Monographs*, 46 (1979): 126–134.

Dexter, L. "Role Relationships and Conception of Neutrality in Interviewing," *American Journal of Sociology*, 62 (1956): 153–157.

Dibner, A. S. "Cue-counting: A Measure of Anxiety in Interviews." *Journal of Consulting Psychology*, 20 (1956): 475–478.

Dinges, N. G. and R. R. Oetting "Interaction Distance Anxiety in a Counseling Dyad." *Journal of Consulting Psychology*, 19 (1972): 146–149.

Dipboye, R. L., H. L. Fromkin and K. Wiback "Relative Importance of Applicant Sex, Attractiveness and Scholastic Standing in Evaluation of Job Applicant Resumes." *Journal of Applied Psychology*, 60 (1975): 39–43.

Dipboye, R. L., R. D. Arvey and D. E. Terpstra "Equal Employment and the Interview." *Personnel Journal*, 55 (1976): 520–524.

Dittman, A. T. "The Relationship Between Body Movements and Moods in Interviews." *Journal of Consulting Psychology*, 26 (1962): 480.

Dittman, A. T. and L. G. Llewellyn "Relationship Between Vocalizations and Head Nods as Listener Responses." *Journal of Personality and Social Psychology*, 9 (1968): 79–84.

Dittman, A. T. and L. C. Wynne "Linguistic Techniques and the Analysis of Emo-

tionality in the Interview." *Journal of Abnormal and Social Psychology*, 63 (1961): 201–204.

Doherty, P. C. "The Rhetoric of the Public Interview." *College Composition and Communication*, 20 (1969): 18–23.

Dohrenwend, B. S. "An Experimental Study of Payment to Respondents." *Public Opinion Quarterly*, (Winter, 1970): 621–624.

Dohrenwend, B. S. "Some Effects of Open and Closed Questions on Respondent's Answers." *Human Organization*, 24 (1965): 175–184.

Dohrenwend, B. S. and S. A. Richardson "A Use for Leading Questions in Research Interviewing." *Human Organization*, 23 (1964): 76–77.

Doster, J. A. and B. R. Strickland "Disclosing of Verbal Material as a Function of Information Requested, Information About the Interviewer, and Interviewee Differences." *Journal of Consulting and Clinical Psychology*, 37 (1971): 187–194.

Downs, C. W. "A Content Analysis of Twenty Selection Interviews." *Personnel Administration and Public Personnel Review*, (September, 1972): 25.

Downs, C. W. "Perceptions of the Selection Interview." Personnel Administration (May, 1969): 11.

Downs, H. and M. Wallace "The Craft of Interviewing." *Television Quarterly*, 4 (1965): 10.

Dwyer, J. C. and Dimitroff "The Bottoms Up/Tops Down Approach to Performance Appraisal." *Personnel Journal*, 55 (1976): 349–353.

Ehat, D. M. and M. Schnapper "What Your Employees' Non-Verbal Cues Are Telling You." *Administrative Management*, 35 (Aug., 1974): 64–66.

Eisenstadt, A. "Interview-Taking—A Neglected Skill." *Journal of Communication*, 5 (1955): 16–20.

Ekman, P. "Body Position, Facial Expression, and Verbal Behavior During Interviews." *Journal of Abnormal and Social Psychology*, 48 (1964): 295–301.

Ekman, P. and W. V. Friesen "Detecting Deception from the Body and Face."

Journal of Personality and Social Psychology, 29 (1974): 288–298.

Ekman, P., W. V. Friesen and K. R. Scherer "Body Movement and Voice Pitch in Deceptive Interaction." *Semiotica,* 16 (1976): 23–27.

Embrey, W. R., R. W. Mondy and R. M. Noe "Exit Interview: A Tool for Personnel Administration." *The Personnel Administrator,* 24 (1979): 43–48.

Emerick, L. "Interviewing in Speech Pathology and Audiology." *Central States Speech Journal,* 19 (1968): 40–45.

Exline, R. V., D. Gray and D. Schuette "Visual Behavior in a Dyad as Affected by Interview Content and Sex of Respondents." *Journal of Personality and Social Psychology,* 1 (1965): 201–209.

Exline, R. V. and D. Messick "The Effects of Dependency and Social Reinforcement Upon Visual Behavior During an Interview." *British Journal of Social and Clinical Psychology,* 6 (1967): 256–266.

Fidell, L. S. "Empirical Verifications of Sex Discrimination in Hiring Practices in Psychology." *American Psychologist,* 25 (1979): 1094–1098.

Figgins, R. "How to See If a Job Is Right." *Personnel Journal,* 57 (1978): 691–693.

Fischer, M. J. and R. A. Apostal "Selected Vocal Cues and Counselor's Perceptions of Genuineness, Self-Disclosure, and Anxiety." *Journal of Consulting Psychology,* 22 (1975): 92–96.

Flynn, P. T. "Effective Clinical Interviewing." *Language Speech and Hearing Serv. Sch.,* 9 (1978): 265–271.

"Focus Group Interviews: Consumers Rap About Today's Shopping, Buying." *Advertising Age,* (1975): 37–40.

Forbes, R. "Reliability of the Selection Interview." *Personnel Management,* (1979): 37–39.

Freedman, N. "The Analysis of Movement Behavior During the Clinical Interview." in A. W. Siegman and B. Pope, (eds.). *Studies in Dyadic Communication.* Elmsford, N.Y.: Pergamon Press, (1972): 153–175.

Freeman, J. and E. W. Butler "Some Sources of Interviewer Variance in Surveys." *Public Opinion Quarterly,* 40 (1976): 79–91.

Fretz, B. R. "Postural Movements in a Counseling Dyad." *Journal of Counseling Psychology,* 13 (1966): 335–343.

Fox, W. F. "A Job Seeker's View." *The Personnel Administrator,* 20 (1975): 51–54.

Fuller, C. H. "Effects of Anonymity on Return Rate and Response Bias in a Mail Survey." *Journal of Applied Psychology,* 59 (1974): 292–296.

Fuller, C. H. "Weighting to Adjust for Survey Nonresponse." *Public Opinion Quarterly,* 38 (Summer, 1974): 239–246.

Galassi, J. P. and M. D. Galassi "Preparing Individuals for Job Interviews: Suggestions from More Than 60 Years of Research." *Personnel and Guidance Journal,* 57 (1978): 188–192.

Gallup, G. "The Quintamensional Plan of Question Design." *Public Opinion Quarterly,* 11 (Fall, 1947): 385.

Garrison, L. and J. Ferguson "Separation Interviews." *Personnel Journal,* 56 (1977): 438–442.

Gatewood, R. D. and J. Ledvinka "Selection Interviewing and EEO: Mandate for Objectivity." *The Personnel Administrator,* 24 (1979): 51–54.

Giedt, F. H. "Cues Associated with Accurate and Inaccurate Interview Impressions." *Psychiatry,* 21 (1958): 405–409.

Gildersleeve, T. R. "Conducting Better Interviews." *Journal of Systems Management,* 27 (1976): 24–28.

Glasser, G. J. and G. D. Metzger "Random Digit Dialing as a Method of Telephone Sampling." *Marketing Research,* 9 (1972): 59–64.

Goldman, A. E. "The Group Depth Interview," *Journal of Marketing,* 26 (1962): 61–68.

Goldman-Eisler, F. "Speech-breathing Activity: A Measure of Tension and Affect During Interviews." *British Journal of Psychology,* 46 (1955): 53–63.

Goodale, J. G. "8 Ways to Make the Selection Interview Work," *Journal of College Placement,* 39 (1979): 32–38.

Goodale, J. G. "Tailoring the Selection Interview to the Job." *Personnel Journal,* 55 (1976): 62–65.

Graham, P. J. "Interviewing Process: Some Suggestions for Eliminating Bias." *Physical Education,* 35 (1978): 137–140.

Greenwald, R. A. and S. Wiener "A Standardized Interviewing Technique for Evaluating Postgraduate Training Applicants." *Journal of Medical Education,* 51 (1976): 912–918.

Haase, R. F. and D. J. DiMattia "Proxemic Behavior: Counselor, Administrator and Client Preference for Seating Arrangement in Dyadic Interaction." *Journal of Counseling Psychology,* 17 (1970): 319–325.

Haase, R. F. and D. T. Tepper "Nonverbal Components of Empathic Communication," *Journal of Counseling Psychology,* 19 (1972): 417–424.

Hakel, M. D. "Similarity of Post-Interview Train Rating Intercorrelations as a Contributor to Interrater Agreement in a Structured Employment Interview." *Journal of Applied Psychology,* 55 (1971): 443–448.

Hakel, M. D., T. W. Dobmeyer and M. D. Dunnette "Relative Importance of Three Content Dimensions in Overall Suitability Ratings of Job Applicant's Resumes." *Journal of Applied Psychology,* 54 (1970): 65–71.

Hammerback, J. C. "William F. Buckley, Jr., On Firing Line: A Case Study in Confrontational Dialogue." *Communication Quarterly,* 22 (Summer, 1974): 23–30.

Hanck, M. and M. Cox "Locating a Sample by Random Digit Dialing." *Public Opinion Quarterly,* 38 (Summer, 1974): 253–260.

Hargrove, D. S. "Verbal Interaction Analysis of Empathetic and Unempathetic Responses of Therapists." *Journal of Consulting and Clinical Psychology,* 42 (1974): 305.

Harris, C. L. "Exit Interview." *NASSP Bulletin,* 63 (1979): 112–115.

Hatchett, S. and H. Schuman "White Respondents and Race-of-Interviewer Effects." *Public Opinion Quarterly,* (Winter, 1975): 523–528.

Hatfield, J. D. and Gatewood "Nonverbal Cues in the Selection Interview." *The Personnel Administrator,* 23 (1978): 30 & 35–37.

Hawes, L. C. "Development and Application of an Interview Coding System." *Central States Speech Journal,* 23 (1972): 92–99.

Hawes, L. C. "The Effects of Interviewer Style on Patterns of Dyadic Communication." *Communication Monographs,* 39 (1972): 114–123.

Hawes, L. C. and J. M. Foley "A Markov Analysis of Interview Communication." *Communication Monographs,* 40 (1973): 208–219.

Hawk, D. L. "Effective Attitude Surveys." *Personnel Journal,* 57 (July, 1978): 384–389.

Haynes, M. "Developing an Appraisal Program: Part I." *Personnel Journal,* 57 (1978): 14–19.

Haynes, M. "Developing an Appraisal Program: Part II." *Personnel Journal,* 57 (1978): 66–67.

Hays, E. R. and J. E. Mandel "Interviewing: A Definition and Description," *Central States Speech Journal,* 21 (1970): 126–129.

Heller, K. "Interview Structure and Interviewer Style in Initial Interviews," in A. W. Siegman and B. Pope (eds.). *Studies in Dyadic Communication.* New York: Pergamon Press, (1972): 9–28.

Heller, K., J. D. Davis and R. A. Myers "The Effects of Interviewer Style in a Standardized Interview." *Journal of Consulting Psychology,* 30 (1966): 501–508.

Hilb, M. "The Standardized Exit Interview." *Personnel Journal,* 57 (1978): 327–336.

Hill, N. C. "Listening: Searching for a Meaning in the Message." *The Personnel Administrator,* 20 (Oct., 1975): 17–19.

Hinrichs, J. R. "Employees Coming and Going: The Exit Interview." in R. C. Huseman, et al., (eds.). *Readings in Interpersonal and Organizational Behavior.* Boston: Holbrook Press, (1977): 454.

Hoffman, A. M. "Reliability and Validity

in Oral History." *Communication Quarterly,* 22 (Winter, 1974): 23–27.

Holley, W. H. and H. Field "Equal Employment Opportunity and Its Implications for Personnel Practices." *Labor Law Journal,* 27 (May, 1976): 278–286.

Holley, W. H. and H. Field "Performance Appraisal and the Law." *Labor Law Journal,* 26 (July, 1975): 423–430.

Holley, W. H., H. Field and N. J. Barnett "Analyzing Performance Appraisal Systems: An Empirical Study." *Personnel Journal,* 55 (1976): 457–463.

Hopkins, J. T. "The Top Twelve Questions for Employment Agency Interviewers." *Personnel Journal,* 59 (1980): 379–380.

Hopper, R. "Language Attitudes in the Employment Interview." *Communication Monographs,* 44 (1977): 346–351.

Hopper, R. and F. Williams "Speech Characteristics and Employability." *Communication Monographs,* 40 (1973): 296–302.

Hubble, M. A. and C. J. Gelso "Effect of Counselor Attire in an Initial Interview." *Journal of Counseling Psychology,* 25 (1978): 581–584.

Hughes, C. L. "If It's Right for You, It's Wrong for Employees." *The Personnel Administrator,* 58 (1979): 39–44.

Hunt, B. "The New You—Researched, Resumed and Rarin' to Go." *Management World,* 7 (1978): 5–7.

Ivancevich, J. M. "Changes in Performance in a Management by Objectives Program." *Administrative Science Quarterly,* 19 (1974): 563–574.

Iversen, S. M. "Microcounseling: A Model for Teaching the Skills of Interviewing." *Journal of Nursing Education,* 17 (1978): 12–16.

Jacoby, J. "Consumer Research: A State of the Art Review." *Journal of Marketing,* 42 (April, 1978): 87–95.

Jaffe, J. "An Objective Study of Communication in Psychiatric Interviews." *Journal of the Hillside Hospital,* 6 (1957): 207–215.

Jaffe, J. "Dyadic Analysis of Two Psychotherapeutic Interviews." in L. A. Gottschalk (ed.). *Comparative Psycholinguistic Analysis of Two Psychotherapeutic Interviews.* New York: International Universities Press, 1961: Ch. 5.

Jaffe, J. "Language of the Dyad: A Method of Interaction Analysis in Psychiatric Interviews." *Psychiatry,* 21 (1958): 249–258.

Jaffee, C., J. Bender and O. L. Calvert "The Assessment Center Technique: A Validation Study." *Management of Personnel Quarterly,* 9 (1970): 9–14.

Janes, H. D. "The Cover Letter and Resume." *Personnel Journal,* 48 (1969): 732–733.

Jensen, J. V. "Communicative Functions of Silence." *ETC* 30 (1973): 249–257.

Johannesen, R. L. "The Functions of Silence: A Plea for Communication Research." *Western Speech,* 38 (1974): 25–35.

Jolson, M. A. "How to Double or Triple Mail-Survey Response Rates." *Journal of Marketing,* 41 (Oct., 1977): 78–81.

Jones, S. E. "Directivity vs. Non-directivity: Implications of the Examination of Witnesses in Law for Fact-Finding Interviews." *Journal of Communication,* 19 (1969): 64–75.

Jourard, S. M. and P. E. Jaffee "Influence of an Interviewer's Disclosure on the Self-Disclosing Behavior of Interviewees." *Journal of Consulting Psychology,* 17 (1970): 252–257.

Kahn, G., B. Cohen and H. Jason "The Teaching of Interpersonal Skills in U. S. Medical Schools." *Journal of Medical Education,* 54 (1979): 29–35.

Kalton, G., M. Collins and L. Brook "Experiments in Wording Opinion Questions." *Applied Statistics,* 27 (1978): 149–161.

Kanfer, F. H. "Verbal Rate, Eyeblink, and Content in Structured Psychiatric Interviews." *Journal of Abnormal and Social Psychology,* 61 (1960): 341–347.

Kanuk, L. and C. Berenson "Mail Surveys and Response Rate: A Literature Review." *Journal of Marketing Research,* 12 (1975): 440–453.

Kasl, S. V. and G. F. Mahl "A Simple Device for Obtaining Certain Verbal Activity Measures During Interviews." *Journal of Abnormal and Social Psychology,* 53 (1956): 388–390.

Kay, E. H., H. Meyer, and R. P. French, Jr. "Effects of Threat in a Performance Appraisal Interview." *Journal of Applied Psychology,* 49 (1965): 311–317.

Kearney, W. J. "The Value of Behaviorally Based Performance Appraisals." *Business Horizons,* 18 (1975): 75–83.

Kearney, W. J. "Behaviorally Anchored Rating Scales—MBO's Missing Ingredient." *Personnel Journal,* 58 (1979): 20–25.

Keenan, T. "Recruitment on Campus: A Closer Look at the Tools of the Trade." *Personnel Management,* (1980): 43–46.

Kegeles, S., C. F. Fink, and J. P. Kirscht "Interviewing a National Sample by Long Distance Telephone." *Public Opinion Quarterly,* 33 (1969–1970): 412–419.

Killenberg, G. M. and R. Anderson "Sources Are Persons: Teaching Interviewing as Dialogue." *Journalism Educator,* 31 (1976): 16–20.

Kindall, A. F. and J. Gatza "Positive Program of Performance Appraisal." *Harvard Business Review,* 41 (1963): 153–160.

Kirchner, W. and D. Reisberg "Differences Between Better and Less Effective Supervisors in Appraisal of Subordinates." *Personnel Psychology,* 15 (1962): 295.

Kirk, E. B. et al. "Appraisee Participation in Performance Review." *Personnel Journal* (1965): 23.

Kleinke, C. L., R. A. Staneski, and D. E. Berger "Evaluation of an Interviewer as a Function of Interviewer Gaze, Reinforcement of Subject Gaze, and Interviewer Attractiveness." *Journal of Personality and Social Psychology,* 31 (1975): 115–122.

Knapp, M. L., R. P. Hart and H. S. Dennis "An Exploration of Deception as a Communication Construct." *Human Communication Research,* 1 (1974): 15–29.

Knight, P. H. and C. K. Bair "Degree of Client Comfort as a Function of Dyadic Interaction Distance." *Journal of Counseling Psychology,* 23 (1976): 13–16.

Koellner, P. "Planning and Communication: Building Blocks for Effective Interviewing." *Personnel Journal,* 57 (1978): 11–13.

Kornhauser, A. and P. B. Sheatsley "Questionnaire Construction and Interview Procedure," in C. Selltiz, M. Jahoda, M. Deutsch, and S. W. Cook (eds.). *Research Methods in Social Relations.* New York: Henry Holt, (1959): 546–587.

Kraut, R. and J. McConahay "How Being Interviewed Affects Voting: An Experiment." *Public Opinion Quarterly* (Fall, 1973): 398–406.

Kravetz, D. J. "Counseling Strategies for Involuntary Terminations." *The Personnel Administrator,* 23 (1978): 49–54.

LaCrosse, M. B. "Nonverbal Behavior and Perceived Counselor Attractiveness and Persuasiveness." *Journal of Consulting Psychology,* 22 (1975): 563–566.

Laitin, Y. J. "How to Make Employee Surveys Pay Off." *Personnel,* 38 (1961): 23–33.

Lambert, S. "Reactions to a Stranger as a Function of Style of Dress." *Perceptual and Motor Skills,* 35 (1972): 711–712.

Lassen, C. R. "Effect of Proximity and Anxiety and Communication in the Initial Psychiatric Interview." *Journal of Abnormal Psychology,* 81 (1973): 226–232.

Latterell, J. D. "Planning for the Selection Interview." *Personnel Journal,* 58 (1979): 466–467.

Leap, T. L., W. H. Holley and H. S. Field "Equal Employment Opportunity and Its Implications for Personnel Practices in the 1980's." *Labor Law Journal,* 31 (November, 1980): 669–682.

Lefebvre, L. "Encoding and Decoding of Ingratiation in Modes of Smiling and Gaze." *British J. Soc. Clin. Psychology,* 14 (1975): 33–42.

Lefkowitz, J. and M. Katz "Validity of Exit Interviews." *Personnel Psychology,* 22 (1969): 449.

Leuthold, M. and R. Scheele "Patterns of

Bias in Samples Based on Telephone Directories." *Public Opinion Quarterly*, 35 (1971): 249–257.

Levine, E. L. "Legal Aspects of Reference Checking for Personnel Selection." *The Personnel Administrator*, 22 (1977): 14–28.

Levinson, H. "Management by Whose Objectives?" *Harvard Business Review*, 48 (1970): 125–134.

Lewis, C. et al. "Interview Training." *Personnel Management*, 8 (1976): 29–33.

Lichtenberg, J. W. and E. J. Heck "Interactional Structure of Interviews Conducted by Counselors of Differing Levels of Cognitive Complexity." *Journal of Counseling Psychology*, 26 (1979): 15–22.

Likert, R. "Motivational Approach to Management Development." *Harvard Business Review*, 36 (1959): 75.

"Listen with Your Eyes." *Industry Week*, 178 (July 16, 1973): 37–39.

Locke, E. A., N. Cartledge and C. S. Knerr "Studies in the Relationship Between Satisfaction, Goal-setting and Performance," *Psychological Bulletin*, 70 (1968): 474–485.

Loffreda, R. "Employee Attitude Surveys: A Valuable Motivating Tool," *The Personnel Administrator*, 24 (July, 1979): 41–43.

London, M. and M. Hakel "Effects of Applicant Stereotypes, Order and Information on Interview Impressions." *Journal of Applied Psychology*, 59 (1974): 157–162.

Lubliner, M. "The Advantages of Open Communications with Employees," *The Personnel Administrator*, 24 (July, 1979): 23–26.

Lykken, D. T. "The Detection of Deception," *Psychological Bulletin*, 86 (1979): 47–53.

Mahl, G. F. "Measures of Two Expressive Aspects of a Patient's Speech in Two Psychotherapeutic Interviews," in L. A. Gottschalk (ed.). *Comparative Psycholinguistic Analysis of Two Psychotherapeutic Interviews.* New York: International Universities Press, 1961: Ch. 6.

Mahl, G. F. "Measuring the Patient's Anxiety During Interviews from 'Expressive' Aspects of His Speech." *Transactions of the New York Academy of Sciences*, 1959: 249–257.

Marsden, G. "Content-Analysis Studies of Therapeutic Interviews: 1954–1964." *Psychological Bulletin*, 63 (1965): 298–321.

Matarazzo, J. et al. "Interviewer Influence of Durations of Interviewee Speech." *Journal of Verbal Learning and Verbal Behavior*, 1 (1963): 451–458.

Matarazzo, J. D. and A. N. Weins "Speech Behavior as an Objective Correlate of Empathy and Outcome in Interview and Psychotherapy Research." *Behavior Modification*, 1 (1977): 453–480.

Matarazzo, J. D., A. N. Weins, and G. Saslow "Studies of Interview Speech Behavior," in L. Krasner and L. P. Ullmann (eds.). *Research in Behavior Modification: New Developments and Implications.* New York: Holt, Rinehart and Winston, 1965.

Mathis, R. L. and R. H. Sutton "Performance Appraisal—Part I." *Journal of Systems Management*, (1979): 16–18.

Mayfield, E. "The Selection Interview—A Re-evaluation of Published Research." *Personnel Psychology*, 17 (1964): 239–260.

Mayfield, H. "In Defense of Performance Appraisal." *Harvard Business Review*, 37 (1960): 82.

McConkey, D. D. "MBO—Twenty Years Later, Where Do We Stand?" *Business Horizons*, 16 (1973): 25–36.

McFillen, J. M. and P. G. Decker "Building Meaning into Appraisal." *The Personnel Administrator*, 23 (1978): 75–84.

McGovern, T. V. and H. E. A. Tinsley "Interviewer Evaluations of Interviewee Nonverbal Behavior." *Journal of Vocational Behavior*, 13 (1978): 163–171.

McGovern, T. V. et al. "Comparison of Professional Versus Student Ratings of Job Interviewee Behavior." *Journal of Counseling Psychology*, 26 (1979): 176.

McGregor, D. "An Uneasy Look at Performance Appraisal." *Harvard Business Review*, 35 (1957): 89–94.

McKenzie, J. R. "An Investigation into Interviewer Effects in Market Research." *Journal of Marketing Research*, 14 (1977): 330–336.

McMahan, E. M. "Nonverbal Communication as a Function of Attribution in Impression Formation." *Communication Monographs*, 43 (1976): 287–294.

McMaster, J. B. "Designing an Appraisal System That Is Fair and Accurate." *Personnel Journal*, 58 (1979): 38–40.

Mehrabian, A. "Orientation Behaviors and Nonverbal Attitude Communication." *Journal of Communication*, 17 (1967): 324–332.

Mehrabian, A. and M. Williams "Nonverbal and Concomitants of Perceived and Intended Persuasiveness." *Journal of Personality and Social Psychology*, 13 (1969): 37–58.

Meyer, H. E. "The Science of Telling Executives How They're Doing." *Fortune*, 89 (1974): 102.

Meyer, H. H. "The Annual Performance Review Discussion—Making It Constructive." *Personnel Journal*, 56 (1977): 508–511.

Michaels, D. T. "Seven Questions That Will Improve Your Managerial Hiring Decisions." *Personnel Journal*, 59 (1980): 199–200.

Millard, C. W. and S. Pinsky "Assessing the Assessment Center." *Personnel Administrator*, 25 (1980): 85–88.

Milmoe, S., R. Rosenthal, H. T. Blane, M. E. Chafetz and I. Wolf "The Doctor's Voice: Postdictor of Successful Referral of Alcoholic Patients." *Journal of Abnormal Psychology*, 72 (1967): 78–84.

Minter, R. L. "Human Rights Laws and Pre-Employment Inquiries." *Personnel Journal*, 52 (1972): 431–433.

Mitchell, C. "Things Carl Rogers Never Told Me." *The Personnel Administrator*, 24 (May, 1979): 76–78.

Molde, D. A. and A. N. Weins "Interview Interaction Behavior of Nurses with Task Versus Person Orientation." *Nursing Research*, 17 (1967): 45–51.

Morgan, E. G. "The Right Interviewer for the Job." *Journal of Marketing*, (October, 1951): 201–202.

Morris, J. R. "Newsmen's Interview Techniques and Attitudes Toward Interviewing." *Journalism Quarterly*, 50 (1973): 539–542.

Morton-Williams, J. "The Use of Verbal Interaction Coding for Evaluating a Questionnaire." *Quality and Quantity*, 13 (1979): 59–75.

Murray, D. C. "Talk, Silence and Anxiety." *Psychological Bulletin*, 75 (1971): 244–260.

Murray, R. P. and H. McGinley "Looking as a Measure of Attraction." *Journal of Applied and Social Psychology*, 2 (1972): 267–274.

Murray, W. A. "Tips on Screening Executives." *The Personnel Administrator*, 24 (1979): 39–40 & 46–53.

Natarajan, V. "On the Reliability of Rating in Interviews." *New Frontiers in Education*, 8 (1978): 11–18.

Nehrbass, R. G. "Psychological Barriers to Effective Employment Interviewing." *Personnel Journal*, 55 (1976): 598–600.

Nehrbass, R. G. "Psychological Barriers to Effective Employment Interviewing." *Personnel Journal*, 56 (1977): 60–63.

Nemesh, A. "The Interviewing Process." *Business Education Forum*, 33 (1979): 19–20 & 23.

Nichols, R. G. "Do We Know How to Listen?" *The Speech Teacher*, 10 (1961): 120–124.

Nichols, R. G. "Listening Is a 10-Part Skill." in Huseman, R. C., C. M. Logue and D. L. Freshley. *Readings in Interpersonal and Organizational Communication* (3rd ed.). Boston: Holbrook (1967): 554–560.

Nilsson, N. G. "The Origin of the Interview." *Journalism Quarterly*, 48 (1971): 707–713.

Noelle-Neumann, E. "Wanted: Rules for Wording Structured Questionnaires." *Public Opinion Quarterly*, 34 (1970): 191–201.

Novick, S. and J. Nussbaum "Using Interviews to Probe Understanding." *Science Teacher*, 45 (1978): 29–30.

Oberg, W. "Make Performance Appraisal Relevant." *Harvard Business Review*, 49 (1972): 61.

Odiorne, G. S. "An Application of the

Communication Audit." *Personnel Psychology*, 7 (1954): 235–243.

Odiorne, G. S. "Management by Objectives: Antidote to Future Shock." *Personnel Journal*, 53 (1974): 258–263.

Ofsanko, F. J. and C. C. Paulson "Who Interviews the Interviewer—and How." *The Personnel Administrator*, 22 (Feb., 1977): 27–29.

Olsen, F. A. "Corporations Who Succeed Through Communication—Three Case Studies." *Personnel Journal*, 58 (Dec., 1979): 858–874.

Onoda, L. and L. Gassert "Use of Assertion Training to Improve Job Interview Behavior." *Personnel and Guidance Journal*, 56 (1978): 492–495.

Patterson, M. L. "Compensation and Nonverbal Immediacy and Impression Formation." *Journal of Personality*, 38 (1970): 161–166.

Patterson, M. L. "Stability of Non-Verbal Immediacy Behaviors." *Journal of Experimental Soc. Psychology*, 9 (1973): 97–100.

Pearson, R. E. "Segmented Counseling Interview: A Training Procedure." *Counseling Education and Supervision*, 18 (1978): 153–157.

Peterson, R. A. "An Experimental Investigation of Mail-Survey Responses." *Journal of Business Research*, 3 (1975): 199–209.

Petry, G. H. and S. F. Quakenbush "The Conservation of the Questionnaire as a Research Resource." *Business Horizons*, 17 (1974): 43–50.

Phillips, D. L. and K. Clancy "Modeling Effects in Survey Research." *Public Opinion Quarterly*, (Summer, 1972): 246.

Pope, B. and A. W. Siegman "Interviewer Warmth in Relation to Interviewee Verbal Behavior." *Journal of Consulting and Clinical Psychology*, 32 (1968): 588–595.

Pope, B., A. W. Siegman and T. Blass "Anxiety and Speech in the Initial Interview." *Journal of Consulting and Clinical Psychology*, 35 (1970): 233–238.

Pope, B., S. Nudler, M. Vonkorff and J. P. McGee "The Experienced Professional Interviewer Versus the Complete Novice." *Journal of Consulting and Clinical Psychology*, 42 (1974): 680–690.

Powell, W. J., Jr. "Differential Effectiveness of Interviewer Interventions in an Experimental Interview." *Journal of Consulting and Clinical Psychology*, 32 (1968): 213–214.

"Pre-Planned Question for Efficient Interviewing." *Personnel Journal*, 21 (1976): 8–10.

Pyron, H. C. "The Use and Misuse of Previous Employer References in Hiring." *Management of Personnel Quarterly*, (1970): 15–22.

Rabinowitz, P. A. "Reference Auditing: An Essential Management Tool." *The Personnel Administrator*, 24 (1979): 34–38.

Rahiya, J. "Privacy Protection and Personnel Administration: Are New Laws Needed?" *The Personnel Administrator*, 24 (1979): 19–21.

Resser, C. "Executive Performance Appraisal—The View From the Top." *Personnel Journal*, 54 (1975): 42–66.

Rice, Jr., G. P. and R. H. Staton "The Attorney-Client Interview." *Communication Quarterly*, 6 (January, 1958): 10–11.

Rice, J. D. "Privacy Legislation: Its Effect on Pre-Employment Reference Checking." *The Personnel Administrator*, 23 (1978): 46–51.

Richardson, S. A. "The Use of Leading Questions in Nonscheduled Interviews." *Human Organization*, 19 (1960): 86–89.

Ringle, W. M. "Get the Interview as Readers Surrogate." *The Gannetter*, 30 (1974): 1–3.

Roalman, A. R. "Ten Manytimes Fatal Mistakes Top Executives Make in Press Interviews." *Management Review*, 64 (1975): 4–10.

Robinson, T. "Ask (the right way) and It Shall Be Given: New Approaches in Journalism Courses." *Times Higher Education Supplement*, 335 (April 14, 1978): 11.

Rochester, S. R. "The Significance of

Pauses in Spontaneous Speech." *Journal of Psycholinguistic Research*, 2 (1973): 51–81.

Rogers, T. F. "Interviews by Telephone and in Person: Quality of Response and Field Performance." *Public Opinion Quarterly*, 39 (Spring, 1976): 51–65.

Rosegrant, T. J. and J. C. McCroskey "The Effects of Race and Sex on Proxemic Behavior in an Interview Setting." *Southern Speech Communication Journal*, 40 (1975): 408–418.

Roseman, E. "People Reading: The Art of Recognizing Hidden Messages." *Product Marketing*, 6 (June, 1977): 36–39.

Rosenberg, H. G. "Which Door Should Students Choose: Placement or Personnel?" *Journal of College Placement*, 39 (1978): 63–65.

Rosenfeld, L. B. and G. M. White "Clothing as Communication." *Journal of Communication*, 27 (1977): 24–31.

Sainesbury, P. "Gestural Movement During Psychiatric Interviews." *Psychosomatic Medicine*, 17 (1955): 458–469.

Schlachtmeyer, A. S. and F. Halperin "Criteria-Based Planning for Employee Communication." *The Personnel Administrator*, 24 (Aug., 1979): 77–81.

Schneider, A. E., W. C. Donaghy and P. J. Newman "Communication Climate Within an Organization." *Management Controls* (1976): 159–162.

Schneier, C. E. and R. W. Beatty "Combining BARS and MBO: Using an Appraisal System to Diagnose Performance Problems." *The Personnel Administrator*, 24 (1979): 51–60.

Schneier, C. E. and R. W. Beatty "Developing Behaviorally-Anchored Rating Scales (BARS)." *The Personnel Administrator*, 24 (1979): 59–68.

Schneier, C. E. and R. W. Beatty "Integrating Behaviorally-Based and Effectiveness-Based Methods." *The Personnel Administrator*, 24 (1979): 65–76.

Schuler, R. S. "Effective Use of Communication to Minimize Employee Stress." *The Personnel Administrator*, 24 (1979): 40–44.

Schuman, H. and J. Converse "The Effects of Black and White Interviewers on Black Responses in 1968." *Public Opinion Quarterly*, (Spring, 1977): 44–48.

Searles, J. R. "Top Three/Bottom Three: A Personnel Evaluation Technique." *The Personnel Administrator*, 20 (1975): 50–53.

Serafini, C. P. "Interview Listening." *Personnel Journal*, 54 (1975): 398–399.

Shaw, E. A. "Differential Impact of Negative Stereotyping in Employee Selection." *Personnel Psychology*, 25 (1972): 333–338.

Sheatsley, P. B. "Closed Questions Are Sometimes More Valid Than Open End." *Public Opinion Quarterly*, 12 (1948): 12.

Sheppard, H. L. "Asking the Right Questions on Job Satisfaction." *Monthly Labor Review*, 96 (1973): 51–52.

Sheridan, J. H. "Are You a Victim of Nonverbal 'Vibes'?" *Industry Week*, 198 (July 10, 1978): 36–42.

Sheth, J. N., A. LeClaire, Jr. and D. Wachspress "Impact of Asking Race Information in Mail Surveys." *Journal of Marketing*, 44 (Winter, 1980): 67–70.

Siegman, A. W. "Do Noncontingent Interviewer Mm-Hums Facilitate Interviewee Productivity?" *Journal of Consulting and Clinical Psychology*, 44 (1976): 171–182.

Sigband, N. "Listening for the Whole Message." *Supervisory Management*, 44 (1970): 29–31.

Simon, Jr., W. A. "A Practical Approach to the Uniform Selection Guidelines." *The Personnel Administrator*, 24 (1979): 75–80.

Sims, Jr., H. P. "Tips and Troubles with Employee Reprimand." *The Personnel Administrator*, 24 (1979): 57–61.

Sjoberg, G. "A Questionnaire on Questionnaires." *Public Opinion Quarterly*, (Winter, 1954): 423–427.

Smith, E. W. L. "Postural and Gestural Communications of A and B 'Therapist Types' During Dyadic Interviews."

Journal of Consulting and Clinical Psychology, 39 (1972): 29–36.

Spirita, A. A. and D. S. Holmes "Effects of Models on Interview Responses." *Journal of Consulting Psychology*, 8 (1971): 217.

Stackpole, C. and R. Widgery "Interviewing as Taught in American College and University Speech Departments." *Communication Education*, 20 (1971): 184–191.

Stauffer, A. J. "Information Derived from an Objectivity Study of an Interview Schedule." *Education and Psychological Monographs*, 38 (Summer, 1978): 501–505.

Stephens, D. C. "Developing Interviewing Experts." *Instructor*, 88 (1979): 118.

Sterrett, J. H. "Job Interview: Body Language and Perceptions of Potential Effectiveness." *Journal of Applied Psychology*, 63 (1978): 388–390.

Summers, G. F. and E. M. Beck "Social Status and Personality Factors in Predicting Interviewer Performance." *Sociological Method and Research*, 2 (1973): 111–122.

"Survey Finds Testing Less Important in Employee Selection." *Personnel Management—Policies and Practices*, 24 (1977): 3.

Sutton, R. H. and R. L. Mathis "Performance Appraisal—Part II," *Journal of Systems Management*, (1979): 9–13.

Tate, E., E. Hawrish and S. Clark "Communication Variables in Jury Selection." *Journal of Communication*, 24 (1974): 130–139.

Teel, K. S. "Performance Appraisal: Current Trends, Persistent Progress." *Personnel Journal*, 59 (1980): 296–301.

Tessler, R. and L. Sushelsky "Effects of Eye Contact and Social Status on the Perception of a Job Applicant in an Employment Interviewing Situation." *Journal of Vocational Behavior*, 13 (1978): 338–347.

"The Impact of EEO Legislation on Performance Appraisal." *Personnel*, 55 (1978): 24–34.

Thompson, P. H. and G. W. Dalton "Performance Appraisal: Manager Beware." *Harvard Business Review*, 48 (1979): 149–157.

Thompson, R. C. "A Placement Standards Check List." *Personnel Journal*, 58 (1979): 685 & 714.

Timney, B. and H. London "Body Language of Persuasiveness and Persuadability in Dyadic Interaction." *International Journal of Group Tension*, 3 (1973): 48–67.

Tucker, D. H. and P. M. Rowe "Relationship Between Expectancy, Causal Attributions, and Final Hiring Decisions in the Employment Interview." *Journal of Applied Psychology*, 64 (1979): 27–34.

Tull, D. S. and G. S. Albaum "Bias in Random Digit Dialed Surveys." *Public Opinion Quarterly*, 41 (1977): 389–395.

Turnbull, G. "Some Notes on the History of the Interview." *Journalism Quarterly*, 13 (1936): 272–279.

Tschirgi, H. D. and J. M. Huegli "Monitoring the Employment Interview." *Journal of College Placement*, 39 (1979): 37–39.

Urich, L. and D. Trumbo "The Selection Interview Since 1949." *Psychological Bulletin*, 63 (1965): 100–116.

U.S. Government "Guidelines on Employee Selection Procedures." *Federal Register*, 35 (Aug. 1, 1970).

Vocino, T. "Three Variables in Stimulating Responses to Mailed Questionnaires." *Journal of Marketing*, 41 (Oct., 1977): 76–77.

Voorhis, S. C. "Is Anybody Listening—Now?" *Personnel Administration*, 6 (1961): 16–20.

Wagner, R. "The Employment Interview: A Critical Summary." *Personnel Psychology*, 2 (1949): 17–46.

Washburn, P. V. and M. D. Hakel "Visual Cues and Verbal Content as Influences on Impressions Formed After Simulated Employment Interviews." *Journal of Applied Psychology*, 58 (1973): 137–141.

Watt, D. F. and D. T. Campbell "A Study of Interviewer Bias as Related to Interviewer's Expectations and Own Opinions." *International Journal of Opinion and Attitude Research*, 4 (1950): 77–83.

Webb, E. J. and J. Salancik "The Interview or the Only Wheel in Town." *Journalism Quarterly*, II (November, 1966): 1.

Webster, E. C. "The Selection Interview: Hopeless or Hopeful?" *Studies in Personnel Psychology*, 1 (1972): 6–18.

Weins, A. N. "The Assessment Interview," in I. B. Weiner (Ed.). *Clinical Methods in Psychology*. New York: Wiley Interscience, 1976: 3–60.

Weins, A. N., G. Saslow and J. D. Matarazzo "Speech Interruption Behavior During Interviews." *Psychotherapy: Theory, Research, and Practice*, 3 (1966): 153–158.

Weins, A. N., J. D. Matarazzo, G. Saslow, S. M. Thompson and R. G. Matarazzo "Interview Interaction Behavior of Supervisors, Head Nurses, and Staff Nurses." *Nursing Research*, 14 (1966): 322–329.

Westin, A. F. "What Should Be Done About Employee Privacy?" *The Personnel Administrator*, 25 (1980): 27–30.

"What Businessmen Look for in the Resume." *Personnel Journal*, 54 (1975): 516–519.

"What Recruiters Watch for in College Graduates." *Nation's Business*, 64 (1976): 34–38.

Wheatly, B. C. and W. B. Cash "The Employee Survey: Correcting Its Basic Weaknesses." *Personnel Journal*, 52 (1973): 456–459.

Wiggins, J. D. "Comparison of Counselor Interview Responses and Helpee Behavioral Changes." *Counsel Educ. and Sup.*, 18 (1978): 95–99.

Wildman, R. C. "Effects of Anonymity and Social Setting on Survey Responses." *Public Opinion Quarterly*, 41 (1977): 74–79.

Williams, A. B. "How to Improve Listening Ability." *Business Education Forum*, (Dec., 1978): 22–23.

Williams, D. "Basic Instructions for Interviewers." *Public Opinion Quarterly*, 6 (1942): 634–641.

Williams, H. E. "Eight Question Interview." *Management World*, 7 (1978): 17–18.

Williams, J. A. "Interviewer-Respondent Interaction: A Study of Bias in the Information Interview." *Sociometry*, 27 (1964): 338–352.

Wiseman, F. "Methodological Bias in Public Opinion Surveys." *Public Opinion Quarterly*, (Spring, 1972): 105–108.

Wright, O. R., Jr. "Summary of Research on the Selection Interview Since 1964." *Personnel Psychology*, 22 (1969): 394.

Yates, T. L. "Interviewing: Foundation of Fact Finding." *Journal of Systems Management*, 26 (1975): 14–16.

Young, D. M. et al. "Beyond Words: Influence of Nonverbal Behavior of Female Job Applicants in the Employment Interview." *Personnel and Guidance Journal*, 57 (1979): 346–350.

Zalkowitz, A. "When I Give Instructions, My Patients Take Notes." *Medical Economics*, 18 (1980): 133–138.

Zawacki, R. A. and R. L. Taylor "A View of Performance Appraisal from Organizations Using It." *Personnel Journal*, 55 (1976): 290–299.

Index

Credits continued